Regionalism and globalization

Over the last three decades there has been a phenomenal integration of the world economy. This volume brings together articles written by some of the most eminent researchers in the field to cover the three main dimensions of the globalization process:

- the reduction of barriers to international trade through multilateral agreements such as successive GATT Rounds;
- the proliferation of regional trading arrangements, such as the EU and NAFTA;
- the unilateral actions taken by many countries to open up their economies.

Within these broad areas, essays cover the substantive issues relating to commodity trade, capital movements and monetary and fiscal policies, addressing the subject from both theoretical and empirical perspectives. This comprehensive work will prove invaluable to economists, researchers, policy makers, and anyone with an interest in international economics.

Sajal Lahiri obtained his PhD from the Indian Statistical Institute in 1976, and is currently Professor of Economics at the University of Essex, where he has been a faculty member since 1978. He has published numerous articles in prestigious economics journals, including *Econometrica, Economic Journal, Journal of International Economics, Journal of Development Economics, International Economic Review, Canadian Journal of Economics, European Economics Review*, and *Oxford Economic Paper*. He is one of the founding editors of the *Review of Development Economics*.

Routledge Contemporary Economic Policy Issues
Series editor Kanhaya Gupta

This series is dedicated to new works that focus directly on contemporary economic policy issues. It aims to include case studies from around the world on the most pressing questions facing economists and policy makers at both a national and international level.

Regionalism and globalization
Theory and practice

Edited by Sajal Lahiri

London and New York

First published 2001
by Routledge
11 New Fetter Lane, London EC4P 4EE

Simultaneously published in the USA and Canada
by Routledge
29 West 35th Street, New York, NY 10001

Routledge is an imprint of the Taylor & Francis Group

Typeset in Times by Wearset, Boldon, Tyne and Wear
Printed and bound in Great Britain by University Press, Cambridge

British Library Cataloguing in Publication Data
A catalogue record for this book is available from the British Library

Library of Congress Cataloging in Publication Data
Regionalism and globalization : theory and practice / edited by Sajal
Lahiri.
    p. cm.
  Includes bibliographical references and index.
  1. International economic integration. 2. International trade.
  3. Regionalism. 4. Globalization. I. Lahiri, Sajal.
HF1418.5 .R4436 2001
337.1-dc21

00-047052

ISBN 0-415-22075-0

In memory of my parents
Dipali and Samarendra Nath Lahiri

Contents

Figures

Tables

Contributors

Philip Arestis is Professor of Economics at South Bank University, London. His research interests are in the areas of macroeconomics, monetary economics, applied econometrics and applied political economy. He has published widely in academic journals and, as author or editor, a number of books.

Eric Bond is a Professor of Economics at Pennsylvania State University. He has published articles on international trade theory and microeconomics in a number of professional journals, including the *American Economic Review*, *Journal of Political Economy*, *International Economic Review* and *Journal of International Economics*. He is an associated editor of the *Journal of International Economics*.

V.N. Balasubramanyam is Professor of Development Economics at Lancaster University. His publications include articles and books on foreign direct investment, technology transfer, and the Indian economy.

Rupa Duttagupta is an economist at the International Monetary Fund. She holds a PhD in Economics from the University of Maryland at College Park.

Panicos Demetriades is Professor of Financial Economics at Leicester University and Consultant at the World Bank. He has published extensively on financial liberalization and economic growth.

Wilfred J. Ethier has been a faculty member of the Department of Economics of the University of Pennsylvania since 1969, is a Fellow of the Econometric Society, and for eleven years was Editor of the *International Economic Review*.

Bassam Fattouh is a Research Fellow at the Centre for Financial and Management Studies, the School of Oriental and African Studies, University of London. He has published on financial liberalization and economic growth. He obtained his PhD in Economics from the University of London.

Helena Gaytán-Fregoso is Director of Multilateral Technical and Scientific Cooperation at the Mexican Institute for International Cooperation of the Ministry of Foreign Affairs of Mexico. She has worked as consultant for the OECD and economic advisor at the National Bank of Mexico. She obtained her PhD from the University of Essex.

David Greenaway is Professor of Economics and Pro-Vice-Chancellor at the University of Nottingham. He is also joint managing editor of *The World Economy*. His current research interests are globalization and labour markets.

Andreas Haufler has completed his dissertation and habilitation theses at the University of Konstanz and is now an Associate Professor of Public Finance and Social Policy at the University of Goettingen, Germany. His research interests focus on international taxation, fiscal aspects of economic integration, and the financing of the welfare state.

Sajal Lahiri is a Professor of Economics at the University of Essex. He is one of the founding editors of the *Review of Development Economics*. He obtained his PhD from the Indian Statistical Institute, Calcutta (now Kolkata).

Peter J. Lloyd is the Ritchie Professor of Economics and the Director of the Asian Economics Centre at the University of Melbourne. He is a Fellow of the Academy of Social Sciences in Australia. He specializes mostly in international economics, microeconomic theory and the economics of Asia.

Chris Milner is Professor of International Economics and currently Head of the School of Economics at the University of Nottingham. He is also one of the managing editors of the *Journal of Development Studies* and co-editor (with Peter Lloyd) of *The World Economy annual 'Global Trade Policy'* review.

Ijaz Nabi is a Lead Economist at the World Bank, currently works on structural reform and international competitiveness in Thailand and Malaysia. Previously, he taught at Quaid-i-Azam University in Islamabad and at the Lahore University of Management Sciences. In 1996–7, he advised the government of Pakistan on trade policy. His publications include several books and articles in academic journals on agriculture, industry, finance and the social sectors.

Anjum Nasim is a Professor of Economics at the Lahore University of Management Sciences. He was a member of the economics faculty at the Quaid-i-Azam University, Islamabad during 1974–86 and a Research Advisor with the State Bank of Pakistan in 1995–6. His publications are in the areas of applied econometrics, agriculture price policy and international trade.

Yoshiyasu Ono is a Professor at the Institute of Social and Economic
Research, Osaka University, and has advised the government of Japan
on macroeconomic management. He has published extensively in
international trade and macroeconomics. His books (in English and
Japanese) on stagnation have been warmly received by policy makers in
Japan.

Arvind Panagariya is a Professor of Economics and Co-director, Center
for International Economics, University of Maryland at College Park.
He holds a PhD in economics from Princeton University. He has been a
consultant to various international institutions including the World
Bank, Asian Development Bank, IMF, WTO, and UNCTAD. He has
written or edited half a dozen books on international economics. He is
an editor of the *Journal of Policy Reform* and an associate editor of
Economics and Politics. The journals in which he has published include
the *American Economic Review*, *Quarterly Journal of Economics,
Review of Economic Studies*, *Journal of International Economics*, *International Economic Review*, *The World Economy*, *Journal of International Affairs*, and *Finance and Development.*

Martin Richardson is Professor of Economics at the University of Otago,
Dunedin, New Zealand. He earned his PhD from Princeton University
in 1989 and has taught in the United States of America and Australia as
well as New Zealand. He has published on a variety of international
trade and microeconomic issues, most prominently on the economics of
preferential trading arrangements.

Mohammed A. Salisu is Lecturer in Economics at the Department of Economics, Management School, Lancaster University. His publications
include papers on foreign direct investment, the food and drink industry
of the UK, and the Nigerian economy. He is currently working on a
book on Nigeria.

Arja Turunen-Red is a graduate of University of Helsinki and University
of British Columbia. She is Professor of Economics at the University of
New Orleans. She has contributed to numerous major journals and is a
member of the Editorial Board of the *Journal of International Trade
and Economic Development.*

Kerrin Vautier is an Auckland-based consulting research economist specializing in competition policies. She is also a company director, Chair
of the New Zealand Committee of the Pacific Economic Cooperation
Council (PECC) and teaches competition law and policy at the University of Auckland.

L. Alan Winters is Professor of Economics at the University of Sussex. He
was previously Research Manager for International Trade at the World
Bank, and has taught at the Universities of Cambridge, Bristol, Wales

(Bangor) and Birmingham. He is a Research Fellow of the Centre for Economic Policy Research, London, and Senior Visiting Fellow at the Centre for Economic Performance, LSE.

Alan D. Woodland is Professor of Econometrics at the University of Sydney in Australia, previous posts being held at the University of British Columbia in Canada and the University of New England in Australia. He has long-standing research interests in international trade and applied econometrics. His current research interests in international trade theory have a focus upon the welfare implications of both unilateral and multilateral reforms of tariffs and quotas.

Acknowledgement

I am grateful to the series editor Professor Kanhaya Gupta for his kind advice and encouragement, to all the contributors for their cooperation, and to my wife Dipa for her patience.

Preface

Over the last three decades, there has been a phenomenal integration of the world economy, and the speed of such integration is increasing all the time. This is not simply about commodity trade: foreign investment, both direct and portfolio, have been playing a major role in the integration process. There are three broad, not necessarily independent, elements in this globalization process. First, the multilateral reductions of trade barriers under the auspices of the General Agreement on Tariffs and Trade (GATT) made major inroads into reducing trade restrictions, increasing the scope of such negotiations through the eight post-war rounds of negotiations. More recently, the World Trade Organization (WTO) is preparing for the Millennium Round to take trade negotiations into hitherto uncharted territories. Second, preferential trading arrangements, after some grand failures, have recently proliferated, reducing trade barriers within the member countries. Some estimates suggest that currently there are nearly one hundred regional arrangements. The word 'preferential' is the key word here, and it necessarily implies that countries not belonging to a particular regional arrangement are discriminated against. Finally, many developing countries have recently realised the futility of inward-looking policies and have started to remove trade restriction unilaterally. These three elements are not independent of each other. In particular, regional integration can in principle and practice undermine the multilateral arrangements.

The debate on the desirability of regionalism is not a new one. The discriminatory aspect of regional agreements led Jacob Viner to question, in his famous 1950 book,[1] the then conventional wisdom that such agreements are necessarily welfare improving by drawing attention to the possibility of significant 'trade diversion'. Subsequent formation of the European Common Market gave fresh impetus to the debate in the 1950s and the 1960s when many attempts were made in different parts of the world to form regional trading blocks. Most of these agreements, with the notable exceptions of the European Common Market, did not really get off the ground. Those attempted arrangements are sometimes called the 'old' or 'first' regionalism.

The debate remained latent for nearly two decades and came back with a vengeance in recent years with the advent of 'new' or 'second' regionalism. In this second phase of regionalism, preferential trading agreements are being formed at unprecedented speed with the explicit blessings of influential political forces (the US administration, for example). This is the 'new' or 'second' regionalism.

The old issues, such as trade diversion, have not been forgotten in the debate on new regionalism. Recent works by some economists at the World Bank have found evidence of significant trade diversion in the case of the MERCOSUR in Latin America. However, the old and the new regionalism have many important differences and these differences may explain why new regionalism could prove to be more successful than the old one. In the time of the old regionalism, the multilateral trading system was in its infancy. In contrast, today the WTO has wide ranging powers with an explicit goal of multilateral free trade, not only in commodities, but also in services and capital. The simultaneous existence of regionalism and multilateralism has obviously led to a new debate. Various questions are being asked. Will the spread of regionalism undermine the progress of multilateralism? Does the success with multilateralism necessarily lead to the spread of regionalism? Should the developing countries form regional agreements of their own? Are the developing countries getting a good deal from the multilateral agreements? All these and many other questions are essentially dynamic in nature and their analyses require endogenizing many of the issues that were treated as exogenous in the old controversy.

Although there are numerous preferential trading arrangements, the actual agreements vary very significantly from one another. For example, in the European Single Market agreement free mobility of workers between the member states is an important element, but in the North American Free Trade Agreement (NAFTA) no such provision is made. In fact, some people believe that one of the reasons for bringing Mexico into NAFTA was to stem the flow of (illegal) workers from Mexico to the USA. Regional integration also brings in many new issues for the member countries. For example, the questions of policy harmonization and cross-border shopping often lead to heated debate on the question of national sovereignty. The issues of exchange rate coordination and common monetary policy are even more contentious.

It is true that during the current decade there has been a proliferation of regional agreements. However, in some sense the reverse has also happened in some regions. For example, the demise of the Soviet Union also saw the end of the East European economic block, namely the COMECON. Casual empiricism suggests that trade between many of the former members of COMECON has more or less collapsed. Presumably, they were trading 'too much' (compared to the 'ideal' situation) between themselves before the break-up, and now it seems that they are trading 'too little'. One wonders if this significant diversion of trade in favour of the countries in the European Union (EU) is a strategic move on the part of the East and Central European countries to influence future decisions by the EU on new membership. Another example can be found in South Asia. In spite of the formation of the South Asian Association for Regional Cooperation (SAARC) in the mid-1980s, intra-regional trade between the member countries remains negligible even in absolute terms. Trade between India and Pakistan is restricted by numerous quantitative and administrative measures. This can be called inverse regionalism. The political processes in the two countries have a lot do with this inverse regionalism. Clearly such restrictions to trade can be reduced by regional agreements without necessarily imposing trade restrictions against countries outside South Asia. Such reversals of inverse regionalism could only reinforce the multilateral trading system.

This volume brings together articles—written by eminent researchers in the field—on three aspects of globalization: multilateralism, regionalism, and unilateralism. The articles are varied not only in terms of their coverage, but also in style. Some are written for academic economists and some for policy makers, and there are articles which should appeal to both groups. In Chapter 1, Wilfred Ethier first of all identifies the important differences between the old and the new regionalism. He then examines the role of political economy, direct investment, economic reforms etc. in the regional aspect of regionalism, i.e. why neighbouring countries often form regional arrangements. In Chapter 2, Eric Bond develops a four-country model to compare the welfare effects of multilateral and preferential trading arrangements. In the absence of transport costs, multilateral arrangement dominates. However, the inclusion of transport costs makes the case for preferential trading arrangement somewhat stronger. Arvind Panagariya and Rupa Duttagupta take a critical look in Chapter 3 at some of the computable general equilibrium analysis of preferential trading arrangements and conclude that preferential liberalization is likely to be hurtful to the countries undertaking such liberalization. In Chapter 4, Arja Turunen-Red and Alan Woodland develop a multi-country, multi-good model of international trade to examine the welfare effect of multilateral trade policy reforms. They derive conditions under which such reforms are strictly Pareto improving, both in the presence and in the absence of concurrent lump-sum transfers. In Chapter 5, Helena Gaytán-Fregoso and Sajal Lahiri examine the effects of multilateral tariff reforms on the incidence of illegal immigration in a two-country model where immigration decisions are endogenous.

Chapters 6–9 focus on the developing countries. In Chapter 6, Alan Winters discusses how to assess the costs and benefits of regionalism in the developing countries. He emphasizes the importance of considering potential downward risks of regionalism. He argues that regionalism can potentially be harmful by arresting progress towards multilateral agreements.

David Greenaway and Chris Milner, in Chapter 7, look at the evolution of GATT, particularly from the point of view of the role of the developing countries in the successive GATT Rounds. They also analyse the reasons behind the recent upsurge in regionalism and its potential impact on multilateralism. Looking forward, they identify some key issues in which the developing countries will have a major stake. In Chapter 8, Ijaz Nabi and Anjum Nasim look at the specific case of trade between Pakistan and India. In particular, they identify the key areas in which the two countries can gain significantly by removing barriers to regional trade. In Chapter 9, V.N. Balasubramanyam and M.A. Salisu analyse the role of foreign direct investment in the growth process of the developing countries, and how trade liberalization can affect the flow of such investment into these countries.

As is well known, the globalization process had a major set back recently because of the financial crisis in some of the Asian countries. In Chapter 10, Philip Arestis, Panicos Demetriades and Bassam Fattouh examine why financial liberalization has worked so well in some countries, but not in others. They identify the potentials and the pitfalls of the globalization of the financial sector. Comparing the experiences of Hong Kong with other Asian countries, they highlight the role of orderly development of the banking sector in the success or otherwise of the liberalization of the financial sector.

In Chapter 11, Martin Richardson brings together the arguments for unilateral liberalizations in a world where both regionalism and multilateralism are gaining in popularity. He analyses why unilateral reforms have increased at the same time as multilateral liberalizations.

The last three chapters examine the issue of policy coordination between sovereign countries. In Chapter 12, Andreas Haufler looks at the issue of tax policy coordination in the European Union. He considers both commodity and capital taxes, and the historical evolution of the theories and policies on tax levels and tax rules. In Chapter 13, Peter Lloyd and Kerrin Vautier examine why competition policies are at the heart of many bilateral, regional and multilateral agreements. Finally, in Chapter 14, Yoshiyasu Ono develops a theoretical model of an asymmetric world with unemployment to examine the effect of exchange rate coordination.

Note

1. Viner, J. (1950) *The Customs Union Issue* (New York: Carnegie Endowment for International Peace).

Part I
Gains from regionalism and multilateralism

1　Regional regionalism

Wilfred J. Ethier

Regionalism is regional. Preferential trading arrangements since World War II have almost always involved nations that are geographic neighbours, or near neighbours. This chapter investigates why. A second distinguishing feature of these arrangements is their occurrence over time: many attempts at integration—most ultimately futile except in Europe—during the 1950s and 1960s, followed by years of relative inactivity, with a dramatic resurgence of new initiatives beginning in the late 1980s. Geographic proximity of neighbours characterizes both the 'old regionalism' and the 'new regionalism', but this chapter concerns the latter.

1 Introduction

Because the world economy has changed in dramatic and fundamental ways during the past half-century the temporal gap between the old and the new initiatives is essential. They have taken place in very different environments for very different reasons.

The following section summarizes those changes in the world economy that are most important for regional integration, and the third section describes the stylized facts of the new regionalism, contrasting them with those of the old regionalism. This strongly suggests that the theoretical framework developed in response to the old regionalism is likely to be inadequate to deal with central features of the new. Armed with this background, I then advance four distinct, but complementary, explanations of why preferential trading arrangements might feature geographic neighbours: regional regionalism.[1]

Countries tend to trade a lot with their neighbours, so it is sometimes said that current regional initiatives, often involving neighbours, are therefore likely to be benign.[2] However the geographical nature of regional arrangements, like the arrangements themselves, has been treated as exogenous in the literature. Understanding why neighbours integrate should be prior to asking whether it is a good thing or not.

2 The world of the new regionalism

The world economy has undergone fundamental changes in the last half century. The following are the most important ways in which the world of the new regionalism differs from that of the old.

- The multilateral liberalization of trade in manufactured goods among the industrial countries is much more complete now than it was during the advent of the old regionalism.
- Most countries of the East and of the South have abandoned the basically autarkic, anti-market policies of the days of the old regionalism and are now actively trying to join the multilateral trading system. For these countries the old regionalism was a *substitute* for such entry; the new regional initiatives are intended as *complements*.
- Direct investment is much more prominent now than in the days of the old regionalism, is much more multilateral, and has been surging since the advent of the new regionalism.
- Consistent with the above, the most dramatic changes in the costs of international transactions have been those dealing with information processing, communications, etc., suggesting that costs of foreign direct investment may have fallen relative to the costs of trade (other than the man-made costs).

All this suggests that the new regionalism might be a quite different animal from the old. The next step is to look at the basic properties of the former.

3 The stylized facts of the new regionalism

The following six features are not exhaustive and do not characterize all recent regional initiatives, which are very diverse, but they do apply to most of the more important ones.

- The new regionalism typically has one or more small countries linking up with a big country.

In NAFTA (North American Free Trade Agreement), Mexico and Canada are each small economically, relative to the United States; the new members of the EU (European Union) are tiny compared with the EU itself; the same is true of the central European adherents to the Europe Agreements with the EU; Brazil is dominant in Mercosur.

- Usually the small countries have recently made, or are making, significant unilateral reforms.

This is dramatically true of the Europe agreements' central European participants, who had abandoned communism, and of the members of

Mercosur and of Mexico; but it also characterizes, to a lesser degree, the small industrial country participants in various regional initiatives. Canada had turned away from Trudeau-style economic nationalism as it negotiated a free trade agreement with the USA, and the Scandinavian applicants to the EU (except for Norway, which declined to join) had made significant reforms in some sectors (e.g. agriculture).

- A dramatic move to free trade between members is *not* central: the degree of liberalization is usually modest.

NAFTA actually gave only moderate liberalization: US tariffs were already low and NAFTA hedges sensitive sectors in all sorts of ways. Canada and Mexico have done somewhat more, but the most significant measures (largely Mexican) were unilateral and not part of NAFTA. The situation with new members of the EU is even more glaring: the trade relations of Austria, Finland and Sweden with the EU are virtually identical to what they would have been had they decided not to join. The Europe agreements provide for little concrete liberalization. Even the more ambitious Mercosur features liberalization which is modest relative to the members' unilateral liberalizations.

- The liberalization is due primarily to concessions by the small countries, not by the large country: the agreements are one-sided.

NAFTA liberalization is more 'concessions' by Mexico and Canada than by the United States. In negotiations the EU is flexible on financial responsibilities and periods of adjustment, but maintains a take-it-or-leave-it attitude over the nature and structure of the EU itself. The Europe agreements involve virtually no 'concessions' by the EU; indeed the EU instituted antidumping measures against some of its new partners even as the initial agreements were coming into effect! Partly this asymmetry reflects how the world has changed since the days of the old regionalism; one reason small countries get only small tariff advantages is that large countries have small tariffs to begin with.

- Regional arrangements often involve 'deep' integration: partners address diverse economic policies beyond tariff barriers.

The EU is an obvious example. The USA–Canada free-trade agreement and the subsequent NAFTA included a host of economic reform commitments by Canada and by Mexico. Sometimes partners in regional arrangements exempt each other from acts of administered protection (such as antidumping duties), but often they do not (e.g. NAFTA). Sometimes partners are in effect granted rights of appeal denied to non-partners (NAFTA again). The latest three GATT (General Agreement on

6   *Wilfred J. Ethier*

Tariffs and Trade) rounds tried, with significant success, to broaden the
scope of multilateral arrangements. However, a major attraction of the
new regionalism seems to be that negotiations with a small number of
partners broadens the range of instruments over which fruitful negotiation
is feasible.

Finally, for completeness, the feature central to this chapter is listed,
even though it does not distinguish the new regionalism from the old.

- Regional arrangements are regional in a geographic sense: the
  participants are neighbours.

In summary, regional integration typically involves reform-minded
small countries 'purchasing', with moderate trade concessions, links with a
large, neighbouring country that involve 'deep' integration but confer
minor trade advantages.

The new regionalism differs fundamentally from the old. It is the
product of a different world, addresses different needs, and possesses different characteristics. The theoretical literature, however, is caught in a
time warp. Following Viner (1950), old-regionalism theory emphasizes the
tension between trade creation and trade diversion—important for the
1950s. Recently, game theoretic considerations have been introduced and
attention has shifted to the implications of regional integration for multilateral liberalization, but the distinctive features of the new regionalism
and of the world to which it belongs have been ignored.[3] Successful multilateral liberalization, widespread fundamental reform and the prominence
of direct investment still play no role in most of the theory, which continues to be driven by trade creation and trade diversion. I shall therefore
try to give central roles to the distinctive features of the world in which we
live.[4]

4 The common framework

I shall describe four alternative, but complementary, theories of why
regionalism might be regional. Although they are distinct, the theories are
built on formal structures that overlap significantly. The following are
common components.

- Countries are identical, except that they are spatially separated: countries are grouped into N continents of n countries each; the distance
  between any two countries in the same continent is equal to d and the
  distance between any pair in different continents is D, with $d < D$.
- Trade flows between pairs of countries are predicted by a *gravity
  equation*, in which the amount of bilateral trade is positively related to
  the economic sizes of the countries and negatively related to a
  measure of the gross distance between them.

The gravity equation has consistently been shown to describe actual trade patterns well. In this model, gross distance is all that matters since countries are otherwise identical.[5] Gross distance is determined by geographic distance (just described) and by tariff barriers. These barriers comprise tariffs and the tariff-equivalents of other instruments and, initially, are given by past history. Assume that, if each of a pair of countries imposes a tariff-equivalent barrier of t on products from the other, the total trade between the two is given by $\alpha/(t + d)$ if they are in the same continent, and by $\alpha/(t + D)$ if they are in different continents, for some parameter $\alpha > 0$.

Let $T(t)$ denote the ratio of each country's intra-continental trade to inter-continental trade, if all countries impose the tariff equivalent t on all trade:

$$T(t) = \frac{(n-1)\,\dfrac{\alpha}{t+d}}{n(N-1)\,\dfrac{\alpha}{t+D}}$$

Now,

$$\frac{A}{T}\frac{dT}{dt} = \frac{t}{t+D} - \frac{t}{t+d}$$

since $D > d$. Thus, if $t° > 0$ denotes the initial level of trade barriers, $T(t°) < T(0)$.

5 A political-economy perspective

Consider now how successive rounds of trade negotiations might develop in the framework described above. To this end, add the following structure.

- The government of each country may negotiate a mutual reduction in trade barriers with other governments, but each government is constrained by negotiating costs. In subsequent periods there will be new rounds of negotiations, with the governments constrained by the same costs in negotiating further reductions in trade barriers.

At the outset of each negotiating round, each government decides whether to negotiate *regionally* (only with other countries in the same continent) or *multilaterally* (with all other countries); because of the symmetry, all governments make the same choice. The negotiating costs reflect the government's political support, which is not modelled explicitly. I assume that larger reductions in trade barriers incur greater costs, further inflaming adversely affected special interests, and that a reduction in the number of negotiating partners lowers costs. The reason for the latter is twofold.

1   With fewer negotiating partners the reduction in barriers applies to a smaller range of goods and so harms fewer special interests.
2   The fewer the number of partners, the easier it is to reach agreement, enabling deeper integration, that is, agreement over a wider range of policies; this allows a country to achieve a given reduction of trade barriers in more diverse ways, and thus find a way to minimize the harm done to powerful special interests.

I assume the total cost a government is willing to incur in a negotiating round is exogenously given. Let γ denote the amount by which reducing the number of negotiating partners by one allows a government to increase the rate of trade-barrier reduction at unchanged cost.

•   In its negotiations, each government strives to maximize, subject to the constraint on costs, an index of benefits. Benefits are greater the greater the reduction in trade barriers and the greater the number of partners to which those reductions apply.

Let δ denote the amount by which reducing the number of negotiating partners by one must be matched by an increase in the rate of trade-barrier reduction to leave unchanged the perceived benefit.

•   The parameter δ is a decreasing function of the ratio of aggregate trade with negotiating partners to aggregate trade with non-partners.

The government, for political reasons, wants to reduce the 'tax' on as much trade as possible, and existing trade matters more than trade that would exist if barriers were lower. Also, a higher partner–to–non-partner trade ratio may also imply a higher trade creation–to–trade diversion ratio.

With δ a decreasing function of its argument, there are three possibilities.

1   $\delta(T(t^\circ)) > \delta(T(0)) > \gamma$. Multilateral negotiation is initially more tempting than regional, and remains so after each successive round. The world continues to approach free trade with regional blocs never emerging: the *multilateral outcome*.
2   $\gamma > \delta(T(t^\circ)) > \delta(T(0))$. Regional negotiation is initially better than multilateral negotiation, and remains so after each successive round. The world splits up into continental regional blocs, and no multilateral negotiation can even begin until all the regions have free internal trade: the *Vinerian outcome*.
3   $\delta(T(t^\circ)) > \gamma > \delta(T(0))$. Multilateral negotiation is initially more tempting than regional negotiation, but eventually successful multilateral liberalization will cause regional negotiation to become more attractive. Regional blocs then emerge, and multilateral negotiation cannot resume until regional integration is complete. Call this *induced regionalism*.

The basic message is that the success of multilateral tariff reduction can generate regional integration by neighbours. The explanation has used reduced-form representations of a trade model and of a political-economy model. The former (the gravity equation[6]) is compatible with a sufficiently wide class of structural models to inspire hopes of generality, although such a structure would be needed to draw normative conclusions. The political economy representation, though intended to mimic historical experience crudely, is more special. For example, governments must choose either a multilateral strategy or a regional strategy; they are not allowed to pursue both simultaneously while choosing relative emphasis.

The assumption that δ is decreasing in the ratio of partner trade to non-partner trade plays a key role. It is not hard to build structural models with this property. However it is also possible (though not easy) to build structural models where the reverse is true. In this case, the outcome with a switch will involve the initial formation of regional blocs whose partial success will eventually induce the commencement of multilateral negotiations. The multilateral and Vinerian outcomes will remain, but they will now correspond to cases (2) and (1) respectively.

Thus far I have utilized only one of the changes in the world economy (significant multilateral liberalization) and touched on only two of the stylized facts of the new regionalism (deep integration and neighbourhood arrangements). This suggests the possibility of additional explanations exploiting additional features.

6 A reduction-in-communications-costs perspective

I now amend the common framework to incorporate additional stylized facts and features of the world of the new regionalism.

- In addition to the n countries described (henceforth called *richer* countries), each continent also contains m countries (*poorer* countries). The distance between any two countries in the same continent is still d and that between any pair in different continents is D, with $d < D$.
- The richer countries are all alike, except that their final products are differentiated—the basis for trade between them. These goods are produced in multiple stages, with the more labour-intensive stages candidates for transfer to subsidiaries in the poorer countries.
- Operating a multinational enterprise is costly because of the added need for communications, information processing, etc.

Now suppose that multilateral negotiation succeeds in lowering trade barriers, *and* that technological improvements also lower the costs of operating a multinational enterprise and make it easier to disperse stages of production around the globe. Then the following consequences are immediate.

1   The reduction of trade barriers, by making distance relatively more important as a determinant of trade flows, increases intra-continental trade relative to inter-continental.
2   The lower costs of communication, information processing and so on induce firms in the richer countries to fragment production by establishing subsidiaries in the poorer countries; because distance has become relatively more important for trade, source country firms will look for hosts in the same continent.
3   The establishment of foreign subsidiaries in the same continents as their source countries will further magnify the increase in intra-continental trade relative to inter-continental trade.

The basic conclusion is that the reduction in costs of communication, information processing and so on, interacting with trade, will produce a geographic concentration of economic activity—direct investment correlated with international trade. As a result, regional integration with neighbouring poorer countries becomes more attractive for the richer countries relative to further multilateral liberalization.

7 A fundamental-economic-reform perspective

The previous section focused on potential sources of direct investment and argued that regional integration with neighbouring potential hosts could be the result. Now I focus on incentives for the latter themselves to desire such integration. So, I now *replace* the amendments, given in the preceding two sections, to the common framework with the following.

*   In addition to the n countries hitherto described (henceforth called *inside* countries), each continent also contains m countries (*outside* countries) initially in autarky. The distance between any two countries in the same continent is still d and that between any pair in different continents is D, with $d < D$.
*   Inside countries are alike, except that their final products are differentiated—the basis for trade between them. These are produced in multiple stages, with labour-intensive stages candidates for transfer to subsidiaries in reforming countries.
*   Outside countries will attempt reform (i.e., allow foreign trade and inward foreign direct investment) if the rewards of successful reform overcome special interests. These rewards depend upon the size of the multilateral economy.
*   Reform will be more successful the more foreign direct investment is attracted: direct investment transfers technology, modern business practices, etc. So, reform is assumed to succeed if and only if some direct investment is attracted.
*   Reforming countries in each continent are alike so, other things equal,

inside-country firms are indifferent about where to locate foreign subsidiaries. But they will tend to locate together, because direct investment is lumpy and because of positive externalities between foreign subsidiaries.

With sufficiently successful multilateral liberalization, many outside countries will undertake fundamental reform to try to join that multilateral system. Since they see direct investment as key to successful reform, they compete to attract it.

Since outside countries differ only in location, inside-country firms will never locate their foreign subsidiaries, producing intermediate goods, in continents different from those in which they reside as that would raise the cost of those intermediate goods by $D - d$. They will locate subsidiaries in the same continent if the cost advantage of doing so exceeds d plus whatever tariff the inside countries levy on the intermediate goods. Presumably multilateral liberalization lowers such tariffs. Outside countries in each continent are identical, so a reforming country can improve its prospects if it can distinguish itself from its rivals.

Consider the potential role of regional arrangements. Define a regional agreement as the following.

> An agreement between one inside country and one reforming outside country in which:
>   the reforming outside country commits
>   • to the details of an attempted reform,
>   • to give the goods of its partner preferential treatment;
>   the inside country commits
>   • to make a *small* reduction in the duty applicable to goods imported from its partner country.

This definition reflects the fact that regional arrangements involve one or more small reforming countries linking up with a large country in an arrangement characterized by asymmetrical concessions and deep integration.

Suppose for simplicity that each potential reformer regards the products of all inside countries as perfect substitutes. With the assumptions already made, this will wipe out the possibility of negative welfare effects due to trade diversion. This oversimplification will highlight the changed world and the distinctive features of the new regionalism that have made the old Vinerian concerns less important, and it will also reveal the new concerns.

Consider first the effects on a potential reformer. The trade preference implies that all imports will come from the partner country. However, this (possibly massive) trade diversion is of no consequence in this model. However, the preference granted by the inside-country partner, though

only marginal, is much more significant. To firms considering direct investment to provide intermediate-stage inputs for the inside-country partner's
products, all reforming countries in the continent are equivalent, except
for this marginal preference. Thus it attracts all such investment.[7] This
ensures the reform will succeed because of the 'investment diversion'
implied by the regional arrangement. Furthermore, $D>d$ causes inside
countries to prefer regional arrangements with reformers in the same continent and to have no use for arrangements in other continents: regionalism will be regional.

This explains why reforming countries find one-sided regional arrangements attractive. They compete with other *similar* countries for direct
investment, *not* to attract from their partners direct investments that
would otherwise not be made.

A regional arrangement is not uniformly benign. Other reformers will
suffer. Suppose a country that would reform anyway enters into a regional
arrangement. Direct investment producing intermediate goods for that
country's partner will all be diverted there, and the country still remains a
potential host for other direct investment. Less direct investment remains
for other reformers, reducing their prospects for success and perhaps even
deterring some of them from embarking upon reform: 'reform destruction'. However, the country with the regional arrangement may instead
not itself have attempted reform in its absence: 'reform creation'. So the
number of countries attempting reform may either rise or fall.

With regionalism ubiquitous, consider the general equilibrium if all
countries freely negotiate such regional arrangements, allowing a single
country to enter multiple relationships.[8]

If several reforming countries establish regional arrangements with
a single inside country (presumably in the same continent), the value
of the arrangements to the former will be eroded because direct investment may cluster mainly in some subset of them all. So the reforming
countries will spread themselves out in their choices of partners. If
there are at least as many inside countries as potential reformers, each
of the latter can find a partner to guarantee the success of reform. This
may or may not be true if there are fewer inside countries, depending
upon the amount of direct investment. Nevertheless, the ability to enter
freely into regional arrangements will maximize the extent and the
probability of successful reform, and also the number of countries that
attempt reform.

The global interest is for successful reform to be widespread. This will
maximize the multilateral trading system, accentuating its benefits and the
number of nations receiving those benefits, but this global externality will
be ignored by multinational firms. A single regional arrangement may be
either good or bad in its results. But the *regional general equilibrium* will
internalize the global externality with an outcome unambiguously superior
to that without regionalism.

8 An 'enforcer' perspective

The basic idea of the preceding section is that reforming outside countries compete among themselves to attract direct investment from inside countries. In this competition, outside countries in the same continent as those inside countries which that direct investment is intended to serve have an advantage over outside countries in different continents. Regional integration enters as a means of competition between those in the same continent, where only a small advantage, such as that provided by a one-sided agreement, can be decisive. However, countries can compete for direct investment in many ways; if only a small advantage is needed, why resort to regional integration? This has to do with another role such agreements can play.

Regardless of whether other incentives are present, direct investment will be sensitive to the credibility of the announced reform effort, as well as to the credibility of any other announced incentives. A regional arrangement establishes an external commitment to reform that (weakly, perhaps) binds future governments, thereby making the future preservation of reform (slightly, perhaps) more credible. This in turn makes the country more attractive for direct investment, relative to similar countries without such external commitments. Deep integration allows reforming countries to write a commitment to reform into an arrangement with a big country that is a natural enforcer and which, as a result of the investment induced by the arrangement, has an interest in enforcing it. Only regionalism has this property, so it can be expected to be employed even if other tools are used as well. The best enforcer is the country with the most incentive to punish deviations and the most ability to do so. This is presumably an inside country in the same continent, given the gravity-equation description of bilateral trade. Furthermore, liberalization of any type, by making distance more important for trade relative to protective barriers, will make inside countries in the same continent even more attractive, relative to those in other continents, as enforcers. So, once again, regionalism can be expected to be regional.

Such an external commitment in turn makes the country more attractive for direct investment, relative to similar countries without such external commitments. Thus the ability of a regional arrangement to bind the government to reform can be important for the success of that reform even when it confers only modest direct benefits.

9 Concluding remarks

This chapter has investigated why preferential trading arrangements almost always involve geographical neighbours. It has been concerned with the 'new regionalism' of the last decade. I first argued that the new regionalism is taking place in a world fundamentally different from that of the old regionalism, so that old-regionalism theory is not necessarily relevant. I then described the prominent stylized facts of the new regionalism.

I then set out four alternative, but complementary, reasons why neighbours might integrate. These gave prominent roles to political economy, direct investment, and fundamental economic reform, and de-emphasized the tired trade creation versus trade diversion tradeoff that thoroughly dominates the existing literature.

These explanations might appear to cast regionalism in a very favourable light. I want to close by cautioning against such an interpretation. My analysis has been positive rather than normative, and I have proceeded by positing a sub-optimal world.

Notes

1. Ludema (1999) creatively uses some of the same ingredients to advance yet another potential explanation.
2. But see Bhagwati and Panagariya (1966) for a contrary view.
3. For old-regionalism theory, see Kemp and Wan (1976), Ethier and Horn (1984), Krugman (1991), McMillan (1993), Baldwin and Venables (1995), Bond and Syropoulos (1996), and Bagwell and Staiger (1997a, 1997b). Many important contributions to old-regionalism theory are conveniently collected in Bhagwati, Krishna, and Panagariya (1999).
4. Other attempts along this line are in Ethier (1998a, 1998b, 1998c, 1998d and 1999).
5. The gravity equation can be thought of as a reduced form consistent with many trade models, so that its empirical success reveals little about the underlying causes of trade. See Deardorff (1995).
6. See Garriga and Sanguinetti (1995, 1997) for an application to Mercosur.
7. But if the externalities between foreign subsidiaries—which induce them to locate together—are strong enough, more than 'small' concessions may be required by the industrial partner.
8. These are sometimes called 'hub and spoke' arrangements. See Wonnacott (1996).

References

Bagwell, K. and Staiger, R.W. (1997a) 'Multilateral tariff cooperation during the formation of customs unions', *Journal of International Economics*, 42: 91–124.
—— (1997b) 'Multilateral tariff cooperation during the formation of free trade areas', *International Economic Review*, 38 (2): 291–320.
Baldwin, R.E. and Venables, A.J. (1995) 'Regional economic integration', in G.M. Grossman and K. Rogoff (eds), *Handbook of International Economics, Vol. 3*, Amsterdam: Elsevier: 1597–1644.
Bhagwati, J., Krishna, P. and Panagariya, A. (eds), (1999) *Trading Blocs: Alternative Approaches to Analyzing Preferential Trade Agreements*, Cambridge: MIT Press.
Bhagwati, J. and Panagariya, A. (1996) 'Preferential trading areas and multilateralism: Strangers, friends or foes?', University of Maryland Center for International Economics Working Paper, No. 22.

Bond, E. and Syropoulos, C. (1996) 'Trading blocs and the sustainability of inter-regional cooperation', in M. Canzoneri, W.J. Ethier and V. Grilli (eds), _The New Transatlantic Economy,_ Cambridge: Cambridge University Press: 118–41.

Deardorff, A.V. (1995) 'Determinants of bilateral trade: Does gravity work in a neoclassical world?', Discussion Paper No. 382, Research Forum on International Economics, University of Michigan.

Ethier, W.J. (1998a) 'Regionalism, international trade and multinational firm location', in J.-L. Mucchielli (ed.), _Multinational Location Strategy: Economic Management and Policy,_ Greenwich, Connecticut: JAI Press: 3–28.

—— (1998b) 'The new regionalism', _Economic Journal_ 108 (449): 1149–61. Reprinted in Dixon, H. (ed.), (1999) _Controversies in Macroeconomics: Growth, Trade and Policy,_ Oxford: Blackwell Publishers: 150–62.

—— (1998c) 'The international commercial system', _Essays in International Finance_ No. 210, September, Princeton: International Finance Section.

—— (1998d) 'Regionalism in a multilateral world', _Journal of Political Economy_ 6 (106), December: 1214–45.

—— (1999) 'Multilateral roads to regionalism', in J. Piggot and A. Woodland (eds), _International Trade Policy and the Pacific Rim,_ New York: St. Martin's Press: 131–52.

Ethier, W.J. and Horn, H. (1984) 'A new look at economic integration', in H. Kierzkowski (ed.), _Monopolistic Competition and International Trade,_ Oxford: Oxford University Press: 207–29. Reprinted in A. Jacquemin and A. Sapir (eds) (1989), _The European Internal Market: Trade and Competition,_ Oxford: Oxford University Press.

Frankel, J.A., Stein, E. and Wei, S.-J. (1996) 'Regional trading arrangements: natural or supernatural?', _American Economic Review_ 86 (2), May: 52–6.

Garriga, M. and Sanguinetti, P. (1995) '¿Es el Mercosur un bloque natural? Efectos de la política comercial y la geografía sobre el intercambio regional', _Estudios_ 18 (73): 59–68.

—— (1997) 'The determinants of regional trade in Mercosur: geography and commercial liberalization', unpublished manuscript, Departamento de Economìa, Universidad Torcuato Di Tella, Buenos Aires, Argentina.

Kemp, M.C. and Wan, H. (1976) 'An elementary proposition concerning the formation of customs unions', _Journal of International Economics_ 6: 95–8.

Krugman, P. (1991) 'Is bilateralism bad?', in E. Helpman and A. Razin (eds), _International Trade and Trade Policy,_ Cambridge: The MIT Press.

Ludema, R.D. (1999) 'Increasing returns, multinationals and geography of preferential trade agreements', unpublished manuscript, Georgetown University, Department of Economics.

McMillan, J. (1993) 'Does regional integration foster open trade? Economic theory and GATT's article XXIV', in K. Anderson and R. Blackhurst (eds), _Regional Integration and the Global Trading System,_ New York: Harvester Wheatsheaf.

Viner, J. (1950) _The Customs Union Issue,_ New York: Carnegie Endowment for International Peace.

Wonnacott, R.J. (1996) 'Free-trade agreements: For better or worse?', _American Economic Review_ 86 (2), May 1996: 62–6.

2 Multilateralism versus regionalism

Tariff cooperation and inter-regional transport costs

Eric Bond

1 Introduction

Substantial attention has recently been focused on whether regional trade agreements have favourable effects on the world trading system and should be encouraged, or whether new initiatives for trade liberalization should be restricted to multilateral trade agreements that apply the most-favoured nation (MFN) principle. This chapter addresses the question by examining a model in which countries cannot write enforceable contracts on tariffs, so that trade agreements must be self-enforcing agreements that are supported through repeated interactions between the countries. Although a number of papers have examined the effect of preferential arrangements on the multilateral trading system under the assumption that multilateral trade agreements must be self-enforcing (e.g. Bagwell and Staiger 1997a and b, 1999, Bond and Syropoulos 1996b, Bond, Syropoulos and Winters 2001)[1], all of these papers have assumed that member countries can commit to tariff rates in the preferential trading arrangement. Thus, a fundamental asymmetry in commitment power is assumed between preferential agreements and the multilateral trading system.

The purpose of this chapter is to compare preferential and multilateral trade agreements in an environment where both types of agreements must be self-enforcing in a repeated game between the participating countries, so there is no exogenous difference in commitment ability between preferential and multilateral agreements. A simple four-country trade model is examined. A multilateral agreement is a trade agreement between all four countries that is required to satisfy the MFN principle, with a deviation by any country being punished by reversion to the one-shot Nash equilibrium by all participating countries. A preferential agreement equilibrium is one in which two pairs of countries form preferential trade agreements that give a discriminatory tariff reduction to member countries, with deviations punished by reversion to the Nash equilibrium of the one-shot game by the member countries. The question to be examined is whether the level of world welfare that can be sustained under the multilateral trading system is higher than can be attained if instead the world were divided into symmetric preferential trade areas (PTAs).

Two basic sources of difference between multilateral and regional agreements will be examined. The first is due to difference between the deviation and punishment effects under the respective types of agreements where all countries are symmetric. It will be shown that in the case where the punishment under each type of trade agreement is the reversion to the Nash equilibrium of the one-shot tariff game, the minimum sustainable tariff on trade between the countries is always lower under a preferential trade agreement than under a multilateral agreement. This ability to sustain lower tariffs under the preferential agreement results from strategic spillovers between the preferential trade groups during the punishment and deviation phases. However, this ability must be weighed against the fact that the discriminatory nature of these agreements results in lower welfare at a given agreement rate. It is shown that when both of these factors are combined, multilateral agreements will dominate unless discount factors are quite low. The case in which minmax punishments are used to support the trade agreements will also be examined. It is shown that a multilateral system is able to impose sufficiently more severe punishments in the minmax case that it can sustain lower tariffs for any level of the discount parameter.

The second source of asymmetry between multilateral and regional agreements is obtained by giving the trade model a regional structure: the four countries are divided between two continents, with transport costs incurred on trade between continents but not within continents. It is shown that in this case the existence of transportation costs gives an advantage to preferential agreements over multilateral agreements when the discount parameter is low, because of the requirement that multilateral agreements satisfy the MFN principle. Multilateral agreements satisfying the MFN principle must impose the same tariff on all countries, even though deviation incentives may differ across the partner countries, which makes sustaining of multilateral agreements more difficult. However, when the weight placed on the future is high this effect is dominated by the superior welfare effects of the multilateral agreement.

The case with regional differences in trade costs also raises the question of whether the preferential trade equilibrium is better when there are regional partners or distant partners. It is shown that the equilibrium with regional trade blocs yields higher welfare. This result is due to the fact that the regional agreement has lower external tariffs than does the preferential agreement with a distant country. This analysis contributes to the literature on 'natural trading blocs', which has been concerned with whether there is a presumption that tariff reductions with nearby partners are welfare improving. Krugman (1991), Frankel, Stein and Wei (1995) and Bhagwati and Panagariya (1996) have examined this question by considering whether exogenously given preferential tariff reductions are welfare improving in a model where there are differing levels of transport costs between trading partners. The analysis in this chapter differs in that attention is focused on preferential reductions that are self-enforcing agreements.

The second section of the chapter presents the basic trade model. The third section compares regional and multilateral trade agreements when reversion to the Nash equilibrium is used to punish deviators. The fourth section compares regional and multilateral agreements when minmax punishments are used. The fifth section compares preferential and multilateral agreements in the presence of inter-continental transport costs, and the welfare obtained in a PTA with a near partner against that with a distant partner. The final section offers some concluding remarks.

2 The trade model

We examine a four-country, four-good endowment model of trade in which countries are symmetric. The endowment pattern is chosen so that each country exports one good and imports the others from the rest of the world. The four-country framework is adopted because it is the simplest framework in which to compare multilateralism with regionalism when there is more than one regional trading bloc. In this section we present the model and characterize the equilibrium in the one-shot Nash equilibrium when there are no trade agreements.

The demand for good j in country i is $D_j^i = \alpha - p_j^i$, where p_j^i is the price of good j in country i. Each country i has an endowment of X of good i and 0 of goods $j \neq i$, so country i will export good i and import goods $j \neq i$ in any trading equilibrium. Letting t_j^i denote the specific tariff imposed by country i on imports of good j, $p_j^i = p_j^j + t_j^i$ for $j \neq i$. It will be assumed that countries cannot levy export taxes, so $t_i^i \equiv 0$ for all i. Under these assumptions, the equilibrium prices will be

$$p_j^j = \alpha - \left(X + \sum_i t_j^i\right)/4$$

and

$$p_j^i = \alpha - \left(X - 3t_j^i + \sum_{k \neq i} t_j^k\right)/4 \text{ for } i \neq j.$$

Under this specification, a tariff imposed by country i on country j will worsen the terms of trade of country j but will improve the terms of trade of the other importing countries.

In an importing country, the social surplus obtained from imports of good j is the sum of consumer surplus and tariff revenue:

$$S_j^i\left(t_j^i, \sum_{k \neq i} t_j^k\right) = \int_{p_j^i}^{\alpha}(\alpha - u)du + t_j^i(\alpha - p_j^i) = \frac{\left(X + \sum_k t_j^k\right)^2 - 16(t_j^i)^2}{32}$$

for $3t_j^i - \sum_{k \neq i} t_j^k \leqslant X$ \hfill (1)

The bound on tariffs in (1) ensures that t_j^i is not prohibitive. Surplus in the importable sector is concave in the country's own tariff, t_j^i, and increasing and convex in the tariff of other importing countries for tariffs are less than the prohibitive value. The surplus in the exporting country in sector j is the sum of consumer surplus and endowment income

$$S_j^i\left(\sum_{k \neq j} t_j^k\right) = \int_{p_j^i}^{\alpha}(\alpha - u)du + Xp_j^i = \alpha X + \frac{\left(\sum_{k \neq j} t_j^k\right)^2 - 6\left(\sum_{k \neq j} t_j^k\right)X - 7X^2}{32}$$

for $\sum_{k \neq j} t_j^k \leqslant 3X$ \hfill (2)

Surplus in the export sector is convex and decreasing in the tariffs of importing countries for tariffs below the prohibitive level.

Letting $\mathbf{t}^i$ be the vector of tariffs imposed by country k on goods $j \neq k$, welfare of country i can be expressed as

$$W_i(\mathbf{t}^1, \mathbf{t}^2, \mathbf{t}^3, \mathbf{t}^4) = \sum_{j=1}^{4} S_j^i\left(t_j^i, \sum_{k \neq j} t_j^k\right)$$ \hfill (3)

The free trade welfare level is $\alpha X - X^2/8$. In the absence of a trade agreement, countries are assumed to play a one-shot tariff setting game. Country i will choose $\mathbf{t}^i$ to maximize W_i, given $\mathbf{t}^k$. The tariff t_j^i will be chosen to maximize (1), which yields the optimal tariff formula

$$\tilde{t}_j^i = \left(X + \sum_{k \neq i} t_j^k\right)/15$$ \hfill (4)

Using the symmetry of countries, (1)–(4) can be solved for the unique Nash equilibrium tariff and welfare levels,

$$t^N = \frac{X}{13} \quad W^N = \alpha X - \frac{X^2 + 3(t^N)^2}{8}$$ \hfill (5)

These welfare functions generate the usual prisoner's dilemma feature of trade negotiations: unilateral tariff reductions will be welfare reducing, but bilateral or multilateral tariff reductions have the potential to benefit all countries.

3 Trade agreements with Nash punishments

It is well known that repeated interactions between parties can be used to support payoffs to the parties that Pareto dominate those obtained in the one-shot game. A trade agreement will be modelled here as a coordination mechanism in which parties choose tariffs that are to be sustained under the agreement and punishments that are to be imposed on any member countries that deviate from the agreement. A particular choice of tariffs in a trade agreement will be incentive compatible if the payoff to setting the tariffs specified under the agreement exceeds that obtained by deviating and then suffering the specified punishment.

A multilateral agreement will be a four-player repeated game in which each country i chooses $\mathbf{t}^i$ to maximize W_i. It will be assumed that the tariff rates chosen under a multilateral trade agreement satisfy the MFN principle, which requires country i to extend tariff reductions to all trading partners (i.e. $t^i_j = t^i_k$ for all i and k, $j \neq i$). This restriction is imposed because it has been a cornerstone of the GATT negotiation process. It will be assumed that among the sustainable trade agreements satisfying the MFN principle, multilateral negotiations result in the selection of the symmetric trade agreement that maximizes the welfare of a representative member country. The assumption that the tariff agreement chosen is not Pareto dominated seems natural in an environment where the choice of tariff rates is made in a public forum where countries can negotiate. The symmetry of payoffs to countries under the agreement reflects the underlying symmetry of the model, and can be thought of as resulting from the symmetric bargaining power of the countries. Finally, it is assumed that in the event of deviation by a member country, the country is punished by infinite reversion to the one-shot Nash equilibrium of the tariff game.

A preferential trade agreement, on the other hand, will be a two-player repeated game involving two partner countries. In order to maintain symmetry of the preferential agreements, we will restrict attention to the case in which each country is involved in a preferential agreement with one other country. The purpose of this is to abstract from market power issues that result when preferential arrangements create an asymmetry in the relative size of countries or trading blocs.[2] It will be assumed that the preferential trading arrangement takes the form of a free trade agreement (FTA), rather than a customs union, so that countries do not coordinate in their choice of external tariffs.[3] Denoting the partner countries by i and p, the choice of internal tariffs in the FTA is modelled as an infinitely repeated game in which country i chooses t^i_p and country p chooses t^p_i in each period. The payoff to country i in each period is

$$S^i_p\left(t^i_p, \sum_{k \neq i,p} \tilde{t}^k_p\right) + S^i_i\left(t^p_i + \sum_{k \neq i,p} \tilde{t}^k_i\right) \tag{6}$$

The tariffs of the rest of the world against the partner countries, $\{\tilde{t}^k_p, \tilde{t}^k_i\}$, are assumed to be chosen as best responses in a one-shot tariff-setting game according to the optimal tariff formula (4). The payoff of country i from trade with the rest of the world,

$$\sum_{j \neq i,p} S^i_j\left(t^i_j, \sum_{k \neq i,j} t^k_j\right),$$

is treated as a one-shot game in which i chooses its tariff according to the optimal tariff formula (4).

It is assumed that the FTA will involve a pair of tariffs on internal trade that is symmetric, $t^i_p = t^p_i$, and that is not Pareto dominated by another pair of sustainable tariffs. The punishment phase of the FTA will involve the infinite reversion to a strategy of choosing the optimal tariff against the imports from the former partner country. These assumptions involving the choice of tariffs from the set of supportable agreements and the choice of punishment phase are made so that the structure of preferential trade agreements will be similar to that of multilateral agreements; this facilitates comparisons of the two systems.

With these definitions of multilateralism and preferential trading agreements, we can now turn to an analysis of the respective cases.

3.1 Multilateral trade agreements

Under a multilateral trade agreement, the assumption that trade agreements are symmetric and satisfy the MFN principle means that a trade agreement will consist of a single tariff rate which applies to all imported goods for all countries, $t^i_j = t$ for all i, j and i ≠ j. Substituting these assumptions into (1)–(3), the payoff to a representative country under a multilateral trade agreement that specifies an import tariff of t will be

$$W^m(t) = \alpha X - (X^2 + 3t^2)/8 \tag{7}$$

Since welfare is decreasing in the tariff rate, the member countries will choose the lowest tariff rate that is incentive compatible.

An agreement with tariff t will be incentive compatible if the gain to a country from deviating during the current period is less than the present value of the loss during the punishment phase. If country i were to deviate from this agreement, it would impose the optimal tariff (4) on all of its importables and receive a payoff of $S^i_j(\tilde{t}^i_j(2t), 2t)$ for each j ≠ i. The export sector payoff would be unaffected by the deviation. The gain from deviation in the current period is $G^m(t) = (X - 13t)^2/160$. Following a deviation, the deviating country will receive the Nash equilibrium payoff in all subsequent periods. This yields a loss of $L^m(t) = 3((t^N)^2 - t^2)/8$. Incentive compatibility requires that $G^m(t) \leqslant \delta L^m(t)/(1 - \delta)$ where δ is the discount rate.

The function $G^m(t)$ is decreasing and convex on $[0, t^N]$, with $G^m(t^N) = 0$ and $G^{m'}(t^N) = 0$. $L^m(t)$ is decreasing and concave on $[0, t^N]$, with $L^m(t^N) = 0$ and $L^{m'}(t^N) < 0$. It then follows that for $\delta > 0$, there will exist an interval of tariffs contained in $[0, t^N]$ at which the incentive compatibility constraint is satisfied. If $\delta \geqslant 169/229$, free trade will be incentive compatible. For lower values of the discount parameter, the minimum level of the tariff that is incentive compatible can be obtained by solving for the value of t at which the incentive constraint holds with equality,

$$t^m_{min} = \max\left[\frac{X(169 - 229\delta)}{13(169 - 109\delta)}, 0 \right] \tag{8}$$

Note that the minimum sustainable tariff will be an increasing function of the magnitude of the gains from trade, as represented by X. Although the losses during the punishment phase are increasing in X, the gains from deviation are also increasing in X and the latter effect is dominant.

3.2 Free trade agreements

We now compare the sustainability of tariffs under the multilateral trade system with that in which the world is divided into two free trade areas consisting of two countries each. The pattern of tariffs when there is an FTA between countries 1 and 2 is illustrated in Figure 2.1, which uses solid lines to denote the trade (and corresponding tariffs) between country 1 and the rest of the world. By our assumptions regarding choice of tariffs under an FTA, countries 1 and 2 (3 and 4) will choose a common tariff $t^f_a(t^f_b)$ to support on trade with each other. In trade with the outside countries, 1 and 2 will individually choose optimal external tariffs on trade with the outside countries, 3 and 4, denoted t^{of}_a. In the market for good 3, there will be a tariff of t^f_b imposed by country 4 and optimal tariffs imposed by countries 1 and 2. By the symmetry of the countries, the optimal tariff of each non-member country will be identical, so the tariff imposed on non-

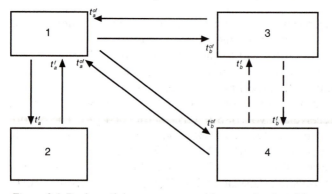

Figure 2.1 Preferential arrangement with countries 1 and 2.

member countries will be the solution to $t^{of} = \tilde{t}(t^f + t^{of})$. Substituting from (4) yields

$$t^{of}(t^f) = \frac{t^f + X}{14} \qquad (9)$$

A similar solution is obtained in the market for good 4, so the external tariffs of the FTA between 1 and 2 are denoted $t_a^{of} = t^{of}(t_b^f)$ and the external tariff imposed by countries 3 and 4 is $t_b^{of} = t^{of}(t_a^f)$. Note that (9) indicates a favourable spillover of FTA liberalization to the world trading system, since reductions in internal tariffs will result in declines in external tariffs by the rest of the world.

Country 1 will receive $S_2^1(t_a^f, 2t^{of}(t_a^f))$ on imports from its partner and $S_1^1(t_a^f + 2t^{of}(t_a^f))$ on exports. On trade with outside countries, 1 receives a surplus of $S_k^1(t^{of}(t_b^f), t_b^f + t^{of}(t_b^f))$ for $k = 3, 4$. Substituting into these expressions from (1), (2), and (7) yields a payoff of

$$W^f(t_a^f, t_b^f) = \alpha X + \frac{-25X^2 - 24t_a^f X - 82(t_a^f)^2 + 30t_b^f + 15(t_b^f)^{2^2}}{196} \qquad (10)$$

Welfare of country 1 will be decreasing and concave in the tariff that it negotiates with country 2, and will be increasing and convex in the tariff set by the other FTA. The latter result follows from the fact that increases in t_b^f increase the supply of goods 3 and 4 to country 1. This results in a terms-of-trade improvement to country 1, and also results in an increase in its tariff on imports from 3 and 4. The fact that W^f is decreasing in t_a^f means that the partner countries will always choose the lowest sustainable internal tariff in their negotiations, since the tariff of the other FTA would be treated as given in any tariff negotiations between the partner countries.

We now examine the sustainability of an internal tariff t^f. If country 1 deviates from its FTA, it will impose its optimal tariff on imports from country 2, given that countries 3 and 4 are charging a tariff of $t_b^{of}(t_a^f)$. Tariffs by country 1 on imports from 3 and 4 are unaffected, because these tariffs are already best responses to t_b^f. This yields a gain from deviation of $G^f(t_a^f) = S_2^1(\tilde{t}(2t^{of}(t_a^f)), 2t^{of}(t_a^f)) - S_2^1(t_a^f, 2t^{of}(t_a^f)) = 2(X - 13t_a^f)^2/735$. In the punishment phase, the FTA between countries 1 and 2 has collapsed, so that these countries revert to charging static optimal tariffs on imports from the former partner. Since countries 3 and 4 are also imposing optimal tariffs on these goods, the markets for goods 1 and 2 will be characterized by a trade war in which all countries impose $t^N = X/13$ in these markets. Even though countries 3 and 4 are not parties to the FTA between 1 and 2, they will contribute to the punishment indirectly because the increase in tariffs by the partner countries will lead to a rise in tariffs by the outside countries from (9). The markets for goods 3 and 4 are unaffected by this trade war, because 1 and 2 are already imposing optimal tariffs in these markets. The loss to the deviating country during the punishment phase is $L^f(t_a^f) = [S_2^1(t_a^f, 2t^{of}(t_a^f)) - S_2^1(t^N, 2t^N)] + [S_1^1(t_a^f + 2t^{of}(t_a^f)) - S_1^1(3t^N)] = t^N - t_a^f)(197X + 533t_a^f)/1274$. Note that since both G^f and L^f are independent of t_b^f, the sustainability of one FTA is independent of the tariff chosen by the other FTA.[4] An FTA equilibrium will be sustainable if $G^f(t) \leqslant \delta L^f(t)/(1 - \delta)$. Using arguments similar to those for the multilateral case, there will exist a value t_{min}^f for $\delta > 0$ such that an FTA is incentive compatible for all $t \in [t_{min}^f, t^N]$.[5] Solving for the value at which the incentive constraint holds with strict equality, we obtain

$$t_{min}^f(\delta) = \max\left[\frac{X(676 - 3631\delta)}{13(676 - 61\delta)}, 0\right] \tag{11}$$

For $\delta > 676/3631$, free trade between the FTA members is incentive compatible.

Since the sustainability problem is symmetric for both FTAs and each will choose the minimum level sustainable tariff, the level of world welfare that is sustainable with FTAs is obtained by evaluating (10) at $t_a^f = t_b^f = t_{min}^f(\delta)$. The resulting welfare level can then be compared to that sustainable under a multilateral agreement, obtained by evaluating (7) at $t_{min}(\delta)$. There will be two conflicting effects present in the comparison of world welfare under the two regimes. The first is that for a given level of the tariff under the trade agreement, the multilateral system yields higher world welfare than does the FTA. If we evaluate (10) at a common agreement for each FTA, we obtain

$$W^f(t^f, t^f) = \alpha X + \frac{-25X^2 + 6t^fX - 67(t^f)^2}{196} \tag{12}$$

Comparing (12) with (7) yields $W^m(t) > W^f(t, t)$ for $t \in [0, t^N]$. Welfare of the representative country with FTAs is concave in t and is maximized at $t^f = 3X/67$. This contrasts with the multilateral case, where the welfare of the representative country is maximized at $t = 0$. This follows from the fact that when an FTA reduces its internal tariff, the external tariff decreases, but by a smaller amount. The average level of tariff falls but the difference between the tariffs increases. The former effect raises world welfare, but the latter effect decreases welfare. For sufficiently low tariffs, the latter effect will dominate and world welfare will fall when internal tariffs are reduced. In particular, the welfare level with free internal trade will be $\alpha X - 25X^2/196$, which is less than the Nash equilibrium level of welfare from (4).

On the other hand, it can be seen by comparison of (6) and (9) that $t_{min}^f(\delta) \leqslant t_{min}^m(\delta)$ for $\delta \in [0, 1]$. The benefit of deviating from an FTA is less than that of deviating from a multilateral agreement because the country is also deviating in only one market. However, the losses in the punishment phase are also lower because the punishment occurs in only one market. This result suggests that the punishment is relatively more severe in the FTA case. A contributing factor to the severity of the punishment in the FTA is that the non-member countries will also increase their tariffs in the punishment phase. There is thus a favourable punishment phase spillover from the other countries.

It is clear that for values of $\delta \geqslant 169/229$ the multilateral system must dominate the regional one, because global free trade will be sustainable. On the other hand, it can be established using (7), (8), (11) and (12) that

$$\left(\frac{\partial W^f(t^N, t^N)}{\partial t_a^f} + \frac{\partial W^f(t^N, t^N)}{\partial t_b^f} \right) \frac{\partial t_{min}^f(0)}{\partial \delta} > \frac{dW^m(t^N)}{dt_{min}^f} \frac{\partial t_{min}^m(0)}{\partial \delta} > 0$$

This ensures that the FTA system must yield higher welfare than the multilateral system for values of δ in the neighbourhood of 0, where cooperation is very difficult to sustain. Figure 2.2 illustrates $W^m(t_{min}^m)$ and $W^f(t_{min}^f)$ for the case where $X = 13$ and $\alpha = 5$, which yields $t^N = 1$ and $W^N = 44.5$.[6] In this case, the FTA yields a higher welfare level for $\delta < 0.15$.

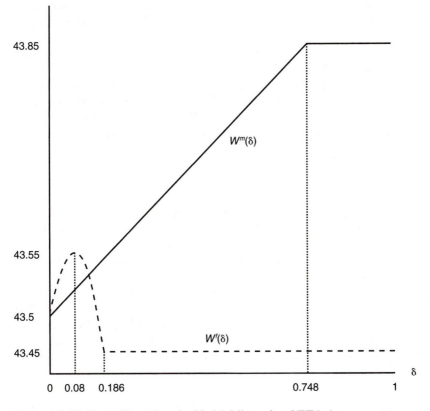

Figure 2.2 Welfare of Best Sustainable Multilateral and ETA Agreements.

The fact that the payoff under the FTA is decreasing for $\delta \in [0.1, 0.19]$ results from a coordination failure associated with the FTA case. The maximum payoff under preferential arrangements is attained when $t^f = 2X/13 = 0.58$ in this case, which is supportable for $\delta > 0.1$. The FTA equilibrium would yield higher payoffs if the internal tariffs were held at 0.58 for $\delta > 0.1$. However, each FTA will treat the internal tariff of the other FTA as given and will choose the lowest sustainable tariff. Similar conclusions were obtained for other values of X.

4 Trade agreements with minmax punishment schemes

One might expect that a multilateral agreement has greater power to punish a defector, because it uses the agreement to coordinate punishment schemes using the power of all countries. However, one of the results of the previous section was that when an FTA member punished a defecting partner, the outcome in that market was the same as if the country had deviated from a multilateral agreement. This occurred because the punishment by the partner induced higher tariffs by the non-member countries, so that the outside countries were being induced to participate in the punishment because of the complementarity among import tariffs in (4). The purpose of this section is to determine whether multilateral agreements have punishments that are relatively more effective than FTAs when punishments more severe than the Nash equilibrium are chosen. One way to capture this notion is to assume that agreements punish defectors by holding them to their minmax payoffs, which means that member countries choose tariffs that result in the lowest possible payoff to the defecting country.[7]

In the case of a multilateral agreement, the minmax payoff is

$$\min_{t^2, t^3, t^4} \left[\max_{t^1} W_1(t^1, t^2, t^3, t^4) \right]$$

The tariffs for country 1 are given by the optimal tariff formula (4), given the tariffs chosen by the rest of the world. It is clear from differentiation of (1) that tariffs on goods $j \neq 1$ by the rest of the world serve to raise the welfare of country 1 by improving its terms of trades. Therefore, $t_j^k = 0$ for $k, j \neq 1$ in the minmax solution. The welfare of country 1 will be decreasing in t_1^k for $k \neq 1$, so these tariffs will be set at the prohibitive level of $t_1^k = X$. Evaluating the welfare of country 1 at this solution yields a payoff of $W^m_{minmax} = \alpha X - 2X^2/5$. Defining $L^m_{minmax} = W^m(t) - W^m_{minmax}$, the minimum discount parameter that can support the tariff rate t will be one at which the incentive constraint holds with strict equality. Solving this equation yields

$$\delta^m_{minmax}(t) = \frac{G^m(t)}{G^M(t) + L^m_{minmax}(t)} = \frac{(X - 13t)^2}{45X^2 - 26Xt + 109t^2} \tag{13}$$

Free trade can be supported using minmax punishments in the multilateral case for $\delta \geqslant 1/45$, which is substantially lower than the value obtained for the case with the Nash equilibrium punishments.

In the case of an FTA between countries 1 and 2, the minmax payoff is

$$\min_{\mathbf{t}^2} \left[\max_{\mathbf{t}^1} W_1(\mathbf{t}^1, \mathbf{t}^2, \mathbf{t}^3, \mathbf{t}^4) \right]$$

The tariff vectors of the outside countries 3 and 4 are given by (9) for trade with countries 1 and 2, and are given by the cooperative rate on trade with each other. The tariffs of country 1 are chosen according to the optimal tariff formula (4) for trade with all countries, as in the multilateral case. For country 2, tariffs on goods 3 or 4 will raise the welfare of country 1 from (1), so the optimal tariff on these goods is zero. The welfare of country 1 is decreasing t_1^2, so country 2 will set this tariff as high as possible. The maximum tariff that can be imposed by 2 is the prohibitive tariff on imports from 1, which is $t_1^2 = 2X/5$. Note that the punishment strategy by 2 will have a spillover on the tariffs imposed by the outside countries by (9), as in the case of Nash punishments, because the optimal tariffs of the outside countries are increasing in the tariff of 2. However, the punishment tariffs in this case are below those imposed in the multilateral case because country 2 cannot coordinate with the outside countries to force country 1 to the autarky level in its export market. Utilizing these tariffs in the welfare function (3) yields a payoff to country 1 under minmax punishment in the FTA case of $W_{minmax}^f = \alpha X - (164867X^2)/828100 > W_{minmax}^m$. Defining $L_{minmax}^f = W^f(t) - W_{minmax}^f$, the minimum discount parameter for this case will be

$$\delta_{minmax}^f(t) = \frac{G^f(t)}{G^f(t) + L_{minmax}^f(t)} = \frac{(X-13t)^2}{(184486X^2 - 99710Xt + 293215t^2)/6760}$$

(14)

It can be shown that the denominator of (14) is no greater than that of (13) for $t \in [0, x]$, so that $\delta_{minmax}^f(t) \geqslant \delta_{minmax}^m(t)$. Thus, cooperation is easier to maintain for all tariff rates under multilateralism than under an FTA when minmax punishments are used as part of the agreement.

These results suggest that multilateralism has the potential to be more successful at maintaining trade agreements when it is able to make use of its power to impose the most severe punishments. Maggi (1999) shows the benefits of multilateral punishments in a three-country world in which relations between trading partners are asymmetric because a country imports more from one trading partner than the other. A country is less able to punish a deviation by a trading partner from which it imports a small quantity, so that the multilateral trading system coordinates punishment by having a country that imports a large quantity from the deviator punish the deviation. In the present context the trade patterns are balanced, so that each country has the same ability to punish a deviant. The advantages of multilateral punishment in this case arise from the ability to push a deviating country to very low welfare. In the case of regionalism, severely punitive tariffs by one country cause the deviator to switch trade to outside countries that impose less severe punishment. Multilateral punishments prevent this from taking place.

It should be noted however that the existing World Trade Organization (WTO) structure does not seem to take advantage of these severe punishment schemes. Punishments for deviations involve the withdrawal of equivalent concessions against the deviating party, which seems more consistent with the notion of static Nash punishments.

5 Transportation costs between continents

The analysis of the preceding sections assumed that the countries had symmetric trading relations with all partner countries. In this section we introduce a regional structure with an asymmetry in trade relations due to transportation costs. The world is assumed to be divided into two continents, with two countries located on each continent. There is a cost of c per unit on any goods imported from a country on the other continent, but zero transport cost on goods coming from the country on the same continent. In this section we analyse how the results of the third section, regarding the relative benefits of multilateral trade agreements and FTAs, are affected by this transport cost structure.

The demand and supply structure for each good is assumed to be identical to that in previous sections. Since each exporter sells to two countries on the other continent, the price of good j in the exporting country will be

$$p_j^i = \alpha - (X + \sum_i t_j^i + 2c)/4.$$

The price in the importing country will be $p_j^i = p_j^j + t_j^i + c_j^i$, where $c_j^i = c$ if i and j are on different continents and 0 otherwise. Substituting these results into the definitions of surplus in (1) and (2)

$$S_j^i\left(t_j^i, c_j^i, \sum_{k \neq i}(t_j^k + c_j^k)\right) = \frac{u(u - 8t_j^i)}{32} \text{ for } u \equiv X + \sum_{k \neq i}(t_j^k + c_j^k) - 3(t_j^i + c_j^i) \geq 0$$

$$S_j^i\left(2c + \sum_{k \neq j} t_j^k\right) = \alpha X + \frac{\left(2c + \sum_{k \neq j} t_j^k\right)^2 - 6\left(2c + \sum_{k \neq j} t_j^k\right)X - 7X^2}{32}$$

for $2c + \sum_{k \neq j} t_j^k \leq X$ (15)

where the inequality constraints reflect the requirement that trade barriers and transport costs not be so high that trade is eliminated. National welfare will be the sum of the sectoral surpluses.

The optimal tariff formula with transport costs is obtained by maximizing S_j^i with respect to t_j^i, yielding

$$\tilde{t}_j^i\left(c_j^i, \sum_{k \neq i}(t_j^k + c_j^k)\right) = \left(X - 3c_j^i + \sum_{k \neq i}(t_j^k + c_j^k)\right)/15 \tag{16}$$

Comparing with (4), it can be seen that the existence of transport costs leads to higher tariffs on goods from the same continent and lower tariffs on goods from the other continent, for a given level of tariffs by other countries. This follows because the transport costs tend to lower (raise) the elasticity of demand for goods from the same (other) continent by increasing (decreasing) the volume of trade at given tariffs. Since there is an asymmetry between countries in this case, the Nash equilibrium tariffs imposed on the regional trading partner (denoted by r) will differ from those on the distant partner (d). Solving for the equilibrium tariffs yields

$$t^{Nr} = \frac{X}{13} + \frac{3c}{26}; t^{Nd} = \frac{X}{13} - \frac{7c}{52}; W^N = \alpha X + \frac{1293c^2 - 344X^2 - 1344cX}{2704}$$

$$\tag{17}$$

Nash equilibrium tariffs on regional trading partners will be higher than those on the distant partners.

5.1 Multilateral trade agreements

Under a multilateral trade agreement, we continue to impose the requirement that the same tariff be imposed on imports from all partner countries. Utilizing (15) for the case of $t_j^i = t$ for all $i \neq j$ yields an expression for welfare under a multilateral trade agreement

$$W^m(t, c) = \alpha X - \frac{X^2 + 3t^2 - 4c(X - c)}{8} \quad \text{for } t < X - 2c \tag{18}$$

Tariff levels exceeding $X - 2c$ would never be chosen under a multilateral agreement, because they would eliminate trade with the distant country.

A deviating country will impose optimal tariffs on imports, with the optimal tariffs differing between regional and distant partners. If these optimal tariffs are substituted into the import surplus expressions, we obtain a gain from deviation of $G^m(t, c) = [3(X - 13t)^2 + 4c(3c + 13t - X)]/480$. The effect of transport costs is to reduce the gains from deviation iff $t < (X - 6c)/13$, which implies that increases in transport costs raise the incentives for multilateral deviations when tariffs are close to the Nash equilibrium values. In particular, note that in the previous examples the gains from deviation were equal to zero at the Nash equilibrium tariff. In the present case the Nash tariff differs across countries, so with the MFN principle in place the gains from deviation are minimized at $t = X/(13 + c/9)$. Under the assumption of reversion to the one-shot Nash equilibrium in the punishment phase, the per period loss punishment phase is the difference between (17) and W^N, $L^m(t, c)$ $= [3(X^2 - 169t^2)/1352] + c(59c - 8X)/2704$. Increases in transport costs will reduce the losses from punishment iff $c < 4X/59$.

These results on deviation and punishment phases suggest a non-monotonic relationship between transport costs and the sustainability of cooperation. When tariffs are high (i.e. in the neighbourhood of the non-cooperative Nash equilibrium) and transport costs are low, the gains from deviation are increased and the losses from punishment are decreasing in the level of transport costs. Both of these forces will tend to make cooperation harder to sustain as transport costs rise. These effects are reversed for low tariffs. They can be formalized by solving for the minimum discount parameter for which a tariff t can be supported under multilateralism

$$\delta^m(t, c) = \frac{G^m(t, c)}{L^m(t, c) + G^m(t, c)}$$

$$= \frac{169(3(13t^2 - X)^2 + 4c(3c + 13t - X))}{(687X^2 + 13182tX + 55263t^2) + c(3798c + 8788t - 916X)} \quad (19)$$

It may be easier to see the relationship between transport costs and the minimum discount parameter by plotting (19) for several different tariff levels. Figure 2.3 illustrates the minimum discount parameter for the case

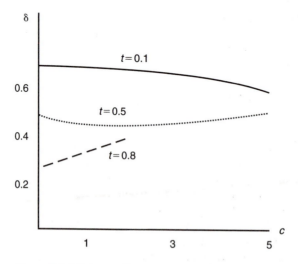

Figure 2.3 Minimum discount rates as function of inter-continental transport costs.

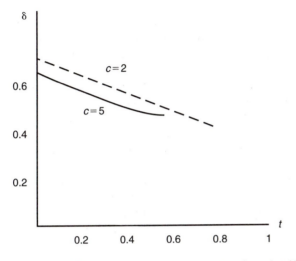

Figure 2.4 Minimum discount factors as function of tariffs.

in which $X = 13$ and $c \in [0, 5]$, which yields a Nash tariff of 1 when there are no transport costs. For a relatively low tariff of 0.1, the minimum discount factor is monotonically decreasing in c. For higher tariffs of 0.5 and 0.8, the minimum discount factor initially decreases in c and then increases in c.

A second point to note regarding (19) is the sustainability of tariffs for very low values of the discount parameter. In the expressions for minimum sustainable tariffs in (8) and (11), the minimum sustainable tariff approaches the Nash equilibrium tariff as $\delta \to 0$. This follows because both the gains from deviation approach zero more rapidly than do the losses from punishment as t approaches the Nash level. However, with transport costs there is a difference between the Nash tariffs imposed on distant and regional partners. Since multilateral agreements must utilize an MFN principle, there is no single tariff that will drive the gains from deviation to zero. This results in the minimum discount factor being bounded away from zero when transport costs are positive. This is illustrated in Figure 2.4, which shows the relationship between the minimum discount parameter and the level of tariffs for alternative levels of transport costs. With $c = 0.1$, there is no single tariff level that can be supported for $\delta < 0.05$. When $c = 5$, multilateral cooperation cannot be supported for $\delta < 0.49$. Thus, multilateral cooperation becomes increasingly difficult to sustain for high levels of transport costs because the MFN principle becomes a significant constraint on the ability to sustain cooperation.

5.2 Free trade areas

We next examine the sustainable tariffs between member countries in the case where countries pair up and form free trade areas. Under an FTA, a member country plays a repeated game with the partner country, while imposing an optimal tariff against non-member countries. In the absence of transport costs, it did not matter how the countries paired up because the trade flows were symmetric between all pairs of countries. When inter-regional transport costs are introduced, the agreement will differ depending on whether the partner country is on the same or a different continent. Therefore, we will consider sustainability of cooperation for both types of FTAs.

First consider the optimal tariff imposed on trade with outside countries. If country 1 forms an FTA with country 2, which is located on the same continent, then it will impose an optimal tariff on trade with both of the distant countries as illustrated in Figure 2.1. Using the same logic as in the derivation of (9), we obtain

$$t^{ofr}(t^f, c) = \frac{t^f + X - 2c}{14} \tag{20}$$

The external tariffs of regional FTA partners are decreasing in the level of transport costs. Using (20), the payoff to country 1 under a regional FTA can then be derived as in (10), where t_a^f is the internal tariff of country 1's FTA and t_b^f is the tariff of the other country's FTA.

$$W^{fr}(t_a^f, t_b^f, c) = \alpha X +$$
$$\frac{-25X^2 - 24t_a^f(X - 2c) - 82(t_a^f)^2 + 30t_b^f(X - 2c) + 15(t_b^f)^2 + 96c(c - X)}{196}$$

$$\tag{21}$$

Welfare of a bloc is decreasing in its own tariff for $X \geqslant 2c$, a condition which is required for inter-continental trade to occur, so a bloc will always choose the lowest sustainable internal tariff. Welfare is decreasing in the internal tariff of the other bloc.

This welfare level can be compared with that obtained if country 1 chooses to form an FTA with a country 3, which is located on the other continent. This case is slightly more complicated because the external tariff of 1 on imports from country 2, t_2^{ofd}, will differ from that on imports from 4, t_4^{ofd}, because of the difference in transport costs. In the market for good 2, country 1's tariff is a best response to the agreement tariff between 4 and 2 and the optimal tariff imposed by 3 on 2. By the symmetry between 1 and 3, 3's tariff on 2 will be the same as 1's tariff on 4, so $t_2^{ofd} = \tilde{t}(0, t_b^f + t_4^{ofd} + 2c)$. In the market for good 4, country 1's tariff on a distant non-member is the best response to the agreement tariff imposed by 2 on 4 and the optimal tariff on a regional non-member imposed by 3 on 4 (which will equal t_2^{ofd} by the symmetry between 1 and 3). This yields $t_4^{ofd} = \tilde{t}(c, t_b^f + t_2^{ofd} + c)$. Solving these two equations simultaneously, we have

$$t_2^{ofd}(t^f, c) = \frac{t^f + X}{14} + \frac{c}{8}, \quad t_4^{ofd}(t^f, c) = \frac{t^f + X}{14} - \frac{c}{8} \tag{22}$$

The external tariff on the regional non-member will be higher in equilibrium than that on the distant non-member. Note that for a given level of an agreement tariff between the partners, all external tariffs are higher under an FTA with a distant partner than with a regional partner. This results from the fact that countries impose higher tariffs against nearby countries in this model, and this effect spills over to affect all external tariff levels under FTAs with distant partners due to the complementarities between tariffs. In the case of an FTA with a distant country, country 1 receives a surplus of $S_3^1(t^f, 0, t_2^{ofd}(t_a^f, c) + t_4^{ofd}(t_a^f, c) + c)$ on imports from the partner country, $S_2^1(t_2^{ofd}(t_b^f, c), 0, t^f + t_4^{ofd}(t_b^f, c) + 2)$ from the regional non-member, $S_3^1(t_4^{ofd}(t_b^f, c), c, t_2^{ofd}(t_b^f, c) + t^? + c)$ from the distant non-member, and $S_1^1(t^f + t_2^{ofd}(t_a^f, c) + t_4^{ofd}(t_a^f, c) + 2c)$ from the export sector. Solving yields

$$W^{fd}(t_a^f, t_b^f, c) = \alpha X + \frac{-25X^2 - 24t_a^f X - 82(t_a^f)^2 + 30t_b^f X + 15(t_b^f)^2}{196}$$

$$+ \frac{c(1519c - 1568X)}{3136} \tag{23}$$

W^{fd} also has the property of being decreasing and concave in t_a^f and increasing and convex in t_b^f.

Due to the symmetry of the incentive constraints between the two FTAs and the fact that each FTA will choose the minimum sustainable tariff, we will have $t_a^f = t_b^f$ in any FTA equilibrium involving either regional or distant FTAs. One way to illustrate the difference between the two types of FTAs is to compare the welfare of a representative country under the two different types of preferential arrangements, holding the internal tariff constants across the two regimes. Subtracting (23) from (21) yields $W^{fr}(t^f, t^f, c) - W^{fd}(t^f, t^f, c) = c(32X + 17c - 192t^f)/3136$. With $c > 0$, the welfare under an FTA with a regional partner will be higher than that for a distant partner for any agreement tariff that is less than $X/6 + 17c/192$. Since this will hold for any tariffs that are below the Nash equilibrium level, FTAs with regional partners dominate those with distant partners at a given agreement tariff. The reason for the dominance of regional agreements is that the external tariffs imposed when countries form FTAs with distant partners are higher than those when countries form FTAs with regional partners. This increase in world tariffs will make regional FTAs more attractive, given the level of the internal tariff.

We now turn to the sustainability of tariffs under the respective types of FTAs. It can be shown using similar arguments to those in the derivation of (11) that the minimum sustainable tariff with a regional FTA will be[8]

$$t^{fr}_{min}(\delta) = \max\left[\frac{52X + 78c - (7262X - 5487c)\delta/26}{676 - 618\delta}, 0 \right] \qquad (24)$$

Tariffs below the Nash equilibrium tariff rate will be sustainable for very low discount parameters because (23) is decreasing in δ with $t^{fr}_{min}(0) = t^{nr}$. For the case of an FTA with a distant partner, the minimum sustainable tariff is

$$t^{fd}_{min}(\delta) = \max\left[\frac{52X - 91c - (14524X - 9037c)\delta/52}{676 - 618\delta}, 0 \right] \qquad (25)$$

t^{fd}_{min} is decreasing in δ with $t^{fd}_{min}(0) = t^{nd}$. Subtracting (24) from (23) yields $t^{fr}_{min}(\delta) - t^{fd}_{min}(\delta) > 0$. The difference reflects the fact that in general it is more attractive to deviate from a trade agreement when c is lower, so cooperation is easier (i.e. lower tariffs are sustainable) with a distant partner.

These results suggest conflicting effects in the evaluation of the attractiveness of regional and distant FTAs. The FTA with a regional partner provides a higher payoff at a given internal tariff, but at a given discount parameter the regional FTA will not be able to support as low a tariff rate. Substituting (24) and (25) into the respective welfare functions (21) and (23), we can derive the difference in welfare between the regional and distant FTA at given δ to be

$$\Gamma(\delta) = W^{fr}(\delta) - W^{fd}(\delta) =$$
$$\frac{15c\delta[(146692 + 209338\delta)X - (107315 + 141858\delta)c]}{52(618\delta - 676)^2} \qquad (26)$$

$\Gamma(0) = 0$ because both types of FTAs yield the Nash equilibrium payoff at $\delta = 0$. For $\delta > 0$, the sign of this expression will be determined by the sign of the term in brackets. By (15), $X \geq 2c$ is required for there to be imports from distant countries. This condition is sufficient to ensure that the bracketed expression in (26) will be positive for all $\delta \in [0, 1]$, so that FTAs with regional partners will always be preferred to FTAs with a distant partner.

These results are consistent with the notion that 'natural trading blocs' between neighbouring countries are more likely to be welfare improving. It should be noted that the exercise considered here differs from that performed by Frankel, Stein and Wei (1995) and Bhagwati and Panagariya (1996), who consider the effect of preferential reductions from an initial point of equal tariffs. Frankel, Stein and Wei utilize a general equilibrium model with constant elasticity of substitution models and find a significant range of parameter values for which regional agreements are preferred. Bhagawati and Panagariya, on the other hand, use a model with linear excess demands and find a preference for tariff reductions with a distant partner. In the exercise considered in this chapter, tariffs against regional and distant countries would not be the same in the initial equilibrium because of the different degree of market power created by transport costs. The regional FTA has the advantage of eliminating what would otherwise be relatively high tariffs against nearby partners.

Figure 2.5 illustrates the difference in payoffs between the regional FTA, distant FTA and multilateral system utilizing the same parameter values as in Figure 2.3, but with an inter-continental transport cost of $c = 2$; it shows how the regional FTA dominates the FTA with distant partners. Second, it illustrates how the existence of transport costs between countries expands the range of discount parameters for which preferential agreements yield higher welfare, since multilateral agreements cannot be sustained for $\delta < 0.39$ in this case.

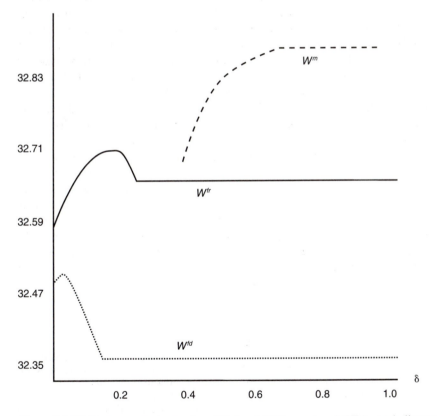

Figure 2.5 Welfare comparison of multilateral FTA, regional FTA, and distant FTA with transport costs.

6 Conclusion

This analysis has departed from previous work by comparing the ability of preferential trade agreements and multilateral agreements to sustain trade agreements. The results illustrated a tradeoff between greater sustainability of internal tariffs under preferential agreements against the losses resulting from discrimination in tariffs against non-member countries. The advantage in sustainability of tariffs under preferential agreements was obtained in the case where punishment took the form of reversion to the Nash equilibrium of the one-shot game, and resulted from the fact that an FTA could impose relatively severe punishment in the event of deviation in partner markets because punishment induced higher tariffs by outside countries.

A second point concerned the relative advantages of regional and distant preferential trade agreements. In the presence of transport costs, countries will have higher optimal tariffs against nearby countries. One might anticipate that this fact would make it more difficult to support trade liberalization with nearby countries, because the incentive to deviate at a given agreement tariff would be higher. However, it was shown that this effect was more than offset by the fact that the welfare level under regional FTAs is higher than that with a distant partner (with given internal tariffs). This is due to the fact that FTAs with distant partners have higher external tariffs against all countries, which leads to lower world welfare under distant FTAs. Also, the results indicated that multilateral trade agreements with the MFN principle become more difficult to sustain in the presence of transport costs because deviation against some trading partners is more attractive than deviation against others.

These results suggest several directions for future work. One is to examine interactions between multilateral and regional agreements when the degree of enforceability of both agreements is endogenous. A second issue concerns the role of other factors which may affect the enforceability of regional agreement relative to multilateral agreements. For example, the incorporation of side agreements involving environmental standards, competition policy, and infrastructure investments in regional agreements may reflect the bundling of issues among regional trading partners to enhance the enforceability of agreements.

Notes

1. Bond and Syropoulos (1996b) examine how an increase in the size of trading blocs affects multilateral cooperation in a many-country world. Bagwell and Staiger (1997a, 1997b) examine changes in trade relations over time between two countries when preferential trading agreements with outside countries, either free trade areas or customs unions, are anticipated in the future. Bagwell and Staiger (1999) and Bond, Syropoulos and Winters (2001) examine how the existence of preferential arrangements between two countries affects trade relations with a third.

2. Bond and Syropoulos (1996a) focus on the difference in market power effects between expansion in the absolute size of trading blocs (holding relative size constant) and increases in relative size of trading blocs in the case where blocs take the form of customs unions.

3. If instead the countries chose to form a customs union, they would cooperate in the choice of external tariff as well. Since the customs union would choose the external tariff to maximize union welfare, the union will take advantage of its market power and set higher external tariffs than would a customs union, as emphasized by Kennan and Riezman (1990). While this effect is favourable for a customs union for a given level of the external tariff imposed by the other union, the Nash equilibrium when both unions are setting their external tariffs will involve higher external tariffs for both unions. It can be shown that when both customs unions can commit to internal and external tariffs, the Nash equilibrium external tariffs is $X/6$. Since this tariff level is substantially higher than in the Nash equilibrium (5), it results in a world welfare level that is lower than W^N. In light of this negative aspect of customs unions, we will concentrate here on the case of FTAs.

4. In particular, we do not have to worry about the possibility that a collapse of one FTA creates a domino effect on the other FTA in the following period.

5. The function $G^a(t^f)$ is non-increasing and convex for $t \in [0, t^N]$ with $G^f(t^N) = G^{f_1}(t^N) = 0$. $L^{fa}(t)$ is a decreasing and concave function for $t \in [0, t^N]$ with $L^{fa}(t^N) = 0$. If $G^f(0) > L^f(0)$, then there will be a unique value $t \in (0, t^N)$ at which the constraints hold with equality when $\delta > 0$. If $G^f(0) \leq L^f(0)$ then free trade is sustainable.

6. These parameter values yield a Nash equilibrium tariff rate of 100 per cent and a welfare loss of the Nash equilibrium relative to free trade of approximately 1 per cent.

7. While these punishments are more severe than the Nash punishments, they have the disadvantage that they are not subgame perfect. They are used here because they are relatively simple to calculate, and they illustrate how coordinated punishments can be used to yield payoffs to the deviator that are below the static Nash level. If we restrict attention to punishments that are subgame perfect, we could utilize the subgame perfect payoff that yields the deviator the lowest payoff of any subgame perfect payoff following Abreu (1986). Such payoffs, even if attention is restricted to symmetric punishment schemes, are difficult to calculate in this case.

8. With a regional FTA, there is a deviation gain of $G^{mr}(c, t^r) = 338(t^{nr} - t^f)^2/735$ and a punishment loss of $L^{mr}(c, t) = (t^{nr} - t^f)(394X + 1066t^f - 501c)/2548$. With a distant partner FTA, the deviation gain is $G^{fd}(c, t^f) = 2704(t^{nd} - t^f)^2/5880$ and the punishment loss is $L^{fd}(t^f, c) = (t^{nr} - t^f)(788X + 2132t^f - 287c)/5096$. In each case, there will be an interval of sustainable tariffs $[t^f_{min}, t^N]$ for any $\delta > 0$ with (25) and (26) being the minimum values in the respective cases.

References

Abreu, D. (1986) 'Extremal equilibria of oligopolistic supergames', *Journal of Economic Theory*, 39: 191–225.

Bagwell, K. and Staiger, R.W. (1997a) 'Multilateral tariff cooperation during the formations of customs unions', *Journal of International Economics* 42: 91–123.

—— (1997b) 'Multilateral tariff cooperation during the formation of regional free trade areas', *International Economic Review*, 38: 291–320.

—— (1999) 'Regionalism and multilateral tariff cooperation', in J. Piggot and

A. Woodland (eds), *International Trade Policy and the Pacific Rim*, New York: St Martins Press.

Bhagwati, J. and Panagariya, A. (1996) 'Preferential trading areas and multilateralism—strangers, friends, or foes?', in *The Economics of Preferential Trading Arrangements*, J. Bhagwati and A. Panagariya (eds); American Enterprise Institute, Washington, DC: 1–78.

Bond, E.W. and Syropoulos, C. (1996a) 'The size of trading blocs: market power and world welfare effects', *Journal of International Economics*, 40: 411–38.

—— (1996b) 'Trading blocs and the sustainability of inter-regional cooperation', in M. Canzoneri, W.J. Ethier and V. Grilli (eds), *The New Transatlantic Economy*, London: Cambridge University Press.

Bond, E.W., Syropoulos, C. and Winters, L.A. (2001) 'Deepening of regional integration and multilateral trade agreements, *Journal of International Economics*, 53: 335–61.

Frankel, J., Stein E. and Wei S.-J. (1995) 'Trading blocs and the Americas: the natural, unnatural, and the super-natural', *Journal of Development Economics*: 61–95.

Kennan, J. and Riezman, R. (1990) 'Optimal tariff equilibria with customs unions', *Canadian Journal of Economics*, 23: 70–83.

Krugman, P. (1991) 'Is bilateralism bad?', in E. Helpman and A. Razin (eds), *International Trade and Trade Policy*, Cambridge: MIT Press.

Maggi, G. (1999) 'The role of multilateral institutions in international trade cooperation', *American Economic Review*, 89, 190–214.

3 The 'gains' from preferential trade liberalization in the CGE models

Where do they come from?

Arvind Panagariya and Rupa Duttagupta

1 Introduction

In a series of papers, Bhagwati and Panagariya (1996), Bhagwati, Greenaway and Panagariya (1998) and Panagariya (1996, 1997a, 1998) have argued forcefully that a tariff preference by a country is likely to hurt itself and benefit its union partner. If the union members are small in relation to the rest of the world and the country giving the tariff preference imports the good from the partner as well as the rest of the world, the tariff preference has no impact on the country's internal price and hence the allocation of resources. Instead, to the extent of the tariff preference, the tariff revenue collected previously on the imports from the partner is transferred to the latter's exporting firms as additional profit. If the union members are large in relation to the rest of the world, the tariff preference leads to a deterioration of the country's terms of trade. In either case, the presumption is that the country loses from its own preferential trade liberalization.

A key implication of this argument is that, as a result of the North American Free Trade Agreement (NAFTA), which effectively amounted to one-way preferences by Mexico to the United States, Mexico was hurt and the United States benefited. However, this view has not gone uncontested, in fact, many Computable-General-Equilibrium (CGE) modellers, among others, have reached exactly the opposite conclusion. They contend that repeated exercises have shown that preferential liberalization is beneficial to the country undertaking such liberalization and that the trade-creation effect far outweighs trade-diversion effect. Robinson and Thierfelder (1999, 2) have promoted this view as follows:

> The results from a large number of model-based empirical studies strongly support a few robust conclusions about RTAs [Regional Trade Agreements]: (1) they increase welfare of participating countries; (2) aggregate trade creation is much larger than aggregate trade diversion...

To be sure, not everyone agrees with this summary of model-based studies. Thus, not too long ago, after a careful survey of both *ex post* empirical studies and CGE models, Srinivasan, Whalley and Wooton (1993, 72) had reached quite a different conclusion:[1]

> We, therefore, see these studies as shedding somewhat incomplete and at times conflicting light on the effects of post-war RIAs [Regional Integration Agreements] on trade and welfare, to say nothing of what might be the likely effects of prospective RIAs. There seems to be near unanimity that trade creation occurred in Europe, but its size and the precise contribution of the RIAs relative to other factors is unclear. Nor is it clear that significant trade creation from RIAs has occurred elsewhere.

This very different conclusion notwithstanding, the issue remains as to the source of the gains from preferential liberalization in the group of CGE studies surveyed by Robinson and Thierfelder (1999). In this chapter, we subject the CGE models, based on *conventional* theory, to a critical examination.[2] We argue that when these models generate benefits to a country from its own preferential liberalization, they do so by recourse to models characterized by internally inconsistent assumptions. Further, even within the wrong model structure, the gains are generated by choosing questionable values of some key parameters. If a theoretically correct *conventional* model is chosen, the CGE models are unlikely to generate positive benefits to a country from its own preferential liberalization. We hypothesize that in addition to the structure of the model and parameter values, investigators can abuse the specific functional forms used to operationalize the models. We do not investigate this hypothesis here, however.

Unearthing the features of CGE models that drive them is often a time-consuming exercise. This is because their sheer size, facilitated by recent advances in computer technology, makes it difficult to pinpoint the precise source of a particular result. They often remain a black box. Indeed, frequently, authors are themselves unable to explain their results intuitively and, when pressed, resort to uninformative answers such as 'trade creation dominates trade diversion', or vice versa. Cognizant of this problem, in this chapter, we will provide our numerical examples using very simple and stylized models, which are strictly in conformity with theory and are fully transparent. The challenge to CGE modellers is to offer similar stylized counterparts of their models, so that others can examine the assumptions underlying them.

The chapter is organized as follows. In section 2, we present some simple, partial-equilibrium theory, which must form an integral part of any model of preferential liberalization. Relying on a homogeneous-good, small-union model, we already establish here a strong presumption that preferential liberalization by a country hurts itself and benefits the recipient of the preference. In section 3, we argue that many CGE models from which Robinson and Thierfelder (1999) have drawn their conclusions are fundamentally flawed, in that they combine the Armington assumption with fixed terms of trade. The Armington assumption says that goods are differentiated by the country of origin. If that is the case, the goods produced by a country, no matter how small, are not supplied by any other country. The country necessarily has market power in these goods. Using stylized numerical examples, we then demonstrate that, with appropriate closure of the model, the results of section 2 remain valid in the presence of product differentiation according to the Armington assumption.[3] In section 4, we show that many of the CGE models generate benefits from preferential liberalization by recourse to a wrong model and wrong parameter values. Using the right parameter values, even within this wrong model, is likely to lead to losses from preferential liberalization. Section 5 concludes the chapter.

2 The small-union, homogenous-goods model: a partial equilibrium analysis

When goods are assumed to be homogeneous, the analysis of FTAs—as distinct from customs unions (CUs)—is more complicated than normally realized. Under a customs union arrangement, both producer and consumer prices are equalized within the union. But under an FTA, as Richardson (1994) has noted, while producer prices equalize, consumer prices do not. Free mobility of goods produced within the union ensures there is a single union-wide price for them. However, the goods imported from outside pay a different duty, depending on the country in which they are consumed, leading to differences in consumer prices between member countries. This feature of FTAs gives rise to effects that are more complicated than those obtained under a customs union arrangement. This is shown below, building on the analyses of Grossman and Helpman (1995) and Bhagwati and Panagariya (1996).

Consider the usual three-country setting, with A, B and C denoting the three countries. Countries A and B are potential members in a union while C represents the rest of the world. In this section, we assume that A and B are small in relation to C. Given the assumption that goods are homogeneous, the 'small-union' assumption translates into 'price-taking' behaviour by A and B.

In this section, we limit ourselves to a partial-equilibrium model in which the FTA consists in country A removing a single tariff on B but not C. We begin with the assumption that the good under consideration, called steel, is imported by A and exported by B. We further assume that, being an exporter, B does not impose a tariff on steel. The cases in which B levies a tariff (even as an exporter) or is an importer of the product in the initial equilibrium are discussed later. Based on the pattern of trade among A, B and C before and after trade, three analytically distinct cases must be considered.

2.1 Case 1. Country A imports steel from C before and after the FTA

In this case, since the pre-FTA tariff continues to apply to imports from C and the latter's supply price is fixed via the small-country assumption, the internal price of steel in A is unchanged. Consequently, the tariff preference has no impact on the output, consumption and total imports into A. The change brings about no trade creation. At the same time, the tariff preference allows B to partially replace C as the source of imports, even though its marginal cost of production is higher than that of the latter. This trade diversion leads to a net loss to the union as a whole.

As far as country A alone is concerned, its losses exceed those arising solely from trade diversion. In particular, they equal the tariff revenue foregone on the imports coming from B; the more A imports from B in the post-union equilibrium, the more it loses. Country B, in turn, benefits from the union, since its exporters capture the tariff revenue not collected by A. Effectively, intra-union terms of trade shift in favour of B by the full amount of the tariff preference. Country B's net gain equals the revenue transfer, via improved terms of trade, minus the welfare cost of trade diversion.

These results are derived in Figure 3.1. The left-hand panel in the figure shows the market for steel in country B and the right-hand panel the

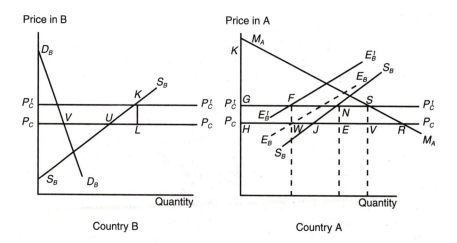

Figure 3.1 Effects of preferential removal of tariff by A when imports continue to come from C: A loses GNEH, B gains GNJH and the Union loses JNE (=UKL in the left-hand panel).

import-market in country A. D_BD_B and S_BS_B represent the demand for and supply of steel, respectively, in country B. P_C represents the price of steel in the rest of the world. In the absence of a tariff preference, the export-supply curve of B is given, as usual, by the difference between its supply and demand curves. This is represented by E_BE_B in the right-hand panel.

Curve M_AM_A in the right-hand panel represents country A's import-demand curve, obtained by subtracting its domestic supply from demand. The horizontal line P_CP_C is C's perfectly elastic supply curve. Initially, A imposes a non-discriminatory tariff at rate $P_CP_C^t$. Consequently, export supply curves of B and C, as perceived by agents in A, are given by $E_B^tE_B^t$ and $P_C^tP_C^t$, respectively. The domestic price in A is established at P_C^t. The country imports quantity GS, of which GF comes from B and FS from C. Country A collects $P_CP_C^t$ per unit in tariff revenue, leaving a net price of P_C for both B and C.

Suppose now that A eliminates the tariff on B but not C. Steel producers in B now have access to A's internal price. Since the price in their own home market is P_C, they have no incentive to sell steel there: they divert their entire quantity of steel to A. Therefore, after the tariff preference, the export supply from B shifts all the way to S_BS_B rather than E_BE_B, where S_BS_B resembles B's *total* supply curve of B as shown in the left-hand panel. All of B's demand for steel is now satisfied by imports, while all of its domestic supply is sold in A at the improved terms of trade, P_C^t.

By assumption, B's total supply of steel at P_C^t is less than A's demand for imports, so that imports continue to come from C. With the original tariff still applied to country C, the internal price in A remains unchanged. This means that the total imports of steel are also unchanged at GS. The union is wholly trade diverting: A's imports from B rise from GF to GN, without any expansion of total imports.

It is readily verified that the tariff preference by A results in a loss of rectangle GNEH to itself, a gain of trapezium GNJH to B, and a net loss of triangle NEJ ($=$ UKL in the left-hand panel) to the union as a whole. Country A loses GFEH because it is no longer able to collect tariff revenue on steel imports from B, GN. Alternatively, we can view the loss as resulting from a deterioration of A's intra-union terms of trade: rather than P_C, it now pays P_C^t on imports from B. Country B gains area GNJH because its exporters are able to get A's higher internal price. The tariff revenue on the import quantity GF, previously collected by A, becomes a part of export revenue earned by B's firms. Of this, area NEJ constitutes a net deadweight loss due to the higher cost of production of quantity JE in B than in C. This area is the net cost to the union as a whole of extending A's protection to B's firms.

An important point that deserves noting is that, though the total quantity of trade diverted from C to B is WE $=$ WJ $+$ JE, the diversion of WJ imposes no welfare cost on the union. This is simply because imports from the rest of the world into the union as a whole decline by JE (= UL in the left-hand panel), not WE. With all of B's supply diverted to A, the former now satisfies its domestic demand entirely through imports. By construction, these imports, represented by $P_C V$ in the left-hand panel of Figure 3.1, equal WJ in the right-hand panel.

This analysis is extended easily to the cases in which (i) B is an exporter of steel in the initial equilibrium but happens to keep a tariff on imports on its books, and (ii) A and B are both importers of steel and impose tariffs on imports. Thus, assume that the tariff in B is lower than that in A. In case (i), the tariff in B is redundant initially, yielding the same pre-preference equilibrium as in Figure 3.1. However, in the post-preference equilibrium, as steel producers in B divert their supply to A (since, given the higher tariff, the price is higher there) and domestic demand has to be satisfied by imports, the tariff becomes effective. There is an increase in the price of steel in B, a decline in its consumption, and a concomitant loss of welfare. This loss is over and above triangle JNE in the right-hand panel of Figure 3.1 (= KLU in the left-hand panel).

In case (ii), the tariff is effective in the pre-preference equilibrium, with the price in B exceeding that in C by the amount of tariff per unit. Under the FTA, both A and B remove the tariff on steel on each other. Since the external tariff and, hence, the price of steel is higher in A, B's output is diverted to A as before. The difference with the original case, however, is that the height of the triangle representing the loss from trade diversion in the right-hand panel in Figure 3.1 is now measured by the difference between tariff rates in A and B. Moreover, there is no additional loss in consumption in B that occurs in case (i). Both results follow from the fact that the pre-preference price in B is already equal to the world price plus its tariff.

In concluding this case, it is important to emphasize that, as far as the welfare of an individual union member is concerned, the redistributive effect of a tariff preference is likely to overwhelm the efficiency effect. Whereas the redistributive effect is represented by a rectangle whose base is the *total* quantity of intra-union trade, the efficiency effect is represented by a triangle whose base is the *change* in trade. Country A, which gives the tariff preference, loses potential tariff revenue on the entire quantity of steel imported from B. If it imports a large quantity of steel from its partner, this loss will be large. Even if the preference was to give rise to trade creation (see the next case below), because the corresponding welfare gain will be a triangle built on the *increase* in intra-union trade over and above the diverted quantity, the net effect on A is likely to be negative. More generally, in a many-goods setting, if one partner has high tariffs and the other low tariffs (Mexico and USA, respectively, in NAFTA) and bilateral trade between them is approximately balanced, an FTA is likely to hurt the former and benefit the latter.

2.2 Case 2. Country A imports steel from C before but not after the FTA

The results in the previous subsection notwithstanding, the consensus view in the literature is that a preferential reduction in tariff has an ambiguous effect on the welfare of the country giving the preference and the union as a whole. What is surprising, however, is that in the small-union context, this ambiguity almost always relies on the assumption that the good subject to the preference is either not imported from the rest of the world or the preference eliminates the latter as a source of imports. The pioneering contributions of both Viner (1950) and Meade (1955) implicitly make use of this property. Recall that in the Vinerian formulation, the supply price of the rest of the world as well as the union partner is assumed to be constant. In this setting, if the good is initially imported from the rest of the world, a tariff preference has no impact unless it eliminates the latter as a supplier. Similarly, the Meade model explicitly assumes that the good imported from the partner is not imported from the rest of the world in either pre- or post-FTA equilibrium.

Figure 3.2 shows formally how the elimination of the rest of the world as a source of imports opens the door to beneficial effects of a tariff preference. In this figure, we reproduce the right-hand panel of Figure 3.1, with the difference that B's supply curve, $S_B S_B$, crosses A's import-demand curve, $M_A M_A$, below the tariff-inclusive price of C (point S). Given its large supply of steel, B now eliminates C as a source of imports into A in the post-FTA equilibrium. Steel price in A is, thus, delinked from P_C^t. Instead, the price is determined by the intersection of A's import-demand curve and B's supply curve.

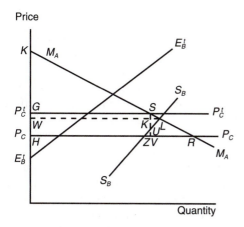

Figure 3.2 Effects of preferential removal of tariff by A when C is eliminated as source of imports: A gains SKL and loses WKVH, B gains WLZH, and the union gains SLU and loses UZV.

It is a straightforward matter to see that the net effect of the tariff preference by A is now ambiguous on itself and the union as a whole and, as
before, non-negative on B. With the decline in the internal price, new
trade in the amount KL is created, which is associated with a rise in the
union's welfare equal to triangle SLU. At the same time, since A's protection is extended to B's firms, there is harmful trade diversion: the cost of
production of units ZV (previously imported from C) in B exceeds that in
C by area UVZ. The union as a whole gains or loses as area SLU is larger
or smaller than area UVZ. The farther to the right S_BS_B lies, the larger is
SLU and smaller UVZ. In the limit, if S_BS_B crosses P_CP_C at or to the right
of V, area UVZ disappears altogether and the union as a whole necessarily benefits.

The effect of the tariff preference on A is also ambiguous. In Figure 3.2,
it gains area SKL from trade creation but loses area WKVH due to tariff-
revenue transfer. The farther to the right B's supply curve lies, the closer is
A's internal price to P_C and the more likely that it will be a net gainer. In
the limit, if the internal price drops to P_C, no revenue transfer to B takes
place and there is benefit from trade creation, implying a net gain.

The effect on B's welfare is non-negative. As drawn in Figure 3.2, the
price received by its exporters as well as the quantity of exports rises. It
benefits on both counts, receiving a net gain of WLZH. In the limiting case
when B's supply is sufficiently large that the price in A drops to P_C, it
makes no gain but it also does not lose.

2.3 Case 3. Country B exports steel to C before and after the FTA

The analysis of the previous two cases shows that the possibility of positive
gains from preferential liberalization for A and the union as a whole arises
only when the rest of the world is eliminated as A's trading partner. This
suggests an even more extreme case as a candidate for welfare-improving
preferential liberalization: if the partner exports the product to the rest of
the world both before and after the union is formed, intra-union terms of
trade cannot change as a result of preferential liberalization by A. And if
intra-union terms of trade do not change, the revenue-transfer effect is
eliminated entirely. Any tariff preference, granted by A, results in an
equivalent decline in its domestic price, with tariff revenue transferred to
its own consumers rather than B's exporters.

As can be readily verified, this case arises when $E_B^tE_B^t$ in Figure 3.2
crosses M_AM_A at or below point R. In this case, both in the initial and
final equilibrium, B exports steel to country C. The price received by
firms in B never rises above P_C and there is no revenue transfer from A
to B. Preferential liberalization essentially mimics nondiscriminatory
liberalization with country A benefiting and country B remaining
unaffected.

To anticipate the analysis in the following sections, especially section 4, it may be noted that, in general equilibrium, the assumption that the partner exports its good to the rest of the world before as well as after the tariff preference is not sufficient to rule out trade diversion. There may be goods that are imported from the rest of the world that are not imported from the partner and are substitutes for the latter's good. In such a situation, a tariff preference to the partner lowers the imports from the rest of the world and, thus, gives rise to trade diversion indirectly. Since the good imported from the rest of the world is likely to be subject to a tariff, such trade contributes negatively to welfare.

3 A general-equilibrium model with product differentiation by country of origin

In assessing the effects of FTAs, CGE analysts rarely use homogeneous-goods models. Instead, they resort to the so-called Armington assumption, according to which products are differentiated by the country of origin. For example, Mexican, US and the rest of the world's steel are modelled as different products. Correspondingly, in consumer preferences, the three types of steel are represented as substitutes via a constant-elasticity-of-substitution (CES) function.

It would seem that once goods have been redefined this way, the revenue-transfer effect, which played the dominant role in the previous section, would disappear altogether. For in this case, country B must export its steel to both A and C before as well as after the formation of the FTA. Assuming the prices in the rest of the world to be fixed via the small-country assumption, we are effectively in the realm of case 3 of the previous section. The revenue-transfer effect cannot arise.

However a moment's reflection shows that this conclusion is based on an incorrect application of the small-country assumption. The key point, which the CGE modellers under review overlook, is that product differentiation by country of origin is incompatible with fixed terms of trade; if goods are assumed to be differentiated by the country of origin, the terms of trade in the rest of the world or the union cannot be assumed to be fixed. If the terms of trade are not fixed, the revenue-transfer effect re-enters the analysis through a deterioration of intra-union terms of the country extending the tariff preference.

The logic behind why product differentiation is incompatible with fixed terms of trade is simple: by assumption, each country is the sole producer of its products and, hence, enjoys monopoly power over it. This point has been made formally in the context of the monopolistic-competition model in an important paper by Gros (1987), and is reproduced in the recent textbook by Bhagwati, Panagariya and Srinivasan (1998).

Since many CGE modellers have continued to ignore this important point in their applications to preferential trading, it is worth making it explicitly in the context of the Armington assumption. This is done most simply in a two-good, two-country model in which each country produces one good. Call the two countries A and B and label their products 1 and 2, respectively. Assume, as the CGE models do, that preferences are CES.

We know that, in this setting, the optimum tariff of A on B equals $1/(\eta_1^* - 1)$, where η_1^* is B's elasticity of demand for imports of good 1. Of course, since good 1 is not produced in B, the import-demand elasticity coincides with the total-demand elasticity of good for the good. What we need to do to obtain the optimum tariff, therefore, is to derive the elasticity of demand for good 1 in B in the Armington model. This is readily done by recourse to country B's first-order condition of utility maximization and the budget constraint.

Distinguishing B's variables by superscript B, let p_i^B and C_i^B, respectively, represent the price and consumption of good i (i = 1, 2) and σ^B the elasticity of substitution in consumption between the two goods in B. Assume that good b is the numeraire so that $p_2^B \equiv 1$. Using a hat ($^$) to denote the proportionate change in a variable, the first-order condition of utility maximization and the budget constraint, respectively, may be written in deferential form as

$$\hat{C}_1^B - \hat{C}_2^B = -\sigma^B \hat{p}_1^B \tag{1}$$

$$p_1^B C_1^{*B}(\hat{p}_1^B + \hat{C}_1^B) + C_2^B \hat{C}_2^B = 0 \tag{2}$$

Solving these equations for the proportionate change in C_1^B due to a change in p_1^B, we obtain

$$\eta_1^B \equiv -\frac{\hat{C}_1^B}{\hat{p}_1^B} = \frac{\sigma^B C_2^B + p_1^B C_1^B}{p_1^B C_1^B + C_2^B} \tag{3}$$

From this expression, we can write the optimum tariff of country A as

$$t_{opt}^A = \frac{1}{\eta_1^B - 1} = \frac{p_1^B C_1^B + C_2^B}{C_2^B} \frac{1}{\sigma^B - 1} \tag{4}$$

The first fraction in the last equality remains larger than unity, no matter how small country A becomes. In the limit, as A becomes infinitesimally small, the fraction approaches unity and the optimum tariff approaches $1/(\sigma^B - 1)$. If we assume $\sigma^B = 2$, not an unusual assumption in the CGE models, the optimum tariff for a small country in this set up is 100 per cent; this is far from the fixed terms-of-trade interpretation of the small-country assumption employed by CGE analysts!

The feature that the Armington assumption necessarily implies market power on the part of each country, no matter how small, has far-reaching implications for the analysis of FTAs. For, with union members' goods not even produced in the rest of the world, we can no longer fix their prices in the latter. Any liberalization by a country, preferential or otherwise, alters its terms of trade, which must be taken into account in the calculation of the welfare effects.

Once we bring the terms-of-trade changes into our calculations, the revenue-transfer effect, emphasized in the previous section, comes back to haunt us. For even a preferential reduction in the tariff worsens a country's terms of trade *vis-à-vis* its partner, thereby partially redistributing the tariff revenue to the union partner. If the initial tariff on the partner is lower than the 'optimum' tariff, as is likely to be the case in view of the substantial unilateral liberalization in recent years, the deterioration in the terms of trade will also be accompanied by a deterioration in the country's welfare.

Mundell (1964) recognized this fact in a somewhat neglected paper, published more than three decades ago.[4] Assuming substitutability and low initial tariffs, Mundell (1964: 78) reached the following dramatic conclusions:

1   A discriminatory tariff reduction by a member country improves the terms of trade of the partner country with respect to both the tariff reducing country and the rest of the world, but the terms of trade of the tariff reducing country might rise or fall with respect to third countries.

2   The degree of improvement in the terms of trade of the partner country is likely to be larger the greater is the member's tariff reduction; this establishes the presumption that a member's gains from a free trade area will be larger the higher are initial tariffs of partner countries.

These conclusions closely resemble those derived in the previous section for the small-union, homogeneous-goods, partial-equilibrium model.

To gain insight into how this 'large-union' effect matters in determining the effects of preferential liberalization, we can simulate a three-country version of the model just discussed. The model itself can be summarized by a handful of equations, using the dual approach. Throughout, use superscript j (j = A, B, C) to denote a country and subscript i (i = 1, 2, 3) to denote a good. By assumption, good 1 is produced exclusively by A, good 2 by B and good 3 by C. All goods are consumed in all countries. Denote by p_i the price of good i in the country where it is produced. Thus, p_1 is the price of good 1 in country A, p_2 of good 2 in B, and p_3 of good 3 in C. Domestic prices can then be computed with the help of tariff rates. Thus, letting t_i^j (i = 1, 2, 3 and j = A, B, C) denote the ad valorem tariff rate on good i in country j, where $t_1^A = t_2^B = t_3^C = 0$, the domestic price of good i in country j is given by good $(1 + t_i^j)p_i$.

Assuming CES preferences that are identical across individuals within a country but can differ between countries, the expenditure function of the representative individual in country j can be written

$$E^j(.) = \left[\sum_{i=1}^{3}\{(1+t_i^j)p_i\}^{1-\sigma}\right]^{1/1-\sigma}.u^j \qquad j = A, B, C \qquad (5)$$

where u^j is the (endogenous) level of utility of the representative individual in country j and σ is the common elasticity of substitution in consumption. The same elasticity of substitution is assumed across countries. Since the purpose here is to focus on the role of the terms-of-trade effects, no asymmetries are introduced in tastes across products or countries. The next section will focus on some of these differences in a model which abstracts from the terms-of-trade effects.

$E^j(.)$ contains all the relevant information on the representative individual's demand. In particular, its first partials with respect to domestic prices give his compensated demand functions. Thus, the compensated demand for good i of the individual in country j is given by

$$E_i^j(.) = \{(1+t_i^j)p_i\}^{-\sigma}\left[\sum_{i=1}^{3}(a_i^j)^{\sigma}\{(1+t_i^j)p_i\}^{1-\sigma}\right]^{\sigma/1-\sigma}.u^j \qquad j = A, B, C \qquad (6)$$

$$= \{(1+t_i^j)p_i\}^{-\sigma}.\{E^j(.)\}^{\sigma}u^j \qquad j = A, B, C$$

Turning to the supply side, assume that labour is the only factor of production and that each individual supplies one unit of labour. Thus, country size varies directly with the size of total number of individuals, which we denote by L^j. Assume further that one unit of labour produces $\bar{x}_1$ of good 1 in A, $\bar{x}_2$ of good 2 in B and $\bar{x}_3$ of good 3 in C. Letting tariff revenue be redistributed equally across individuals, the representative individual's income in country j, at domestic prices, can be written

$$Y^j(.) = p_k\bar{x}_k + \sum_{i=1}^{3}t_i^jp_iE_i^j(.) \qquad j = A, B, C \qquad (7)$$

The first of these terms is the value of output, produced by the individual, and the second one is his share of tariff revenue. By assumption, country A produces only good 1, B only good 2 and C only good 3. This fixes subscript k in the first term of (7) to k = 1, 2, 3, respectively as j = A, B, C.

The budget constraint of the representative individual requires $E^j(.) = Y^j(.)$. Therefore, after substitution from (6) into (7) and combining the resulting equation with (5), we can write the budget constraint of country j as

$$\left[\sum_{i=1}^{3}\{(1+t_i^j)p_i\}^{1-\sigma}\right]^{1/1-\sigma}.u^j = p_k\bar{x}_k^j + \sum_{i=1}^{3}t_i^jp_i\{p_i(1+t_i^j)\}^{-\sigma}\{E^j(.)\}^{\sigma}u^j$$

$$j = A, B, C \qquad (8)$$

We let good 1 be the numeraire and set $p_1 = 1$. This leaves p_2 and p_3 as the only prices to be determined endogenously. Once again, making use of (5), market-clearing conditions for goods 2 and 3 can be written

$$\sum_{j=A,B,C} [L^j\{p_i(1+t_i^j)\}^{-\sigma}\{E^j(.)\}^\sigma u^j] = \bar{x}_i L^h \qquad i=2,3 \qquad (9)$$

On the right-hand side, we set h = B, C, respectively, as i = 2, 3. Thus, recalling that L^h represents the total supply of labour in country h, for i = 2, the right-hand side represents the total world supply of good 2 and when i = 3, it gives the total world supply of good 3. Since L^j also represents the total number of individuals in country j, $L^j E_i^j(.)$ represents that country's *total* demand for good i. Summing these over j and taking account of (6), as in the left-hand side of (9), we obtain the total world demand for good i. Thus, (9) equates the total demand for good 2 with its supply and similarly for good 3. We do not write the market-clearing condition for good 1 since it is redundant by Walras' Law and can be derived using (8) and (9).

We have five equations in (8) and (9) (with $E^j(.)$ defined by equation (5)), which can be solved for five endogenous variables, p_2, p_3, u^A, u^B, and u^C. Thus, duality allows us to summarize a three-country model in just five equations. Taking specific parameter values of σ, per-worker outputs, labour supplies, and tariff rates, we can solve the model numerically.

In Table 3.1, we present the results of several simulations exploring the role played by different tariff rates. To fix the context, we choose the relative values of L^j and $\bar{x}_i$ so that the relative sizes of A, B and C approximately resemble those of Mexico, the USA and the rest of the world, respectively. We report several simulations for $\sigma = 2$ and 10 and tariff rates of 15 per cent and 30 per cent.

Cases 1–3 consider preferential liberalization by A alone. In case 1, only A has a tariff initially, in case 2, both A and B have a tariff and in case 3, all countries have a tariff. Within our stylized model, case A1 best approximates NAFTA. For, under NAFTA, Mexico gave virtually all tariff preferences. An FTA in this case simply amounts to A eliminating its tariff on B, holding the tariff on C unchanged. In all four cases ($\sigma = 2$, 10 and $t_2^A = t_3^A = 0.15, 0.30$), A loses from the change. For $\sigma = 2$, the reduction in A's income from preferential liberalization is 0.8 per cent at 15 per cent tariff and 2.2 per cent at 30 per cent tariff. For $\sigma = 10$, these reductions become 2.3 per cent and 5.4 per cent, respectively. At the higher value of σ, the terms of trade *vis-à-vis* the rest of the world shift less and the revenue transfer effect is larger. The tariff preference uniformly benefits B and hurts C. However, since both are very large in relation to A, the impact on them is very small. The results are similar in cases 2 and 3, with the largest loss to A of 6.4 per cent arising in case 2 for $\sigma = 10$ and tariff of 30 per cent. These results are contrary to the results CGE modellers reported during the NAFTA debate.

Table 3.1 Effects of preferential liberalization (Compensating variation as percentage of the initial income) (Stylized Representation of NAFTA: A = Mexico, B = USA, C = rest of the world)

	$\sigma = 2$					
Tariff Rate = 15%				*Tariff Rate = 30%*		
Case	A	B	C	A	B	C
1	−0.78	0.51	−0.31	−2.19	0.97	−0.58
2	−0.76	0.52	−0.30	−2.12	1.01	−0.53
3	−0.80	0.51	−0.32	−2.27	0.99	−0.58
4	4.71	0.16	−0.62	8.63	0.28	−1.12
5	4.87	0.11	−0.65	9.23	0.13	−1.23
6	−5.81	−1.33	0.78	−11.16	−3.09	0.67
7	−1.42	3.05	−2.23	−2.78	5.32	−4.25
8	0.75	−0.05	−0.05	1.36	−0.11	−0.11

	$\sigma = 10$					
Tariff Rate = 15%				*Tariff Rate = 30%*		
Case	A	B	C	A	B	C
1	−2.27	0.11	−0.05	−5.39	0.18	−0.08
2	−2.24	0.14	−0.04	−6.44	0.32	−0.05
3	−2.16	0.14	−0.06	−3.32	0.37	−0.05
4	3.18	0.03	−0.08	4.16	0.072	−0.11
5	5.49	−0.03	−0.14	14.07	−0.008	−0.19
6	−8.63	−3.58	−0.65	−18.54	−7.10	−2.48
7	−1.53	1.57	−1.61	−3.46	0.49	−2.73
8	0.066	−0.004	−0.004	−0.65	−0.013	−0.01

Cases 1–3 Only A liberalizes with respect to B (case 1: B and C have free trade before as well as after the preference; case 2: B imposes the MFN tariff before and after the preference but C has free trade; case 3: B and C both impose the MFN tariff before and after the preference)
Cases 4–5 A and B form FTA with mutual tariff preference (case 4: C has free trade before and after the FTA; case 5: C imposes the MFN tariff before and after the preference)
Cases 6–8 The effect of an MFN tariff relative to free trade (initially, free trade everywhere. Case 6: all three introduce the tariffs; case 7: only A and B introduce the tariff; case 8: only A introduces the tariff)

Cases 4 and 5 present the results of mutual tariff preference by A and B. In case 4, only A and B impose tariffs in the initial equilibrium, while C adheres to free trade. In case 5, C also has a tariff. Now the results are exactly the opposite of those in cases 1–3. Gaining a preferential access to B's large market, A is now a big winner. In case 5, with $\sigma = 10$ and initial tariffs in A and B of 30 per cent, mutual preferential liberalization leads to a 14 per cent rise in A's real income. The effect on B is negligible. What may be surprising, however, is that when C also levies a tariff (case 5), B actually loses. This is an entirely plausible outcome: the loss to B from its own preferential liberalization can outweigh the gain from the partner's preferential liberalization. This is more likely when the outside country levies a tariff as well. For in this case, the optimum tariffs of A and B on each other (and C) are also higher.

A final set of simulations (cases 6–8) report on the effects of MFN tariffs relative to multilateral free trade. In case 6, all three countries levy a tariff; in case 7, A and B levy a tariff but not C; and in case 8, only A levies a tariff. Relative to free trade, for $\sigma = 2$, a 30 per cent MFN tariff by all countries results in a loss of GDP of 11.2 per cent for A, 3.1 per cent for B and 0.7 per cent for C. For $\sigma = 10$, these losses jump to 18.5 per cent for A, 7.1 per cent for B and 2.5 per cent for C. At the other extreme, in case 8, a 30 per cent tariff by A results in a gain of 1.4 per cent to itself when $\sigma = 2$ and a loss of 0.7 per cent when $\sigma = 10$. In the former case, A's optimum tariff is higher than in the latter case. A key implication of these results is that, at low tariffs, a one-percentage point reduction in tariffs by other countries is much more valuable to a small country than an equivalent reduction in its own tariffs.

These results should serve as a warning to the reader against taking any CGE results seriously, without carefully examining the underlying structure of the model and parameter values. By choosing a three-country structure in which one country is very small relative to others, even within a conventional model, we are able to generate welfare effects of trade policy that are much larger (a decline of 18.5 per cent in income for country A) than these models are known to generate. Furthermore, by changing the value of just one parameter, σ, we are able to turn a 0.7 per cent loss to C into a 2.5 per cent loss, a six-fold increase.

4 Generating positive gains: wrong model, wrong parameters

The analysis and simulations in the previous two sections establish a very strong presumption in favour of the view that *conventional* models yield the following results at tariff rates that are 30 per cent or lower:

1   Preferential liberalization by a country results in losses to itself and gains to its union partner;
2   If the union is small and the introduction of preferential trading does not eliminate trade with the rest of the world in a large number of products, the union as a whole loses; and
3   The union as a whole can benefit from preferential liberalization if trade diversion leads to an improvement in its terms of trade *vis-à-vis* the rest of the world. In this case, the rest of the world is hurt, making preferential liberalization a 'beggar thy neighbour' policy.

These results lead to the puzzle: how do CGE modellers generate gains from preferential liberalization to the country undertaking such liberalization in the conventional models? We will demonstrate in this section that this is done by recourse to wrong models *and* wrong parameter values.

The first trick the CGE modellers use is to superimpose the small-country assumption on the Armington assumption. We have already argued at length that this is erroneous; within the usual CGE structure with CES preferences, the Armington assumption is incompatible with the small-union assumption, unless we assume that the elasticity of substitution in the rest of the world is infinity. But there is no justification for such an assumption: why should individual preferences exhibit such an extreme property and only in the rest of the world?

It is tempting to invoke the Meade-Lipsey, small-union model (Lipsey 1958) to justify the small-union structure used by the CGE analysts. In this model, union members are assumed to be small and to specialize in the good they export. This justification poses serious dilemmas for CGE modellers. The small-union assumption is validated in the Meade-Lipsey model by assuming that goods are homogeneous and that the products exported by union members are also produced in the rest of the world (Lloyd 1982 and Panagariya 1997a, 1997b). Thus, the model relies on a structure different from that required for validating the Armington assumption. This is a substantive distinction; for, if we assume that the rest of the world produces all goods, the assumption that a union member does not import *any* good from it that it imports from the union partner is quite unrealistic. The CGE modellers cannot have it both ways. If they want to justify the small-union assumption via the assumption that the rest of the world produces all goods, they must admit the possibility that goods imported from a union partner are also imported from the rest of the world. In that case, they will be faced with the revenue-transfer effect discussed in section 2. If they want to avoid this possibility by invoking the Armington assumption, they must give up the small-union assumption and, in turn, incorporate the terms-of-trade effects discussed in section 3.

Indeed, we will argue that if the objective is to measure the effects of preferential liberalization, the Meade-Lipsey, small-union model offers the least attractive setting. It combines fixed terms of trade in the rest of the world with a structure of trade in which the good imported from the partner is not imported from the rest of the world in the initial or final equilibrium. The partner, in turn, exports the good to the union member as well as the rest of the world before and after the introduction of preferential trading. These assumptions lead to the outcome that preferential liberalization by a member has no impact whatsoever on its union partner and vice versa. All effects of preferential liberalization by a country are confined to itself. Under such a setting, why should any country form a preferential trade area in the first place? Whatever liberalization it wants to undertake, it can do on its own.

However, suppose we follow the CGE modellers, make the small-union assumption and even accept the Armington assumption. That is to say, the terms of trade are fixed in C and that A exports good 1 to both B and C, B exports good 2 to both A and C and C exports good 3 to both A and B.

Can we then generate gains from preferential liberalization? We will show that even in this implausible model, for plausible parameter values, preferential liberalization leads to losses and, when positive gains can be generated, they are too tiny to impress anyone.

As explained in Bhagwati and Panagariya (1996) and Panagariya (1997a, 1997b), under the small-union assumption, the central role is assumed by the relative degree of substitutability between different pairs of goods rather than the terms of trade. Before we turn to simulations, it is useful to reproduce this point analytically here. Since a member country is impacted solely by its own liberalization in this model, we need focus on only one country, say, country A. Moreover, since the number of individuals as represented by L^A plays no role in determining the outcome now (recall that the terms of trade are fixed), we can set $L^A = 1$.

By appropriate choice of units, we can set all prices in country C equal to unity. Since A exports good 1, this good's domestic price is also 1. Good 2 is exported by B, for which it receives a price of 1 in C. Therefore, A must pay B the same price for this good at the border. Letting the tariff rate on the good be t_2, this implies a domestic price of good 2 of $1 + t_2$. Finally, good 3 is imported from C at a border price equal to 1 and is, therefore, priced at $1 + t_3$ in A. With prices in A, thus, fixed entirely by its own trade policy, policy changes in the union partner, B, have no impact on it. By symmetry, policy changes in A have no impact on B.

Following the practice in CGE models, assume that the consumer's utility function is linear homogeneous.[5] We can then represent consumer demand via the separable expenditure function $e(1, 1 + t_2, 1 + t_3)u$, where $e(.)$ is concave and linear homogeneous in its arguments and u is the level of utility. Letting $\bar{x}_1$ be the output of good 1 in A, the country's budget constraint can be written as

$$e(1, 1 + t_2, 1 + t_3)u = \bar{x}_1 + t_2 e_2.u + t_3 e_3.u \qquad (10)$$

where e_2 is the first partial of $e(.)$ with respect to $1 + t_2$ and e_3 with respect to $1 + t_3$. Remembering that $e_2.u$ and $e_3.u$, respectively, represent the quantities of goods 2 and 3 consumed and, hence, imported, the last two terms represent tariff revenue. It is assumed, as usual, that tariff revenue is redistributed to the consumer in a lump-sum fashion.

The tariff preference in this model is represented by a reduction in t_2, assuming $t_2 = t_3$ initially. The idea is that goods imported from the potential partner and the outside country are close substitutes on which the initial tariff is the same. To see how such a tariff preference affects A's welfare, differentiate (10) with respect to t_2. After some simplifications, we obtain

$$(e - t_2 e_2 - t_3 e_3)\frac{du}{u} = [t_2 e_{22} + t_3 e_{33}]dt_2 \qquad (11)$$

Remembering that e_2 is homogeneous of degree zero in domestic prices, we have

$$e_{21} + (1 + t_2)e_{22} + (1 + t_3)e_{23} = 0 \tag{12}$$

Solving this equation for e_{22} and substituting into (11), we obtain

$$(e - t_2e_2 - t_3e_3)\frac{du}{u} = -\frac{1}{1+t_2}[t_2e_{21} - (t_3 - t_2)e_{23}]dt_2 \tag{13}$$

This is a familiar expression from the Meade-Lipsey model (Panagariya 1997a, 1997b), which also obtains in the context of piecemeal tariff reform when we consider the effect of a unilateral reduction in a tariff, which is what the current exercise is about (equation (35.5) in Bhagwati, Panagariya and Srinivasan 1998).

If all goods are normal in consumption, which is true for our linear homogeneous preference, the coefficient of du/u in (13) is positive. Therefore, a reduction in t_2 raises or lowers welfare, as the term in square brackets is positive or negative. If good 2 exhibits net substitutability with good 1, e_{21} is positive, so that a small reduction in t_2 at $t_2 = t_3$ raises welfare. But if $t_3 > t_2$ at the initial equilibrium and goods 2 and 3 are also substitutes, the effect is ambiguous. For sufficiently small values of t_2, reductions in t_2 necessarily lower welfare.

The intuitive reason behind these results is well understood (see Bhagwati and Panagariya (1996)) and can be spelt out as follows. The reduction in t_2 expands the imports of good 2, which is beneficial trade creation (see the first term in (11)). But it also leads a contraction of imports of good 3, which is harmful trade diversion (second term in (11)). The net effect depends on the relative magnitudes of the two effects. Net substitutability between goods 1 and 2 ensures that, at world prices, the tariff reduction expands the value of exports. Via the trade balance condition, this fact, in turn, implies that the value of imports of good 2 expands more than the value of imports of good 3 contracts. If the two tariff rates are equal, the beneficial effect of trade creation necessarily dominates the harmful effect of trade diversion. However, if t_3 is larger than t_2, the greater expansion in the value of imports of good 2 is not sufficient to guarantee a favourable outcome. For sufficiently low t_2, the beneficial effect of the expansion of imports of good 2 is necessarily outweighed by the harmful effect of the contraction of good 3.

These results imply that, given substitutability, small reductions in t_2 first raise welfare but eventually lower it. Therefore, in general, there is no guarantee that lowering t_2 all the way to zero is welfare improving. This analytic ambiguity assigns a critical role to parameters determining the degree of substitutability between goods 2 and 1 on the one hand and goods 2 and 3 on the other.

Therefore, we need to allow a more general utility function in the simulations than the standard CES utility function used in the previous section. In particular, the utility function must allow us to distinguish between elasticities of substitution across different pairs of goods. This is accomplished most easily by representing preferences by a nested utility function.

$$u = [a_1 C_1^\alpha + b\chi^\alpha]^{1/\alpha} \tag{14}$$

where C_1 is the consumption good 1, produced and exported by A, and χ is a composite good defined over goods 2 and 3, imported from B and C, respectively. The composite good is assumed to have the form

$$\chi = [a_2 C_2^{\alpha*} + a_3 C_2^{\alpha*}]^{1/\alpha*} \tag{15}$$

Observe that the degree of substitutability between C_1 and χ is $\sigma = 1/(1 - \alpha)$, while that between C_2 and C_3 is $\sigma* = 1/(1 - \alpha*)$. Thus, the present specification allows the degree of substitutability to differ across different pairs of goods. A priori, we will expect $\sigma*$ to be larger than σ. The US goods, imported into Mexico, are likely to be better substitutes for goods imported from the European Union and Japan than those produced within Mexico. This feature plays a crucial role in determining the outcome in the simulations.

The price of the composite good, defined in (14), is represented by

$$\pi(1 + t_2, 1 + t_3) = [a_2^{\sigma*}(1 + t_2)^{1-\sigma*} + a_3^{\sigma*}(1 + t_3)^{1-\sigma*}]^{1/1-\sigma*} \tag{16}$$

Similarly, the expenditure function, corresponding to (15), is given by

$$e(1, 1 + t_2, 1 + t_3)u \equiv [a_1^\sigma + b^\sigma \pi^{(1-\sigma)}]^{1/1-\sigma}u \tag{17}$$

In defining $e(.)$, we take advantage of the fact that π is a function of $1 + t_2$ and $1 + t_3$, as shown in (16).

Given explicit forms of $e(.)$ and $\pi(.)$ as in (17) and (16), respectively, equation (10) can be simulated to yield the effects of changes in the values of various parameters on u. Before we do so, however, a likely key result can already be anticipated from our theoretical analysis. In the specific case under consideration, we can obtain

$$e_{21} = \sigma \frac{e_2 e_1}{e} = \sigma e_2 \theta_1 \tag{18a}$$

$$e_{23} = e_2 \left[\sigma \frac{e_3}{e} + (\sigma* - \sigma) \frac{\pi_3}{\pi} \right] = e_2 \left[\sigma \theta_3 + (\sigma* - \sigma) \frac{\pi_3}{\pi} \right] \tag{18b}$$

In (18b), π_3 represents the first partial of π with respect to $(1 + t_3)$. In addition, we use θ_i to denote the expenditure share of good i. Combining these equations with equation (13), we can conjecture the following results:

1   The larger σ^* is in relation to σ, the less likely that the formation of a free trade area between A and B will improve A's welfare. In the extreme case of $\sigma = 0$, any finite tariff preference must lower A's welfare.
2   If $\sigma = \sigma^*$, critical parameters determining the outcome are expenditure shares of goods 1 and 3. The larger the proportion of income spent on home goods relative to outside country's good, the more likely that tariff preference will benefit A.
3   To produce significant gains from preferential liberalization, it must be assumed that σ substantially exceeds σ^*.

We may now look at some simulations. Table 3.2 reports the effects of a removal of the tariff on good 2, amounting to a tariff preference to B, with the external tariff at 15 per cent or 30 per cent. The results do not report on cases with the elasticity of substitution above 2 since the effects are extremely small. In the first two cases for each tariff rate, we assume $\sigma = \sigma^* = 0.3$ and 2, successively. The net gain is positive, with the maximum gain of 0.41 per cent of the income arising with the external tariff set at 30 per cent and $\sigma = \sigma^* = 2$. If the tariff rate is set at 15 per cent and $\sigma = \sigma^* = 0.3$, the gain is 0.018 per cent of the income.

More strikingly, suppose we assume a low elasticity of substitution between imports from the partner and A's home good and a high elasticity between the two imports. Setting $\sigma = 0.3$ and $\sigma^* = 2$, the removal of tariff on good 2 leads to a loss of 0.052 per cent and 0.145 per cent of income as the tariff on good 3 is set at 15 per cent and 30 per cent, respectively. Switching these elasticities of substitution turns the loss into a gain in each case.

Table 3.2 Small-union, imperfect-substitutes model Effect of a unilateral tariff preference by A on itself (Compensating variation as a percentage of income)

σ^*	σ	Tariff preference	
		15%	*30%*
0.3	0.3	0.018	0.062
2	2	0.127	0.405
2	0.3	−0.052	−0.145
0.3	2	0.102	0.315

5 Conclusion

In this chapter, we have questioned the results of CGE models demonstrating that preferential liberalization by a country benefits itself. We have argued that these results have been derived from models based on theoretically wrong assumptions. The models combine product differentiation with fixed terms of trade. There is a fundamental tension between these assumptions: if a country is the sole producer of its products, it necessarily has market power. If correct assumptions are made, both theory and numerical simulations are shown to generate losses to the country liberalizing preferentially.

Notes

1. *Ex post* studies refer to empirical analyses based on data before and after the formation of preferential trade arrangements and include assessments using the gravity equation.
2. This means that we do not examine the CGE models that rely on economies of scale, imperfect competition or changes in ex-efficiency to generate gains from preferential liberalization. We suspect, however, that the critique in this chapter will apply partially to the models in this category as well.
3. Alternatively, we can introduce product differentiation via the Krugman (1980) model, which is theoretically more satisfactory. Our results are preserved in this case.
4. Panagariya (1997a, 1997b) further elaborates on Mundell's (1964) analysis.
5. For our analytic results, this assumption is not required, but it helps connect the model more directly to the specific CES utility function used in the CGE models.

References

Bhagwati, J., Greenaway, D. and Panagariya, A. (1998) 'Trading preferentially: theory and policy', *Economic Journal*, 108 (449): 1128–48.
Bhagwati, J. and Panagariya, A. (1996a) 'Preferential trading areas and multilateralism: strangers, friends or foes?', in J. Bhagwati and A. Panagariya (eds), *The Economics of Preferential Trade Agreements*, Washington, DC: AEI Press.
Bhagwati, J., Panagariya, A. and Srinivasan, T.N. (1998) *Lectures on International Trade*, Cambridge, MA: MIT Press.
Gros, D. (1987) 'A note on the optimal tariff, retaliation and the welfare loss from tariff wars in a framework with intra-industry trade', *Journal of International Economics*, 23: 357–67.
Grossman, G. and Helpman, E. (1995) 'The politics of free trade agreements', *American Economic Review*, 85 (4), September: 667–90.
Krugman, P. (1980) 'Scale economies, product differentiation, and the pattern of trade', *American Economic Review*, 79: 950–9.
Lipsey, R. (1958) *The Theory of Customs Unions: A General-Equilibrium Analysis*, University of London, PhD thesis.
Lloyd, P.J. (1982) '3 × 3 theory of customs unions', *Journal of International Economics*, 12: 41–63.
Meade, J.E. (1955) *The Theory of Customs Unions*, Amsterdam: North-Holland.
Mundell, R.A. (1964) 'Tariff preferences and the terms of trade', *Manchester School of Economic and Social Studies*: 1–13.
Panagariya, A. (1996) 'The free trade area of the Americas: good for Latin America?', *World Economy*, 19, no. 5, September: 485–515.
—— (1997a) 'Preferential trading and the myth of natural trading partners', *Japan and the World Economy*, 9 (4): 471–89.

—— (1997b) 'The Meade model of preferential trading: history, analytics and policy implications', in B.J. Cohen (ed.), *International Trade and Finance: New Frontiers for Research. Essays in Honor of Peter B. Kenen*, New York: Cambridge University Press: 57–88.

—— (1998) 'The regionalism debate: an overview', Center for International Economics Working Paper No. 40, Department of Economics, University of Maryland; (forthcoming in *World Economy*)

Richardson, M. (1994) 'Why a free trade area? The tariff also rises', *Economics and Politics*, 6, no. 1, March: 79–95.

Robinson, S. and Thierfelder, K. (1999) 'Trade liberalization and regional integration: the search for large numbers', International Food Policy Research Institute, Trade and Macroeconomics Division, Working Paper No. 34.

Srinivasan, T.N., Whalley, J. and Wooton, I. (1993) 'Measuring the effects of regionalism on trade and welfare', in K. Anderson and R. Blackhurst (eds), *Regional Integration and the Global Trading System*, New York: St. Martin's Press.

Viner, J. (1950) *The Customs Union Issue*, New York: Carnegie Endowment for International Peace.

4　The anatomy of multilateral trade policy reform

Arja Turunen-Red and Alan D. Woodland

1 Introduction

Throughout the post-World War II period international trade policy reform has seldom been absent from the mind of policy-makers. The formation of the General Agreement of Tariffs and Trade (GATT) as a forum for the discussion of international trade and policy issues and the resolution of disputes, and as a sponsor of regular rounds of multilateral negotiations leading to a substantial drop in the average level of tariff protection, has ensured that trade policy issues have retained currency. More recently, there has been considerable focus on bilateral and regional trade agreements with the expansion of the customs union of the European Community and the advent of organizations such as the North American Free Trade Agreement (NAFTA), the Asia-Pacific Economic Cooperation Conference (APEC) and Mercusor. Nevertheless, cooperative trade policy remains an important part of the international landscape.

This chapter is concerned with some theoretical issues in cooperative multilateral trade policy reform. It provides a partial, and perhaps somewhat idiosyncratic, review of some recent approaches to the analysis of multilateral policy reform. The focus, as its title implies, is on the structure or *anatomy* of the policy reform problem, particularly as it applies to piecemeal policy reform.

The first task of the chapter is to set out a simple competitive model of world trade that involves tariff distortions, and hence yields an equilibrium that is not Pareto optimal. What is meant by the concept of trade policy reform in the context of this model is a primary concern. For our purposes, the policy reform problem is one of making small changes to the policy parameters (piecemeal policy reform) and the appropriate criteria are that the reforms should generate a strict Pareto improvement in welfare.

Three separate but related issues are dealt with. The first concerns the basic structure of the model: its anatomy. The structure of that model is discussed, including the restrictions imposed by Walras' Law and the homogeneity properties of the equilibrium. Of major concern is the notion of what constitutes a tariff distortion in the model. We see that the existence of tariffs is not sufficient for a distortion to exist; distortions involve not only the policy instrument but also the effect of that instrument upon the equilibrium. We also discuss the different approaches that can be taken to the analysis of policy reform: the direct comparative static approach, and the alternative approach that uses various theorems of the alternative to characterize Pareto improving reforms.

The second issue, taking up the major part of the chapter, is concerned with the mechanism by which efficiency gains arising out of trade policy reforms can be distributed among countries to achieve a strict Pareto improvement in welfare. Traditionally, trade theorists have assumed the existence of lump sum income transfers to distribute efficiency gains. Most models have lump sum transfers between countries, and between governments and households. Recently, however, some authors have given more serious attention to cases where such transfers are not feasible. Here we focus upon a connection between international income transfers and tariffs. Turunen-Red and Woodland (2000) have shown that, under a mild condition on the world trade matrix, transfer reforms accompanying quota reforms can be replaced by suitable multilateral tariff reforms to achieve the same welfare outcome. In this chapter, we generalize this idea to deal with *discrete* policy reforms; we also develop several applications to enhance understanding of the connection between tariffs and transfers.

The third and final issue concerns the structure of actual tariff reforms that generate strict Pareto improvements in welfare. Here again we focus on the general structure or anatomy of the reforms rather than on the specific details of the reforms. The chapter concludes with some remarks about possible future directions of this type of analysis of trade policy reforms.

2 The multilateral policy reform problem

2.1 General structure of policy reform

Suppose that the equilibrium conditions for the world economy can be written in the form

$$F(u, p, \tau) = 0 \tag{1}$$

where F is a vector of functions, u is a vector of endogenous variables of direct interest to the policy-makers, p is a vector of endogenous variables of no special interest, and τ is a vector of policy variables to be chosen by the policy-makers. These equilibrium conditions for the world economy determine the endogenous variables as functions of the exogenously chosen policy variables. In the context of this chapter, we can think of u as a vector of utility levels for single-consumer national economies, p as the world price vector for goods, and τ as the vector of tariffs for all countries.

However, such an assignment is not necessary for what follows; models can differ, but the basic policy reform problem may be viewed in a common way.

The policy reform problem concerns the relationship between the policy instruments, given by vector τ, and the endogenous variables of special interest, given by vector u. Starting from an initial equilibrium (solution to the model), the policy maker wishes to change the values of the policy instruments to generate a change in u that is regarded by the policy maker as beneficial. The policy reform problem is to come up with changes in policy that are beneficial. The well known theorem of the second best indicates that this is generally a non-trivial task. The issue of tax policy reform in a closed economy has been well surveyed by Myles (1995: 167–95). Here we concentrate on open economies in a multilateral context.

2.2 A specific trade model

To make our discussion more concrete, we now consider a particular model of world trade. In this competitive equilibrium model, K nations engage in international trade in N goods that are subject to a set of trade taxes by each nation. The world price vector for goods is denoted as p and the trade tax ('tariff') vector imposed by country k on net imports is given by τ^k. Hence, the domestic price vector in country k is $p^k = p + \tau^k$. The production sector in country k is characterized by a revenue or GDP function $G^k(p^k)$, while the single household has an expenditure function $E^k(p^k, u^k)$, where u^k denotes the level of utility. The net revenue function $S^k(p^k, u^k) \equiv G^k(p^k) - E^k(p^k, u^k)$ provides a convenient summary characterization of the price-taking behaviour of the household and production sectors.

Following Turunen-Red and Woodland (1991), the model may be expressed as:

$$\sum_{k \in K} S_p^k(p + \tau^k, u^k) = 0 \tag{2}$$

$$p^T S_p^k(p + \tau^k, u^k) = b^k, k \in K \tag{3}$$

$$\sum_{k \in K} b^k = 0 \tag{4}$$

These are the market equilibrium conditions (2), the budget constraints for each country (3) and the world budget constraint (4). The market equilibrium conditions express the requirement that the net exports of countries, $x^k \equiv S_p^k(p + \tau^k, u^k) \equiv \partial S^k/\partial p$, sum to the zero vector, meaning that world markets clear. The budget constraints state that the value (at world prices) of net exports (the balance of trade) must be matched by a transfer of income abroad, b^k. In our atemporal world, the national budget constraints are simply the requirements of zero current account balances. The world budget constraint requires these transfers abroad to sum to zero over all countries.[1]

It is implicit in this formulation of the model that there is just one consumer in each country, who gets or receives a transfer from the government. To see this, the national budget constraints may be written as

$$E^k(p + \tau^k, u^k) = G^k(p + \tau^k) + \tau^{kT} (E_p^k(p + \tau^k, u^k)$$

$$- G_p^k(p + \tau^k)) - b^k, k \in K \tag{5}$$

which states that expenditure by the household equals income from production, plus net tariff revenue, minus transfers abroad. The latter two terms constitute the government's net receipts (net budget surplus), assumed to be passed on to the household in a lump sum.

It is assumed that, for given policy variables $b = (b^1, \ldots, b^K)$ and $\tau = (\tau^1, \ldots, \tau^K)$, the market equilibrium and national budget constraint equations determine the endogenous variables of the model, namely the world price vector $p \geqslant 0$ and the vector of national utilities $u = (u^1, \ldots, u^K)$.[2]

2.3 Variations

This model is special in many respects and can be extended in various ways. First, we can easily modify the model to deal with quota restrictions on trade, as is done by Anderson and Neary (1992) and Turunen-Red and Woodland (2000). This extension is dealt with further in the discussion of the redistribution of efficiency gains. Second, the assumption that there is just one household in each country is for simplicity and can be easily dropped. In this case, each national expenditure function can be written as a sum of household expenditure functions,

$$E^k(p + \tau^k, u^k) = \sum_{h \in H^k} E^k(p + \tau^k, u^{hk}),$$

where $u^k = (u^{1k}, \ldots, u^{H^k k})$ is a vector of household utilities in country k. Diewert, Turunen-Red and Woodland (1989) provide a detailed account of tariff reform in such a model, but for a small open economy only. Third, the government only acts as a redistributor in this model. If the government produces public goods, it needs revenue and so cannot be simply concerned with redistributing tariff revenue to consumers. The government must either use tariff revenues or revenues from the domestic taxation of consumers and producers to finance its provision of public goods. The model of Diewert, Turunen-Red and Woodland (1989) includes a government sector that produces fixed quantities of public goods, while Abe (1995) and Anderson (1999) consider the optimal choice of public goods production in small open economies.

Fourth, the existence of lump sum taxes or transfers between each national government and its household can be dispensed with by introducing a set of domestic taxes, creating a wedge between producer and consumer prices. Thus, the net revenue function would now be of the form $S^k(p_P^k, p_C^k, u^k) \equiv G^k(p_P^k) - E^k(p_C^k, u^k)$, where consumer and producer prices differ by the domestic tax vector $t^k = p_C^k - p_P^k$. If no lump sum taxes are permitted, the government budget constraint and the individual household constraints need to be incorporated explicitly into the model. Households can then only benefit from a multilateral tariff reform if consumer prices move in their favour, and the government can only pass on tariff revenue to households via alterations in the domestic tax vector. For a small open economy concerned with unilateral tariff reform, this has been explicitly modelled by Diewert, Turunen-Red and Woodland (1989). Fifth, the model can be readily extended to deal with non-traded goods. This extension may be achieved by separating non-traded (N) and traded goods (T), and explicitly incorporating in the model the market equilibrium conditions for each non-traded good in each country as $S_i^k(p_T + \tau_T^k, p_N^k, u^k) = 0$, $k \in K$, $i \in N_N$ (non-traded goods), which determine the domestic prices p_i^k of the non-traded goods. Alternatively, these market equilibrium conditions may be solved for the prices of non-traded goods, which may then be substituted out of the net export functions to yield 'reduced form' net export functions for traded goods that depend only upon the prices of traded goods and the level of utility.[3] In this case, our model (2)–(4) handles non-traded goods if the net export functions are interpreted as reduced form net export functions. Essentially, this approach is equivalent to the introduction of quotas into the model (as briefly discussed above), since non-traded goods can be regarded as having a zero quota on trade.

2.4 Piecemeal policy reform

The multilateral policy reform problem is to find changes in the policy variables that yield a strict increase in the level of utility for each national household. Several points of clarification are in order. First, while the initial tariff-distorted equilibrium may be the consequence of a non-cooperative strategic policy game, it is implicitly assumed that the policy reform itself is cooperative; the national governments are not engaged in non-cooperative, strategic policy games during the reform process. This, of course, raises the question of whether the solution to the policy reform problem will be incentive compatible, that is whether each participant will continue to honour the cooperative agreement. This issue is not addressed here and is ignored by assuming a reversion to the initial equilibrium, if any country should deviate from the agreement. Second, the requirement that all national households experience a strict increase in welfare is the definition of a strict Pareto improvement in welfare (SPI). Countries will not agree to a multilateral policy change unless they benefit. Accordingly, it is implicitly assumed that unanimous support is required for a cooperative agreement to proceed. While a weak Pareto improvement (no household loses and some gain) could be contemplated, this raises technical issues for differential policy changes, as explained by Diewert (1978).[4] Third, it is assumed that it is not feasible to move directly from a distorted equilibrium to a Pareto optimal equilibrium. Accordingly, policy changes are assumed to be 'small' in some sense. We can contemplate differential or small discrete policy changes; most of the literature is devoted to the former since it allows analysis by differential calculus methods. One reason for greater interest in differential policy reforms is that they have less stringent informational requirements than discrete policy reforms; differential reforms simply require knowledge of the values of variables and all responses at the initial equilibrium, whereas discrete reforms demand knowledge of the response surfaces at the initial and final equilibrium.

3 Some preliminary observations

3.1 Normalizations and Walras' Law

Two aspects of the general equilibrium model of the world economy need to be discussed briefly. The first is known as Walras' Law and the second concerns the homogeneity properties of the solution set.

Walras' Law

Walras' Law arises because each country in our world economy has a budget constraint and its net export choices reflect this budget constraint. This means that there is a dependency between the world market equilibrium conditions and the national budget constraints. Multiplying the left-hand side of the market equilibrium conditions (2) by the world price vector p, subtracting the result from the sum of the national budget constraints (3) and the world budget constraint (4), we obtain the identity

$$-p^T \sum_{k \in K} S_p^k(p + \tau^k, u^k) + \sum_{k \in K} p^T S_p^k(p + \tau^k, u^k) - b^k) + \sum_{k \in K} b^k \equiv 0 \qquad (6)$$

Because of this identity, there is a linear dependence among the equations of the model and, consequently, one of the equations is redundant, in the sense that any one equation can be dropped from the model without loss. Put differently, if all but one of the equations of the model are satisfied then the remaining equation is automatically satisfied. The equilibrium can be determined from any $M - 1 = N + K$ equations, where $M = N + K + 1$ is the total number of equations. It is normal practice to drop one of the market equilibrium equations, but this is not a necessary choice.

Homogeneity

It is clear from the equations of the model that the solution for the real variables of the model, namely u, is independent of the scale of the nominal variables $(p, \tau^1, \ldots, \tau^K, b^1, \ldots, b^K)$. This result follows from the homogeneity properties of the net revenue functions and their derivatives, namely that the net revenue functions S^k are positively linearly homogeneous, and hence the net export functions are homogeneous of degree zero, in domestic prices, $p^k \equiv p + \tau^k$. Thus, for example, a doubling of all domestic prices will double the net revenue function S^k and leave net exports S_p^k unchanged.[5] In general, if all the nominal variables $(p, \tau^1, \ldots, \tau^K, b^1, \ldots, b^K)$ in a competitive equilibrium are multiplied by a positive constant but utility levels are not altered, domestic prices $p^k \equiv p + \tau^k$ will be multiplied by the same constant but net exports will be unchanged (due to homogeneity); thus all equilibrium conditions continue to hold. Thus, the real solution is unaffected by an equi-proportional change in all the nominal variables. For example, if world prices, tariffs and transfers are all doubled, domestic prices are doubled and net exports are unchanged at constant utility levels, so the new nominal variables and the same utility levels also constitute an equilibrium. Moreover, if it is the case that there are no international income transfers in a particular equilibrium (i.e. $b = 0$), then the real solution is homogeneous of degree zero in prices and tariffs $(p, \tau^1, \ldots, \tau^K)$ alone.

The homogeneity property implies that the equilibrium conditions cannot determine the *levels* of the nominal variables of the model. Accordingly, the homogeneity property yields the important implication that the nominal variables in the model may be normalized without loss of generality. In particular, the world price vector, provided it is positive, can be normalized by setting the price of any one good (called the *numeraire*) equal to unity without loss of generality. In this case, vector p can be interpreted as the vector of price ratios (relative to the price of the numeraire). If we allow non-zero international transfers when the world price vector is normalized as just described, b^k must now be interpreted as a *real* variable representing the amount of the transfer expressed in terms of the amount of the numeraire good that the transfer will buy at world prices. It is customary to choose the first good as the numeraire, whence $p_1 = 1$ is the normalization rule.

Since consumer and producer choices of consumptions and supplies depend only upon relative domestic prices, it also means that one of the tariff rates in each country can be set to zero without loss of generality. It is customary to choose as the numeraire the good whose tariff rate is set to zero. In this case, both p and p^k can be interpreted as world and domestic relative prices, with all prices relative to that of the first commodity.

While these normalizations to the tariff vectors can be made without loss of generality, they do not have to be made in a description of an equilibrium. What the normalizations do is eliminate the non-uniqueness in the solution for the nominal variables caused by the homogeneity of the net revenue functions in the model. Without the normalizations, there is a (proportional) arbitrariness to the solution. This is not generally a problem, but a property of the model. Thus, while there is no loss of generality in setting a tariff rate for one good in each country equal to zero, there is no necessity to do so and no problem is created if no such normalization is made. Similarly, no difficulty is created if we fail to normalize the world price vector, provided that international income transfers are treated as nominal variables.

Explicit use of Walras' Law and homogeneity

Nevertheless, models are often specified by explicitly incorporating the restrictions arising from Walras' Law and the homogeneity properties. Specifically, the model described above is amended by dropping the market equilibrium condition for the numeraire good, setting the world price of the numeraire good equal to unity, and setting the national tariffs on the numeraire equal to zero. If we define the resulting world price vector as $p^T = (1, q^T)$, the national tariff vectors as $\tau^{kT} = (0, \tau_q^{kT})$ and the national net export functions as $S_p^{kT} = (S_1^k, S_q^{kT})$ the model may be rewritten as

$$\sum_{k \in K} S_q^k(1, q + \tau_q^k, u^k) = 0 \tag{7}$$

$$S^k(1, q + \tau_q^k, u^k) - \tau_q^{kT} S_q^k(1, q + \tau_q^k, u^k) = b^k, \; k \in K \tag{8}$$

$$\sum_{k \in K} b^k = 0 \tag{9}$$

This model includes the market equilibrium conditions for non-numeraire goods only, and determines the world price vector for the non-numeraire goods, q, given the national tariff vectors for non-numeraire goods, $(\tau_q^1, \ldots, \tau_q^K)$. With these features, the model's notation can be simplified, of course. On the other hand, it is important to realize that it is no different in any essential way from the previous model that deals with all goods; we have simply made the restrictions explicit rather than implicit.

3.2 Tariff distortions

The model under consideration allows only for tariff distortions. We now characterize formally what precisely is meant by a tariff distortion. The budget constraint for country k can be totally differentiated to yield the relationship between changes in tariffs, transfers and world prices and the consequent change in utility as:[6]

$$(-p^T S^k_{pu}) du^k = S^{kT}_p dp + p^T S^k_{pp}(dp + d\tau^k) - db^k$$

$$= (S^{kT}_p + p^T S^k_{pp}) dp + p^T S^k_{pp} d\tau^k - db^k \tag{10}$$

The left-hand side gives the change in utility (multiplied by a coefficient that is positive under assumed normality of preferences).[7] The middle expression shows the determinants of this change in terms of world prices, domestic prices and transfers; the last expression decomposes the domestic price effect and shows the separate effects of world prices, tariffs and transfers.

For a small open economy, only the term $p^T S^k_{pp} d\tau^k$ is relevant when undertaking tariff reforms; a large open economy has also to take account of the terms of trade effects of its tariff reforms. In a multilateral setting, international income transfers might also have to be taken into account.

Measures for a small open economy

It is evident from the right-hand side of (10) that the welfare change is related to tariff changes via the term $p^T S^k_{pp} d\tau^k$. If $p^T S^k_{pp} \neq 0$, then it is possible to find a tariff reform $d\tau^k$ for a small open economy (world prices given) to increase welfare. Accordingly, we can take the vector $\epsilon^k \equiv p^T S^k_{pp} \equiv -\tau^{kT} S^k_{pp}$ as a measure (one element for each good) of existing tariff distortions for a small open economy. If element i is positive (negative), a small increase (decrease) in the tariff on good i will raise welfare. The bigger this measure of distortion for good i, the smaller the change in the tariff will be required to achieve a given increase in utility.

A scalar measure of distortion is obtained by creating the positive semi-definite quadratic form $\delta^k \equiv p^T S^k_{pp} p \equiv \tau^{kT} S^k_{pp} \tau^k \geq 0$. This scalar measure can be interpreted as the increase in utility (strictly, the left-hand side of (10)) arising from the tariff reform $d\tau^k = -\tau^k$, in which each tariff is proportionately reduced. While this is a very special reform, it is one that is guaranteed to be welfare improving in a small open economy and leads towards free trade. It therefore has the intuitive appeal of measuring the welfare consequences of a proportionate reduction in tariffs.

When will our two measures of distortion be zero? One situation is where the world price vector, the domestic price vector and the tariff vector are proportional to one another, meaning that *relative prices* are the same domestically as they are abroad. If $p^k = \alpha p$ for some $\alpha > 0$, then $\tau^k = (\alpha - 1)p$ and, since $p^{kT} S^k_{pp} \equiv 0$, it follows that $p^T S^k_{pp} = \tau^{kT} S^k_{pp} = p^{kT} S^k_{pp} \equiv 0$. Thus, even though there may be non-zero tariffs, there is no tariff distortion because relative domestic prices are not affected by the tariff structure.

A second situation where there is no distortion is in the trivial case where the substitution matrix vanishes, i.e. $S^k_{pp} = 0$. Since this matrix

summarizes all the substitution possibilities around the production possibilities frontier and around the household's indifference curve, a null substitution matrix means that there are no substitution possibilities at the
prices and utility level in question.[8] The indifference curve and the production possibilities frontier are both pointed; small changes in prices do not
affect consumptions or productions. Accordingly, tariffs do not create a
distortion at the margin (that is, for small changes).

A third situation is more subtle and occurs when the substitution matrix
has more than one zero eigenvalue. In this case, the substitution matrix has
rank less than $N-1$ and so the equation system $\tau^T S_{pp}^k = 0$ is satisfied for a set
of potential tariff vectors $\tau \neq 0$. This case might occur when S^k is a 'lined
surface', consisting of an infinity of straight lines of continuously varying
slopes (so the surface is linear in one direction but nonlinear in others).

In general, the vector $\epsilon^k \equiv p^T S_{pp}^k$ gives a local measure of tariff distortion for each good. If the vector ϵ^k is the zero vector then there are no
tariff distortions at the margin, deviations from zero measuring the extent
of distortions. If this vector is non-zero, then there are tariff distortions.
The scalar measure $\delta^k \equiv p^T S_{pp}^k p \equiv \tau^{kT} S_{pp}^k \tau^k$ is similarly interpreted.

An alternative measure of distortion for a small open economy has
been developed by Anderson and Neary (1996). They use as their measure
the uniform ad valorem tariff rate that would yield the same utility level as
the existing tariff schedule. Their measure has the advantages of an intuitive interpretation and validity for non-marginal analysis. Further discussion of the Anderson-Neary measure, and an extension to a quantity
measure, has been provided by Anderson and Neary (1999) and Chau,
Fare and Grossopf (1999).

Measures for the world economy

Measures of tariff distortion for our world economy may be obtained
simply as the sums of the individual economy measures. Thus, we can
define the following vector and scalar world distortion measures

$$\epsilon \equiv \sum_{k \in K} \epsilon^k \equiv p^T S_{pp} \equiv -\sum_{k \in K} \tau^{kT} S_{pp}^k \tag{11}$$

$$\delta \equiv \sum_{k \in K} \delta^k \equiv p^T S_{pp} p \equiv \sum_{k \in K} \tau^{kT} S_{pp}^k \tau^k \geq 0 \tag{12}$$

where

$$S_{pp} \equiv \sum_{k \in K} S_{pp}^k$$

is the *world substitution matrix*. This matrix may be expressed as
$S_{pp} = \partial S_p / \partial p^T = [\partial S_i / \partial p_j]$, so its elements are the pure substitution effects of
prices upon the world compensated net export function,

$$S_p \equiv \sum_{k \in K} S_p^k.$$

That these are suitable measures of tariff distortions (at the margin) is confirmed by the following proposition.

Proposition 1   The vector measure $\epsilon \equiv p^T S_{pp} = 0$ if, and only if, $p^T S_{pp}^k = 0$ for every $k \in K$. Similarly, the scalar measure $\delta \equiv p^T S_{pp} p = 0$ if, and only if, $p^T S_{pp}^k = 0$ for every $k \in K$. That is, each of these aggregate measures of distortion is zero if, and only if, each country has zero tariff distortions.

An implication of this proposition is that each measure is non-zero if there is at least one country that exhibits a tariff distortion, characterized by $\epsilon^k \equiv p^T S_{pp}^k \equiv -\tau^{kT} S_{pp}^k \neq 0$. Another implication is that if $\epsilon = 0$ (equivalently, $\delta = 0$) then there is no country that exhibits a tariff distortion. In short, these aggregate measures truly reflect tariff distortions (at the margin) in our model.

3.3 Motzkin's theorem of the alternative

Before proceeding to the analysis of tariff reforms, it is worth considering the mode of analysis. Here we focus on differential policy reform rather than discrete reforms. There are basically two modes of analysis, both based on the comparative statics methodology. The idea is to totally differentiate the equations of the model, thus obtaining the differential equations or system. One method is to completely solve these linear equations for the changes in the endogenous variables. Then, answers to questions about policy reform can be answered by direct inspection of the complete solutions; we can try to determine reforms that will be strict Pareto improving. The second method does not solve the comparative statics equations. Rather, this method uses various 'theorems of the alternative' to determine conditions under which a SPI exists.

The general model represented by (1) can be used to make this distinction clearer. Its total differentiated form may be written as

$$A du + B dp + C d\tau = 0 \tag{13}$$

where A, B and C are matrices of derivatives evaluated at the initial solution to (1). The first method solves these linear equations for changes in the endogenous variables as

$$(du^T, dp^T)^T = -(A, B)^{-1} C d\tau \tag{14}$$

provided the matrix inverse exists. The solution is normally very complex since it involves the inverse of a matrix. Consequently, the search for conditions yielding a solution involving $du \geqslant 0$ can be very difficult.

The method often employed in policy reform research is to use theorems of the alternative. This approach is to ask for solutions to the system

$$Adu + Bdp + Cd\tau = 0, \ du \gg 0 \tag{15}$$

That is, we ask whether we can find changes in all of the variables (du, dp, $d\tau$) that are consistent with the equilibrium conditions of the model and yield a strict Pareto improvement in welfare, $du \gg 0$.

The answer is provided by Motzkin's theorem of the alternative.[9] For the present problem, this theorem states that either (15) has a solution or another system of equations and inequalities, which we refer to as Motzkin's alternative, has a solution for a vector λ, but not both. In other words, a SPI exists if, and only if, there does *not* exist a solution to Motzkin's alternative (MA). Formally, the theorem is expressed in the present context as follows.

Theorem 1 (Motzkin's Theorem of the Alternative) Either (15) has a solution (du, dp, $d\tau$), or the following Motzkin's Alternative

$$\lambda^T A < 0, \ \lambda^T B = 0, \ \lambda^T C = 0 \tag{16}$$

has a solution for vector λ, but not both.

Thus, the strategy employed under this approach is to make assumptions about the model that ensure that MA does not have a solution, in which case we can be assured by Motzkin's theorem that there is a solution to (15), meaning that a SPI exists. It is often the case that assumptions expressed in economically meaningful and easily interpreted ways lead in a reasonably straightforward way to a demonstration that MA has no solution. This strategy also has the advantage of not having to solve the complete set of linear comparative static equations of the model.

This second approach will be illustrated further below in the context of our concrete model of world trade. However, it is a general method that can be usefully applied whenever a solution to a set of comparative statics equations with sign restrictions on some of the changes in variables is required.

4 Redistribution of efficiency gains

One of the major issues in trade policy reform concerns the way efficiency gains can be distributed to ensure a SPI. To obtain a SPI, we need an increase in economic efficiency created by reducing the distortions in the world economy, but we also need some mechanism of distributing these gains. An assumption that there exists the possibility of employing lump sum transfers between countries allows the separation of these two objectives, since lump sum transfers can always be used to distribute the gains successfully. If lump sum transfers are not allowed, however, distortionary taxes and tariffs have to accomplish both tasks and this can be difficult.

In this section, we present some results that establish a clear relationship between tariff reforms and lump sum transfers. This relationship allows us to demonstrate that tariffs can sometimes be used to redistribute efficiency gains in lieu of lump sum transfers.

4.1 Propositions regarding discrete policy choice

The model used in this demonstration may be expressed as:

$$\sum_{k \in K} S_p^k(p + \tau^k, \theta, u^k) = 0 \tag{17}$$

$$p^T S_p^k(p + \tau^k, \theta, u^k) = b^k, k \in K \tag{18}$$

$$\sum_{k \in K} b^k = 0 \tag{19}$$

This is an extension of the model discussed above to include a vector of policy parameters other than tariffs. This vector is denoted by θ, which can be given a variety of interpretations depending upon the particular model under discussion. Examples include θ being a vector of quota restrictions on trade (a case dealt with below) and domestic commodity taxes. Of course, we can get back to the original model (given by equations (2)–(4)) by simply ignoring the existence of θ.

In the initial equilibrium, the policy parameters (τ^0, θ^0, b^0) determine the endogenous variables (p^0, u^0). Now consider a new situation that involves a *discrete change in policy* to (τ^1, θ^1, b^1) with a solution for the endogenous variables given by (p^1, u^1).

The question posed is: can we choose the new tariffs so that the initial utility vector is attained, but without any transfers? That is, given that there is a solution $(\tau^0, \theta^0, b^0, p^0, u^0)$ to the equilibrium conditions (17)–(19), is there also a solution of the form $(\tau^1, \theta^0, 0, p^1, u^0)$? Specifically, this new solution $(\tau^1, \theta^1, b^1, p^1, u^1)$ proposed involves $\theta^1 = \theta^0$, $u^1 = u^0$ and $b^1 = 0$. This new solution therefore involves the same θ policy and yields the same utility vector as the first solution, but there are no transfers. However, the tariff policy and world price outcomes are different. The answer to the question of whether such a solution is possible is 'yes', under suitable conditions.[10]

The strategy for the proof is, first, to postulate a new solution involving tariffs chosen carefully to keep domestic prices unchanged by 'neutralizing' the domestic price effects of any new world price vector and, second, to demonstrate that the world price vector can be determined such that all of the equilibrium conditions are satisfied. The existence of a world price vector that is consistent with our multilateral choice of tariffs depends upon a mild condition on the world trade matrix.

To prove this proposition, therefore, we choose the new tariffs so that initial domestic prices in each country are retained, that is, $p^1 + \tau^{k1} = p^0 + \tau^{k0}$. Since domestic prices, the θ policy vector, and utility levels are unchanged, consumers and producers make the same choices as they did initially. Accordingly, the market equilibrium conditions (17) remain satisfied since

$$\sum_{k \in K} S_p^k(p^1 + \tau^{k1}, \theta^0, u^{k0}) = \sum_{k \in K} S_p^k(p^0 + \tau^{k0}, \theta^0, u^{k0}) = 0 \qquad (20)$$

The world balance of trade conditions (19) hold trivially, since transfers are zero.

Will the individual country balance of trade conditions (18) hold? This requires the new world price vector p^1 to satisfy the equations

$$p^{1T} S_p^k(p^0 + \tau^{k0}, \theta^0, u^{k0}) = b^{k1} \equiv 0, \, k \in K \qquad (21)$$

Defining the initial equilibrium world trade matrix as $X \equiv [x^1, \ldots, x^K]$, where $x^k = S_p^k$ is the net export vector for country k, these equations may be written compactly in matrix form as

$$p^{1T} X = 0 \qquad (22)$$

Since the world trade matrix has dimension $N \times K$, this is a set of K linear equations in N unknowns given by the elements of vector p^1.

What is required in order to complete our demonstration is that this set of homogeneous linear equations has a positive solution for the world price vector, since market clearing is assumed. By a version of Motzkin's theorem of the alternative, such a solution is assured under the following assumption.

Assumption A   There is no solution λ to the inequality system $X\lambda > 0$.

This system may be expressed as

$$\sum_{k \in K} x^k \lambda^k > 0.$$

If this system does have a formatting solution, it is possible to expand or contract each economy (multiply its trade vector by some number) such that no good is in excess demand and at least one good is in excess supply. Such a solution exists, for example, if there is some country k for which $x^k > 0$, meaning that country k exports every good (or has zero trade in some goods).[11] In this case, it will clearly not be possible to find a positive vector p^1 such that $p^{1T}x^k = 0$. Assumption A rules out such cases and therefore guarantees that we *can* find a vector of positive prices that satisfies the national budget constraints (22).

Given this solution, we find the appropriate tariffs vectors from the required relation $p^1 + \tau^{k1} = p^0 + \tau^{k0}$. Thus

$$\tau^{k1} = p^0 + \tau^{k0} - p^1 \tag{23}$$

where p^1 is any positive solution to the equation system (22). This completes our demonstration. The result may be conveniently recorded in the following proposition.

> *Proposition 2* If $(\tau^0, \theta^0, b^0, p^0, u^0)$ solves the equilibrium conditions (17)–(19) and assumption A holds, then we can construct another solution of the form $(\tau^1, \theta^0, 0, p^1, u^0)$. That is, any equilibrium involving income transfers can be replaced by an equilibrium without transfers, but with the same welfare outcome, by an appropriate choice of tariffs. Appropriate tariffs are given by (23), where p^1 is any positive solution to the equation system (22).

While we have chosen $b^1 = 0$ in this proposition, there is no need to do so. If we choose the transfers in the new situation arbitrarily, the same argument follows except that now the requirement for satisfaction of the budget constraints is that p^1 is a positive solution to the equation system

$$p^{1T}X = b^{1T} \tag{24}$$

The assumption that guarantees a positive solution to these equations for the world price vector is the following.

> *Assumption B* There is no solution λ to the inequality system $\lambda^T(X^T - b^1) > 0$.[12]

The solution to this set of linear equations determines the new world price vector and then the required tariffs in the new situation are given by (23). Thus, we get the following slightly more general proposition.

> *Proposition 3* If $(\tau^0, \theta^0, b^0, p^0, u^0)$ solves the equilibrium conditions (17)–(19) and assumption B holds, then we can construct another solution of the form $(\tau^1, \theta^0, b^1, p^1, u^0)$. That is, any equilibrium involving income transfers can be replaced by an equilibrium with a different set of transfers, but with the same welfare outcome, by an appropriate choice of tariffs. Appropriate tariffs are given by (23), where p^1 is any positive solution to the equation system (24).

4.2 Discussion

What these propositions establish is an 'equivalence' between transfers and tariffs. Specifically, the utility vector that arises from any equilibrium involving a set of international income transfers can be attained from another equilibrium that does not involve any such transfers (proposition 1). This new equilibrium is achieved by the imposition of a carefully selected set of tariffs for each country. In this sense, a set of transfers can be replaced by a suitably chosen set of tariffs; transfers are redundant policy instruments. In the case of proposition 2, what we have shown is that any new set of income transfers can be 'neutralized' by a careful choice of tariffs, in the sense that the initial utility vector will remain the equilibrium outcome.

While these propositions show that any transfer can be replaced by tariffs to get the same welfare outcome, the reverse is not true in general. Thus, we cannot change all tariffs arbitrarily and replace them by a set of transfers to get the same welfare outcome, in general. The exception is where the change in tariffs is the same for each country. Thus, transfers can be replaced by suitable tariffs, but a general structure of tariffs cannot be replaced by transfers.

It is noteworthy that the tariff reforms required to go from one equilibrium to the other are the *same* for every country. This follows from our requirement that domestic prices remain the same under the two policy regimes. Accordingly, the *change* in each country's tariff vector is given by $\tau^{k1} - \tau^{k0} = p^0 - p^1$, which is clearly the same for every country. Also noteworthy is the fact that the net export vectors for each country are unchanged by the change in policy from transfers to tariffs, so the volume and pattern of trade is unaffected. Thus, all real variables in the model are unchanged by this change of policy, as are domestic prices. The only differences in the two scenarios are in the tariff and transfer policy instruments and the world price vector. This arises from a dependency that exists between these variables of the model.

Figure 4.1 contains an offer curve diagram to illustrate proposition 2. The figure shows offer curves for two countries (in net export space for one country). These offer curves have their origin at point T, which represents the initial transfer in terms of good 2. The initial equilibrium is at E. The initial world price vector is p^0, which is normal to the line TE, the domestic price vector for country 1 is $p^0 + \tau^{10}$ and the trade vector for country 1 is OE. The same trade vector can be supported with the same utilities and the same domestic price vectors, but with no transfers, if the new world price vector is p^1, which is normal to the trade vector OE. In the new equilibrium, the tariff vectors adjust to ensure that the domestic prices are unchanged and the new trade balances are zero, implying zero transfers.

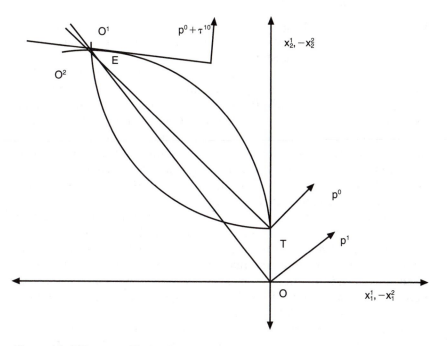

Figure 4.1 Offer curve illustration.

4.3 Two special cases

The development above is reasonably general. Understanding of the general result will be enhanced by considering two interesting special cases.

Tariffs replace transfers

Here we consider that scenario 0 has no tariff reform; a θ reform, accompanied by transfers, yields a SPI. Thus we have $\Delta\tau^0 = 0$, while $\Delta\theta^0$ and Δb^0 are non-zero and generate a SPI given by $\Delta u^0 \gg 0$. The new equilibrium is therefore $(\tau^0, \theta^0, b^0, p^0, u^0)$. In scenario 1 there are no transfers and no change in transfers $(b^1 = \Delta b^1 = 0)$, but a tariff reform $\Delta\tau^1$ is now permitted to accompany the same θ reform $\Delta\theta^0$. By proposition 2, we know that the new tariff structure can support the same utility vector as in scenario 0. The new scenario 1 equilibrium is therefore $(\tau^1, \theta^0, 0, p^1, u^0)$. A comparison of the two equilibria reveals that the difference in tariffs in the two equilibria, given by $\tau^1 - \tau^0$, has simply replaced transfers as a means of achieving utility vector u^0 when policy reform $\Delta\theta^0$ is undertaken.[13] That we can get the same change in utility means that the tariff reform effectively replaces the transfer reform as a redistributive device.

Tariffs replace tariffs and transfer

In this second special case, we do not allow a θ reform in either policy scenario and hence consider only a tariff reform with (in scenario 0) and without (in scenario 1) transfers.

Now consider two policy reforms ($\Delta\tau^0$, $\Delta\theta^0 = 0$, Δb^0, Δp^0, Δu^0) and ($\Delta\tau^1$, $\Delta\theta^1 = 0$, $\Delta b^1 = 0$, Δp^1, Δu^0) leading to equilibria (τ^0, θ^0, b^0, p^0, u^0) and (τ^1, θ^0, $b^1 = 0$, p^1, u^0) with $\Delta u^1 = \Delta u^0 \geqslant 0$. Thus, both reforms yield the same welfare outcome but with different policy settings. Given that (τ^0, θ^0, b^0, p^0, u^0) is an equilibrium for the model, proposition 2 can be used to demonstrate that (τ^1, θ^0, $b^1 = 0$, p^1, u^0) is also a viable equilibrium. Scenario 0 involves a reform of tariffs and transfers that leads to a SPI in welfare. Scenario 1 also involves a tariff reform and leads to the same SPI in welfare, but does not involve any income transfers.

Accordingly, we have been able to show that the transfer reform accompanying the tariff reform in scenario 0 can be dispensed with, provided the tariff reform is altered appropriately from $\Delta\tau^0$ to $\Delta\tau^1$. The difference between this result and that obtained for the previous special case discussed above is that in this second special case there is no reform of the policy parameter vector θ. Thus, the second special case applies to a model where the focus is completely on tariff reform.

The result yielded by this second special case is rather strong. Suppose that we have a discrete tariff and transfer policy reform that yields a strict Pareto improvement in welfare. Then our result tells us that we can dispense totally with the income transfers and can construct another tariff reform that provides for exactly the same SPI welfare change. In other words, there is an equivalence between transfers and tariffs in the sense that transfers can be replaced by a suitable multilateral reform of tariffs. The reason for this result is that there are sufficient tariffs in the world described by our assumptions to replicate any welfare outcome that transfers are able to achieve.[14]

This suggests a two-step approach to tariff reform. The first step involves finding a tariff reform that, alone with a suitable set of multilateral transfers, is able to generate a strict welfare gain. This problem has been addressed by several authors and various suggested tariff reforms are available. Step two involves the use of the first solution to the tariff reform problem to create a new tariff reform, from the same initial equilibrium, that involves no transfers (the special case of $\Delta b^1 = 0$). This new reform could be the one implemented if transfers are not permitted. This two-step procedure is, of course, a purely analytical device that helps to understand the anatomy of tariff reform; it is not put forward as a procedure to be followed in the actual practice of multilateral negotiations for tariff reform.

4.4 Some applications

Here some applications of the propositions are discussed.

Transfer problem

In the context of the model of trade under discussion here, Turunen-Red and Woodland (1988) showed that it was possible to establish a SPI by a pure redistribution of income via international lump sum transfers, provided that some country exhibits a consumption inferiority. While their analysis is for a SPI arising from a differential change in transfers, it obviously implies the existence of a SPI arising from a (possibly small) discrete change in transfers. Assume that the required conditions hold for such a SPI to occur and that the equilibrium following a discrete change in transfers is (τ^0, b^0, p^0, u^0), in which we ignore policy vector θ.[15] Thus, the change in the equilibrium is $(\Delta\tau^0, \Delta b^0, \Delta p^0, \Delta u^0) = (0, \Delta b^0, \Delta p^0, \Delta u^0)$ with $\Delta u^0 \gg 0$.

Now consider an alternative discrete policy change (from the original initial equilibrium) that achieves the same welfare change as the pure transfer reform just described. The change is to be $(\Delta\tau^1, 0, \Delta p^1, \Delta u^0)$, which involves a tariff reform (but no change in transfers) and the same welfare change $\Delta u^0 \gg 0$. The new equilibrium is therefore (τ^1, b^0, p^1, u^0). By proposition 2, we know that such an equilibrium is possible, provided that assumption B on the world trade matrix is satisfied.

Thus, it has been shown that, instead of using a pure transfer reform to obtain a SPI as did Turunen-Red and Woodland (1988), we can use a carefully chosen multilateral tariff reform to achieve exactly the same welfare outcome. Of course, the equilibrium is not the same since, for example, the world price vector will be different under the two different policies. Nevertheless, tariffs can be used to achieve the same welfare outcome that transfers were able to achieve. Thus, we have been able to extend the Turunen-Red and Woodland result on the existence of SPI transfer reforms to the existence of equivalent SPI uniform tariff reforms.

This result occurs because each country has a full set of tariffs at its disposal to ensure that domestic prices are kept unchanged even though the world prices are affected. By a 'full set of tariffs' we mean $N-1$ tariffs, since the tariff on any one of the N goods can be set to zero without any loss of generality (as discussed above). If we choose this good conveniently to be the numeraire (whose world price can be set to unity, again without loss of generality), the $N-1$ tariffs can be used to neutralize any change the world price vector would otherwise have upon the domestic price vector.

Commodity taxes

Next, we consider the consequences for the above propositions if some countries have a set of domestic commodity taxes in place. In this case there is a distinction between consumer and producer prices and the net export functions depend separately upon these two sets of prices. Accordingly, for the above argument to proceed in the same way, both consumer and producer prices have to be maintained at their initial values even though world prices change. This is possible, since producer prices can be maintained at the initial levels by an adjustment of tariffs, while consumer prices can be maintained by an adjustment of commodity taxes. Then the market equilibrium conditions will hold and the appropriate choice for the world price vector comes from solving the balance of trade conditions as described above. Thus, the propositions can be readily extended to handle domestic taxes.

Quota reforms

Turunen-Red and Woodland (2000) develop results concerning the 'equivalence' between differential quota and transfer reforms on the one hand, and differential quota and tariff reforms on the other. Here we show that this equivalence, established in the differential policy reform context, also applies to discrete policy reforms.

The model of Turunen-Red and Woodland (2000) may be expressed in compact form as

$$\sum_{k \in K^1} S_p^k(p_t + \tau_t^k, p_q + \tau_q^k, u^k) + \sum_{k \in K^2} S_p^k(p_t + \tau_t^k, x_q^k, u^k) = 0 \tag{25}$$

$$p^T S_p^k(p_t + \tau_t^k, v_q^k, u^k) = b^k, \ k \in K \tag{26}$$

$$\sum_{k \in K} b^k = 0 \tag{27}$$

where $v_q^k \equiv (p_q + \tau_q^k)$, $k \in K^1$ and $v_q^k \equiv x_q^k$, $k \in K^2$. In this model, net exports of traded goods are given by $x^k = S_p^k(p_t + \tau_t^k, p_q + \tau_q^k, u^k)$ for countries $k \in K^1$ without any quota restrictions; for countries $k \in K^2$ that have quota restrictions on net trades of the subset of goods labelled by the subscript q, net exports are given by $x^k = S_p^k(p_t + \tau_t^k, x_q^k, u^k)$, where x_q^k is the vector of quotas. As previously, the equations of the model are the market equilibrium conditions, the budget constraints for each country, and the world budget constraint.

Turunen-Red and Woodland (2000) showed that a differential reform of quotas and transfers that yields a SPI can be replaced by the same differential reform of quotas and an appropriate multilateral, differential reform of tariffs that yields exactly the same welfare improvement. Here we show that the same result obtains when we consider discrete policy reforms. The demonstration of this result follows from observing that the models (25)–(27) correspond exactly to the general model given by (17)–(19) above, where $\theta = x$ is the vector of all quotas on trade. Accordingly, the propositions established above apply to the current model of quotas. Therefore, assuming that there is a solution $(\tau^0, x^0, b^0, p^0, u^0)$ to the equilibrium conditions (25)–(27), there is another solution of the form $(\tau^1, x^0, 0, p^1, u^0)$ that has no transfers but the same set of quotas and utility levels. The tariffs that achieve this outcome are chosen (in the same way as above) to keep domestic prices unchanged.

4.5 The differential policy reform case

The discussion above has focused on a comparison of discrete policy reforms. Here the case of small or differential policy reforms is briefly discussed and compared to the discrete policy reform case.

The main proposition

For concreteness, we present the ideas in the context of the extended model dealt with above for the discrete reform case. The proposition and proof follow those provided by Turunen-Red and Woodland (1999) for the specific model of trade (given above) in which both tariff and quota distortions occur. However, the proposition stated below is more general in that it allows for tariff reforms in both policy scenarios.

The total differential of system (17)–(19) may be written as:

$$\sum_{k \in K} dS_p^k(p_t + \tau_t^k, \theta, u^k) = 0 \tag{28}$$

$$p^T dS_p^k(p_t + \tau_t^k, \theta, u^k) + S_p^{kT}(p_t + \tau_t^k, \theta, u^k)dp = db^k, \quad k \in K \tag{29}$$

$$\sum_{k \in K} db^k = 0 \tag{30}$$

Consider two alternative policy reforms enacted at a common initial equilibrium. We assume a solution for policy 0 of the form $(d\tau^0, d\theta^0, db^0, dp^0, du^0)$ with $du^0 \gg 0$. We now propose a solution policy of the form $(d\tau^1, d\theta^1, db^1, dp^1, du^1) = (d\tau^1, d\theta^0, 0, dp^1, du^0)$ with $db^1 = 0$ and $du^0 \gg 0$. In this new solution, the same θ policy change is enacted and the same welfare outcome is required as in the original policy reform, there are no transfers, and the tariff policy and world price changes are different. We wish to show that such a policy change is indeed possible under a particular rank condition on the world trade matrix.

The demonstration that the new solution to the comparative statics equations is feasible proceeds by choosing a tariff reform that ensures that the *changes* in domestic prices are the same under the two policy scenarios, that is, that $dp^1 + d\tau^{k1} = dp^0 + d\tau^{k0}$. By ensuring that the differential changes in domestic prices are the same under both policy scenarios, along with the same θ reform and the same change in utilities, it is easy to see that the changes in the net export vectors are also the same in both scenarios. Hence, market equilibrium is preserved under policy 1. Since changes in the transfers are zero by assumption, the world budget constraints are satisfied.

Therefore, it remains to be checked whether the national budget constraints will be satisfied. The total differentials of the national budget constraints under the two scenarios are

$$p^T dS_p^{k0} + S_p^{kT} dp^0 = db^{k0}, k \in K \tag{31}$$

$$p^T dS_p^{k1} + S_p^{kT} dp^1 = db^{k1} = 0, k \in K \tag{32}$$

where initial values of variable have no indicator and changes in variables for the two policies are indicated by superscripts 0 and 1. Since $dS_p^{k1} = dS_p^{k0}$, it follows that policy 1 is viable if, and only if, the change in world prices satisfies the equations

$$S_p^{kT}(dp^0 - dp^1) = db^{k0}, k \in K \tag{33}$$

This set of K linear equations in N unknowns given by $(dp^0 - dp^1)$ may be written in matrix form as

$$X^T(dp^0 - dp^1) = db^0 \tag{34}$$

Let us assume a suitable condition that ensures a non-trivial solution to these equations.

Assumption C   The world trade matrix $X \equiv [x^1, \ldots, x^K]$ has rank equal to $K - 1 \le N - 1$.

Under this assumption, a non-trivial solution to (34) for $(dp^0 - dp^1)$ is assured.[16] Once determined, this solution yields the required tariff reform given by

$$d\tau^{k1} = dp^0 - dp^1 + d\tau^{k0} \tag{35}$$

Thus, we obtain the following result.

Proposition 4   Let the world trade matrix at the initial equilibrium, X, satisfy assumption C (Rank Condition) above. If $(d\tau^0, d\theta^0, db^0, dp^0, du^0)$ solves the comparative statics equations (28)–(30) then we can construct another solution of the form $(d\tau^1, d\theta^0, db^1 = 0, dp^1, du^0)$. That is, if there exists a differential reform of policy parameters θ and transfers $(d\theta^0, db^0)$ that yields a SPI in welfare, then there also exists a differential reform of policy parameters θ and tariffs $(d\theta^0, d\tau^1)$ with no accompanying transfer reform, that yields the same SPI in welfare. That is, the reform of transfers accompanying the reform of θ can be replaced by a suitable multilateral reform of tariffs. The appropriate tariff reform is given by $d\tau^{k1} = dp^0 - dp^1 + d\tau^{k0}$, where $dp^0 - dp^1$ is any solution to the equation system $X^T(dp^0 - dp^1) = db^0$.

This proposition is a generalization of a result developed in Turunen-Red and Woodland (1999) for the case where θ is a vector of quotas on trade. In their theorem 1, the scenario 0 reform does not involve a reform of tariffs, whence $d\tau^0 = 0$. The present proposition is a generalization by allowing a tariff reform to be part of scenario 0. Apart from this, the outline of the proof provided above follows that in Turunen-Red and Woodland (2000).

In the special case where the $d\tau^0 = 0$, this proposition shows that an accompanying differential transfer reform can be dispensed with and replaced by a suitable multilateral differential tariff reform; the differential welfare gain is the same under either policy. In the more general case, when scenario 0 involves a tariff reform, a further suitable multilateral change in tariffs can compensate for the differential removal of transfers.

It is clear from the above demonstration that the differential reform case is very similar to the discrete reform case. While the differential case has been discussed in detail by Turunen-Red and Woodland (2000), it has been presented here in order to show a difference that relates to the conditions on the world trade matrix required for the appropriate propositions to hold. It is to this difference that attention is now turned.

Comparison of discrete and differential reforms conditions

The question arises as to why the condition on the world trade matrix is apparently different depending on whether we are dealing with discrete policies or differential policy changes. Assumption C, our rank condition required to solve (34), is weaker (more easily satisfied) than assumption A, already made, to ensure a positive solution to (24). The reason lies in the fact that the discrete case requires a solution for the new world price vector, which has to be positive to be consistent with the market clearing conditions. By contrast, the differential analysis is undertaken at the initial price vector, which is positive. The differential comparative statics results are valid in a sufficiently small neighbourhood of the initial positive price vector and so the new price vector will be positive in this neighbourhood.

In short, the differential analysis demands less than the discrete analysis and so the required conditions for the validity of our results are less stringent in the differential policy reform case.

5 Multilateral tariff reforms

Here we consider the anatomy of tariff reforms under several different situations. First, we briefly look at reforms in small open economies to set the stage. Then we examine multilateral reforms when transfers are available as redistributive instruments. Finally, some attention is given to reforms when international income transfers are not permissible instruments of policy. Our discussion is not intended to be a comprehensive survey; rather, the focus is on the structure or anatomy of the expressions leading to welfare changes.

5.1 Unilateral tariff reforms

Although this chapter is concerned with multilateral trade policy reform, it will be useful for comparison purposes to briefly review some basic results that have come out of the literature on tariff reform in small open economies. The small open economy case is much easier to analyse because there are no terms of trade effects to take into account and each country can be considered in isolation.

Equation (10) above simplifies to give the welfare effects for a small open economy as

$$(-p^T S_{pu}^k) du^k = p^T S_{pp}^k d\tau^k \tag{36}$$

Assuming that the coefficient on the left-hand side is positive (the normality case), the tariff reform problem in a small open economy is one of finding tariff changes that make the right-hand side of (36) positive. The right-hand side may be expressed as $p^T S_{pp}^k d\tau^k = -\tau^{kT} S_{pp}^k d\tau^k$ due to homogeneity, and it is noted that the substitution matrix is positive semidefinite. Consequently, the reform $d\tau^k = -\alpha\tau^k$, $\alpha > 0$, will be successful since then $-\tau^{kT} S_{pp}^k d\tau^k = \alpha\tau^{kT} S_{pp}^k \tau^k > 0$ whenever $\epsilon^k = -\tau^{kT} S_{pp}^k \neq 0$ (a distortion exists). This is the well-known result that a proportional reduction in tariffs will be welfare improving.

Another well-known result is that a small open economy will benefit from a reduction in the tariff of the good with the highest ad valorem tariff rate, provided that good is a net substitute for all other goods (meaning that $S_{ij}^k < 0$ for all $j \neq i$, where good i is the good in question). It will also benefit if the good with the lowest ad valorem tariff rate is increased. These results (collectively known as the *concertina theorem*) are obtained by showing that the right-hand side of (36) is positive. Hatta (1977a, 1977b) and Fukushima (1979) provide these and other results, while a review of this early literature can be found in Woodland (1982) and Neary (1995).

5.2 Tariff reforms with transfers

With this brief review of tariff reform in a small open economy in hand, we now direct attention to multilateral tariff reforms that have to take into account consequent changes in the terms of trade facing all countries. First, consider reforms when there exist a set of multilateral lump sum transfers between countries. In this case, individual budget constraints are not important, since they can be satisfied by appropriate transfers. The analysis proceeds by totally differentiating the model, solving the market equilibrium conditions for the change in the prices for non-numeraire goods dq, substituting this result into the world budget constraint to get a relationship between changes in utilities and changes in tariff vectors. We proceed in two separate steps.

First, summing the national budget constraints, totally differentiating the sum and making use of the market equilibrium conditions, we obtain

$$\sum_{k \in K} (-p^T S_{pu}^k) du^k = \sum_{k \in K} p^T S_{pp}^k (dp + d\tau^k) = p^T S_{pp} dp + \sum_{k \in K} p^T S_{pp}^k d\tau^k \qquad (37)$$

Since the left-hand side is a positively weighted sum of utilities (under the normality assumption), a necessary condition for a strict Pareto improvement, $du = (du^1, \ldots, du^K)^T \geqslant 0$, is that the right-hand side of (37) be positive.[17] The middle expression shows the dependence of this on the change in the domestic prices in relation to the national substitution matrices. The right-hand side expression separates this into a world-wide terms of trade effect and separate national terms involving changes in national tariff vectors. Clearly, the terms of trade effect given by the term $p^T S_{pp} dp$ will be important in determining whether the right-hand side is positive.

Second, by totally differentiating the market equilibrium conditions, solving the resulting equations (excluding the numeraire's equation) for the change in the prices for non-numeraire goods dq, and substituting this result into (37), we obtain

$$\sum_{k \in K} (-\tilde{p}^T S_{pu}^k) du^k = \sum_{k \in K} \tilde{p}^T S_{pp}^k d\tau^k \qquad (38)$$

where $\tilde{p}^T \equiv p^T - (0, p^T S_{pq} S_{qq}^{-1})$ is defined as the *world shadow price vector*. This expression gives the relationship between changes in utilities and changes in each country's tariff vectors.

This expression bears a strong resemblance to the previous expression (37) and the expression (36) for a small open economy. There are two main differences. First, the terms of trade effect in the previous expression (37) has been eliminated in (38) by making use of the market equilibrium conditions. Second, the remaining parts of each expression are very similar, differing only in that the world price vector p appearing in (37) has been replaced by the world *shadow* price vector $\tilde{p}$ in (38). This shadow price vector takes account of the changes in the world market price vector needed to restore market equilibrium and is the appropriate price vector for the evaluation of tariff reforms, as (38) shows. When world price changes are taken into account, tariff distortions in country k may be measured by $\tilde{p}^T S^k_{pp}$ (vector form) or $\tilde{p}^T S^k_{pp} \tilde{p}$ (scalar form); corresponding aggregate measures are $\tilde{p}^T S_{pp}$ (vector form) and $\tilde{p}^T S_{pp} \tilde{p}$ (scalar form). These extended concepts allow for distortion measures similar in structure to those applicable for small open economies; shadow prices simply replace market prices in the formulae.

The shadow price vector is equal to the world market price vector, p, if and only if there are no tariff distortions $(p^T S_{pp} = 0)$. The difference between the two price vectors, $\tilde{\tau}^T \equiv \tilde{p}^T - p^T = (0, -p^T S_{pq} S^{-1}_{qq})$, may be interpreted as a world *shadow* tariff vector and it will be zero if and only if there are no tariff distortions.

If it is assumed that the coefficients $\tilde{\beta}^k \equiv (-\tilde{p}^T S^k_{pu})$ on the left-hand side of (38) are positive, then it follows from a simple application of Motzkin's theorem that a strict Pareto improvement in welfare occurs if and only if at least one country's distortion vector is non-zero, that is $\gamma^{kT} \equiv \tilde{p}^T S^k_{pp} \neq 0$ for at least one $k \in K$.[18] If there are no distortions, the right-hand side must be zero for all possible tariff reforms and so du cannot have all positive elements, since $\tilde{\beta}^T du = 0$ and $\tilde{\beta} \gg 0$. Conversely, if a distortion exists then a tariff change can always be found to make the right-hand side positive and $du \gg 0$.

Thus the cooperative, multilateral tariff reform problem (when there are international income transfers available) reduces to finding directions of changes in national tariffs to make the right-hand side of (38) non-zero. Clearly, as explained above, this can be done provided $\gamma^{kT} \equiv \tilde{p}^T S^k_{pp} \neq 0$ for some country k. If we go further and specify a *particular direction of reform*, given by $d\tau^k = a^k d\alpha$ where a^k is the direction and $d\alpha > 0$ is the step length, then the condition for a strict Pareto improvement is that[19]

$$\theta \equiv \sum_{k \in K} \tilde{p}^T S^k_{pp} a^k > 0 \qquad (39)$$

Formally, these results may be recorded as the following proposition.

Proposition 5   Assume that (a) the world substitution matrix S_{pp} has maximal rank $N-1$ and (b) all generalized normality terms $\tilde{\beta}^k \equiv -\tilde{p}^T S^k_{pu}$, $k \in K$, are positive. Then there exists a multilateral tariff and transfer reform that yields a strict Pareto improvement in welfare $(du \gg 0)$ if and only if some nation k has a tariff distortion characterized by $\tilde{p}^T S^k_{pp} \neq 0$. The multilateral tariff reform $d\tau^k = a^k d\alpha$, $d\alpha > 0$, yields a strict Pareto improvement in welfare if and only if

$$\theta \equiv \sum_{k \in K} \tilde{p}^T S^k_{pp} a^k > 0.$$

Turunen-Red and Woodland (1991) develop several examples of tariff reforms that satisfy this criterion. Most, but not all, are based upon the strategy of choosing the direction vectors a^k to ensure that θ is a sum of positive definite quadratic forms.

It is noteworthy that the expressions to be evaluated in the multilateral tariff reform case, such as $\tilde{p}^T S^k_{pp} d\tau^k$, are similar to those to be evaluated in the case of unilateral tariff reform in a small open economy, such as $p^T S^k_{pp} d\tau^k$. The difference is that the multilateral case uses the world shadow price vector $\tilde{p}$ to evaluate the tariff change rather than the world market price vector. Thus, the use of the world shadow price vector enables us to see the similarities between multilateral and small open tariff reform. This shadow price vector embodies the terms of trade effects of reforms that need to be taken into account in multilateral tariff reforms.

5.3 Tariff reforms without transfers

Now briefly consider tariff reforms when multilateral lump sum transfers between countries are not permitted.

The first, and important, point to note is that, if the rank condition (assumption C) on the net world trade matrix is satisfied, reforms that can be shown to be SPI under transfers will also be SPI when transfers are not permitted in many instances.[20] This follows from the above discussion on the equivalence between transfers and tariffs as redistributive devices in the analysis of differential tariff reforms. These results have been demonstrated by Turunen-Red and Woodland (2000) for the case of quota reforms, for example.

If this result cannot be applied (due to the rank condition not holding), then a direct demonstration of SPI reforms of tariffs is needed. On this approach, see Turunen-Red and Woodland (1993) and earlier work by Mayer (1981). Recently, Bagwell and Staiger (1999) have examined tariff reform without transfers in a two-commodity model.

6 Conclusion

Multilateral policy reforms have particular importance because of the role of the GATT (now the World Trade Organization (WTO)) in the international trade negotiations over the post-war period. This chapter has concentrated on some particular aspects of the multilateral policy reform problem. In particular, attention has focused on the *anatomy* of the competitive trade model used to analyse the problem and of the structure of the solutions. In addition to reviewing the role of the well-known homogeneity properties of the solution, we have discussed how theorems of the alternative can be used to analyse models where interest centres on obtaining strict Pareto improvements in welfare. We have also proposed two measures of what constitutes a distortion for both an individual and the world economy, one a vector and the other a scalar, that reflect the welfare consequences of changes in tariffs: each depends upon the tariff vector and the substitution matrix, which embodies responses to tariffs. Once general equilibrium responses to changes in world prices are taken into account, appropriate measures of distortions can be obtained using the concepts of a world shadow price vector and a world shadow tariff vector. Results on multilateral policy reform are characterized using the concepts of world shadow prices and our measures of distortion, and reflect these homogeneity properties, as well as curvature properties of revenue and expenditure functions arising from optimizing behaviour by producers and consumers.

The model structure also has implications for the important theoretical and practical question of how efficiency gains arising from trade policy reform can be distributed to countries to ensure that all countries benefit in a welfare sense. If lump sum transfers (employed by most trade analysts) are not available policy instruments, the achievement of a strict Pareto improvement must depend on changes in distortionary taxes, such as domestic taxes or tariffs on trade. Our results developed in this chapter (extending the ideas presented previously in Turunen-Red and Woodland (2000)) show that, under a mild condition on the world trade matrix, it does not matter whether lump sum transfers are available. An equilibrium with transfers can be replaced by an equilibrium with no transfers if tariffs are appropriately adjusted. This ability to replace transfers by tariffs is a result of the structure or anatomy of the model of international trade, whereby the terms of trade effects for a country and a lump sum transfer are equivalent and whereby there are sufficient tariff instruments to enable countries to neutralize the domestic price effects of terms of trade movements.

While many possible extensions to the multilateral trade reform literature can be contemplated, two particular ones come to mind. First, rather than starting from an arbitrary initial competitive equilibrium, it would be potentially productive to start from a Nash equilibrium for a trade policy game. This would provide added structure to the initial equilibrium that could be profitably exploited. A second extension would be to consider a restricted set of policy reforms. For example, following the ideas in Bagwell and Staiger (1999) concerning the reciprocity rules of the WTO, tariff reforms that are world price preserving as well as welfare increasing may constitute interesting research.

Notes

1. Throughout the chapter, we use the symbol K to denote the set of countries (as well as the number) of countries in the world.
2. The notational convention used regarding vector inequalities is as follows: $x = (x_1, \ldots, x_n) \geq 0$ means $x_i \geq 0$, $i = 1, \ldots, n$; $x \gg 0$ means $x_i > 0$, $i = 1, \ldots, n$; and $x > 0$ means $x \geq 0$ and $x \neq 0$.

3. See Woodland (1982: 218–23) for further details on these reduced form functions.
4. If each household's utility is increasing in a particular direction of policy change, then there is a, possibly small, discrete policy change that will yield higher utility. On the other hand, if a household's utility is stationary with respect to a policy change (derivative is zero), there is no guarantee that a small discrete policy change will raise that household's utility.
5. See Woodland (1982) for further details on the homogeneity and other properties of the net revenue functions and their derivatives.
6. Second derivatives are indicated by the subscripts so, for example, $S^k_{pu} = \partial^2 S^k/\partial p \partial u^k = \partial S^k_p/\partial u^k$ and $S^k_{pp} = \partial^2 S^k/\partial p \partial p^T = \partial S^k_p/\partial p^T$.
7. If preferences are normal then $-S^k_{pu} = E^k_{pu} \geqslant 0$ and so $(-p^T S^k_{pu}) > 0$ at positive world prices. Even without normality of all goods, sufficient normality can yield the Hatta normality condition $(-p^T S^k_{pu}) > 0$. This condition ensures that a gift from abroad is welfare improving.
8. Since $S^k = G^k - E^k$, it follows that $S^k_{pp} \equiv \partial S^k_p/\partial p^T = G^k_{pp} - E^k_{pp}$. The matrix $G^k_{pp} = \partial G^k_p/\partial p^T$ consists of the effects of prices upon net production (movements around the production possibilities frontier), while $E^k_{pp} = \partial E^k_p/\partial p^T$ consists of pure substitution effects of prices (around the indifference curve).
9. See, for example, Mangasarian (1969: 34).
10. We are grateful to Kala Krishna for raising the question of whether our previous results on the equivalence of differential changes in tariffs and transfers could be extended to discrete changes.
11. This could happen if that country has a positive trade balance, $b^k > 0$.
12. The inequality system in assumption B may be expressed as

$$\sum_{k \in K} \binom{x^k}{-b^{1k}} \lambda^k > 0$$

A solution to this system means that it is possible to expand or contract each economy (multiply its trade vector and trade deficit by some number) so that no good is in excess demand and there is no world payments surplus, and that either some good is in excess supply or there is a world payments deficit. The existence of a positive solution for prices to the national budget constraints requires that such anomalies do not exist.
13. This is made even clearer if there are no tariffs in the initial equilibrium, in which case $\tau^0 = 0$. Then (τ, b) is $(0, b^0)$ in scenario 0 equilibrium and $(\tau^1, 0)$ in scenario 1 equilibrium.
14. In an extension of scenario 1, we can simply contemplate a *different* transfer reform $\Delta b^1 \neq 0$ that involves $b^1 \neq 0$. Then, for any such arbitrary change of transfers, we can construct another tariff reform that provides for exactly the same welfare change. Thus, the change in transfers from b^0 to b^1 can be accommodated by the change in tariffs from τ^0 to τ^1.
15. The model used by Turunen-Red and Woodland (1988) is that of (2)–(4), which corresponds to (17)–(19) if the policy parameter vector θ is ignored.
16. The solution allows us to set $dp^i_1 = 0$, as required by the assumption that the price of the numeraire is fixed at unity, and hence to have the tariffs on the numeraire equal to zero in every country.
17. The equation may be written as $\beta^T du = \theta$, where $\beta^k \equiv -p^T S^k_{pu}$ and θ is the right-hand side. If $\beta \gg 0$ and $du \geqslant 0$ then $\theta > 0$.
18. Write equation (38) as $\tilde{\beta}^T du = \Sigma \gamma^{kT} d\tau^k$, where $\gamma^{kT} \equiv \tilde{p}^T S^k_{pp}$. According to Motzkin's theorem, this equation has a solution with $du \geqslant 0$ if and only if there is no scalar λ such that $\lambda \tilde{\beta} < 0$ and $\lambda \gamma^{kT} = 0$ for all $k \in K$. If all elements of vector $\tilde{\beta}$ are positive (as assumed), a solution to the Motzkin's alternative is

assured if and only if $\gamma^{kT} \equiv \tilde{p}^T S_{pp}^k = 0$ for all $k \in K$. Thus, if $\tilde{\beta} \geqslant 0$, a necessary and sufficient condition for a SPI is that $\gamma^k \equiv \tilde{p}^T S_{pp}^k \neq 0$ for some $k \in K$.

19. Write equation (37) as $\tilde{\beta}^T du = \theta d\alpha$, where scalar $\theta \equiv (\Sigma \gamma^{kT} a^k)$. According to Motzkin's theorem, this equation has a solution with $du \geqslant 0$ and $d\alpha > 0$ if and only if there is no scalar λ such that $\lambda[\tilde{\beta}^T - \theta] < 0$. If all elements of vector $\tilde{\beta}$ are positive (as assumed), a solution to the Motzkin's alternative is assured if and only if $\theta \leq 0$. Thus, if $\tilde{\beta} \geqslant 0$, a necessary and sufficient condition for a SPI is that $\theta > 0$.

20. The earlier literature on multilateral reforms with transfers includes Hatta and Fukushima (1979) and Fukushima and Kim (1989).

References

Abe, K. (1995) 'The target rates of tariff and tax reform', *International Economic Review*, 36: 875–85.

Anderson, J.E. (1999) 'Trade reform with a government budget constraint', in J. Piggott and A.D. Woodland (eds) *International Trade Policy and the Pacific Rim*, London: Macmillan: 217–36.

Anderson, J.E. and Neary, P.J. (1992) 'Trade reform with quotas, partial rent retention and tariffs', *Econometrica*, 60: 57–76.

—— (1996) 'A new approach to evaluating trade policy', *Review of Economic Studies*, 63: 107–25.

—— (1999) 'A mercantilist index of trade policy', National Bureau of Economic Research Working Paper 6870.

Bagwell, K. and Staiger, R.W. (1999) 'An economic theory of GATT', *American Economic Review*, 89: 215–48.

Chau, N.H., Fare, R. and Grossopf, S. (1999) 'Trade restrictiveness and efficiency', unpublished paper.

Diewert, W.E. (1978) 'Optimal tax perturbations', *Journal of Public Economics*, 10: 139–77.

Diewert, W.E., Turunen-Red, A.H. and Woodland, A.D. (1989) 'Productivity and Pareto improving changes in taxes and tariffs', *Review of Economic Studies*, 56: 199–216.

Fukushima, T. (1979) 'Tariff structure, nontraded goods and theory of piecemeal policy recommendations', *International Economic Review*, 2: 427–35.

Fukushima, T. and Kim, N. (1989) 'Welfare improving tariff changes: a case of many-good and many-country', *Journal of International Economics*, 26: 383–88.

Hatta, T. (1977a) 'A theory of piecemeal policy recommendations', *Review of Economic Studies*, 44: 1–12.

—— (1977b) 'A recommendation for a better tariff structure', *Econometrica*, 45: 179–202.

Hatta, T. and Fukushima, T. (1979) 'The welfare effect of tariff rate reductions in a many country world,' *Journal of International Economics*, 9: 503–11.

Mangasarian, O. (1969) *Nonlinear Programming*, New York: McGraw-Hill.

Mayer, W. (1981) 'Theoretical considerations on negotiated tariff adjustments', *Oxford Economic Papers*, 33: 135–53.

Myles, G.D. (1995) *Public Economics*, Cambridge: Cambridge University Press.

Neary, J.P. (1995) 'Trade liberalization and shadow prices in the presence of tariffs and quotas', *International Economic Review*, 36: 531–54.

Turunen-Red, A.H. and Woodland, A.D. (1988) 'On the multilateral transfer problem: existence of Pareto improving international transfers', *Journal of International Economics*, 25: 249–69.

—— (1991) 'Strict Pareto improving reforms of tariffs', *Econometrica*, 59: 1127–52.

—— (1993) 'Multilateral reforms of tariffs without transfer compensation', in N.V. Long and H. Herberg (eds), *Trade, Welfare and Economic Policies: Essays in Honor of Murray Kemp*, Ann Arbor: University of Michigan Press: 145–66.

—— (2000) 'Multilateral policy reforms and quantity restrictions on trade', *Journal of International Economics*, 52: 153–68.

Woodland, A.D. (1982) *International Trade and Resource Allocation*, Amsterdam: North-Holland.

5 Regionalism and illegal immigration in North America

A theoretical analysis[1]

Helena Gaytán-Fregoso and Sajal Lahiri

1 Introduction

Regionalism takes various forms. In most regional agreements liberalization in the movement of goods and services forms the cornerstone of such agreements. The flexibility with regard to the movement of factors of production and firms varies from agreement to agreement, and the liberalizations on these fronts are typically phased in. For example, in the European Union, since the introduction of the single market, there are no institutional restrictions on the movement of either labour or capital. Although the mobility of capital has increased significantly because of the removal of all restrictions, the mobility of labour has been disappointingly limited.

In the North American Free Trade Agreement (NAFTA)—which is the focus of this chapter—the mobility of labour is not allowed.[2] In fact, it is commonly believed that the sceptics of NAFTA in the USA were won over by the argument that free trade of commodities between USA and Mexico would reduce the flow of illegal immigrants from the latter.

The theoretical underpinning for the above argument lies in the classic paper by Mundell (1957) who showed in the Heckscher–Ohlin framework that trade and international factor mobility are substitutes, in the sense that either achieves the same world equilibrium and that an increase in one lowers the other one. Several subsequent papers added to Mundell's seminal work by modifying the underlying assumptions.

Two important points need to be made about the supposed substitutability between goods and labour. First, although there exists a voluminous trade theory literature (see Ruffin (1984) for a survey) on international migration of labour, most authors, with a few notable exceptions, assume that labour is not different in any essential way from other factors, such as capital. This is a serious drawback of the existing trade literature, as labour has many characteristics, such as family ties, which are fundamentally different from other factors. Migration is not just a result of rewards differentials, it is a result of a cost-benefit analysis undertaken to maximize *expected* income through international movement. That is, differences in income (net of the cost of migration) expected at the destination and at the origin which, if positive, promotes migration. A household, and not an individual, is often at the heart of a decision on labour migration.

The second point is that the substitutability *à la* Mundell is true provided, among other things, there are no impediments to factor movements. Thus, in a distorted world with factor mobility restrictions, commodity trade and factor mobility can be complements. That is to say, illegal immigration, which is by definition subject to frictions, can in principle rise with liberalization of commodity trade.

By ignoring some of the key characteristics of labour and ignoring frictions in the mobility of labour, the traditional trade theory literature ignored the possibility that workers could attempt to migrate by illegal means as in fact often occurs. This possibility is explored in earlier contributions by Ethier (1986a, 1986b); in both articles he not only took explicit account of the fundamental characteristics of labour mobility, he also presented models where labour migration is restricted through a Harris-Todaro type equilibrium. Here, the probability of success at illegal immigration is a function of the level of expenditure on anti-immigration policies, and potential migrants make their migration decision on the basis of expected income differentials. Subsequently, Bond and Chen (1987), Yoshida (1993), Schulze (1995) and Djajić (1987) offered different extensions to the model. Although those are very important contributions to the literature, none of these models explicitly consider commodity trade, and consequently the important interactions between commodity trade and factor movements are missing from their analysis.[3]

In the existing theoretical literature on illegal migration there is a common key assumption that differentiates this model from those where labour mobility is untrestricted. This key assumption is that labour movements are restricted by some degree of enforcement of migration controls, so that the probability of success in entering the host country illegally is a function of the resources spent on enforcement. Taking into account this established assumption, this chapter develops a general equilibrium two-country model of international trade, where both countries, namely the North and the South, trade in a number of (unspecified) commodities and such trade is distorted by the presence of trade taxes in both countries. In this two-country world, international factor movements are disallowed. However, labour from the South attempts with some probability of success to emigrate to the North by illegal means, and this probability is, as in Ethier (1986a, 1986b), a function of the expenditure on enforcement. Apart from the general equilibrium nature of our model which distinguishes it from other models in the literature, we also model migration equilibrium in a somewhat different conceptual framework. In contrast to the existing literature where *individuals* make migration decisions, in the present case *families* make such decisions—although not all members of a family necessarily attempt illegal migration. The cost of failed migration is also modelled somewhat differently: here expenditures are incurred before attempts at illegal migration are made. In most other models, expenditures are incurred only if attempts are unsuccessful. These differences in modelling international migration will be seen to have serious implications for the properties of the model.

Our framework enables us to analyse the interaction between commodity trade and illegal immigration. In particular, we examine the effect of multilateral tariff reductions on the flow of illegal migration, and on the welfare levels of the families in the South and the North. The present analysis is of immediate relevance to many of the recent developments in the world today. Recent years have seen very rapid integration of the international commodity markets while at the same time immigration policies are being tightened up in most developed countries. This chapter attempts to synthesize these two developments in the field of policy making.

The chapter is organized as follows. The next section introduces the basic framework. The third section focuses primarily on the effect of multilateral tariff reductions on the flows of illegal immigration to the North. The welfare effects are analysed in the fourth section. The final section presents some concluding remarks.

2 The model

We consider a general equilibrium two-country model where international movements of factors of production are disallowed. In spite of the restrictions on labour migration, some workers from one of the two countries (called the South) attempt, with some probability of success, to emigrate to the other country (called the North) by illegal means.

The total endowment of labour in the North and the South are denoted by $\bar{L}$ and $\bar{l}$ respectively. The total supply of labour in the South is equal to the total endowment of factor in that country, $\bar{l}$, minus the volume of illegal immigration, I. That is,

$$l = \bar{l} - I \tag{1}$$

The total supply of legal residents (nationals) in the North is denoted by $\bar{L}$, and are employed in the production of a private good (L^p), and a club good in the public sector (L^g). That is,

$$\bar{L} = L^p + L^g \tag{2}$$

These residents and the illegal migrants are assumed to be non-homogenous. Moreover, illegal immigrants only take jobs in the private sector.

The probability of successful migration, π, is given by[4]

$$\pi = \frac{I}{C+I} \tag{3}$$

where C is the number of people who are caught while attempting to migrate, and who are sent back to the country of origin as a result of the enforcement of migration deterrence policies.[5]

From (3) the relationship between C and I can be expressed as

$$C = I\left(\frac{1-\pi}{\pi}\right), I = C\left(\frac{\pi}{1-\pi}\right) \tag{4}$$

We assume that wages are the only cost on the production of the club good, and that this cost is met by lump-sum taxation of the earnings of the legal residents of the North, so that

$$\bar{W}L^g = \tau = (\bar{L}+I)g \tag{5}$$

where $\bar{W}$ is the wage paid in the public sector, g is the per capita consumption of the club good, and τ is the tax, which is assumed to be constant. Implicitly, we have assumed that the club good is consumed by both the legal residents and the illegal immigrants. The constancy of τ is assumed to highlight crowding in the consumption of the club good.

The expenditure functions for the representative consumer in the North, for an illegal resident in the North, and for a representative consumer in the South are given respectively by $E(P, g, U)$, $\tilde{E}(P, g, \tilde{U})$, and $e(p, u)$ where the terms U, $\tilde{U}$, and u are the respective utilities.[6] Domestic price vectors (exclusive of the numeraire good) are denoted by P and p.[7] It is to be noted that $-E_g(>0)$ and $-\tilde{E}_g(>0)$ are the willingness to pay for the club good by respectively the legal workers and the illegal residents in the North. Clearly, $P = P^w + T$ and $p = P^w + t$, where P^w is the world price vector, and T and t are the vectors of specific tariffs. Similarly, the revenue functions of the North and the South are given by $R(P, \bar{L}-L^g, I)$ and $r(p, l)$.[8] For simplicity we assume that all other factors of production in the North are owned by the legal residents.

We assume that some nationals in the North actively help people in the South to migrate illegally and receive from each person who decides to make an attempt to migrate an amount F, which is paid in advance of the attempt to migrate.[9] Since $C+I$ is the number of people who attempt to migrate, the amount $F(C+I)$ can be viewed as a lump-sum transfer from the household in the South to those in the north.

It is known from the properties of revenue functions that R_I is the wage rate of the migrants in the North so that $R(\cdot)-IR_I$ is the factor income of the legal residents in the North from the productive sector. The government in the North spend ϵ on the enforcement of anti-immigration control. Assuming also that tariff revenues in each country are transferred to its legal residents in a lump-sum manner, and that the illegal immigrants repatriate a fraction of their incomes α to their families in the South, the budget constraints for each representative household of each country are[10]

$$\bar{L}E(P, g, U) = R(P, \bar{L} - L^g, I) + T'M - \epsilon + F(C + I) - IR_I \qquad (6)$$

$$I\tilde{E}(P, g, \tilde{U}) = (1 - \alpha)IR_I \qquad (7)$$

$$le(p, u) = r(p, l) + t'm - F(C + I) + \alpha IR_I \qquad (8)$$

where the imports of each country are[11]

$$M = (\bar{L}E_P + I\tilde{E}_P - R_P) \qquad (9)$$

$$m = (le_p - r_p) \qquad (10)$$

We also assume that the two countries are small open economies in the commodity markets so that the vector of international prices P^w is exogenously given.[12]

It only remains to specify how the number of illegal immigrants is determined. In conventional migration analysis, migration decisions are assumed to be made by individuals and not families. However, there are empirical micro-level migration analyses which have emphasized the role of family in migration decisions (see, for example, Banerjee (1981) for a study of rural-urban migration in India, and Stark and Lucas (1988) for the case of Botswana). In this chapter, we assume that decisions to migrate are made at the family level. We also assume that the family size is large so that, by appealing to the Strong Law of large Numbers, we can assume away the existence of aggregate uncertainty for the family, although individuals face the risk of getting caught at the border.[13] For conceptual convenience we assume that the South consists of one household with $\bar{l}$ members and the family decides how many of its members would make an attempt to migrate, and how much of their income is to be repatriated to the family. In making such a decision, family welfare is maximized, and for simplicity we assume a utilitarian family welfare function, i.e. family welfare ω is given by the total sum of individual utilities. That is[14,15]

$$\omega = I\tilde{U} + (\bar{l} - I)u \qquad (11)$$

The number of illegal immigrants is then determined from the following optimality rules[16]

$$\frac{\partial \omega}{\partial I} = 0; \; \frac{\partial \omega}{\partial \alpha} = 0$$

Differentiating (7), (8) and (10) with respect to I, and doing the appropriate substitutions we obtain

$$\frac{\partial \omega}{\partial I} = \tilde{U} - u - \frac{\theta}{\Delta} = 0 \tag{12}$$

$$\frac{\partial \omega}{\partial \alpha} = -IR_I \left[\frac{1}{\tilde{E}_{\tilde{U}}} - \frac{1}{\Delta} \right] \tag{13}$$

where

$$\theta = -(e - r_l) + \alpha R_I + IR_{II} - t'(e_p - r_{pl}) + \frac{F}{\pi}$$

and

$$\Delta = e_u - t' e_{pu}$$

The second order conditions for the optimization problem of the family from the South can be written as[17]

$$\frac{\partial^2 \omega}{\partial I^2} = \frac{1}{\Delta} (r_{ll} + 2R_{II} + IR_{III} - t' r_{pll})$$

$$- \frac{\theta^2 - \theta(1 - \alpha)IR_{II}}{I\Delta^3} \cdot (e_{uu} - t' e_{puu}) < 0 \tag{14}$$

$$\frac{\partial^2 \omega}{\partial \alpha^2} = - \frac{IR_I^2}{I\tilde{E}_{\tilde{U}}^3} [I(e_{uu} - t' e_{puu}) + I\tilde{E}_{\tilde{U}\tilde{U}}] < 0 \tag{15}$$

From (13) the repatriation equilibrium can be written as

$$\tilde{E}_{\tilde{U}} = \Delta$$

which states that the marginal utilities of the illegal immigrants and their family members back at home are equalized.

From (12) the migration equilibrium condition can be written as

$$\tilde{U} - u = \frac{\theta}{\Delta} \tag{16}$$

That is, in equilibrium the utility differential for the migrants is equal to the cost of migration, given that such costs are shared between family members. The cost of migration includes indirect costs (given by the first and the second term in the right-hand side of the expression for θ) on top of the direct cost, F.

It can be shown that $\Delta > 0$ if the numeraire good is a normal good in the South. However, the value of θ can be either positive or negative.[18] If the value for θ turns out to be negative, it follows from (12) that the migrant would be worse off in the post-migration equilibrium than his or her family members who stay behind (or are caught while attempting to migrate). This is an interesting possibility which does not arise in other models of migration found in the literature (see, for example, Ethier 1986a) and it occurs in the present context because we assume migration decisions to be family based rather than individual based. Therefore, our assumption that migration decisions are family, rather than individual, based has important implications for the properties of the model.[19]

This completes the description of the model. We shall conclude this section by interpreting (16) in terms of the Harris-Todaro type equilibrium condition. For this, we rewrite (16) as

$$u = \pi \tilde{U} + (1 - \pi)\left(u - \frac{\pi \theta}{(1 - \pi)\Delta}\right) \tag{17}$$

The right-hand side of (17) is the expected utility of a potential migrant. If he or she is successful, the utility obtained is $\tilde{U}$ and the probability of its occurrence is π. On the other hand, if the attempt is unsuccessful (the probability of that happening is $1 - \pi$), he or she simply returns to the family and enjoys a utility u, minus the cost which has already been incurred. The left-hand side of (16) is the utility of not making an attempt at migration. This equation is quite similar to the migration equilibrium specified in Ethier (1968a, 1968b).

3 Tariff reductions and illegal immigration

Using the framework described in the previous section, we shall now analyse the effect of uniform reduction in all tariffs (in both countries) on the volume of illegal immigration.

First of all we note that $dP = dT$ and $dp = dt$. Then denoting the family welfare in the South, ω, by a function of I, T, t and α we rewrite (12) as

$$\omega_I = \omega_I(I, t, T, \alpha)$$

Totally differentiating this equation we get

$$\omega_{II} dI = -\omega'_{It} dt - \omega'_{IT} dT - \omega'_{I\alpha} d\alpha \tag{18}$$

where $\omega_{II} < 0$ from (14).

Totally differentiating (1), (3), (7), (8) and (10) we obtain

$$l\Delta du = t' s dt + \alpha I R'_{Ip} dT - \theta dI + I R_I d\alpha \tag{19}$$

$$\tilde{E}_{\tilde{U}}d\tilde{U} = ((1-\alpha)R_{IP} - \tilde{E}_P)'dT + (1-\alpha)R_{II}dI + \frac{g}{\tilde{L}+I}\tilde{E}_g dI - R_I d\alpha \quad (20)$$

where s is the substitution matrix, $le_{pp} - r_{pp}$, in the South. It is well known that the matrix s is negative definite.

Equation (19) states that tariff reform has two effects on per capita utility in the South. The first term on the right-hand side represents the direct effect of tariff reform on welfare, and this expression can be found in the literature on tariff reform (see, for example, Dixit and Norman 1980: 187). This effect works via changes in import levels. The second term is the direct effect of the tariff reform on the illegals' level of wage and the repatriation factor. The third term is the indirect effect via changes in the level of illegal immigration, and the fourth term works via changes in the amount of income remitted to the South. Changes in tariffs in the North have two effects on the utility level of the immigrants. It changes their wage rate, given by $R'_{IP}dT$, and it affects the level of consumers' surplus, given by $\tilde{E}'_P dT$. At the same time, changes in the number of new illegal immigrants coming to the North affect their wage level and their per capita consumption of the club good. These two effects are given by the second and third terms in the right-hand side of (20). Finally, the reductions have an indirect effect on welfare via changes in income remitted to the residents in the South, and this is given by the fourth term in (20).

Partial differentiation of (12) with respect to T, and using (20) and (19) gives

$$\omega'_{IT}dT = \frac{1}{\Delta}(R_{IP} + R_{IIP} - \tilde{E}_P)'dT + \frac{\theta}{l\Delta^3}\cdot(e_{uu} - t'e_{puu})\alpha IR'_{IP}dT \quad (21)$$

Similarly, from differentiating (12) with respect to t and using (20) and (19) we obtain

$$\omega'_{It}dt = -t'sdt - \frac{\partial\left(\frac{\theta}{\Delta}\right)}{\partial t}dt$$

$$= -t'\hat{s}dt \quad (22)$$

where

$$\hat{s} = \frac{1}{\Delta}(e_{pp} - r_{ppl}) - \frac{\theta}{l\Delta^3}[(e_{uu} - t'e_{puu})s - l\Delta e_{ppu}] \quad (23)$$

Doing the same with respect to α gives

$$\omega_{I\alpha} = \frac{\theta}{l\Delta}\cdot(e_{uu} - t'e_{puu})IR_I \quad (24)$$

In order to study the effects of multilateral tariff reductions on the flow of illegal immigrants we will analyse two cases in turn. Before proceeding to the two cases, we need to specify a rule for tariff reduction. The one that we consider is a uniform percentage reduction of all the tariffs in both countries, viz.,

$$dt = -\lambda t, \, dT = -\lambda T \tag{25}$$

where λ is a small positive fraction. Moreover, we also need to assume that the preferences of people originating in the South exhibit diminishing marginal utility of income, i.e.[20]

$$e_{uu} > 0, \, \tilde{E}_{\tilde{U}\tilde{U}} > 0 \tag{26}$$

3.1   Case 1. Exogenous repatriation

In this section, we shall assume that the fraction of income repatriated by the illegal immigrants, α, is exogenous.

From substituting (21) and (22) in (18) we obtain

$$\omega_{II} dI = t' \hat{s} dt - \frac{1}{\Delta} (R_{IP} + IR_{IIP} - \tilde{E}_P)' dT$$

$$- \frac{\theta}{l\Delta^3} \cdot (e_{uu} - t' e_{puu}) \alpha IR'_{IP} dT \tag{27}$$

Substituting (25) in (27) we obtain

$$- \frac{\omega_{II}}{\lambda} dI = t' \hat{s} t - \frac{1}{\Delta} (R_{IP} + IR_{IIP} - \tilde{E}_P)' T$$

$$- \frac{\theta}{l\Delta^3} \cdot (e_{uu} - t' e_{puu}) \alpha IR'_{IP} T \tag{28}$$

Uniform tariff reductions affect the volume of illegal immigration via a number of channels. First, they increase income in the South because of the efficiency gain associated with tariff reductions.[21] This makes it less attractive for the people in the South to attempt illegal migration. Second, it lowers (raises) wages of the immigrants in the North if R_{IP} is positive (negative), and this reduces (increases) migration; this is the Stolper–Samuelson effect of changes of output prices on factor prices, if we make the Heckscher–Ohlin assumption that the non-numeraire good uses intensive labour. Third, tariff reductions in the North reduce domestic prices in the North and therefore increase the real income of the immigrants. This effect, given by $\tilde{E}'_P T$, increases the level of migration. Finally, tariff reductions change the cost of migration, θ/Δ, and therefore, the expected income of migration. The first and the last effect are captured by the first and third terms on the right-hand side of (28). There are thus many opposing effects of tariff reductions on the volume of illegal immigration, and the net effect can be either positive or negative. Ignoring the third order cross derivatives, the following proposition establishes a sufficient condition for the net effect to be negative.

Proposition 1 Uniform percentage reductions in all tariffs in both countries reduce the volume of illegal immigration if (i) the matrix $\hat{s}$ (defined in (23)) is negative definite, and (ii) $(R_{IP} - \tilde{E}_P)'T$ is positive.

The conditions in proposition 1 simply ensure that the negative effects described above dominate the positive ones, and an inspection of the conditions suggests that they are plausible.

3.2 Case 2. Endogenous repatriation

We now turn to the case where α is endogenous. This endogeneity introduces an extra term in the determination of the level of illegal immigration, viz. the third term in the right-hand side of (18). From (24) and (26) we know that $\omega_{I\alpha} > 0$, therefore we need to examine what happens to $d\alpha$. For this, we differentiate (15) and using (19)–(20), we obtain

$$\frac{I\tilde{E}_{\tilde{U}\tilde{U}} + I(e_{uu} - t'e_{puu})}{I\Delta} R_I d\alpha = \frac{\tilde{E}_{\tilde{U}\tilde{U}}}{\tilde{E}_{\tilde{U}}}((1-\alpha)R_{IP} - \tilde{E}_P)'dT + E_{UP}dT$$

$$+ t'e_{ppu}dt - \frac{(e_{uu} - t'e_{puu})}{I\Delta}(t'sdt + \alpha IR_{IP}dT)$$

$$+ \frac{(e_{uu} - t'e_{puu})}{I\Delta}(\theta + (1-\alpha)IR_{II})dI$$

$$+ \frac{\tilde{E}_{\tilde{U}\tilde{U}}}{\tilde{E}_{\tilde{U}}}(1-\alpha)R_{II}dI$$

$$- \frac{g}{\overline{L}+I}\left(\tilde{E}_{\tilde{U}g} - \frac{\tilde{E}_{\tilde{U}\tilde{U}}}{\tilde{E}_{\tilde{U}}}\tilde{E}_g\right)dI \qquad (29)$$

Rewriting (29) as

$$\alpha = \alpha(t, T, I)$$

where

$$\frac{I\tilde{E}_{\tilde{U}\tilde{U}} + I(e_{uu} - t'e_{puu})}{I\Delta} R_I\alpha_t = t'e_{ppu} - \frac{(e_{uu} - t'e_{puu})}{I\Delta}t's \qquad (30)$$

$$\frac{l\tilde{E}_{\tilde{U}\tilde{U}} + I(e_{uu} - t'e_{puu})}{l\Delta} R_I \alpha_T = \frac{\tilde{E}_{\tilde{U}\tilde{U}}}{\tilde{E}_{\tilde{U}}} ((1-\alpha)R_{IP} - \tilde{E}_P)' + E_{UP}$$

$$- \frac{(e_{uu} - t'e_{puu})}{l\Delta} (\alpha I R_{IP}) \tag{31}$$

$$\frac{l\tilde{E}_{\tilde{U}\tilde{U}} + I(e_{uu} - t'e_{puu})}{l\Delta} R_I \alpha_I = \frac{(e_{uu} - t'e_{puu})}{l\Delta} (\theta + (1-\alpha)IR_{II})$$

$$+ \frac{\tilde{E}_{\tilde{U}\tilde{U}}}{\tilde{E}_{\tilde{U}}} (1-\alpha)R_{II}$$

$$- \frac{g}{\bar{L}+I} \left(\tilde{E}_{Ug} - \frac{\tilde{E}_{\tilde{U}\tilde{U}}}{\tilde{E}_{\tilde{U}}} \tilde{E}_g \right) \tag{32}$$

Reductions in tariffs affect the proportion of income repatriated in a number of ways. Increased income associated with efficiency gains in the South decreases marginal utilities of the people in the South and thus increase the fraction of income repatriated. Similarly, reduced tariff in the North will increase the income of the illegal immigrants if $R_{IP} > 0$. Therefore, if $R_{IP} > 0$, tariff reductions in the North will reduce the marginal utility of the immigrants and thus increase α. Increased level of illegal immigration will reduce wages of the illegal immigrants and reduce their consumption of the club good (due to crowding). Both these effects will raise marginal utility of the illegal immigrants, and thus reduce α.

From (18) we get

$$(\omega_{II} + \omega_{I\alpha}\alpha_I)\, dI = -(\omega_{It} + \omega_{I\alpha}\alpha_t)dt - (\omega_{IT} + \omega_{I\alpha}\alpha_T)dT \tag{33}$$

Applying (24), (25) and (30)–(32) to (33), we obtain

$$- \frac{\omega_{II} + \omega_{I\alpha}\alpha_I}{\lambda}\, dI = t'\bar{s}t - \frac{1}{\Delta}(R_{IP} + IR_{IIP} - \tilde{E}_P)'T$$

$$- \frac{\theta}{l\Delta^3} \gamma(e_{uu} - t'e_{puu})\alpha IR'_{IP}T + \frac{\theta l\tilde{E}_{\tilde{U}\tilde{U}}}{l\Delta^2\tilde{E}_{\tilde{U}}} \hat{\gamma}\alpha R'_{IP}T$$

$$- \frac{\hat{\gamma}\theta}{\Delta^2} \left[\frac{\tilde{E}_{\tilde{U}\tilde{U}}}{\tilde{E}_{\tilde{U}}} (R_{IP} - \tilde{E}_P)'T + \tilde{E}'_{\tilde{U}P}T \right] \tag{34}$$

where

$$\omega_{II} + \omega_{I\alpha} \cdot \alpha_I = -\frac{\gamma\theta^2}{l\Delta^3}(e_{uu} - t'e_{puu}) + \frac{g}{\bar{L}+I}\left[\frac{1}{\Delta} + \frac{\hat{\gamma}\tilde{E}_{\tilde{U}\tilde{U}}\theta}{\Delta^2}\right]\tilde{E}_g$$

$$-\frac{\theta\hat{\gamma}g}{\Delta^2(\bar{L}+I)}\tilde{E}_{\tilde{U}g}$$

$$+\frac{1}{\Delta}(r_{II} + 2R_{II} + IR_{III} + t'r_{pII}) < 0 \qquad (35)$$

$$\bar{s} = \frac{1}{\Delta}(e_{pp} - r_{ppl}) - \gamma\frac{\theta}{l\Delta^3}[(e_{uu} - t'e_{puu})s - l\Delta e_{ppu}] \qquad (36)$$

and

$$\hat{\gamma} = \frac{I(e_{uu} - t'e_{puu})}{l\tilde{E}_{\tilde{U}\tilde{U}} + I(e_{uu} - t'e_{puu})} > 0; \quad \gamma = \frac{l\tilde{E}_{\tilde{U}\tilde{U}}}{l\tilde{E}_{\tilde{U}\tilde{U}} + I(e_{uu} - t'e_{puu})} > 0$$

From the repatriation equilibrium (15) and the definitions of γ and $\hat{\gamma}$ the third and fourth terms in (34) cancel out, simplifying the equation to

$$-\frac{\omega_{II} + \omega_{I\alpha}\alpha_I}{\lambda}dI = t'\bar{s}t - \frac{1}{\Delta}(R_{IP} + IR_{IIP} - \tilde{E}_P)'T$$

$$-\frac{\hat{\gamma}\theta}{\Delta^2}\left[\frac{\tilde{E}_{\tilde{U}\tilde{U}}}{\tilde{E}_{\tilde{U}}}(R_{IP} - \tilde{E}_P)'T + \tilde{E}'_{\tilde{U}P}T\right] \qquad (37)$$

The first three terms in the right-hand side of (34) are similar to those in the case of exogenous repatriation (see (28)), the only difference is that some of the terms are multiplied by γ (or $\hat{\gamma}$) because of the endogeneity of α. The final two terms are new and appear only because α is endogenous.

Since $\omega_{II} + \omega_{I\alpha} \cdot \alpha_I < 0$, it follows from (37) that multilateral tariff reductions reduce the volume of illegal immigration if the following conditions are satisfied.

Proposition 2 When the proportion of income repatriated by the illegal immigrants is endogenous, uniform percentage reductions in all tariffs in both countries reduce the volume of illegal immigration if (i) the matrix $\bar{s}$ (defined in (36)) is negative definite, and (ii) $(R_{IP} - \tilde{E}_P)'T$ is positive.

In the next section we analyse the welfare effects of the tariff reductions.

4 Tariff reforms and welfare

Having analysed the effect of tariff reductions on the level of illegal immigration in the preceding section, we now turn our attention to the effects of such reform on the welfare level of the legal nationals in the North and on the family welfare in the South. For simplicity, we shall only consider the case of exogenous income repatriation in this section.

Turning first to the welfare of the nationals of the North, totally differentiating (6), (7) and (9), and substituting (25) we obtain:

$$\bar{L}E_U(1 - T'C_Y)dU = -\lambda T'ST + \lambda I(1 - T'\tilde{C}_{\tilde{Y}})(R_{PI} - \tilde{E}_P)'T$$

$$+ \lambda T'\tilde{C}_{\tilde{Y}}\alpha R_{IP}T$$

$$- (R_{PI} - \tilde{E}_P)'TdI + \frac{g}{\bar{L}+I}(\bar{L}E_g + IT'\tilde{C}_{\tilde{Y}}\tilde{E}_g)dI$$

$$- [(1 - T'\tilde{C}_{\tilde{Y}}(1 - \alpha))IR_{II}]dI + \left(\frac{F}{\pi}\right)dI \qquad (38)$$

where S $(= E_{PP} - R_{PP})$ is the substitution matrix for the nationals in the North, and PC_Y $(= PE_{PU}/E_U)$ and $P\tilde{C}_{\tilde{Y}}$ $(= P\tilde{E}_{P\tilde{U}}/\tilde{E}_{\tilde{U}})$ are the marginal propensities to consume the non-numeraire good for the nationals in the North and the illegal immigrants respectively. The term $1 - T'\tilde{C}_{\tilde{Y}}(1 - T'C_Y)$ is positive if the numeraire good is normal for the illegal immigrants (nationals) in the North.

Since the matrix S is negative definite, the first term on the right-hand side of (38) is positive. This is the standard welfare effect tariff reform in a small open economy. The remaining terms are present here only because of the presence of illegal immigration. The second term is the direct effect of tariff reductions on the tariff revenue via changes in import demands from the illegal immigrants. The third term indicates the direct effect of the tariff reduction on the illegal wage. Since we assumed that $R_{IP}>0$, that is, as the tariff in the North reduces the illegal wage is reduced as well, this clearly improves the welfare in the North as lower wages are paid to the illegals.

To analyse the rest of the terms in (38) we assume that migration is reduced as a result of tariff reductions. The fifth term is the indirect effect on tariff revenue via changes in the level of illegal immigration. The sixth reflects a positive effect on the per capita availability of the club good which increases as migration is reduced. The effect of reduced immigration on the illegal wage level is given by the seventh term, which is negative as $IR_{II}<0$. Finally, the last term represents the change in income of the agents in the North who help illegal immigrants to migrate, which reduces as migration decreases.

If the conditions in proposition 1 are satisfied, i.e. $(R_{PI} - \tilde{E}_P)'T>0$ and

$t'\hat{s}t' < 0$, tariff reductions reduce illegal immigration, therefore the fifth and the sixth terms on the right-hand side of (38) are also positive.

Only the last two terms have a negative effect on welfare, and this negative effect is small if the illegal wage is inelastic to reductions in the supply of illegal labour, and if the direct cost of migration (which accrues to the nationals in the North) is not very high. These results can be summarized as follows.

> *Proposition 3* Uniform percentage reductions in all tariff in both countries raises the welfare of the nationals in the North if (i) the matrix $\tilde{s}$ (defined in (36)) is negative definite, (ii) $(R_{PI} - \tilde{E}_P)'T$ is positive, (iii) the illegal wage is not very sensitive to changes in the supply of illegal immigrants, and (iv) the direct cost of migration F is not very high.

Having analysed the welfare effect for the residents of the North, we analyse the same effect for the residents of the South. Since $\partial w/\partial I = 0$ from the family optimization rule and $\partial u/\partial T = \partial \tilde{U}/\partial t = 0$, from (11), and using (19), (20) and (27), the family welfare in the South can be written as

$$\Delta dw = -\lambda t'st - \lambda I(R_{IP} - \tilde{E}_P)T + \frac{g}{\bar{L}+I} I\tilde{E}_g dI \tag{39}$$

The first term is the terms of trade effect produced by the tariff reduction, and this term is positive since the matrix s is negative definite. The second term is an indirect effect on the family of the South welfare via the tariff reduction in the North. This is a negative effect if one of the conditions in propositions 1 and 2, viz. $(R_{IP} - \tilde{E}_P)'T > 0$, is satisfied. This is because, as already explained, the tariff reform reduces the illegals' wage, but at the same time increases the real income of the immigrants still resident in the North. The final term is a positive effect for the illegal migrants resident in the North, who face an increased availability of the public good if illegal migration is reduced.

The net effect of the tariff reform on the welfare of the families in the South is ambiguous. However, a necessary condition for welfare improvement is that the matrix s is negative definite and the valuation of the club good by the illegal residents in the North is high. We conclude our analyses by noting that it is possible for tariff reforms to reduce illegal immigration and increase the welfare of the nationals in the North and that of the families in the South.

5 Conclusion

In this chapter we developed a general equilibrium two-country international trade model of illegal immigration and analysed the effects of multilateral tariff reductions on illegal immigration, and on the welfare in the two countries. In contrast to the existing migration models where migration decisions are assumed to be made by individuals, migration here was modelled as the result of family based decision-making process.

We found that coordinated tariff reductions in the two countries have several opposing effects on welfare. First, the standard welfare improving effects via the reduction of trade distortions are present here as well. Second, there are a number of indirect effects via changes in the level of illegal immigration and some of these effects could be negative. However, we have found sufficient (or necessary) conditions for the positive effects to outweigh the negative ones. In fact, it has been shown that it is possible for uniform tariff reductions in both the countries to be strictly Pareto improving. Similarly, tariff reductions also have opposing effects on the level of illegal immigration, and one can find a set of plausible conditions under which the level of illegal immigration in fact reduces as a result of the reforms.

Therefore, when illegal immigration between two trading partners, such as Mexico and the USA, puts a particular strain on the relationship between the two countries, placing further restrictions on trade is perhaps the wrong way to deal with the situation. Some politicians in the USA do not like free trade agreements, such as NAFTA, between the USA, Canada and Mexico, and at the same time they are very concerned about the extent of illegal Mexican immigration into the USA. One of the messages of the present chapter is that free trade agreements should perhaps be encouraged by people who are seriously concerned about the extent of illegal immigration. It is however not the purpose of this chapter to suggest that direct anti-illegal immigration policies, such as policing the borders should be scaled down. All possible instruments need to be applied if the problem is viewed as really alarming. However, trade reforms may strike at the root cause of the problem, viz. the huge welfare differentials between the two countries, more effectively than some other instruments.

Notes

1. The views expressed in this chapter are the authors' own and not necessarily of their employers. An earlier version of this chapter was presented at the European Science Foundation and the Euroconferences Activity of the European Union co-sponsored conference on 'Migration and Development', held in Mont Sainte Odile, Alsace during 31 May–5 June 1996. The authors are grateful to the participants of that conference for helpful comments.
2. Although the North American Free Trade Agreement does not envisage the free movement of people, it does consider in Chapter 12 the temporary entry of business persons into each member country. It is acknowledged that their temporary entry contributes to business realization, as well as facilitating ideas,

technology and general knowledge exchange, helping by this means to stretch communication links among nationals of all three countries. However, the agreement does not consider free movement of any other kind of workers.

3. Faini and Venturini (1993) and Faini and de Melo (1995) point out that empirically there is a link between trade policy and international migration. Bandyopadhyay and Bandyopadhyay (1998) is the only analytical paper that explicitly considers the simultaneous existence of commodity trade and illegal immigration.

4. π is a function of expenditure on the enforcement of anti-immigration policies in the North. However, since this expenditure is taken as exogenous in our analysis, π effectively is a constant parameter in our model.

5. Those policies could range from border interdiction to internal detection, and deportation.

6. All the variables and functions in the North (South) will henceforth be denoted by upper (lower) case letters, and a tilde will refer to the variables for the illegal residents.

7. All vectors are column vectors, and for a vector x, the transpose of it is denoted by x'.

8. Since the factors of production other than labour do not vary in our analysis, without any loss of generality, they are omitted from the arguments of the revenue functions.

9. We implicitly assume that the people in the North who receive such payments are some naturalized or legal immigrants who have developed a social network and act as contractors for the employers of illegal labour.

10. Factor income $\tilde{W}L^g$ from the public sector and τ, the lump-sum tax, cancel each other out in the budget constraint for the legal residents, as the latter finances the former.

11. It is well-known that the derivative of the revenue (expenditure) function with respect to the domestic price vector gives the vector of domestic productions (compensated demands).

12. We can relax this assumption by introducing another equation, $m + M = 0$, which states that the world demand is equal to world supply for the non-numeraire good. However, for the sake of the tractability of analysis, we retain the small open economy assumption.

13. For a similar assumption in a different context, see Shi (1997).

14. The following analysis will go through without much added complication even if we consider a more general family welfare function of the type $\omega = \omega(I\tilde{U}, (\bar{l} - I)u)$.

15. Faini and Venturini (1993), for instance, state that the crucial hypothesis for this type of specification of expected welfare is that, *ceteris paribus*, people would rather live in their home country to avoid the social and psychological costs of settling into a new unfamiliar milieu, the loss of social relationships, and the costs implied by the risk of being caught in the attempt to enter the North illegally, and so forth. Here we assume that such costs are implicit in $\tilde{U}$.

16. In fact, the decision variable is $C + I$, the number of people who attempt to migrate. However, because of (4), for analytical purposes, the decision variable can be taken to be I, the number of people who succeed in migrating.

17. Since we assume an additively separable family welfare function (defined in (11)), we have to impose restrictions on preferences in the South in order to have an interior solution to the family's welfare maximization problem.

18. The possibility of a negative value for θ arises because the per capita consumption in the South, e, is, by construction, larger than the wage rate, r_l, in the

South. As should be clear from (14), a negative value for θ is consistent with the second order condition for the family welfare maximization problem.

19. It should be noted that per capita family welfare in the South may well be less than $\tilde{U}$ if the family had decided not to make any attempt at illegal migration.
20. See Dixit and Norman (1980: 61).
21. Note that tariffs are pure distortions in our model.

References

Bandyopadhyay, S. and Bandyopadhyay, S.C. (1998) 'Illegal immigration: a supply side analysis', *Journal of Development Economics*, 57: 343–60.

Banerjee, B. (1981) 'Rural-urban migration and family ties: an analysis of family considerations in migration behaviour in India', *Oxford Bulletin of Economics and Statistics*, 43: 321–8.

Bond, E.E. and Chen, T.-J. (1987) 'The welfare effects of illegal immigration', *Journal of International Economics*, 23: 315–28.

Dixit, A.K. and Norman, V. (1980) *Theory of International Trade*, Cambridge: Cambridge University Press.

Djajić, S. (1987) 'Illegal aliens, unemployment and immigration policy', *Journal of Development Economics*, 25: 235–49.

Ethier, W.J. (1986a) 'Illegal immigration: the host country problem', *American Economic Review*, 76: 56–71.

—— (1986b) 'Illegal immigration', *American Economic Review*, 76: 258–62.

Faini, R. and Venturini, A. (1993) 'Trade, aid and migrations: some basic policy issues', *European Economic Review*, 37: 435–42.

Faini, R. and de Melo, J. (1995) 'Trade policy, employment and migration: Some simulation results from Morocco', CEPR Discussion paper, No. 1198 (August) London.

Harris, J. and Todaro, M.P. (1970) 'Migration, unemployment and development', *American Economic Review*, 60: 126–42.

Hillman, A. and Weiss, A. (1995) 'Why illegal immigration is illegal', Israel: Department of Economics Bar-Ilan University.

Jahn, A. and Straubhaar, T. (1995) 'On the political economy of illegal immigration', Paper presented at the CEPR-Workshop on Illegal Immigration in Greece, organized by the Centre for Economic Policy Research.

Levine, P. (1995) 'The welfare economics of legal and illegal migration', Paper presented at the CEPR-Workshop on Illegal Immigration in Greece, organized by the Centre for Economic Policy Research.

Mundell, R.A. (1957) 'International trade theory and factor mobility', *American Economic Review*, 47: 321–35.

Ruffin, R. (1984) 'International factor movements', in R. Jones and P. Kennen (eds), *Handbook of International Economics*, Vol. I, Chapter 5, Amsterdam: North-Holland.

Schulze, G.G. (1995) 'Capital export, unemployment and illegal immigration', Paper presented at the CEPR-Workshop on Illegal Immigration in Greece, organized by the Centre for Economic Policy Research.

Shi, S. (1997) 'A divisible search money of fiat money', *Econometrica*, 65: 75–102.

Stark, O. and Lucas, R.E.B. (1988) 'Migration, remittances, and the family', *Economic Development and Cultural Change*, 36: 465–81.

Todaro, M.P. and Maruszko, L. (1987) 'Illegal immigration and US immigration reform: a conceptual framework', *Population and Development Review*, 13: 101–14.

Yoshida, C. (1993) 'The global welfare of illegal immigration: a note', *Indian Economic Review*, 28: 111–15.

Part II

Regionalism and globalization for the developing countries

6 Regionalism for developing countries

Assessing the costs and benefits[1]

L. Alan Winters

1 Introduction

Trade liberalization is an important and complex issue—albeit one governed by simple principles—and regional trade liberalization is even more so. Thus in no sense can a single paper claim to give definitive answers about whether and, if so, how and with whom regional preferential integration should be pursued. I have therefore set myself a less ambitious goal of discussing not regionalism among developing countries, but rather how we might go about making such an assessment. I do not claim to be comprehensive, but rather to focus on some of the less obvious and more recent aspects of the assessment of regionalism.

First, some terminology: economists and policy makers have increasingly come to recognize the economic benefits of integration between the economies of different nations, e.g. Sachs and Warner (1995), World Bank (1996). Thus the issue is not whether regional integration per se is desirable, but whether regional integration explicitly pursued and fostered by discriminatory policy interventions is desirable. In discussing such policies, I shall use the studiedly neutral term 'Regional Integration Arrangements' (RIAs), for as Martin Wolf (*Financial Times*, Tuesday, 29 October 1996: 14) has noted, terminology can affect the way we think about something: 'Names matter. Who but a staunch protectionist could have anything against a "free trade agreement?" "Preferential trade agreements" sound less benign, while "discriminatory trade agreements", yet another name for the same thing, sound nasty...' I should also note that while most RIAs are regional in the geographic sense this is not necessary for most analytical discussion. Thus I shall use the term RIA for any reciprocally preferential or discriminatory arrangement between two or more countries.

This chapter restricts itself to the 'direct effects' of RIAs—those that follow immediately and causally from the initiation of the RIA, rather than those that occur indirectly because the RIA induces other changes in economic policy. Thus I consider some of the so-called static effects, through which RIAs affect trade patterns, the changes in economic welfare emanating from such effects, and the dynamic effects on economic growth felt through factors such as investment and the relocation of industry. What I exclude is the fascinating and rapidly growing analysis of the effects of RIAs on other countries' trade policy and on the multilateral trading system. This limitation is primarily for reasons of space and because I have analysed 'regionalism versus multilateralism' elsewhere (Winters 1999). It also, however, reflects the fact that for individual governments and policy makers the direct effects, especially those on their own countries, are likely to be the more important: that is, only very rarely will systemic considerations reverse conclusions for developing countries made on the basis of direct effects.[2]

Before starting it is salutary to recall that discussions of RIAs are always complex and frequently diffuse. One requires at least three countries and everything occurs in a 'second-best' world, in which distortions and policy interventions are present in every outcome we consider—specifically, restrictions on trade with non-member countries.[3] As a consequence there are few general and unambiguous economic results to appeal to; each case is *sui generis*. Additionally, many of the alleged costs and benefits of RIAs are in areas which economists understand relatively poorly, even without regional complications, for example, growth, technology transfer, political economy, and political benefits. Even worse, there are few cases of significant regional integration on which to base empirical studies (Foroutan 1997), a fact which increases the burden borne by our already inadequate theory.

2 Standards of comparison

We all know the joke about the economist who, when asked 'how is your husband?' replied 'relative to what?'[4] She worked on RIAs. The most difficult part of assessing the effects of an RIA is to work out what would have happened in its absence—the *anti-monde*, or counterfactual. Indeed, for *ex post* studies using the residual imputation method, this is the only question. These studies take actual data on some phenomenon after an RIA has been created and attribute the difference between them and an *anti-monde* to the RIA. *Anti-mondes* vary from the simple (and frequently implicit) 'no change from pre-RIA values' to complex model-based predictions based on exogenous data.

For *ex ante* studies of the sort that must be used for discussions of future policy options, the *anti-monde* has to be constructed, but again 'no change' is the most frequent choice. Thus, for example, modellers such as Haaland and Norman (1992) or Harrison, Rutherford and Tarr (1997) calibrate their models to actual data for a historical ('base') year and then shock it with changes to represent the RIA they are investigating. Thus their estimates are as if '1992' happened in 1985, and the *anti-monde* is the base-year actual values.

If economies are developing very rapidly 'no change' is inadequate, and we must be more explicit about the *anti-monde*. This inevitably involves judgement. Thus, for example, if we are assessing the effects of the creation of Mercosur since 1991, what should we assume about tariffs in the absence of Mercosur? We could assume

- that Mercosur has made no difference to the evolution of tariffs, so that in the absence of the agreement, all Mercosur countries' imports would have paid the same rates as extra-Mercosur trade currently does (*anti-monde* tariff = current actuals on non-members);
- that all tariff changes would have stopped in 1991 (*anti-monde* = 1991 actuals); or
- that some non-discriminatory (most-favoured nation (MFN)) liberalization would have continued (*anti-monde* based on trends of liberalization over, say, 1988–91).

Our decision makes a huge difference. Once we move beyond simple tariffs, *anti-mondes* become even more complex. If we believe that RIAs foster the credibility of policy reforms, how do we represent credibility in their absence?

Hence, we should always be explicit about the *anti-monde* and be prepared to justify (if only within our own heads) our choice. Moreover, we should always be conscious of the epistemological difficulty that *anti-mondes* cannot be judged true or untrue, but rather merely persuasive or unpersuasive. This has led some commentators to argue that, rather than assessing RIAs against a necessarily hypothetical benchmark, we should measure them only against their stated objectives. Such a standard is interesting, because policy so often fails to deliver the expected or promised results and we want to know why. However, it is not sufficient, because unintended effects are just as real as intended ones, and economists should, anyway, not be debarred from asking whether stated objectives are consistent or sensible.

A second issue regarding standards of comparison concerns the indicator we examine. An economics profession of the current size can be justified only in terms of making life better; that is, in terms of someone's welfare. We might still debate whose welfare, i.e. what welfare weights to use (including those of future generations), and whether and how to incorporate supposedly non-economic dimensions of welfare, such as security or culture. We should also be clear whether results refer to the welfare (suitably aggregated) of the citizens of one or all of the member countries in the RIA, those of non-members, or those of the world as a whole. In practice, of course, many discussions of RIAs are conducted in terms of intermediate variables, such as aggregate output (GNP) or levels of trade. This is quite legitimate, for we must simplify to make problems manageable, but it requires care. The mere observation that international trade has increased—still less that intra-RIA trade has increased—is not sufficient to prove that an RIA is desirable; think of the European Union's (EU) Common Agricultural Policy. Thus we should always bear in mind the links between the variable under examination and welfare.

A particular example of the way in which intermediate stages of analysis can confuse us is the use of the term 'natural trading partners'. If this term has any role in the assessment of RIAs it requires (a) that we can, as a general proposition, equate 'natural' with 'desirable' and (b) that, for the RIA in question, we cannot make a direct assessment of its desirability, for otherwise we could jump straight to the latter without worrying about 'naturalness'. As a practical matter of discourse we also need (c) to be able to define and measure 'naturalness'.

In fact neither requirement (a) nor (c) is very secure. Some commentators define 'natural' in terms of outcomes (volumes of trade between potential partners) (Summers 1991) while others focus on transportation (or transactions) costs (Krugman 1991). In the former case, large flows are far from sufficient to render preferential liberalization beneficial (Panagariya 1997, Schiff 1997), while in the latter, relative transportation costs may not matter (Amjadi and Winters, 1999) or may have perverse effects (Nitsch 1997). Overall, therefore, I believe that we would be better off not using the term 'natural trading partners' or 'natural integration', except in the sense I used in the introduction as meaning without any policy inducements.[5]

The rest of the chapter considers some of the arguments that have been advanced for and against creating RIAs. It obviously cannot do them justice in a single paper, but I hope to give a feeling for the nature of the arguments, identify their critical components, particularly in the dimensions just noted, and comment briefly on empirical or practical aspects of their application. I start by considering aspects of the simple static effects of regional integration which, despite a huge and venerable literature, still appear to generate some confusion, and then move onto dynamic and political dimensions.

3 Static analysis

3.1 A priori *analysis*[6]

The traditional tools for RIA analysis—Viner's (1950) trade creation and trade diversion—are marvellous heuristic devices for illustrating the fundamental effects of RIAs. If, as a result of a preferential tariff reduction, imports from a partner displace higher-cost local production, real resources are saved in satisfying local consumption, and the domestic economy benefits accordingly. This is trade creation. If, alternatively, the preferences allow partner supplies to displace those from non-members that would otherwise have been purchased because they were cheaper when both faced equal tariffs, the domestic economy ends up paying more real resources for imports and loses accordingly. This is trade diversion and it amounts to diverting part of what would have been tariff revenue on imports from non-members to producers in the partner country who now face no tariffs.

Unfortunately, except in the very simple case explored by Viner, the mapping from trade creation and diversion to economic welfare is treacherous.[7] For example, pure trade diversion can be beneficial if its effect of lowering consumer prices is sufficiently important to welfare. The benefits of trade creation for a single country can be outweighed by the losses of tariff revenue on the pre-RIA volume of imports from the partner country, i.e. by having to return to partner producers the tariff revenue on those imports that would have been purchased from them even in the absence of preferences (Bhagwati and Panagariya 1996 and Schiff 1997). Thus, ultimately, simple creation/diversion exercises are indicative rather than definitive. Nonetheless, because they are so pervasive and intuitively appealing it is worth thinking briefly about their empirical basis. Before doing so, however, I consider two other aspects of static behaviour.

One of the early puzzles about why small countries adopted RIAs was that in neoclassical analysis they could always do better by an MFN liberalization. Wonnacott and Wonnacott (1981, 1992) offered a neat solution by observing that, if trade with the rest of the world was costly because of their tariffs or transactions costs, two partners might both be able to make terms-of-trade gains by removing tariffs on their mutual trade and trading only with each other. This requires that trade with the rest of the world ceases, for otherwise internal prices would remain anchored to world prices plus the tariff. Overall, such changes in trade patterns do not seem very realistic.[8] Amjadi and Winters (1999) explore the possibilities of these sorts of gains in Mercosur. Transport costs with the rest of the world are high enough for there to be substantial savings by switching to intra-bloc trade, but the requirement that trade with the rest of the world completely cease seems unlikely to be fulfilled in any but a few commodities.

Transportation costs also matter in the models based on differentiated goods, such as Frankel, Stein and Wei (1995) and Nitsch (1996). As in Wonnacott and Wonnacott, this is because they rely on corner solutions, in which there is no trade with the rest of the world; this means that even marginal changes in trade result in changes in internal prices. In models of this kind each good from each supplier is unique, and hence faces a downward-sloping demand curve. As a consequence, all changes in tariffs or other trade barriers are partially passed through to consumers; this results in changes in consumer welfare and, through changes in consumption bundles, pressures on other (domestic and non-preferred) suppliers to adjust their prices and quantities. This gives much more scope for RIAs to have real welfare effects than do homogeneous good models in which world prices, assumed fixed, tend to anchor domestic prices. A problem with many differentiated goods models, however, is that through their assumptions of symmetry (all goods compete equally with all others), they ignore comparative advantage and/or 'home preference', and hence overemphasize trade diversion (see Srinivasan 1993 and Jones 1993). Symmetry also means in these models that results depend on relative intra- and extra-bloc transport costs rather than absolute transport costs. Amjadi and Winters (1999) suggest that, for the Mercosur countries and Chile, this relativity is sufficiently small that only minor benefits from RIAs are likely.

Once products are differentiated we open the way to consider models of RIAs under imperfect competition. Starting from Smith and Venables (1988), a huge literature has emerged in which RIAs are generally pre- dicted to have much larger effects than perfectly competitive models suggest.[9] Market integration changes the nature of competition: it almost always reduces market power by enlarging the scope of each market and removing some (domestic) players' special privileges. This generates gains additional to the usual allocative ones. The existence of rents in imperfect competition which get shifted about by trade changes also make RIAs more strongly redistributive, usually with larger benefits to small previ- ously oligopolized economies. Important advances in this genre are reported by several authors in Winters (1992), and a more recent survey is given by Baldwin and Venables (1995).

The imperfect competition literature has given RIAs a new lease of intellectual life (as it has international trade theory in general), but it should not be accepted completely uncritically. For example, the perma- nence of oligopolistic positions is not guaranteed even without RIAs, especially in the face of a determined government. If RIAs dominate MFN liberalization—as is possible in these models—it is at the expense of the rest of the world. It is not guaranteed that intra-bloc competition really will be fiercer (see Haaland and Wooton (1992) in theory and Jacquemin and Sapir (1991) in practice). The latter found that French, German, Italian and UK profit margins were significantly squeezed by extra-EC imports but not by intra-EC imports. It is not clear that the EU has really shifted from being fifteen segmented markets to a single unified one as is assumed in most analyses, and it is certainly not clear that Mercosur or SADC will do so. Finally, we have, to date, no empirical tests of these models at all.[10]

3.2 Estimating static effects ex post

The simplest approach to *ex post* estimates of creation and diversion is to look at the evolution of partner and non-partner shares of total imports. The typical *anti-monde* is that, without the RIA, these shares would not have changed. However, even putting aside the potential weaknesses of the *anti-monde*, this approach cannot separate trade creation from trade diversion. Writing M_N for imports from non-members and M_P for imports from partners, one is examining $M_P/(M_P + M_N)$. Clearly this can increase if M_P rises in isolation (creation), or if M_P rises as M_N falls by the same amount (diversion).

To identify creation and diversion one requires an extra piece of information. One approach, emanating from Truman (1969), is to add sales of domestic output (D) into the equation and look at shares in apparent consumption, which is assumed constant. Thus if $S_P \equiv M_P/(M_P + M_N + D)$ rises at the expense of $S_D \equiv D/(M_P + M_N + D)$ we have creation, whereas if it rises at the expense of S_N we have diversion. For applications of this approach on Europe see, for example, Winters (1983) and Sapir (1992). At an aggregate level these shares are often approximated by corresponding shares in GDP (relying on the fact that $M_P + M_N \approx X$, where X is total exports).

A novel alternative approach to identifying trade diversion is due to Yeats (1998). He recognizes that intra-bloc imports, M_P, equal intra-bloc exports, X_P, and uses X_N to suggest an *anti-monde* for X_P. Yeats illustrates his method on Mercosur, and focuses on the compositions of X_P and X_N. He finds that the strongest increases in X_P occur in products for which protection is high and performance in X_N very weak. Since members' exports are competing with the same third-country exports in P and in N, Yeats infers that the much greater relative success for some of them in P is due to preferences. That is, X_P ($\equiv M_P$) displaces M_N in Mercosur because of preferences, i.e. there is trade diversion. Note that the *anti-monde* here is based on world markets, and thus is closer to non-discriminatory trade than to the members' pre-Mercosur situations.

A problem with *anti-mondes* based just on changes in import (or export) shares is that they fail to take account of changes in the relative sizes of economies as they grow at different rates. For example, the huge growth of the East Asian economies in the last three decades would lead us to expect that, *ceteris paribus*, their shares in partners' trade would grow strongly. One solution is to look at trade intensity ratios—the share of i in j's imports relative to the share of i in the world's imports. The level of this index is obviously influenced by factors such as geographical proximity and i's and j's comparative advantages, as well as by trade policies, but changes in the index will primarily reflect changes in the last because the other factors are so static. Anderson and Norheim (1993) show how dramatically these indices changed during European integration and Yeats (1998) shows dramatic changes for Mercosur countries after 1991.

The third way to establish an *anti-monde* for an RIA is by reference to the trade patterns of other countries. The *locus classicus* for this is Aitken's (1973) use of the gravity model on the EEC, but see also, for example, Braga, Safadi and Yeats (1994) on developing countries. In Aitken's model it is again impossible to separate trade diversion from trade creation (that, *ceteris paribus*, imports from partners exceed those from non-partners is consistent with either). However, later scholars have done so by seeking separate RIA-effects on trade with members (if M_P is significantly higher than the norm, we have trade creation) and on non-members (if M_N is significantly lower we have trade diversion). Recently, Bayoumi and Eichengreen (1997), Frankel and Wei (1996) and Sapir (1997) use this sort of approach to suggest that the creation or enlargement of the EC did, after all, cause material amounts of trade diversion, a significant change in the conventional wisdom.

Soloaga and Winters (1999) extend the gravity model even further, to estimate different effects for intra-bloc trade, bloc imports from outside countries and bloc exports to outside countries. They also formally test whether these effects change when RIAs are introduced or modified.[11] They replicate the finding of trade diversion in Europe, and find that the Latin American blocs apparently became more open to both members and non-members over the 1990s, but otherwise they find rather small effects from regionalism.

3.3 A diversion on the rest of the world

The discussion so far has focused on the effects of RIAs on their members, but equally important are their effects on non-members. Even the simple comparative static issue of how an RIA affects non-member trade and welfare has caused a good deal of confusion. The traditional approach has been to consider the evolution of the share of non-members in each member's imports, i.e. $M_N/(M_N + M_P)$, or apparent consumption, i.e. $M_N/(M_N + M_P + D)$. This is not an implausible approach to the trade effects. The *anti-monde* is that, *ceteris paribus*, shares would have been constant, which is probably reasonably accurate over the short run. As the time period of investigation increases, however, it becomes less relevant, as factors such as different partners' ability to supply imports and the different income elasticities of demand for different imports become more significant. In these circumstances—just as for members' own trade shares—a more sophisticated view of *anti-monde* shares is required, such as that provided by trade intensity indices, trade propensity indices, more complex import functions or a gravity model.

While the shares of different suppliers in members' total imports offer some insight into the effect of RIAs on members' welfare as well as on their trade, they offer virtually none into non-member welfare (Winters 1997a, 1997b). First, even if exports to the RIA were the correct driver of non-member welfare, it is the absolute level, not its ratio to total RIA imports, that affects the evolution of welfare through time. The ratio is informative only relative to the gains that non-members would have made if the same expansion of members' imports had been made in a non-discriminatory fashion, that is, relative to an MFN liberalization.

Second, and much more importantly, the level of exports is a poor indicator of non-members' welfare. At the extreme, if *ceteris* are strictly *paribus*, more exports imply that fewer goods are left at home for non-member consumption, i.e. it correlates with lower welfare! Of course, exports are actually a means to obtaining imports, which do raise welfare, but then we should consider the effects of the RIA on non-members' *imports* or strictly, see below, their terms of trade. To my knowledge, non-members' imports have never been investigated *ex post*, although in Winters (1985), I noted that British exports of manufactures to certain non-EEC markets fell below expected levels following British accession to the EEC. Even this is not particularly informative if British exports were replaced by other supplies of equivalent quality and price.

The observation that a non-member's imports from members of an RIA might easily be substituted by imports from other countries is essentially a comment on the economic size of the RIA. If the RIA is small, in the technical sense of having no perceptible influence on the prices at which other countries trade, non-members should be indifferent to its creation. It is true that if the RIA cuts its exports to the rest of the world (RoW) the shortfall must end up somewhere (not every member of RoW can replace the lost imports), but the loss is so marginal that it is effectively zero.[12] Thus the critical question about the effect of an RIA on non-members must be its effect on prices, or the terms of trade.[13]

Again, to my knowledge, there are no published studies of the terms-of-trade effects of regionalism, although recent work by Gupta and Schiff (1997), Winters and Chang (2000) and Chang and Winters (1999) is starting to address this lacuna. The first argues that unusual tastes or barriers to trade with RoW can make even a small RIA large to certain neighbours, and it shows how the formation of the Andean Pact led to price increases for members' exports of beef and price decreases for non-members'. Winters and Chang find that the prices of European Community (EC) exports of machinery to Spain increased relative to those of non-EC exports following the Spanish accession in 1986, evidence that is consistent with non-EC suppliers receiving lower prices. Chang and Winters find strong evidence that the prices of US exports to Brazil fell relative to those of other US exports following the creation of Mercosur. These studies all suggest that regionalism has significant effects on the terms of trade— potentially beneficial for members and adverse for non-members. Further work on the price effects of RIAs seems a high priority, although as Winters and Chang observe, it is not easy to do.

3.4 Deep integration and security of access

The standard discussion of RIAs proceeds as if tariffs were the only barrier to trade and as if once these had been set to zero within the bloc, that was the end of the story. Of course, this is far too simple. First, there are myriad other costs to international trade, for example, currency exchange and its associated uncertainty, customs formalities, industrial standards, unfamiliar legal structures. Unfortunately, we know very little about these even for industrial countries, but experience suggests they are real enough. Herin (1986) estimates that such costs average 3 per cent of the gross value of a trade flow and most analyses of the EC's '1992' programme assume that they are 2½ per cent; see, for example, Smith and Venables (1988) or Winters (1992). McCallum (1995) shows that trade between Canada and the United States, among the most integrated of partners, is over twenty times less than inter-provincial trade within Canada with equivalent incomes and distances, while Engel and Rogers (1996) show that crossing the Canadian–US border creates frictions equal to adding an extra 2,000 miles to an equivalent intra-US trade. Helliwell (1998) extends their analyses and confirms these results.

Reducing transaction costs should be an important objective of policy, for they not only segment markets and reduce competition but typically waste real resources in doing so. In some cases both partner and non-partner suppliers will benefit, e.g. from RIA-wide design requirements, but in others deep integration is feasible only in a discriminatory, i.e. geographically limited, way. For example, for so long as different currencies and standards exist within the world economy, harmonizing with one partner automatically precludes harmonization with another. Thus this sort of 'deep integration' seems ideally suited to RIAs. 'Discriminatory' deep integration can have trade-creation and trade-diversion effects, just as can discriminatory tariff reductions, but with one crucial difference: if the trade barriers addressed under 'deep integration' entail the expenditure of real resources rather than the creation of rents, reducing them saves those resources and is thus, at least in simple models, welfare improving even if it diverts trade. It is just that lower gains result if there is diversion than if the cost reduction is non-discriminatory. Overall, therefore, discriminatory deep integration seems unlikely to be harmful, except in the opportunity cost sense of foregoing the greater gains from non-discriminatory integration.[14]

If deep integration is so benign, why do we not see more of it? The reason is that it is formidably difficult and sensitive to achieve. It requires great mutual trust and confidence between partners, as well as a perception that their interests in various issues are compatible. For example, achieving a single currency entails surrendering a fundamental element of sovereignty, and foregoing a major tool of (short-run) economic management. Harmonizing standards entails agreeing about the tradeoffs between, say, costs of production and safety, on which views might genuinely differ, and always appears to favour the partner whose standard is adopted by the group. Experience in the EU amply illustrates the difficulties and slow pace of deep integration (see, for example, European Commission 1996), although it may be easier to achieve among developing countries with less long-lived traditions of this sort of economic management and more fluid institutions.

In assessing RIAs *ex post*, deep integration is not conceptually difficult, except when one tries to separate the integration that would occur 'naturally' and via global forces (e.g. through network economies or via the WTO), from that which is induced by the RIA. In *ex ante* assessments it is easy to assume that transactions costs will be reduced, and to quantify the effects of those reductions, but actually one needs to exercise the self-discipline of asking exactly how and in what areas deep integration will be achieved: who will surrender what and how? If deep integration is necessary for an RIA to be beneficial it is clearly desirable to answer such questions before embarking upon it.

One final question warrants some thought: are trade preferences necessary to the achievement of deep integration? In some cases, clearly not: countries already share some standards (e.g. electrical power and compatible railway gauges and timetables) but nonetheless impose tariffs on each other's goods. In other cases, probably not: even if countries use the same currency they could tax mutual trade. In yet other cases, preferences are necessary: it is hard to abolish frontier formalities if you wish to levy taxes on cross-border trade. Schiff and Winters (1998) explore a further connection in which the additional trade generated by preferences is required to build up the trust necessary to proceed to deep integration. One might also imagine cases where the private benefits of trade preferences are used as a way of compensating firms for the private costs of deep integration.

Deep integration concerns reducing the costs of facilitating market access, but in the real world the security or reliability of access is nearly as important, for both exporters and importers. RIAs enhance security by making it more difficult to increase tariffs on partner trade. Even a bound tariff can be raised under GATT rules so long as the increase is negotiated and compensation is offered, and an RIA may offer more direct routes for retaliation than does the GATT (see section 4.3 below). But, in fact, raising bound tariffs is relatively rare under the GATT because governments can achieve similar results without renegotiation via safeguards actions, and without either renegotiation or compensation via antidumping actions. How do RIAs affect these instruments?

Between members of the EU (as between US states), allegations of dumping would be investigated under the auspices of competition policy. This imposes more rigorous standards of proof than does antidumping law—so rigorous that misconduct is rarely claimed or identified; it is also administered by a super-national body, eliminating the strong 'them versus us' rhetoric of dumping. Under these circumstances, RIAs more or less assure market access, although on occasion *ad hoc* restrictions on access have emerged within the EU, e.g. on cars made by Japanese firms in EU countries. Also, EU members exercise antidumping against third countries collectively, through EU organs, as is required by a common trade policy.

Among less deep RIAs, three have eschewed antidumping: Australia-New Zealand, Canada-Chile, and the European Economic Area. In NAFTA and in the EU's agreements with Eastern European and Mediterranean countries, the northern partners have maintained the right to institute antidumping actions against their partners. In both cases the institutional arrangements have been changed somewhat, but not in ways that have obvious effects on the frequency or rigour of the use of the instrument. In the EU cases, the parties have to refer cases of alleged dumping to Association Councils (relatively high-level joint political bodies) to seek a 'solution acceptable to the two parties'. This approach arguably encourages managed trade outcomes to complaints of dumping, but possibly gives the developing country partner more power in negotiation.[15] While the EU's use of antidumping against Eastern European countries seems to have declined since the RIAs were signed, it is still the subject of bitter complaint among the latter. NAFTA, building on CUSFTA, has established a new review process for antidumping actions, based on bilateral panels. However, the panels' terms of reference are linked to procedural rather than substantive issues, and it is too recent for its effects on antidumping to be isolated.

Security of market access figured prominently in the aims of the developing partners to NAFTA and the Europe Agreements, and the issue of antidumping was negotiated vigorously in both cases. In neither case did the developing partners gain much on paper, but one might plausibly assume that their treatment has become a little gentler *de facto*—certainly it is not likely to have got worse. However, I know of no formal demonstration of such effects. For prospective members of RIAs the brutal truth is that the major industrial users of antidumping are unlikely to give up much of their discretion, and thus that one should not expect too much in this direction even from far-reaching RIAs. For RIAs among developing countries, which are newer converts to the delights of antidumping, it may be feasible to reach mutual disarmament agreements, but it is probably necessary that these be formally part of the agreement before much reliance can be placed on them. Experience in Mercosur is not particularly encouraging, for members have used antidumping and other trade measures against each other (Rowat, Lubrano and Porrata 1997 and *The Economist* August 12–19 1999).

Finally, some commentators have hoped that RIAs will also earn their members more sympathetic treatment under sanitary and phytosanitary regulations: for example, Chilean views on joining NAFTA, see Schiff and Sapelli (1996). Except in so far as an RIA opens new routes to disputes settlement or facilitates closer cooperation in standards and testing, there is no evidence to encourage this view.

4 Dynamics

Dynamics play an almost mystical role in many discussions of economic integration. Having found that the static benefits are usually rather small or possibly even negative, advocates of regional integration arrangements (RIAs) typically appeal to the dynamic benefits. However, what these constitute and how they come about are frequently rather vague, and the evidence linking dynamic benefits to particular instances of integration is very difficult to pin down.

This section defines dynamics as anything that affects a country's rate of economic growth over the medium term. Thus it includes both permanent increments to the rate of growth and temporary but long-lived increases of, say, over five years, as countries move from one growth path to another. It then briefly introduces some of the arguments made about dynamics and seeks to isolate their critical components. As with the previous section, the aim is to try to put discussion of dynamic costs and benefits on a more objective basis, to force us to be explicit about what we expect of RIAs.

Economic growth generally stems from accumulation: either of a factor of production—specifically capital, physical or human—or of knowledge. Traditional growth theory suggests that merely accumulating factors will eventually run out of steam, for, as one adds ever more units of physical and human capital to a fixed stock of land and labourers, their rates of return decline to such an extent that further accumulation appears unprofitable. Some recent endogenous growth theorists have sought to avoid these constraints by arguing that production exhibits constant returns to scale in capital and increasing returns to scale overall. On the whole, however, this is quite difficult to believe and recent work by Jones (1995) has provided a fairly strong refutation in the case of the United States. The accumulation of knowledge, on the other hand, could lead to permanent increases in rates of growth, for as an economy grows the return to an increment in knowledge (which is basically a public good) increases, and as knowledge accumulates the base for further advances expands.

The direct evidence that RIAs stimulate growth is actually rather weak. Henrekson, Torstensson and Torstensson (1997) use a cross-section regression to suggest that European integration has enhanced members' growth rates, but other commentators, e.g. de Melo, Panagariya and Rodrik (1993) and Vamvakidis (1998a), have failed to do so with similar approaches. Part of the difference lies in the treatment of openness. Vamvakidis (1998a) identifies an EU growth effect if he excludes openness from his equation, but finds it insignificant if openness is included. He does find beneficial effects on a country's growth rate from large open neighbours, but this is quite independent of RIAs.

Attractive as the sweeping generalizations from cross-section regressions are, they are not wholly persuasive. They offer no information on the mechanisms through which growth occurs and may well be subject to simultaneity problems. Thus the rest of this section looks at alternative, less direct, arguments and evidence.

The most direct approach to identifying the growth effects of non-European RIAs is Vamvakidis (1998b). He uses panel data to explore whether countries' growth rates changed when they liberalized their trade, comparing the ten years before the liberalization with the ten years after. He finds quite strong evidence that non-discriminatory liberalizations boosted growth, while discriminatory ones (i.e. RIAs) did not. Vamvakidis did not explore the effects of the RIAs created or revived in the 1990s because we do not yet have ten years' 'after' data, but with that exception (namely that things are better now), he has provided quite convincing evidence that RIAs are not good for growth.

Whether we are talking about permanent changes in the rate of growth or only temporary ones, we must remember the distinction between output and welfare. Accumulation is not free, so while an RIA might raise the growth rate of output, total economic welfare will not increase by as much, because the investment in plant, education or knowledge has to be paid for in terms of foregone consumption. Not every increase in the rate of growth, still less in investment, is welfare-improving.

4.1 Convergence and spillovers

Convergence is the phenomenon by which countries' incomes per head converge towards each other over time. Over the last ten years a huge amount of effort has been devoted to describing and explaining convergence; the classic references include Baumol, Blackman and Wolf (1989), Lucas (1988), Mankiw, Romer and Weil (1992), and Barro and Sala-i-Martin (1995). The evidence suggests rather strongly that the world's economies do not converge unconditionally, but many economists maintain that they do so conditionally, such that, after allowing for a series of other explanatory variables, the remaining unexplained component of growth shows poorer economies growing more rapidly than richer ones and thus converging. The explanatory variables are used either to explain the steady state levels of income per head towards which each country is converging, or to explain differences in growth rate for a given level of steady state income. Among the variables which are used for these purposes are human capital, the rate of investment, political stability and the openness of the economy. For a recent survey the reader is referred to de la Fuente (1997).

Since this chapter is concerned with economic integration, I shall concentrate on the work of just one economist who has focused on trade links: Ben-David (1993, 1994, 1995, 1996). Ben-David (1993) offers very striking evidence that, after they signed RIAs, the EEC, the European Free Trade Association and the United States and Canada, each displayed a marked increase in trade between members and a dramatic fall in the standard deviation of incomes per head across countries. Ben-David (1994) suggests that this convergence is upwards, i.e. it increases the growth rates of poorer members.

Ben-David (1995) extends the analysis to explore the role of trade in creating so-called convergence clubs, small groups of countries (not necessarily linked by RIAs) which appear to display convergence. He finds that if we create clubs between countries that are each other's major trading partners, convergence is a very common phenomenon, whereas if we create similar sized clubs by drawing countries randomly convergence is very rare. This appears to reinforce the view that international trade is the mechanism through which convergence occurs, although it might equally well be other elements of international commerce, such as foreign direct investment (FDI), which are strongly correlated with trade.

Finally Ben-David (1996) uses the same set of countries as in his previous article to demonstrate that the convergence clubs appear to owe more to convergence in rates of total factor productivity growth than to convergence in rates of investment. This suggests that convergence arises from contact and spillovers rather than from incentives to accumulate physical capital. It might also be due to the stimulating effect of overseas competition on economic performance, to the direct consequences of technology improvements through FDI, or even to the mobility of highly skilled labour, be it permanently or temporarily.

It would be comforting to infer from all this that a developing country has only to sign an RIA with a richer country in order to experience a rapid catch-up. Unfortunately, however, this conclusion might be premature. First, while convergence appears between OECD countries, it is not generally evident between them and other countries (Ben-David 1994). Second, Ben-David's recent work includes very few developing countries—in fact, only middle-income countries in Latin America. Thus, we do not know how well the experience will translate to developing countries in general. Third, it is likely to matter whether the increase in trade is generated by preferences or by more 'natural' integration such as a reduction in real trade costs. Fourth, nothing in these results promotes RIAs above unilateralism, concerted or not, as the engine of trade growth. Overall, however, Ben-David's work does offer some encouragement for expecting dynamic benefits, especially from North–South RIAs.

A separate stream of work which is also maintained to show the role of international trade in convergence is Coe, Helpman and Hoffmaister (1997), who seek to explain the rate of increase in total factor productivity across a wide range of countries. They construct an index of total knowledge capital (measured by accumulated investment in R and D) in each industrial country, and then assume that trading partners get access to a country's stock of knowledge in proportion to their imports of machinery and transport equipment from that country. Using import-weighted sums of industrial countries' knowledge stocks to reflect developing countries' access to foreign knowledge, they seek to explain the latters' total factor productivity (TFP) growth. They find that access to foreign knowledge is statistically significant.

In the case of developing countries, Coe, Helpman and Hoffmaister find that TFP growth is related to the interaction between the openness of the economy (imports/GDP) and its access to foreign knowledge. Thus an economy benefits from foreign knowledge, first, according to how open it is and, second, according to whether it is open to those countries which have the largest knowledge stocks. These results are intuitively very attractive and suggest, again, that trade is a major conduit for spillovers between countries. Unfortunately, however, the conclusion is not wholly secure because Coe, Helpman and Hoffmaister assume rather than test that imports from industrial countries provide the correct weights with which to combine stocks of knowledge in order to reflect importers' access to foreign knowledge. Keller (1998) has suggested that, in fact, the results are no better than would be obtained from a random weighting of countries' knowledge stocks.

A further implication of the Coe, Helpman and Hoffmaister model, if we believe it, is that trade policy which switches a country's imports of machinery and equipment away from the USA and Japan, which have the highest stocks of knowledge, towards other economies, which have lower stocks, may be harmful to the rate of TFP growth. Winters (1997d) explores this possibility for an EU–Lebanon RIA and finds, fortunately, that, provided it increases general openness a little, its net effect will be positive despite the trade diversion. For other RIAs, however, where trade may be diverted to less knowledge-intensive suppliers than the EU (e.g. Argentina and Chile switching from US to Brazilian capital goods) it could be important. The static analysis of RIAs has long observed that trade diversion is potentially harmful. What I have described here is a dynamic version of trade diversion. Like its antecedent, it is a result about trade, not welfare; we cannot immediately conclude that subsidizing trade with the United States would be desirable.

4.2 Accumulation

Growth results from accumulation. Hence, if RIAs affect the incentives for accumulation they will have at least temporary effects on growth. An early and striking application of this insight is Baldwin (1989, 1992), who models the effects of integration on accumulation to generate a '*medium-term* growth bonus'. An RIA makes trade easier and hence tends to raise the returns to at least some factors of production. If the cost of capital is unchanged, the response to increasing rates of returns is to invest more and thus to increase the capital stock. This leads to a temporary, but generally rather long-lived, increase in growth rates as the accumulation shifts the economy onto a higher trajectory: once the new steady-state level of capital stock has been achieved there will be higher levels of output per head, but growth will return to its original level. Baldwin (1989) suggests that the medium-term bonus could double or treble the static efficiency effects of an RIA on output.

If we accept the basic model, the first question to ask is whether an RIA will raise or lower a developing country's rate of return to capital. A simple application of the Heckscher–Ohlin model might lead us to expect that the latter would fall in a North–South arrangement. For example, comparing the EU and, say, Morocco, the EU is capital-abundant and Morocco capital-scarce. Since international trade tends to reduce the returns to the scarce factor, increased trade with the EU seems likely to reduce the returns to capital in Morocco.[16] This is a salutary thought, but perhaps the basic Heckscher-Ohlin model is too simple for this purpose.

First, it applies only to a so-called square model with equal numbers of factors of production and goods; there is no indication that this is the way the real world is. Second, the Euro-Med Agreement is not a complete liberalization of trade but a partial liberalization, which could have rather different effects (see Falvey 1995). Third, the Heckscher–Ohlin model presumes homogeneous products, whereas experience suggests that many markets are better represented by a model of differentiated products and intra-industry trade. In the latter case it becomes very important how substitutable domestic and foreign goods are for each other. Building on these complications Baldwin and a number of collaborators have suggested a series of reasons why one might expect economic integration to raise the rates of returns on capital in both partners regardless of capital abundance.[17] I will briefly sketch four of them.

First, an RIA typically reduces the transactions cost on tradeable goods more than those on non-tradeable goods. If, as is commonly believed, non-tradeables are labour intensive and tradeables capital intensive, trade liberalization will increase the demand for capital relative to labour, and thus increase the rate of return on capital. Relatedly, increased competition in tradeable goods sectors may induce improvements in efficiency and declines in markups in this sector. This will cause increased demand for inputs into the tradeable sector, and thus reinforce the transactions cost effect just noted.[18]

Second, an RIA may reduce tariffs and trading costs on imports of capital equipment. This would reduce the prices which industry has to pay for imported investment goods, and may stimulate the domestic capital goods industry to greater efficiency and/or less monopolistic behaviour. This effect is more likely for middle-income than for low-income countries, because the latter, having no capital goods sector, typically do not tax imports highly. Third, an RIA that goes beyond tariff reductions could improve efficiency in the financial sector. If this led to reductions in lending margins it would stimulate investment by reducing the cost of funds. Fourth, an RIA may improve the atmosphere for investment by inducing greater credibility in the government's willingness or ability to pursue sound policies (see section 4.3).

There is at least circumstantial evidence that RIAs can generate investment booms, as is evidenced in the investment data for the 'Six' after the creation of the EEC, the Iberian enlargement of the EC, EC '1992', NAFTA and Mercosur. Thus there is support for this as a route to a temporary spurt of growth relative to no liberalization at all. However, given the well-known possibilities of immiserizing investment in the presence of other distortions, one needs to be clear that such investment is economically warranted before declaring such RIAs successful. The result of de Melo, Panagariya and Rodrik (1993) that investment is responsive to RIA-formation but growth is not, could indicate problems of this kind.

An important element of accumulation in some RIAs is believed to be FDI. Many economists see inflows of FDI, first, as harbingers of confidence in the economy and, second, as the route through which an economy can modernize, for example, through access to modern technology, modern management, marketing networks and sources of inputs. If inflows of FDI are to be beneficial, such advantages are essential, for FDI is an extremely expensive way of borrowing capital if that is all that is obtained. Also, while FDI might boost GDP, it does less for GNP, because many of the benefits of FDI will accrue abroad. If the local economy is to reap benefit from FDI, we have to identify the route through which incomes, as well as output, are stimulated. Among the most obvious of such routes are the ability to tax foreign companies (although sometimes governments are prone to forego this right in order to attract the companies); benefits to employment if there are pre-existing unemployed resources (but then we need to know why labour that was potentially employable was unemployed in the first place); and spillovers, mainly of the sort which we discussed briefly under the heading of convergence.

The literature on spillovers from FDI is somewhat ambiguous (see Blomstrom and Kokko 1997a) but there is evidence in favour of their existence. FDI appears in some cases to have stimulated productivity in local firms. In the same industry as the FDI, this may be due to demonstration effects—local firms see that things can be managed better than they currently are—or a competition effect—local firms are obliged to adjust or go under. In other industries it may reflect forward linkages—other firms using better inputs from the multinational corporation (MNC)—or backward linkages—the MNC requiring and helping local suppliers to produce better inputs for *all* their customers. It may also arise from the mobility of labour as the multinational corporation trains labour and managers who then move on to other parts of the economy. The fact that the multinationals seem to pay efficiency wages, that is, wages above the going market rate, suggests that they are conscious that such spillovers are possible and that it is to their advantage to try to hang on to the skilled labour which they have trained.

The evidence suggests that the principal requirement for attracting FDI is sound policies at home, including macroeconomic stability, good labour relations and open borders. One has only to consider China and Indonesia to realize that RIAs are not necessary for strong FDI flows, and Greece to realize that they are not sufficient.

A simple RIA may reduce FDI flows between member countries because it makes trade a more attractive option. On the other hand, FDI from outside the bloc may increase as foreigners seek to exploit new investment opportunities and to use one member as a platform for serving the whole bloc. Blomstrom and Kokko (1997b) suggest that while the US–Canada FTA had little investment effect, Mercosur and NAFTA (Mexico) both coincided with increased FDI inflows. Intra-RIA flows may be stimulated—as, for example, with the EC's Iberian expansion—by flows in non-traded sectors (e.g. several services) and, if they are made, by provisions for capital inflows, the repatriation of profits, and enhanced dispute settlement.

The changing patterns of FDI under an RIA sometimes attract the sobriquets 'investment creation' and 'diversion'. As mere descriptors of rising and falling shares these terms are unexceptionable, but then we hardly need new vocabulary to describe increases and decreases. However, as parallels to trade creation and trade diversion, and especially their welfare implications, these terms are dangerous. Advocates of the view that RIAs increase FDI rarely argue that it displaces domestic investment (the parallel with creation) or that member flows displace non-member flows (diversion). Still less do they argue that member flows are less desirable than non-member flows. Moreover, new FDI from any source could go into the production of goods for trade diversion and thus worsen the RIA's welfare overall. Thus my advice is that we should drop the terms investment creation and diversion from our vocabulary and spell out directly the phenomenon we are interested in.

However, in immediate violation of my own advice, let me identify one very close investment parallel to trade diversion. Rules of origin (ROOs) within FTAs require substantial shares of the value of a good to originate in member countries before the good qualifies for the RIA's trade preferences.[19] In some sectors, e.g. vehicles, this severely handicaps potential investors from outside the bloc who would, at least initially, probably wish to source considerable shares of their inputs from their traditional (non-bloc) suppliers. That is, ROOs give member investors an artificial advantage. If members are less suitable sources of FDI than non-members, we have essentially investment diversion. This might be the case if members are less efficient producers than non-members: consider, for example, the advantages that US and EU vehicle producers receive in Mexico and Eastern Europe relative to Japanese firms. It could also occur if member firms offer fewer opportunities for spillovers than non-member ones. The ability of local firms to assimilate information may decrease as the gap in knowledge and experience between partners widens. Thus, for example, Mediterranean producers may learn more from Korean or Taiwanese (China) firms than German ones, but the ROOs in the Euro-Med Agreements will favour the latter.

It is easy to argue that RIAs will generate new investment and, in particular, increased inflows of FDI, but it is difficult to prove either such a view or its desirability. RIAs have clearly been associated with such changes, but to establish the advantages of the RIAs on these grounds one needs to show that: the RIA and not, say, MFN liberalization generated the incentives; the investment is not immiserizing; spillovers occur; and 'better' investment was not displaced by 'worse' investment.

4.3 Credibility[20]

A common claim for RIAs is that they enhance policy credibility, e.g. Whalley (1998). On the narrow issue of the instruments negotiated under the RIA, e.g. tariffs on intra-bloc trade, this seems reasonable, although one must still consider the incentives and ability for one partner to discipline another. An RIA probably focuses the incentives better than the WTO: under the WTO there is a large 'public goods' element to retaliation. If A retaliates against B for increasing a tariff (a) other suppliers benefit directly from the lower tariff, and (b) if, as a result, B becomes less prone to such anti-social behaviour in future, the likely major beneficiaries are C, D.... Within an RIA the spillover is smaller, being restricted to other member countries. On punishment, if an RIA delivers benefits beyond the WTO in the form of, say, increased investment, punishment for defection can be correspondingly heavier.

Whether RIAs discipline trade policy towards third parties, however, is moot. Clearly if trade policy is common across RIA members, as in a customs union, individual countries have less ability to impose their own barriers, but, on the other hand, any that do emerge are spread more widely (see Winters 1994). Thus, for example, the creation of Mercosur led to Brazil's tariffs on capital goods being extended to other members (Olarreaga and Soloaga 1998).

Where members set their own trade policies on third country trade (an FTA), there is no formal discipline; the issue then is whether internal and external tariffs are strategic substitutes or complements, and two offsetting forces are at work. If tariffs on partner imports are fixed at zero, those on other suppliers will be lowered by the incentives to minimize distortions between different sources of imports and capture tariff revenue from partners (Richardson 1995) but raised by the desire to protect domestic output more vigorously against supplies from third parties if one cannot protect it against those from partners. The latter effect depends on goods being differentiated by supplier, but, given this, which effect dominates depends on the degrees of substitutability between different goods.

It is equally difficult to identify the effect of RIAs on trade policy towards third countries empirically, because the *anti-monde* for policy is so difficult to define. For example, Mexico responded to the peso crisis of 1994/5 by raising tariffs on 503 items against non-NAFTA suppliers. Bhagwati and Panagariya (1996) see this as diverting protectionist pressure onto third parties. Others argue that previous crises have witnessed far worse protectionism and thus that NAFTA has induced restraint. Bhagwati and Panagariya respond that the intellectual atmosphere was far more liberal in 1995 than previously (consider, for example, India) and, less convincingly, that vigorous protectionism, such as seen in the 1980s, sows the seeds of its own demise; thus by permitting a partial response now NAFTA could slow down ultimate progress towards multilateral liberalism. Similarly, how did the existence of Mercosur factor into the Argentinian and Brazilian decisions to raise all tariffs by one-quarter to head off contagion from East Asia in November 1997?

Turning to policies that are not part of an RIA, it is even more difficult to see where credibility comes from. Two possibilities are identified by Fernandez and Portes. First, an RIA may raise the cost of macroeconomic laxity because it typically increases marginal leakages to imports, although, as Fernandez and Portes note, the RIA also increases the (temporary) returns to competitive devaluation which pushes the opposite way. Second, if entering an RIA entails (political) sunk costs, and if it requires liberal or sound policies to make sense, entry provides the government with a signalling device, for only a government with liberal intentions would sign. Thus in the presence of asymmetric information about the government's type, an RIA could improve credibility.

I find the last argument quite a persuasive explanation for the recent interest of developing country governments in RIAs. There has clearly been a shift in perceptions of the policy requirements for economic growth, and after several decades of pursuing inward looking policies, governments clearly require means of signalling genuine changes in attitudes. Whether RIAs are the best means of such signalling, however, and whether signalling is sufficient to justify RIAs are less clear. First, there is an element of circularity in the argument. If an RIA is genuinely liberal, i.e. it increases domestic competition and creates trade, it is beneficial (relative to the status quo) in those terms alone. Thus credibility is just icing on the cake. If, however, the RIA is not liberal, it will presumably not induce much credibility. Thus credibility is, in some sense, not an independent characteristic of RIAs. Second, there are other means of signalling and winning credibility: for example, binding trade policy with the WTO, accepting Article VIII of the IMF, domestic rhetoric, and constitutional limitations. These do not have the trade-diverting risks of RIAs.

To summarize, 'locking-in' and the credibility of policy reform do seem to have been closely linked with RIAs over the last few years. It is also true that many developing countries have liberalized both globally and regionally. Whether that confers on RIAs an independent ability to grant credibility I doubt, however. Greece has been a member of the EU since 1981 and yet is subject to serious macroeconomic shortcomings: it shows that RIAs are not sufficient for sound policy and hence presumably not particularly good sources of credibility in themselves.[21] Hence overall, if we are to believe that a prospective RIA enhances a government's credibility, I believe we should spell out quite clearly why and how.

4.4 Location

A major issue in RIAs among developing countries has been the location of industry, often loosely equated with the location of the benefits of integration. Indeed, in previous decades when governments felt they could and should manage location this was sufficiently contentious to destroy some RIAs. Now governments profess greater faith in the market to distribute industry efficiently, but they still worry about outcomes and wonder whether they can nudge the process their way.

Recent analysis has suggested that there may be some truth to worries that RIAs and the deepening of integration within them could lead to some regions losing, or at least failing to gain. These analyses depend on the interactions between economies of scale and transactions costs. Krugman and Venables (1990) provided the first, elegant, example, which showed how industry's preferred location between a high-cost large-market 'centre' and a low-cost small-market 'periphery' would vary with transactions costs between them. Briefly, at very high (prohibitive) transactions costs industry locates in both places just in order to serve both. At intermediate costs it is feasible to trade and, if scale effects are strong enough, it pays to concentrate production in one place and export to the other. Obviously, if it is not 'too much more expensive' in production terms, firms choose the (large-market) centre because there they avoid transactions costs on the larger part of their sales. At zero transactions costs location is determined solely by production costs, so now firms prefer the (low-cost) periphery for all their production.

This model had a salutary effect in simply disproving the notion that low-cost peripheries would automatically attract industrial activity. However, it offered little practical guidance for predicting the effects of RIAs. First, it was partial equilibrium in nature—costs of production were independent of the volume of industry. Second, the exercise is comparatively static: it does not actually refer to firms relocating. Third, we have no idea whether the irreducible minimum transactions cost between two countries—perhaps best thought of as that between two states in the United States—is high, low or intermediate. Brulhart and Torstensson (1996) have found suggestive evidence for the EU that industry has concentrated and along the lines predicted by Krugman and Venables, but, on their own admission, it is not strong.

Economic geography has advanced a lot since 1991, but it is still a long way from producing testable or quantitative predictions, because the models it uses are so far removed from reality. Among the most relevant advances are the studies by Puga and Venables (1997, 1998) who have a model in which industry is both attracted to large markets to avoid sales costs and repelled from them by their higher production costs. They use this in the latter paper to explore how industrialization in two identical developing (Southern) countries might be affected by various forms of integration arrangements. Among their conclusions are that even if the two countries liberalize their trade at the same rate, they will take off at different times, because, at low levels of southern industrial development, agglomeration economies make it inefficient to split industry between two sites. Although eventually both developing countries fare the same, there are clear (discounted) benefits to being the first to industrialize. Moreover, the lagging developing country can actually lose before it industrializes itself. Thus developing countries are at least partly competing against each other for industry.

Puga and Venables also suggest that while unilateral liberalization by a developing country stimulates its industrialization, signing an RIA is even better for the member developing country. While precise results depend on parameter values and the level of remaining trade costs, about both of which we have almost no information in the real world, their results suggest that North–South RIAs dominate South–South RIAs. Multilateral liberalization dominates all options for a developing country except for a North–South RIA outside which the excluded developing country refuses to liberalize.

These models are stimulating and challenging for they capture better than most the common perception that countries compete and that development can be uneven. However, they do not yet constitute practical tools for predicting the effects of RIAs for they lie so far from measurable reality. Thus, while it is now clear that an RIA *could* have locational effects, we are not able to predict these *ex ante* nor, with confidence, identify them *ex post*.

5 Politics

Regional Integration Agreements (RIAs) are frequently argued to be an important element of diplomacy. The classic case is the precursor to the European Economic Community, the European Coal and Steel Community, 1951, which was quite explicitly seen as a way of reducing Franco-German tensions—making war not only unthinkable but materially impossible. Similar objectives are said to be present, if not so centrally, in Mercosur and ASEAN. These cases raise at least two sets of questions: why use trade as the diplomatic tool and what implications does this have for regionalism itself?

On the latter, Schiff and Winters (1998) have recently offered a theoretical analysis. Taking as given the premise that trade increases understanding and harmony between partners—a view with a venerable heritage—they show that an FTA could be an optimal policy if actors value these things. They also show that as the FTA grows, and if it pursues deep integration, the optimal degree of preference for intra-bloc trade decreases. This translates into declining external tariffs: exactly the pattern observed in the EU. They also examine the optimal degree of preference as a bloc widens its membership. There is a weak presumption that this could lead to rising tariffs, but this is easily overturned by changes in particular circumstances.

On the question of why use trade diplomacy, i.e. whether trade is the appropriate or optimal tool, little analysis exists. Mansfield (1993) relates politics and RIAs, but with the former 'causing' the latter and a requirement (for his argument to make sense) that the RIA be welfare enhancing. Fawcett and Hurrell (1995) also see causation running in this direction, with RIAs as part of the response of nation states to the erosion of their power by globalism. That is, states pool sovereignty in an RIA in order to achieve sufficient leverage to manage global pressures. From this perspective it is not clear whether RIAs are desirable for developing countries or not, for it is not clear that managed solutions are better than just accepting life as a small open economy.

In the case of European integration Milward (1992) has advanced similar arguments. These clearly have some validity, for Europe has clearly generated material economic power in those areas in which it can act in a concerted fashion. One should also observe, however, that in the European case several other forms of diplomacy/integration were tried and failed, e.g. the Political and Defence Communities in the 1950s. Thus in a sense trade diplomacy was all that was left.

The political dimension of RIAs does seem an important one, but one over which the analyst needs to exercise caution. Cooperation without tariff preferences seems perfectly possible if one wishes it, and free trade does not guarantee peace—witness the American Civil War which was partially caused by disagreements over trade policy. Thus to justify an RIA on political grounds one needs to show how preferences contribute to the political rapprochement and show that such a rapprochement is valuable. The latter requires (a) that rapprochement is real and (b) that it would not have happened anyway.

6 Conclusion

The challenge is not in thinking up how RIAs *could* be beneficial, but in offering convincing reasons why, in particular cases, they *will be* or *have been*. I have argued elsewhere (Winters 1999) that, as well as generating trade diversion, regionalism can be harmful in terms of arresting progress towards liberal multilateral outcomes. Hence, while they may well provide benefits relative to the status quo, RIAs also entail a potential downside risk.

In discussing RIAs I believe that there is no alternative to the careful exploration of the various sources of costs and benefits. By this I am most definitely *not* saying that we should conduct careful trade creation/diversion exercises and ignore everything else on the grounds that it cannot be measured. Rather, we should spell out the benefits that we have in mind and their channels of causation, so that their bases can be discussed and examined explicitly. Even if we cannot quantify and add up the various effects we can, at least, be clear and identify areas of agreement and disagreement. I hope this chapter helps us to do this.

Notes

1. This chapter is based on 'Assessing Regional Integration Arrangements', Chapter II of Burki, J., Perry, G. and Calvo, S. (eds) *Trade: Towards Open Regionalism*, The World Bank, Washington, DC, 1998. I am grateful to Robert Devlin and Maurice Schiff for comments on an earlier draft. I am also grateful, for discussions on regionalism in general, to the many contributors to the programme on 'Regionalism and Development' that Maurice Schiff and I coordinated at the World Bank, 1997–9. Their work figures prominently in the chapter.
2. This is not saying that countries ignore the effects of their policies on other countries, only that the feedbacks via systemic effects are so small and uncertain that few small or medium-sized countries will internalize them in policy decisions.
3. It is true that all policy advice occurs in a second-best context, but in other areas the connection, or degree of interaction, between the remaining (immovable) distortions and those whose removal is being contemplated is rarely as close as that between, say, tariffs on wheat imported from Argentina and wheat imported from Canada. Thus, generally speaking, second-best is a bigger problem in discussions of RIAs than elsewhere.
4. I am grateful to Diane Tussie and Ann Weston for purging the traditional form of this joke of its gender bias!
5. Recently, Schiff (1999) and Venables (1999) have both used the term 'natural' in this context, but only to stress that they are seeking to identify countries with which signing an RIA is welfare enhancing. Although each has made some advance, neither has given the concept *de facto* operational meaning.
6. All the analysis in this subsection compares RIAs with *anti-mondes* in which all members would levy unchanged MFN tariffs against each other in the absence of an RIA. Comparisons of the RIA with concerted unilateralism, in which partners jointly reduce their MFN tariffs to zero, would be less favourable to the RIA.
7. There is actually some dispute about what Viner actually said—see Michaely and Viner and the references therein in the *Journal of International Economics*, February 1976.
8. Wonnacott and Wonnacott's gains depends *only* on there being transport costs on the rest of the world, not, as they claim, on the relative size of these and intra-bloc transport costs (Amjadi, Winters and Yeats 1995).
9. I discount a pioneering effort by Harris and Cox (1986) because it failed to provide a coherent view of imperfectly competitive pricing (see Winters 1992).

L. Alan Winters

10. There are, of course, myriad CGE modelling predictions of the sizes of these gains, but CGE models are not truly empirical; they are numerical manifestations of theoretical equations, not examinations of data on what actually happened.
11. Bloc members may trade more or less than normally with each other for all sorts of non-policy reasons, so it is, again, *changes* in these 'biases' that reveal RIA effects.
12. The loss of imports is matched by a loss of exports, so the welfare cost arises from the (small) decline in the efficiency of transforming one into the other, not from the loss of the whole bundle of imports.
13. The change in the terms of trade is strictly the best indicator of the welfare effects of any trade shock; the problem with examining changes in non-member imports following an RIA, as we did above, is that imports might be reduced endogenously in response to price changes even though welfare increases.
14. This statement is true of simple cases with constant returns to scale and no other distortions. Once the latter are introduced, however, deep RIAs can be harmful—see, for example, Haaland and Wooton (1992) and section 4.4 where costs and economies of scale interact. It is also true that where deep integration involves harmonizing standards or policies, they need to be harmonized at 'sensible' levels if doing so is to be beneficial.
15. Also, signing a Europe Agreement has been the signal for the EU treating an Eastern partner as a market, rather than a non-market, economy, and so relaxing its treatment under anti-dumping law. These issues are neither formally nor conceptually linked, however.
16. Mazumdar (1996) shows that a similar problem arises if liberalization favours the labour-abundant commodity.
17. See Baldwin, Forslid and Haaland (1996), Baldwin and Seghezza (1996a, 1996b, 1996c) and Baldwin and Forslid (1996).
18. In the case of efficiency increases, this effect depends on the elasticity of demand being high enough to increase demand by more than efficiency improvements reduce the inputs required per unit of output.
19. Krueger (1998) provides an analysis of the difficulties caused by ROOs.
20. This section draws freely on Fernandez and Portes (1998).
21. In fact, Alogoskoufis (1995) suggests that EU membership worsened Greece's macroeconomic policy by subsidizing its profligacy—fortunately not a likely outcome in most developing country RIAs.

References

Aitken, N.D. (1973) 'The effect of the EEC and EFTA on European trade: a temporal cross-section analysis', *American Economic Review*, Vol. 63 (5): 881–92.
Alogoskoufis, G. (1995) 'The two faces of Janus: institutions, policy regimes and macroeconomic performance in Greece', *Economic Policy*, Vol. 20: 147–92.
Amjadi, A. and Winters, L.A. (1999) 'Transport costs and "natural" integration in Mercosur', *Journal of Economic Integration*, Vol. 14: 497–52.
Amjadi, A., Winters, L.A. and Yeats, A. (1995) 'Transportation costs and economic integration in the Americas', *Swiss Journal of Economics and Statistics*, Vol. 13 (3): 465–88.
Anderson, K. and Norheim, H. (1993) 'From imperial to regional trade preferences:

its effect on Europe's intra- and extra-regional trade', *Weltwirtschaftliches-Archiv*, Vol. 129 (1): 78–102.

Baldwin, R. (1989) 'The growth effects of 1992', *Economic Policy*, Vol. 9: 247–81.

—— (1992) 'Measurable dynamic gains from trade', *Journal of Political Economy,* Vol. 100: 162–74.

Baldwin, R. and Forslid, R. (1996) 'Trade liberalization and endogenous growth: a q-theory approach', National Bureau of Economic Research, Working Paper Series, No. 5549.

Baldwin, R., Forslid, R. and Haaland, J. (1996) 'Investment creation and diversion: a simulation study of the EU's Single Market programme', *The World Economy*, Vol. 19 (6): 635–59.

Baldwin, R. and Seghezza, E. (1996a) 'Testing for trade-induced investment-led growth', Centre for Economic Policy Research, Discussion Paper Series, No. 1331.

—— (1996b) 'Trade-induced investment led growth', mimeo, Graduate Institute of International Studies, Geneva.

—— (1996c) 'Growth and European integration: towards an empirical assessment', Centre for Economic Policy Research, Discussion Paper Series, No. 1393.

Baldwin, R. and Venables, A. (1995) 'Regional economic integration', in G. Grossman and K. Rogoff (eds), *Handbook of International Economics*, Vol. III, Amsterdam: North-Holland.

Barro, R.J. and Sala-i-Martin, X. (1995) *Economic Growth*, New York: McGraw-Hill.

Baumol, W.J., Blackman, S.A.B. and Wolff, E.N. (1989) *Productivity and American Leadership: The Long View*, Cambridge, Mass.: MIT Press.

Bayoumi, T. and Eichengreen, B. (1997) 'Is regionalism simply a diversion? Evidence from the evolution of the EC and EFTA', in A. Krueger and T. Ito *Regionalism Versus Multilateral Trade Arrangements*, NBER-East Asia Seminar on Economics, Vol. 6, Chicago and London: University of Chicago Press.

Ben-David, D. (1993) 'Equalizing exchange: trade liberalization and income convergence', *Quarterly Journal of Economics*, Vol. 108: 653–79.

—— (1994) 'Income disparity among countries and the effects of freer trade', in L.L. Pasinetti and R.M. Solow (eds) *Economic Growth and the Structure of Long Run Development*, London: Macmillan: 45–64.

—— (1995) 'Convergence clubs and diverging economies', Foerder Institute Working Paper 40/95.

—— (1996) 'Trade and convergence among countries', *Journal of International Economics,* Vol. 40: 279–98.

Bhagwati, J.N. and Panagariya A. (eds) (1996) *The Economics of Preferential Trade Agreements*, Washington, DC: The AEI Press.

Blomstrom, M. and Kokko, A (1998) 'Multinational corporations and spillovers', *Journal of Economic Surveys*, Vol. 12 No. 3: 247–77.

—— (1997a) 'How foreign direct investment affects host countries', World Bank Policy Research Working Paper Series, No. 1745.

—— (1997b) 'Regional integration and foreign direct investment: a conceptual framework and three cases', World Bank Policy Research Working Paper Series, No. 1750.

Bond, E.W. (1997a) 'Using tariff indices to evaluate preferential trading arrangements: an application to Chile', World Bank Policy Research Working Paper Series, No. 1751.

—— (1997b) 'The impact of Canada-U.S. Free Trade Agreement on antidumping filings and decisions', mimeo.

Braga, C.A., Safadi, R. and Yeats, A. (1994) 'Regional integration in the Americas: deja vu all over again?' *World Economy*, Vol. 17 (4): 577–601.

Brulhart, M. and Torstensson, J. (1996) 'Regional integration, scale economies and industry location in the European Union', Centre for Economic Policy Research, Working Paper Series, No. 1435.

Chang, W. and Winter, L.A. (1999) 'How Regional blocs affect excluded countries: the price effects of Mercosur', Policy Research Working Paper No. 2157, The World Bank.

Coe, D.T., Helpman, E. and Hoffmaister, A.W. (1997) 'North–South R&D spillovers', *Economic Journal*, Vol. 107: 134–9.

de la Fuente, A. (1997) 'The empirics of growth and convergence: a selective review', *Journal of Economic Dynamics and Control*, Vol. 21 No. 1: 23–73.

de Melo, J., Panagariya, A. and Rodrik, D. (1993) 'The new regionalism: a country perspective', in J. de Melo and A. Panagariya (eds) *New Dimensions in Regional Integration*, New York: Cambridge University Press: 159–92.

Engel, C. and Rogers, J.H. (1996) 'How wide is the border', *American Economic Review*, Vol. 86 (5): 1112–25.

European Commission (1996) 'Economic evaluation of the internal market', *European Economy*, Reports and Studies, No. 4.

Falvey, R. (1995) 'Factor price convergence', mimeo, International Trade Division, The World Bank.

Fawcett, L. and Hurrell, A. (1995) *Regionalism in World Politics: Regional Organization and International Order*, New York: Oxford University Press.

Fernandez, R. and Portes, J. (1998) 'Returns to regionalism and evaluation of non-traditional gains from RTA', *World Bank Economic Review*, Vol. 12: 197–220.

Foroutan, F. (1997) 'Does membership in an FTA make a country more or less protectionist?' *The World Economy*, Vol. 21: 305–36.

Frankel, J.A. and Wei, S.-J. (1996) 'Regionalization of world trade and currencies: economics and politics', Chapter 7 of J.A. Frankel (ed.) *The Regionalism of the World Economy*, Chicago University Press.

Frankel, J.A., Stein, E. and Wei, S.-J. (1995) 'Trading blocs: the natural, the unnatural, and the super-natural', *Journal of Development Economics*, Vol. 47: 61–95.

Gupta, A. and Schiff, M. (1997) 'Outsiders and regional trading arrangements among small countries: the case of regional markets', World Bank Policy Research Working Paper, No. 1847, Washington, DC.

Haaland, J.I. and Norman, V. (1992) 'Global production effects of European integration', in L.A. Winters (ed.) *Trade Flows and Trade Policy After '1992'*, CEPR and Cambridge University Press: 67–88.

Haaland, J.I. and Wooton, I. (1992) 'Market integration, competition and welfare', in L. Winters (ed.) *Trade Flows and Trade Policy After '1992'*, CEPR and Cambridge University Press: 125–46.

Harris, R. and Cox, D. (1986) 'Quantitative assessment of the economic impact on Canada of sectoral free trade with the United States', *Canadian Journal of Economics*, Vol. 19: 377–94.

Harrison, A., Rutherford, T.F. and Tarr, D. (1997) 'Trade policy options for Chile', World Bank Policy Research Working Paper Series, No. 1783, Washington, DC.

Helliwell, J.W. (1998) *How Much Do National Borders Matter?* Washington, DC: Brookings Institution.

Henrekson, M., Torstensson, J. and Torstensson, R. (1997) 'Growth effects of European integration', *European Economic Review*, Vol. 4, No. 8: 1537–57.

Herin, J. (1986) 'Rules of origin and differences between tariff levels in EFTA and the EC', EFTA Occasional Paper, No. 13, EFTA, Geneva.

Jacquemin, A. and Sapir, A. (1991) 'Competition and imports in the European market', L.A. Winters and A.J. Venables (eds) *European Integration: Trade and Industry*, Cambridge, New York and Melbourne: Cambridge University Press: 82–91.

Jones, C. (1995) 'Time series tests of endogenous growth models', *Quarterly Journal of Economics*, Vol. 110 (2): 495–525.

Jones, R. (1993) 'Regionalism vs. multilateralism: analytical notes' comment', in J. de Melo and A. Panagariya (eds) *New Dimensions of the Regional Integration*, New York: Cambridge University Press: 79–83.

Keller, W. (1998) 'Are international R&D spillovers trade-related? Analyzing spillovers among randomly matched trade partners', *European Economic Review*, Vol. 42 No. 8: 1469–81.

Krueger, A.O. (1997) 'Free trade agreements versus customs union', *Journal of Development Economics*, 54: 169–87.

Krugman, P. (1991) 'The move towards free trade zones', in *Policy Implications of Trade and Currency Zones*, Federal Reserve Bank of Kansas City, Kansas City: 7–42.

Krugman, P. and Venables, A.J. (1990) 'Integration and the competitiveness of peripheral industry', in C. Bliss and J. de-Macedo (eds) *Unity with Diversity in the European Community: The Community's Southern Frontier*, Cambridge: Cambridge University Press.

Lucas, R.E. (1988) 'On the mechanics of economic development?', *Journal of Monetary Economics*, Vol. 22: 3–42.

Mankiw, G., Romer, D. and Weil, D. (1992) 'A contribution to the empirics of economic growth', *Quarterly Journal of Economics*, Vol. 107: 407–37.

Mansfield, E. (1993) 'Effects of international politics on regionalism in international trade', in K. Anderson and Blackhurst (eds) *Regional Integration and the Global Trading System*, New York: St. Martin's Press: 191–217.

Mazumdar, J. (1996) 'Do static gains from trade lead to medium-run growth?' *Journal of Political Economy*, Vol. 104 (6): 1328–37.

McCallum, J. (1995) 'National borders matter: Canada-U.S. regional trade patterns', *American Economic Review*, Vol. 85 (3): 615–23.

Michaely, M. (1976) 'The assumptions of Jacob Viner's theory of customs unions', *Journal of International Economics*, Vol. 6: 75–93.

Milward, A.S., (1992) *The European Rescue of the Nation-State*, London: Routledge.

Nitsch, V. (1997) 'Do three trade blocs minimize world welfare?' *Review of International Economics*, Vol. 4: 355–63.

—— (1996) 'Natural trading blocs: a closer look', *Journal of Economic Integration*, Vol. 12 No. 4: 433–55.

Olarreaga, M. and Soloaga, I. (1998) 'Endogenous tariff formation: the case of Mercosur', *The World Bank Economic Review*, Vol. 12: 297–320.

Panagariya, A. (1997) 'Preferential trading and the myth of natural trading partners', *Japan and the World Economy*, 9: 471–89.

Puga, D. and Venables, A.J. (1997) 'Preferential trading arrangements and industrial location', *Journal of International Economics*, Vol. 43: 347–68.

—— (1998) 'Trading arrangements and industrial development', *World Bank Economic Review*, Vol. 12: 221–50.

Richardson, M. (1995) 'Tariff revenue competition in a free trade area', *European Economic Review*, Vol. 39: 1429–37.

Rowat, M., Lubrano, M. and Porrata Jr., R. (1997) *Competition Policy in Mercosur*, World Bank Discussion Paper, No. 385, Washington, DC: The World Bank.

Sachs, J.D. and Warner, A. (1995) 'Economic reform and the process of global integration', *Brookings Papers on Economic Activities*, No. 1: 1–118.

Sapir, A. (1992) 'Regional integration in Europe', *Economic Journal*, Vol. 102 (415): 1491–506.

—— (1993) 'The European Community: a case of successful integration? Discussion', in J. de Melo and A. Panagariya (eds) *New Dimensions in Regional Integration*, Cambridge University Press: 230–3.

—— (1997) 'Domino effects in West European trade: 1960–92', CEPR Discussion Paper Series, No. 1576.

Schiff, M. (1997) 'Small is beautiful: preferential trade agreements and the impact of market size, market share, efficiency, and trade policy', *Journal of Economic Integration*, Vol. 12 (3): 359–87.

—— (1999) 'Will the real natural trading partner please stand up?' mimeo, Development Research Group, The World Bank.

Schiff, M. and Sapelli, C. (eds) (1996) *Chile en el NAFTA*. Centro Internacional para el Desarrollo Económico, San Francisco and Santiago.

Schiff, M. and Winters, L.A. (1998) 'Regional integration as diplomacy', *World Bank Economic Review*, Vol. 12: 271–96.

Smith, A. and Venables, A.J. (1988) 'Completing the internal market in European Community: some industry simulations', *European Economic Review*, Vol. 32: 1501–25.

Soloaga, I. and Winters, L.A. (1999) 'Regionalism in the nineties: what effect on trade', CEPR Discussion Paper, No. 2183.

Srinivasan, T.N. (1993) 'Regionalism vs. multilateralism: analytical notes' comment', in J. de Melo and A. Panagariya (eds) *New Dimensions of the Regional Integration*, New York: Cambridge University Press: 84–9.

Summers, L. (1991) 'Regionalism and the world trading system', in *Policy Implications of Trade and Currency Zones*, Kansas City: Federal Reserve Bank of Kansas City: 295–302.

Truman, E.M. (1969) 'The European Community: trade creation and trade diversion', *Yale Economic Essays*, No. 9: 201–57.

Vamvakidis, A. (1998a) 'Regional integration and economic growth', *World Bank Economic Review*, Vol. 12 No. 2, 1998: 251–70 (mimeo). International Trade Division, World Bank, Washington, DC.

—— (1998b) 'Regional trade agreements versus broad liberalization: which path leads to faster growth? Time series evidence', IMF Working Paper No. 98/40.

Venables, A.J. (1999) 'Regional integration agreements: a force for convergence or divergence?', mimeo, Development Research Group, The World Bank.

Viner, J. (1950) *The Customs Unions Issue*, New York: Carnegie Endowment for International Peace.

Whalley, J. (1998) 'Why do countries seek regional trade agreements?' in J. Frankel (ed.) *The Regionalization of the World Economy*, Chicago University Press.

Winters, L.A. (1983) 'British imports of manufactures and the Common Market', *Oxford Economic Papers*, Vol. 36: 103–18.

Winters, L.A. (1985) 'Separability and the modelling of international economic integration: UK exports to five countries', *European Economic Review*, Vol. 27: 335–53.

—— (1992) *Trade Flows and Trade Policies After '1992'*, Cambridge University Press.

—— (1993) 'The European Community: a case of successful integration', in J. de Melo and A. Panagariya (eds) *New Dimensions in Regional Integration*, New York: Cambridge University Press: 202–28.

—— (1994) 'The EC and protection: the political economy', *European Economic Review*, Vol. 38: 596–603.

—— (1997a) 'Integration and the rest of the world: the irrelevance of the Kemp-Wan Theorem', *Oxford Economic Papers*, Vol. 49: 228–34.

—— (1997b) 'Regionalism and the rest of the world: theory and estimates of the effects of European integration', *Review of International Economics*, Supplement to Vol. 5: 134–47.

—— (1997c) 'What can European experience teach Latin America about integration?', *The World Economy*, Vol. 20: 889–912.

—— (1997d) 'Lebanon's Euro-Mediterranean agreement: possible dynamic effects', Chapter 3 in W. Shahin and K. Shehadi (eds) *Pathways to Integration: Lebanon and the Euro-Mediterranean Partnership*, Beirut: The Lebanese Centre for Policy Studies.

—— (1999) 'Regionalism versus multilateralism', Chapter 2 of R. Baldwin, D. Cohen, A. Sapir and A. Venables (eds) *Market Integration, Regionalism and the Global Economy*, Cambridge University Press: 7–48.

Winters, L.A. and Chang, W. (2000) 'Regional integration and the prices of imports: an empirical investigation', *Journal of International Economics*, Vol. 51: 363–78.

Winters, L.A. and Wang, Z.K. (1994) *Eastern Europe's International Trade*, New York: Manchester University Press, distributed by St. Martin Press in US and Canada.

Wonnacott, P. and Wonnacott, R. (1981) 'Is unilateral tariff reduction preferable to a customs union? The curious case of the missing foreign tariffs', *American Economic Review*, Vol. 71 (4): 704–14.

Wonnacott, P. and Wonnacott, R. (1992) 'The customs union issue reopened', *Manchester School of Economics and Social Studies*, Vol. 60 (2): 119–35.

World Bank (1996) *Global Economic Prospects*, Washington, DC: World Bank.

Yeats, A. (1998) 'Does Mercosur's trade performance raise concerns about the effects of regional trade arrangements', *World Bank Economic Review*, Vol. 12 No. 1: 1–28.

7 Multilateral trade reform, regionalism and developing countries

David Greenaway and Chris Milner*

1 Introduction

The second half of the twentieth century has seen a remarkable increase in integration affecting all parts of the global economy, including much of the developing world. The exchanges that result in integration of economies are triggered by similar economic stimuli as those which trigger exchanges within economies, namely declines in transactions costs. These are associated both with natural and man-made barriers. With regard to the former, there have been declines in the costs of transportation and even more so in the costs of communication which have proved to be an enormous stimulus to globalization. Declines in man-made barriers have been no less dramatic, as governments have reduced or removed impediments to cross-border commerce. This has taken place unilaterally (i.e. unreciprocated actions by a single trading nation), multilaterally (i.e. reciprocated reductions in trade barriers which extend to all trading partners) and minilaterally (i.e. reciprocated reductions in trading barriers which extend to some subset of trading partners). All three forms of liberalization have been in evidence over the post-war period.

In this chapter we concentrate on the way in which multilateral integration has affected the developing countries and the tensions between multilateral and regional integration. Both sources of integration have been advanced over the last fifty years to a very considerable degree and developments in both have been extensively documented and analysed. The aims of this chapter are fourfold: first, to assess past and recent developments in both multilateral and regional integration; second, to investigate the interests of developing countries in multilateral liberalization over this period and in future Rounds of multilateral trade negotiations; third, to explore the compatibility of multilateral and minilateral trade reforms from the point of view of the developing countries; finally, to explore some of the major unresolved issues affecting the integration of the global trading system and the developing countries.

The chapter is organized as follows. In the second section we focus on multilateralism under the General Agreement on Tariffs and Trade

(GATT) prior to the Uruguay Round. The third section provides an analysis of the Uruguay Round and its implications for the developing countries. The fourth section evaluates regional integration forces and their implications for multilateralism, while the fifth section considers the future agenda of the developing countries into the next Round and next century. The sixth section concludes.

2 GATT and the developing countries

The General Agreement on Tariffs and Trade (GATT) had its origins in the Anglo-American vision for post-war reconstruction, which rested on three multilateral institutions: one to provide an orderly framework for monetary relations—the International Monetary Fund (IMF); one to mobilize resources for development—the World Bank Group; and one to bring order to commercial trade. The last of these was meant to be the International Trade Organization (ITO), but turned out to be the Enabling Treaty for that organization, i.e. the GATT.

The over-riding objective of the GATT was to provide a framework for the orderly conduct of trade, as well as a process within which trade liberalization could take place. To this end, the key principles which underlay the Charter were non-discrimination, reciprocity and transparency. The first was important because it discouraged the swapping of favours between trading partners and thereby encouraged Contracting Parties (CPs) to the negotiating table—countries negotiating in the knowledge that the agreements reached applied to all parties. The principle of reciprocity states that if one CP makes a trade concession to another (e.g. by cutting a tariff), the beneficiary is obliged to reciprocate with an equivalent concession. As we know from basic trade theory, in the absence of distortions, reciprocity is not necessary for a tariff cutting country to benefit. However, it is important to the liberalization process. From the outset it sought to encourage negotiators who were instinctively mercantilist to believe that 'fairness' was being achieved by both parties making concessions; it also encouraged them to claim that there were double benefits from any agreement: lower prices of imports for consumers and better market access for exporters. Transparency dictates that when intervention is necessary it should be via visible, rather than opaque, instruments.

The mechanism instituted by GATT to promote trade liberalization was the 'Rounds' system. Rather than negotiating continually, CPs came together periodically and agreed a package of measures which were then implemented. Eight Rounds of MTNs have been completed so far. Over time the number of countries involved has expanded dramatically, especially over the last two Rounds. This is a reflection on the success of GATT and the multilateral liberalization process which has become more encompassing through time. In addition, the value of trade involved has grown dramatically in real terms; this clearly came about by more and more countries being involved and also by more and more trade impediments being addressed. More countries and more multi-layered negotiations have also meant that Rounds have become more protracted as time has gone on. Crudely, the early Rounds were essentially about tariff liberalization in manufactures and nothing else. Recent Rounds, and in particular the Uruguay Round, have involved negotiations on tariffs, non-tariff barriers (like voluntary export restraints or VERs), contingent protection, new issues, such as intellectual property protection, and new sectors, such as agriculture and services. This has resulted in longer and more complicated negotiations. As we shall see later, this is a possible contributory factor in explaining the upsurge of interest in the 1990s in regional trade arrangements (RTAs).

Developing country involvement in the GATT, and in GATT negotiations, can usefully be thought of in three phases: pre-Kennedy Round, post-Kennedy Round and Uruguay Round. Prior to the Kennedy Round there were five GATT Rounds in which developing country involvement was minimal. This was due in part to the orientation of the negotiations and, in particular, their focus on tariff liberalization in manufactures, and in part to the absence of a reciprocity requirement on less developed countries (LDCs). In the period during and immediately after the Kennedy Round, LDCs assumed a higher profile and more active role. Some of this effort was directed at the formation of the United Nations Conference on Trade and Development (UNCTAD), and some was aimed at making the case for special and differential treatment (S and D). This was affirmed on two separate grounds: a right to protect, and a right to preferential market access. Both were underpinned by arguments based on relatively poor growth prospects.[1] Table 7.1 provides a summary of the S and D features of the GATT. As can be seen, some Articles in the original Charter affirmed S and D, in particular Article 18. Clause 18b sanctions protection in support of the balance of payments as does Article 12. However, the conditions attaching to recourse to Article 18 are less stringent than those associated with Article 12. Clause 18c offers a right to protect in support of infant industries. This is a right which does not extend to industrialized countries. Together, Clauses 18b and 18c are the cornerstone of LDCs 'right to protect' preferences.

As noted above, S and D treatment also manifests itself in a 'right to access' form. Part 4 of the GATT, which was added in 1965, makes an explicit commitment to preferential access (Article 36), as well as formally waiving the reciprocity obligation. Preferential access was subsequently delivered through the various Generalized System of Preferences (GSP) schemes which came into force after 1971. These constituted a formal derogation from the GATT principle of non-discrimination in permitting access to LDC imports on preferential terms. The GSP schemes were subsequently given a full legal basis by the Tokyo Round Framework Agreement.

Table 7.1 Special and differential treatment in GATT

Article 18	18b Balance of payments
	18c Infant industry
Article 28	LDC needs and MTNs
Part IV	improved market access
	prioritization in MTNs
	non-reciprocity
Generalized system of Preferences	improved market access
Tokyo Framework Agreement	legal basis for generalized system of preferences

S and D treatment constitutes a non-trivial exception to the key GATT principles of non-discrimination, transparency and reciprocity. Why were such important exceptions sanctioned, and did they achieve their objectives? Finger (1991) addresses the first question at length and emphasizes three factors: the prevailing orthodoxy regarding the role of trade policy in development; the evolution of GATT; and the institutional rivalry between GATT and UNCTAD. When the GATT charter was drafted, and in the period through to the addition of Part 4, the prevailing orthodoxy was, broadly speaking, structuralist. Planning was seen as performing a key role, and this applied as much to tradeable as non-tradeable sectors. Dependence on primary products, it was argued, could be relieved only via fostering infant industries behind protective barriers. In other words, what we now refer to as import substitution industrialization was widely seen as providing the foundation for successful industrialization. As GATT evolved and the number of LDC contracting parties increased, so too did the lobby in favour of S and D. Finger argues that the relatively poor trade performance of developing countries in the 1950s was taken by LDCs as evidence of a failure of existing S and D provisions. The creation of UNCTAD in 1964 helped push the GATT into providing more by way of 'affirmative action', as manifested in Part 4: 'GATT rules were being shaped by an our-organization-versus-their-organization competition for membership, and not by any concern to guide or push countries to choose the most effective trade policies' (Finger 1991: 215).

Has S and D 'worked'? To provide a convincing answer one needs a well specified counterfactual, and an appropriate geographical and product breakdown. Although we do not have an overall evaluation of S and D, we do have quite a lot of evidence on the consequences of protective regimes in developing countries and the effects of the GSP. The evidence on the former suggests that pervasive and indiscriminate protection was in general damaging to growth (see, for example, Greenaway and Nam 1988 and Krueger 1997); the evidence on the latter suggests that GSP schemes have been of minimal benefit, given their product exclusions, rules of origin, small margins of preference and use of trigger price mechanisms (see, for example, Langhammer and Sapir 1987). As a result, widespread disillusionment with S and D increased in both developed and developing countries. Many developing countries retreated during the 1980s from import substitution industrialization (ISI) strategies, often under pressure from the Bretton Woods institutions, and initiated unilateral liberalization. As we shall see, this had implications for their interests in the Uruguay Round. For their part, many industrialized countries took the view that greater constraints should pertain to the application of S and D, and in particular that the criteria for graduation should be more explicit.

To summarize, then, prior to the Uruguay Round, developing countries in general saw their interests in GATT as being best served by acquiring and extending special and differential treatment. However, the evidence suggests that S and D was not necessarily in their best interests, in the sense that there is little evidence that it delivered much in terms of a growth bonus. Although, as we shall see in the next section, a case for S and D continued to be put within the Uruguay Round, developing country interests were by this stage much more diverse, and this was reflected in both the agenda setting and actual negotiations within the Uruguay Round.

3 The Uruguay Round and the interests of developing countries

Launched in 1986, the Uruguay Round is rightly regarded as having been the most ambitious, and most difficult, of all of the Rounds so far. The Agreement was seven years in the making, at the end of which the negotiators delivered a package (finally signed in April 1994) which was certainly comprehensive and in some areas at least, quite radical.[2] Given the phased implementation of some of the components and the lags in effects feeding through, we will not really know what has been achieved for some years yet. It is only after new disciplines and institutional arrangements have been tried and tested, and after liberalization measures have been fully implemented, that we can make unambiguous assessments of its consequences and implications. Notwithstanding this, however, many features of the Agreement are sufficiently clear to permit analysis from the perspective of the developing countries. Indeed from a developing country perspective, two things stand out about the Round. First, from the outset, LDCs were actively involved in shaping the agenda. Second, developing countries were noticeably more active in the negotiations themselves than in previous Rounds—in building coalitions and shaping draft agreements

Table 7.2 Uruguay Round negotiating groups

Trade barriers	
Tariffs	Reduction/elimination; bindings; credit
NTMs	Elimination; equivalence; GATT consistency
Sectors	
NRB products	Tariff escalation; QRs; access
Tropical products	Liberalization; GSP V. MFN (most-favoured nation); Reciprocity
Textiles + clothing	Integration into GATT
Agriculture	Market access; subsidies
GATT System	
Safeguards	Criteria; conditions; GATT compatibility
Subsidies + CVDs	Review of VI + XVI; disciplines
GATT articles	II, XXIV, XXVII, XVII, XXV, XXXV, XII, XVIII
MTNs	Codes; developing countries
Functioning of the GATT system	Surveillance; ministerial activity; IMF/IBRD
Dispute settlement	Effectiveness; enforcement
New Issues	
Trade-related intellectual property rights	Disciplines; disputes; WIPO
Trade-related investment measures	Disciplines
Services	Coverage; approach; investment; migration

(see Whalley 1989 for a detailed evaluation). Where exactly did the interests of developing countries lie in the Round? Table 7.2 details fifteen Uruguay Round negotiating groups, categorized across four broad areas: trade barriers, sectors, GATT system, and new issues.

Market access There were essentially three ingredients to the tariff agreements: a zero for zero component to achieve tariff-free trade in some eleven sectors; a liberalization component to reduce mean tariffs on industrial goods by some 38 per cent; and a harmonization component which resulted in higher tariffs being subject to deeper cuts. As a result, the trade-weighted average tariff in industrial countries should decline from 6.4 per cent to 4 per cent and some 40 per cent of imports enter duty free within a 7 year period. Another crucial outcome was that the proportion of tariffs to become bound in industrial countries increased from 78 per cent to 97 per cent, and that in developing countries from 21 per cent to 65 per cent.

Sectors Agriculture was the single most contentious issue in the Round. The market access agreement required the tariffication of existing non-tariff barriers (NTBs), the binding of the resultant tariffs and their reduction by 36 per cent over 6 years in developed market economies (DMEs) and over 10 years in LDCs, with the least developed being exempted. Domestic support measures are to be reduced by 20 per cent in DMEs and 13.3 per cent in LDCs, with an exemption for interventions which were decoupled from production, or which had a minimal impact on trade. Export subsidies are to be reduced by 36 per cent in value terms and 21 per cent in volume terms (on 1986–90 bases) in DMEs. Lower reductions of 24 per cent and 14 per cent are required of LDCs, with no further concessions for the least developed. Although these reforms will be phased in over a 6–10 year period, they represent a potentially very significant liberalization in an erstwhile completely sheltered sector.

Trade in textiles and clothing has been subject to a legal derogation from non-discrimination requirements for over 30 years. The web of quotas which comprised the MFA imposed significant costs on 'northern' consumers and 'southern' producers (see Silberston 1989, Trela and Whalley 1990). The Uruguay Round agreement commits Contracting Parties to a phased rundown of the MFA over the period 1995–2005 and the complete integration of textiles and clothing into the GATT system. Four phases were envisaged: 1995–8, 1999–2002, 2003–5, post 2005. At the beginning of Phases I, II and III, Contracting Parties are required to have integrated products accounting for not less than 16 per cent, 17 per cent and 18 per cent respectively of their total imports of textiles and clothing. After 2005, all products will be fully integrated. Annual growth rates for quotas of products still subject to MFA provisions within each phase were set at 16 per cent, 25 per cent and 27 per cent above the growth rates in each of the previous phases. There was a limited safeguard provision available for a maximum 3 year duration, in instances where serious injury could be established.

GATT system   This was the least glamorous area of the negotiations, yet the agreements reached were among the most important. On safeguards, several commitments were made to strengthen Article XIX and encourage its use, in preference to extra legal interventions. First, there was an outright prohibition of grey-area measures, a vitally important outcome given the proclivity of DMEs towards instruments like VERs. Second, the criteria for recourse to Article XIX were tightened, with tougher injury tests and a scheduled commitment to phase out. Third, explicit arrangements for the termination of existing measures were agreed. Fourth, discriminatory action was only to be permitted under certain tightly defined circumstances. The last was a fundamental departure from the principle of non-discrimination and one which many LDCs were uneasy about. The potential for abuse was intended to be circumscribed by tougher criteria for application, a shorter termination date of 4 years and careful monitoring by the Safeguards Committee. Subsidies and countervailing duties (CVDs) have been contentious for some time. For the first time the

Uruguay Round agreement actually defined subsidies and identified three categories: prohibited, actionable and non-prohibited. This 'traffic light' approach is expected to prove more effective than the Tokyo Round Code. Moreover, it is to be complemented by strengthened disciplines on the use and termination of CVDs.

A whole series of GATT Articles were reviewed and in some cases amended. Potentially the most important development was the strengthening of antidumping provisions in Article VI. A growing body of evidence (e.g. Finger and Murray 1990, Messerlin 1989, 1990), indicates that the USA and EU are using antidumping procedures as an instrument of protection, rather than a fair trade measure, and in a discriminatory fashion against Japan and the newly industrialized countries (NICs). The agreement strengthened the procedures for calculating the dumping margin, as well as strengthening the injury test. The Functioning of the GATT system (FOGs) group was also 'unglamorous', yet delivered two constitutional changes which will have a profound impact: the Trade Policy Review Mechanism (TPRM) and the World Trade Organization (WTO). The TPRM gave GATT an explicit audit function. All Contracting Parties now have their trade policies reviewed on a regular basis, from every two years in the case of the 'large' CPs (the EU, Japan and USA), through to every 7 years in the case of the smallest.

The WTO was the first serious systemic reform since the GATT's inception. At its heart is a Ministerial Conference which meets at least biannually. It embraces GATT, General Agreement on Trade in Services (GATS), the new bodies like the Safeguards Committee and the Textile Surveillance Body, and all of the UR agreements. The organization is only open to those GATT CPs which signed up to the Uruguay Round. As with GATT it continues to seek to adopt resolutions by consensus, but is able to take a wide range of decisions on the basis of qualified majority. Unlike some other regimes (e.g. the European Union or International Monetary Fund (IMF)) voting rights are not weighted; it is a one vote per CP system. From a developing country standpoint this is important. Although the WTO will have enhanced powers over the GATT these do not include sanctions; enforcement is to be effected by authorization of MFN withdrawal.

New issues   Here, trade related investment measures (TRIMs) have been dealt with by an affirmation of the applicability of existing disciplines, notably Articles III and XI. Those TRIMs which are inconsistent with these are to be prohibited. Pre-existing measures had to be phased out within 2 years (DMEs), 5 years (LDCs) or 7 years (least developed). There is also a commitment to evaluate the role of TRIMs in the wider context of competition policy. By contrast, the agreement on trade related intellectual property (TRIPs) is more complicated. The general provisions and basic principles do include national treatment and MFN. In addition specific provisions relate to: copyrights, trademarks, geographical indications, industrial designs, patents, layout designs of integrated circuits and trade secrets. The obligations on the part of governments to ensure enforcement are set out in each case. The transition period for DMEs was short (1 year), the assumption being that most had pre-existing regimes. The transition is somewhat longer for LDCs (at 5 years) and longest for the least developed (at 11 years).

Services were controversial from the launch of the Round. Given the diversity of philosophies and regulatory regimes, it was also a complicated area. GATS is more limited in scope than seemed possible but took an important first step in bringing disciplines to the area. The agreement specifies a range of basic obligations which include national treatment and MFN commitments. A schedule was established for progressive liberalization and the specific institutional provisions required to accomplish this. Finally, for a number of sectors (financial services, telecommunications, and air transport services) detailed schedules were agreed.

3.1 Market access for the developing countries

The starting point for any evaluation should obviously be the average percentage reductions agreed in the Round, as applying to products of special export interest to LDCs. These range from 18 per cent in the case of leather, footwear, rubber and travel goods, through to 69 per cent in the case of wood, pulp, paper and furniture. Superficially, these are impressive. However, they are average cuts, not reductions which apply only to LDCs. To gain some insight into this, an UNCTAD study has examined more closely the tariff reforms by reference to the detailed tariff offers of the so-called Quad, i.e. USA, EU, Japan and Canada which collectively account for some 90 per cent of total LDC exports. As a result of the Round, the proportion of non-fuel imports from LDCs which enters these countries duty-free increased considerably. In the USA it tripled, it doubled in Japan, and in the EU and Canada increased by a half. In addition, the proportion of imports facing tariffs in excess of 10 per cent fell significantly: by up to 50 per cent (in Japan and Canada). This looks impressive. However, closer inspection of data which lie behind it raises some serious qualifications. First, the reduction in trade-weighted average tariffs was less for LDCs than for all countries, against the backcloth of initial trade-weighted averages which were higher for LDCs. Thus, the extent to which there was protection from LDC imports in industrialized countries relative to imports from elsewhere has increased. As Stevens and Kennan (1994) show in an analysis of EU tariff reductions, this may be especially pronounced for sub-Saharan Africa. Moreover, the distribution of tariff reductions was non-random. The highest trade-weighted averages where LDCs are concerned continue to apply to textiles and clothing, leather and footwear, chemical and agricultural products. These are the commodities of greatest export interest to most developing countries. A further qualification relates to GSP margins. GSP concessions do make a difference to the tariff rates faced by LDCs, though arguably not a dramatic one. However, a considerable erosion of margins resulted from the reductions, in particular for sub-Saharan African countries. Finally, it is worth noting that industrialized country tariff structures continued post-Uruguay to show a marked degree of escalation. It is true that the harmonization component of the agreement had an impact on this and some reduction in escalation was better than none. The fact remains, however, that only a modest change occurred.

To further sharpen the focus of the analysis, the UR reforms can be evaluated by reference to changes in market access in specific sectors. For example, natural resource based products (NRBs) and tropical products (TPs) remain of great interest to developing countries. Even diversified economies like Malaysia have an interest in these product areas. Clearly, however, NRBs and TPs are of greatest interest to many small and low-income LDCs, where dependence on these commodities amounts to 70 per cent or more of total merchandise exports. Import tariffs on many of these products were zero prior to the Uruguay Round. Those which were positive have in general been reduced. MFN tariff averages on tropical agricultural products fell by around 40 per cent as a consequence of the Round, those on tropical non-agricultural products declined by 50 per cent and those on NRBs by 20 per cent to 40 per cent. Post-Uruguay Round averages for non-agricultural products are now at very low levels; those for agricultural products are also very low in the USA and Canada, but exceed 10 per cent in Japan and the EU. There are therefore real improvements in market access for developing countries which offer scope for improved export performance.

For most developing countries, exports of temperate zone agricultural products (TZAs) were of minimal importance pre-UR and remain so. Such crops may be grown, but typically for domestic consumption. This is of course a product range where the major markets have been very heavily protected. This certainly applies to the large DMEs (USA, EU and Japan) and to a greater extent in many of the smaller DMEs. The capacity to produce for export does exist in quite a number of developing countries but, given the power and influence of agricultural lobbies in the major DMEs, it is no more than potential. For example, it is interesting to note that even those countries which have Association Agreements with the EU, e.g. Cyprus and Malta, and which permit free trade in manufactures, have been unable to extend product coverage to products under the common agricultural policy (CAP). There were superficially significant changes flowing from the agriculture agreement, but in practice improvements in access will be limited (Stevens and Kennan 1994, Rayner and Ingersent 1999). Historically this sector has been very effectively sheltered and we are unlikely to witness a rapid transition to free trade.

Textiles and clothing are invariably the first rung on the ladder of comparative advantage. For the most part the technology in question is transferable internationally and production does not require significant prior investment in human capital. Since it can be a fairly labour intensive activity, relatively labour abundant/low wage economies have a clear advantage. Following more than 30 years of trade restraints, there is now a commitment, as a result of the UR, to phase out the MFA. If all goes according to plan, the only restraints applying to textiles and clothing after 2004 will be MFN tariffs. The eventual elimination of quantitative restraints will affect developing countries differentially. Those newly industrialized countries (NICs) and new exporting countries (NECs), like Hong Kong, Singapore and Malaysia, which have enjoyed relatively large quotas under the MFA will in due course be subject to free and unfettered competition from lower wage economies like India, Indonesia and China. Not only will this mean that the rents presently enjoyed by those producers are dissipated, it will also mean that they need to upgrade into higher value-added products and invest in increasingly capital-intensive techniques to remain competitive. By contrast, eventual abolition will make market entry, and a build up of market share, easier for new producers. Under the MFA new entrants have found that their market share has quickly been capped. The absence of historically determined quotas is very good news for many of the least developed: it will allow them to exploit an obvious area of comparative advantage more readily. This is a point which has also been emphasized by Page and Davenport (1994) and Sorsa (1995).

Of course, there is a transitional period during which existing quotas are being gradually relaxed. There are two potential difficulties. First, importing countries have discretion over which products are included in the relaxation at each stage of the process. It appears that this discretion is being used strategically. For example, Stevens and Kennan (1994) claim that 'the EU's strategy ... confirms that the most sensitive products will be tackled later rather than sooner'. It seems that the EU proposals for Phase I of the phase-out integrate into GATT only 0.12 per cent of trade which was previously restricted and developing countries will benefit to only a very limited degree. The second potential difficulty is that the transitional arrangements allow for temporary intervention when domestic injury is threatened by a sudden increase in imports. Realistically, new suppliers are more likely to be subject to this particular provision than established producers. There is, therefore, a real danger that this will be used to restrain imports from new entrants. In summary, eventual abolition of the MFA will result in a loss of rents to the NICs and we can expect them to be pushed into further upgrading. Where the least developed are concerned, there is the potential for improved penetration. However, benefits of UR are unlikely to be realized quickly and a watchful eye will have to be kept on the use of transitional measures. Like many features of the settlement, the Uruguay Round agreement is end-loaded, with developing countries having to wait some time to reap the benefits.

Only a limited number of developing countries have well developed and diversified bases for manufactured exports. Where countries have progressed beyond low-tech manufactures (crudely low value-added garments and footwear), and have developed some capacity in intermediate capital goods, machinery and transport equipment, chemicals, toys and sports equipment, consumer electronics, the tariff reductions agreed in the Uruguay Round are clearly likely to be of benefit. At least as significant, certainly for the NICs, are the commitments on VERs and antidumping. There is an overwhelming body of evidence which shows that these have been used in a discriminatory way against NICs. VERs have now been explicitly proscribed, although the ability of vote maximizing governments, under pressure from protectionist lobbies, to devise close substitutes should not be underestimated. Provisions relating to antidumping have been tightened and should constrain the proliferation of contingent protection. For many other LDCs the tariff reductions on manufactures are at present superfluous. These countries do not have the capacity to produce the products concerned and therefore the tariff cuts are currently irrelevant. In time, of course, that will alter. As and when export capacity is developed, the key UR changes are those relating to VERs and antidumping since they tend to have most effect on new entrants.

Most developing countries regarded the inclusion of services on the agenda with suspicion, as it was seen as the preserve of industrialized countries. This, however, is an over-simplification. Quite a number of developing countries earn in excess of 20 per cent of foreign exchange from exports of services. Admittedly in quite a number of countries this is predominantly from tourism. However, some are diversifying into financial services, communications and transportation. Under the GATS, about 100 countries have submitted schedules of specific commitments. Generally they provide for a standstill on existing arrangements but also include offers to liberalize. Further negotiations have also continued after the agreement on offers in financial services, telecommunications, maritime services and movement of people. Given its limited and on-going nature, it is difficult to assess the impact of the services agreements with any real precision. Unless and until agreements relating to movement of people are concluded, the GATS will have a limited impact on the LDCs.

3.2 Erosion of preferential access

There are a number of bilateral or multilateral preferential access schemes of the industrial countries from which developing countries may benefit. Since all of these schemes frame their preferences by reference to MFN tariffs, any reduction in the latter must erode the value of preferences; the degree of erosion of margins depends upon the impact of final cuts in MFN rates and the volume of imports which benefit from GSP under the different schemes. Other things being equal, this would leave developing countries worse off. Calculations by GATT suggest that the reductions in preference margins would be significant (82 per cent in Canada, 61 per cent in Japan, 50 per cent in the USA and 32 per cent in the EU, with the highest losses occurring for agricultural products) leaving many LDCs worse off. The analysis by Stevens and Kennan (1994) of the impact of the EU changes suggested that this would certainly be the case in sub-Saharan Africa. Sorsa (1995), however, feels that this possibility is exaggerated, because the degree to which developing countries benefit from GSP is limited by product specification restrictions, rules of origin, quantitative limits and so on. In practice, therefore, little by way of preferential imports would actually be taken, especially in agricultural products.

3.3 Graduation and the right to protect

The Final Act affirmed quite explicitly the principle of special and differential treatment at various points throughout the Agreement. In contrast to GATT 1947, however, two important points should be noted. First S and D was affirmed explicitly in various contexts throughout, as well as being affirmed as a specific principle. In that sense, the Round did not diminish the 'right to protect' of developing countries, indeed it may actually have extended it. However, this extension refers to the routes through which S and D can be accessed.

The second feature of the Agreement which should be highlighted was an explicit graduation provision. This is a profound change: for the first time a distinction is being made between the least developed and other developing countries. For the subsidies agreement, the least developed were identified as the United Nations group of forty-seven least developed countries, with the addition of: Bolivia, Cameroon, Congo, Côte d'Ivoire, Dominican Republic, Egypt, Ghana, Guatemala, Guyana, India, Indonesia, Kenya, Morocco, Nicaragua, Nigeria, Pakistan, Philippines, Senegal, Sri Lanka and Zimbabwe. The criterion used to identify this group is income per capita, with the cut-off being a GDP per capita of US$1,000 (nominal). Moreover, this was not a cosmetic distinction; it affected the privileges from which the countries concerned could benefit. The distinction is especially important in agricultural support, technical barriers, subsidies and safeguards. In some areas, the least developed will enjoy privileges which 'other' developing countries will not; in other cases they are being given a longer period over which to phase out specific measures.

3.4 Future evolution of S and D

Both dimensions of S and D were affected by the Uruguay Round. The right to access was eroded by the liberalization; the right to protect has been constrained. However, one should not think of these as unambiguously threatening from the standpoint of the developing countries.

Although one can find cases where preferential access under GSP or Lomé had been successful, in general these schemes have been so constrained by qualification criteria, quotas, rules of origin and so on, as to have been of limited usefulness. A strong case can be made to the effect that many LDCs would be better off facing lower MFN tariffs and fewer NTBs, than they were with (apparent) preferential access. Regarding the right to protect, if this did indeed confer benefits then the introduction of a graduation criterion enhances the relative position of the least developed. As a consequence they should find it easier to nurture infant industries and gain world market share than when competing on level terms with 'other' developing countries, especially NICs.

Having established a graduation principle it is safe to assume that it will be a permanent feature of the GATT infrastructure. It should be viewed actually as a helpful development from the standpoint of targeting concessions and assistance, and a multilaterally agreed and transparent criterion is preferable to the likely alternative, namely opaque criteria being unilaterally applied by the major trading nations/blocs.

3.5 The new issues and the developing countries

Developing countries make more extensive use of TRIMs than industrialized countries (see Greenaway 1992). They are often seen as an important instrument of investment policy. As we have seen, the TRIMs agreement outlawed the more trade distorting and most widely deployed measures (local content requirements, trade balancing requirements, minimum export requirements). It is plausible that the use of TRIMs by developing countries has emerged out of a desire to redistribute rents from multinational enterprises (MNEs) and to counter the use of restrictive business practices by MNEs. Admittedly, the need to do so may often have been created by other aspects of the policy regime: trade barriers that created rents and reduced competition on the domestic market. Although many developing countries now pursue more liberal trade policies, non-negligible trade barriers remain in many of the less and least developed countries. Constraining the use of TRIMs will certainly constrain policy options and alter relative bargaining positions with foreign investors, especially multinational enterprises. Thus, developing countries could lose as a result of this part of the Agreement (see Morrissey and Rai 1995) if GATT was to remain out of the competition policy field and/or if the developing countries do not explore new approaches to policy in this area.

The TRIPs Agreement unambiguously required major policy changes by all countries, within 5 years in the case of developing and 11 years for the least developed. Members are required to apply the principles of MFN and national treatment to the protection of intellectual property rights (IPRs), which covers copyright and related rights, trademarks, geographical indications, industrial designs, patents, layout designs of integrated circuits and the protection of undisclosed information. Most of the areas are covered by the provisions already administered by the World Intellectual Property Organization (WIPO) and the Agreement contains cross-references to these; but the TRIPs Agreement extended the country and instrument coverage of the provisions. Thus most developing countries were required to introduce and revise existing national laws in the area of IPRs, so as to enforce the provisions of the TRIPs Agreement.

For many small and least developed countries the TRIPs agreement requires legislative revisions or extension which will have little immediate impact on trade and development strategies, but could have a more significant impact longer term. For example, an UNCTAD study estimated recurrent costs of $750,000 per annum in Bangladesh to comply with the TRIPs agreement, with no immediate offsetting benefits. However, one obvious benefit will be the avoidance of the kind of unilateral action which the USA launched against China. For those countries with diversified industrial bases (e.g. India) or trade strategies directed towards the exporting of more technologically intensive goods (e.g. Malaysia), the protection of IPRs could be expected to have a more immediate impact. This group of countries have already invested in technologies which will now embody a new distribution and pricing of intellectual property. Import substitution of generic pharmaceutical products in countries such as India will become more costly. Similarly, the export competitiveness of 'imitated' products (designs or trademarks) in some of those markets where the NICs have moved up the ladder of comparative advantage (e.g. textiles, electrical and electronic goods, software) will be eroded by the additional cost of acquiring technology. There is clearly a complex balance of issues involved here. Reverse engineering has been a key element in technology transfer and therefore the weak protection (or its absence) of IPR obligations by developing countries has contributed positively to industrialization efforts. The correct 'pricing' of technology may, however, encourage in future the adoption of appropriate technologies and induce greater allocative efficiency and, in the longer term, improved export performance.

The GATS sets out principles to govern trade in services, extending the general principle of MFN. However, actual commitments were confined to the specific sectors or types of 'trade' that were included in each of their Schedules of Commitment. The types of 'trade' or modes of supply most often covered in the offers of the developed countries are commercial presence, movement of consumers and movements of persons in the form of intra-corporate transferees (i.e. managers and specialists) linked to commercial presence. Most developing countries are not in a position to benefit from this mode of exporting, when faced with high costs of establishment in developed countries and disadvantages in terms of endowments and technologies. The sectors of particular interest to developing countries, e.g. tourism, construction, business services and maritime services, were included among developed country offers but few countries offered access to categories of persons beyond intra-corporate transferees. Movement of persons other than executives and specialists is required (and has been repeatedly requested) by the developing countries if they are to provide services in these sectors. The absence of improved access for non-executive labour does not mean, however, that there is little scope for significant future gains for developing countries arising from the present GATS agreement. Of course there would have been much greater potential for gains from a more ambitious set of offers, but the entry of services into the GATT framework provides greater opportunities for reaping these benefits in future. Additionally, growth in international trade and production arising out of the Agreements on trade in goods will bring about an increase in the demand for labour services from lower wage developing countries. Thus there are significant opportunities for gains for developing countries, even from the relatively limited multilateral liberalization implied by the UR Agreement on services. This is in terms both of the cost of imported services and of the scope for growth of exporting in services in line with comparative advantage.

3.6 Overall assessment

Overall what were the implications of the Uruguay Round Agreement and the creation of the WTO for the interests of developing countries? The first point to make is that the WTO has a more secure legal status than GATT 1947 and, where commercial relations are concerned, a somewhat broader scope. The Final Act viewed the WTO as creating an environment within which trade, employment and income growth is facilitated. To this end, it explicitly endorsed the liberal principles of GATT in 'contributing to these objectives by entering into reciprocal and mutually advantageous arrangements directed to the substantial reduction of tariffs and other barriers to trade and to the elimination of discriminatory treatment in international trade relations'. This 'mission statement' was clearly helpful to developing countries aiming to pursue liberal policies as well as avoiding discriminatory treatment.

The Final Act also ratified the commitment to the TPRM which is now a fully functioning, and fully integrated, feature of the WTO. This is an important development for all contracting parties but especially developing countries. While there had always been an obligation on contracting parties to notify trade measures and changes therein, to the Secretariat, the GATT never at any point had the authority, nor the mechanisms, to review systematically the trade policies of its signatories. What the TPRM does is to provide the WTO Secretariat with a basis for systematic audit of trade and industrial policies, which has brought greater transparency and credibility to trade policy. Although there are no explicit enforcement criteria written into the TPRM agreement, there can be little doubt that its existence has raised the possibility of stronger third-party enforcement. This is especially desirable for smaller CPs in general and developing countries in particular. An independent audit of this form makes it easier to resist the predations of domestic interest groups. Second, independent audit of the large CPs makes discriminatory interventions on their part all the more obvious, thereby offering the offended party the prospect of due recourse. Moreover, because the audits are conducted on a regular basis, failure to remove/reduce illegal or extra legal interventions can be exposed more readily. (For a review of the operation of TRPM, see Laird 1999.)

The interests of developing countries are diverse, given their range and structure. The eventual deals which were struck were inevitably fashioned more by the major protagonists than by developing countries individually or collectively. Nevertheless there is much to be welcomed from a developing country perspective. Chief among these are potential improvements in market access, commitments to reduce dependence on source specific quotas in DMEs, commitments to phase out the MFA and reduce protection in temperate zone agricultural products and the general tightening up of disciplines, including those relating to dispute settlement. Equally there are some threats or challenges, particularly those which could arise from a sanctioning of discriminatory intervention under Article XIX, the erosion of preferences for some of the LDCs and the greater competitive pressures resulting from the TRIPs and services agreements. Ultimately, however, the agreements and the WTO can be viewed as strengthening the multilateral disciplines and obligations governing world trade to the benefit of small, developing countries.

4 Regionalism and multilateralism: the policy options

Despite the positive assessment of the overall progress made by the Uruguay Round towards reinforcing multilateralism, it is easy to criticize the Rounds process and focus on GATT's shortcomings. Rounds have become slow and cumbersome, sectors like agriculture and textiles and clothing have been sheltered from liberalization, NTBs have proliferated as tariffs declined, contingent protection measures have become more widespread than desirable. It is right and proper that deficiencies and shortcomings are highlighted. It is no less important to draw attention to the system's accomplishments. These number at least five.

First, average nominal tariffs have declined dramatically in industrialized countries from an average of over 40 per cent in the early post-World War II years to around 4 per cent now. This is entirely an outcome of multilateral trade negotiations (MTNs). Second, average tariffs have fallen sharply in the NICs and developing countries more generally. These declines are not as dramatic as in the industrialized countries, nor are they solely attributable to the MTNs: there has been a wave of unilateral liberalization since 1980 in developing countries. Third, the sectoral and instrument coverage of GATT has extended rather dramatically in recent Rounds. Fourth, the institutional infrastructure underpinning the world trading system has been strengthened through improved audit, dispute settlement and a range of strengthened disciplines. Finally, the number of Members of the WTO has continued to grow. Newly independent states in Central and Eastern Europe and the former Soviet Union have rather quickly signed up to GATT/WTO in the same way as newly independent developing countries did in the 1960s and 1970s.

Against this background of ongoing multilateralism there has also been an ongoing process of minilateralism, in the form of regional trading arrangements (RTAs). These have been a feature of the global economy for centuries and should not be thought of only as a post-World War II phenomenon; however, there has been a remarkable proliferation in RTAs during the second half of the twentieth century. As we shall see, more than 100 agreements have been ratified. This raises the obvious question of how this could have occurred since, over the same period, the GATT has been in existence, which has as one of its key pillars a commitment to non-discrimination. In a strictly legal sense, there is no inconsistency between GATT and RTAs; Article XXIV in effect offers a waiver to Article I and sanctions RTAs, subject to certain conditions. It was included in the Agreement, largely for political reasons; given pre-existing RTAs, some major GATT signatories would not have signed up without it. It was also the case, however, that pre-Vinerian customs union theory did not hold forth strong arguments against RTAs: regional liberalization was more confidently viewed at that time as a stepping stone to multilateral liberalization.

The key conditions of Article XXIV are that members eliminate restraints on 'substantially-all-trade' between them, and have a trade policy towards non-members which ensures that restraints are not 'on the whole' more restrictive than those which prevailed prior to the RTA. Article XXIV has turned out to be an extremely important exception to the non-discrimination clause and has been complemented by the Enabling Clause of Part IV added by the Tokyo Round Agreement, which sanctions preferential trading arrangements between developing countries. Finally, it should be noted that Article V of GATS offers trade in services an equivalent waiver to Article XXIV of GATT.

Over 100 RTA agreements were notified to GATT under Article XXIV or the Enabling Clause over the period 1947 to 1994. They vary in the degree of actual integration achieved but it is nonetheless a remarkable number. Essentially there were two waves, the first in the 1970s, the second in the 1990s. The 1990s wave is often referred to as 'the new regionalism'. As with its analogue, 'the new protectionism', new can be taken as a chronological reference. However, it also refers to a number of distinctive characteristics of the phenomenon. First, while the old regionalism of the 1950s/1960s typically involved RTAs that were 'North–North' or 'South–South', the new regionalism has been typified by many 'North–South' arrangements like NAFTA and APEC. This characteristic offers obvious potential in terms of gains from trade. However, it also creates the potential for adjustment problems and trade tensions. Second, whereas with the old regionalism RTAs typically involved contiguous countries or near neighbours, many recent arrangements have been intercontinental. Third, many recent arrangements are not inclusive: multiple membership is not problematic. Finally, whereas all arrangements under the 'old regionalism' promoted shallow integration, i.e. liberalization of border measures, many recent agreements have aspired to deep integration with commitments to harmonization of regulatory measures, freeing up of factor movements and so on. Since around one third of all of the post-war RTAs have been signed since 1990, the first issue to address is: what has triggered this dramatic growth in RTAs?

4.1 Causal factors behind the new regionalism

There are a range of explanations for the resurgence of popularity of RTAs. A common view sees their proliferation as a reaction to frustrations with the GATT in general and the Uruguay Round in particular. This sees RTAs as a reaction to concerns that the Rounds process would ultimately fail with the Uruguay Round and some kind of insurance was required in the form of membership of an RTA. It is true that the timing of some recent RTAs is consistent with the prolongation of the Round. It is equally true, however, that some are not! A more sophisticated version of this explanation is associated with, among others, Krugman (1993) along the lines that RTAs are easier to negotiate and implement than multilateral agreements, partly as a consequence of the number of negotiating parties involved. Multilateral agreements mean more parties, lower costs associated with non-cooperation and therefore more protracted negotiations. It is also a consequence of the fact that MTNs are no longer simply about tariffs but a much wider range of border and non-border measures. The combination of more parties and a more complex array of issues is a recipe for protracted negotiation. By contrast, he argues that RTAs typically involve fewer negotiating parties endeavouring to reach agreement on a narrower range of issues.

Bhagwati (1993) advances a related argument in putting the new regionalism down to US interests in RTAs. He argues that US hegemony was vital not only to the sustenance of GATT, but also to multilateralism more generally. As its dominance in the process waned and negotiations became more plurilateral, US policy makers were drawn to a more overt 'results oriented' approach to international trade policy. This manifested itself in two ways. First, 'aggressive unilateralism', i.e. legislation which activated Super 301 and Special 301 instruments permitting the United States Trade Representative (USTR) to initiate unilateral action against alleged unfair trading and alleged breaches of US Intellectual Property Rights respectively. Second, a greater regional focus to trade negotiations where the putative benefits were superficially more transparent and more immediate. This then resulted in the Canada–US Trade Agreement (CUSTA) and NAFTA.

Baldwin (1997) contends that these explanations are not supported by the facts. He points out that many RTAs go beyond simple tariff deals and confront liberalization and harmonization of non-tariff measures which, by definition, are much more difficult to negotiate. He also argues that many of the key agreements precede rather than lead any apparent US conversion to the cause—EC92 and negotiations on CUSTA being good examples. As an alternative explanation, Baldwin puts forward his 'domino theory', which builds on Viner's (1950) classic analysis and exploits the fact that any RTA results in some trade and investment diversion, which in turn generates pressures in excluded nations to be included. The greater the number of nations included, the greater the pressures on non-participants. Thus, a single initial agreement, if it is important enough, triggers a domino effect that stimulates expansion of that agreement and/or proliferation of others. In the context of the 'new regionalism', EC92 and NAFTA are the key agreements in stimulating further rounds of regionalism in these areas.

A similar, though not identical explanation, is often cast in terms of defensive regionalism. This can be found, for example, in Whalley's (1991) analysis of western hemispheric regionalism and Greenaway's (1999) analysis of regionalism in Asia. Here it is not trade and investment diversion from growing blocs which is the threat, but the fear of market exclusion and the need to provide countervailing bargaining power. The 'Fortress Europe' fears surrounding the Single Market discussions are a nice example, as is APEC in the Asia Pacific region.

4.2 Minilateralism and multilateralism

Is minilateralism in conflict with multilateralism? Put differently, are RTAs a stepping stone or a stumbling bloc to free trade? This is a crucial question from an efficiency and political economy standpoint. If one believes, as theory suggests, that global free trade maximizes global welfare and RTAs are an impediment to global free trade, then there are clear welfare costs associated with the phenomenon. If this is indeed the case, then from a political economy standpoint one would wish to raise the costs of negotiating RTAs relative to those of negotiating multilateral agreements. One way of coming at the issue is to think of regional integration as a dynamic process. Following Bhagwati, Greenaway and Panagariya (1998), this can be approached through two analytical questions. If the time paths of multilateral trade negotiations (MTNs) and RTAs are completely independent, will a given RTA have expanding membership such that it will eventually equate to worldwide membership? If the MTN and RTA time paths, on the other hand, are embraced simultaneously, they will interact. This being so, will the policy undertakings in the RTA have a benign or malign impact on the progress along the MTN time path?

Most analyses ignore the time path issue and treat expansion of membership as exogenous. However, some recent work has begun to address the question of incentives to add members. We have already mentioned Baldwin (1997), who demonstrates that the incentive facing non-members will be positive. The RTA will create a 'domino' effect, with outsiders wanting to become insiders. The argument is basically driven by the fact that the RTA implies a loss of cost-competitiveness by imperfectly competitive non-member firms, whose profits in the RTA markets decline because they face tariffs that inside firms do not have to pay. These firms then lobby for entry, tilting the political equilibrium towards entry demands in their countries. The countries closest to the margin will then enter the bloc, assuming that the members have open entry, enlarging the market and thereby increasing the cost of non-membership and pulling in countries at the next margin.

Some recent work also addresses the second question, i.e. whether the RTA possibility and/or time-path helps or harms the MTN time-path; examples are Krishna (1997) and Levy (1997), both of whom reach the 'malign-impact' conclusion. Krishna models the political process as government acting in response to lobbying by firms as a 'clearing house', and shows that the RTA reduces the incentive of member countries to liberalize tariffs reciprocally with the non-member world. With sufficient trade diversion, this incentive could be so reduced as to make impossible an initially feasible multilateral trade liberalization. Levy, who models the political process instead in a median-voter model, works with scale economies and product variety to demonstrate that bilateral RTAs can undermine political support for multilateral free trade. At the same time, a benign impact is impossible in this model: if a multilateral free trade proposal is not feasible under autarky, the same multilateral proposal cannot be rendered feasible under any bilateral RTA.

If there are potential dangers and potential costs associated with RTAs, how can we improve the 'fit' with multilateralism? Since RTAs are unlikely to cease being a feature of the international trading environment, the key clearly lies in the approval and supervision arrangements, which brings us back to Article XXIV of the GATT, the WTO and the Millennium Round (to be discussed in the next section). One of the leading commentators on the GATT described Article XXIV and the 1979 Enabling Clause as 'woefully inadequate for the tasks required of a multilateral trading system to provide some sort of adequate supervision and discipline on certain of the more dangerous tendencies of trading blocs' (Jackson 1993). It is clear from experience that the review process for endorsement of new agreements requires strengthening beyond that agreed in the Uruguay Round, a necessity acknowledged by WTO (1995).

It is equally clear, however, that third parties need some kind of WTO recourse to challenge 'nullification and impairment' commitments which RTA members sign up to when they commit to an agreement. At present there are no embedded arrangements for taking action against third party damage; WTO dispute settlement procedures are the obvious mechanism. Finally, Jackson (1993) makes the interesting suggestion that RTAs could be subject to periodic reviews along the lines of the TPRM. As we argued earlier, this has turned out to be a useful mechanism for periodically auditing the trade policies of Contracting Parties and could in principle be extended to the RTA arena.

5 Implementing the Uruguay Round and preparing for the Millennium Round

As we saw in the third section, the Uruguay Round was a long and slow process, given the breadth of the agenda and the number of countries involved. As we also saw, it was the first Round where developing countries really 'engaged', in the sense of having a serious negotiating position on and interest in quite a large number of the agenda issues. Having had this involvement, what is next from a developing country standpoint? In this section we set out the priorities on two fronts: first, the implementation of the Uruguay Round agreements; second, the priorities for the next (Millennium) Round of multilateral trade negotiations.

5.1 Implementing the Uruguay Round

We covered the Uruguay Round settlement and its implementation earlier in the chapter. Rather than repeat the details we will simply remind ourselves here of areas where implementation will not be straightforward and/or protracted, since these will no doubt influence the agenda for the next Round.

Both agriculture, and textiles and clothing have lengthy implementation schedules; real liberalization in both will be strongly resisted by domestic interest groups in the industralized countries. Liberalization in both is important for developing countries in general and the least developed in particular. In neither case can the liberalization commitments made be said to be 'deep', nor do the implementation timetables offer prospects for substantial improvements in market access.

With regard to systemic issues, two issues stand out where developing countries are concerned: the roll back of grey-area measures, and tightened disciplines for antidumping; proliferation and persistence of so-called grey-area measures has been very well documented and their relative inefficiency extensively analysed. The evidence clearly points to discriminatory use against developing countries. While the Uruguay commitments to proscribe some NTBs are a welcome first step, they have limited potential for reducing the stock, as opposed to the flow of NTBs. Future negoti-ations will have to return to this issue. The same can be said of antidump-ing. Inclusion on the Uruguay Round agenda did recognize there was a problem. However, little has been done to resolve the problem. This too will need to feature again in the next round.

5.2 Preparing for the Millennium Round

At the time of writing, exploratory discussion are underway with a view to initiating a Millennium Round of multilateral trade negotiations at the WTO Ministerial Conference in Seattle in November 1999. In addition to the 'unfinished business' we have just discussed, there are a number of major issues of particular interest to developing countries and which could ultimately figure on the agenda. These are: competition policy, environ-mental regulation and labour standards.[3]

Some components of competition policy figured in the Uruguay Round: subsidies, TRIMs and, indeed, antidumping. As border measures become relatively less significant, so differences in regulatory regimes become more transparent. In turn, this is engendering pressures for a more holistic approach which goes beyond the rather partial and piecemeal targeting of particular policy instruments. This is a complex and complicated area raising quite profound extraterritoriality issues. The same can be said of environmental regulation, although the drive for inclusion here is a little different. On the one hand, some contracting parties have concerns about the capture of environmental policies as quasi-trade policies; on the other hand there is quite a widespread push to ensure that multilateral trade lib-eralization does not accelerate the process of global environmental degra-dation. Finally, there is the issue of labour standards, which is equally contentious and complex. The so-called 'social dumping' debate had been used by some developed market economies as a foundation for arguing that differentials in labour costs between countries should be a WTO issue. This is a difficult argument to sustain on economic grounds (Milner 1997). Nevertheless, it may very well find itself on the agenda.

6 Conclusion

The focus of this chapter has been multilateralism and regionalism. We began by reviewing the evolution of the GATT system and the interests of developing countries in that system, paying particular attention to special and differential treatment. We then turned our attention to the Uruguay Round. We dwelt on this at some length, in part, because it was the first Round in which developing countries were fully engaged in the negotiation process. We then reviewed the factors behind the recent upsurge in region-alism, our emphasis being on the key issue of whether this is consistent with continued multilateralism. Finally, we commented briefly on potential 'big issue' negotiating areas of particular interest to developing countries, which are likely to feature prominently in the next Round of MTNs.

The conclusions which we would reach from this analysis are as follows. First, the GATT infrastructure has attempted to acknowledge the special needs of developing countries via a range of 'S and D' provisions. These have, however, been of limited value. Second, until the most recent Round, GATT negotiations have largely been focused on tariff liberalization; this has paid insufficient attention to non-tariff protection in general, and (tariff) and non-tariff protection in sensitive sectors like textiles and clothing and agriculture, in which developing countries have a particular interest. Third, the Uruguay Round made important steps forward in broadening the negotiating agenda and in involving developing countries more fully in the process. Fourth, the upsurge in regionalism in the late 1980s/1990s does constitute a potential threat to multilateralism, since multilateralism is likely to serve the longer-term needs of developing countries more effectively than minilateralism, keeping the Rounds' momentum going is vitally important. Finally, the Millennium Round, when it is launched, should progress a range of unfinished business from the Uruguay Round and a number of new issues of potentially greater significance than those of the Uruguay Round.

Notes

* The authors gratefully acknowledge financial support from The Leverhulme Trust under Programme Grant F114/BF.
1. The rationale for, and mechanisms of, S and D have been thoroughly analysed by Whalley (1990).
2. For a review of the negotiations and outcomes see Schott (1966).
3. For a thorough overview of the issues likely to be of interest to developing countries, see Krueger (1999). For a detailed analysis of the S and D agenda, see Whalley (1999).

References

Balasubramanyam, V.N. (1989) 'ASEAN and regional trade cooperation in South East Asia', in D. Greenaway, T. Hyclak and R. Thornton (eds) *Economic Aspects of Regional Trading Arrangements*, London: Wheatsheaf.

Baldwin, R.E. (1997) 'The causes of regionalism', *The World Economy*, Vol. 20: 865–88.

Bhagwati, J. (1993) 'Regionalism and multilateralism: an overview', in J. de Melo and A. Panagariya (eds). *New Dimensions in Regional Integration*, Cambridge: Cambridge University Press.

Bhagwati, J., Greenaway, D. and Panagariya, A. (1998) 'Trading preferentially: theory and policy', *Economic Journal*, Vol. 107: 1128–48.

Ethier, W. (1999) 'Regionalism in a multilateral world', in J. Piggott and A. Woodland (eds) *Trade Policy and the Pacific Rim*, Macmillan, for the International Economic Association.

Finger, J.M. (1991) 'Development economics and the general agreement on tariffs and trade', in J. de Melo and A. Sapir (eds) *Trade Theory and Economic Reform*, Oxford: Basil Blackwell.

Finger, J.M. and Murray, T. (1990) 'Policing unfair imports: the United States experience', *Journal of World Trade*, Vol. 24: 39–53.

Foroutan, F. (1998) 'Does membership in a regional preferential trading arrangement make a country more or less protectionist?', *The World Economy*, Vol. 21: 305–36.

GATT (1994) 'An analysis of the Uruguay Round Agreement', mimeo, Trade Negotiations Committee.

Greenaway, D. (1992) 'Trade related investment measures and development strategy', *Kyklos,* Vol. 45: 139–60.

—— (1993) 'The Uruguay Round: agenda, expectations and outcomes', in K.A. Ingersent, A.J. Rayner and R.C. Hine (eds) *Agriculture in the Uruguay Round*, London: Macmillan.

—— (1999) 'Current issues in trade policy and the Pacific rim', in J. Piggott and A. Woodland (eds) *International Trade Policy and the Pacific Rim*, London: Macmillan.

Greenaway, D. and Nam, C.H. (1988) 'Industrialisation and macroeconomic performance in developing countries under alternative liberalisation scenarios', *Kyklos*, 41: 419–35.

Ingeraent, K.A. and Raynes, A.J. (1999) *Agricultural policy in Western Europe and the United States*, Edward Elgar.

Jackson, J (1993) 'Regional Trade Blocs and the GATT', *The World Economy*, Vol. 16: 121–32.

Krishna, P. (1997) 'Regionalism and multilateralism: a political economy approach', mimeo, Economics Department, Columbia University, *Quarterly Journal of Economics*.

Krueger, A.O. (1997) 'Trade policy and economic development: how we learn', *American Economic Review*, Vol. 87: 1–22.

—— (1999) 'Developing countries and the next round of multilateral trade negotiations', *The World Economy*, Vol. 22: 909–32.

Krugman, P.R. (1993) 'Growing world trade: causes and consequences', Brookings Papers, No. 1: 327–77.

Laird, S. (1999) 'The WTO's trade policy review mechanism: from through the looking glass', *The World Economy*, Vol. 22: 741–64.

Langhammer, R. and Sapir, A. (1987) 'Economic impact of generalised tariff preferences', Thames Essay 49, London: TPRC.

Levy, P. (1997) 'A political economic analysis of free trade agreements', *American Economic Review*, Vol. 87, No. 4: 506–19.

Messerlin, P.A. (1989) 'The EC Anti-Dumping Regulations: a first economic appraisal', *Weltwirtschaftliches Archiv*, Vol. 125: 563–87.

—— (1990) 'Anti-dumping regulations or pro-cartel law?', *The World Economy*, Vol. 13: 465–92.

Milner, C.R. (1997) 'New standards issues and the WTO', *Australian Economic Review*, Vol. 30: 90–7.

Morrissey, W.O. and Rai, Y. (1995) 'The GATT Agreement and trade related investment measures: implications for developing countries and their relationship with transnational corporations', *Journal of Development Studies*, Vol. 31, No. 5: 702–24.

Page, S. and Davenport, M. (1994) 'World trade reform: do developing countries gain or lose?', ODI Special Report, London: ODI.

Rayner, A.J., Ingersent, K.A. and Hine, R.C. (1993) 'Agriculture in the Uruguay Round: an assessment', *Economic Journal*, Vol. 103: 1513–27.

Schott, J.J. (1996) *The Uruguay Round: An Assessment*, Washington: Institute for International Economics.

Sorsa, P. (1995) 'The burden of Uruguay Round commitments in sub-Saharan Africa: myth or reality?', *The World Economy*, Vol. 19: 287–306.

Silberston, Z.A. (1989) *The Future of the Multifibre Arrangement: Implications for the UK Economy*, London: HMSO.

Stevens, C. and Kennan, I. (1994) 'The Uruguay Round, EU and sub-Saharan Africa', IDS Discussion Paper.

Trela, I. and Whalley, J. (1990) 'Global effects of developed country trade restrictions in textiles and apparel', *Economic Journal*, Vol. 100: 1190–205.

Viner, J. (1950) *The Customs Union Issue*, New York: Carnegie Endowment for International Peace.

Whalley, J. (1989) *The Uruguay Round and Beyond*, London: Macmillan.

—— (1990) 'Non-discriminatory discrimination: special and differential treatment under the GATT for developing countries', *Economic Journal*, Vol. 100: 1318–28.

—— (1991) 'Recent trade liberalisation in developing countries: what is behind it and where is it headed', D. Greenaway (ed.) *Global Protection Issues*, London: Macmillan, 225–52.

—— (1999) 'Special and differential treatment in the Millennium Round', *The World Economy*, Vol. 22: 1065–94.

WTO (World Trade Organization) (1995) *Regionalism and the World Trading System*, WTO.

8 Trading with the enemy

A case for liberalizing Pakistan–India trade

Ijaz Nabi and Anjum Nasim*

1 Introduction

It is natural for neighbours to trade for a number of reasons. The foremost
of these is that transportation costs are low. Furthermore, language similarities lower communication barriers and reduce transaction costs. Cultural affinity among neighbours also influences tastes, which causes
profitable complementarities to emerge. Trade in turn fosters growth
through economies of scale, innovation, knowledge spillover and other
channels identified in the recent literature on growth and trade. Indeed,
the regional trade alliances forged in many parts of the world (e.g.
NAFTA, ASEAN, EC and Mercosur) reflect attempts to exploit the
advantages of geography and trade. Several subregional trading 'triangles'
have also spawned in Southeast Asia, and more recently there is talk of a
new trading triangle involving Bangladesh, India and China.

Neighbours, of course, can also be enemies: proximity results in
territorial disputes and human beings can nurture old hatreds. Inward
oriented autarkic economic systems are perfect breeding grounds for this
destructive worldview. However, the recent trend towards globalization,
or continuing integration of the world economy presents a new paradigm.[1]
By focusing energies on trade and investment as opposed to border tensions and wars, welfare enhancing growth opportunities can be increased
many fold. This is converting old enemies into mutually advantageous
trading partners. Many vicious hatchets are being buried, e.g. Japan and
Korea, China and India, France and Germany.

India and Pakistan, until recently both closed economies, fit the old
paradigm for conducting relations among neighbours. A year ago both
countries celebrated hatred by exploding nuclear devices and this summer
they took each other to the brink over the Kargil affair. This chapter seeks
to demonstrate that there is much to be gained by the citizens of the countries (the poorest one-fifth of humanity) from shifting to the new paradigm
of neighbourly relations anchored in investment and trade liberalization.

The chapter consists of six sections. The second section summarizes the
structure of the economies of India and Pakistan. In section three the

history of bilateral trade between India and Pakistan is outlined. The fourth section analyses the economic impact of trade liberalization on Pakistan from the perspective of the three principal players likely to be affected by such liberalization, viz. the government, the consumers and the producers. Section V suggests safeguards that need to be put in place to minimize the risk of any short-run damage to the economy following removal of restrictions on trading with India. Conclusions are presented in the sixth section.

2 Overview of the economies of India and Pakistan

India and Pakistan have a combined population of about 1.1 billion, which is about one-fifth of the world population. Table 8.1 provides a comparison of the population, per capita incomes, and HRD indices of the two countries. India has a per capita income of $430 and Pakistan $480, but the ranking in terms of per capita income changes if measured in purchasing power parity terms. There is a high incidence of poverty in the region. Poverty rates (per cent of population below national poverty lines) are about 35 per cent in both countries. For most of the last decade, the Indian economy grew at an average of 6 per cent, while Pakistan's economy, which historically had a higher rate of growth than India's, grew at a considerably slower rate of 4 percent.

Both countries are similar in terms of the GDP share of agriculture in the economy (25 percent). The share of industry is 30 per cent in India and 25 per cent in Pakistan. The services sector contributes 45 per cent to the GDP in India and 50 percent in Pakistan (Table 8.2).

Macroeconomic indicators for the two economies are given in Table 8.3. During 1990–8, the rate of inflation was on average 7.5 per cent per annum in India and 11.2 per cent in Pakistan. Fiscal deficit in 1997 was 5 per cent for India and 8 per cent for Pakistan. The rates of domestic saving and investment in India are considerably higher compared with Pakistan. The external debt-to-GDP ratio is about 25 per cent in India compared with 48 per cent for Pakistan. Macroeconomic indicators are thus much more robust in the case of India compared with Pakistan.

The share of international trade in GDP is 27 per cent in India and 37 per cent for Pakistan. Weighted average tariff is 28 per cent in the case of India compared with 18.5 per cent for Pakistan (Table 8.4)

The total trade between the two countries is of the order of $200–$250 million (Tables 8.5 and 8.6) compared to their total world-wide trade (imports plus exports) of about $128 billion.

Table 8.1 Country profiles: India and Pakistan

Country	Population (millions) (1998)	GNP (US dollars) (1998)	GNP per capita (1998) (US dollars)	GNP per capita (PPP) (1998) (US dollars)	GDP growth rate (average annual) (%) (1990–8)	Poverty (percentage of population below national poverty line)	Human Development Index (1999)
India	980	421.0	430	1,700	6.1	35.0	132
Pakistan	132	63.0	480	1,560	4.1	34.0	138

Sources: 1. World Development Report 1999–2000, The World Bank. 2. Human Development Report, 1999, UNDP, United Nations.

Table 8.2 Structure of output

| Country | (% of GDP) | | |
	Agriculture	Industry	Services
India	25	30	45
Pakistan	25	25	50

Source: World Development Report 1999–2000, The World Bank.

Table 8.3 Macroeconomic indicators

Country	GDP deflator (% change) (1990–8)	Fiscal surplus/ deficit (% of GDP) (1997)	Gross domestic saving (% of GDP) (1998)	Gross domestic investment (% of GDP) (1998)	Debt (% of GDP) (1997)
India	5.5	−4.9	18.0	23.0	24.7
Pakistan	11.4	−7.9	13.0	17.0	48.1

Source: 1. World Development Report 1999–2000, The World Bank. 2. 1999 World Development Indicators, The World Bank.

Table 8.4 Degree of openness, 1997

Country	Imports of goods and services (% of GDP)	Exports of goods and services (% of GDP)	Total trade (% of GDP)	Weighted average tariff (%)
India	15.2	11.5	26.7	27.7
Pakistan	21.0	16.2	37.2	18.5

Sources: 1. 1998, World Development Indicators, The World Bank. 2. Economic Survey 1999, Government of Pakistan.

Note
NA stands for 'Not available'.

Table 8.5 Pakistan–India trade, 1997 (US dollars in millions)

| | India | | Pakistan | |
	Exports	Imports	Exports	Imports
India			33	142
Pakistan	186	21		

Sources: 1. Direction of Trade Statistics Yearbook 1998, International Monetary Fund. 2. Direction of Trade Statistics Quarterly, June 1999, International Monetary Fund.

Note
The matrix of trade flows should ideally be symmetric, but for a number of reasons it is not. For an explanation see International Monetary Fund (1998: x1).

Table 8.6 Pakistan–India trade flows (Rs million)

	Exports to India	Imports from India	Balance
1953–54	114.5	39.0	75.5
1954–55	136.4	36.8	99.6
1955–56	209.8	41.1	168.7
1956–57	141.4	66.7	74.7
1957–58	87.6	87.8	−0.2
1958–59	41.8	77.4	−35.6
1959–60	96.1	82.3	13.8
1960–61	105.0	129.7	−24.7
1961–62	151.5	107.1	44.4
1962–63	194.5	105.3	89.2
1963–64	111.4	94.5	16.9
1964–65	219.8	127.7	92.1
1965–66	18.0	26.2	−8.2
1966–67	0.8	2.2	−1.4
1967–68	0.4	3.2	−2.8
1968–69	—	0.1	—
1969–70	0.1	—	—
1970–71	—	—	—
1971–72	—	—	—
1972–73	0.1	—	—
1973–74	—	—	—
1974–75	92.3	—	—
1975–76	149.5	12.7	136.8
1976–77	1.2	235.5	−234.3
1977–78	347.3	441.4	−94.1
1978–79	166.7	208.8	−42.1
1979–80	478.7	129.7	349.0
1980–81	962.3	21.9	940.4
1981–82	601.6	79.0	522.6
1982–83	340.0	60.3	279.7
1983–84	343.3	147.6	195.7
1984–85	498.1	261.3	236.8
1985–86	465.0	197.0	268.0
1986–87	324.4	166.4	158.0
1987–88	483.4	340.9	142.5
1988–89	940.0	614.0	326.0
1989–90	757.0	816.0	−59.0
1990–91	933.0	1,026.0	−93.0
1991–92	2,814.0	1,213.0	1,601.0
1992–93	2,175.0	1,748.0	427.0
1993–94	1,288.0	2,126.0	−838.0
1994–95	1,284.0	1,974.0	−690.0
1995–96	1,379.2	3,172.2	−1,793.0
1996–97	1,412.4	7,980.3	−6,567.9
1997–98	3,912.5	6,675.1	−2,762.6

Sources: 1. Ministry of Commerce, Government of Pakistan. 2. Foreign Trade Statistics of Pakistan, Federal Bureau of Statistics, Government of Pakistan (various issues). 3. Statistical Bulletin, State Bank of Pakistan, September 1999.

2.1 History of the Pakistan–India trade relationship

Immediately following independence in 1947, India was the most important trading partner of Pakistan. In 1948–9, 56 per cent of Pakistan's total exports were destined for India and 32 per cent of imports originated in India. Currency devaluation by India in 1949, not reciprocated by Pakistan, led to a decline in Pakistan's exports. This was followed by import restrictions by Pakistan. Trade with India fell drastically and the stage was set for Pakistan to orient its trade to the global economy.

Soon after the 1965 war, even this low volume of trade dried up and for several years there was virtually no trade between the two countries. The protocol of 1974 attempted to restore commercial relations on a government-to-government basis and shipping services were resumed in 1975. Trading between the private sectors of the two countries resumed in 1976. Between 1979–86, the two governments talked of expanding trade but no new agreements or protocols were signed. In 1986, the government of Pakistan permitted the import of 42 items, which was expanded to 249 items in 1987. Another 328 items were added to the list in 1989. Even though the list has continued to expand, 90 per cent of the trade was concentrated in 42 items. India contends that Pakistani exports to India are governed by its normal, global, import policy procedures.

Between 1953–4 and 1997–8 (see Table 8.6 for flow of trade flows and Table 8.7 for a chronology of recent trade agreements between India and Pakistan), Pakistan and India have traded for 38 years (trade was virtually suspended between 1968–9 and 1973–4). Of these, Pakistan enjoyed a trade surplus for 22 years. In the last 5 years, trade balance has shifted in favour of India. In other years when trade balance has been in favour of India, the absolute size of the trade deficit for Pakistan has been relatively small.

The significance of the Pakistan–India bilateral trade balance has to be seen in the context of Pakistan's overall trade. In 1997–8, Pakistan's total imports from India at about US$150 million accounted for 1.5 per cent of Pakistan's total imports. Similarly, Pakistan's exports to India of about US$100 million were 1 per cent of its global exports. Thus, if current trade patterns are not altered dramatically following trade liberalization between the two countries, the size of the bilateral trade balance is unlikely to affect significantly Pakistan's global trade balance.[2] (Note that these balances are for official trade only; smuggling and bilateral trade via third parties is substantial and would alter the bilateral trade structure considerably. However, detailed breakdown of such 'unofficial' trade is not available (see below).)

Table 8.7 Pakistan–India trade: a chronology of recent events

Events	Remarks
Protocol of 1974	Restoration of commercial relations on government-to-government basis.
Protocol of 1975	Resumption of shipping services.
Trade Agreement 1975	Expired in 1978.
Joint Statement of Foreign Secretaries 1975	Exchange of goods/passenger traffic by rail started through Wagah/Attari border.
July 1976	Private sector trade permitted.
1978	Expiry of Trade Agreement of 1978 and trade relations reverted to Protocol of 1974, which envisaged State sector trading only.
1979–86	A series of talks and negotiations continued until 1986 without reaching any consensus.
1986	Government of Pakistan permits imports of 42 items by the private sector from India.
1987	List of items enlarged to 249 items.
1989	A list of 328 items added to the list of permitted imports, which included raw materials and industrial goods.
1996	Exports from Pakistan are governed by normal export (policy) procedures whereas imports are restricted to 577 items.

Source: Ministry of Commerce, Government of Pakistan.

3 The impact of liberalizing Pakistan–India trade on the economy

Three broad categories of economic agents would be affected by Pakistan–India trade liberalization, viz. (i) the government (in its revenue collection capacity), (ii) consumers and (iii) producers. Three principal segments of the economy most likely to be affected from such trade liberalization are agriculture, textiles and the engineering sector.

It is possible to obtain quantitative estimates of the expected impact of a regional trading arrangement using CGE type models. These models have been employed to analyse, *ex ante*, the impact of regional arrangements such as the European Union and NAFTA. These models have also been attempted to study the impact of regional arrangements among less developed countries (see DeRosa (1998) for a review of the empirical literature). While such models yield useful insights into specific impacts, 'they raise some fundamental questions about the appropriate specification of behavioural and technical relationships, and the choice of parameter values in CGE and other analytical models' (DeRosa 1998). Both India and Pakistan have pursued highly distortionary economic policies in the past, which are now being rapidly dismantled through deregulation, privatization and tariff reform. In this setting, simulating the impact of regional trade liberalization in a CGE-type model using parameter values estimated from historical data is subject to considerable margin of error.

We have taken a pragmatic approach to assessing trade liberalization. Quantitative estimates are used where possible. These are supplemented with evidence obtained by talking directly to producers and traders who have detailed knowledge of the market. A broad picture has thus emerged of the likely impact of trade liberalization. But first, it is useful to assess how much additional trade would be generated between Pakistan and India if trade were liberalized.

3.1 The impact on the volume of bilateral trade

Srinivasan and Canonero (1993) show that in a free trade setting, trade between Pakistan and its regional partners could grow to about nine times its present levels. With trade relations characterized by most-favoured nation (MFN) status and maximum tariff of 50 per cent, trade is unlikely to exceed a factor of three.[3] Thus in the post-MFN period, trade between India and Pakistan could increase from its level of US$250 million in 1997–8 to a range between $750–$1000 million (the upper range factors in smuggling but more on this shortly). This could make India a major trading partner for Pakistan.

Three additional factors may result in larger than predicted trade flows. The first two, distance and similarity of tastes, are intertwined; greater exposure after trade liberalization may convert some non-traded goods into traded goods and may result in increased trade flows. The third factor, alluded to above, is that both countries are engaged in deep liberalization of their economies. This may lead to new investments, which would alter the current comparative advantage of both countries and may result in new trade flows in the medium term.

3.2 Impact on the government

A broad spectrum of public opinion cites the greatest benefit of Pakistan–India trade liberalization to be the peace dividend that is likely to accrue to both countries. This would follow from the multidimensional relationship that will emerge which will help ease tensions, allowing both governments greater freedom in orienting their budgetary expenditures towards economic uplift.

The principal focus here is the budgetary impact of Pakistan–India trade liberalization via curtailment of smuggling and the additional import duty revenue that would accrue by legalizing the current illegal trade. This requires an estimation of the current levels of cross-border smuggling. In the absence of data and large-scale surveys, interviews with 'informed' sources suggest two estimates of the value of smuggled goods. The 'low' estimate (based on visits to various markets for smuggled goods) identifies the principal illegal 'imports' from India at around $100 million. The 'high' estimate (based on interviews with customs officials) places the value of smuggled Indian goods at $500 million.[4] For a proper perspective on the extent of smuggling it is useful to keep in view Pakistan's global merchandise imports of US$10.3 billion in 1997–8. The high estimate of smuggling implies that out of every 20 dollars' worth of imports, goods worth 1 dollar originate in India. This is not borne out in casual market surveys.

For the purpose of this chapter, it is assumed that the truth regarding the extent of smuggled Indian goods into Pakistan lies somewhere between these two 'guestimates', i.e. about $250 million. Trade liberalization that converts all the smuggled trade into legal trade and levies an import duty of 18 per cent (the current weighted average import tariff) would result in additional tariff revenues of about Rs 2 billion. This would constitute nearly 2.2 per cent of the customs revenue received by the government in 1997–8, or about a quarter of the total public-sector development expenditure on education in 1997–8.

The revenue gain to the government is, of course, much larger if the value of Indian goods smuggled into Pakistan is taken to be between US$1–1.5 billion, as is commonly believed. However, this value of illegal trade flow would over-estimate the likely revenue benefit, since it includes import of Indian manufactured goods into Pakistan via third countries. This is not smuggling and therefore duty already accrues to the government. The benefit of direct Pakistan–India trade in such goods would accrue largely to consumers of the goods, since transportation costs of imports would be reduced.

3.3 Impact on consumers

Consumers would benefit unambiguously from Pakistan–India trade liberalization. Goods imported from India after trade liberalization may be categorized as follows:

- Goods that India manufactures and whose ex-factory cost is similar to that of any other third-country exporter; here the Pakistani consumer would benefit from increased sourcing and from lower transportation costs of importing from India.

- Goods that are currently non-traded because of high transportation costs, which gives Pakistani manufacturers automatic protection; liberalized import of such goods will reduce protection, increase competition and lower prices for the consumers.
- Goods whose demand is such that only India can supply these such as *paans*, *Banarsi saaris*, Hindi film music etc., and trade restrictions result in smuggling; consumers would benefit from the legalized trade of such goods since smuggling margins will be reduced.

3.3.1 Agricultural products

Because of higher crop yields and generally lower prices (discussed in detail in the next section), Pakistan–India trade liberalization will have a beneficial impact on the Pakistani consumer. The demand-pull inflationary pressure will subside and the consumer will have access to a wide range of products. This would help avoid sharp price increases through unforeseen shortages in local sources of supply of fresh produce of onions, pulses etc. These advantages arise from the fact that Pakistani urban centres are located close to the Indian border states with good farming potential.

3.3.2 Textiles

The consumption profile of Pakistani consumers shows that rural and lower income households spend a relatively larger proportion of total expenditure on textile products compared to the urban and upper income households. These consumers will benefit from trade-related lower prices in cotton products such as cotton fabrics, blended fabrics and made-ups such as *chaddars/duppatas* etc.[5] This will have a beneficial income distribution impact.

Upper income groups in Pakistan have a high demand for Indian silk products, shawls, dresses, suits, ensembles and *saaris* (printed and embroidered). Currently, this demand is met through smuggling that adds on a very high premium to prices. Liberalized import of such items will increase product variety and will also lower prices.

3.3.3 Engineering goods

As a consequence of the high protection provided to domestic auto assemblers (both two- and four-wheelers), prices faced by Pakistani producers are higher than comparable prices internationally. Pakistani produced scooters, motorcycles and passenger cars up to 1000 cc are priced about 50 per cent higher than in India. At the prevalent duty rates in excess of 100 per cent, opening of trade with India will have no impact on the market. However, liberalized Indian imports combined with overall tariff reduction (for transport equipment), would enable consumers to purchase, especially, two-wheelers at lower prices.

Another segment of the engineering goods market where consumers would benefit from low-cost Indian imports is bicycles. In the 1996 the price of bicycles in Pakistan was about 20 per cent higher compared with that in India. India's comparative advantage lies in its lower steel prices (a large component of costs), together with scale economies. About 50 per cent of price differential between prices of bicycles in India and Pakistan can be attributed to differences in steel prices.[6] The remaining may be attributed to scale economies with Indian production at 10 million units compared with 0.5 million in Pakistan. Since this product is used principally by lower income groups, liberalized imports will have a beneficial distributional impact.

3.4 Impact on producers

Three important criteria to assess the impact of liberalized trade with India on Pakistani producers are:

 (i) ability to compete with Indian products in the Pakistani market;
 (ii) ability to compete in the larger world market; and
 (iii) access to the larger Indian market.

To examine these impacts, it is instructive first to make an assessment of the relative competitiveness of Pakistani and Indian exports.

A country's manufacturing exports competitiveness may be assessed by grouping exports according to a fourfold matrix, based on whether exports are 'competitive' in world markets (whether the country's exports are gaining or losing in world market-shares in those products) and whether the products themselves are 'dynamic' in trade (whether the products' shares of world trade are rising). The four possible combinations are:

- 'Rising stars' are exports with strong competitiveness (i.e. rising world market-shares) in 'dynamic' products (which are growing faster than total trade).
- 'Lost opportunities' are exports whose competitiveness is declining (falling market-shares) in dynamic products.
- 'Falling stars' are exports with rising market-shares in non-dynamic products, which indicates competitive vulnerability.
- 'Retreat' are exports that are losing market-shares in non-dynamic products, which is desirable.

Based on this classification, Table 8.8 shows the relative competitiveness of Pakistani and Indian manufactured exports. It appears, overall, that Pakistani exports are more competitive than Indian exports because

Table 8.8 Manufactured exports competitiveness, 1985–92 (percentage of exports)

	Pakistan	India
Rising stars	60.4	52.3
Falling stars	25.3	16.2
Lost opportunity	10.0	29.3
Retreat	4.3	2.2
Total	100	100

Source: Authors' calculations based on United Nations (various issues).

the share of rising stars and retreats (both desirable) is higher than India's. Moreover, there are fewer lost opportunities. However, Pakistan's share in falling stars (exports that are vulnerable) is higher than India's.

Another way to gauge competitiveness is in terms of 'revealed comparative advantage' (RCA) indicators. This is the ratio of a country's world market share in a particular export to the world market share of its total exports. RCA indices range around unity, with figures below unity denoting relative disadvantage in exporting the product and those above unity indicating relative advantage.

RCAs for Pakistan and India are calculated for the products in which the two countries compete internationally. Table 8.9 presents the average RCA (1992–4) for exports at the three digit level and shows that Pakistan enjoys strong revealed comparative advantage *vis-à-vis* India in cotton, cotton-based products, leather and rice.

3.5 Supply-side determinants of competitiveness

A brief review is in order of the supply side determinants of international competitiveness to assess whether Pakistan will compete successfully with India in the medium term. This review will further underline the importance of the timing of liberalizing trade with India, a theme that resurfaces in other parts of this chapter.

A fundamental determinant of a country's competitiveness is the unit labour cost of manufactured goods. Unit labour costs measure wage costs as a share of labour productivity. If this ratio is rising, it implies that the wage cost of producing a unit of output is increasing and the country is losing out in international competitiveness. If we focus on manufacturing exports and assume constant labour, then unit labour depends on the rate of growth of wages and the rate of growth of manufacturing exports. Table 8.10 shows that in 1985–92 manufactured exports have grown more rapidly in Pakistan than in India. However, wages in the export sector may have increased more rapidly in Pakistan. Annual manufacturing wages (measured in US dollars), increased in Pakistan by 5.4 per cent whereas they declined in India. Holding

Table 8.9 Pakistan–India revealed comparative advantage (average 1992–4)

SITC Code	Product	Pakistan	India	RCA(Pak)–RCA(India)
036	Shellfish Fresh-Frozen	3.3	8.8	−5.4
042	Rice	34.1	12.9	21.3
057	Fruits, Nuts, Fresh-Dried	1.0	3.0	−1.9
075	Spices	4.9	15.0	−10.1
122	Tobacco, Manufactured	0.0	0.0	0.0
263	Cotton	21.8	2.6	19.2
291	Crude Animal Materials NES	0.0	0.0	0.0
292	Crude Vegetable Materials NES	1.6	0.0	1.6
333	Crude Petroleum	0.2	0.0	0.2
334	Petroleum Products, Refin	0.1	1.0	−0.9
541	Medicinal Pharmaceutical Products	0.2	1.6	−1.3
611	Leather	11.4	4.9	6.5
651	Textile Yarn	27.6	5.1	22.4
652	Cotton Fabrics Woven	27.8	7.4	20.4
653	Woven Manmade Fibre Fabrics	12.0	1.8	10.1
655	Knitted or Crocheted Fabrics	5.9	1.4	4.6
658	Textile Articles NES	33.1	7.4	25.7
659	Floor Coverings	11.1	11.4	−0.4
671	Pig Iron etc.	0.0	4.7	−4.7
842	Men's Outwear Non-Knit	4.8	0.8	4.0
843	Women's Outwear Non-Knit	3.1	5.9	−2.8
848	Headgear, Non-textile Clothing	19.2	6.3	12.9
851	Footwear	0.5	1.4	−0.9

Source: Authors' calculations based on United Nations (various issues).

productivity growth constant, increasing real wages signals increasing unit labour costs.

Productivity growth is determined crucially by workers' skills; this is where Pakistan's current comparative advantage is vulnerable. Pakistan's education enrolment rates (as a percentage of age groups, in 1992) were 46, 21, and 3 per cent at the primary, secondary and tertiary levels, compared to India's 102, 44 and 10 per cent. Among tertiary level students, those enrolled in the natural sciences, mathematics and computers and engineering in Pakistan were 0.01 per cent and 0.02 per cent compared to

Table 8.10 Growth in manufacturing exports and wages (annual percentages)

	Pakistan	India
Growth of manufactured exports (1985–92)	19.0	16.3
Growth of annual manufacturing wages (measured in current US dollars) (1985–93)	5.4	−0.8

Sources: 1. Economic Survey, Government of Pakistan (various issues). 2. Economic Survey, Government of India (various issues).

India's 0.09 and 0.02 per cent. Furthermore, progress on vocational training that provides workers with specific skills is also not encouraging. Enrolled students as percentage of population in Pakistan in 1990 were 0.04 per cent compared to India's 0.09 per cent.

These skill mix differences between the two countries are beginning to be reflected in the composition of exports and may alter future comparative advantage of the two countries. Between 1980–92, 90 per cent of Pakistan's exports were concentrated in low skill products, while India's were in the upper 70 per cent. A further breakdown of exports by technological categories shows that 4.6 per cent of Indian manufactured exports are science-based compared to 1.7 per cent for Pakistan. These trends have implications for future competitiveness of the two countries. Unless the trends are reversed, Pakistan runs the risk of remaining concentrated in the low skill, slow growth and more vulnerable segments of the international economy, while India moves into more diversified, more skilled and therefore higher value-added segments. Before long, this will impact on living standards in the two economies.

India's better performance in sources of international competitiveness and therefore the potential of India outperforming Pakistan is not an argument for continued restrictive trade. Exposure to competition from a neighbour would encourage policy makers as well as the private sector in Pakistan to focus more sharply on the investments needed to strengthen Pakistan's international competitiveness. The impact of liberalizing trade with India on Pakistani producers in three sub-sectors is discussed next.

3.6 Textiles

It is instructive to explore whether Pakistani textiles products will be able to hold their own in the face of Indian imports. We show that the fear of a deluge of Indian products in the Pakistani market after liberalizing trade is much exaggerated. But first, a brief overview of the textiles sector in India and Pakistan is in order.

Despite its late start Pakistan is as large a player in the world textiles markets as India. Partly, this is due to comparative advantage anchored in geography.[7] Pakistan's cotton yield (593 kg/hectare) is almost twice India's and, despite a cotton cultivated area (2.8 million hectares) that is a third of India's, Pakistan's total cotton output is 8.69 million bales (1994–5) compared to India's 11.69 million. This, combined with sophisticated imported textile machinery, has allowed Pakistan to compete successfully with India in the international market. Table 8.11 captures the importance of textiles in the economies of India and Pakistan.

Table 8.11 Importance of textiles in India and Pakistan, 1994–5

	Pakistan	India
Textiles production (per cent of manufacturing value added)	30.00	20.00
Textiles employment (per cent of manufacturing employment)	39.00	20.50
Textiles investment (per cent of manufacturing investment)	15.00	NA
Cotton yarn output (million metric tons)	1.27	1.51
Cotton fabrics output (million metric tons)	0.71	1.45
Textiles exports (million US$, 1994-5)	5,178.00	6,352.00
Textiles exports (per cent of total exports)	60.00	24.00
Textiles imports (per cent of total imports)	1.20	1.00
Textiles tax as (per cent of total central excise duty)	10.00	12.00

Sources: 1. Economic Survey, Government of Pakistan (various issues). 2. Economic Survey, Government of India (various issues). 3. Handbook of Statistics on Cotton Textile Industry, Indian Cotton Mills Federation (1995).

3.6.1 Competitiveness of textiles producers

If Pakistani textiles manufacturers can compete successfully with Indians in international markets, there is little reason to believe that they will not be able to do so in the domestic market. There is plenty of evidence that allows an assessment of the performance of India and Pakistan in textiles products that are sold in the international markets by both countries.

A criterion for assessing competitiveness is the revealed comparative advantage (RCA) coefficient introduced earlier. RCAs for India and Pakistan for textiles exports at the four digit level are reported in Table 8.12. The table shows that Pakistan is more competitive in cotton yarn, grey woven fabric, bleached woven cotton and hand knotted carpets, while India is more competitive in women's non-knit dresses, non-knit blouses and men's shirts. This is consistent with other evidence that shows India doing better than Pakistan in the value-added clothing sector. The table also shows that in sectors where Pakistan enjoys a comparative advantage, it does considerably better than India. Furthermore, in the two segments where India has greater advantage, the difference is considerably smaller, and in men's shirts the difference is shrinking. In 1991 RCA ratios were 8 and 12 for Pakistan and India respectively in the export of men's shirts: by 1993 the coefficient values were down to 7 and 8.

Direct comparisons of textile costs and productivity also show that the industry in the two countries is more or less equally efficient. Raw cotton costs are similar in the two countries. Low-count yarn is cheaper in Pakistan but high-count yarn is cheaper in India. Wages are lower in India but labour productivity (because of better quality machinery) is higher in Pakistan. The cost of textile machinery is lower in India. However, the quality is poorer and is reflected in lower labour productivity.

In thinking about liberalizing trade with India, the focus must remain

Table 8.12 Revealed comparative advantage of Pakistani and Indian textiles exports (four digit level, average 1990–3)

	Pakistan	India
Raw cotton (2,631)	31	3
Cotton yarn (6,513)	115	14
Grey woven cotton fabric (6,521)	55	18
Woven cotton bleached etc.(6,522)	18	4
Women's non-knit dresses	6	14
Women's non-knit blouses (8,435)	5	14
Men's shirts (8,441)	7	10
Carpets hand-knotted (6,592)	43	12

Source: Authors' calculations based on United Nations (various issues).

on long-term international competitiveness, as illustrated in Table 8.9. Given the evidence reported in the table, how should Pakistan respond to India being relatively more competitive in the value-added segment of the textiles market? Pakistan's textile import regime is fairly restrictive. Treating India at par with other countries will maintain the protection to the clothing sector in the domestic market. However, another way to look at it is that a more liberalized import regime globally, and therefore *vis-à-vis* India as well, will stimulate Pakistan's clothing sector to be more competitive domestically and therefore in the international market. This latter argument has to be seen in the context of Pakistan's global trade liberalization and not just *vis-à-vis* India.

3.7 Engineering sector

Pakistan's engineering sector consists of 2000 units that employ 140,000 workers and produce goods valued at 2 per cent of GDP and 15 per cent of manufacturing output (Table 8.13). But this output constitutes just 24 per cent of total domestic consumption of engineering goods. The rest of the domestic demand is met through imports. This is not because of insufficient domestic production capacity: capacity utilization in firms manufacturing engineering goods ranges between 56 per cent (electrical and electronic equipment) and 69 per cent (basic metals). The large propensity to import is partly because of supply side problems and partly because of the superior quality of imports. Pakistan is not a player in the world market for engineering goods; in 1993, it exported auto-parts worth US$3 million and surgical instruments worth $120 million.

The Indian engineering goods sector is comparatively healthier. In 1992–3 value added in the engineering sector was 40 per cent of the total value added in manufacturing industry and constituted 13 per cent of total exports. The engineering sector also contributes to greater skill intensity of traditional exports. India is still a minor player in the international

Table 8.13 Pakistan's engineering sector: domestic production and imports, 1991–2

	Value added (Rs million)	Value added (% of total)	Output (Rs million)	Capacity utilization (%)	Employment	Imports (Rs million)	Imports ($s thousand)
Basic metals	12,700	49.9	44,800	69	63,600	7,600	308
Metal products	2,200	8.4	6,300	60	18,900	3,400	139
Mechanical equipment and machinery	1,200	4.6	3,550	58	16,600	38,600	1,567
Electrical and electronic equipment	4,200	16.2	11,400	56	22,900	12,500	506
Transport equipment	5,600	21.6	26,000	58	20,800	21,100	855
Total	25,900	100	—	—	142,800	83,200	3,375

Sources: 1. 'A Perspective for Five Year Development Plan (1993-8) for Engineering Goods Industry in Pakistan', National Management Consultants (Pvt) Ltd., December 1993.
2. Economic Survey, Government of Pakistan (various issues).

market for engineering goods; its share in world trade of selected engineering products, such as passenger cars, auto parts, two-wheelers and machine tools, is negligible (it ranges between 0.08 per cent and 2.3 per cent, see Table 8.14). It is unlikely that liberalization of Pakistan–India trade will result in a major market penetration of Indian engineering goods, because of competition from Korean and Taiwanese products with considerable market presence. The impact on domestic producers is now assessed according to product.

3.7.1 Mechanical equipment and machinery

There are two segments of this market: the premium machinery imported from OECD countries, and the non-premium segment dominated by Chinese and Taiwanese imports. Indian imports are unlikely to displace these sources of quality products. Domestic producers play a relatively small role in this category of engineering products. A few large publicly owned firms, such as the Heavy Mechanical Complex and the Pakistan Machine Tool Factory, could be effective players but are not because they lack market orientation. They have captive buyers who, for strategic reasons, are unlikely to displace these sources of supply. At the other end of the spectrum are small firms in the unorganized sector with high levels of craftsmanship, low overheads and low labour costs. They are organized along kinship lines which also influences market access to local clusters. They are confident that they can withstand competition from India.

Table 8.14 Engineering goods exports for selected items and countries, 1995, US$ million

	Passenger cars (SITC 781)	Auto parts (SITC 784)	Two-wheelers (SITC 785)	Machine tools (SITC 731 + 733)
Japan	42,208	19,656	5,804	6,570
Germany	48,602	21,932	548	4,206
Italy	8,021	6,053	1,848	1,774
China	33	378	880	274
India	181	277	323	30
World Total	231,320	119,148	14,038	21,506

Source: International Trade Statistics, UNCTAD/WTO (1999).

3.7.2 Transport equipment

Although the sector has an average tariff rate of 29 per cent due to various concessions under the indigenization policy, in general it has enjoyed high protection (with duties of 100 per cent to 265 per cent). The result is that prices of scooters, motorcycles and cars under 1000 cc are higher than in the international market (prices are 50 per cent higher than in India).

Domestic producers will be unaffected by liberalization of trade with India at the prevalent duty rate in excess of 100 per cent. India will be able to penetrate the market, especially in the *two-wheeler category*, if the overall tariff rates are lowered from the present 100 per cent (Bajaj Autos is reputed to be the world's lowest cost producer of two- and three-wheelers). Indian producers might also gain access to the market for *bicycles*, but only if tariffs are lowered from the current rates.

On the supply side, a principal source of distortion is the tariff structure. Higher duty is levied on raw material for capital goods and lower duty on capital goods themselves, which distorts the incentive for domestic production. For example, while the world price for steel (C & F Karachi) is Rs 11,000 per ton, the market price of domestically produced steel is Rs 19,000.[8] This greatly lowers the international competitiveness of Pakistani producers of engineering goods. This supply side constraint is well illustrated by two products: with an average import duty of only 10 per cent, import of mechanical equipment and machinery goods constitutes 97 per cent of domestic consumption; on the other hand, the average import duty on basic metals is 46 per cent and imports of this item constitute only 37 per cent of total demand.

3.7.3 Electrical and electronic equipment

As a result of low tariffs and high level of smuggling, quality products are being produced by Pakistani manufacturers. In the quality conscious segments they can hold their own in the domestic market. In these segments

Indian products are unlikely to be competitive. In other segments, Pakistani consumer is unlikely to switch demand from the superior products currently imported from the best international suppliers.

3.7.4 Cautionary note

It is important that Pakistani producers of engineering goods are given a level playing field *vis-à-vis* their Indian counterparts. Currently, they face negative protection because statutory duties are lower on finished products than on raw materials. The average duty (including import duty, *iqra*, flood relief fund, regulatory duty and surcharge) in 1994–5 was 46 per cent on raw material (basic metals) and 10, 18, 20 and 29 per cent on finished goods (mechanical equipment and machinery, electrical and electronic equipment, metal products and transport equipment, respectively). This anomaly must be remedied by bringing down the effective duty on raw materials to below the levels on finished goods.

A key factor determining competitiveness of Pakistani producers is the cost of steel. Currently, steel prices in Pakistan are substantially higher than in India. Access to internationally priced steel will lower costs of production.

The negative protection of Pakistani producers of engineering goods is further increased because weak customs administration results in under-declaration of imported finished engineering goods, which further reduces the effective duty. Indian producers of engineering goods, on the other hand, do not suffer from such negative protection. Indeed, they receive substantial overt and hidden subsidies to make them internationally competitive. Thus liberalization of trade with India in engineering goods must be done simultaneously with removing the negative protection given to Pakistani producers, as well as tightening up of customs administration to avoid large inflows of undeclared imports.

3.8 Agriculture

Because land is the principal constraint in agricultural production in India and Pakistan, a useful measure of competitiveness of agricultural producers is farm yield, since it captures the relative efficiency of land use. Direct evidence is available on the yield performance of Pakistani and Indian farm producers and is presented in Tables 8.15a and 8.15b. Table 8.15a shows that Indian farmers have achieved higher yields per hectare than Pakistani farmers for all major crops. The exception is cotton, where Pakistani producers have higher yields. This and larger cropped area result in higher output per capita in India than in Pakistan for rice, maize, gram and sugarcane. In cotton, Pakistan enjoys a considerable yield advantage, so that despite the lower area devoted to this crop (about a third of the Indian area), Pakistan's output is nearly 75 per cent that of India.

Table 8.15a Cropped area, yield and total output of principal crops in Pakistan and India

	Pakistan Cropped area (average 1994–5) (000 hectares)	India Cropped area (average 1994–5) (000 hectares)	Pakistan Yield (average 1992–4) (kg/hectare)	India Yield (average 1992–4) (kg/hectare)	Pakistan Output (average 1993–5) (million ton)	India Output (average 1993–5) (million ton)
	Pakistan	India	Pakistan	India	Pakistan	India
Wheat	8,152	25,600	1,963	2,420	16.00	60.80
Rice	2,125	42,200	1,662	1,851	3.50	78.10
Maize	886	6,100	1,408	1,590	1.20	9.60
Grams	1,063	23,200	420	775	0.40	5.50
Sugarcane	1,009	3,800	44,803	65,667	42.70	238.70
Cotton	2,653	7,900	530	262	1.46	1.94

Sources: 1. Economic Survey, Government of Pakistan (various issues). 2. Economic Survey, Government of India (various issues).

Table 8.15b Efficiency of crop production in Pakistan and India

	Acres per capita India/Pakistan	Yield gap Yield (Pak)–Yield (India) (percentage)	Per capita output India/Pakistan
Wheat	0.44	−23	0.53
Rice	2.76	−11	2.67
Maize	1.00	−47	1.08
Grams	2.89	−13	1.72
Sugarcane	0.50	−85	0.77
Cotton	0.38	51	0.18

Sources: 1. Economic Survey, Government of Pakistan (various issues). 2. Economic Survey, Government of India (various issues).

One predictor of the direction of trade flows in agricultural produce after Pakistan–India trade liberalization is the exportable surplus. Taking per capita crop output as a crude measure of exportable surplus, Table 8.15b shows that India has a distinct advantage in rice, maize and grams, while Pakistan has clear superiority in cotton. However, this predictor of trade flows is crude because it ignores the demand side. Thus, while in Pakistan per capita availability of sugarcane and wheat is higher than in India, so is demand, which results in Pakistan importing these items. Pakistan imports nearly 2 million tons of wheat, annually worth US$250 million. Indian states located near Pakistan's borders such as Punjab and Rajasthan may well be competitive in selling wheat to Pakistan compared to suppliers in the USA, Australia and Canada.

Pakistani *basmati* rice would be in demand in India both for domestic consumption as well as for re-export. Trade in sugar would be sporadic with the two countries trading only to take advantage of unforeseen shortages and surpluses. Lahore would become a major destination for vegetables, fruits and other perishables grown in the border states in India. Pakistani citrus and mango growers with a reputation for high quality produce could tap the large Indian market, but would have to contend with strong price competition from local producers. In processed food, India's industry would dominate Pakistan's. Indian tea exports to Pakistan would be substantial.

Indian manufacturers will have a presence in the Pakistani market for agricultural inputs. India has made good progress in the development of new seed technology, and irrigation and mechanical technology for small farmers.

In the short run, the agricultural trade balance is likely to be in favour of India. The long-run benefits to Pakistani producers are potentially substantial. The largest benefit would be to Pakistani farmers in terms of access to high yield technologies across the whole range of crops. The Indian farm research and extension services have made remarkable progress in recent years and are largely responsible for the gains made by India in its farm output. Pakistan is well endowed with good quality land and its irrigation network is one of the largest in the world. These features, combined with access to Indian research and extension services and quality inputs (seeds and implements) will enable Pakistani farmers to rapidly increase their yields and generate exportable surpluses. Access to Indian food processing technology will contribute to the international competitiveness of Pakistani farmers in this lucrative market.

Dynamics of sub-regional trade

Besides the economy-wide impact of liberalizing trade with India discussed in other sections, there are also likely to be substantial benefits for sub-regions within Pakistan. There are already two sub-regional trade zones in Pakistan. In the west Quetta, located close to the borders with Afghanistan and Iran, has enjoyed good trade relations with those countries. The economy of Quetta has prospered despite being located far from the industrial and urban centres of the rest of the country. Similarly, Peshawar located on the trade routes to Afghanistan and China has benefited from the dynamics of trade beyond the borders in the northwest and the northeast.

Liberalizing trade with India will open two new hubs of commercial/industrial activity. Karachi will establish commerce with Gujrat and Bombay while Lahore will re-establish the old commercial links with regions to its east. The potential for the Lahore trade zone is outlined below.

Before the partition of 1947, Lahore was the hub of commercial/industrial/cultural/political activity for cities in a 100-mile radius. To the northwest, the radius included the old established towns of Gujranwala, Sialkot, Wazirabad and Gujrat (Punjab), to the west were the new canal colonies of Faisalabad (old Lyallpur) and Sargodha, and to the south were smaller canal colonies and towns like Sahiwal (old Montgomery), Khanewal and the commercial centre of the ancient city of Multan. There was an eastern corridor as well consisting of the well developed commercial centres of Amritsar, Gurdaspur, Ferozepur and Ludhiana. A broad trade pattern had been established whereby Lahore was the primary credit and goods clearing centre for the agricultural towns in the western and southern corridors, as well as for the manufacturing towns in the northern and eastern corridors. The entire region, with Lahore at its centre, benefited from these commercial/trading exchanges.

The partition brought about some remarkable changes to this zone. The eastern corridor (Amritsar, Ferozepur, Gurdaspur and Ludhiana) became part of India (the international border between India and Pakistan is about 20 miles to the east of Lahore) and was soon completely cut-off. Meanwhile, Lahore deepened its trade/commerce/credit relations with towns in the other three corridors. Gujranwala, Sialkot, Wazirabad and Gujrat to the north and Faisalabad to the west have become substantial centres of manufacturing activity, initially serving the Lahore market but increasingly exporting directly to the rest of the world. Thus Lahore has been more than compensated for the loss of the manufacturing centres in the east.

Cities in the old eastern corridor have done well, but it has been a struggle. The severe trade restrictions between India and Pakistan imply that the distance to Lahore has become infinite, while Delhi, further to the east, is nearly twice as far as Lahore. In any case, Delhi had its own established secondary hubs and breaking into that market was not easy (although business links were established to some extent since Hindu/Sikh business partners had moved from Lahore to Delhi at partition).

Removal of trade restrictions is tantamount to reducing the distance between the eastern corridor, the epicentre Lahore and the other three corridors commanded by Lahore. This would unleash substantial commercial/manufacturing activity in the entire region. The potential benefits include:

- a large new market for the agricultural produce of western and southern zones;
- a flow of technology from the more advanced agricultural regions in the east to the farming corridors in the west and the south;

- new, potentially large, markets for textiles manufactured in Faisalabad, and cutlery, surgical instruments and sports goods manufactured in Sialkot and Wazirabad;
- building on existing comparative advantage, new clusters would emerge in the eastern and northern corridors specializing in inter-linked processes of the light engineering industry; this would sharpen zone-wide international competitiveness, eventually leading to a flow of investments;
- workers in all regions would benefit from increased employment opportunities and higher wages;
- Lahore would benefit culturally and commercially from being at the hub of increased zone-wide economic activity.

4 Market access and safeguards

After the removal of restrictions on trading with India, and treatment of India at par with other GATT signatories, negotiated solutions will still need to be found to protect the legitimate interests of Pakistani producers. Regarding market access, two aspects would need to be considered: (i) access of Pakistani exports to the Indian market and (ii) the access of Indian exports to the Pakistani market. The latter concern arises in case Indian exporters gain unfair access to the Pakistani market because of GATT inconsistent subsidies. This would require (iii) strengthening the regulatory framework for dealing efficiently with dumping and invoking countervailing duties.

4.1 Accessing the Indian market

In product categories where local producers compete internationally, such as automotive parts and electrical and electronic equipment, Pakistani producers are confident of gaining access to the much larger Indian market. Several vendors of automotive plastic parts have received orders from India, even though the Indian duty rates are 50 per cent. A small share of the rapidly growing Indian market for Pakistani producers of automotive parts will increase capacity utilization, provide scale economies and smooth out fluctuations in local demand. The latter is particularly important since it lowers dependence on monopsonistic buyers.

Internationally competitive producers of engineering goods speak of the importance of timing in gaining access to the Indian market. The argument is that until recently India was a highly protected and closed economy, whereas Pakistan was not. This enabled the surviving Pakistani manufacturers to produce goods to international standards, while Indian producers were less quality conscious in their captive home market.

However, this edge is now rapidly eroding because as India has begun to dismantle protective barriers and liberalize the investment climate, foreign direct investment has started to flow in. The technology that comes with it will soon begin to improve product quality in India. The perception of Indian consumers regarding higher quality of Pakistani consumer durables can be capitalized upon through liberalizing trade now. In a few years, this advantage would be lost.

Despite the competitive advantage enjoyed by Pakistani producers, a protective Indian import regime may thwart access to the Indian market. The incidence of tariff protection is considerably higher in India compared with Pakistan. Although in recent years, trade liberalization in India has resulted in significant lowering of quantitative restrictions and reduction in non-tariff barriers for the capital goods and intermediate goods industry, the import regime for consumer goods items still continues to be quite restrictive. In 1998 India agreed to phase out all quantitative restrictions over the next 6 years; at present this includes about 2200 items. In August 1998, quantitative restrictions were removed on 2000 items for countries in the SAARC region. Although non-tariff barriers have been lowered, tariff barriers continue to be significant. Since the strength of Pakistani industry is believed to lie in consumer goods items, therefore, trade negotiations with India must stress unrestricted market access to Pakistani exports of consumer goods items.

It may well be the case that trade with India on the same basis as with other signatories of GATT may result in Pakistani consumer goods' market being much more open to Indian exports than the Indian market is to Pakistani exports. This would indicate the need for a negotiated solution with Indian counterparts, within the framework of Article XXXIV, Clause 11. Indeed, Pakistan would help pry open the protected Indian consumer regime, which would be beneficial for both bilateral as well as mulitlateral trade.

4.2 Accessing the Pakistani market

The concern here is with protecting the interest of Pakistani producers in case of unfair advantage enjoyed by Indian producers due to GATT/inconsistent subsidies. Significant Indian government financial assistance, in various forms including subsidies, grants, concessional loans, tax concessions, equity investments and R and D funding, is provided to firms in major industrial sectors. Such funding, partly financed by production levies, is usually controlled by ministries/departments responsible for the development of certain industries, such as ministries of chemicals and fertilisers, coal, food processing, industry, mines, petroleum and natural gas, steel and textiles. Structural adjustment assistance is arranged and administered through the Board of Industrial and Financial Reconstruction to rehabilitate declared 'sick' firms.

194 Ijaz Nabi and Anjum Nasim

The cornerstone of India's trade policy is the promotion of Indian exports. This is to be achieved through targeted incentives to selected goods in agriculture, textiles and garments, engineering, electronics, computer software and gem and jewellery product groups. India has also identified export markets in which special efforts would be undertaken to achieve some degree of market penetration. Although not part of the declared strategy, it would be reasonable to presume that Indian exporters could find it profitable to focus on market development efforts in Pakistan.

With regard to trade-related export incentives, Pakistan needs to monitor imports of those Indian goods, which are recipient of two specific schemes; namely, Export Promotion of Capital Goods Scheme and Technology Upgradation scheme. These schemes conflict with the provisions of the GATT 1994 Subsidies Agreement. Another scheme, the Brand Rate Fixation Scheme, which seeks to promote Indian branded manufactured goods, also possibly falls foul of the GATT Subsidies Agreement. Other export incentive schemes are at variance with Pakistani policies. For example, income from exports is fully tax exempt in India. Furthermore, specified categories of industries in India are eligible for Advance License Scheme, which allows exporters to obtain duty-free imports of inputs. Currently, improvements in and expansion of the Advance License scheme is the largest source of incentives to exporters in India.

An analysis of competitiveness of selected Indian industries, based on calculated protection coefficients and their exports, suggests that exporters of items such as some auto and cycle components, computers, TVs, some pharmaceuticals, and plastic products could well engage in dumped sales in overseas markets. Furthermore, subject to future rationalization of Indian tariff structure, the following industries are identified as having a potential to engage in dumping practice: grey iron casting, aluminium casting, polyester filament yarn, components of textile machinery, copper battery cables, components of motor cycles, moped, auto and bicycles components, stereo tape-players with radio, pocket calculators, walkman cassette players, computers, geysers, air conditioners, battery chargers and melamine crockery sets.

4.3 A regulatory and institutional framework for checking unfair trading practices

In the area of administered protection (i.e. antidumping and countervailing laws), Pakistan's Anti-Dumping and Countervailing Measures Act (1995), circulated by the Pakistani National Tariff Commission (NTC), is on the anvil. A number of amendments are needed to make it an effective instrument for protection against unfair international trade practices. In order to deal with the concern that imports from India can, in some cases, cause material injury to industries in Pakistan, a two-tier investigative procedure is proposed. This proposal is motivated by a more general perception that there does not exist an appreciation, among industry associations, of conceptual and procedural issues involved in seeking remedial measures against *unfair* international trade practices. This concern is especially true for small- and medium-sized producers located around industrial clusters in Pakistani Punjab from imports originating from Indian Punjab.

To address these issues, a two-tiered investigative procedure should be followed: an initial examination of the alleged complaint of dumped imports, leading to a *prima facie* decision. This *prima facie* investigation is conceived more in the nature of a consultancy service to the affected industry in order to prepare a more credible presentation for a formal hearing in the second stage by the NTC. Pakistan Customs is tentatively suggested as a possible body where informal advice and assistance is given, and information and data are collated (within a stipulated time period) and provided to the potential complainant industry on antidumping matters. It is proposed that the Government provide the first stage service gratis.

The case for two-tier procedure is further strengthened if the objective in designing institutional rules is also to protect the NTC from admitting petitions and adjudicating cases which are essentially frivolous and motivated by narrow vested interests or narrow nationalistic sentiments. In the event, a two-tier procedure is more likely to take the edge off the use of antidumping and countervailing laws as a means of accomplishing protectionist intentions without compromising the authority or independence of the NTC.

A separate question arises with regard to the nature of the formal or quasi-judicial NTC hearings: an adversarial format would place the burden of proof of alleged dumped imports causing material injury squarely on the complainant industry. Strict evidence should be required to support such a claim. On the other hand, an inquisitorial format would place the burden of detailed investigation, including costly accountancy and legal support, on the NTC. If the NTC adopted such a format, it could be seen as acting as prosecutor and judge simultaneously, which raises the possibility of a denial of natural justice. Seen in this context, it seems that an appropriate solution would be a two-tier investigative procedure, with NTC adopting an adversarial format in undertaking examination of alleged complaints of dumped or subsidized imports.

5 Conclusion

This study finds that, given the current structure of the two economies, removal of restrictions is likely to increase the volume of trade from its present $250 million to $750–1000 million. The economic benefits to Pakistan of liberalizing trade with India are substantial. Two principal economic groups, consumers (lower prices) and the government (greater customs duty revenue from legalizing the illicit border trade), would benefit. Important segments of producers would also benefit because of increased competitiveness and market access to a much larger Indian economy. Inefficient producers would need to restructure and increase competitiveness to stay in the market. However, the tariff regime must be reformed to ensure that Pakistani producers (especially in the engineering sector) do not suffer negative protection *vis-à-vis* Indian competitors.

To facilitate trade and technology exchange (especially in agricultural produce), many more land border crossings would need to be opened up and visa restrictions eased. Customs administration would need to be tightened to ensure that increased entry points and reduced transactions costs do not result in large undeclared trade flows.

GATT consistent procedures (legislation and institutions) need to be put in place to ensure unimpeded access of Pakistani products to the (more restrictive) Indian market and protection of Pakistani markets against subsidized exports and possible unfair trading practices of Indian producers. These safeguards must be in place as trade restrictions are removed.

A 'stop-go' India–Pakistan trade relationship would damage business confidence and must be avoided. A confidence building strategy might well be step-wise removal of restrictions beginning with trade in agriculture and textiles. Meanwhile, the ground rules for market access on both sides could be defined and investments in trade infrastructure made. Following successful completion of this phase, restrictions could be lifted across the board.

Notes

* Views in the chapter are the authors' and not those of the institutions to which they are affiliated. The chapter draws heavily on 'Pakistan–India Trade: Transition to the GATT Regime', a report prepared in 1996 for the Ministry of Commerce, Government of Pakistan, by a team led by Ijaz Nabi and consisting of Mohammad Ahmad, Jawaid Ghani, Zubair Khan, Zareen Naqvi, Anjum Nasim, Salman Shah and K.K. Suri. Some of the conclusions of the empirical analysis presented in the chapter would change with more recent data.

1. See World Development Report 1999–2000 (World Bank 1999) which suggests that globalization is one of 'the two forces, which will be shaping the world' in the twenty-first century and that development policy will have to be conducted in the context of this reality.
2. India's trade with Pakistan was an even less significant share of its total trade. Its imports from Pakistan were 0.2 per cent of its total imports and exports to Pakistan were 0.5 per cent of its global exports.
3. The projections assume a host of quantitative restrictions as well as no preferential treatment *vis-à-vis* the rest of the world. The results from Srinivasan and Canonero (1993) reported here are quoted from Khan (1996).

4. Principal smuggled goods from India are cattle, betel leaves and nuts, spices, tea, tyres, tubes and pharmaceuticals.
5. The expectation is that trade will lower the prices of these products in Pakistan because the import of these items is restricted in Pakistan but there are no restrictions on exports.
6. See Ghani and Nasim (1996) for details.
7. Modern textiles industry started in the 1850s in what are now Indian centres of production. In Pakistan the industry started in the early 1950s.
8. The price of steel refers to the average price of various categories of sheet steel.

References

DeRosa, D.A. (1998) 'Regional integration arrangements: static economic theory, quantitative findings, and policy guidelines', Policy Research Working Paper 2007, Development Research Group, The World Bank, Washington, DC.

Ghani, J. and Nasim A. (1996) 'Impact of India–Pakistan trade on engineering sector', CMER Working Paper Series, Centre for Management and Economic Research, Lahore University of Management Sciences, Lahore.

Government of India (various issues), *Economic Survey*, New Delhi: Ministry of Finance.

Government of Pakistan (various issues), *Economic Survey*, Islamabad: Finance Division.

—— (various issues) *Foreign Trade Statistics*, Islamabad: Federal Bureau of Statistics.

Indian Cotton Mills Federation (1995) *Handbook of Statistics on Cotton Textile Industry*, Bombay: Indian Cotton Mills Federation.

International Monetary Fund (1998) *Direction of Trade Statistics Yearbook 1998*, Washington DC: International Monetary Fund.

—— (1999) *Direction of Trade Statistics Quarterly*, June, Washington DC: International Monetary Fund.

Khan, Z. (1996) 'A review of Pakistan's trade relations with India', paper prepared for the Ministry of Commerce, Government of Pakistan, Islamabad: Processed.

National Management Consultants (Pvt.) Ltd. (1993) *A Perspective for Five Year Development Plan (1993–98) for Engineering Goods Industry In Pakistan.* Islamabad: Processed.

Srinivasan, T.N. and Cononero, G. (1993) 'Liberalisation of trade among neighbours: two illustrative models and simulations', Washington, DC: The World Bank.

State Bank of Pakistan (1999) *Statistical Bulletin*, September, Karachi: State Bank of Pakistan.

United Nations (various issues), *International Trade Statistics*, New York: United Nations Statistical Office.

—— (1999) *Human Development Report 1999*, UNDP, New York: Oxford University Press.

UNCTAD/WTO (1999) 'International Trade Statistics', Geneva: International Trade Centre. Available at <HTTP: http://www.intracen.org> (4 November 1999).

World Bank (1998) *1998 World Development Indicators CD-ROM*, Washington, DC: The World Bank.

—— (1999) *1999 World Development Indicators CD-ROM*, Washington, D.C.: The World Bank.

—— (1999) *World Development Report 1999–2000*, Washington, DC: The World Bank.

9   Foreign direct investment and globalization

V.N. Balasubramanyam and
Mohammed A. Salisu

The phenomenon of globalization has served to rekindle many an old controversy on the contribution of foreign direct investment (FDI) to development. As in the past, its critics assign it centre stage in propagating the perceived evils of globalization, including the demise of the nation state, impoverishment of developing countries, collapse of cherished cultural values and the degradation of the environment. Its advocates reiterate the role of FDI in promoting trade, growth and employment. Indeed, since the 1980s most developing countries have eagerly sought FDI, proposals such as the multilateral agreement on investment (MAI) drafted by the OECD have sought to liberalize rules and regulations governing FDI, and flows of FDI to developing countries have increased appreciably. There is a copious literature on various aspects of FDI. Yet there are very few settled conclusions on the contribution of FDI to the development process, in part due to the complex nature of FDI and in part due to the ideological preconceptions which colour most debates on the issue. Indeed, there may be no other area of economic inquiry where so much has been written and yet we know so little.

It is, however, worth reviewing what little we do know about the relationship between FDI and development, if only to provide a framework and background for the continuing debate on globalization and FDI. This chapter reviews the known facts concerning the experience of developing countries with FDI. It is not intended to be a survey of the vast literature on FDI in developing countries, but a commentary on well established propositions in the literature. The second section of the chapter provides an overview of the volume and dimensions of FDI in developing countries. The third section outlines the main stylized facts in the literature on FDI and available empirical evidence on some of these propositions. The fourth section reviews these propositions in the context of the debate on the relationship between FDI and development. The final section pulls together the main conclusions of the chapter.

1 Statistical dimensions: size, growth and destination of FDI

The total stock of FDI in developing countries at the end of 1996 stood at $918 billion and accounted for 28 per cent of the world stock (Table 9.1). Annual flows of FDI to developing countries from the OECD countries increased substantially from around $20 billion in 1987 to $129 billion by the end of 1996. Latin America and Asia are the principal recipients of these flows. Some three-quarters of the total flows of FDI are received by only ten developing countries. The least developed countries account for less than 1 per cent of the total flows (Table 9.2).

As a proportion of total capital stock in developing countries as a whole, FDI accounts for 8 per cent. In some of the Latin American and Asian countries, however, the ratio is substantially higher. In 1995, for instance, FDI inflows accounted for over 25 per cent of total gross fixed capital formation in Singapore, China, Bolivia and Peru (Table 9.3). It should be noted that this statistic differs substantially from one country to

Table 9.1 Stock of inward foreign direct investment: share of principal countries, 1980–98

	1980	1985	1990	1995	1996	1998
Total World $bn	479.2	745.2	1,726.2	2,865.8	3,233.2	4,088.1
Developed } $bn	372.9	537.7	1,370.6	2,042.1	2,269.3	2,785.4
countries ∫ (%)	77.8	72.2	79.4	71.3	70.2	68.1
USA (%)	22.2	34.3	28.8	27.4	28.4	31.4
UK	16.9	11.9	15.9	15.4	15.2	11.7
France	6.1	6.2	6.3	7.2	7.4	6.4
Germany	9.8	6.9	8.1	8.2	7.5	8.2
EU	49.6	42.1	51.9	54.6	53.7	53.4
Japan	0.9	0.8	0.7	0.9	0.8	1.1
Developing } $bn	106.2	207.3	352.7	789.7	917.6	1,219.3
countries ∫ (%)	22.2	27.8	20.4	27.6	28.4	29.8
Malaysia (%)	5.6	4.1	4.0	4.7	4.6	3.4
Taiwan	2.3	1.4	2.8	2.0	1.9	1.7
Hong Kong	1.6	1.7	3.8	2.8	2.6	7.9
Singapore	5.8	6.3	8.1	7.3	7.3	7.1
Thailand	0.9	1.0	2.3	2.2	2.1	1.6
Korea	1.0	0.9	1.6	1.3	1.4	1.7
Indonesia	9.7	12.1	11.0	14.3	6.3	5.0
China	0.1	1.6	4.0	16.1	18.4	21.4
India	1.1	0.5	0.5	0.7	0.9	1.1
Mexico	7.6	9.1	9.2	8.1	7.8	5.0
Brazil	16.5	12.4	10.5	12.5	11.8	12.9
Chile	0.9	1.1	2.9	2.0	2.0	2.5
Argentina	5.0	3.2	2.5	3.1	3.1	3.7

Source: United Nations, *World Investment Report 1997: Transnational Corporations, Market Structure and Competition Policy,* New York; United Nations, World Investment Report 1999: Foreign Direct Investment and the Challenge of Development, New York.

Table 9.2 Inflows of foreign direct investment, 1985–98

	1985–90	1994	1995	1996	1998
Total World $bn	141.9	238.7	316.5	349.2	643.9
Developed countries $bn	116.7	142.4	205.9	208.2	460.4
USA (%)	41.6	35.0	29.5	40.6	42.0
UK	16.3	7.2	10.7	14.5	13.7
France	6.2	11.7	11.5	10.0	6.1
Germany	2.0	0.6	4.3	1.9	4.3
EU	45.2	50.8	53.9	47.7	50.0
Japan	0.3	0.6	0.02	0.1	0.7
Developing countries $bn	24.7	90.5	96.3	128.7	165.9
Latin America (%)	32.8	29.8	26.4	30.0	43.2
Brazil	5.3	3.4	5.1	7.4	17.3
Mexico	10.5	12.2	7.3	5.8	6.1
South and East Asia	50.2	61.5	67.7	63.1	46.6
Malaysia	4.5	4.8	4.3	4.1	2.2
Taiwan	3.6	1.5	1.7	1.1	0.2
Hong Kong	6.5	2.2	2.2	1.9	1.0
Singapore	12.1	6.1	7.2	7.3	4.3
Thailand	4.0	1.4	2.1	1.9	4.2
Korea	2.9	0.9	1.9	1.8	3.1
Indonesia	2.2	2.3	4.5	6.2	–0.2
China	10.9	37.3	37.3	32.9	27.4
Least developed countries	0.4	0.4	0.3	0.5	

Source: United Nations, *World Investment Report 1997: Transnational Corporations, Market Structure and Competition Policy*, New York; United Nations, World Investment Report 1999: Foreign Direct Investment and the Challenge of Development, New York.

the other. FDI accounts for a sizeable proportion of exports in some developing countries, particularly in East Asia. It is estimated that it accounts for more than 50 per cent of manufacturing exports and more than 40 per cent of total exports in Malaysia. In the case of Indonesia, it accounts for over 40 per cent of total exports (UNCTAD 1998). Exports of foreign affiliates in developing countries as a whole increased from $242 billion in 1982 to $585 billion in 1994 (Table 9.4). It is, however, noteworthy that the share of affiliates in the exports of developing countries has remained stationary at around 32 per cent, although the number of affiliates increased substantially over the period. In terms of geographical distribution of exports of affiliates, there has been a considerable shift away from Latin America towards Asia. Each of the two continents accounted for around 45 per cent of exports of foreign affiliates in developing countries in 1982, but by the end of 1994, the share of Asia increased dramatically to nearly 74 per cent, while that of Latin America declined to 24 per cent (Table 9.4).

The record of FDI on job creation in developing countries is much less impressive than its record on exports. Available data for the year 1992 shows that around 41 per cent (or 12 million) of the 29 million jobs created by the

Table 9.3 Inward stock of FDI as percentage of gross fixed capital formation (percentages)

	1985–90	1993	1994	1995	1997
Total World	5.4	4.4	4.5	5.2	7.7
Developed countries	5.5	3.7	3.5	4.4	6.5
USA	5.3	4.9	4.8	5.9	9.3
UK	13.7	11.0	6.8	13.2	18.6
France	10.3	9.0	6.9	8.6	9.7
Germany	1.6	0.4	0.2	1.7	2.3
EU	9.1	5.9	5.0	6.8	8.5
Japan	0.2	0.2	0.1	NA	0.3
Developing countries	8.0	6.6	8.0	8.2	10.3
Latin America	11.3	7.2	10.3	11.0	16.1
Argentina	13.0	31.0	4.8	11.7	12.7
Bolivia	25.0	14.9	17.6	47.7	53.8
Brazil	3.1	1.3	3.0	4.7	11.9
Mexico	16.9	6.0	14.3	17.1	16.3
Peru	15.5	8.7	37.3	24.7	11.1
South and East Asia	9.7	7.5	8.3	9.0	9.1
Malaysia	43.7	22.5	16.1	17.9	12.2
Taiwan	5.1	1.8	2.5	2.7	3.8
Hong Kong	12.2	7.1	8.2	8.4	9.9
Singapore	59.3	23.0	23.0	24.6	27.3
Thailand	10.2	3.4	2.3	2.9	6.8
Korea	1.9	0.5	0.6	1.1	1.8
Indonesia	7.6	3.8	3.7	6.5	7.0
China	14.5	20.0	24.5	25.7	14.3
Least developed countries	2.3	2.1	1.3	1.3	4.8

Source: United Nations, *World Development Report 1997: Transnational Corporations, Market Structure and Competition Policy*, New York; United Nations, World Investment Report 1999: Foreign Direct Investment and the Challenge of Development, New York.

Table 9.4 Exports of foreign affiliates, 1982–94

Region		Exports of foreign affiliates	
		1982	1994
Total World	($ billion)	**732.0**	**1,850.0**
Developed countries	($ billion)	491.0	1,255.0
	(% of total)	67.0	68.4
Developing countries	(% of total)	33.0	31.6
	($ billion)	**242.0**	**585.0**
of which:	(% of LDCs)		
Africa		9.5	2.5
Latin America		45.0	23.8
Asia		45.5	73.7

Source: United Nations, *World Development Report 1997: Transnational Corporations, Market Structure and Competition Policy*, New York.

Table 9.5 Estimated employment in transnational corporations (millions of employees)

	1975	1985	1990	1992
Total employment	40	65	70	73
Parents companies at home	NA	43	44	44
Foreign affiliates	NA	22	26	29
Developed countries	NA	15	17	17
Developing countries	NA	7	9	12

Source: United Nations (1994) *World Investment Report: Transnational Corporations, Employment and the Workplace*, New York.

foreign affiliates of multinational enterprises (MNEs) the world over were located in developing countries (Table 9.5). This represents a mere 2 per cent of the economically active population in these countries, although in some developing countries MNEs account for more than a quarter of total employment in the manufacturing sector. It is worth noting, however, that while the direct employment effects of FDI in developing countries may be small, the indirect employment effects (through forward and backward linkages and income growth induced multiplier effects) could be substantial.

2 Stylized facts and propositions

2.1 Determinants

As stated in the second section some three-quarters of FDI is received by a select group of ten developing countries. These are countries which possess one or more of the features and endowments sought by multinational enterprises, including natural resources, large domestic markets, endowments of relatively cheap but efficient labour, developed infrastructure, macro economic stability, liberal trade and investment regimes and institutional arrangements, such as export processing zones, designed to promote exports. The extant empirical literature identifies these features as the major determinants of FDI. The stylized facts on the determinants of FDI in developing countries are listed below.

• Countries which pursue liberal trade policies as opposed to foreign trade regimes designed to promote import substituting industrialization tend to receive relatively large volumes of FDI. In its strict version, the proposition is that foreign firms favour locations which are free of policy induced product and factor market distortions. They prefer to exploit the inherent comparative advantage in the production of goods and services host countries possess, rather than profit from short-term and uncertain inducements in the form of protection from import competition provided by tariffs and quotas. Specifically, Bhagwati's hypothesis is that:

With due adjustments for differences among countries for their economic size, political attitudes towards DFI and political stability, both the magnitude of DFI inflows and their efficacy in promoting economic growth will be greater over the long haul in countries pursuing the export promotion (EP) strategy than in countries pursuing the import substitution (IS) strategy.

(Bhagwati 1978: 212)

- In the absence of the type of endowments and investment climate sought by MNEs, various sorts of incentives, including tax concessions, tax holidays and investment subsidies, offered by host countries may not prove effective in attracting FDI. Competition between developing countries on the basis of incentives may not increase the total volume of FDI. As Guisinger (1992) notes, 'once the appropriate volume of investment is attained, further incentives aimed at increasing one country's share may prove to be collectively futile'.
- Political stability of host countries is a factor which influences the investment decisions of foreign firms. Opinion on the relative importance of political stability as opposed to economic stability as determinants of FDI is divided. Some studies assign primacy to economic as opposed to political factors (Root and Ahmad 1979, Levis 1979), others suggest that economic and political factors are equally important determinants of FDI in developing countries (Schneider and Frey 1985, Balasubramanyam and Salisu 1991). Studies based on interviews with managers of foreign firms suggest that it is the stability of policies over time rather than the stability of governments and political regimes which weigh heavily in the FDI decision process of foreign firms.
- Opinion on the relationship between foreign aid and FDI is also divided. Some empirical studies report a positive relationship between the two sorts of capital flows (Schneider and Frey 1985), whilst others report a negative relationship between aid flows and FDI. Those who detect a positive relationship argue that aid donors favour those countries which provide a favourable political climate for the operations of MNEs. Those who detect a negative relationship argue that countries exhibiting a relatively poor economic performance tend to receive relatively large amounts of aid, but their poor economic performance also deters them from receiving large volumes of FDI.

2.1.1 Empirical evidence

There are a number of econometric studies on the determinants of FDI in developing countries (Schneider and Frey 1985, Root and Ahmed 1979, Balasubramanyam and Salisu 1991). Most of these studies identify per capita GDP, the real wage rate, political stability and low inflation rates in the host countries to be the principal determinants of FDI.

Balasubramanyam and Salisu's study specifically tests Bhagwati's hypothesis that countries whose product and labour markets tend to be distortion-free (these are typically countries which follow a neutral or EP trade policy), attract a relatively high volume of FDI. Utilizing standard regression techniques, this study finds statistical support for Bhagwati's hypothesis (Table 9.6). It employs both the distortion index, devised by the World Bank, and the ratio of imports to GDP as proxies for the neutral trade policy identified in Bhagwati's hypothesis. It is also of interest that the study in general does not identify any specific relationship between aid and FDI. It also argues that economic variables such as exchange rate stability, income growth and inflation rate are adequate proxies for political variables and that the usually employed variables, such as strikes and coup d'états, as proxies for political stability may be suspect. This study, which relates to 38 FDI-recipient countries, is for the period 1970–80 and is dated.

Table 9.6 Estimated regression equations (dependent variable: annual average inflows of foreign direct investment per capita for the years 1970–80 for 38 developing countries)

Eq.	GDP/P	GDP_{gr}	AID/P	M/GDP	INFL	WR	DI	R^2
1	0.007[a]	−0.07	−0.13[b]	0.12[a]	−0.05[a]	−0.02[a]		0.65
	(5.02)	(0.58)	(2.04)	(3.01)	(5.26)	(2.55)		
2	0.01[a]	−0.61	0.12[c]		−0.05[a]	−0.03[a]	−2.87[b]	0.58
	(5.35)	(1.40)	(1.85)		(2.98)	(2.59)	(2.11)	
3	0.01[a]	−0.004		0.73[a]	−0.05[a]	−0.02		0.63
	(5.92)	(0.01)		(2.19)	(5.27)	(3.61)		
4	0.01[a]	−0.73[c]			−0.07[a]	−0.01[b]	−2.57	0.62
	(4.38)	(1.67)			(3.45)	(2.24)	(1.38)	

Source: Balasubramanyam and Salisu (1991)

Notes
[a], [b], [c] significant at the 1, 5, 10 per cent levels respectively. All equations were estimated by the ordinary least squares method
Figures in parentheses are absolute values of t-ratios of individual coefficients.
Intercept is suppressed due to space constraints.
Diagnostic tests for heteroscedasticity, model mis-specification and normality of residuals (not reported) show lack of evidence of these problems.

Definition of variables
GDP/P   Real per capita gross domestic product
GDP_{gr} Growth rate of gross domestic product
AID/P   Real aid per capita
M/GDP   Ratio of imports to gross domestic product
INFL   Rate of inflation
WR   Real manufacturing wage rate
DI   Distortion Index, composed by the World Bank

Sources of data GDP/P, GDP_{gr}, INF: World Bank (1984) *World Tables*, Vol. 1, Baltimore and London; M/GDP: International Monetary Fund (1988) *International Financial Statistics Yearbook*; AID/P: Organization for Economic Co-operation and Development, *Development Co-operation* (various issues); WR: UNIDO (1984) *Industrial Statistics*; DI: Agarwala, R. (1985) *Price Distortions and Growth in Developing Countries*, World Bank Staff Working Paper, No. 575, Washington, DC.

A recent study (Balasubramanyam and Salisu 1999) of a sample of 46 developing countries for the period 1982–95, however, confirms the results for the earlier period. These countries are divided into two main categories on the basis of the volume of FDI inflows over the period 1982–95. The first category consists of the top ten principal recipients of FDI[1], and the second group consists of the remaining 36 countries. The aim is to distinguish the characteristic features which enable the top ten countries to attract relatively high volumes of foreign direct investment. Discriminant analysis technique is used to identify the determinants of FDI which best discriminate between the two sets of countries (the top ten principal recipients of FDI and the 36 other developing countries). The results of the discriminant analysis confirm Balasubramanyam and Salisu's earlier findings that growth rate of GDP, per capita income and low inflation are the principal characteristics of the ten host recipients of FDI which distinguish them from the other countries in the sample (Table 9.7).

Table 9.7 Standardized canonical discriminant coefficients of determinants of foreign direct investment in 46 developing countries, 1982–95

	Function
AID/GNP	−0.407
DEBT/X	0.210
GDP gr	0.308
GNP/P	0.776
INFL	0.327
M/GDP	−0.337

		Stepwise Statistics			
Step	*Variable entered*	*Wilk's Lambda Exact F*			
		Statistic	*df1*	*df2*	*Sig. Level*
1	GNP/P	86.166	1	641	0.000
2	AID/GNP	65.985	2	640	0.000
3	INFL	47.210	3	639	0.000
4	GDP gr	38.509	4	638	0.000
5	M/GDP	32.684	5	637	0.000
6	DEBT/X	28.078	6	636	0.000

Method of estimation Discriminant Analysis (countries are classified into two distinct groups: the ten largest FDI recipients are classified as group 1 and the other 36 developing countries in the sample classified as group 2).

Definition of variables

AID/GNP	Ratio of foreign aid (AID) to gross national product (GNP)
DEBT/X	Ratio of total external debt (DEBT) to total exports (X)
GDP$_{gr}$	Growth rate of gross domestic product (GDP)
GNP/P	Real per capita GNP
INFL	Inflation rate
M/GDP	Ratio of imports (M) to GDP

Source of data World Bank (1997), World Development Indicators CD ROM Database.

2.2 Impact

During the 1960s and 1970s views on the impact of FDI on the economic welfare of developing countries ranged to extremes. Its left-wing critics charged FDI with many sins, including economic colonialism, exploitation of labour, importation of inappropriate taste patterns and technologies into developing countries. For its right-wing advocates FDI was a potent instrument of development, with a unique ability to transfer capital, know-how and technology to developing countries. The policy makers in these countries, for their part, entertained an ambivalent attitude towards FDI, wooing it for the riches it was supposed to offer and at the same time riling against MNEs for their supposed pernicious activities. There were several attempts at statistical verification of the contribution of FDI to the development process, but most of them were inconclusive. The literature on FDI during the sixties and the seventies mostly consisted of either a long list of benefits FDI could confer on developing countries, aptly dubbed the 'laundry list approach' by Paul Streeten, or a polemical diatribe on the neo-colonialist nature of the MNE and FDI.

By the middle of the 1980s, developing countries were much more sanguine about the contribution of FDI to the growth process. The debt crisis compelled most developing countries to increasingly rely on non-bank sources for their requirements of external capital. Also by then Japan, France, Germany and the Scandinavian countries had emerged as substantial exporters of capital and opened up new sources of FDI in addition to the traditional exporters—the USA and the UK. Paralleling the change in attitude of the developing countries are the much more objective attempts at assessing the contribution of FDI to development. This literature has yielded a useful set of facts and propositions listed below.

- The contribution of FDI to the growth of the national product tends to be relatively high in countries which have instituted liberal as opposed to protectionist trade regimes. Indeed, the tariff jumping variety of FDI imposes a series of social costs on the host countries. This proposition has been elegantly demonstrated with the aid of theoretical models (Bhagwati 1973, Brecher and Allejandro 1977). In the context of a standard $2\times2\times2$ trade model of the Heckscher–Ohlin–Samuelson variety, it is shown that inflows of foreign capital into the relatively capital-intensive importable industry in the presence of a tariff on the importable is immiserizing because of the following factors:
  - (a) the tariff imposes a production cost by distorting the prices faced by producers;
  - (b) inflows of capital increase the production of the capital-intensive good at tariff inclusive prices, à la the Rybczynski effect;
  - (c) the tariff imposes a consumption cost by distorting consumer prices; and

(d) the tariff-induced capital inflow generates increased earnings to foreign capital.

While (b) may serve to increase or reduce welfare in the host country, (a), (c) and (d) necessarily lower welfare.

In addition to these welfare-reducing effects of inflows of FDI into a distortion-ridden environment, there is the 'warm sun' effect of protection on both domestic and foreign owned firms. Protection which seals off competition from international trade provides little incentive for firms to innovate and improve managerial efficiency, they rest content with tried and tested techniques. Competition, however, spurs them to improve X-efficiency.

- FDI has an appreciable impact on growth in countries which have attained a threshold level of development (Blomstrom, Lipsey and Zejan 1996). The more developed of the developing countries are able to provide foreign firms with the sort of growth promoting ingredients they seek and hence their efficacy in promoting growth in these countries. This proposition also endorses the suggestion that foreign firms seek locations with well-developed infrastructure facilities and endowments of efficient labour.
- FDI has an appreciable impact on growth in countries which have accumulated substantial volumes of human capital (Balasubramanyam, Salisu and Sapsford 1995). This proposition elaborates upon the one cited above and isolates human capital endowments of recipient countries as one of the main ingredients which FDI utilizes in promoting growth.
- Productive efficiency tends to be high in the case of sectors of manufacturing activity with relatively high levels of FDI. This proposition is based on statistical evidence relating to the manufacturing sectors of Mexico, Brazil and Uruguay (Blomstrom 1986, Bielschowsky 1994, Kokko, Tansini and Zejan 1996). The case studies on which the proposition is based suggest that there could be technology spillovers from foreign owned firms to the locally owned firms.
- Productivity levels of local firms converge to the levels achieved by foreign owned firms in sectors with a strong foreign presence. This proposition too is based on statistical evidence from Mexico.
- Productive efficiency of foreign owned firms tends to be high in the face of competition from locally owned firms.
- Spillovers of technology from foreign to local firms are unlikely to occur in industries and sectors where the technology gap between the former and the latter is large.
- Evidence on the contribution of foreign firms to growth of exports from developing countries is mixed. In countries such as Malaysia, which have established a number of export processing zones, FDI has been instrumental in promoting exports of labour-intensive products such as electronic goods and clothing. In most other East Asian

countries, perhaps with the exception of Singapore, locally owned firms have been as active in promoting exports as foreign owned firms.

- The contribution of foreign owned firms to direct employment creation in developing countries is not noticeably high, except for firms located in the export processing zones in countries such as China and Malaysia. It is estimated that in 1992 MNEs created a total number of 73 million jobs the world over. Around 60 per cent of these jobs were located in the home countries of the MNEs. Of the other 29 million jobs created by MNEs around 12 million were in developing countries, which accounts for less than 2 per cent of the economically active population in developing countries. It is noteworthy that China alone accounted for 50 per cent of the jobs created by MNEs in developing countries. These estimates do not include the number of jobs indirectly created by MNEs, which are reported to be substantial.
- Evidence on how export processing zones, which are to be found in almost every developing country and heavily populated by foreign firms, have contributed to development is mixed. In some countries, when their costs and revenues are all evaluated at world prices, the social rate of return to investment is found to be very low or negative (Balasubramanyam 1988). In others such as China and Korea the social rate of return to investment is positive and they are reported to make a substantial contribution to employment.
- Trade related investment measures (TRIMs), such as local content requirements and export obligations imposed by host countries on foreign firms, are shown to introduce distortions and reduce consumer welfare (Greenaway 1991). Performance requirements are often tied up with incentives. The former provide a device to ensure that firms which are recipients of incentives do contribute to development objectives in some measure.
- Foreign owned firms in general use a relatively high proportion of imported inputs in the production process.

2.2.1 Empirical evidence

Some of the empirical evidence in support of these propositions has been cited in the foregoing. Two of the propositions which have been verified empirically, however, need elaboration. These relate to the impact of competition on productive efficiency of foreign firms and the proposition that efficient utilization of FDI requires a threshold level of human capital in the host countries.

To recall, Bhagwati's hypothesis states that the productive efficiency of foreign firms and their contribution to growth tend to be relatively high in countries which have pursued a liberal as opposed to protectionist trade regimes. A liberal economic environment free of both domestic and trade policy induced distortions promotes competition and hence static allocative efficiency and dynamic growth generating effects from inflows of FDI.

Balasubramanyam, Salisu and Sapsford's (1996) econometric tests suggest that Bhagwati's hypothesis is robust in the sense that the impact of FDI on growth tends to be relatively high in EP countries as opposed to that in IS countries. Utilizing regression analysis equation (1) was estimated against annual average data relating to a cross-section of 46 developing countries for the period 1970–85:

$$\dot{Y} = \alpha + \beta \dot{L} + \gamma(I/Y) + \varphi(FDI/Y) + \phi \dot{X} \tag{1}$$

where the dot over a variable represents growth rate, Y = gross domestic product, L = labour force, I = gross fixed capital formation and X = exports.

The equation was first estimated for the 46 countries as a whole, and then separately for 18 EP countries and 28 IS countries. The classification of the 46 countries into the EP and IS categories was based on the ratio of imports to GDP in each of the countries. It is the assumption here that countries with relatively high imports to GDP ratio are likely to be EP countries, as a relatively high ratio indicates low levels of import protection. Also, in the absence of import protection, investments in domestic market oriented industries are likely to be guided by market forces and comparative advantage, and in the absence of import protection there would be little need for artificial policy inducements designed to entice firms away from import substitution industries into export oriented industries. In sum, investments in the two categories are likely to be based on comparative advantage rather than policy induced. Conversely, in countries with a low ratio of imports to GDP, import protection tends to be high and investments in export industries require inducements such as export subsidies.

The results of the exercise are reported in Table 9.8. Briefly the results suggest that:

(a) the growth enhancing effects of FDI are stronger in countries which pursue an EP policy than in those following an IS regime;
(b) foreign capital in both sets of countries is more important than domestic capital in terms of its contribution to economic growth, as measured by the beta (standardized) regression coefficients.

Empirical findings of a recent study by Blomstrom and Sjoholm (1999) are worth noting here as it sheds additional light on the role of competition in promoting the productive efficiency of FDI. The study suggests that spill over effects of FDI are likely to be higher in the case of non-exporting local firms than in the case of export oriented local firms. This is because export oriented firms already face competition in world markets, but domestic market oriented firms face no such competition. Competition

Table 9.8 Estimated regression coefficients of determinants of growth rate of real GDP, 1970–85 (annual averages)

Eq. No.	Sample	Cons	FDI/Y	I/Y	l	x	R^2
1.1	All Countries (n = 46)	−0.20 (0.16)	1.84** (3.86)	−0.004 (0.09)	1.07** (2.73)	0.22** (4.74)	0.57
1.2	EP Countries (n = 18)	−0.63 (0.39)	1.84** (3.71)	0.01 (0.19)	0.95 (1.67)	0.30** (4.45)	0.79
1.3	IS Countries (n = 28)	−0.73 (0.34)	1.77 (1.39)	−0.03 (0.45)	1.07* (1.85)	0.16** (2.35)	0.37
1.4	All Countries (n = 46)	−0.18 (0.14)	1.65** (2.68)	−0.002 (0.05)	1.07** (2.73)	0.22** (4.76)	0.57
1.5	EP Countries (n = 18)	−0.52 (0.32)	1.68** (3.20)	0.01 (0.21)	0.93 (1.62)	0.30** (4.49)	0.79
1.6	IS Countries (n = 28)	−2.14 (0.40)	−10.16 (0.90)	0.22 (0.79)	1.21 (0.94)	0.30 (1.52)	0.01
1.7	EP Countries[a] (n = 10)	−3.25 (1.66)	1.54* (3.43)	0.06 (0.86)	2.09* (3.83)	0.22 (2.31)	0.90
1.8	IS Countries[a] (n = 24)	1.57 (0.83)	−0.14 (0.08)	−0.05 (0.71)	0.90 (1.61)	0.21 (2.02)	0.33
1.9	EP Countries[a] (n = 10)	−3.27 (1.66)	1.43* (2.93)	0.06 (0.91)	2.11* (3.83)	0.22 (2.28)	0.90
1.10	IS Countries (n = 24)	0.81 (0.21)	−13.71 (0.96)	0.18 (0.67)	0.32 (0.25)	0.35 (1.37)	0.01

Notes

FDI/Y is the ratio of FDI to GDP, I/Y is the ratio of domestic investment to GDP, l is the growth rate of labour force, x is the growth rate of real exports and Cons is an intercept term. Figures in parenthesis are absolute 't' values.
* estimated coefficient which is significantly different from zero at the 5 per cent level
** significance at the 1 per cent level
[a] Based on World Bank classification

Sources of data World Bank (1997) *World Development Indicators CD ROM Database.*

from foreign firms, however, compels locally owned firms to improve their productive efficiency. Statistical tests of the proposition in the context of the Indonesian manufacturing sector appear to support the proposition. Blomstrom and Sjoholm's caveat that this proposition does not endorse protection-induced inflows of FDI is worth noting; for protection induced welfare costs may outweigh the spill over effects of FDI.

The second proposition, which states that for FDI to be an effective growth promoting ingredient it requires a threshold level of human capital, has also received some empirical support. A study by Balasubramanyam, Salisu and Sapsford (1999) suggests that a certain threshold level of human capital endowments is necessary for FDI to impact on growth. The threshold level of human capital which enables FDI to be an effective ingredient of growth was identified in a group of forty-six developing

countries by first ranking the countries according to the prevailing level of
real wage rate in the manufacturing sectors of each of these countries. The
assumption here is that the level of the real wage indicates the relative
endowments of human capital in each of these countries. In other words,
the real wage is an output measure of human capital; the higher the level
of the real wage rate, the higher would be the volume of human capital in
the country. The threshold level of human capital was identified to be
slightly below the median real wage rate. A zero-one dummy variable
(DUM) was then constructed to represent the threshold level of human
capital. A value of zero was assigned to countries with a real wage rate
below the threshold level and a value of one was assigned to countries
whose real wages exceed the threshold.

Having identified the threshold level of human capital for the cross-
section of countries, equation (2) was estimated for the sample of forty-six
countries for the period 1970–85.

$$\dot{Y} = \alpha + \beta \dot{L} + \gamma(I/Y) + \varphi(FDI/Y) + \phi\dot{X} + \psi HC + \delta(FDIHCDUM) \quad (2)$$

where HC is human capital, proxied by growth in the real wage rate,
FDIHCDUM is the interaction term between foreign direct investment
(FDI/Y), human capital (HC), and the threshold level of human capital
(DUM).

The estimated coefficient of the FDI-human capital interaction term in
equation (2) is found to be positive and statistically significant at the 0.05
level (equation 1 of Table 9.9). Balasubramanyam, Salisu and Sapsford

Table 9.9 Estimated regression coefficients of determinants of growth rate of real
GDP, 1970–85 (annual averages) for 46 developing countries

Eq.	Cons	FDI/Y	I/Y	L̇	Ẋ	HC*	FDIHCDUM	R^2
1	−0.52	1.31[a]	0.001	0.95[a]	0.18[a]	0.20[a]		0.64
	(0.45)	(2.72)	(0.04)	(2.62)	(4.03)	(2.83)		
2	2.39	0.12	−0.04	0.77[b]	0.10[b]	0.22[a]	0.11[b]	0.76
	(1.19)	(0.12)	(1.21)	(2.38)	(2.20)	(3.57)	(2.60)	
3	1.54	0.96	−0.04	0.92[a]	0.17[a]	−0.10	0.17[b]	0.65
	(1.05)	(0.95)	(1.04)	(2.33)	(3.13)	(0.39)	(1.81)	
4	1.08	0.19	−0.04	0.84[b]	0.10[b]	0.22[a]	0.09[b]	0.76
	(0.84)	(0.17)	(1.20)	(2.42)	(2.09)	(3.53)	(1.93)	

Notes
[a], [b] denote 1 and 5 per cent levels of significance.
Figures in parentheses are 't' ratios of individual coefficients.
*Equations 1 and 2 HC = growth rate of real wage rate
  Equation 3, HC = secondary school enrolment rate
  Equation 4, HC = educational attainment (Barro and Lee measure)
Lagrangean multiplier tests indicate that the estimates are free of econometric problems of
heteroscedasticity, functional form and normality of residuals.

Sources of data World Bank (1997) *World Development Indicators CD ROM Database.*

(1999) also explore other measures of human capital and test for the interaction term between FDI and these alternative measures of human capital. As is well known, a number of studies have used school enrolment rates (Levine and Renelt 1992) and educational attainment (Barro and Lee 1993) as input measures of human capital. An interaction variable between FDI and each of these alternative proxies of human capital was entered into the above growth equation. Equations 2 and 3 in Table 9.9 show the estimated coefficients of the interaction terms between FDI and school enrolment rate, and FDI and educational attainment respectively. Both coefficients are positive and statistically significant at the 0.05 level. The results therefore provide support to the FDI-human capital interaction hypothesis.

3 Assessment

3.1 Growth

What do all these stylized facts and propositions add up to? The most striking feature of FDI in developing countries is that much of it is located in only ten countries, most of which are middle income countries. These are also the countries which are endowed with relatively high volumes of human capital and infrastructure facilities. FDI appears to be a rich country good, in a sense it finds its way to he that hath. This should be of little surprise, as the MNE which is the major purveyor of FDI is a profit maximizing entity; its mandate from its owners and shareholders is not to engage in altruistic development activities but to maximize profits. It can best deliver that which is expected of it in locations which provide an investment climate conducive to its operations. It could, however, be argued that the very act of FDI generates and promotes labour skills, technological change and investments in infrastructure. In fact, whether FDI promotes growth or growth promotes FDI is a much discussed proposition in the literature. To the extent that FDI is attracted to countries which possess one or more of the growth ingredients, it is to be concluded that growth promotes or attracts FDI rather than the other way round.

The other stylized facts concerning the impact of FDI also suggest as much. FDI appears to be an effective instrument of growth in countries which have achieved a threshold of growth and human capital. The inference to be drawn from this finding is that FDI educates and trains the available human capital, it does not add to the existing stock. If this is the case, the claim that the Multilateral Agreement on Investment (MAI) would somehow promote inflows of FDI into the poorer of the developing countries or the least developing countries rings hollow. It would be illogical to believe that profit maximizing firms would invest in countries with relatively low endowments of human capital, inadequate infrastructure and limited domestic markets. This would be so whether or not these countries accept a binding multilateral agreement.

The necessary condition for attracting FDI appears to be the possession of growth promoting ingredients. Poor countries, with their low levels of income and savings, are hardly in a position to afford the volume of investments required for the generation of substantial amounts of human capital and infrastructure facilities. But could not increased foreign aid enable these countries to equip themselves with the human capital and infrastructure facilities attractive to foreign firms? The Fitzgerald Report (1998) acknowledges the need for assistance from the OECD countries to the poor countries if they are later to embrace the MAI. The report, however, is concerned with the external debt overhang of the poor countries and their lack of legal and negotiating experience. It is in these areas that it enjoins the OECD countries to assist the poor countries. Admittedly, poor countries do need such assistance if they are to be credible signatories of the MAI, but assistance which enables them to equip themselves with the sort of institutions and growth ingredients attractive to foreign firms may be much more important.

Would the OECD countries offer increased aid to the poor developing countries without demanding a *quid pro quo*? Their demands could be for unhindered access to the markets of the poor countries for their MNEs. There is some though not conclusive evidence, as stated earlier, that countries which are favourably disposed to FDI and MNEs from the rich countries receive substantial amounts of aid. However, many developing countries which regard the MAI as no more than a neo-colonial design of the rich countries to delimit their economic sovereignty are likely to look upon foreign aid coupled with the MAI as a poisoned chalice.

3.2 Trade and FDI

The propositions concerning trade and FDI are also of interest in the context of the MAI and developing countries. The proposition that countries with liberal foreign trade regimes receive relatively large volumes of FDI is now well established; and in recent years several developing countries, including India, have liberalized their trade and investment regimes. However, liberalization of the trade regime alone may not attract large volumes of FDI, it has to be accompanied by the institution of a favourable economic environment for the operations of foreign firms. Such an environment has to be fostered with investments in infrastructure and promotion of labour skills. Moreover, efficient utilization of FDI requires coordination of trade policy with the policy framework governing FDI. In the absence of a coherent trade and FDI policy host countries may unwittingly give away incomes to MNEs, income levels which may be incommensurate with their contribution to the social product.

India's programme of liberalization instituted in 1991 is a case in point.

While the programme has reduced tariffs and quotas on a variety of capital goods and intermediates, most consumer goods imports are prohibited or subject to steep tariffs. However, restrictions on inflows of FDI into the consumer goods sector have been lifted, allowing foreign firms a protected market for consumer goods unhindered by import competition. The social costs of FDI in protected sectors referred to earlier have been rehearsed time and again in the literature. Such lack of coordination between trade and FDI policies may arise for a number of reasons. In the Indian case it is explained by the valiant attempts of policy makers at attracting increased volumes of FDI and at the same time appeasing local business and sectional interests, which argue that imports of luxury goods should not be allowed and that the interests of domestic firms producing consumer goods should be protected.

More generally, such lack of coordination between trade and FDI policies may arise if the agencies formulating the two policies are not one and the same. At the global level, if the WTO is the body charged with formulating trade policy and the OECD formulates FDI policy, coordination between the two may turn out to be problematical. Indeed, one of the objections of the developing countries to the MAI is that they would be unable to seek a *quid pro quo* for acceding to the MAI in the form of increased market access for their manufactured exports, if the MAI is formulated and administered by the OECD which has no mandate to regulate trade. This is a point of view which has merit for a number of reasons. First, most developing countries are not members of the OECD, in any case it does not provide a forum for negotiations on trade which is the preserve of the WTO. Second, there is no presumption that FDI necessarily generates and promotes exports save in the case of a select few developing countries. Although technology spillovers and other externalities arising from the operations of foreign owned firms do assist the promotion of exports, it is the locally owned firms which are the prime movers of exports. Ways and means of gaining negotiated access to the markets of the developed countries is, therefore, essential for developing countries. Third, the growth in regionalism in the West has posed severe obstacles to the exports of developing countries, especially for the Asian countries.

3.3 Labour and environmental standards and FDI

Various proposals concerning labour and environmental standards discussed in the MAI have far-reaching implications for the trade of developing countries. Institution of high standards would impact on both foreign owned and locally owned firms, whether or not the principle of non-discrimination is applied. If the principle of non-discrimination is applied, locally owned firms which are unable to comply because of the resource costs involved may find themselves at a competitive disadvantage *vis-à-vis* foreign firms. If the principle of non-discrimination is not enforced, locally owned firms which do not comply with high standards may be denied access to the markets of developed countries. The demands by sectional interests in the developed countries for the inclusion of a social clause covering labour and environmental standards in the articles of the WTO suggests as much. The wisdom of incorporating a social clause in the WTO is a much debated issue (Brittan 1995, Bhagwati 1995), but the thought that fears of competition from cheap labour imports, rather than concern for labour and the environment, may underlie the demands for a social clause cannot be dismissed.

All this is not to say that developing countries should be exempt from labour and environmental standards. Destruction of the environment and exploitation of labour ought not to be condoned. It is just that developing countries must be assured of access to resources required to implement high standards. Trade and not foreign aid may be an efficient and reliable method of providing such access. The developing countries may be justified in demanding a *quid pro quo* in the form of liberal access to the markets of developed countries for their exports of labour intensive goods in return for instituting high standards. Here again the need is for coordination of trade and FDI policies which can only be achieved by an organization such as the WTO.

It is often argued that in the absence of a mandate requiring developing countries to institute high labour and environmental standards they may successfully attract low quality FDI. In other words, they may lower standards and attract FDI which contributes to the destruction of the environment and the exploitation of labour (Fitzgerald 1998). The underlying assumption of this argument is that foreign firms are ever eager to seek locations with low environment and labour standards. The facts of the matter are that most MNEs are eager to promote high standards if for no other reason than that it is good business practice, it promotes their image and it is socially acceptable. The problem resides in the inability of resource starved poor countries to comply with high standards, not with either the desire of MNEs, or for that matter the desire of poor countries to promote flows of low quality FDI. As stated earlier, the challenge facing international organizations which are wrestling with the task of formulating a multilateral agreement on investment is one of providing the developing countries with the resources required for instituting high labour and environmental standards.

3.4 Import-intensity of foreign firms

The other trade related stylistic fact which has a bearing on the MAI is the observed relatively high-import intensity of foreign owned firms. Here, the one issue which any agreement has to consider is the much-discussed transfer pricing practices by MNEs. It is difficult to ascertain the extent to which the high-import propensity of foreign owned firms reflects transfer pricing practices; but the fact that such practices do contribute to their high import propensity cannot be denied. Provisions for the mitigation of transfer pricing practices in the MAI would be in the interests of developing countries. One other proposition which has a bearing on the import propensity of foreign firms has to do with local content requirements instituted by most developing countries. Admittedly, such requirements along with several other TRIMs are to be phased out following the Uruguay Round Trade negotiations. Again, as most foreign firms, including the Japanese firms, argue they would source imports from local sources if only they were available. Also many MNEs have successfully promoted local suppliers of inputs, in some cases these are subsidiaries of the MNEs, in others they are locally owned but have access to markets and technical help from the MNEs. Even so, local content requirements, judiciously used, may influence the foreign firms to bear the search and development costs involved in establishing local suppliers of components and parts (Balasubramanyam 1991).

It is noteworthy here that there is no suggestion in the empirical literature on FDI that performance requirements imposed by host governments have either deterred inflows of FDI or impaired their efficiency. Admittedly, both IBM and Coca-Cola withdrew from India during the early 1970s rather than comply with the requirement that they should shed a certain proportion of equity in favour of local investors. However, their withdrawal was in response to equity sharing requirements and not performance requirements. Most MNEs seem to comply with requirements concerning employment of local nationals and local content requirements. It should, however, be noted that such regulations may impose social costs on host countries if they are instituted indiscriminately without heed to the stage of development of host countries. Here again the strong suggestion is that FDI contributes to development objectives in countries which are able to provide it with the sort of environment and ingredients it requires for efficient operations.

Indeed, the one strong message in the empirical literature is that in the presence of appropriate policies and investment climate, FDI could be a potent instrument of development; it not only provides capital but, more importantly, it is also a channel for transfer of technology and know-how from the rich to the poor countries; it is not, however, a panacea for the development problem. As stated earlier, efficient utilization of FDI requires a threshold of human capital, well developed infrastructure facilities, a competitive market environment, stability of economic policy and allegiance to a liberal foreign trade regime. It is only a select few developing countries which can boast of all these endowments and policy orientation. Admittedly, China is now the recipient of large volumes of FDI, but China has registered a growth rate in excess of 10 per cent in recent years, she is relatively well endowed with human capital and has attempted to follow economic policies designed to maintain economic stability. But not

218   *V.N. Balasubramanyam and Mohammed A. Salisu*

all developing countries can measure up to the exacting demands made by foreign firms. Those which do not possess these attributes and proffer either various sorts of incentives or protection from competition as a sort of a compensation for the attributes they lack, only succeed in transferring incomes from their citizens to foreign firms.

One attribute of host countries which is essential for the efficient utilization of FDI is competition in product markets from locally owned firms. Such competition compels foreign firms to engage in product market innovations and cost cutting exercises, and such research and development is beneficial to host countries. It is also competition which provides for the generation of externalities much talked about as a major gain to host countries from the operation of foreign firms. In the face of competition, foreign firms would invest in labour training and new product innovations and competing locally owned firms may successfully copy such innovations and entice skilled labour without having to pay for such training. Recent press reports from India suggest such competition for trained labour in the soft drinks producing industry, which includes both Pepsi and Coca-Cola and locally owned producers of soft drinks.

In sum, the literature on the impact of FDI suggests that, while it does contribute to growth, technological development and employment, the conditions required for its efficient utilization are fairly stringent. It is not a recipe for development which each and every developing country can hope to adopt. It can augment existing human resources, it can provide new technologies, it can supply capital, but it cannot assure the efficient utilization of all these ingredients. In the absence of cooperand factors and an economic environment conducive for their operation, foreign firms may augment their private profits but do little for the growth of the social product of their host countries.

4 Conclusion

The main conclusions of this chapter can be briefly summarized. First, FDI is attracted to a select number of developing countries which possess the sort of ingredients and economic environment sought by foreign firms. Several other countries which do not possess such endowments have attracted relatively low volumes of FDI, but they have paid a price for it, both in the form of fiscal incentives and low social rates of return from foreign investments. Second, FDI can be a potent instrument of development, but only in the presence of a threshold level of human capital, well developed infrastructure facilities and a stable economic climate. These are, however, features exhibited by the more developed of the developing countries, for this reason the chapter has argued that FDI is a rich country's good. Until and unless developing countries are able to reach a threshold level of development, they may neither attract large volumes of FDI nor efficiently utilize that which they attract. Third, trade and FDI are intertwined. Efficient utilization of FDI requires coordination of trade and FDI policies. International agreements relating to FDI should recognize this interdependence between trade and FDI, and such agreements should be negotiated in fora which have a mandate to negotiate on both FDI and trade. Fourth, there is no evidence to suggest that judiciously formulated performance requirements impair efficient operations of foreign firms.

Besides these and other conclusions, the chapter has argued that the premise underlying the MAI—that a legal framework governing the rights and obligations of foreign firms in developing countries will serve to increase FDI flows to developing countries and also promote its efficient utilization—is false. An agreement enforceable by law will no doubt be reassuring to potential investors, but a binding agreement alone is unlikely to lure foreign firms to the relatively poor developing countries. The sort of ingredients and economic environment foreign firms seek in these countries would have to be developed with considerable amounts of investments. Resources required for such investments have to be provided through foreign aid and increased access to the markets for the labour-intensive exports of developing countries. FDI is a catalyst of development, not its prime mover. A catalyst will work only in the presence of other elements which can instigate the process of development. Attempts at formulating multilateral agreements on FDI should recognize this basic fact.

Notes

1. The top ten developing country hosts to FDI, as identified by the United Nations' (1997) World Investment Report, are: Argentina, Brazil, Chile, China, Colombia, Indonesia, Malaysia, Mexico, Peru and Singapore.
2. The study concentrates on the period 1970–85 because during this period most countries in the sample consistently followed a single trade policy strategy (either EP or IS), but after 1985 a number of them switched over from IS to EP.

References

Balasubramanyam, V.N. (1988) 'Export processing zones in developing countries', in D. Greenaway (ed.) *Economic Development and International Trade*, London: Macmillan.
—— (1991) 'Putting trims to good use', *World Development*, Vol. 19, No. 9: 1215–24.
Balasubramanyam, V.N. and Salisu, M.A. (1991) 'Export promotion, import substitution and direct foreign investment in less developed countries', in A. Koekkoek and L.B.M. Mennes (eds) *International Trade and Global Environment: Essays in Honour of Jagdish Bhagwati*, London: Routledge.
Balasubramanyam, V.N., Salisu, M.A. and Sapsford, D. (1995) 'Foreign direct investment and growth', Discussion paper, Department of Economics, Lancaster University.

—— (1996) 'Foreign direct investment and growth in EP and IS countries', *The Economic Journal*, Vol. 106, No. 434: 92–105.

—— (1999) 'Foreign direct investment as an engine of growth', *Journal of International Trade and Economic Development*, Vol. 8, No. 1: 27–40.

Barro, R.J. and Lee, J.W. (1993) 'International comparisons of educational attainment', *Journal of Monetary Economics*, Vol. 32, No. 3: 363–94.

Bhagwati, J. (1973) 'The theory of immiserizing growth' in A.K. Swoboda and B. Connoly (eds) *International Trade and Money*, London.

—— (1978) 'Anatomy and Consequences of Exchange Control Regimes', New York: National Bureau of Economic Research.

—— (1995) 'Trade liberalisation and "fair trade" demands', *The World Economy*, Vol. 18, No. 6: 745–59.

Bielschowsky, R. (1994) 'Two studies on transnational corporations in the Brazilian manufacturing sector: the 1980s and early 1990s', Division of Production, Productivity and Management Discussion Paper, No. 18, ECLAC.

Blomstrom, M. (1986) 'Foreign investment and productive efficiency', *Journal of Industrial Economics*, Vol. 35, No. 1: 97–110.

Blomstrom, M., Lipsey, R.E. and Zejan, M. (1994) 'What explains growth in developing countries', NBER Discussion Paper, No. 1924.

Blomstrom, M. and Sjoholm, F. (1999) 'Technology transfer and spillovers: does local participation with multinationals matter?', NBER Working Paper, No. 6816.

Brecher, R. and Alejandro, C. (1977) 'Tariffs, foreign capital and immiserising growth', *Journal of International Economics*, Vol. 7: 317–22.

Brittan, L. (1995) 'How to make trade liberalisation popular', *The World Economy*, Vol. 18, No. 6: 760–7.

de Mello, L.R. (1996) 'Foreign direct investment, international knowledge transfers and endogenous growth: time series evidence', mimeo, Department of Economics, University of Kent, UK.

Fitzgerald, E.V.K. (1998) *The Development Implications of the Multilateral Agreement on Investment*, London: DFID.

Greenaway, D. (1991) 'Why are we negotiating on trims', in D. Greenaway, R.C. Hine et al. (eds) *Global Protectionism*, London: Macmillan.

Guisinger, S. (1992) 'Rhetoric and reality in international business: a note on the effectiveness of incentives', *Transnational Corporations*, Vol. 1: 111–23.

Kokko, A., Tansini, R. and Zejan, M.C. (1996) 'Local technological capability and productivity spillovers from FDI in the Uruguayan manufacturing sector', *Journal of Development Studies*, Vol. 32: 602–11.

Lal, D. (1975) *Appraising Foreign Investment in Developing Countries*, London: Heinemann.

Levine, R. and Renelt, D. (1992) 'A sensitivity analysis of cross-country growth regressions', *American Economic Review*, Vol. 82, No. 4: 942–63.

Levis, M. (1979) 'Does political instability in developing countries affect foreign investment inflows? An empirical examination', *Management International Review*, Vol. 19: 59–68.

Root, F. and Ahmad, A. (1979) 'Empirical determinants of manufacturing direct foreign investment in developing countries', *Economic Development and Cultural Change*, Vol. 27: 751–67.

Schneider, F. and Frey, B.S. (1985) 'Economic and political determinants of foreign direct investment', *World Development*, Vol. 13, No. 2: 161–73.

Part III
Globalization and capital markets

10 Financial liberalization and the globalization of financial services

Two lessons from the East Asian experience

Philip Arestis, Panicos Demetriades and Bassam Fattouh

1 Introduction

One of the most important developments in the financial services industry in the last decade or so has been the massive increase in the volumes of cross-border capital flows, both between developed countries and between developed and developing countries. Although there was a substantial decline in capital flows to developing countries during most of the 1980s, the 1990s witnessed the resurgence of capital flow to many developing countries. IMF (1999: 1) cites some interesting figures: 'Net private capital flows to developing countries trebled to more than $150 billion a year during 1995–7 from roughly $50 billion a year during 1987–9. At the same time the ratio of private capital flows to domestic investment in developing countries increased to 20 per cent in 1996 from only 3 per cent in 1990.' To a large extent these increased flows, which no doubt contributed to the increased globalization of the industry, were the result of financial reforms that were implemented as part of international agreements. In the case of the European Union (EU), the creation of the single market led to the abolition of all remaining capital controls in the late 1980s. In the case of emerging market economies these reforms were usually implemented with the encouragement of the Bretton Woods institutions, in some cases being part of structural adjustment programmes.

Simple textbook models suggest that the free movement of capital across borders should raise consumer welfare by allowing a smoother consumption path, and should result in a more efficient allocation of resources as world's savings are directed towards the world's most productive investment opportunities. However, the reality has been much more complex than simple textbook models would suggest, especially given the informational asymmetries which accompany financial transactions of any kind. These asymmetries have meant that where prudential regulation has been weak, moral hazard-type problems resulted in excessive risk-taking by financial institutions or investors, which then led to financial fragility or banking crises.

In this chapter we tell two different, but complementary, stories from the East Asian region which help demonstrate both the potential and pitfalls of the globalization of financial services. These are the story of Hong Kong, where the globalization of the financial services industry went hand-in-hand with regional economic development, and the story of the Asian financial crisis of 1997, where premature capital account liberalization destabilized the economies of the region and led to contagion effects throughout East Asia.

2 Banking centres and regional development: the case of Hong Kong[1]

A recent survey on financial centres by *The Economist* (1998) considers Hong Kong as one of the leading financial centres in the world and a major player in the global financial industry. Hong Kong's financial markets are highly developed. As an important financial centre for foreign exchange, Hong Kong had, for example in 1998, an average daily turnover of more than US$78 billion (BIS 1998). Its stock exchange plays an important role in raising capital for Chinese firms (Fattouh 1999). Hong Kong had also become an active centre for fund management with more than 1,800 unit trusts and funds registered. In fact, most international fund managers run their Asian business from Hong Kong. Furthermore, Asian corporate-finance teams of international banks run their main operation from Hong Kong. This can be partly attributed to the large number of multinational firms' offices located in Hong Kong. More than 2,000 multi-national firms, as well as the largest accounting companies and legal advisers, maintain regional offices there (*The Economist* 1998). Hong Kong is also emerging as an important centre for derivative instruments trading. In 1998, it ranked third in the region (after Japan and Singapore) with a daily average of OTC foreign exchange contracts and interest rate contracts of US$3.8 billion dollars (BIS 1998).

In terms of banking development, Hong Kong has managed over the years to attract a large number of foreign bank offices. Table 10.1 presents some evidence on the importance of foreign bank presence in Hong Kong. In 1990, 213 of the top 500 banks in the world had a physical presence in Hong Kong. This number increased to 236 in 1994, but declined later to 215 in 1997. A broader measure is the number of overseas banks in Hong Kong. By the end of 1996, 337 foreign banks had some form of representation in Hong Kong. Table 10.2 shows that Japan by far had the largest representation with 92 bank offices, followed by China (35), Indonesia (20) and South Korea (19). Germany has the largest European representation in Hong Kong (16), followed by France and the UK (12). The presence of US banks in the Hong Kong market is also substantial with a total

Table 10.1 Presence of world's largest 500[b] banks in Hong Kong (end of December 1997)

World Ranking[a]	1990	1991	1992	1993	1994	1995	1996	1997
1–20	18	19	19	18	19	19	19	19
21–50	26	22	24	26	28	27	26	26
51–100	37	34	35	37	38	39	36	36
101–200	55	53	53	58	65	57	57	51
201–500	77	78	80	71	86	86	75	83
Sub total	213	206	211	210	236	228	213	215
Others	110	107	99	101	93	109	121	122
Total	323	313	310	311	329	337	334	337

Source: Hong Kong Monetary Authority Annual Report 1997.

Note
[a] Top 500 banks in the world ranked by total assets less contra items.
[b] The figures exclude banks incorporated in Hong Kong.

Table 10.2 Foreign banks in Hong Kong by country of origin (end of 1996)

	Licensed banks	Restricted licensed banks	Deposit taking companies	Total number of banks in Hong Kong
Australia	4	0	0	4
China	18	3	14	35
India	4	0	3	7
Indonesia	3	1	16	20
Japan	46	11	35	92
Malaysia	3	2	3	8
Pakistan	1	0	2	3
Philippines	2	1	6	9
Singapore	6	2	2	10
South Korea	3	6	10	19
Thailand	1	4	1	6
Vietnam	0	0	1	1
Austria	2	0	0	2
Belgium/Luxembourg	3	0	0	3
Denmark	1	0	1	2
France	9	3	4	16
Germany	10	1	1	12
Italy	6	0	0	6
Netherlands	3	2	0	5
Spain	3	0	0	3
Sweden	2	0	0	2
Switzerland	3	1	0	4
UK	7	4	1	12
Bahrain	1	0	1	2
UAE	0	1	1	2
Canada	6	1	1	8
USA	14	11	7	32
South Africa	0	3	1	4

Source: Hong Kong Monetary Authority Annual Report 1997.

of 32 bank offices. Notice that despite Hong Kong's success in attracting a large number of banks from all over the world, Asian banks constitute the largest share of the Hong Kong market (around 70 per cent) in terms of number of overseas banks.

There is little doubt that financial and capital account liberalization and regulations that encouraged foreign banks entry contributed enormously to Hong Kong's current position as one of the leading financial centres. In fact, it could be argued that the emergence of Hong Kong as an important banking centre can be mainly attributed to differences in regulatory and tax structures within the East Asian region (Cassard 1994).[2] One interesting issue to explore is whether Hong Kong's financial centre played a significant role in enhancing its economic performance and that of the region, or whether deregulation of Hong Kong's financial structure and the globalization of its banking industry destabilized its financial system and generated negative shocks to other parts in the region. In this section, we provide empirical evidence which shows that the orderly development of banking centres such as Hong Kong can play a significant positive role, not only in financing domestic economic development, but also in financing regional economic development. Furthermore, our empirical evidence suggests that the globalization of Hong Kong's banking system has contributed significantly to its financial development.

Before we discuss our empirical results, we present some evidence which shows the importance of links between Hong Kong's financial system and the rest of the East Asia and Pacific region. The regional and international role of Hong Kong becomes evident when we examine the external position of Hong Kong's financial system against geographical regions (see Table 10.3). In 1997, net external claims against Asia and the Pacific *vis-à-vis* all sectors amounted to HK$550 billion. The bulk of net external claims are against Japan, China, South Korea and Thailand. It is interesting to note that Japan is the major supplier of funds to banks in Hong Kong. These funds are mainly intermediated through the inter-bank market. Despite this fact, Hong Kong still has total net claims of HK$229 billion against Japan. This position is achieved through lending to non-bank customers in Japan. In a sense, there is some sort of circular flow of funds by which Hong Kong attracts funds from Japan through the inter-bank market and then re-lends these funds to Japanese non-bank customers (Fattouh 1999). In the Asia and Pacific region, Singapore and, to a lesser extent, Macau and Vanuatu are net suppliers of funds to Hong Kong. Unlike the Japanese position, both banks and non-banks in these economies channel funds to Hong Kong. The fact that the bulk of external claims are against economies in the region reflects the regional lending role of Hong Kong. Hong Kong also plays an important role in channelling foreign capital from the rest of the world to the region through arrangement, syndication and management of Eurocredits to Asia Pacific borrowers (Fattouh 1999). This becomes evident when we examine the position of banks in Hong Kong

Table 10.3 Geographical distribution of external assets of banks in Hong Kong
vis-à-vis banks and non-banks (end of 1997, HK$ billions)

	Net claims on (liabilities to) banks outside Hong Kong	Net claims on (liabilities to) non-banks outside Hong Kong	Total net claims (liabilities)
Asia and Pacific	**−1,105**	**1,655**	**550**
Japan	−1,288	1,517	229
South Korea	54	53	107
Mainland China	47	54	101
Thailand	57	25	82
Australia	36	11	47
Indonesia	5	16	21
New Zealand	10	10	20
Taiwan	32	−15	17
Philippines	6	4	10
India	0	8	8
Malaysia	−1	3	2
Vanuatu	−4	−3	−7
Macau	−15	−4	−19
Singapore	−41	−25	−66
Others	−4	0	−4
North America	**−16**	**27**	**11**
Canada	4	14	18
United States	−20	13	−7
Caribbean	**−69**	**−178**	**−247**
Panama	−1	18	17
Bahamas	14	0	14
Bermuda	−1	5	4
Netherlands Antilles	0	−57	−57
Cayman Islands	−81	−122	−203
Others	−2	−21	−23
Western Europe	**−276**	**−15**	**−291**
Italy	1	7	8
Sweden	0	4	4
Switzerland	4	−1	3
Finland	0	1	1
Denmark	−3	2	−1
Austria	−9	0	−9
Germany	−30	12	−18
Luxembourg	−25	0	−25
Netherlands	10	−46	−36
Belgium	−47	3	−44
France	−65	5	−60
United Kingdom	−105	−9	−114
Middle East	**−15**	**−2**	**−17**
Bahrain	−2	−1	−3
Saudi Arabia	−3	0	−3
UAE	−8	−1	−9
Others	−2	−2	−4

Source: Monetary Authority of Hong Kong Annual Report.

against the rest of the world. Western Europe, the Caribbean, and the Middle East are important net suppliers of funds to banks, with the Cayman Islands and the United Kingdom being by far the major supplier of funds to Hong Kong. Western Europe, France, Belgium and Netherlands are also important net suppliers of funds.

This evidence clearly suggests that there are some important links between Hong Kong's banking system and the regional economies on the one hand, and Hong Kong and the rest of the world on the other.[3] Using two different data sets and various econometric techniques, Fattouh (1999) shows that the large number of foreign banks in Hong Kong is related to regional and international trade rather than merely to Hong Kong's trade activity. Specifically, trade links between a host country and Hong Kong cannot explain the number of banks from that country to Hong Kong. On the other hand, trade links with the region are found to be a major determinant of the number of banks there. In what follows, we provide some empirical evidence on the importance of these links in terms of the relationship between financial developments in Hong Kong and the economic performance of the region, drawing on Fattouh (1999) and Deidda and Fattouh (2000). Specifically, we show that instead of destabilizing the banking system, the globalization of Hong Kong's financial industry, reflected mainly in its cross-border lending activity, contributed significantly to Hong Kong's financial development.

We start our empirical analysis by observing that various models aimed at assessing the contribution of the banking system to economic development are based on the assumption that the banking system is linked to the domestic economy (Arestis and Demetriades 1997). Although this feature characterizes banking systems of most economies in the world, there are few financial systems, Hong Kong being a prime example, that also specialize in financing foreign production and international trade. This fact is likely to have a bearing on the relationship between economic and financial development in Hong Kong. Specifically, in the case of banking centres, it is no longer necessary that financial development is linked to domestic economic development. Instead, it may be possible that financial development is determined by regional economic activity (Deidda and Fattouh 2000). In order to explore this hypothesis, we first explain our empirical methodology, and then examine the relationship between a broad measure of financial development, which includes the level of external and domestic lending to GDP, and economic development. We then proceed to investigate the relationship between financial development and regional economic activity.

2.1 Empirical methodology

The empirical investigation is carried out in a vector autoregression (VAR) framework, using the maximum likelihood approach of Johansen

(1988) to estimate long-run relationships (cointegrating vectors) between the variables in question. This technique allows the identification of multiple long-run relationships and is an efficient method of testing causality (see Toda and Phillips 1993; Hall and Milne 1994). The Johansen method is based on a vector error correction (VECM) representation of VAR(p) model, which can be written as:

$$\Delta x_t = \Gamma_1 \Delta x_{t-1} + \Gamma_2 \Delta x_{t-2} + \ldots + \Gamma_{p-1} \Delta x_{t-p+1} + \Pi x_{t-p} + \Psi D_t + u_t \tag{1}$$

where x is an $n \times 1$ vector of the first order integrated variables, $\Gamma_1, \Gamma_2,$ $\ldots \Gamma_n$, are $n \times n$ matrices of parameters, D is a set of I(0) deterministic variables such as constant, trend and dummies and u is a vector of normally and independently distributed errors with zero mean and constant variance. The steady state (equilibrium) properties of equation (1) are characterized by the rank of Π, a square matrix of size n. The existence of a cointegrating vector implies that Π is rank deficient. Johansen (1988) derives the maximal eigenvalue and trace statistics for testing the rank of the Π. If Π is of rank $(0 < r < n)$ then it can be decomposed into two matrices α $(n \times r)$ and β $(n \times r)$ such that:

$$\Pi = \alpha \beta' \tag{2}$$

The rows of β are interpreted as the distinct cointegrating vectors whereby $\beta'x$ form stationary processes. The α's are the error correction coefficients which indicate the speeds of adjustment towards equilibrium. Substituting (2) into (1), we get:

$$\Delta x_t = \Gamma_1 \Delta x_{t-1} + \Gamma_2 \Delta x_{t-2} + \ldots + \Gamma_{p-1} \Delta x_{t-p+1} + \alpha(\beta' x_{t-p}) + \Psi D_t + u_t \tag{3}$$

This is a basic specification for the test of long-run causality. A test of zero restriction on the α's is a test of weak exogeneity when the parameters of interest are long-run (Johansen and Juselius 1992). We employ weak exogeneity tests to examine the issue of long-run causality between the variables in the system. The null of $\alpha = 0$ can be tested by standard likelihood ratio test.

2.2 Empirical results

Following the empirical literature on finance and growth (Arestis and Demetriades 1997), we first test for the existence of a stable relationship between a broad measure of financial development, which includes the level of external and domestic lending to GDP, and economic development proxied by real GDP using the Johansen procedure (Table 10.4).[4] Utilizing different lag structures, we cannot reject the null hypothesis of no cointegrating vector. Both the eigenvalue and the trace statistics indicate

Table 10.4 Financial and economic development in Hong Kong (Johansen
procedure) (sample period: 1975 Q1–1996 Q4)

Variables entered			
LBCLAIMY = Logarithm of the level of domestic claims and external claims to nominal GDP			
LRGDP = Logarithm of real GDP			

Lag Length of VAR = 8 *(based on Sim Likelihood Ratio Test)*

Ho: Rank = p	Trace Statistics	Eigenvalue Stat	
$p = 0$	13.05	$p = 0$	9.85

Lag Length of VAR = 12

$p = 0$	17.70	$p = 0$	9.53

that there is no stable relationship between broad financial development
and domestic economic development. In fact, this is partly reflected in the
size of Hong Kong's banking system, which is six times larger than the size
of the domestic economy. Despite the fact that Hong Kong experienced
rapid economic growth, such economic performance alone cannot explain
the high level of Hong Kong's financial development. In other words,
broad financial development cannot be solely attributed to economic
trends within Hong Kong itself.

Due to the special features of banking centres, the relationship between
financial and economic development needs special treatment and attention. Specifically, the econometric approach should differentiate between
domestic and external lending activity as well as introduce regional economic activity to the analysis. We account for this by including four variables in the cointegration analysis. We employ two different measures of
financial development: domestic financial development, measured by
claims on private sector in Hong Kong to nominal GDP, and external
financial development, measured by external claims to nominal GDP. In
addition to real domestic GDP, we include the level of regional exports to
proxy the level of regional economic activity. While domestic economic
and financial development are likely to be linked, external financial development is likely to be linked with regional economic activity, as proxied by
the region's exports to the rest of the world. We test for these hypotheses
using the Johansen procedure.

The results of applying Dickey-Fuller (DF) and Augmented Dickey-
Fuller (ADF) to the level of the series indicate that the null hypothesis of
a unit root cannot be rejected for the level-series. Applying the DF and
ADF test on the first differenced series indicates that the null hypothesis
can be rejected at conventional levels and hence we conclude that all the
variables are integrated of degree I(1).[5] The variables are therefore
analysed using Johansen's (1988) cointegration analysis. Table 10.5 reports
the maximal eigenvalue and the trace statistics which suggest the existence
of two cointegrating vectors at the 5 per cent level. Hence, a cointegration
rank of two is imposed upon the system and further tests are carried out in

Table 10.5 Banking and economic development in Hong Kong (Johansen procedure) (sample period: 1975 Q1–1996 Q4)

Variables entered
LDFD = Logarithm of the ratio of claims on domestic private sector to nominal GDP
LFFD = Logarithm of the ratio of external claims to nominal GDP
LRGDP = Logarithm of Hong Kong's GDP in real terms
LREXP = Logarithm of regional exports in real terms

Lag Length of VAR = 8

Ho: Rank = p	Trace Statistics	Eigenvalue Stat	
$p = 0$	115.42*	$p = 0$	75.93*
$p <= 1$	39.49**	$p = 1$	24.60**
$p <= 2$	14.90	$p = 2$	12.17

Analysis assuming two cointegrating vectors

System exogeneity test: *chi squared* (2)	LR test	*p*-value
LDFD exogenous to the system	36.63	0.00
LFFFD exogenous to the system	6.55	0.04
LRGDP exogenous to the system	14.46	0.00
LREXP exogenous to the system	9.01	0.01

Exclusion of variables in the long run	LR test	*p*-value
LDDFD included in the system	38.62	0.00
LFFD included in the system	26.88	0.00
LRGDP included in the system	31.66	0.00
LREXP included in the system	5.94	0.05
Constant included in the system	39.54	0.00

2 cointegrating Vectors:
LDFD = −21.330* + 2.261 LRGDP*
LFFD = −19.019 + 2.172 LDFD* + 0.704 LREXP**

	LR test	*p*-value
Joint test on over-identifying restrictions *Chi-squared* (1)	0.95	0.33

	T-test	*p*-value
LRGDP exogenous to the first vector	3.870	0.00
LDFD exogenous to the second vector	7.128	0.00
LREXP exogenous to the second vector	1.231	0.20

Notes
A dummy variable is included to take into account the banking crisis of 1983.
* significant at the 1 per cent level; ** significant at the 5 per cent level.

order to reduce the system to economically interpretable relationships (Pesaran and Smith 1995). The first step is a test for weak exogeneity of each of the variables in the system, which corresponds to a notion of long-run causality (Johansen 1992). This involves testing whether the speed of the adjustment coefficient (α) is significantly different from zero. If α which is related to variable x_1 is zero, then when estimating the parameters of the model there is no loss of information of not including Δx_1. Tests for weak exogeneity on each of the variables show that none of the variables are weakly exogenous to the system at the 10 per cent level. Hence, no restrictions are imposed on the system. The next step is to test zero restrictions on the parameters of the cointegrating vector. These tests show that none of the variables should be excluded from the system.

After imposing normalization and exclusion restrictions on the β vectors, we obtain the two cointegrating vectors shown in Table 10.5. The estimates show some interesting patterns. The first cointegrating vector shows that the level of domestic financial development (or the extent of domestic financing) is positively linked to the level of economic development, with causality running from the latter to the former. This piece of evidence is consistent with the empirical literature which persistently finds a stable relationship between financial and economic development, although the direction of causality can differ across countries (Demetriades and Hussein 1996; Arestis and Demetriades 1997). Interestingly, this result clearly shows that in the context of financial centres it is important to differentiate between the domestic and external lending activity of the centre. A broad measure of financial development based on these two aspects of lending activity cannot be solely attributed to economic trends within Hong Kong itself and hence we are unlikely to find an overall meaningful relationship between financial and economic development. On the other hand, if we consider a narrower measure of financial development based on domestic lending activity only, then we are likely to find links between the level of domestic economic development and banking activity.

The second cointegrating vector reveals some interesting patterns regarding regional trade activity and Hong Kong's external lending activity. Given Hong Kong's position as a financial centre which not only attracts deposits from abroad, but also arranges and extends Euroloans for its region, we expect that Hong Kong's external lending activity to depend positively on the region's economic activity. The empirical results show that external banking development (or the extent of external lending activity) is positively associated with the region's trade activity. Hence, Hong Kong's cross border lending activity, rather than destabilizing its banking system, contributed significantly to its development. The cointegrating vector also shows a positive relationship between the extent of domestic and external lending activity, with causality running in both directions. This evidence is consistent with the notion of complete transferability of knowledge in which the financial centre finances both domestic and regional economic activity (Deidda and Fattouh 2000). Specifically, in their paper, the evolution of the lending activity of a financial centre depends on the transferability of knowledge across countries. When transferability of knowledge is complete, the financial centre would finance both domestic and foreign production. In this case, we expect foreign and domestic financial activity to move together. On the other hand, when technology is not transferable, polarization of financial activity, by which the centre finances either domestic or foreign activity, can occur.

In short, the evidence presented in this section shows that globalization of the banking industry contributed positively to Hong Kong's financial development. Furthermore, globalization of Hong Kong's banking industry has contributed positively to regional economic development by channelling funds from outside the region to countries in the East Asia Pacific region. Both theory and empirical evidence vividly confirm that conclusion. By contrast, financial and capital account liberalization in East Asian countries produced financial instability. We move on in what follows to explore recent East Asian experience.

3 Premature capital account liberalization and the East Asian financial crisis

It has been argued (Fischer and Reisen 1992: 3) that 'dismantling capital controls is generally presumed to generate economic benefits through increased opportunities for intertemporal trade and cross-border diversification in both assets and liabilities, by imposing macroeconomic discipline on national governments, and from the rising costs and ineffectiveness of controls as economic development proceeds'. However, the recent financial crisis in East Asia has vividly demonstrated that the liberalization and globalization of capital flows in the presence of institutional weaknesses in parts of a region may destabilize the whole region through the transmission of financial fragility across borders. These weaknesses ranged from inadequate or ineffective prudential regulation of financial institutions, especially those engaged in cross-border transactions, to cronyism and corruption. In more general terms, the following stylized facts of financial markets in developing countries are pertinent: 'credit markets are segmented, competition among banks is weak, joint ownership between the corporate sector and financial institutions predominates, asset quality in banks' balance sheets is low, and institutional arrangements for prudential supervision and regulation are inadequate' (Fischer and Reisen 1992: 14).

While there is an ongoing debate on the exact causes of the East Asian financial crisis, there is now widespread agreement that the freedom and ease with which massive amounts of capital flowed across borders played a major part in it (Demetriades and Fattouh 1999a). During the financial liberalization of the 1990s, East Asian countries removed or loosened controls on companies' foreign borrowing, abandoned coordination of borrowing and investments, while failing to strengthen bank supervision. Banks were thus able to borrow from abroad, directly or indirectly through offshore branches, without government control. This activity was further enhanced by the fact that they could borrow abroad much more cheaply than they could domestically. Table 10.6, which shows the amount of inflows intermediated through the banking system in the 'crisis'

Table 10.6 External position of reporting banks[1] *vis-à-vis* individual countries (*vis-à-vis* all sectors, US$ millions)

	Indonesia	Korea	Malaysia	Thailand
1990	29,632	32,219	8,444	15,997
1991	34,213	39,155	9,166	22,705
1992	40,086	42,653	11,094	27,430
1993	37,203	45,216	16,034	34,738
1994	41,626	60,973	14,484	54,465
1995	48,932	83,260	18,756	92,178
1996	57,850	109,148	25,908	99,274
1997	62,786	103,787	29,077	79,655
1998	57,626	87,257	26,165	70,789

Source: BIS, International Banking and Financial Market Developments (various issues).

Note
[1] Reporting banks include European, North American (Canada and USA), Japanese and banks in reporting offshore centres (Bahamas, Bahrain, Cayman Islands, Hong Kong, Netherlands Antilles and Singapore) with significant international banking business.

economies (Thailand, Indonesia, Malaysia and Korea), suggests that these countries witnessed a dramatic increase in the amount of inflows intermediated through the banking system during the 1990s. The increase in capital flows caused an expansion in domestic banks' balance sheets which permitted the acceleration of bank credit. The credit boom was also facilitated by western investors who transferred vast amounts of capital to East Asian countries. The better returns in these countries when markets elsewhere offered less profitable opportunities, especially in the industrialized countries owing to slow economic growth there, was a significant contributory factor. Low interest rates in the industrialized world led investors to search for higher returns, and these East Asian countries offered fertile ground. The high growth rates and high interest rates of these countries produced large interest rate differentials which international investors exploited. The 10-year experience of currency pegs, which implied fluctuations relative to dollar of less than 10 per cent, was another significant contributory factor.

3.1 Credit-asset booms in Thailand, Malaysia and Indonesia, but not in Korea

Prior to 1996 those developments did not appear to have caused any obvious problems. In 1996 and 1997, however, problems started arising in many countries, as much of the capital flow was directed towards cyclical sectors such as the real estate sector, equity markets, and towards activities which could be considered very risky. What is of some interest in this context, however, is the different experience across these countries. While in Thailand, Malaysia and Indonesia, the banking system was heavily exposed to the real estate sector, thus becoming susceptible to their downward price movements, existing evidence suggests that South Korean

Table 10.7 Banking risks

	Indonesia	Malaysia	Thailand	South Korea
Property sector risks	*High*	*High*	*High*	*Moderate*
Exposure (% of total loans)	25–30	30–40	30–40	10–15
Loans/Collateral (%)	80–100	80–100	80–100	60–100

Source: JP Morgan (1998: 5) *Asian Financial Markets: Second Quarter 1998*, JP Morgan
Economic Research Group.

banks' exposure to real estate sector was moderate (see Table 10.7). In fact,
examining the allocation of credit across sectors in South Korea shows that
the share of real estate sector of total lending declined during 1996 and 1997.
Real domestic credit growth also slowed down from 11.46 per cent per
annum in the 1980s to 9.69 per cent during 1990–5, accelerating to 15.43 per
cent in 1996 (Demetriades and Fattouh 1999b). In short, there is little evidence to suggest that the South Korean crisis was triggered by the collapse of
an asset price bubble caused by a lending boom.

3.2 Korean banks and cross-border lending activity

Although, in principle and in practice, net capital inflows are usually associated with a rapid expansion of domestic credit and asset price bubbles,
there are some cases in which increases in capital inflows may not
necessarily result in domestic lending or investment booms. For instance,
Folkerts-Landau et al. (1995) argue that if the expansion of bank liabilities
is met by extension of loans to importers, then the increase in domestic
credit can be minimal, since these inflows are used to finance current
account deficits. Capital inflows can also be sterilized by imposing reserve
requirements on foreign deposits or by resorting to indirect monetary
instruments. A number of East Asian economies, especially Malaysia and
South Korea, resorted to such policies in an attempt to sterilize capital
inflows (Folkerts-Landau et al. 1995). A third channel which could also
help sterilize capital inflows is related to domestic banks' cross-border
banking activity. Specifically, if the expansion in foreign liabilities caused
by an increase in capital inflows is met by an expansion in foreign assets,
then a lending–investment boom may not necessarily occur. This channel
seems to have been in operation in South Korea. Monetary authorities in
South Korea also attempted to sterilize capital inflows through encouraging capital outflows by early repayment of external debt (Folkerts-Landau
et al. 1995).

Over the second half of the 1990s, South Korean banks witnessed a dramatic increase in the size of their balance sheets against a background of a
decline in domestic liabilities. One striking feature in the financial data for
1992–6 is the decline in inter-bank operations, reflected in the severe
decline in the rate of growth of Certificate of Deposits (CDs) and bank

Table 10.8 Real growth rates of various types of bank deposits in South Korea
(commercial banks) (percentage)

	Total demand deposits	Time and saving deposits	Deposits in foreign currency	CDs	Foreign liabilities	Deposits from other banks	Deposits denominated in foreign currency
1991	6.79	6.02	−4.70	27.02	30.75	−59.01	10.58
1992	−11.29	7.71	2.23	9.69	3.44	−32.90	2.64
1993	−16.03	10.40	30.34	33.68	−2.69	56.29	12.97
1994	0.45	19.67	8.10	23.73	33.27	−2.96	18.57
1995	23.70	34.82	6.76	27.82	38.95	46.18	19.21
1996	5.98	15.75	1.43	−2.12	40.57	133.27	16.92
1997	−20.26	32.43	203.54	−10.67	26.53	−54.69	91.35

Source: Bank of Korea.

deposits with other banks (Table 10.8). Since banks are likely to assess the creditworthiness of their counterparts more accurately than depositors, a decline in inter-bank market activity reflects perceived deterioration of some banks' balance sheets. In fact, this was reflected in the real interest rates: rates on CDs increased from 3 per cent in 1995 to 9.75 per cent in 1997. The increase in bad credit and non-performing loans is also a clear indication of deterioration in the banks' position. The decrease in the domestic deposit base, however, was offset by an increase in foreign liabilities. In 1997, real growth in foreign currency denominated deposits amounted to 91 per cent.[6] Most of these funds were obtained from international banks, which reflects the poor quality of international banks' risk assessment, and South Korean deposits in foreign currency mainly raised in international capital markets.

Faced with an expansion of foreign liabilities, low investment opportunities at home and increased deterioration of domestic borrowers, South Korean banks tried to minimize the currency risk both by increasing their loans in foreign currency as well as increasing their share of foreign assets. The first option is quite tricky: although banks can shift the currency risk to customers, in reality they are simply substituting currency risk, with credit risk, as devaluation can hit borrowers hard, creating a large pool of non-performing loans. In all cases, loans in foreign currency remained low compared to foreign denominated deposits which indicates that banks could not completely shift the currency risk. The second option of increasing the share of foreign assets can be more viable under certain conditions. In principle, this increase in cross-border assets can both ease the pressures on exchange rate and asset prices caused by capital inflows, and provide domestic banks with greater opportunities for diversification. Furthermore, if managed properly, investing abroad could reduce or even eliminate currency risk although maturity mismatch risks are likely to remain. Finally, if the expansion in foreign liabilities caused by an increase in capital inflows is met by an expansion in foreign assets, then a country could avoid a lending–investment boom. However, this practice may expose the banking system and domestic investors to a number of serious problems, especially in the absence of international banking expertise and the proper financial infrastructure, as the South Korean experience has shown.

In South Korea, capital account liberalization contributed to a large increase in banks' foreign assets. Although total assets of commercial banks increased during 1995–7, the growth of foreign assets more than doubled the growth in total assets over the same period (Table 10.9). In principle, one would expect such a practice to be effective in diversifying away from projects with low productivity and away from cyclical sectors, such as real estate. This practice can also be partly responsible for avoiding a lending boom to the extent witnessed in Thailand, Indonesia and Malaysia. However, given the institutional weaknesses of the South Korean financial system and the lack of international banking expertise, most of these inflows were directed towards very risky foreign assets. A JP Morgan (1998: 5) report suggests that Korean banks' overseas investments were highly risky. In fact, there is some evidence that South Korean banks invested heavily in Russian junk bonds (Chote 1998). Given the established links of South Korean companies with its region, it is very possible that South Korean banks have also invested in the other crisis countries. Hence, instead of minimizing the problems associated with capital inflows, the practice of investing abroad increased the riskiness of banks' portfolios and magnified the existing weaknesses in the financial system. It is important to note that, even if South Korean banks have invested in relatively safe assets, cross-border banking activity would have not necessarily eliminated maturity mismatch risk. Hence, a change in sentiment which causes capital outflows and capital flights could still have generated serious problems of illiquidity and insolvency.

Table 10.9 Increasing importance of foreign assets of commercial banks in South Korea (percentage)

Year	Real growth of total assets of commercial banks	Real growth of foreign assets of commercial banks	Real growth in loans in foreign currency of commercial banks
1991	9.02	8.09	13.74
1992	5.19	16.82	−6.49
1993	3.05	21.72	−4.91
1994	10.55	18.02	22.14
1995	20.66	27.25	26.10
1996	12.79	25.36	23.79
1997	35.49	90.21	63.93

Source: Bank of Korea.

The conclusion following the discussion in this section is that the recent East Asian crisis may very well have been caused by premature capital account reforms which always run a high risk of being counter-productive. While short-term capital inflows may in principle supplement domestic savings and lead to higher levels of investment and growth rates, this benefit is likely to be small in East Asian economies because of the already high savings and investment ratios. Thus, it may not be possible to invest short-term capital inflows in domestic productive investments. This may push domestic banks to invest domestically in unproductive projects and/or to invest these short-term inflows abroad. The last option can be very costly if banks and domestic investors do not have the required banking expertise and the infrastructure which allow them to identify profitable investment opportunities abroad. In South Korea, the existing evidence suggests that banks invested their funds in risky cross-border assets which magnified the underlying structural problems of the banking system. This is in contrast with Hong Kong, where cross-border lending activity contributed to the banking system's development.

4 Summary and Conclusions

Recent movements towards the globalization of financial services have posed major benefits and risks to developing countries. This chapter discussed the potential and pitfalls of such changes on the domestic banking system with special reference to banks' investment decisions abroad. While Hong Kong's banking system, with its developed financial infrastructure and international banking expertise over a long period of time, was able to benefit from the globalization of financial flows, the banking systems of other countries in the region exhibited weaknesses that did not allow them to benefit from the full integration into global markets. Instead, capital flows magnified the existing weaknesses of the banking system and increased the riskiness of East Asian banks' portfolios and led to asset price bubbles. Although South Korean banks have managed to avoid an asset price bubble, partly by encouraging gross outflows and investment abroad, this policy proved costly. In the absence of an adequate regulatory and supervisory framework and international banking expertise which permits the identification of profitable investment opportunities abroad, Korean investors ended up funding risky foreign investments. This led to a further deterioration in banks' portfolios, increasing the banking system's vulnerability to speculative attacks.

Notes

1. This section draws on Fattouh (1999) and Deidda and Fattouh (2000).
2. Deidda and Fattouh (2000) build a model in which comparative advantage, in terms of regulatory and tax concessions, does not determine emergence on its own. Instead, they emphasize the importance of economies of scale in financial

intermediation as being the major determinant of emergence of banking centres.
3. Deidda and Fattouh (2000) explore more explicitly these links in terms of emergence of banking centres and the evolution of their lending activities.
4. Precise definitions of the variables and data sources are provided in the appendix.
5. The results of the DF and ADF exercises are not reported here but can be obtained from the authors upon request.
6. The South Korean authorities use the notion of residency to differentiate foreign from domestic liabilities. A more broad definition is to use the concept of residency and currency of denomination (Bryant 1987).

Data appendix

Broad financial development (LBFD)

Broad financial development is measured by the sum of banks' claims on private sector in Hong Kong and external claims to nominal GDP. Data for claims on private sector in Hong Kong and external claims were obtained from *Hong Kong Monthly Digest of Statistics* (various issues). Data on nominal GDP were obtained from *Census and Statistics Department, Estimates of GDP 1961 to 1995* and *Hong Kong Monthly Digest of Statistics* (various issues).

Real GDP (LRGDP)

Data on quarterly GDP data were obtained from *Census and Statistics Department, Estimates of GDP 1961 to 1995* and *Hong Kong Monthly Digest of Statistics* (various issues). The data were transformed into US dollars using the exchange rate data from the *IMF, International Financial Statistics* (CD-ROM 1998: 6).

Domestic financial development (LDFD)

Domestic financial development refers to the ratio of claims on domestic private sector to nominal GDP. Data for claims on private sector in Hong Kong and were obtained from *Hong Kong Monthly Digest of Statistics* (various issues). Nominal GDP data were obtained from *Census and Statistics Department, Estimates of GDP 1961 to 1995* and *Hong Kong Monthly Digest Statistics* (various issues).

External financial development (LFFD)

External financial development is measured by the ratio of external assets to nominal GDP. Data for external claims were obtained from *Hong Kong Monthly Digest of Statistics* (various issues). Nominal and real GDP data were obtained from *Census and Statistics Department, Estimates of GDP 1961 to 1995* and *Hong Kong Monthly Digest of Statistics* (various issues).

Regional exports (LREXP)

Regional exports refer to the Asian countries' exports to the rest of the world deflated by the regional consumer price index. Data for regional exports and consumer price index were obtained from *IMF, International Financial Statistics* (CD-ROM 1998: 6).

References

Arestis, P. and Demetriades, P.O. (1997) 'Financial development and economic growth: assessing the evidence', *The Economic Journal*, Vol. 107: 783–99.

BIS (1998) 'Central Bank survey of foreign exchange and derivatives market activity in April 1998: preliminary global data', Bank for International Settlements, press release.

Bryant, R.C. (1987) *International Financial Intermediation*, Washington, DC: Brookings Institution.

Cassard, M. (1994) 'The role of offshore centers in international financial intermediation', IMF Working paper, No. 94/107, Washington, DC: International Monetary Fund.

Chote, R. (1998) 'Financial crises: the lessons of Asia', *CEPR Conference Report*, No. 6, London: Centre for Economic Policy Research.

Deidda, L. and Fattouh, B. (2000) 'The emergence and evolution of banking centres', Centre for Financial and Management Studies Working Paper, SOAS, University of London, February.

Demetriades, P. and Fattouh, B. (1999a) 'The South Korean financial crisis: competing explanations and policy lessons for financial liberalization', *International Affairs*, Vol. 75, No. 4, October.

—— (1999b) 'Unproductive credit and the South Korean crisis', paper presented at Royal Economic Society Annual Conference, University of Nottingham, 29 March–1 April 1999.

Demetriades, P. and Hussein, K. (1996) 'Financial development and economic growth: cointegration and causality tests for 16 countries', *Journal of Development Economics*, Vol. 51: 387–411.

Eaton, J. (1994) 'Cross border banking', Institute for Economic Development, Discussion Paper, No. 42, Boston University.

The Economist (1998) 'A survey of financial centres', *The Economist*, Vol. 347, No. 8067.

Fattouh, B. (1999) *On the Determinants of Competitiveness, Emergence and Evolution of Financial Centres*, Unpublished PhD thesis, Economics Department at the School of Oriental and African Studies, University of London.

Hall, S.G. and Milne, A. (1994) 'The relevance of P-star analysis to UK monetary policy', *The Economic Journal*, Vol. 104: 587–604.

IMF (1999) 'Liberalizing capital movements: some analytical issues', *Economic Issues*, No. 17, Washington, DC: International Monetary Fund.

Fischer, B. and Reisen, H. (1992) 'Towards capital account convertibility', *OECD Development Centre*, Policy Brief No. 4.

Folkerts-Landau, D. et al. (1995) 'Effect of capital flows on the domestic financial sectors in APEC developing countries', in M.S. Khan and C.M. Reinhart (eds)

Capital Flows in the APEC Region, Washington, DC: International Monetary Fund.

Johansen, S. (1988) 'Statistical analysis of co-integrating vectors', *Journal of Economic Dynamics and Control*, Vol. 12: 231–54.

—— (1992) 'Testing for weak exogeneity and the order of cointegration in the UK money demand data', *Journal of Policy Modeling*, Vol. 14: 313–34.

Johansen, S. and Juselius, K. (1992) 'Some structural hypotheses in a multivariate cointegration analysis of purchasing power parity and uncovered interest parity for the UK', *Journal of Econometrics*, Vol. 53: 211–44.

JP Morgan (1998) *Asian Financial Markets: Second Quarter 1998*, JP Morgan Economic Research Group.

Pesaran, M.H. and Smith, R.P. (1995) 'Estimating long-run relationships from dynamic heterogeneous panel', *Journal of Econometrics*, Vol. 68: 79–113.

Toda, H.Y. and Phillips, P.C.B. (1993) 'Vector autoregression and causality', *Econometrica*, Vol. 61: 1367–93.

Part IV

Globalization via unilateral actions

11 Unilateral liberalization in a multilateral world

Martin Richardson

1 Introduction

Recent years have seen a great deal of trade liberalization worldwide, particularly via the vehicles of regionalism and bilateralism. Certainly, the focus of analysts and policy economists has been firmly on these means of liberalization. At the same time, however, many countries have also chosen to liberalize their international trade regimes unilaterally. Only recently have analysts begun to focus on unilateralism as a means of trade liberalization: (see Bhagwati 1999).

What effects, if any, does liberalization through other multilateral[1] means have on the incentive to liberalize unilaterally? We argue that one of the most important sets of reasons for unilateral reforms is precisely that it occurs in an environment of multilateral liberalization. We discuss some theoretical reasons for this before looking briefly at two recent cases. The first is the APEC experience, which we argue is best thought of as a qualified unilateralism; the second is recent experience in New Zealand where unilateralism has been a leading means of liberalization. We suggest that unilateralism has been almost necessary for New Zealand, by virtue of the breadth of its microeconomic reform programme. A final section concludes.

2 What is unilateralism?

The defining feature of unilateral as opposed to multilateral trade liberalization is the absence of reciprocity. Classification of reforms would then seem to be a simple exercise, but several commentators have noted that what appears to be a fairly straightforward notion is in fact rather complicated. McCulloch (1997) talks of 'soft' reciprocity—apparently unilateral reductions in trade barriers actually executed in return for non-trade-related benefits, such as loans. We might also talk of 'soft unilateralism', in which apparently unilateral actions are taken in the expectation that they benefit the reforming country through a non-obvious reciprocity. McCulloch (1997), for instance, notes that the aggressive practices of one country might induce apparently unilateral reforms from trading partners, where in fact it is the threat of actions in the *absence* of such reforms that triggers them: she suggests that many recent reforms in Latin America are attributable to this sort of soft unilateralism.

Nevertheless, there are notable cases in which countries have liberalized their international trading regimes without being subject to these pressures and without any obvious reciprocity. A good example is the liberalization of New Zealand's trade policy since 1984.[2] The World Trade Organization (WTO 1996: 1) has commented: 'New Zealand has transformed its economy from one that was highly protected and regulated to one that is among the most market-oriented and open in the world', and New Zealand is very explicit in recognizing unilateralism as a means of liberalization separate from, if complementary to, alternative routes. 'The overall goal of New Zealand's trade policy ... is simultaneously pursued through four interrelated policy tracks. (i) Domestic policy: the unilateral track ... (ii) The bilateral track ... (iii) The regional track ... (iv) The WTO: the multilateral track.' (WTO 1996: 144.) This suggests another aspect of unilateralism: that it may be only partial and discriminatory. I discuss below a number of reasons why preferential tariff reductions against a partner might lead a country unilaterally to reduce trade barriers against other countries. This sort of unilateralism appears non-discriminatory on its face, but is *de facto* preferential in that previously favourably treated partners now no longer get preferential treatment.

3 Why unilateralism?

3.1 In a neoclassical setting

The case for unilateralism in a competitive, neo-classical world is very clear, but probably of little use as a guideline to trade reforms in practice. Essentially, a country's optimal unilateral tariff is increasing in the country's size (measured in terms of its ability to affect its terms of trade.) Accordingly, the only case for unilateral free trade is when a country has no price-making ability at all in its international markets.[3] Even then, the timing of moves is relevant. Raimondos-Moller and Woodland (2000) show that a perfectly small country may have a non-zero optimal tariff when it is a first mover in a tariff-setting game. Second, in richer models in which countries produce differentiated products, no country is ever small in the sense of having a zero optimal tariff (Gros 1987). Third, in practice most countries have some degree of price-setting power in their actual international markets, if only because of rigidities in contractual arrangements, transport costs and so on. Fourth, there are some notable historical episodes of large countries unilaterally liberalizing their trade, an observation which casts some doubt on the relevance of terms-of-trade effects in driving tariff-setting. Fifth, and perhaps most significant for our purposes, this simple observation says nothing on the *process* of liberalization, that is, on the *transition* from high tariffs to lower tariffs. In general, if low tariffs are optimal for a small country, why do we not observe them at all times? More particularly, why should a global environment of multilateral reforms trigger this realization of a country's best interests?

One possible response to the first of these questions is that policy makers are mistaken about their country's best interests and something happens to correct their faulty perceptions; that something could be multilateral reforms. In itself this is an unsatisfactory answer, of course, as it leaves policy makers' ignorance unexplained, but it is possible to construct rather more sophisticated stories in which there is a 'demonstration effect' from tariff reforms in other countries—perhaps through multilateralism— which convinces a country to reform. This has been argued as a practical matter. Garnaut (1998b: 9) writes concerning the 'far-reaching trade liberalization' of many countries in the Western Pacific since the mid-1980s that '[t]he fact that many have followed this course at the same time has supported the process in each ... through demonstration of the domestic gains of unilateral liberalization'. In the standard terms-of-trade setting of the optimal tariff argument, one might suppose that policy makers are unsure of a country's impact on world prices but downgrade their beliefs about their own market power on observing the consequences of liberalization by similar, neighbour countries.

3.2 Political economy

An alternative context to the neo-classical one in which to examine unilateralism is one in which we consider the political economy of actual tariff-setting. The rationale for non-zero tariffs in a small country is then much greater, potentially. Tariffs and other trade restrictions may be used for income-distributional reasons (see Hillman (1989) and the references therein) and may be the outcome of a voting procedure (Mayer 1974) or a political lobbying game (Grossman and Helpman 1994), for instance. Reforms can then be triggered by changes in the underlying policy setting mechanism, such as a change in the governing political party or shifts in political support.

The New Zealand (NZ) experience fits well with this model where it was a change of government in 1984 that triggered trade, and other, reforms (see Evans and Richardson (1999). However, in the decades prior to its reforms, NZ evolved an elaborate system of 'tariff compensation' as its manufacturing protection grew—it was recognized that this protection hurt exporters (notably in the agricultural sector) and various governments, committed to keeping protection in place, introduced assorted policies (export subsidies, minimum price schemes, fertilizer subsidies etc.) to 'offset' its damage. Both the original system of protection in NZ and the tariff 'compensation' were driven largely by income-distributional concerns and together they constituted some political equilibrium, one propping up the other. However, the compensation aspect of the package came under fire from trading partners when the USA leaned on NZ in 1981 to sign the GATT code on Countervailing Duties (CVDs) (see Lattimore and Wooding 1996: 329). The 'stick' to induce this was the threat that otherwise no injury test would be applied in the USA for CVD complaints against subsidized NZ exports. Once the compensation was dismantled through the agency of this external pressure, the political equilibrium maintaining the protection was upset. So, in this view, NZ's apparently unilateral trade reforms were at least in part a political adjustment as an elaborate house of cards was dismantled by external pressure.[4]

In the political economy setting we could again model uncertainty by a policy maker, perhaps over the income-distributional consequences of trade policy, which is reduced on observation of reforms by similar countries, again generating a demonstration effect of trade liberalization. Another route to unilateral reform here is through the political activity of foreign producers.

4 Unilateralism in a multilateral setting

One can also argue that *preferential* liberalization might also serve a 'demonstration effect' purpose and lead to non-discriminatory liberalization. Certainly this has been suggested in the New Zealand case, where preferential tariff reductions against Australia did not lead to the collapse of the manufacturing sector and so emboldened reformers to liberalize all external tariffs.

We can, however, tell richer stories that explain unilateral liberalization. The effect we have noted is the idea that one country's liberalization demonstrates to others that liberalization may be beneficial. If they then liberalize in turn this can benefit the original liberalizer: the initial reform might then be perceived as soft unilateralism, in the sense defined earlier. Coates and Ludema (1997) construct a model which illustrates precisely this effect. Two large countries are involved in a process of negotiations over tariff reductions. In this model policy makers are interested in maximizing national welfare as usually understood but domestic political interests may, with some probability, be able to block a prospective bilateral trade agreement that one government negotiates with another. If this happens in one of the countries then the government of the other country, although free to set its standard 'optimal' tariff, may prefer instead to reduce its tariffs unilaterally.

Such a reduction serves two purposes. First, such an equilibrium action reduces the probability of the agreement being blocked in the first place. Import-competing producers in a country benefit from high tariffs no matter which of the countries imposes them (by Lerner symmetry a foreign tariff is equivalent to a foreign export tax which benefits domestic import competing firms). So import-competers in one country who are hurt by the tariff cuts in the agreement and thus oppose it will have less to gain if foreign tariffs will be cut anyway, even if the agreement is defeated. Opposition is costly in terms of lobbying resources, so the lower is the expected gain from such opposition, the smaller will be the resources devoted to it. (Coates and Ludema also consider the case of competing lobby groups in a country where export interests are also represented and show that, under fairly weak restrictions on the lobbying game, this result still goes through.)

The second motivation for a unilateral tariff reduction is that it encapsulates some degree of risk-sharing between the two countries. As the ratification of an agreement is subject to risk in one of the two countries, so there is scope for mutually welfare-improving sharing of this risk across the countries. One can think of the country where the agreement may fail as buying insurance against that outcome from the other country (where failure is less costly) and the unilateral tariff reduction as being the payout to that insurance in the 'bad state'. What keeps the 'insurer' from reneging is the ongoing relationship between the two parties—it wishes to keep alive the prospect of beneficial trade agreements in the future. Coates and Ludema demonstrate that the tradeoff between the incentive to renege (and set a high tariff) and the incentive to preserve the relationship (and unilaterally cut the tariff) depends on the 'insuring' country's size in a surprising way: the larger is the country (and so the greater its power to affect its terms of trade) the greater may be the tariff reduction! The reason is that the greater its size the more valuable is the 'insurance contract' to the other country, as total failure of the agreement would have more severe consequences. Accordingly, the other country is willing to pay a higher premium in the form of more favourable terms to the 'insurer' in any agreement that might be reached.

The Coates and Ludema argument is an insightful one and captures formally some common notions surrounding earlier historical episodes of unilateral liberalization by large countries. In particular, British policy makers arguing for tariff reforms in the mid-nineteenth century were very clear that one potential benefit would be the likely reforms in other countries on the coat-tails of Britain's own 'magnanimity' (although on this point it is also clear that proponents of reform perceived it to be in Britain's own best interests, even if no other countries followed: see Bhagwati 1988: Chapter 2).

There is a large literature on the possible effects of regional or bilateral agreements on the multilateral trading system (see Bagwell and Staiger (1999) and the references therein), and many of the arguments apply symmetrically to the situation considered here of the interaction between multilateralism and unilateralism. There are some additional issues, however. Ethier (1999: 132) suggests that one of the stylized facts of the new regionalism is that it typically involves a large country linking up with one or more small countries and that:

> [t]ypically, the small countries have recently made, or are making, significant unilateral reforms. This is dramatically true of the EA's central European participants ..., of the members of Mercosur ... and of Mexico. But it also characterizes, to a lesser degree, the small industrial-country participants in various regional initiatives ... Canada ... and the Scandinavian applicants to the EU.

We noted above that some episodes of unilateral reform involve *de facto* liberalization of tariffs against only a subset of partners and this quote suggests that this is a matter of some practical significance. There are a number of reasons why, when a country joins a preferential free trade area (FTA), it may then wish also to liberalize its trading regime *vis-à-vis* non-member countries. To the extent that the FTA leads to trade diversion to the partner country that is harmful, a decrease in the external tariff against non-members has approximately zero consequences for domestic producers or consumers but can replace duty-free imports from the partner with revenue-earning imports from the rest of the world (Richardson 1993). Thus whether in a political economy setting or not, one would anticipate declining external tariffs when a country joins a FTA.[5]

Another force leading to unilateral external liberalization following membership of a FTA stems from the ability of domestic producers to sell duty-free in the partner country post-FTA, even if the country is a net importer (Richardson 1995). In such a case a small external tariff reduction below the level levied by the partner country will again have approximately zero effect on domestic producers (who divert their sales from the home market to the partner market) and consumers, but replaces duty-free imports with imports subject to tariffs. This incentive, if recognized by governments, leads to a Bertrand paradox type of outcome in tariff-setting: both members' external tariffs are driven to zero by each one's desire to undercut the other. In this case we get quite the opposite of soft unilateralism: both countries would prefer to bind themselves *not* to liberalize as their unilateral behaviour leads to a Prisoners' dilemma outcome of tariffs that are too low.

Aside from these arguments, there are other reasons why preferential liberalization of tariffs might lead to unilateral liberalization of trade policy *vis-à-vis* other countries. While there is no theoretical justification for any presumption that countries' tariffs are strategic substitutes rather than complements or vice versa, one might argue that the latter is the 'usual' case when we are considering a single country's tariffs against different import sources (see Bagwell and Staiger 1999)—but see Mayer (1981) for the 'standard' case of strategic substitutability in a two-country tariff war setting. Accordingly, preferential trade policy liberalization would lead to unilateral liberalization in a strategic policy setting. This need not be the case, of course, and there are many models of customs union formation (so we are outside the realm of unilateralism in the determination of external tariff policy, of course) where quite the opposite occurs. Perhaps the best known is that of Krugman (1991) in which the expansion of a trading bloc leads to a higher external tariff to exploit its increased monopoly power. Subsequent work has shown this to be a fragile result, however (see Bond and Syropoulos 1996), and as noted, it is difficult to conclude that increasing external tariffs is at all a likely effect of preferential trading arrangements.

What is the empirical evidence? In a word, it is mixed. Winters (1996) provides a brief but useful review and suggests, for example, that Canada's accession to the CUSFTA was accompanied by external liberalization whereas Mexico's accession to NAFTA was not. It is worth noting his argument that in some cases external liberalization is characterized by lesser *increases* in trade restrictions than might have occurred in the absence of a preferential agreement.

So far we have discussed reasons why membership of a preferential agreement might lead to unilateral reforms; there are also reasons why the causality might run in the other direction. Ethier (1999: 147) notes one such argument: in a world of transport and other trade costs a reform-minded government might wish to liberalize unilaterally and non-preferentially in order to heighten the relative importance of regional trade and thus render a regional agreement more attractive.

What of strict multilateralism, in particular, multilateralism in the most-favoured nation, non-discriminatory GATT context? Unilateralism is defined by the absence of reciprocity and an immediate consequence of GATT-style liberalization is that it proscribes the nature of reciprocity. A common argument made to explain bilateral trade agreements is that they involve some politically optimal exchange of market access (see Hillman and Moser 1996). Consequently, a criticism of unilateral liberalization is that it 'wastes' the bargaining chip of access to the domestic market: this could be parlayed, in a bilateral or multilateral deal, into access to others' markets. The retort to this in a small country is immediate, of course: this 'chip' has no value. However, it should also be noted that the chip may be less valuable to a large country in a GATT world than it appears because of GATT's twin principles of MFN and reciprocity. Bagwell and Staiger (1997: 40ff) note that reciprocity has been taken in GATT to mean matching liberalizations that lead to equal increases in the value of import volumes. Suppose a country wishes to exchange only partial access to its markets. This 'chip' cannot be used in a bilateral deal as Article XXIV of the GATT limits permissible bilateral deals to those that involve complete internal liberalization. Further, any reciprocity granted by partners if the country liberalizes in the GATT setting must be granted to all *other* GATT members as well by MFN, so the 'cost' of granting reciprocal access is greater than it would be in a world of unilateral decisions. That is, a country that wishes to lower its trade barriers may find it difficult to use that as a lever for foreign reductions when those reductions must be made on an MFN basis.

5 Two recent cases of liberalization

So far we have considered the theoretical case for unilateral trade liberalization in both standard neoclassical and political economy settings. We have suggested that there are a number of cases for soft unilateralism operating through demonstration effects as well as political repercussions, and we have noted that there are important interactions between unilateral and other forms of trade liberalization. We conclude by looking at two notable recent instances of reforms: the APEC grouping founded on 'open regionalism' and the largely unilateral liberalizations that have occurred in the last 15 years or so in New Zealand.

5.1 Asia-Pacific Economic Cooperation: APEC

A great deal of ink has been spilled in discussing exactly what is meant by APEC's 'open regionalism', but if we take our earlier definition of unilateralism then it is perhaps best understood as 'coordinated' unilateralism. Member countries have scheduled a tariff reform programme for each—at different speeds—which is executed on a non-discriminatory MFN basis with extra-regional countries as well as other APEC members. Garnaut (1998b: 7–9) notes three elements of this liberalization. First is 'regional cooperation in multilateral and other extra-regional trade negotiations to secure non-discriminatory trade liberalization at home and abroad.' Second is coordinated unilateralism, and third is non-discriminatory liberalization in sectors in which intra-regional trade is important. The rationale for this latter element is clear: it provides a *de facto* reciprocity of a sort in that large member countries which might otherwise prefer explicit reciprocity (the bargaining chip argument) will find that regional MFN liberalization favours their export sectors as a practical matter.

The big question regarding APEC that arises from our earlier discussion is what binds participants to abide by the agreed liberalization? Garnaut (1998a: Chapter 2) argues that trade liberalization in the Western Pacific contains elements of a 'Prisoners' Delight' game, as opposed to its usual Prisoners' Dilemma conception. That is, liberalization is a dominant strategy and achieves the highest payoff for players when all do it. In such a case, of course, any international agreement to liberalize is unnecessary in the first place. One exception to this might be where policy makers are unaware of the payoffs and we get back to the earlier demonstration effect argument. Coordinated unilateralism here amounts to an agreement to all jump into unknown waters together. Garnaut (1998a: 31) places some stress on this in the APEC setting: 'observation that trade liberalization has been associated with economic prosperity, historically at home, or contemporaneously abroad, strengthen perceptions that support the "prisoners' delight". This has been important to the emergence and sustenance of open regionalism in East Asia.'

The question remains, however, of what happens to APEC liberalization if one or more members renege on their undertakings? Recent and current events are likely to put some countries under internal domestic pressures to slow down or even halt their promised external liberalization and this question may become of more than academic interest. The 'prisoners' delight' view of APEC suggests that one member's failings will have no effect on others. A more cynical view, however, might see APEC itself as another example of soft unilateralism: 'unilateral' reforms are undertaken only in the expectation that they will reinforce reforms elsewhere and this is the *quid* for the initial reforming *quo*. Under this view, backtracking by some members on their specific undertakings would lead to backtracking by others and the institution would fail. Which of these views is more realistic? The answer to that probably depends on which country we consider: we finish by reviewing briefly the experience of one APEC member which illustrates some of the arguments we have made concerning unilateralism, and raises some more.

5.2 The New Zealand experience: some brief remarks

As noted, New Zealand has since 1984 pursued a programme of extensive reforms, including trade policy liberalization. These reforms are well catalogued elsewhere (see Evans and Richardson 1999, Evans, Grimes, Wilkinson and Teece 1996, and Lattimore and Wooding 1996) and we shall not review them here. For our purposes it is important to note, however, that trade reforms were primarily through two means: unilateralism and bilateralism, the latter in the form of Closer Economic Relations (CER), a deep FTA with Australia. NZ has been an ardent supporter of multilateral reforms, particularly through the Cairns interest group in the Uruguay Round of GATT and as a member of APEC, but most progress on trade reform has been achieved through CER and unilateralism.

We have already suggested that the success of CER had an important demonstration effect in NZ. Given NZ's comparative advantage as a small, primary producing country, one might anticipate that the manufacturing sector would suffer under a programme of trade reforms. However, manufactured exports to Australia have been very significant in recent years, due in no small part to CER, and this has certainly helped maintain political support for ongoing unilateral reforms.

NZ has undertaken to achieve full free trade by the year 2006, 4 years earlier than its 2010 commitment under the APEC agreements. How would this goal be affected if other countries were to slow down their reforms? In the current political climate the answer is probably not at all. NZ's unilateral reforms have been so extensive that APEC, in some ways, appears much like the Uruguay Round of the GATT: an opportunity to 'get credit' for actions which would be taken anyway. Certainly the latest GATT Round was seen as a free good by NZ. It is one of the countries estimated to gain most significantly from the Uruguay Round's achievements in terms of per capita income, largely because of the agricultural reforms brought into the GATT in this round. Nevertheless, NZ had very little to do itself in terms of meeting multilateral reciprocity obligations, simply because it had already achieved so much unilaterally. One might argue that NZ's commitment to APEC is similar, in that it stands to gain a lot from APEC's success but is committed to doing little that it would not otherwise do.

Why did NZ choose unilateralism as the main vehicle of trade reforms? Partly it can be attributed to a realization of economists' reasoning about trade policy for small countries. Partly, however, it can be attributed to the fact that trade reforms were nested in a broader web of policy reforms. In particular, Evans and Richardson (1999) have argued that reforms of NZ's competition policy made unilateralism an ideal, even necessary, means of trade liberalization. In the Commerce Act of 1986 NZ removed almost all sector-specific regulatory bodies and imposed a system of what has been termed 'light-handed regulation'. In this regime, certain general principles of competitive behaviour are laid down in the Act (such as a proscription against a dominant firm using its position to deter entry) and a Commerce Commission is empowered to administer the Act. A crucial element is the focus on the 'public benefit' in assessing apparently anti-competitive behaviours and that benefit has generally been construed as an economist would construe it.

> NZ policy-makers drew on the economic arguments of contestability and ... forged a strong link between competition and efficiency— efficiency being regarded as the essential foundation for inter-national competitiveness and competition being the preferred ... means of achieving this. Indeed, it is the competition–efficiency– economic welfare paradigm that has governed the New Zealand government's approach ... to domestic policy reforms and deregulation in particular.
>
> Vautier and Lloyd (1997: 42)

Thus great stress was placed on openness to competition as a means of regulation; but that openness would be meaningless in the absence of liberalized trade (and, indeed, foreign investment) so NZ's liberal trading regime can be thought of as an essential underpinning to its light-handed competition policy.

Why does this favour unilateralism? Simply because bi- or mini-lateral negotiation of trade agreements would (1) be more limited in scope and (2) make NZ's openness contingent on the actions of cosignatory countries. The first of these stems from the observation that bilateral deals invariably exempt certain sectors considered by partners to be sensitive in some fashion. The second follows from the very nature of bilateral agreements: they are a mutual exchange of 'concessions'. Country A agrees to open its markets to country B's firms if B will reciprocate. Accordingly, if B does *not* abide by the agreement in some fashion and ignores any dispute settlement procedures, the agreement only has any content if A is prepared to withdraw its concessions. That is, a bilateral (or any) trade deal ultimately derives its enforceability from the power of signatories to withdraw from their obligations; but that power itself undermines the commitment to openness that is essential for NZ's competition policy to be credible.

6 Conclusion

This chapter commenced by asking a number of questions. Why would countries wish to liberalize their international trading regimes unilaterally? In particular, why would large countries wish to sacrifice some 'bargaining power'? What effects, if any, does liberalization through other multilateral means have on the incentive to liberalize unilaterally? We have reviewed a number of existing arguments—as well as provided some novel ones—which attempt to answer these questions. We have also briefly considered two recent trading regimes (APEC and New Zealand) which illustrate certain aspects of unilateralism.

Two important conclusions follow from our discussion. First, perhaps the most significant rationale for unilateralism in big and small countries alike is the demonstration effect it can have on other countries. This supports an argument made strongly by many authors: what we have termed 'soft' unilateralism could be significant for large countries in that the benefits from unilateral trade liberalization may stem as much from the flow-on effects it has on others' trade policies as from its direct consequences. Second, there are a number of reasons why multilateralism (taken still to include agreements of all sizes from bilateral up to global) may sensibly induce unilateralism. To the extent that these two observations interact, one might reasonably feel confident that the future of a liberal global trading regime is bright.

Notes

1. Typically the word 'multilateralism' is used in this chapter to include all forms of agreement regardless of the number of participants. Thus it includes bilateralism and regionalism. This is in contrast to its current usage, which tends to refer solely to large-group agreements (typically the WTO).
2. But see our discussion below suggesting that the reforms may have been attributable in part to external pressure on some political *consequences* of the initial protection.
3. In a dynamic setting, of course, a large country might recognize the possibility of retaliation and thus choose a zero tariff sustained by the threat of punishment; see Bagwell and Staiger (1999) and references therein for the extensive literature on this argument. This is hardly unilateralism, however.
4. I am grateful to Paul Wooding for this interpretation and line of argument.
5. Again, this describes well the experience of New Zealand although the issue of causality is unclear in that example.

References

Bagwell, K. and Staiger, R. (1997) 'GATT-Think', mimeo, Columbia University, available at <http://www.columbia.edu/~kwb8/gatt-think.pdf>.
—— (1999) 'Regional and multilateral tariff cooperation', in J. Piggott and A. Woodland (eds) *International trade policy and the Pacific rim*, London: The Macmillan Press (for the International Economic Association).
Bhagwati, J. (1988) *Protectionism*, Cambridge, MA: MIT Press.
—— (ed.) (1999) *Relaxed reciprocity: historical and modern experience with unilateral trade liberalization*, MIT Press, under review.
Bond, E. and Syropoulos, C. (1996) 'The size of trading blocs: market power and world welfare', *Journal of International Economics*, 40: 411–37.
Coates, D. and Ludema, R. (1997) 'Unilateral trade liberalization as leadership in trade negotiations', Working Paper, No. 97-23, Washington, DC: Department of Economics, Georgetown University.
Ethier, W. (1998) 'The international commercial system', Princeton Essays in International Finance No. 210, Princeton, NJ: Princeton University.
—— (1999) 'Multilateral roads to regionalism', in J. Piggott and A. Woodland (eds) *International trade policy and the Pacific rim*, London: The Macmillan Press (for the International Economics Association).
Evans, L., Grimes, A., Wilkinson, B. and Teece, D. (1996) 'Economic reform in New Zealand 1984–95: the pursuit of efficiency', *Journal of Economic Literature*, 34: 1856–902.
Evans, L. and Richardson, M. (1999) 'Trade reforms in New Zealand: unilateralism at work', in J. Bhagwati (ed.) *Relaxed reciprocity: Historical and modern experience with unilateral trade liberalization*, MIT Press, under review.
Garnaut, R. (1998a) 'Open regionalism: its analytic basis and relevance to the international system', in R. Garnaut (ed.) *Open regionalism and trade liberalization*, Sydney, Australia: Allen & Unwin (for Institute of Southeast Asian Studies).
—— (1998b) 'Open Regionalism: reality shapes an idea', in R. Garnaut (ed.) *Open regionalism and trade liberalization*, Sydney, Australia: Allen & Unwin (for Institute of Southeast Asian Studies).

Gros, D. (1987) 'A note on the optimal tariff, retaliation and the welfare loss from tariff wars in a framework with intra-industry trade', *Journal of International Economics*, 23, 3/4: 357–67.

Grossman, G. and Helpman, E. (1994) 'Protection for sale', *American Economic Review*, 84: 833–50.

Hillman, A. (1989) *The Political Economy of Protection*, Chur, Switzerland: Harwood Academic Publishers.

Hillman, A. and Moser, P. (1996) 'Trade liberalization as politically optimal exchange of market access', in M. Canzoneri, W. Ethier and V. Grilli (eds) *The New Transatlantic Economy*, Cambridge, UK: Cambridge University Press (for CEPR).

Krugman, P. (1991) 'Is bilateralism bad?', in E. Helpman and A. Razin (eds) *International Trade and Trade Policy*, Cambridge, MA: MIT Press.

Lattimore, R. and Wooding, P. (1996) 'International trade', in A. Bollard, R. Lattimore and B. Silverstone (eds) *A Study of Economic Reform: The Case of New Zealand*, Amsterdam: North-Holland.

Mayer, W. (1974) 'Endogenous tariff formation', *American Economic Review*, 74, 5: 970–85.

—— (1981) 'Theoretical considerations on negotiated tariff adjustments', *Oxford Economic Papers*, 33: 135–43.

McCulloch, R. (1997) 'Unilateral and reciprocal trade reforms in Latin America', mimeo, Waltham, MA: Graduate School of International Economics and Finance, Brandeis University.

Raimondos-Moller, P. and Woodland, A. (2000) 'Tariff strategies and small open economies', *Canadian Journal of Economics*, 33: 25–40.

Richardson, M. (1993) 'Endogenous protection and trade diversion', *Journal of International Economics*, 34: 309–24.

—— (1995) 'Tariff revenue competition in a free trade area', *European Economic Review*, 39: 1429–37.

Vautier, K.M. and Lloyd, P.J. (1997) *International Trade and Competition Policy: CER, APEC and the WTO*, Wellington: Institute of Policy Studies.

Winters, L.A. (1996) 'Regionalism versus multilateralism', Policy Research Working Paper, No. 1687, Washington, DC: World Bank.

WTO (World Trade Organization) (1996) *Trade Policy Review: New Zealand*, Geneva: World Trade Organization.

Part V

Regionalism

Monetary, fiscal, and industrial policy coordination

12 Regional integration and the development of tax systems in the European Union

Andreas Haufler

1 Introduction

Within the past 10 to 15 years, the conditions for the funding of public sectors have changed worldwide through the increasing integration of capital markets. Within the European Union (EU), this development has been reinforced by the abolition of remaining capital controls as part of the internal market programme. At the same time, the completion of the internal market encompassed the abolition of border controls between EU member states, resulting in increased trans-border mobility of consumers. These simultaneous changes in factor and commodity markets pose a number of challenges for tax policy in the European Union, which are of relevance for other integrating regions.

International differences in the rates (and sometimes also the bases) of individual taxes distort either consumer or producer prices across countries. This leads to inefficiencies in the international allocation of resources, which reduce the gains from the increased mobility of factors and the free flow of goods. Furthermore, tax differentials affect the international redistribution of tax revenues and induce countries to strategically adjust national patterns of taxation. Tax competition models predict that the burden of taxation will be shifted away from the most mobile tax bases to the ones which are (still) relatively immobile internationally. In general this implies that capital taxes will decrease while labour taxes will rise, in relative terms, with commodity taxation ranging somewhere in between. Meanwhile, there is increasing empirical evidence that this pattern has indeed been broadly followed since the 1980s.

Recent EU initiatives in the field of both value-added taxation (European Commission 1996) and interest income taxation (European Commission 1998) aim at increasing the overall level of taxation on these two tax bases, in order to reduce the tax burden on labour and reverse the trend that has been observed over the past years. However, the desirability and the effectiveness of these harmonization proposals is far from clear. For value-added taxation, the empirical evidence suggests that member states still enjoy a large degree of tax rate autonomy which would be given up under the Commission's proposals for an 'upward harmonization' of tax rates. For corporate taxation as well as interest income taxation, a regional agreement between EU member states that raises effective tax rates is faced by the problem that capital may flee the EU altogether and locate in third countries.

This chapter tries to combine some core results derived from the theoretical literature on both capital and commodity tax competition with recent evidence on the development of European tax systems. On the basis of these results we ask whether the changes in the tax structures of EU member states can be, and should be, counteracted by a coordinated EU tax policy. The plan of the chapter is as follows. Section 2 discusses the taxation of capital income, while section 3 is concerned with commodity taxation in the internal market. In each section we first introduce the relevant institutional setting and then turn to a simple tax competition model. This is followed by a brief survey of empirical studies before, finally, current harmonization proposals are evaluated. Section 4 briefly sums up our conclusions.

2 Capital taxation

2.1 The dominance of source-based capital taxation

In principle, taxes on capital income (as well as taxes on other factor incomes) can be levied in the source country of the investment, in the residence country of the investor, or in both countries. International tax relations are governed by a heterogeneous net of bilateral double taxation treaties which are usually based on the recommendations in the OECD model double taxation convention (OECD 1977). This convention avoids the double taxation of international capital incomes, but it leaves countries the option to apply either the residence principle or the source principle for any particular transaction.

Under the *residence principle*, capital income is taxed in the country where the investor resides, irrespective of where the capital income has originated. Let the gross returns to capital in two countries $i \in \{1, 2\}$ be denoted by f'_i. From the profit-maximizing input choices of competitive producers these gross returns will equal the marginal productivities of capital in the two countries. A capital owner in country 1 comparing the net returns from domestic and foreign investments thus faces the international arbitrage condition

$$f'_1(1 - t_1) = f'_2(1 - t_1) \Rightarrow f'_1 = f'_2 \tag{1}$$

Since tax rates are equal for domestic and foreign investments, arbitrage by capital owners will equalize gross-of-tax returns, and thus the marginal productivities of capital across countries. This leads to an efficient allocation of investment worldwide.

In contrast, under the *source principle*, capital incomes are taxed in the country where the investment takes place, irrespective of the nationality of the investor. The international arbitrage condition for capital owners in each country is then given by

$$f'_1(1 - t_1) = f'_2(1 - t_2) \tag{2}$$

When tax rates differ across countries, gross-of-tax returns and hence marginal productivities of capital will also differ internationally so that investment decisions are distorted.[1]

The important difference between these two principles is thus that only source-based capital taxes fall on internationally mobile investment and hence will lead to international tax competition. Therefore it is important to see which tax principle applies to different forms of capital taxation. We confine our treatment here to the taxation of corporate profits on the one hand, and interest income on the other (neglecting other sources of capital income, such as dividends or capital gains).

Turning first to the corporation tax, the source country generally levies a tax on the profits of all firms that operate within its territory, while the residence country avoids international double taxation by either exempting the foreign-earned income from domestic tax, or by granting a (limited) tax credit for the taxes paid in the source country. If the residence country exempts foreign-source profit or dividend income from tax, then it is clearly the source country's tax rate which is relevant for an international investment. In contrast, if the source tax is credited in the residence country against the tax liabilities incurred there, then it is in principle the tax rate of the residence country which is relevant from the perspective of the international investor. However, residence-based taxes are generally deferred until profits are repatriated, so that an element of effective source taxation is introduced even under the tax credit method. Furthermore, residence countries generally do not offer a tax refund if the tax payment in the source country exceeds the tax liability on the same income in the country of residence. In this case the tax paid in the source country is the final tax liability for the international investor. In sum, most commentators agree that the effective taxation of foreign direct investment closely follows the source principle of international taxation (see Tanzi and Bovenberg 1990, Keen 1993, Sørensen 1995).

Matters are somewhat different for the taxation of international interest income. All OECD countries adopt a (limited) tax credit system for foreign-source interest income; hence, the international taxation of interest income legally follows the residence principle. However, residence-based taxes on capital income can be easily evaded as home countries are unable to monitor the foreign interest earnings of their residents. In this case, the withholding tax levied in the source country again constitutes the relevant tax rate from the perspective of the investor. Furthermore, since most countries levy a zero withholding tax on foreign investors, there is a widespread belief that international interest income may escape taxation altogether.

2.2 Capital tax competition: theory

This section introduces in an informal way some of the core analytical results derived from a standard model of capital tax competition.[2] Consider a static model of n identical countries, where $n \in \{1, \ldots \infty\}$. Hence the share of country i in the world population is $1/n$. Each individual in each jurisdiction supplies one unit of labour and owns k^* units of capital. Capital is perfectly mobile between countries, whereas labour is immobile. Denoting the amount of capital employed in each region by k_i, capital market clearing implies

$$\sum_i^n k_i = \sum_i^n k^* \equiv \bar{K} \tag{3}$$

All countries produce a single, homogeneous output good whose price is normalized to unity. The production function is identical across countries and is given by $f(k_i)$ where the fixed labour input is suppressed. It is twice differentiable in k_i, with the usual properties $f'(k_i) > 0$, $f''(k_i) < 0$. Output and factor markets are perfectly competitive.

We assume that capital taxation follows the source principle (see section 2.1). Each country levies a source tax at rate t_i on each unit of capital employed in its jurisdiction (specific taxes are assumed purely for analytical convenience). Arbitrage by investors is based on a comparison of net-of-tax returns, $f'(k_i) - t_i$, across countries. From the perspective of a typical country i, the arbitrage condition is

$$f'(k_i) - t_i = r(t_i) \quad \forall \quad i \in \{1, \ldots, n\} \tag{4}$$

where r is the net interest rate, which is equalized worldwide. It is a function of t_i whenever country i is not small in the world economy (i.e. n is finite).

From the arbitrage condition (4) we get through implicit differentiation

$$\frac{\partial k_i}{\partial t_i} = \frac{1 + (\partial r/\partial t_i)}{f''(k_i)}, \quad \frac{\partial k_j}{\partial t_i} = \frac{(\partial r/\partial t_i)}{f''(k_j)} \quad \forall \quad i, j, i \neq j \tag{5}$$

We now adopt the perspective of one particular country i. Differentiating the capital market clearing condition (3) and using the assumption that all other countries j are identical, we get

$$\frac{\partial k_i}{\partial t_i} + (n-1)\frac{\partial k_j}{\partial t_i} = 0 \quad \forall \quad i, j, i \neq j \tag{6}$$

Substituting (5) in (6) and rearranging yields the effect of a change in country i's tax rate on the world interest rate:

$$\frac{\partial r}{\partial t_i} = \frac{-1}{n} \quad \forall \quad i \tag{7}$$

Hence, by reducing the domestic demand for capital, a tax increase in country i will also lower the world interest rate. Given the assumption that all countries (including country i) are identical, this effect will be the stronger the fewer countries there are in the world economy.

Finally, substituting (7) in (5) gives the effect of a change in t_i on country i's equilibrium capital stock, and hence its tax base:

$$\frac{\partial k_i}{\partial t_i} = \frac{[1 - (1/n)]}{f''(k_i)} \quad \forall \quad i \tag{8}$$

The effect of a change in t_i on country i's tax base is the mirror image to the effect on the world interest rate: if n is large, then the world interest rate will fall only slightly and the tax increase will primarily raise the gross-of-tax return in country i. This implies a large reduction in country i's capital stock and hence a large elasticity of the domestic tax base.

We can now turn to the determination of the optimal capital tax rate. Each government maximizes the (identical) utility function $u(c_i, g_i)$ of a representative individual in its jurisdiction, where c_i and g_i denote private and public consumption, respectively. The private and the public good represent different uses of the same output so that the marginal rate of transformation between c_i and g_i is equal to one.

The government budget constraint of each country is

$$g_i = t_i k_i \quad \forall \quad i \tag{9}$$

The representative resident in each country receives rent income (the value of production less the payments for the mobile factor capital) plus the net return r on her capital endowment (no matter where the latter is invested; see equation (4)):

$$c_i = f(k_i) - f'(k_i)k_i + k*r \quad \forall \quad i \tag{10}$$

Each government takes the tax rate in the other regions as given and the first-order conditions for the optimal source tax on capital are determined by

$$\frac{\partial u}{\partial t_i} = \frac{\partial c_i}{\partial t_i} + m_i(c_i, g_i)\frac{\partial g_i}{\partial t_i} = 0 \quad \forall \quad i \tag{11}$$

where we have inserted the marginal rate of substitution $m_i(c_i, g_i)$ = $(\partial u/\partial g_i)/(\partial u/\partial c_i)$. Differentiating (9)–(10) with respect to t_i, substituting the results along with (8) into the first-order condition (11), and using again the symmetry assumption gives the best-response function of each government[3]

$$k^*(m_i - 1) + m_i t_i \frac{[1 - (1/n)]}{f''(k^*)} = 0 \quad \forall \ i \tag{12}$$

Under the usual assumptions that the second-order conditions are fulfilled and that reaction functions are continuous, equation (12) describes a symmetric Nash equilibrium in capital tax rates. Based on this equation, we can now consider some of the fundamental results derived in the tax competition literature.

As a benchmark, let us first consider the case of a closed economy $(n = 1)$. In this case the second term in (12) is zero and the first-order condition (12) reduces to $m_i = 1$. This implies that the marginal rate of substitution between the private and the public good equals the marginal rate of transformation and public goods will be efficiently provided in this case. For $n > 1$, the second term in (12) will be negative, hence $m_i > 1$ must hold in the Nash equilibrium. This is the fundamental result that tax competition leads to an *underprovision of public goods*, relative to an autarky situation where the capital tax base is immobile.

As n is continuously raised, the fraction in the second term becomes larger in absolute terms, indicating that the domestic tax base becomes more elastic from the perspective of each competing government. The first-order condition is maintained by a combination of an increase in m_i (which makes both the first and the second term larger in absolute value) and a reduction in t_i (which reduces the absolute value of the second term). Clearly, this is consistent with the budget constraint (9), since an underprovision of public goods must be accompanied by an *undertaxation of capital*, relative to the closed economy benchmark.

It is then straightforward to extend the basic intuition gained from the case of a variable number of symmetric countries to more complex scenarios that have been analysed in the literature. The first concerns the case where two countries of different size compete for internationally mobile capital. The smaller of the two countries faces the more elastic tax base, and hence it will act as if it faces a larger number of competitors. Hence the small country will choose the lower capital tax rate in the Nash equilibrium. In contrast to the case of symmetric countries this implies, however, that capital will flow from the large (high-tax) to the small (low-tax) region in equilibrium, implying a tax base gain for the small region. Hence, if per capita endowments in the small and the large region are identical, it can be shown that the small country will always have the larger per-capita utility in the non-cooperative Nash equilibrium (Bucovetsky 1991, Wilson 1991).

It is even possible to show that the welfare level of an *infinitely small* country must be higher in the Nash equilibrium as compared to the welfare level in either autarky or under full tax coordination.[4] To see this, note that if one country is infinitely small then the other (large) country faces essentially the same problem as under autarky and will accordingly choose the autarky tax rate. Hence the small country can always replicate the autarky equilibrium. However, given that its tax base is highly elastic this cannot be an optimal policy for the small country. Hence, by a simple revealed preference argument, there must be a critical size below which the small country prefers the noncooperative Nash equilibrium to the case of tax coordination. This finding is in many respects analogous to the well known result in international trade theory that sufficiently large countries can win a 'tariff war' (Johnson 1953/54, Kennan and Riezman 1988).

A still different scenario arises when each government has a wage tax at its disposal in addition to the source-based capital tax. Labour supply is elastic in each country so that the wage tax is distortive, but labour continues to be immobile internationally. Returning to the assumption that countries are symmetric it is then intuitive that, as n increases, the capital tax base becomes more elastic, whereas the elasticity of labour supply is unaffected by the openness of the economy. Hence, for large values of n the conventional inverse-elasticity rule implies that countries will rely relatively more on wage as opposed to capital taxation. In the extreme, if each country is infinitely small in the world economy ($n \to \infty$), then the optimal capital tax rate is zero and only wage income is taxed in the Nash equilibrium (Gordon 1986, Bucovetsky and Wilson 1991).

2.3 Capital tax competition: empirical evidence

The theoretical results sketched in the previous section obviously call for empirical work to determine whether the clear-cut predictions are borne out by real-world data. The empirical implementation of the theory is, however, by no means straightforward.

The first problem is to find an appropriate measure for capital taxation. This in turn first requires a more precise definition of what 'capital taxation' means. Many empirical studies confine themselves to the corporation tax, which can easily be separated from other taxes.[5] A first look at the statutory corporate tax rates indeed shows a significant drop in most EU countries, with the EU average falling from 48.2 per cent in 1985 to 33.9 per cent in 1998 (see Table 12.1).

However, it is well known that statutory tax rates give only a very incomplete picture of the effective taxation of corporate profits. Effective tax rates will also depend on all policy variables that affect the corporate tax base (depreciation rules, inventory valuation, loss offset provisions etc). The incorporation of tax bases is particularly important for the time period under consideration, where income tax reforms have generally followed a pattern of tax rate cut with base broadening.

Table 12.1 Corporation tax rates and value-added tax rates in the EU

Country	Corporation tax rate		Standard VAT rate	
	1985	1998	1987	1998
Austria[a]	61.5	34	20	20
Belgium	45	39	19	21
Denmark	50	32	22	25
Finland[a]	50	28	19.5[d]	22
France	50	33.33	18.6	20.6
Germany	56[b]	45[b]	14	16
Greece	49	40	18	18
Ireland	50	28[c]	25	21
Italy	47.8	37	18	20
Luxembourg	45.5	30	12	15
Netherlands	42	35	20	17.5
Portugal	51.2	34	16	17
Spain	33	35	12	16
Sweden[a]	52	28	23.5[d]	25
United Kingdom	40	30[c]	15	17.5
EU average	48.2	33.9	18.2	19.4

Sources: European Tax Handbook 1999 (International Bureau of Fiscal Documentation, Amsterdam), p. 10 and p. 14; Ruding Report (1992), Table 8.5; European Communities (1988), The economics of 1992, European Economy 35, Table 3.5.1; Coopers & Lybrand (1988), International Tax Summaries.

Notes
[a] EU member since 1995
[b] tax rate on retained profits
[c] 1999/2000
[d] effective tax rate (no VAT in 1987)

Two different measures of the effective corporate tax burden have been used in the literature. The *effective marginal tax rate* (EMTR) measures how a marginal adjustment to the capital stock in a given country is taxed, taking into account both the nominal tax rate and the definition of the tax base (e.g. depreciation rules). On the other hand, the *effective average tax rate* (EATR) measures total taxes paid, as a fraction of the relevant tax base (capital income or profits).

Recent empirical evidence suggests that both marginal and average effective tax rates have fallen moderately in the average of EU and other OECD countries. An initial calculation in the Ruding Report (1992) for the European Commission found that during the period 1980–91, reductions in the EMTRs have been caused largely by tight monetary policies, whereas discretionary fiscal policy changes have played only a minor role. More detailed studies find a moderate fall in effective marginal tax rates in the EU average. Chennells and Griffith (1997: Table 4.2) report for the period 1979–94 that the average of domestic EMTRs has fallen by approximately 5 per cent (from 21.7 per cent to 20.5 per cent). Comparable results are obtained by Schaden (1995: Table 5.9) for German direct investment in other EU countries.

This is roughly consistent with recent empirical evidence on average effective tax rates. Applying this method to the G7 countries for the period 1965–88, Mendoza, Razin and Tesar (1994: 313, Fig. 4) find a stable or even increasing trend in the corporate income tax burden, but reductions in effective average tax rates are visible in some countries towards the end of their sample. A recent study using a similar methodology (Genser, Hettich and Schmidt 1999) shows that effective average corporation tax rates have developed quite differently in eight selected EU countries during the period 1980–96, and an unweighted average of these figures yields a fall in the average effective corporate tax burden in the range of 15 per cent (from 43 per cent to 36 per cent).

The papers by Mendoza, Razin and Tesar (1994) and Genser, Hettich and Schmidt (1999) also compute effective average tax rates on all capital income (including personal capital income taxes), as well as on wage income. The overall development of effective capital income taxes is not very different from the development of effective corporate tax rates, exhibiting a moderate downward trend in the EU average with large country-specific fluctuations. On the other hand, effective taxes on labour income (including social security contributions) show a marked upward trend in most countries since the 1960s; this trend continues in the 1990s in most EU countries, with the notable exception of the United Kingdom.

Overall then, the calculations of effective tax rates on capital versus labour give some first support for the predictions of theoretical models which posit that increasing capital mobility leads to a shift in the tax mix away from the taxation of capital and towards the taxation of wage income.[6] A logical next step is to set up an econometric analysis that tries to link changes in the observed tax mix to the increasing liberalization of capital markets, while controlling for changes in other relevant variables.

Some first attempts in this direction have been undertaken. Rodrik (1997) performs a pooled cross-section, time-series analysis based on the calculations of effective average tax rates in Mendoza, Razin and Tesar (1994), but uses an extended data set that incorporates developments in eighteen OECD countries during the period 1965–92. Effective capital and labour tax rates are regressed on a variable for the 'openness' of the economy, per capital GDP and—in some regressions—a variable for capital account restrictions. The 'openness' variable relates to commodity trade and is constructed from the sum of exports and imports in relation to GDP. If capital account restrictions are not controlled for, the relationship between labour tax rates and the 'openness' variable is positive and statistically significant, while the effect of 'openness' on capital tax rates is negative and also statistically significant. If the variable for capital account restrictions is introduced, then a lifting of the restrictions has a negative and statistically significant effect on the capital tax rate.

Other econometric analyses by political scientists seem to find directly opposing evidence that the liberalization of capital markets is associated with an *increase* in capital taxation (Garrett 1995, Quinn 1997). Garrett (1995) interprets this result as showing that governments do not choose tax levels so as to minimize the excess burden of taxation (what is called the 'efficiency hypothesis'), but rather set taxes so as to compensate those who lose from increased market integration (i.e. the workers: the 'compensation hypothesis'). However, a closer look at these studies shows that the dependent variable is corporate tax *revenue*, either in relation to GDP or to some other tax measure. Since the share of operating profits in GDP (the 'profitability' of companies) has risen since the early 1980s (see, for example, Ruding Report 1992: 154), this simultaneous shift may lead to a spurious correlation between increased capital mobility and rising corporate taxation, even though the effective capital tax rate (i.e. tax revenue divided by the *tax base*) has simultaneously fallen. This shows that the conflicting results between these two studies and the one by Rodrik (1997) can be fully explained by the different ways of measuring the dependent variable, and that the 'efficiency hypothesis' derived from the literature on capital tax competition is not refuted by the empirical work of Garrett and Quinn.[7]

In addition, there is substantial econometric evidence that taxes are an important determinant for the location decision of firms, both in a national and in an international setting (see, for example, Papke 1991, Grubert and Mutti 1996, Devereux and Griffith 1998). Devereux and Griffith (1998) show that differences in effective capital tax rates across EU countries are important for the decision of a US-based corporation in which EU country to invest, once the fundamental decision for foreign direct investment in the European Union has been made. Grubert and Mutti (1996) also combine national measures of effective capital tax rates with regional dummy variables, and show that location decisions within the EU are more sensitive to a given tax differential than if the same differential arises in other parts of the world. This can be seen as evidence for the general proposition that tax differentials matter more when countries are both open to world markets and relatively similar in structure, a proposition that is also supported by the elastic response of investment decisions to tax differentials across different US states (see Papke 1991).

2.4 Harmonization proposals and the 'third-country problem'

The empirical evidence surveyed in the preceding section indicates that some of the theoretically predicted shift in the direct tax mix – away from the more mobile factor capital and towards the less mobile factor labour – has indeed taken place empirically. Therefore, a basic argument can be made for the coordination of capital tax rates in the EU, in order to prevent a further bias in national tax patterns towards the taxation of labour. Nevertheless, the European Commission has been very reluctant so far to initiate explicit harmonization measures for corporate taxation, despite the strong recommendations in favour of a stepwise harmonization process made in the Ruding Report (1992).[8] With respect to the taxation of interest income accruing to individuals, the Commission has proposed EU-wide minimum withholding tax rates in 1989 and 1998, but neither of these proposals won the required unanimous support in the Council of Ministers.

Clearly, the veto right that each EU member possesses in matters of tax policy makes the adoption of coordination measures difficult, since it is indeed possible that individual (small) countries gain from capital tax competition (see section 2.2). This is particularly visible in the case of Luxembourg, which has blocked all efforts to introduce minimum interest withholding taxes in the EU. It was also apparent, however, that other member states were unwilling either to exert political pressure or to offer compensating benefits in order to buy Luxembourg's support.

Arguably, a core issue behind this reluctance to adopt binding harmonization measures in the field of capital taxation is the fear of capital flight to third (non-member) states. In its strongest form, the argument against tax coordination between a sub-group of small countries has been made by Razin and Sadka (1991). They show that as long as the EU is unable to exert any substantial (downward) influence on world interest rates, a coordinated capital tax increase will be fully shifted into higher interest rates in Europe. Hence, in their view, the argument that it is inefficient for a small country to levy source-based taxes on capital (see section 2.2) carries over to any coordinated EU tax on capital income.

Several arguments can be brought forward against this simple analysis. First and most obvious, the EU as a whole is not small in the world economy, so that some of the tax increase would be shifted into lower world interest rates (see the analysis in section 2.2). Second, the analysis by Razin and Sadka assumes that there are no transaction costs for capital transactions worldwide. If such transaction costs exist, and if they are smaller within the EU than for investments from and to third countries (e.g. because of differences in exchange rate uncertainty), then it can be shown that a mandated rise in the capital tax rate of the low-tax country(ies) is welfare-improving for the EU as a whole (see Huizinga and Nielsen 2000). However, rapid developments in financial markets, including the spread of financial derivatives (see Alworth 1998), make it questionable how much weight the transaction cost argument will carry in the future.

Another departure from the simple framework of Razin and Sadka (1991) concerns the existence of pure rents or profits, which is usually associated with foreign direct investment. Here it is important to distinguish between a purely national rent and a general EU location rent which may arise, for example, from access to the single European market. National rents can be taxed by the individual member state without causing mobile firms to leave and hence do not constitute an argument for a coordinated corporate tax policy in the EU. In contrast, it has been

shown in the new trade literature that, in the presence of either transportation costs or agglomeration effects, the reduction of internal barriers to trade
in an integrated region will increase the incentives of firms from outside the
EU to build a branch plant in *any* country of the integrating region (e.g.
Norman and Motta 1993). Since no single EU country will be able to appropriate this rent, non-cooperative tax policy between member states will drive
the taxation of the common EU rent to zero. In this case, there is a basic efficiency argument for a binding minimum corporate tax rate (Keen 1993).

In practice, however, the distinction between national rents and a
common EU rent may not be a very clear one. European integration may
change existing national rents (e.g. by redefining the relevant 'home
market') rather than create an additional EU rent. Furthermore, the rents
earned from locating in Europe will not be the same for individual firms.
Instead, firms will generally differ in their attachment to the EU and hence
in the degree of international mobility that they exhibit towards increased
taxation in Europe (see Osmundsen, Hagen and Schjelderup 1998, for
such a modelling strategy). Any increase in EU corporation taxes, either
through a rise in statutory tax rates or through a closing of tax loopholes,
will thus have two counteracting effects. On the one hand, to the extent
that tax competition between EU members currently leads to an 'undertaxation' of corporate income, it will allow a more effective taxation of
those firms which derive relatively high rents from locating in a particular
EU country. On the other hand, the same measure will drive some internationally mobile firms (with low firm-specific EU rents) out of production
in Europe and thus impose some costs on the EU as a whole. Which of
these effects is the dominant one for a particular harmonization proposal
seems to be very difficult to ascertain. These fundamental ambiguities are
probably one of the core reasons for the reservations held by both academics and policy makers against far-reaching measures of capital tax
coordination in Europe.

3 Commodity taxation

3.1 A mixed tax principle in the EU internal market

World trade is generally taxed under the *destination principle*. Under this
scheme, goods are exempted from tax in the country of production and
value-added tax (VAT) levied at earlier processing stages is fully rebated
when the good is exported. At the same time, commodity taxes are levied
on imports in the country of final consumption, with tax revenue also
accruing to this country. Since the same tax rate applies to imported and
domestically produced goods, international arbitrage by consumers equal-
izes producer prices (p_i) across countries:

$$(1 + t_1)p_1 = (1 + t_1)p_2 \Rightarrow p_1 = p_2 \qquad (13)$$

Integration and tax systems in the EU

As in the case of the residence principle of factor taxation, different tax rates imposed under the destination principle will thus not distort production decisions and will not redistribute tax revenues between countries. Hence, under a pure destination principle, there will be no tax competition for commodity purchases.

The problem in an internal market like the European Union is, however, that the destination principle generally requires the existence of border controls in order to carry out the necessary border tax adjustments. In the absence of border controls, the destination principle can no longer be administered for all intra-EU purchases. Given the desirable properties of this tax scheme the EU has nevertheless decided to maintain the destination principle for all purchases between VAT-registered traders. Under the current 'transitional system', border tax adjustments are implemented 'in the books': exporters are required to report the VAT identification number of their customer when claiming the tax rebate, allowing tax authorities to check whether importers have lawfully paid tax to their government for all imports from other EU member states.[9] This method, however, cannot be applied to direct across-the-border purchases by final consumers. Hence final consumer purchases in an internal market can only effectively be taxed in the country of origin.

Under the *origin principle* goods are taxed in the country of production and revenue accrues to the exporting country. International arbitrage by consumers then implies

$$(1 + t_1)p_1 = (1 + t_2)p_2 \tag{14}$$

Hence production decisions will be distorted if transaction (transportation) costs for consumers are absent and if the value-added tax is not completely general, in the sense that the same tax rate applies to all goods and services.[10] If transaction costs for cross-border shopping exist, producer prices need not be distorted at the margin, but tax differentials nevertheless cause welfare losses and countries have an incentive to compete for cross-border purchases. This is the scenario that underlies the analytical treatment in the following section.

3.2 Commodity tax competition: theory

In this section we briefly review the issue of commodity tax competition in a simple one-good, two-country model ($i \in \{1, 2\}$) where cross-border shopping is the only reason for trade.[11] The single private good is simultaneously imported by the consumers of country 1, which we take to be a high-tax country, and exported by its producers in order to balance trade. Since trade between registered traders occurs under the destination principle (see section 3.1), producer prices are equalized across countries and, without loss of generality, can be normalized to unity.

The representative consumer in the home country (country 1) derives utility from the consumption of a single private good c and a public good g, so that $u(c, g)$. Private goods purchased at home (c_1) and abroad (c_2) are perfect substitutes hence $c = c_1 + c_2$. Consumer purchases in the foreign country are subject to transaction costs $\tau(c_2)$, which are a convex function of the level of cross-border shopping. One way to rationalize this specification is to assume a continuum of consumers who live at varying distances from the border (Kanbur and Keen 1993). For simplicity we use a quadratic transportation cost function of the type

$$\tau(c_2) = \frac{\alpha}{2}(c_2)^2, \quad \alpha > 0 \tag{15}$$

Arbitrage by country 1's residents equates consumer prices across countries so that $(1 + t_1) = (1 + t_2) + \tau'(c_2)$. Hence the tax gain from shopping abroad equals the marginal transaction costs incurred. Using (15) we can then determine the equilibrium level of cross-border shopping

$$c_2 = \frac{t_1 - t_2}{\alpha} \tag{16}$$

Transportation costs incurred by consumers represent a 'pure waste', reducing the consumption possibilities of the representative household. Denoting by x the fixed endowment of the home country, the *private* budget constraint is given by

$$(1 + t_1)c_1 + (1 + t_2)c_2 + \tau(c_2) = x \tag{17}$$

Since only goods purchased in the home jurisdiction are part of the home country's tax base the *public* budget constraint is

$$g = t_1 c_1 \tag{18}$$

Substituting (15)–(18) into the utility function gives

$$u = u\left\{ \frac{\beta}{(1 + t_1)}, t_1\left[\frac{\beta}{(1 + t_1)} - \frac{(t_1 - t_2)}{\alpha} \right] \right\} \tag{19}$$

where the income measure

$$\beta = x + \frac{(t_1 - t_2)^2}{2\alpha}$$

includes the private tax savings, net of transportation costs. Assuming that the benevolent home government maximizes the welfare of the representative citizen (eq. (19)) with respect to the domestic tax rate, the first-order condition reads

$$\frac{t_1}{\alpha} = \frac{c_1}{(1+t_1)}\left(1 - \frac{1}{m}\right) \tag{20}$$

where we have introduced the marginal rate of substitution $m = (\partial u/\partial g)/(\partial u/\partial c)$. Since the left-hand side of equation (20) is positive, $m > 1$ must hold in the non-cooperative equilibrium, indicating an under-supply of public goods. Alternatively, the commodity tax is 'underused', relative to the closed-economy benchmark, as a result of inter-country competition for cross-border shopping.

Again we can link our basic equation (20) to some of the results obtained in the literature on commodity tax competition. First, recall that our argument has been made for a high-tax country only. Hence, in the general case all we can say is that the high-tax country will definitely underprovide the public good in equilibrium (see Mintz and Tulkens 1986). A stronger result can be obtained if it is assumed that the government maximizes tax revenue. In this case it can be shown that both countries strictly underuse the commodity tax in the Nash equilibrium, relative to their objective (Kanbur and Keen 1993).

Furthermore, it is easily seen that a reduction in the transaction cost parameter α will increase cross-border shopping for any given tax differential (compare equation (16)) and will also increase the left-hand side of (20). The equality will be maintained by a reduction in t_1 and a simultaneous increase in the bracketed term on the right-hand side of (20). Analogous to our discussion in section 2.2, a reduction in the costs of cross-border shopping makes the commodity tax base more elastic, leading to a lower commodity tax rate and a more severe underprovision of public goods in the non-coordinated tax optimum.

Note also the special case when the transportation cost parameter α approaches zero. In this case cross-border shopping is not bound by (16), implying that all purchases are made in the low-tax foreign country ($c = c_2$). This implies from (18) that the tax base in the home region shrinks to zero. This scenario has been emphasized in the context of trade deflection under the restricted origin principle (Shibata 1967, Georgakopoulos and Hitiris 1992) to which we will return in section 3.4.

3.3 Commodity tax competition: empirical evidence

As we saw in the preceding section, the basic theoretical analysis of commodity tax competition for cross-border purchases runs parallel in many ways to the competition for internationally mobile capital (section 2.2). This need not imply, however that commodity tax competition is equally important in practice. After all, the transaction cost schedule may be quite steep, implying that cross-border shopping is not a worthwhile form of tax saving for most households.

Indeed, a look at the development of standard value-added tax rates shows that these have risen, in the EU average, from 18.2 per cent in 1987 to 19.4 per cent in 1998 (see Table 12.1). In comparison to statutory corporate tax rates, this nominal rate is a much better indicator in the case of value-added taxation, since tax bases are harmonized and have remained unchanged in the relevant time period. Overall effective tax rates on consumption (including excises) have also remained stable, or even increased, in the EU average since the 1980s (Genser, Hettich and Schmidt 1999).

These tax responses by national governments are consistent with the results of empirical studies showing that, despite the existence of VAT differentials of up to 10 per cent between neighbouring countries (Germany and Denmark), cross-border shopping has not increased significantly after 1992 (Bode, Krieger-Boden and Lammers 1994, FitzGerald, Johnston and Williams 1995, Ratzinger, 1998). In fact, a detailed empirical study for Denmark has shown that the marginal excess burden of the VAT, as caused by cross-border shopping, is still substantially below the marginal excess burden caused by income tax evasion (Gordon and Nielsen 1997). On the other hand, these studies also show that differences in excise tax rates, in particular for cigarettes and spirits, are a cause of concern and have led, for example, to significant tax revenue losses in Britain as a result of increased Channel trade (Price Waterhouse 1994).

To be sure, there are several caveats to these empirical results since most studies were conducted before or shortly after the opening of internal borders in 1992, and most of them do not include estimates for fraud or tax evasion by commercial operators. Evidence from the post-1992 period is still preliminary and subject to the general argument that price elasticities may gradually increase over time as both consumers and firms discover new and cheaper ways of tax arbitrage. Nevertheless, on the basis of the existing evidence on either cross-border shopping or member states' tax policy adjustments, the distortions caused by cross-country tax differentials under the present system of value-added taxation seem to be rather small in practice.

3.4 Harmonization proposals and external trade relations

The empirical results sketched in the preceding section have indicated that the distortions of the EU's internal trade caused by commodity tax differentials are likely to be small. Nevertheless, the Commission pursues a further harmonization of member states' VAT rates, beyond the EU-wide minimum for the standard VAT rate of 15 per cent agreed upon in 1992. As a final objective, it is envisaged that VAT rates are fully equalized between EU member states (see European Commission 1996). Furthermore, the Commission plans to link the harmonization issue to a coordinated increase in VAT rates above the current EU-average, in exchange for a reduction in direct taxes:

> ...the debate is not limited to identifying the rate of tax necessary to guarantee a level of revenues comparable to the present one, but it might also include other political considerations. In particular, it might be envisaged to provide, by way of the VAT, the budgetary resources needed to reduce other contributions and charges.
>
> European Commission 1996: 19

This proposal for a coordinated rise in value-added tax rates obviously contrasts with the cautious approach to policy coordination that the EU Commission adopts in the area of capital income taxation. Interestingly, this is true even though the fiscal externalities involved in capital income taxation seem to be much larger than those associated with commodity tax differentials. It still remains to be seen, however, whether the EU's external trade relations constitute either an additional argument for tax rate harmonization or a constraint, as in the case of the 'third country problem' discussed in section 3.4.

Possible interactions between the EU's internal and external trade relations have been discussed in the literature on the 'restricted origin principle' (Shibata 1967, Whalley 1979, Berglas 1981, Georgakopoulos and Hitiris 1992). In particular it has been stressed that if trade deflection (i.e. the re-exporting of imported goods) is permitted and costless, then the high-tax country within the union will lose its entire tax base through triangular tax arbitrage. If this finding were found to be relevant for the European Union, it would clearly constitute a very strong argument for tax rate harmonization. At the same time it has also been shown that trade deflection will counteract existing tariff distortions in the high-tax country, hence leading to a welfare gain for the Community as a whole (Georgakopoulos and Hitiris 1992).

However, this literature generally assumes that *all* trade in the EU (including trade between registered traders) follows the origin principle. Intra-union commodity tax differentials will then lead to diverging producer prices between EU member states (compare equation (14)). In contrast, our previous analysis has shown that when trade between registered traders follows the destination principle and cross-border shopping by consumers is subject to transaction costs, producer prices will be equalized world-wide. In this case there is neither an additional tax base loss in the high-tax union country through triangular tax arbitrage, nor does the welfare loss from intra-EU tax differentials (the pure waste caused by the 'excess' transportation cost incurred by consumers) interact with an existing tariff distortion at the union's external borders (see Haufler 1996b).

This shows that—in contrast to the case of capital tax coordination—

the arguments for and against commodity tax harmonization in the EU can be safely discussed without taking account of the EU's external trade relations. On the one hand, this implies that the case for tax harmonization remains weak in the area of commodity taxation. It may well be argued that substantial changes in value-added tax rates, and in the direct-indirect tax mix, have strong distributional effects which critically affect the political equilibrium in individual member states. Hence, on grounds of the 'subsidiarity principle', a switch towards a heavier reliance on value-added taxation should be left to the discretion of individual member states. On the other hand, it is also clear that commodity tax coordination at the EU level is more effective than the coordination of capital income taxes, because there is no risk of tax base flight to non-member states.

4 Conclusion

In this chapter we have surveyed some of the theoretical and empirical literature that is concerned with the effects of increasing market integration on national tax patterns, with a particular application to the European Union. While theoretical work has stressed the similarities between tax competition for internationally mobile capital and commodity tax bases, some empirical evidence can be found only for capital tax competition. In general, there is a moderate, but visible, downward trend in the effective taxation of capital income, while effective tax rates on labour (including social security contributions) and, to a lesser extent, consumption have gone up in the EU average.

From this finding we have drawn some conclusions for the need and the effectiveness of tax policy coordination in the EU. Comparing the recent proposals for a coordinated increase in the taxation of capital income on the one hand and of value-added taxation on the other, it can be concluded that the desirability of both sets of coordination measures is uncertain, but for different reasons. In the area of capital income taxation, fiscal externalities between EU countries are present and a basic argument for tax coordination clearly exists. However, the *effectiveness* of such a policy is severely constrained by the integration of the European Union into world capital markets and the resulting possibility of capital flight to third countries. In contrast, trade relations with non-member states do not constrain commodity tax harmonization in the EU. However, the *necessity* of such a policy is far from clear, given the empirical evidence of relatively small disruptions caused by tax differentials in the internal market.

Notes

1. In contrast, the source principle ensures an efficient allocation of world savings whereas the savings decision will be distorted under the residence principle if tax rates differ internationally. For a more detailed introduction to the proper-

ties of international principles of capital taxation, see Frenkel, Razin and Sadka (1991: ch. 2).

2. The analytics in this section is adopted from Hoyt (1991). The initial contributions in the literature on capital tax competition are Wilson (1986) and Zodrow and Mieszkowski (1986). A comprehensive recent survey is given by Wilson (1999).

3. Note that from the symmetry assumption $k_i = k^* \, \forall \, i$ in the Nash equilibrium.

4. Note that there is no motive for trade if the per-capita endowments of all countries are identical. Hence the best that a coordinated tax policy can do is to replicate the (efficient) allocation under autarky.

5. In contrast, the taxation of capital income at the level of individuals (interest, dividends, capital gains) is generally incorporated in the personal income tax. While withholding taxes on certain types of capital incomes can be isolated in the tax statistics, these need not be a close approximation for the final taxation of this capital income, which depends on the personal marginal income tax rate of the investor.

6. Note, however, that the rise in the effective taxation of labour is due primarily to increasing social security contributions. This increase, in turn, is caused by the fact that expenditures on old age pensions and health care have risen more than gross wages and hence may have little connection with differences in the international mobility of labour versus capital.

7. For a more detailed critical evaluation of the econometric literature on this issue, see Schulze and Ursprung (1999: 312–17).

8. In 1997 the European Council, however, adopted a so-called 'Code of Conduct in business taxation'. Under this code member states pledge not to apply discriminatory tax rules that favour internationally mobile firms over less mobile domestic firms. See Genser and Haufler (1999) for a more detailed evaluation of this policy measure.

9. The European Commission plans to replace this 'transitional system' by an international tax credit scheme that grants a full tax credit in the importing country for all taxes levied in the country of exportation (see European Commission 1996). From the perspective of traders, this implies that the tax rate of the home country is relevant for all purchases, so that an international tax credit scheme is very similar to the present destination principle. However, the distribution of tax revenues across member states will change under this scheme, requiring a clearing mechanism that is at the centre of ongoing debates between EU member states.

10. In the special case where the tax is levied at a uniform rate on all goods and services, tax rate differentials can be equalized across countries by an adjustment in the general price level or, alternatively, the exchange rate. This 'exchange rate argument' has received much attention in the literature, but most observers agree that the conditions for it to hold are not met in practice, mostly because the VAT base is less than comprehensive. For more detailed treatments of this issue, see Genser, Haufler and Sørensen (1995) and Keen and Smith (1996).

11. The treatment in this section is adapted from Haufler (1996a). The fundamental contributions in this area are Mintz and Tulkens (1986) and Kanbur and Keen (1993). A first contribution that analyses commodity tax competition under imperfect competition in product markets is Keen and Lahiri (1998). For recent surveys of the relevant literature see Lockwood (1998) and Wilson (1999).

References

Alworth, J. (1998) 'Taxation and integrated financial markets: The challenges of derivatives and other financial innovations', *International Tax and Public Finance*, 5: 507–34.

Berglas, E. (1981) 'Harmonization of commodity taxes', *Journal of Public Economics*, 16: 377–87.

Bode, E., Krieger-Boden, C. and Lammers, K. (1994) *Cross-border activities and the European Single Market*, Kiel: Institut für Weltwirtschaft.

Bucovetsky, S. (1991) 'Asymmetric tax competition', *Journal of Urban Economics*, 30: 167–81.

Bucovetsky, S. and Wilson, J.D. (1991) 'Tax competition with two tax instruments', *Regional Science and Urban Economics*, 21: 333–50.

Chennells, L. and Griffith, R. (1997) *Taxing profits in a changing world*, London: Institute for Fiscal Studies.

Devereux, M.P. and Griffith, R. (1998) 'Taxes and the location of production: evidence from a panel of US multinationals', *Journal of Public Economics*, 68: 335–67.

European Commission (1996) 'A common system of value added taxation. A programme for the Internal Market', Document COM (96) 328, Brussels.

—— (1998) 'Proposal for a Council Directive to ensure a minimum of effective taxation of savings income in the form of interest payments within the Community', Document COM (98) 295, Brussels.

FitzGerald, J., Johnston, J. and Williams, J. (1995) 'Indirect tax distortions in a Europe of shopkeepers', Working Paper 56, Dublin: The Economic and Social Research Institute.

Frenkel, J., Razin, A. and Sadka, E. (1991) *International taxation in an integrated world*, Cambridge, Mass: MIT Press.

Garrett, G. (1995) 'Capital mobility, trade, and the domestic politics of economic policy', *International Organization*, 49: 657–87.

Genser, B. and Haufler, A. (1999) 'Harmonization of corporate income taxation in the EU', *Aussenwirtschaft*, 54: 319–48.

Genser, B., Haufler, A. and Sørensen, P.B. (1995) 'Indirect taxation in an integrated Europe: is there a way of avoiding trade distortions without sacrificing national tax autonomy?', *Journal of Economic Integration*, 10: 178–205.

Genser, B., Hettich, F. and Schmidt, C. (1999) 'Messung der effektiven Steuerbelastung. Eine vergleichende Analyse ausgewählter OECD-Staaten', unpublished manuscript, University of Konstanz.

Georgakopoulos, T. and Hitiris, T. (1992) 'On the superiority of the destination over the origin principle of taxation for intra-union trade', *The Economic Journal*, 102: 117–26.

Gordon, R.H. (1986) 'Taxation of investment and savings in a world economy', *American Economic Review*, 76: 1086–102.

Gordon, R.H. and Nielsen, S.B. (1997) 'Tax avoidance and value-added vs. income taxation in an open economy', *Journal of Public Economics*, 66: 173–97.

Grubert, H.A. and Mutti, J. (1996) 'Do taxes influence where US corporations invest?' paper presented at the Trans-Atlantic Public Economics Seminar (TAPES), Amsterdam.

Haufler, A. (1996a) 'Tax coordination with different preferences for public goods: Conflict or harmony of interest?', *International Tax and Public Finance*, 3: 5–28.

—— (1996b) 'Tax differentials and external tariffs in a trade deflection model', *Finanzarchiv*, 53: 47–67.

Hoyt, W.H. (1991) 'Property taxation, Nash equilibrium, and market power', *Journal of Urban Economics*, 30: 123–31.

Huizinga, H. and Nielsen, S.B. (2000) 'The taxation of interest in Europe: A minimum withholding tax?', in S. Cnossen (ed.) *Taxing Capital income in the European Union*, Oxford: Oxford University Press: 135–60.

Johnson, H.G. (1953/54) 'Optimum tariffs and retaliation', *Review of Economic Studies*, 21: 142–53.

Kanbur, R. and Keen, M. (1993) 'Jeux sans frontières: Tax competition and tax coordination when countries differ in size', *American Economic Review*, 83: 877–92.

Keen, M. (1993) 'The welfare economics of tax co-ordination in the European Community: a survey', *Fiscal Studies*, 14: 15–36.

Keen, M. and Lahiri, S. (1998) 'The comparison between destination and origin principles under imperfect competition', *Journal of International Economics*, 45: 323–50.

Keen, M. and Smith, S. (1996) 'The future of value-added tax in the European Union', *Economic Policy*, 23: 375–420.

Kennan, J. and Riezman, R. (1988) 'Do big countries win tariff wars?', *Journal of International Economics*, 29: 81–5.

Lockwood, B. (1998) 'Tax competition and tax co-ordination under destination and origin principles: a synthesis', unpublished manuscript, University of Warwick.

Mendoza, E., Razin, A. and Tesar, L. (1994) 'Effective tax rates in macroeconomics: cross-country estimates of tax rates on factor incomes and consumption', *Journal of Monetary Economics*, 34: 297–323.

Mintz, J. and Tulkens, H. (1986) 'Commodity tax competition between member states of a federation: equilibrium and efficiency', *Journal of Public Economics*, 29: 133–72.

Norman, G. and Motta, M. (1993) 'Eastern European economic integration and foreign direct investment', *Journal of Economics and Management Strategy*, 2: 483–507.

OECD (1977) *Model double taxation convention on income and on capital*, Paris.

Osmundsen, P., Hagen, K. and Schjelderup, G. (1998) 'Internationally mobile firms and tax policy', *Journal of International Economics*, 45: 97–113.

Papke, L.E. (1991) 'Interstate business tax differentials and new firm location', *Journal of Public Economics*, 45: 47–68.

Price Waterhouse (1994) 'VAT and excise duties: Changes in cross-border purchasing patterns following the abolition of fiscal frontiers on 1 January 1993.' Final Report to the Commission of the European Communities, Brussels.

Quinn, D. (1997) 'The correlates of change in international financial regulation', *American Political Science Review*, 91: 531–51.

Ratzinger, J. (1998) *Die Bedeutung privater Direktimporte für die Güterbesteuerung in der Europäischen Union*, München: ifo-Studien zur Finanzpolitik, 65.

Razin, A. and Sadka, E. (1991) 'International tax competition and gains from tax harmonization', *Economics Letters*, 37: 69–76.

Rodrik, D. (1997) 'Trade, Social Insurance, and the limits to globalization', National Bureau of Economic Research Working Paper 5905, Cambridge/Mass: NBER.

Ruding Report (1992) *Report of the committee of independent experts on company taxation*, Brussels and Luxembourg.

Schaden, B. (1995) *Effektive Kapitalsteuerbelastung in Europa. Eine empirische Analyse aus deutscher Sicht*, Heidelberg: Physica.

Schulze, G. and Ursprung, H. (1999) 'Globalisation of the economy and the nation state', *The World Economy*, 22: 295–352.

Shibata, H. (1967) 'The theory of economic unions: a comparative analysis of customs unions, free trade areas and tax unions', in C.S. Shoup (ed.) *Fiscal harmonization in common markets*, New York: Columbia University Press: 145–264.

Sørensen, P.B. (1995) 'Changing views of the corporate income tax', *National Tax Journal*, 48: 279–95.

Tanzi, V. and Bovenberg, L.A. (1990) 'Is there a need for harmonizing capital income taxes within EC countries?', in Siebert, H. (ed.) *Reforming capital income taxation*, Tübingen: Mohr: 171–97.

Whalley, J. (1979) 'Uniform domestic tax rates, trade distortions and economic integration', *Journal of Public Economics*, 11: 213–21.

Wilson, J.D. (1986) 'A theory of interregional tax competition', *Journal of Urban Economics*, 19: 296–315.

—— (1991) 'Tax competition with interregional differences in factor endowments', *Regional Science and Urban Economics*, 21: 423–51.

—— (1999) 'Theories of tax competition', *National Tax Journal*, 52: 269–304.

Zodrow, G. and Mieszkowski, P. (1986) 'Pigou, Tiebout, property taxation and the underprovision of local public goods', *Journal of Urban Economics*, 19: 356–70.

13 Regional approaches to cross-border competition policies*

Peter J. Lloyd and Kerrin Vautier

Competition policies are a part of some regional trading arrangements (RTAs). The World Trade Organization (WTO) has elements of competition law in its trade law, chiefly in the General Agreement on Trade in Services (GATS), and there are a growing number of bilateral competition cooperation agreements. Consequently, this is an area of cross-border policy which is being developed at the bilateral, regional and multilateral levels. This raises the questions of why it is being developed simultaneously at all levels, and what are the advantages and disadvantages of the regional level *vis-à-vis* the bilateral and multilateral levels? And why have some regional trading arrangements developed competition policies while others have not?

This chapter addresses these questions. The first section discusses the issues of cross-border competition as an area of deep integration. The second section distinguishes between bilateral, regional, and multilateral levels of cross-border policies to promote cross-border competition. The third section outlines the evolution of competition policies in regional trading arrangements. Examples of competition policies which are included in regional trading arrangements are discussed in the fourth section; these are antidumping actions, subsidies and countervailing duties, cartels, and mergers. This leads to an examination of the question of why some RTAs have progressed further in this area than others. Some views on the contribution of regional level policies to promote competition are presented in section 5.

1 The issues

Until recently, competition policies were regarded as a matter of national policy in all countries other than those in the EU. The recent inclusion of these policies in regional trading arrangements is usually regarded as an example of what Lawrence (1996) called 'deep integration'. 'Deep integration' refers to policies which are 'beyond the border', in contrast to 'shallow integration' which refers to the traditional border protection measures, tariffs and non-tariff measures. Other examples of deep integration are standards relating to industrial products or safety or health or the environment, policies relating to particular sectors, such as agriculture or industry or transport, and business laws.[1]

Competition policies have come to be regarded as important in RTAs for several reasons. First, they impinge on international trade. It came to be realized that removing all border restrictions on cross-border trade in goods and services did not assure non-discriminatory market access for foreign supplies if other regulations within borders discriminated against them. The removal of the border barriers to foreign trade itself highlighted the importance of non-border regulations, such as industrial standards and business laws. There is therefore a natural progression from the removal of border restrictions to the removal of non-border regulations and laws which discriminate against supplies from other countries. In the area of competition policies, this is often expressed in terms of ensuring that anti-competitive private behaviour does not deny the benefits of government trade liberalization. This trade-effects motivation is most important in the case of the EU but it is also important in other RTAs. At the multilateral level, concern that private practices might nullify the benefits of trade liberalization was expressed in the Uruguay Round; it led to the establishment of the Working Group on the Interaction between Trade and Competition Policy at the First Ministerial Meeting of the WTO in 1996.

Another link between trade policies and competition policies is provided by the taking of antidumping actions. There has been a rapid growth in the incidence of antidumping actions since the conclusion of the Uruguay Round. Some trade economists see the establishment of multilateral rules relating to cross-border competition as a means of constraining unilateral antidumping action.

However, the reasons for developing competition policies at the regional (and multilateral) level should go beyond concern over trade liberalization. Competition in markets is desirable independently of trade liberalization because of its contribution to efficiency and welfare. Welfare economics teaches us that competitive behaviour and free international trade are two separate conditions required for the efficient allocation of resources in the world economy.[2] Governments around the world are adopting more pro-competitive policies in areas such as deregulation, privatization and foreign direct investment. These trends reflect the convergence of view towards competition in markets as a means of improving the efficiency in individual economies. Concern over cross-border competition can be seen as a reflection of the more general concern with competition. This belief in competition as a means to the efficient production and allocation of goods and services is the primary reason for also developing competition policies at the regional level.

'Competition policy' is a rather vague term. It should encompass all government policies which promote competition among producers. Policies relating to such areas as international trade, foreign direct investment and intellectual property are all relevant to the promotion of competition.

We prefer to use the term policies that promote competition, or 'competition-promoting policies' for short.

The set of competition-promoting policies is very broad. Figure 13.1 sets out the major policies that are used to promote competition. The literature on contestability of markets emphasizes that competition requires freedom of market entry and exit. At the level of competition across national borders, foreign firms enter or have access to other countries by two modes. The first mode is the traditional method of competition by means of production in the home country and exporting to the foreign country. This mode requires free trade in goods and services. The second mode is establishment of an affiliate in the foreign country. This mode requires the right of establishment and national treatment in the country in which the affiliate is established in order to compete on equal terms with national producers. Thus, this mode highlights the importance of foreign direct investment regulations. Freedom of capital movements is especially important in the case of service industries that require a commercial presence, such as electricity and gas generation and distribution, and telecommunications. Freedom of labour movement may also be important in those goods and services which require the movement of natural persons, such as managers and technical personnel. Other policies will also impact on competition in markets for goods and services.

Competition (antitrust) law is a subset of the competition-promoting policies. In fact, it is really the last resort. Trade and investment liberalization and other policies are intended to promote competition but in case producers still act anti-competitively, laws have been put in place to prohibit them from doing so. A few countries, such as Hong Kong and

Government policies	Business conduct (public and private)

- free trade in goods and services
- free trade in capital
- free trade in labour
- intellectual property
- standards
- deregulation
- privatization
- competition law

- unilateral conduct
- collusive conduct
- mergers and takeovers

Figure 13.1 Policy framework for promoting competition.

Singapore, believe that they have no need for comprehensive competition laws as their markets are completely open to traders and investors, although they have not ruled out industry-specific regulation. The WTO (1997: 51) explicitly rejected this argument on the grounds that there are natural monopolies and other natural barriers to entry, and producers will still seek to collude and restrict competition by introducing artificial restrictions on trade and competition. Certainly, RTAs such as the EU and NAFTA which have accomplished or will soon accomplish virtually completely free trade in goods and services and in foreign direct investment (FDI) do not regard these freedoms as adequate to ensure competition.

Actually, the distinction between 'border' and 'beyond-the-border' policies is not accurate in the case of competition policies, as these include policies that cover both competition within national borders and cross-border business practices, such as export cartels, market allocation and mergers. At the regional level, there are three dimensions of competition policies. These are:

- the development and convergence of national competition policies;
- the development of policies dealing with competition problems that cross national borders but which are within the area of the regional trading arrangement;
- the development of policies to deal with intra-regional competition problems involving countries outside the region.

Elements of one or more of these dimensions are present in regional-level competition policies in each RTA.

2 The choice among levels of action

As markets have become globalized and competition across national borders increases, there is a general case *in principle* for some form of concerted action to address competition problems involving the producers of two or more countries (see Lloyd and Vautier 1999: Ch. 2 and WTO 1997: Ch. IV for the general case and examples). Such problems arise in all areas of competition law, that is, in areas of unilateral conduct, collusive conduct and in mergers and acquisitions.

There is a multiplicity of ways in which concerted multi-country action against anti-competitive behaviour may be taken. It is usual to distinguish between four approaches to these problems. These will be called the *bilateral, regional, non-binding multilateral* and *binding multilateral* approaches.[3]

In this context, the term bilateral refers to agreements between two parties in the form of bilateral cooperation agreements or mutual legal assistance treaties. These agreements are usually between the governments of two countries, but in the case of the 1991 and 1998 bilateral competition cooperation agreements between the USA and the European Community, they are agreements between the RTA as a party and the government of another country as the second party. The term 'regional agreement' refers to an agreement among the countries which are members of some RTA,[4] that is, a free trade area or customs union under the rules of the GATT/WTO. The distinction between bilateral and regional agreements is made on the basis of the nature of the agreements, not the number of parties to the agreement. One of the RTAs which is relevant here involves only two countries, namely the CER Agreement between Australia and New Zealand, but the agreement on competition is a part of the RTA. All of the other RTAs involve more than two members.

There are several non-binding multilateral agreements in the area of competition policies,[5] notably the OECD Recommendations for Bilateral Cooperation and the OECD Guidelines for Multinational Enterprises, the GATT 1960 Decision on Arrangements for Consultation on Restrictive Business Practices, and the UN Set of Multilaterally Agreed and Equitable Principles and Rules for the Control of Restrictive Business Practices. The only multilateral agreements relevant to this area which is binding on its members or signatories are the agreements made by the GATT and the WTO. (For detailed description and analysis of each of these types of agreements in the area of competition-promoting policy or law, see Lloyd and Vautier 1999: Parts 2, 3, 4 and 5.)

Non-binding agreements are codes of good behaviour, either for governments (as in the case of the OECD Recommendations) or for the producing enterprises themselves (as in the case of the OECD Guidelines) or for both (as in the case of the UN Set). These agreements were developed from 1960 when the GATT Decision was made and during the 1970s. At this time there was hope that these codes and guidelines might induce the governments and enterprises to act to promote competition in markets, but it is widely believed that they have not had a substantial effect on market behaviour. This is a result of their non-binding nature, though other features such as the lack of any institutional capacity to investigate business conduct may have contributed. The exception is the OECD Recommendations. These provide a framework for bilateral agreements that are increasing in number and scope.

There is one general issue of economic analysis that affects the choice between regional and other approaches to resolving cross-border competition problems. This is the issue of seeking a centralized or a decentralized solution to the problems. Both centralized and decentralized solutions are forms of concerted action but they differ fundamentally in their approach. A centralized solution involves the establishment of a centralized authority with powers of enforcement in the countries concerned. A decentralized solution relies instead on the powers of enforcement of the individual nations aided by cooperation among them through such means as comity and bilateral agreements.

The most centralized solution is the establishment of a supranational authority which would operate at the global level, much like the national competition authorities operate at the national level. It would investigate business conduct in whatever countries were involved, consider the interests of all countries, and enforce its law. It would presumably act to maximize global welfare, the sum of the welfare of all nations, rather than the welfare of individual nations. Such an authority was recommended during the Uruguay Round negotiations by the International Antitrust Draft Code Working Group (1993) and by the Group of Experts commissioned by the European Commission in the lead up to the Singapore Ministerial Meeting of the WTO (European Commission 1996). The least centralized solution is the continued reliance on action by national authorities supplemented by voluntary cooperation among the governments involved. Between these extremes there are several alternatives.

At the level of regional action, there is also a choice between centralized and decentralized action. This has been recognized explicitly in the EU where the debate about the principle of subsidiarity has posed this choice clearly. This principle was first laid down explicitly in the Maastricht Treaty, though it has evolved throughout the history of the European Community. It divides between the national government level and the EU-level functions which are not the exclusive competence of the Community. Article 3B of the Treaty declares:

In areas which do not fall within its exclusive competence, the Community shall take action, in accordance with the principle of subsidiarity, only if and in so far as the objectives of the proposed actions cannot be sufficiently achieved by the member States and can therefore, by reason of the scale or effect of the proposed action, be better achieved by the Community.

This principle does not, contrary to a common belief, lay down which areas of policy shall be dealt with at the regional level and which at the national level. Rather, it lays down principles which shall determine the division of responsibilities between these levels. Its main concern is that the objectives of the policies be achieved efficiently. (CEPR 1993 and Pelkmans 1997: Chs 4 and 12 provide excellent discussions of the principle.)

The choice between a multilateral approach, say under the WTO, on the one hand, and regional approach or a combination of regional and bilateral approach, on the other, may also be regarded as an issue of subsidiarity. Thus, subsidiarity is a general principle that can be applied at all levels to determine the optimum division of responsibilities between multilateral, regional and bilateral authorities.

Several factors will determine the costs and benefits of a centralized versus a decentralized solution and the allocation of powers between the levels. These include the extent of powers of national, regional or supranational authorities to gather information and investigate private actions, and to enforce any decision. They may also include the risks of capture of these authorities by private producer interests, which may be greater in one form of action than in others, and the difficulty of agreeing upon the objectives of the laws and the methods of analysis of competition cases. A more centralized solution may have advantages of greater uniformity and lower risk of capture, but it may have the disadvantages of greater difficulty in agreeing upon objectives and analysis, and of weaker enforcement.

One may expect that opinions about the relative advantages of bilateral, regional and multilateral approaches will differ among countries or groups of countries. This is in fact the case. The EU has been more inclined to centralized solutions at both the regional and multilateral levels, whereas the USA is committed to the bilateral approach and strongly opposed to the development of binding regional or multilateral anti-trust laws. These opinions have been a major force in shaping the characteristics of the approach in each region.

The next section outlines the main features of the competition-promoting policies of the RTAs.

3 Evolution of competition-promoting policies in RTAs

The first regional agreement relating to competition was that of the 1957 Treaty of Rome, principally Articles 85–92. The treaty established the European Economic Community (which became the European Union after the Maastricht Treaty). Subsequently the EEC/EU rules have been extended to the new members of the EEC/EU, and to the European Economic Area (EEA), and the states associated with the EU in Central and Eastern Europe and the Mediterranean. This now involves a total of thirty-three countries (the fifteen full members of the EU, the three remaining members of the EEA, the ten Central and East European countries, and the five Mediterranean countries). Six other regional trading agreements have incorporated some agreement relating to competition; these are the 1990 extension to the Closer Economic Relations Agreement between Australia and New Zealand; the 1991 Andean Group comprising Bolivia, Colombia, Ecuador, Peru and Venezuela; the 1992 North American Free Trade Agreement comprising the USA, Canada and Mexico; the 1994 Group of Three Treaty (G-3) comprising Mexico, Colombia and Venezuela; the 1996 MERCOSUR Agreement comprising, Argentina, Brazil, Paraguay and Uruguay; and the 1996 Canada–Chile Free Trade Agreement. Counting only once those countries in more than one regional agreement, forty-nine countries are currently involved in regional competition agreements. With the exception of the EU, the development of regional competition-promoting policies is a feature of the 1990s.

The Free Trade of the Americas process was initiated at the Summit of the Americas in 1994 and formal negotiations were launched at the Second Summit in Santiago in April 1998. One of the nine Negotiating Groups is Competition Policy but the negotiations among the thirty-four countries are not due to be completed until 2005. If and when completed, the FTAA will represent a major advance in competition-promoting policy at the Hemisphere level.

Of the RTAs which contain explicit competition policies, the EU is by far the most important in the area of competition-promoting policies (as in most other areas). (For a description of the competition policy in the EU, see Pelkmans 1997: Ch. 12). First, it involves the most countries. The country coverage of competition policies and competition law extends beyond the fifteen full members of the EU to the members of the EEA and the Associated States of the Central and East European countries (CEECs) and the Mediterranean states. All of these countries have been obliged to accept the *acquis communautaire* of the EU, including its competition law. Not all of the features of the competition policies and competition law apply currently to these countries; for example, they are not subject to the authority of the DG IV, and there is no freedom of movement of labour between these countries and the full members of the EU. However, all may eventually become members of the EU and therefore subject to its policies and laws in full. Consequently, we shall confine our description to the policies that apply to full members only. Second, it has pioneered many features of regional rules and cooperation among members. For example, the EU established a supranational regional authority, developed the principle of subsidiarity, established detailed rules of cooperation and information sharing between the regional level and the national authorities, and developed extensive principles of positive comity in the 1998 bilateral agreement with the USA. Third, regional competition policies has been developed to a much greater extent in the EU with respect to all three dimensions than in any other RTA.

Each of the seven existing RTAs which have provisions relating to competition policies differs in terms of the extent of harmonization of national policies, the extent of region-wide rules, and the extent of regional level policies to deal with competition problems involving countries outside the region. It is not possible to even summarize the features of the competition policies of each region in this chapter, but some qualitative properties are noted. (For a general review of the properties of the RTA's competition policies, see Lloyd and Vautier 1999: Part 3.)

Table 13.1 provides a broad summary of the main provisions of these policies in all seven RTAs. In most cases, the answers with respect to each feature are a straightforward 'yes' or 'no', but in some instances there are degrees of achievement of the relevant feature. 'Substantial' indicates a greater degree of competition promotion than 'significant'; for example, CER is recorded as having a 'substantial' degree of liberalization of trade

Table 13.1 Summary of competition-promoting policies in RTAs

	EU	CER	NAFTA	Canada–Chile	Group of Three	MERCOSUR	Andean Community
1. General competition-promoting policies							
Free trade in goods	Yes	Yes	Yes	Yes	Yes	Yes	Yes
Free trade in services	Yes	Subst	Sign	Sign	Sign	Subst	Subst
Free trade in capital	Yes	No	Subst	Subst	Sub	Subst	Subst
Free trade in labour	Yes	Yes	No	No	No	No	No
2. Competition-promoting provisions in RTAs							
Common competition policies	Yes	No	No	No	No	No	No
Harmonization of competition laws	Subst	Subst	No	No	No	No	No
Regional competition law	Yes	Sign	No	No	No	Yes[1]	Yes[1]
Supranational competition authority	Yes	No	Yes[2]	No	No	Yes[1]	Yes[1]
Agreements between authorities	NA	Yes	No	No	No	No	No
Elimination of intra-area antidumping	Yes	Yes	No	Yes	No	No	No
3. Agreements with outside countries							
Bilateral agreements	Yes	No	No	No	No	No	No

NA = not applicable, Subst = substantial, Sign = significant

Notes
1. Both the Andean Community and MERCOSUR contain area-wide competition law and supranational provisions, but the powers are unclear and not yet tested.
2. There is an agreement between the governments of the USA and Canada concerning competition law.

in services, as this agreement has a negative list which lists those areas where free trade does not apply and this list is now small, whereas NAFTA, the Canada–Chile Agreement and the Group of Three are recorded as having only a 'significant' degree of liberalization as these agreements have a larger number of exclusions. In some cases, a measure to promote competition may not yet be implemented in full but, where there is a definite commitment, it has been recorded in the affirmative. This applies, for example, to the liberalization of free trade in goods in NAFTA, the Canada–Chile Agreement and the Group of Three which are following schedules of tariff elimination.

These results should be interpreted with caution. In some cases, the answers are approximate and hide a considerably richer detail. For example, in the case of NAFTA, the Canada–Chile Agreement and the Group of Three, the table records that there is no harmonization of national competition laws. In fact, the first paragraph of the first article of NAFTA Chapter 15 declares that each member 'shall adopt or maintain measures to proscribe anticompetitive business conduct', and this language is replicated in the other two regional agreements. That is, they provide for a comprehensive competition law in each member country, and it was the desire to join NAFTA which induced Mexico to accept this (and other) conditions. The introduction of national laws might be regarded as the first step in harmonization, but these regional agreements have not yet resulted in any amendment of the substantive provisions of the laws of one or more of its members to bring about convergence in these national laws in the ways in which this has occurred in both the EU and CER. Similarly, these three agreements all contain provisions for the mobility of business persons. However, this applies only to executive and professional employees, and it is temporary. Consequently, the table records 'No' regional labour mobility. MERCOSUR, too, has a long-term objective of liberalizing labour movements, and the Andean Group established a Labor Consultative Council. Moreover, one should bear in mind that the competition-promoting policies of all of the agreements are constantly evolving.

Even in terms of the broad features recorded in the table, there are major differences in the treatment of competition-promoting policies among the seven areas. Broadly speaking, the countries fall into four groups. The first two groupings consists of the EU and of the CER Agreement singly. The second distinct grouping consists of the NAFTA, Canada–Chile and the Group of Three. The third grouping comprises MERCOSUR and the Andean Community.

The EU has developed broad policies to promote intra-area competition, as well as specific area-wide competition law. From the time of the Treaty of Rome in 1957, the Four Freedoms of the Common Market have guaranteed freedom of movement of goods, services, capital and labour. In relation to competition law in the region, 'competition policy' has been one of the areas of so-called common policies from the outset. The EU has brought about the introduction of national competition laws in its full (and associated) members, and there has been a considerable convergence of these laws and their enforcement procedures. Subsequently, the coverage of competition law has been steadily extended in the EU. The principles of competition-promoting policies were strengthened further in the Maastricht Treaty which laid down the general principle of an open market economy with free competition. The EU has a powerful supranational authority. In terms of policies dealing with countries outside the EU, the EU as a community has signed two competition cooperation agreements with the USA, the second of which has developed important principles of positive comity for competition law. Thus, the EU provides a standard by which to measure the extent of development of regional policies relating to competition in other RTAs.

In the CER countries too, the scope of policies promoting competition is broad. Both countries have also carried out very extensive programmes of privatization and deregulation during the 1990s which have had the effect of greatly increasing competition in many previously highly regulated industries, especially service industries, such as telecommunications and power generation and distribution. Both countries have greatly liberalized trade in goods and FDI with respect to all trading partners as well as bilaterally. Competition law is seen as a protection against private actions which could undermine the governments' achievements in opening markets. Each country has a comprehensive competition law.

At the regional level, the CER Agreement extends further in its competition law provisions and other competition-promoting policies than any of the other five, but it is not as far-reaching as that of the EU. There have been substantial advances in all three dimensions of competition-promoting policies. The CER Agreement was formed as a free trade area in 1983, with free trade in goods achieved by 1990. Free trade was extended to services through the 1988 Protocol on Services; this protocol contained a negative list but the number of exclusions has been reduced. Uniquely among the RTAs, there is free trade in labour (under an independent agreement known as the Trans-Tasman Travel Arrangements that dates back to the 1920s) but not in capital. However, both countries have greatly reduced restrictions on entry of FDI and national treatment *vis-à-vis* all other countries in recent years, and now rate among the most free markets for capital movements.

In relation to the development of policies dealing with competition problems involving both countries, the CER has adopted a decentralized approach in contrast to the centralized approach of the EU. There is no supranational authority. The national competition laws have been substantially harmonized. In 1986 New Zealand amended its competition statute, the Commerce Act, to conform largely to the Australian Trade Practices Act, though some significant differences remain in areas such as essential services and telecommunications. The table records the CER as having a regional competition law, but it has achieved this in a way very different to that of the EU. In 1990 the two countries enacted what are called the Trans-Tasman Competition Provisions of the CER which deal with certain business conduct in the area. Unlike the EU, these provisions are mostly efficiency-oriented rather than trade-oriented. They extend the prohibitions on the abuse of a dominant or powerful market position in the national legislations by redefining the relevant markets as the combined markets of the two countries. By mutual consent between the two countries, this allows the countries to apply this prohibition to persons in the other country extraterritorially. At the same time the rules of evidence were amended to allow the gathering of evidence by a Court in one CER country from the other and the issuing of subpoenas to be served on persons in the other country and, if appropriate, a court of one country can conduct its proceedings in the other country. These enforcement powers go well beyond those incorporated in any bilateral cooperation agreement or other RTAs. However, they only apply to one form of business conduct and they do not apply to services. Pursuant to the Trans-Tasman competition provisions, the competition authorities of the two countries agreed to cooperate and this is extended by a second competition cooperation agreement, outside the CER, that covers all competition law. (For more detail on these aspects, see Lloyd and Vautier 1999: Ch. 5.)

In relation to the extra-CER dimensions of the competition law in the region, both countries have extraterritorial provisions in their laws and have made bilateral competition cooperation agreements with other countries, but they have done so independently, not under the aegis of the CER Agreement.

The next grouping of RTAs are NAFTA, Canada and Chile, and the Group of Three. These form a group of RTAs because the provisions and the wording of the Canada–Chile Agreement and the Treaty establishing the Group of Three follow very closely those of NAFTA. (The text of each of these is conveniently reproduced in Organization of American States 1997; Organization of American States 1998 provides an analytical summary.) The NAFTA, Canada–Chile FTA and G-3 competition provisions are all much more limited than those of the EU and CER.

NAFTA, Canada–Chile FTA and G-3 have a quite strong set of competition-promoting policies. In addition to freedom of trade in goods and services, there are strong provisions relating to the movement of capital in the regions. All agreements have provisions ensuring MFN and national treatment and unrestricted transfer of capital and a prohibition on the use of performance requirements, however, they do not guarantee rights of establishment.

The competition law provisions are limited to general principles under which competition rules are to apply to firms in the member countries and in particular to state-owned enterprises; but the substantive provisions relate only to monopolies and state trading enterprises. In NAFTA and the Canada–Chile Agreement, they merely require that these shall not nullify or impair the benefits of the free trade area and, in the case of the Group of Three, they require that the monopolies shall not engage in anti-competitive practices.

The third grouping of RTAs is MERCOSUR and the Andean Community. The Andean Community replaced the Andean Group in 1997. It widened its institutional framework and strengthened the movement towards a single market. (The text of each of these is conveniently reproduced in Organization of American States 1997; Organization of American States 1998 provides an analytical summary.) These two agreements have been inspired by the precedents of the EU rather than NAFTA. In relation to general competition-promoting policies, these groups have strong provisions, although they have yet to be implemented. In relation to the competition-promoting provisions of the RTAs, they again have broad provisions but have made little progress in implementing them. Only one of the four MERCOSUR countries, Paraguay, has yet ratified the Protocol of Defence of Competition. Although the Agreement requires all State Parties to adopt 'common rules' for conduct which prejudices free trade or is anti-competitive, Uruguay and Paraguay do not have comprehensive national competition laws. The Protocol lists forms of conduct which limit competition but leaves it up to the national governments to regulate this conduct. The Protocol created a Committee for the Defense of Competition and the 1994 Ouro Preto Protocol created a Trade Commission, but the powers of these bodies are untested. (For further discussion of MERCOSUR, see Tavares and Tineo 1998a.) The experience of the Andean Community is similar. On paper, it has established some common rules and created a supranational Board to investigate business conduct, and follows the EU principle of subsidiarity. The focus of its competition law is on conduct which restricts trade. However, it does not cover vertical restraints and mergers and the Board cannot initiate investigations and has no remedies outside a recommendation to the parties. (For further discussion, see Jatar and Tineo 1998 and Tavares and Tineo 1998b.) At the time of the Agreement only one country, Colombia, has a national competition law but the Agreement may well have stimulated Peru and Venezuela in their introduction of national laws.

4 Some examples of competition policies in RTAs

Further differences among RTAs are revealed if we look in more detail at the ways in which they deal with individual policies. We consider a sample of four particular forms of government action which affect competition or business conduct. The first two are government policies and the second two are standard parts of competition law.

4.1 Antidumping rules

Rules permitting antidumping are an instrument of trade policy, but control of the use of this trade instrument is widely perceived to be significant for the competitive process and hence should be the subject of 'competition policy'.

Three of the seven RTAs have banned the use of antidumping actions within the regions. These are the EU, the CER and the Canada–Chile Agreements.[6]

As part of the Common Market, antidumping action was prohibited by the Treaty of Rome in relation to imports from other EC/EU countries. The rationale appears to be simply that antidumping actions as a form of border trade restriction have no place in a common market with freedom of trade (see Hoekman 1998). (This prohibition has been extended to the three EFTA members of the European Economic Area. In the discussions with Associated States in East Europe and the Mediterranean, the EU made it plain that the cessation of antidumping action can occur only when markets are fully integrated; consequently antidumping actions may still be taken.)

In the CER, the antidumping trade remedy was removed in conjunction with the introduction of the specific Trans-Tasman Competition Provisions. The rationale for the removal of the antidumping remedy was never stated clearly. It appears to be primarily a belief that this remedy is inappropriate in a single market (see Vautier and Lloyd 1997: 78–82). Canada and Chile have followed the EU and CER precedents but, unlike the EU and the CER, they did so without simultaneously providing any cross-border competition law remedy. None of the other four RTAs has yet removed the intra-regional antidumping remedy.

4.2 Subsidies or state aids and countervailing duties

Countervailing duties are commonly bracketed with antidumping duties as two forms of contingent border protection, and subsidies are regarded as non-border instruments of government intervention. They are discussed together here, because control on subsidies and control on the application of countervailing (anti-subsidy) duties are complementary ways of dealing with distortions of international competition due to the payment of subsidies.

Control on subsidies is not normally regarded as a part of competition-promoting policies. The sole but important exception is the EU where 'state aids', as they are called, come within the common competition policy of the EU.

Article 92 of the Treaty of Rome prohibits any state aids which distort or threaten to distort competition in the region, although it does allow designated exceptions to this prohibition. The European Commission has endeavoured to limit state aids which distort intra-regional trade. It has drawn up regional aid guidelines and periodically surveys the extent of state aids in the Union. However, these controls have proven to be weak, competition in some industries being substantially distorted by the use of state aids (Buigues, Jacquemin and Sapir 1995 and Pelkmans 1997: Chs 12 and 14). DG IV itself states in its latest annual report that 'according to a widely-held view, this level [of state aids] is too high'. (Directorate-General IV of the European Commission 1998.) Countervailing duties, as a form of customs duties, are prohibited in the EU.

The CER approach to this area is the reverse to that of the EU. The 1988 Minute on Industry Assistance prohibited subsidies which affect CER's intra-area trade. This action reflects a realization that the removal of all borders barriers to trade is not sufficient to assure non-discriminatory market access. Since 1990 both CER member countries have vigorously reduced overall subsidies and other forms of financial assistance to producers, although New Zealand producers remain concerned over some special incentives to Australian producers. No other regional trading arrangement has succeeded in eliminating production subsidies which distort production and trade within the region. The CER still permits the application of countervailing duties on trans-Tasman trade, but no duties have been imposed since the introduction of the prohibition on subsidies which distort intra-area trade.

4.3 Cartels

Cartels are regarded as one of the most egregious forms of collusive behaviour.

In the EU, Article 85 prohibits cartels and other restrictive agreements. This is the article under which most investigations and cases have taken place. (Article 86 deals with abuse of dominant positions.) Article 85 give particular examples of practices which may restrict competition or abuse a dominant position and are, therefore, prohibited. It lists as prohibited agreements those which:

(a) directly or indirectly fix purchase or selling prices or any other trading conditions;
(b) limit or control production, markets, technical development, or investment;
(c) share markets or sources of supply.

Export cartels organized by EU producers and import cartels in other countries relating to imports from the EU are outside the scope of Article 85 and, therefore, permitted; but import cartels by undertakings in the EU and export cartels among non-EU producers relating to exports to the EU fall within the scope of Article 85.

By contrast, in the CER, there is no provision in the Agreement or any of its protocols which deals with cartels. The Trans-Tasman Competition Provisions deal solely with the abuse of a dominant position (or in Australia the use of a substantial degree of market power). The explanation for this narrow focus is that these provisions arose from the debate about antidumping actions in the region and were in large part a substitute for these actions (see Vautier and Lloyd 1997). Moreover, to date neither of the two national competition authorities has yet taken a prosecution action under these provisions.

None of the RTAs in the NAFTA-MERCOSUR-Andean Community grouping contain provisions dealing with cartels or other forms of collusive cross-border action. Their competition law provisions relate solely to monopolies and state trading enterprises. Both MERCOSUR and the Andean Community competition provisions cover cartels (and other business conduct). However, as noted, the MERCOSUR Protocol of Defence of Competition has been ratified by only one of the four members and the Andean Community Community-wide provisions have been ineffective.

4.4 Mergers

Merger law is one of the important areas of competition law, along with laws dealing with unilateral actions and collusive behaviour.

There are no explicit provisions in the Treaty of Rome relating to mergers. The Merger Regulations were added in 1990 as a result of dissatisfaction with the powers relating to mergers under Articles 85 and 86 and the increase in mergers during the 1980s, and amended in 1997 with effect from 1 March 1998.

In the context of the choice between centralized or decentralized approaches to competition problems, the Merger Regulations are the most explicit attempt to allocate power between the jurisdictions at the levels of the EU and the national governments under the principle of subsidiarity. The 1990 Merger Regulations stipulated that mergers, acquisitions and 'concentrative' joint ventures should be notified to the Commission when they are between parties whose combined world-wide annual turnover exceeds ECU 5 billion, the Community-wide turnover of each of at least two of the undertakings concerned is more than ECU 250 million and 'unless the parties conduct two-thirds or more of their business in one and the same member state'. All three conditions have to be met. The conditions mean that the merger powers do not go exclusively to the EU level, even when they involve cross-border aspects: '[The second condition] is a clear and precise attempt to base centralization upon the extent of the spillovers between member states' (CEPR 1993: 135). The 1998 revised Merger Regulations maintained the thresholds. (The Commission had proposed that the thresholds be lowered but this was not approved by the Council.) They also harmonized the treatment of mergers involving joint ventures and simplified the notification procedures.

CEPR (1993: 135–7) evaluated the net gains from centralizing merger controls at the EU-level compared to the net gains from coordination among the national-level competition authorities. It saw the net gains at each level as a tradeoff between the loss from regulatory capture and gains from the capture of cross-border spillovers. Its conclusion is that:

> Merger control is an area in which cooperation to secure the benefits of policy coordination is a particularly unsatisfactory alternative to centralization, because of the highly discretionary nature of the policy to be implemented and the consequent difficulty for twelve member states in observing whether each is abiding by the terms of a collective agreement. Overall, merger policy is a good illustration of a case where the gains from centralization are high; but it is also a warning that the central institutions need to be designed in such a way as to ensure that these gains are not dissipated through an increase in rent-seeking and regulatory capture.
>
> (CEPR 1993: 136–7)

In practice, however, the merger thresholds, and especially the Community-wide turnover threshold, have meant that more than 90 per cent of proposed mergers in which one or more parties is located in the EU escape EU control (Sleuwaegen 1998). The merger regulations have also been criticized by Sleuwaegen for a lack of transparency and flexibility.

None of the other six RTAs has developed any region-wide laws and procedures for dealing with mergers. This may reflect in part the fact that the investigation by national competition authorities of mergers involving parties located in other countries is widely regarded as adequate.

In summary, the four examples reveal very wide variations among the RTAs in their handling of matters of significance to the competitive process. In relation to the second two examples, only the EU has developed working laws and procedures to deal with region-wide competition problems generally. The CER has developed laws and procedures to deal with the abuse or misuse of market power but these provisions have virtually not been used. MERCOSUR and the Andean Community have provisions modelled on those of the EU but they are ineffective. In relation to the first two examples, the development of laws or actions to deal with these problems is a little more extensive; three RTAs have abolished the use of antidumping actions on intra-area trade and two have restricted the use of subsidies which affect intra-area trade or competition.

Why have some RTAs progressed further in the area of competition-promoting policies than others? The answer to this question appears to be a combination of attitudes or culture and of factors which are favourable to the development of regional level policies to promote competition.

In the case of the grouping comprising MERCOSUR and the Andean

Community, there is an absence of a culture of competition and several of the member countries still do not have comprehensive national competition laws.

Even if the members of an RTA have a competition promotion culture, it is not easy or even perceived as desirable to develop regional level policies. For example, the USA has the best developed and the most aggressively enforced competition law in the world (and Canada also has a well developed and enforced competition law). The USA generally wishes to promote competition across national borders. However, the USA has adamantly opposed the development of regional and multilateral level competition law. NAFTA is confined to the development of national competition laws and provisions relating solely to monopolies and state trading enterprises, with action to police these areas left in the hands of the national competition authorities. It did not succeed in bringing antidumping rules into its 'competition policy' framework. At the WTO Working Group on the Interaction between Trade and Competition Policy, the USA has opposed the development of a multilateral level law. Instead it has advocated the development of national competition law in all countries and the development of a network of bilateral competition cooperation agreements (WTO 1998). The views of the US government have dominated the general direction of policies to promote competition in NAFTA and in the other two RTAs involving countries which are members of NAFTA, the Canada–Chile Agreement and the Group of Three.

By contrast, a common competition policy and a common competition law have been an integral feature of the development of the Common Market in the EU from the outset. In the case of the CER, the two member countries have had both a culture and long history of competition law; Australia has had competition laws since 1906 and New Zealand since 1908, both shortly after the introduction of competition laws in Canada and the USA. They have also had a desire to develop regional level competition policies including laws. There is no official view that the region should be a fully integrated single market, but the two countries have moved in that direction steadily as the removal of barriers to trade in goods and services has increased trade and competition in the area. Competition-promoting policies such as the Trans-Tasman Competition Provisions, the cessation of intra-area antidumping actions and the removal of intra-area trade-distorting subsidies have been seen pragmatically as ways of getting the maximum benefit from trade liberalization in the area.

In both the EU and the CER political factors were favourable to the development of regional competition-promoting policies. The European Community was formed in the aftermath of a devastating war and with a strong desire to form an economic union which would integrate the economies and help to ensure peace in Europe. Australia and New

Zealand have a long shared history as former colonies of the United Kingdom and now dominions of the British Commonwealth, a common tradition of common law and a long history of cooperation in political and economic matters. These circumstances have made the countries in these RTAs willing to cede elements of national sovereignty to aid regional development.

5 Contribution of RTAs to the promotion of global competition

We have found that the development of region-wide competition-promoting policies in the RTAs is limited. The EU has developed a full range of common competition-promoting policies and a full arsenal of competition law at the regional level. However, none of the other RTAs has actually used region-wide competition law and associated supra-national institutional arrangements to overcome regional problems with anti-competitive business conduct. There are more successes in general competition-promoting policies in these RTAs, such as trade liberalization and in other measures such as the abolition of antidumping actions in three regions and strict control of subsidies in the CER, but these are very patchy.

The limited achievements in deeper regional integration in this area should, however, be compared with the achievements of bilateral and multilateral approaches to dealing with competition problems in the global economy, as they are possible alternative approaches. In this perspective, it is notable that the other two approaches also have severe limitations. The country coverage of bilateral agreements is less than that of the RTAs, these agreements rely on voluntary cooperation and there are severe limits on the abilities of the authorities to exchange information and enforce legal actions. (For a review of the bilateral experience, see Lloyd and Vautier 1999: Ch. 3.) The non-binding multilateral agreements are generally agreed to have had little effect on market outcomes. The WTO is the only existing multilateral organization with any role in the area of binding multilateral law and its role is limited to a few rules relating to the international trade of state trading enterprises and monopolies and to the regulation of government actions, chiefly with respect to services. (For reviews of the activities of the WTO in this area, see WTO 1997: Ch. 4 and Lloyd and Vautier 1999: Ch. 10.) Given the diversity among nations of views relating to competition, to the role and scope of 'competition policy' and to the place of competition law within this policy area, there is a marked reluctance on the part of a number of countries to cede powers to the WTO to deal with private business conduct. Further, a traditional market access and trade-related approach to the resolution of competition problems, rather than the tools of competition analysis, would not necessarily be conducive to efficient and welfare-enhancing outcomes.

Probably the main contribution of the regional arrangements in this area of deepening integration is to competition advocacy and the convergence of national laws. The experience of the EC/EU[7], MERCOSUR and the Andean Group/Community have all shown that it is possible to begin the process of forming regional competition policies and laws without pre-existing national laws in all members. After the process has begun, however, these arrangements led rapidly to the development of comprehensive national competition laws in several members where none existed before. In the case of the EU, the development of national laws has been extended to another fifteen associated states in the CEEC and the Mediterranean. Moreover, the laws of these countries all follow similar principles derived from the EU law enshrined in the Treaty of Rome. Similarly, the competition-promoting policies and laws in the CER and the countries which are members of the NAFTA/Canada–Chile/Group of Three grouping and the MERCOSUR and Andean Community grouping have all shown convergence within their regions.

There is an emerging consensus that problems of achieving deep integration in the area of competition are especially complex and that the best feasible way to deal with cross-border competition problems requires the development and convergence of national competition-promoting policies. The international law which may resolve remaining problems will evolve gradually. Bilateral, regional and multilateral approaches are complementary. By freeing trade within regions and adopting other competition-promoting policies and by starting the development of regional competition law in some areas, the regional approach has made a major contribution to the resolution of cross-border competition problems in the global economy.

Notes

* This chapter has drawn on material in the recent book by Lloyd and Vautier (1999). We are grateful to José Tavares for providing additional information on the Latin American groups.
1. This terminology suggests that we might refer to the regional agreements as regional integration agreements. Some economists use this term. However, the agreements were approved under the GATT and WTO as trading agreements. More importantly, only the EU has explicitly adopted a policy of integration in the original form of the Common Market and, more recently, as the Single Market in the Maastricht Treaty.
2. There are other conditions, chiefly the absence of externalities or other sources of market failure.
3. Governments may also take action unilaterally by trying to apply their national laws extraterritorially. Extraterritorial application of national competition laws has been used extensively by the USA and to a lesser extent the EU and other countries. However, it is usually regarded as an infringement of the national sovereignty of the foreign nations involved and has given rise to conflict among nations. These conflicts reduce the effectiveness of the actions. Falvey and Lloyd (1999) demonstrate that, even when effective, the application of laws

extraterritorially may not bring about an efficient allocation of resources in the world as a whole.

4. At the time of writing APEC is considering Competition Principles. These are broad-ranging. However, APEC is not a regional trading arrangement in the sense of a free trade area or customs union notified to the WTO and these principles are non-binding.

5. Lloyd and Vautier (1999) call these non-binding agreements *plurilateral* agreements to distinguish them from (binding) *multilateral* agreements. However, the Uruguay Round Agreement uses the term 'plurilateral' in a different sense, namely an agreement which members may opt to sign but which is binding on those who do sign. The Uruguay Round Agreement included four such agreements in addition to the multilateral agreement but only two of them, the Agreement on Government Procurement and the Agreement on Trade in Civil Aircraft, are now in force.

6. The EU prohibition on antidumping action has been extended to the three EFTA members of the European Economic Area.

7. At the time of the formation of the EC, only two members, the Netherlands and Germany, had comprehensive national competition laws. Italy was the last of the original six members to develop national competition law. It did not do so until 1990. (United Nations Conference on Trade and Development (UNCTAD) (1997), World Investment Report 1997: Transnational Corporations, Market Structure and Competition Policy, New York: UNCTAD.)

References

Buigues, P., Jacquemin, A. and Sapir, A. (1995) *European Policies on Competition, Trade and Industry: Conflict and Complementarities*, Aldershot: Edward Elgar.

Centre for Economic Policy Research (CEPR) (1993) *Making Sense of Subsidiarity: How Much Centralization for Europe?* London: CEPR.

Directorate-General IV of the European Commission (1998) *European Community Competition Policy*, Brussels: European Commission.

European Commission (1996) *Report of the Group of Experts, Competition Policy in the New World Order: Strengthening International Co-operation and Rules*, Directorate-General IV, Brussels: European Commission.

International Antitrust Draft Code Working Group (1993) 'Draft international antitrust code: A GATT-MTO-Plurilateral Trade Agreement', *World Trade Materials*, 5 September: 126–96.

Jatar, A.J. and Tineo, L. (1998) 'Competition policy in the Andean Region: the ups and downs of a policy in search of its place', in M.R. Menoza et al. (eds) *The Andean Community and the United States: Trade and Investment Relations in the 1990s*, Washington, DC: Organisation of American States.

Falvey, R. and Lloyd, P.J. (1999) 'An economic analysis of extraterritoriality', mimeo.

Hoekman, B. (1998) 'Free trade and deep integration: antidumping and antitrust in regional agreements', World Bank Policy Research Paper, No. 1950, Washington, DC: World Bank.

Lawrence, R.Z. (1996) *Regionalism, Multilateralism and Deeper Integration*, Washington, DC: Brookings Institution.

Lloyd, P.J. and Vautier, K. (1999) *Promoting Competition in Multi-national Markets*, Cheltenham: Edward Elgar.

Mendoza, M.R., Correa, P. and Kotschwar, B. (eds) (1998) *The Andean Community and the United States: Trade and Investment Relations in the 1990s*, Washington, DC: OAS.

Organisation of American States (OAS) (1997) *Inventory of the Competition Policy Agreements, Treaties and other Arrangements Existing in the Western Hemisphere*, Washington, DC: OAS.

—— (1998) *Trade and Integration Arrangements in the Americas*, Washington, DC: OAS.

Pelkmans, J. (1997) *European Integration: Methods and Economic Analysis*, London: Addison Wesley Longman.

Sleuwaegen, L. (1998) 'Cross-border Mergers and EC Competition Policy', *The World Economy*, November: 1077–93.

Tavares, J. and Tineo, L. (1998a) 'Harmonization of competition policies among Mercosur countries', *The Antitrust Bulletin*, Spring: 45–70.

—— (1998b) 'Competition policy and regional trade: NAFTA, Andean Community, Mercosur and FTAA', paper presented to the Conference on Multilateral and Regional Trade Issues, Washington, DC, 26–7 May.

Vautier, K. and Lloyd, P.J. (1997) *International Trade and Competition Policy: CER, APEC and the WTO*, Wellington: Institute of Policy Studies.

World Trade Organization (WTO) (1997) *Annual Report 1997*, Vol. I, Geneva: WTO.

—— (1998) Working Group on the Interaction between Trade and Competition Policy, *Communication from the United States*, Geneva: WTO.

14 Multiple steady states with unemployment and exchange-rate coordination*

Yoshiyasu Ono

1 Introduction

Using a two-country two-commodity monetary model with dynamic optimization, this chapter shows a possibility that there is a choice of exchange rates and that both countries' consumption and employment depend on the choice. It finds that, if people have insatiable liquidity preference, one or both countries may face unemployment. In this case, an appropriate choice of the exchange rate can raise both countries' consumption.

In most international macroeconomic models with dynamic optimization, such as Frenkel and Razin (1985), Devereux and Shi (1991), Turnovsky and Sen (1991), Ghosh (1992), Ikeda and Ono (1992), and Ono and Shibata (1992), only market equilibrium paths are examined. This may be because market equilibrium is believed to obtain after all even if prices or wages are sluggish. In fact, in the dynamic optimization model with nominal wage sluggishness presented by Ploeg (1993), market equilibrium is eventually attained.

In such models as consider only market equilibrium paths, real variables are first determined independently of monetary variables, and next monetary variables are determined depending on the real variables. Furthermore, once the nominal money stock is given, the exchange rate is uniquely determined. The possibility that choosing an exchange rate affects employment or consumption cannot be analysed since there is no choice of exchange rates.

Using a competitive closed-economy setting with dynamic optimization, however, Ono (1994, 2001) shows the possibility of stagnation in steady state. He finds that, if people's liquidity preference is insatiable, persistent stagnation occurs even though prices continue to adjust in a sluggish manner, and that market equilibrium is eventually reached if liquidity preference is either satiable or null, as assumed in standard neoclassical models. This chapter extends his model into a two-country two-commodity setting and shows that there are four types of steady state with and without unemployment. These are a steady state with both countries' full employment, a steady state with both countries' unemployment, a steady state where one country faces unemployment and the other realizes full employment, and the state symmetric to the third.

Furthermore, this chapter proves that, if the state with both countries' full employment occurs, the state with both countries' unemployment can never occur, and vice versa. In any case, besides either of the symmetric steady states, both the two asymmetric steady states can occur depending on which exchange rate is chosen. Therefore, by choosing the exchange rate appropriately, both countries can select one of the steady states. It is also found that not only the country with full employment, but also the country with unemployment, enjoys higher consumption in the asymmetric steady states than in the steady state with both countries' unemployment. Thus, when at least one of the two countries has to face unemployment, it is better for both countries to choose an exchange rate at which one faces unemployment and the other realizes full employment.

After section 2 presents the basic structure of the model, section 3 formalizes the dynamics of this economy and obtains steady state conditions. The four steady states with unemployment and full employment are shown in section 4. Section 5 considers the case where the two countries are symmetric in all respects and shows the possibility of multiple states. It also compares each country's consumption levels in various steady states and explores the possibility that exchange-rate coordination enables both countries to enjoy higher consumption. Finally, section 6 summarizes the implications of this chapter.

2 The model

We consider an economy with two countries, which are called countries J and A. Country J produces only commodity J whereas country A produces only commodity A. The firm sector of each country inputs only labour when producing each commodity. Households in both countries consume both commodities. The price of commodity J is P_J yen, and that of commodity A is $\$P_A^*$. As a result of international arbitrage of commodity trade, PPP (purchasing power parity) holds. Thus, when the exchange rate is ϵ [yen/dollar], country J faces prices $(P_J, \epsilon P_A^*)$ and country A $(P_J/\epsilon, P_A^*)$. Anyway, the price of commodity A relative to that of commodity J, denoted by ω, is

$$\omega = \epsilon P_A^*/P_J \tag{1}$$

Variables with and without * imply those of countries A and J respectively.

2.1 Households

To minimize the complexity of the model, all households in both countries are assumed to have the same utility function of the following form:

$$\int_0^\infty [\delta \ln(c_J) + (1-\delta) \ln(c_A) + v(m)] \exp(-\rho t) dt, \quad 1 > \delta > 0$$

where c_i $(i=J, A)$ represents the consumption of commodity i, m real balances, and $v(m)$ the utility of money. We assume that $v(m)$ satisfies

$$v'(m) > 0, \quad v''(m) < 0, \quad v'(\infty) = \beta > 0 \tag{2}$$

namely, households have insatiable liquidity preference and thus $v'(m)$ stays to be strictly positive. This assumption is required for persistent stagnation to occur, as shown by Ono (1994, 1999).[1]

In this case, the general price levels of the two countries are respectively

$$P = P_J^{(1-\delta)} (\epsilon P_A^*)^\delta, \quad P^* = (P_J/\epsilon)^{(1-\delta)} P_A^{*\delta} \tag{3}$$

which yield

$$P = \epsilon P^* \tag{4}$$

From this equation,

$$\pi = \dot{\epsilon}/\epsilon + \pi^* \tag{5}$$

where π (or π^*) is the inflation rate of each country and a dot represents a time derivative. From (1) and (3), the real prices of the two commodities are

$$p_J = P_J/P = \omega^{\delta-1}, \quad p_A = P_A^*/P^* = \omega^\delta \tag{6}$$

which are the same in both countries.[2]

Each household allocates asset a (or a^*) to real balances m (or m^*), which generate only the utility of liquidity, and international bonds b (or b^*), which yield only nominal interest R (or R^*). Since the interest rate of international bonds measured in terms of the same currency must equal each other,

$$R = \dot{\epsilon}/\epsilon + R^* \tag{7}$$

From (5) and (7),

$$r \, (=R - \pi) = r^* \, (=R^* - \pi^*) \tag{8}$$

which implies that the real interest rate is internationally the same.

Each household's income consists of interest earnings and wages. Its labour endowment is normalized to unity, but actual labour supply x (or x^*) may be lower than unity since the possibility of unemployment is considered. Thus, given (8), the flow budget equation and the stock constraint of both countries are

$$\dot{a} = ra + wx - \omega^{\delta-1}c_J - \omega^\delta c_A - Rm, \quad a = b + m,$$
$$\dot{a}^* = ra^* + w^*x^* - \omega^{\delta-1}c_J^* - \omega^\delta c_A^* - R^*m^*, \quad a^* = b^* + m^* \tag{9}$$

where w (or w^*) is the real wage rate.

Since each household maximizes the utility functional subject to (9), the Hamiltonian functions are given by

$$H = \delta\ln(c_J) + (1-\delta)\ln(c_A) + \lambda(ra + wx - \omega^{\delta-1}c_J - \omega^\delta c_A - Rm),$$
$$H = \delta\ln(c_J^*) + (1-\delta)\ln(c_A^*) + \lambda^*(ra^* + w^*x^* - \omega^{\delta-1}c_J^* - \omega^\delta c_A^* - R^*m^*)$$

As a result of the optimization behaviour, each household satisfies the intra-temporal first-order conditions:

$$c_J = \delta c/\omega^{\delta-1}, \quad c_A = (1-\delta)c/\omega^\delta, \quad \lambda = 1/c$$
$$c_J^* = \delta c^*/\omega^{\delta-1}, \quad c_A^* = (1-\delta)c^*/\omega^\delta, \quad \lambda^* = 1/c^* \tag{10}$$

where c and c^* represent each country's real consumption:

$$c = \omega^{\delta-1}c_J + \omega^\delta c_A, \quad c^* = \omega^{\delta-1}c_J^* + \omega^\delta c_A^*$$

and the intertemporal first-order conditions:

$$\rho + \frac{\dot{c}_J}{c_J} + \frac{\dot{P}_J}{P_J} = \rho + \frac{\dot{c}_A}{c_A} + \frac{\dot{P}_J}{P_J} + \frac{\dot{\omega}}{\omega} = R = v'(m)c = v'(m)\omega^{\delta-1}c_J/\delta \tag{11}$$

$$\rho + \frac{\dot{c}_J^*}{c_J^*} + \frac{\dot{P}_A^*}{P_A^*} - \frac{\dot{\omega}}{\omega} = \rho + \frac{\dot{c}_A^*}{c_A^*} + \frac{\dot{P}_A^*}{P_A^*} = R^*$$
$$= v'(m^*)c^* = v'(m^*)\omega^\delta c_A^*/(1-\delta) \tag{12}$$

The transversality conditions:

$$\lim_{t\to\infty} \lambda a\exp(-\rho t) = \lim_{t\to\infty} (1/c)(m+b)\exp(-\rho t) = 0,$$

$$\lim_{t\to\infty} \lambda^* a^*\exp(-\rho t) = \lim_{t\to\infty} (1/c^*)(m^*+b^*)\exp(-\rho t) = 0 \tag{13}$$

must also be valid.

2.2 Firms

The production function of the firm sector of each country is assumed to satisfy constant returns to scale:

$$y_J = \theta_J l, \quad y_A^* = \theta_A l^* \tag{14}$$

where y_J and y_A^* represent the output of commodity J and that of commodity A respectively, and θ_J and θ_A are assumed to be constant. Since in this case each firm's profits are

$$(P_J \theta_J - W)l, \quad (P_A^* \theta_A - W^*)l^*$$

its labour demand is given by

$$l = \infty \text{ if } P_J \theta_J > W, \ 0 \leq l < \infty \text{ if } P_J \theta_J = W, \ l = 0 \text{ if } P_J \theta_J < W,$$
$$l^* = \infty \text{ if } P_A^* \theta_A > W^*, \ 0 \leq l^* < \infty \text{ if } P_A^* \theta_A = W^*, \ l^* = 0 \text{ if } P_A^* \theta_A < W^* \tag{15}$$

Thus, because of the constant-returns-to-scale technology given by (14), firms earn zero profits as long as labour demand has a positive finite value.

2.3 Market adjustments

The money market in each country and the international bond market are assumed to be always in equilibrium.

$$m = M/P, \quad m^* = M^*/P^* \tag{16}$$
$$b + b^* = 0 \tag{17}$$

Note that the total real asset of the world $(b + b^*)$ is zero since firms' profits are zero. The adjustment of each commodity price is so fast that each commodity market is always in equilibrium:

$$\theta_J x = c_J + c_J^*,$$
$$\theta_A x^* = c_A + c_A^* \tag{18}$$

where x and x^* are actual labour supplies.

Nominal wages W and W^* in the two countries adjust in a sluggish manner, as assumed in Ploeg (1993). For simplicity, it is assumed that the adjustment speeds of W and W^* equal each other, and that their dynamics are given by

$$\frac{\dot{W}}{W} = \alpha(l - 1), \quad \frac{\dot{W}^*}{W^*} = \alpha(l^* - 1) \tag{19}$$

where l and l^* represent labour demand given by (15). Thus, if $P_1\theta_1 > W$, labour demand l is ∞ and hence W immediately rises to $P_1\theta_1$. If $P_1\theta_1 < W$, labour demand (= actual employment) is zero and thus commodity supply is zero. Consequently, because of the rapid adjustment of P_1, P_1 immediately rises to W/θ_J. The initial adjustment of W^* is analogously described.

After such instantaneous initial adjustments of W and W^*, they maintain to satisfy

$$P_J\theta_J = W, \quad P_A^*\theta_A = W^* \tag{20}$$

and hence from (6) each real wage is

$$w = W/P = \theta_J\omega^{\delta-1}, \quad w^* = W^*/P^* = \theta_A\omega^\delta \tag{21}$$

Thereafter, they move following (19) in which l and l^* respectively equal x and x^* given by (18).

3 Dynamics and steady state conditions

Using each agent's behaviour and the market adjustment mechanism mentioned above, this section formulates the dynamics of this economy and obtains the steady-state conditions that generally hold whether full employment is attained or not.

3.1 Dynamics

Since (20) is valid throughout the adjustment process, P_J and P_A^* move in parallel to W and W^* respectively. Thus, (10), (18) and (19) generate the dynamics of P_J and P_A^*:

$$\frac{\dot{P}_J}{P_J} = \frac{\dot{W}}{W} = \alpha[\delta(c + c^*)/(\omega^{\delta-1}\theta_J) - 1],$$

$$\frac{\dot{P}_A^*}{P_A^*} = \frac{\dot{W}^*}{W^*} = \alpha[(1-\delta)(c + c^*)/(\omega^\delta\theta_A) - 1] \tag{22}$$

From (7), (11) and (12), the dynamic equation of ϵ is

$$\frac{\dot{\epsilon}}{\epsilon} = v'(m)c - v'(m^*)c^* \tag{23}$$

The time differentiation of (1) yields

$$\frac{\dot{P}_J}{P_J} + \frac{\dot{\omega}}{\omega} = \frac{\dot{P}_A^*}{P_A^*} + \frac{\dot{\epsilon}}{\epsilon} \tag{24}$$

Equations (22)–(24) generate the dynamics of ω:

$$\frac{\dot{\omega}}{\omega} = \alpha[(1-\delta)(c+c^*)/(\omega^\delta\theta_A)-1] - \alpha[\delta(c+c^*)/(\omega^{\delta-1}\theta_J)-1]$$

$$+ v'(m)c - v'(m^*)c^* \qquad (25)$$

From (11), (12) and (22), the dynamics of c_J and c_A^* are given by

$$\frac{\dot{c}_J}{c_J} = v'(m)c - \rho - \alpha[\delta(c+c^*)/(\omega^{\delta-1}\theta_J)-1],$$

$$\frac{\dot{c}_A^*}{c_A^*} = v'(m^*)c^* - \rho - \alpha[(1-\delta)(c+c^*)/(\omega^\delta\theta_A)-1] \qquad (26)$$

(10), (25) and (26) yield

$$\frac{\dot{c}}{c} = \frac{\dot{c}^*}{c^*} = \delta\{v'(m)c - \rho - \alpha[\delta(c+c^*)/(\omega^{\delta-1}\theta_J)-1]\}$$

$$+ (1-\delta)\{v'(m^*)c^* - \rho - \alpha[(1-\delta)(c+c^*)/(\omega^\delta\theta_A)-1]\} \qquad (27)$$

which implies that c and c^* move in parallel.[3] Since from (6) and (16) m and m^* are represented as follows:

$$m = \omega^{\delta-1}M/P_J, \quad m^* = \omega^\delta M^*/P_A^* \qquad (28)$$

(22), (25) and (27) formulate an autonomous dynamic system with respect to c, c^*, P_J, P_A^*, and ω.

The time differentiation of (16) gives

$$\dot{m}/m = -\pi, \quad \dot{m}^*/m^* = -\pi^* \qquad (29)$$

as long as M and M^* are kept constant. From (9), (21) and (29), the dynamics of each country's international bond is

$$\dot{b} = rb + \omega^{\delta-1}\theta_J x - c, \quad \dot{b}^* = rb^* + \omega^\delta\theta_A x^* - c^* \qquad (30)$$

3.2 Steady state conditions

Let us obtain the conditions that generally hold in steady state, whether full employment is eventually realized or not. Since in steady state ω stays constant, from (6), P and P^* move in parallel to P_J and P_A^* respectively. Since c_J and c_A^* also stay constant, from (11),

$$r = \rho \qquad (31)$$

Furthermore, since b and $b*$ stay constant, from (17), (30) and (31), the employment levels of the two countries in steady state are

$$x = (c - \rho b)/(\omega^{\delta-1}\theta_J), \quad x* = (c* + \rho b)/(\omega^\delta\theta_A) \tag{32}$$

(11), (12) and the above properties imply

$$v'(m)c = \rho - \alpha + \alpha(c - \rho b)/(\theta_J\omega^{\delta-1}),$$
$$v'(m*)c* = \rho - \alpha + \alpha(c* + \rho b)/(\theta_A\omega^\delta) \tag{33}$$

Substituting the first equation of (32) into that of (18) and using (10) yield

$$\omega^\delta c_A - \rho b = \omega^{\delta-1}c_J^* \tag{34}$$

The left-hand side of (34) is country J's real import minus interest earnings, and the right-hand side is country A's real import. Thus, (34) implies that the current account is zero. Using (10), (34) is rewritten as

$$(1 - \delta)(c - \rho b) = \delta(c* + \rho b) \tag{35}$$

4 Various steady states

This section explores the possibility of various steady states where full employment or unemployment occurs in the two countries.

4.1 Full employment in both countries

Since the full employment steady state requires

$$x = 1, \quad x* = 1$$

from (32),

$$c = \omega^{\delta-1}\theta_J + \rho b, \quad c* = \omega^\delta\theta_A - \rho b \tag{36}$$

(33), (35) and (36) give

$$\omega = [(1 - \delta)/\delta](\theta_J/\theta_A),$$
$$c = [(1 - \delta)/\delta]^{\delta-1}\theta_J^\delta\theta_A^{1-\delta} + \rho b,$$
$$c* = [(1 - \delta)/\delta]^\delta\theta_J^\delta\theta_A^{1-\delta} - \rho b,$$
$$v'(m)\{[(1 - \delta)/\delta]^{\delta-1}\theta_J^\delta\theta_A^{1-\delta} + \rho b\} = \rho,$$
$$v'(m*)\{[(1 - \delta)/\delta]^\delta\theta_J^\delta\theta_A^{1-\delta} - \rho b\} = \rho \tag{37}$$

For this steady state to exist, the following conditions are required.

$$-[(1-\delta)/\delta]^{\delta-1}\theta_J^\delta\theta_A^{1-\delta}<\rho b<[(1-\delta)/\delta]^\delta\theta_J^\delta\theta_A^{1-\delta},$$

$$[(1-\delta)/\delta]^\delta\theta_J^\delta\theta_A^{1-\delta}-\rho/\beta<\rho b<\rho/\beta-[(1-\delta)/\delta]^{\delta-1}\theta_J^\delta\theta_A^{1-\delta} \tag{38}$$

The two sets of conditions respectively guarantee c and c^* to be positive and m and m^* to exist.

Obviously, in order for b that satisfies the second equation of (38) to exist, it must be satisfied that

$$\beta(\theta_J/\delta)^\delta[\theta_A/(1-\delta)]^{1-\delta}<2\rho \tag{39}$$

4.2 Unemployment in both countries

Since

$$x<1, x^*<1$$

in this state and hence the general price levels continue to decline, (2) implies that $v'(m)$ and $v'(m^*)$ converge to β. Thus, (33) reduces to

$$\beta c=\rho-\alpha+\alpha(c-\rho b)/(\theta_J\omega^{\delta-1}),$$

$$\beta c^*=\rho-\alpha+\alpha(c^*+\rho b)/(\theta_A\omega^\delta) \tag{40}$$

This case occurs since the liquidity premium (the left-hand side of (40)) exceeds the nominal rate of time preference (the right-hand side of (40)) when c is large enough to attain full employment. This condition is represented as

$$\beta\omega^{\delta-1}\theta_J+\beta\rho b>\rho, \quad \beta\omega^\delta\theta_A-\beta\rho b>\rho$$

or equivalently,

$$\{(\beta\theta_J)/[\rho(1-\beta b)]\}^{1/(1-\delta)}>\omega>[\rho(1+\beta b)/(\beta\theta_A)]^{1/\delta} \tag{41}$$

Therefore, in order for the state with both countries' unemployment to exist, there must be a level of b under which the left-hand sides of the two equations of (40) are respectively smaller than the right-hand sides of (40) when c and c^* are zero. This condition is given by[4]

$$\rho>\alpha$$

Note that, although real balances m and m^* diverge to infinity in this state, transversality conditions (13) hold since b, b^*, c and c^* stay constant and (29) and (40) yield

$$\dot{m}/m = -\pi = \rho - \beta c < \rho, \quad \dot{m}^*/m^* = -\pi^* = \rho - \beta c^* < \rho \quad (42)$$

From (40), the solutions for c and c^* are

$$c - \rho b = (\rho - \alpha - \rho\beta b)/[\beta - \alpha/(\omega^{\delta-1}\theta_J)],$$
$$c^* + \rho b = (\rho - \alpha + \beta\rho b)/[\beta - \alpha/(\omega^\delta\theta_A)] \quad (43)$$

Substituting (43) into (35) yields

$$(1 - \delta)(\rho - \alpha - \rho\beta b)/[\beta - \alpha/(\omega^{\delta-1}\theta_J)]$$
$$= \delta(\rho - \alpha + \beta\rho b)/[\beta - \alpha/(\omega^\delta\theta_A)] \quad (44)$$

where the left-hand side is country J's import and the right-hand side is country A's import. ω is determined so that (44) is satisfied. The left-hand side of (44) is an increasing, and the right-hand side is a decreasing, function with respect to ω, as illustrated by Figure 14.1. Thus, ω at the intersection point is uniquely determined. Once ω is determined, from (43), c and c^* obtain.

The second property of (38), which must hold for the steady state with full employment in both countries to exist, reduces to

$$\{(\beta\theta_J)/[\rho(1 - \beta b)]\}^{1/(1-\delta)} < [(1-\delta)/\delta](\theta_J/\theta_A) < [\rho(1+\beta b)/(\beta\theta_A)]^{1/\delta} \quad (45)$$

Comparing (45) with (41), one finds that ω that satisfies (41) does not exist if (45) holds, and equivalently that (45) does not hold if ω that satisfies (41) exists. This property implies the following proposition:

Proposition 1   There is not b under which both countries realize full employment in steady state if there is b under which both countries face unemployment in steady state. Conversely, there is not b under which both countries face unemployment in steady state if there is b under which both countries realize full employment in steady state.

4.3 Unemployment in country J and full employment in country A

In this state

$$x < 1, \quad x^* = 1 \quad (46)$$

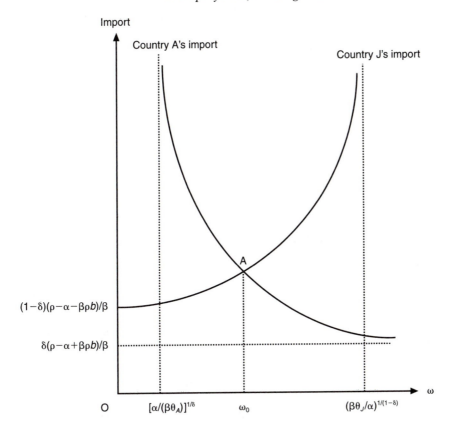

Figure 14.1 The two countries' import under employment.

From (32), the first equation of (33) in which $v'(m)$ is replaced by β, and (46),

$$c - \rho b = (\rho - \alpha - \beta\rho b)/[\beta - \alpha/(\omega^{\delta-1}\theta_J)], \quad c^* = \omega^\delta\theta_A - \rho b \qquad (47)$$

Note that the transversality condition of country J, given by the first equation of (13), holds in this state although m diverges to infinity since the first equation of (42) is valid and b and c stay constant.[5]

(35) and (47) generate the current-account balance condition:

$$(1 - \delta)(\rho - \alpha - \beta\rho b)/[\beta - \alpha/(\omega^{\delta-1}\theta_J)] = \delta\omega^\delta\theta_A \qquad (48)$$

which determines ω. Substituting this ω into (47) gives the steady state levels of c and c^*. Once c^* is given, from the second equation of (33), m^* is determined so that

$$v'(m^*)c^* = \rho \tag{49}$$

From (32), (46) and (49), it must be satisfied that

$$\min(0, \rho b) < c < \omega^{\delta-1}\theta_J + \rho b,$$

$$c^* = \omega^\delta\theta_A - \rho b > 0, \quad \beta c^* < \rho \tag{50}$$

in order for this state to exist.

4.4 Full employment in country J and unemployment in country A

Since

$$x = 1, x^* < 1 \tag{51}$$

(32), the second equation of (33) in which $v'(m^*)$ is replaced by β, and (51) yield

$$c = \omega^{\delta-1}\theta_J + \rho b, \quad c^* + \rho b = (\rho - \alpha + \beta\rho b)/[\beta - \alpha/(\omega^\delta\theta_A)] \tag{52}$$

The transversality condition of country A, given by the second equation of (13), holds in this state although m^* diverges to infinity since the second equation of (42) is valid and b^* and c^* stay constant.
From (35) and (52),

$$(1 - \delta)\omega^{\delta-1}\theta_J = \delta(\rho - \alpha + \beta\rho b)/[\beta - \alpha/(\omega^\delta\theta_A)] \tag{53}$$

which determines ω. Substituting this ω into (52) gives the steady state levels of c and c^*. Once c is given, from the first equation of (33), m is determined so that

$$v'(m)c = \rho \tag{54}$$

From (32), (51) and (54), it must be satisfied that

$$c = \omega^{\delta-1}\theta_J + \rho b > 0, \quad \beta c < \rho,$$

$$\min(0, -\rho b) < c^* < \omega^\delta\theta_A - \rho b \tag{55}$$

in order for this state to exist.

5 Exchange rate coordination

This section shows that there is a range of b under which any of three steady states among the four obtained in the previous section can hold. Thus, by choosing an appropriate exchange rate, a country can realize full employment and make the other face unemployment. It is also examined in which steady state each country's consumption is highest.

In order to show the possibility of multiple steady states, this section considers a simple symmetric case where

$$\delta = 1/2, \ \theta_J = \theta_A = \theta, \ b = 0 \tag{56}$$

In this case, the conditions that hold in each of the four steady states obtained in section 4 reduce to the following:

Full employment in both countries:

$$\omega = 1, \ c = c^* = \theta, \ x = 1, \ x^* = 1, \ v'(m)\theta = \rho, \ v'(m^*)\theta = \rho, \tag{57}$$

$$\beta\theta < \rho$$

Unemployment in country J and full employment in country A:

$$\alpha\omega - \beta\theta\omega^{1/2} + (\rho - \alpha) = 0, \ c = c^* = \theta\omega^{1/2},$$

$$x = \omega < 1, \ x^* = 1, \ v'(m^*)\theta\omega^{1/2} = \rho,$$

$$(\beta\theta)^2 - 4\alpha(\rho - \alpha) > 0, \ \omega^{1/2} < \min(\rho/(\beta\theta), 1) \tag{58}$$

Full employment in country J and unemployment in country A:

$$\alpha(1/\omega) - \beta\theta(1/\omega)^{1/2} + (\rho - \alpha) = 0, \ c = c^* = \theta(1/\omega)^{1/2},$$

$$x = 1, \ x^* = 1/\omega < 1, \ v'(m)\theta(1/\omega)^{1/2} = \rho,$$

$$(\beta\theta)^2 - 4\alpha(\rho - \alpha) > 0, \ (1/\omega)^{1/2} < \min(\rho/(\beta\theta), 1) \tag{59}$$

Unemployment in both countries:

$$\omega = 1, \ c = c^* = (\rho - \alpha)/(\beta - \alpha/\theta), \ x = x^* = (\rho - \alpha)/(\beta\theta - \alpha) < 1,$$

$$\beta\theta > \rho \tag{60}$$

Note that the inequality in (57) contradicts that in (60). This is a special case for proposition 1. In the cases of (58) and (59), replacing ω in (58) by $1/\omega$ yields the same solution in (59). Furthermore, the condition for the case of (58) to exist is the same as that for the case of (59). Thus, if a steady state with unemployment in country J and full employment in country A exists, a steady state with full employment in country J and unemployment in country A exists, and vice versa. The value of ω in one case equals its inverse in the other. Using these properties, we shall examine the possibility of multiple steady states and compare each country's consumption in those states.

5.1 The case where unemployment in both countries can occur

In this case,

$$\beta\theta > \rho \tag{61}$$

and hence full employment cannot simultaneously be realized in both countries. Since the maximum of $4\alpha(\rho - \alpha)$ is ρ^2, which occurs when $\alpha = \rho/2$, the first condition in (58) is valid. Under (61) the second condition of (58) reduces to

$$\omega^{1/2} < \rho/(\beta\theta)$$

Since the two solutions of the equation for $\omega^{1/2}$ in (58) are

$$\omega_1^{1/2} = \{\beta\theta - [(\beta\theta)^2 - 4\alpha(\rho - \alpha)]^{1/2}\}/(2\alpha),$$
$$\omega_2^{1/2} = \{\beta\theta + [(\beta\theta)^2 - 4\alpha(\rho - \alpha)]^{1/2}\}/(2\alpha) \tag{62}$$

and satisfy

$$\omega_1^{1/2} < \rho/(\beta\theta) < \omega_2^{1/2},$$

ω, c and c^* are

$$\omega = \omega_1, \quad c = c^* = \theta\omega_1^{1/2} = \theta\{\beta\theta - [(\beta\theta)^2 - 4\alpha(\rho - \alpha)]^{1/2}\}/(2\alpha) \tag{63}$$

Analogously, the case of (59) is valid under (61) and in this case ω, c, and c^* satisfy

$$(1/\omega)^{1/2} = \omega_1^{1/2},$$
$$c = c^* = \theta\omega_1^{1/2} = \theta\{\beta\theta - [(\beta\theta)^2 - 4\alpha(\rho - \alpha)]^{1/2}\}/(2\alpha) \tag{64}$$

Thus, the levels of c and c^* in the case with unemployment in country J and full employment in country A are the same as those in the case with full employment in country J and unemployment in country A.

By comparing c and c^* in (63) and (64) with those in (60), it is found that under (61)

$$(\rho - \alpha)/(\beta - \alpha/\theta) < \theta\{\beta\theta - [(\beta\theta)^2 - 4\alpha(\rho - \alpha)]^{1/2}\}/(2\alpha)$$

that is, c and c^* in the case where both countries face unemployment are less than those in the asymmetric cases.

Proposition 2 If $\beta\theta>\rho$, any of the steady state with unemployment in both countries, that with full employment in country J and unemployment in country A, and that with unemployment in country J and full employment in country A can occur, depending on the choice of the exchange rate. The two countries enjoy larger consumption in the two asymmetric cases than in the case where both countries face unemployment.

From (58) and (59), in the asymmetric cases the country whose product has a lower relative price realizes full employment while the other country faces unemployment. Thus, if the yen's value is set to be high and hence the price of commodity J is higher than that of country A, country J faces unemployment and country A realizes full employment. However, since the price of commodity J is higher than that of commodity A, the real income and consumption of country J equal the respective values of country A.[6] On the other hand, if the yen is set to be low, country A faces unemployment while country J realizes full employment. In this case the price of commodity A is higher than that of country J, and the two countries have the same levels of real income and consumption.

If the exchange rate has the intermediate level at which the relative price of the two commodities is one, both countries face unemployment. In this case each country realizes lower consumption than in the asymmetric cases. However, each country can realize full employment with the other country remaining in unemployment by inducing the exchange rate so that the price of its own product is lower than that of the other. Thus, under political pressure from the unemployed, both countries may compete for full employment by undercutting its own currency and consequently realize lower real income and consumption.

5.2 The case where full employment in both countries can occur

If

$$\beta\theta<\rho \tag{65}$$

a steady state where both countries realize full employment exists but a steady state where both countries face unemployment does not.

In this case, in order for the first inequality of (58) to hold, α must be close to either θ or ρ and thus it must be satisfied that

$$\rho^2>(\beta\theta)^2>4\alpha(\rho-\alpha) \tag{66}$$

The second inequality of (58) and (65) imply

$$\omega < 1 \tag{67}$$

If

$$2\alpha > \beta\theta \tag{68}$$

both ω_1 and ω_2 given in (62) satisfies (67). If $2\alpha < \beta\theta$, on the contrary, both ω_1 and ω_2 are larger than 1 and hence there is no solution that satisfies (67). Thus, under (66) and (68) there is the steady state in which country J faces unemployment and country A realizes full employment. In this state,

$$\text{either } \omega = \omega_1 \ (<1), \ c = c^* = \theta\omega_1^{1/2} \ (<\theta),$$
$$\text{or } \omega = \omega_2 \ (<1), \ c = c^* = \theta\omega_2^{1/2} \ (<\theta) \tag{69}$$

Therefore, c and c^* in this asymmetric case are smaller than those in the case where both countries realize full employment.

In the steady state where country J realizes full employment and country A faces unemployment, from (59), the solutions for $\omega^{1/2}$ and c and c^* satisfy

$$\text{either } \omega = 1/\omega_1, \ c = c^* = \theta\omega_1^{1/2},$$
$$\text{or } \omega = 1/\omega_2, \ c = c^* = \theta\omega_2^{1/2} \tag{70}$$

where ω_1 and ω_2 are given by (62). Thus, from (69), the level of each country's consumption in this state equals that in the case symmetric to it.

The above analysis implies the following proposition:

> *Proposition 3*   If $\min(2\alpha, \ \rho) > \beta\theta > 2[\alpha(\rho - \alpha)]^{1/2}$, any of the steady state with full employment in both countries, that with full employment in country J and unemployment in country A, and that with unemployment in country J and full employment in country A can occur, depending on the choice of the exchange rate. The two countries face less consumption in the two asymmetric cases than in the case where both countries realize full unemployment.

Proposition 3 implies that, by lowering the value of its own currency, a country can make the other country face unemployment although it is possible for both countries to realize full employment at the same time. In this state, however, not only the home country's but also the foreign country's consumption is smaller than that in the state where both countries realize full employment. Thus, international coordination with respect to the exchange rate can lead to higher consumption and full employment in both countries.

Finally, from (57)–(60), if people's liquidity preference β is small enough, only the steady state with both countries' full employment holds. In this case, there is no room for the two countries to cooperate in deciding the exchange rate.

6 Conclusion

In a two-country monetary economy, if people's liquidity preference is small enough, there is a unique steady state and in this state both countries realize full employment. In this case there is no room for the two countries to cooperate in deciding the exchange rate. The Pareto-optimal situation would automatically be realized.

However, if people's liquidity preference is large enough, at least one of the two countries faces unemployment even if two countries are symmetric in all respects. In this case there are three steady states: a state where both countries face unemployment and two states where one country realizes full employment and the other faces unemployment. One of these three states is reached dependent on choice of the exchange rate. Both countries enjoy larger consumption in the asymmetric steady states than in the case where both countries face unemployment. Thus, the proper choice of the exchange rate enables both countries to enjoy higher consumption although one of the two countries still remains to face unemployment.

In this state the country whose currency is set higher than the other has to face unemployment whereas the other realizes full employment. Thus, it may be difficult for the government of the country with unemployment to persuade its people to accept persistent unemployment. If both countries attempt to undercut its currency so that they realize full employment, both of them eventually face unemployment and lower consumption.

If people's liquidity preference is not so large as discussed above, at least one of the two countries realizes full employment. There are three steady states: a state where both countries realize full employment and two states where one country realizes full employment and the other faces unemployment. One of these three states is reached dependent on the choice of the exchange rate. Contrary to the previous case, each country's consumption in the asymmetric steady states is smaller than that in the case of worldwide full employment. Thus, the exchange rate coordination enables both countries to realize full employment and enjoy higher consumption.

7 Appendix: Stability analysis

This appendix analyses the local stability of the dynamics in the case where at least one of the two countries faces unemployment. The case with full employment in both countries is omitted since it has essentially the same structure as conventional neoclassical models.

7.1 *The asymmetric cases*

We focus on the case where country J faces unemployment and country A realizes full employment. Obviously, the dynamics in the case where country J realizes full employment and country A faces unemployment can be analysed analogously.

From (58),

$$c = c^* = \theta\omega^{1/2} \tag{A1}$$

which yields

$$\frac{1}{2}\frac{\dot{\omega}}{\omega} = \frac{\dot{c}}{c} = \frac{\dot{c}^*}{c^*} \tag{A2}$$

From (25) and (27) in which $v'(m) = \beta$, (56), (A1) and (A2),

$$\frac{\dot{\omega}}{\omega} = \beta\theta\omega^{1/2} - \alpha\omega - (\rho - \alpha) \tag{A3}$$

Note that the two solutions of ω in the steady state of this dynamics equal ω_1 and ω_2 given by (62).

If (61) holds, i.e. $\beta\theta > \rho$, the phase diagram of ω is illustrated in Figure 14.2.

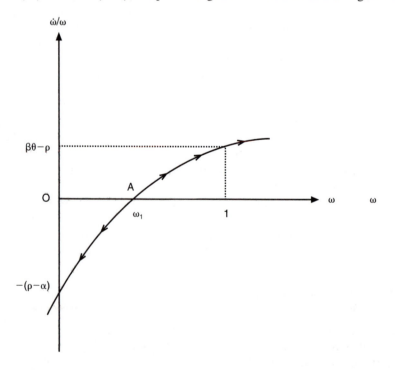

Figure 14.2 Exchange-rate dynamics in the case of proposition 2.

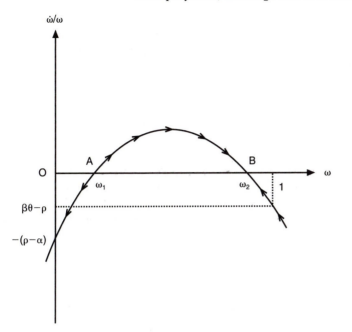

Figure 14.3 Exchange-rate dynamics in the case of proposition 3.

Since ω is jumpable as a result of a jump in exchange rate ϵ, the equilibrium path is such that the economy jumps to A and thereafter stays there.[7] If (66) and (68) hold, i.e. $(2\alpha, \rho) > \beta\theta > 2[\alpha(\rho - \alpha)]^{1/2}$, the phase diagram of ω is illustrated in Figure 14.3.[8] In this case there are the same equilibrium path as above and a continuum of equilibrium paths that approach B.

7.2 The case of unemployment in both countries

In this case,

$$\beta\theta > \rho \tag{A4}$$

Since we treat a symmetric case where both countries have the same consumption level at any point in time, from (25) and (27) in which $v'(m) = v'(m^*) = \beta$ and (56), the following autonomous dynamic system with respect to c and ω are derived.

$$\frac{\dot{c}}{c} = \beta c - (\rho - \alpha) - \alpha c(\omega^{1/2} + 1/\omega^{1/2})/(2\theta),$$

$$\frac{\dot{\omega}}{\omega} = \alpha c(1/\omega^{1/2} - \omega^{1/2})\theta$$

Figure 14.4 illustrates the phase diagram of this dynamics under (A4). This dynamics is viable in the area where supply exceeds demand in both commodity markets. It is represented by the area located below the following two curves:

Market equilibrium of commodity J: $c = \theta\omega^{1/2}$

Market equilibrium of commodity A: $c = \theta(1/\omega)^{1/2}$ (A5)

As shown by Figure 14.4, BA and B′A are the equilibrium paths. Since ω can jump, any point on BA and B′A can be chosen as the initial point and thereafter the economy moves on the saddle path toward A. Steady state A represents the state given by (60). Note that A is located below both the two curves in (A5), which implies that unemployment occurs in both countries.

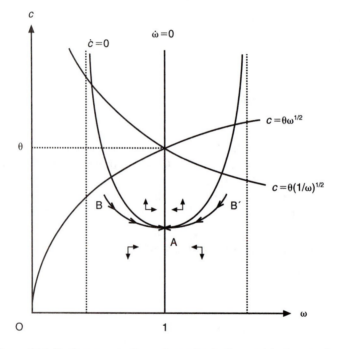

Figure 14.4 Exchange-rate dynamics under both countries' unemployment.

Notes

* This research is financially supported by the Grants-in-Aid for Scientific Research, the Ministry of Education.
1. See Ono (1994: 4–8) for discussions on the insatiable utility of money in the history of economic thought (e.g. Veblen, Marx, Simmel, Keynes) and its economic implications. The validity of this property is empirically supported by

Ono (1994: 34–8) using the GMM (Generalized Method of Moments), and more extensively by Ono, Ogawa and Yoshida (1998) using both parametric and non-parametric methods.
2. This is because there is no distortion such as tariffs and transportation costs.
3. This property holds since the utility function of consumption is log-linear.
4. In order for the steady state with unemployment to exist in a closed economy, the same condition is imposed by Ono (1994, 2001).
5. The transversality condition of country A is obviously valid since all variables of country A including m^* stay constant in this state.
6. Since (56) is assumed to be valid, this property holds.
7. This is the case of proposition 2.
8. This is the case of proposition 3.

References

Devereux, M.B. and Shi, S. (1991) 'Capital accumulation and the current account in a two-country model', *Journal of International Economics*, 30, February: 1–25.

Frenkel, J.A. and Razin, A. (1985) 'Government spending, debt, and international economic interdependence', *Economic Journal*, 95, September: 619–36.

Ghosh, A.R. (1992) 'Fiscal policy, the terms of trade, and the external balance', *Journal of International Economics*, 33, August: 105–25.

Ikeda, S. and Ono, Y. (1992) 'Macroeconomic dynamics in a multi-country economy: a dynamic optimization approach', *International Economic Review*, 33, August: 629–44.

Ono, Y. (1994) *Money, Interest, and Stagnation: Dynamic Theory and Keynes's Economics*, Oxford University Press.

—— (2001) 'A reinterpretation of Chapter 17 of Keynes's *General Theory*: effective demand shortage under dynamic optimization', *International Economic Review*, 42, February: 207–36.

Ono, Y. and Shibata, A. (1992) 'Spill-over effects of supply-side changes in a two-country economy with capital accumulation', *Journal of International Economics*, 33, August: 127–46.

Ono, Y., Ogawa, K. and Yoshida, A. (1998) 'Liquidity preference and persistent unemployment with dynamic optimizing agents', ISER Discussion Paper, No. 461, Osaka University.

van der Ploeg, F. (1993) 'Channels of international policy transmission', *Journal of International Economics*, 34, May: 245–67.

Turnovsky, S.J. and Sen, P. (1991) 'Fiscal policy, capital accumulation, and debt in an open economy', *Oxford Economic Papers*, 43, January: 1–24.

Index

demic circles also, most of the research attention to adult-child incest has emerged in the last ten years.

PURPOSE

The primary purpose of this book is to critically evaluate what is now a very large but scattered literature of research findings on adult-child incest, integrating these findings into a coherent picture and drawing applied implications from them. Because research uninformed of history and devoid of theoretical guidance is disjointed and myopic, we precede this effort at synthesizing the "facts" about adult-child incest with a brief history of the recognition of child abuse as a social problem and a comprehensive survey of theories concerning incest and the incest taboo. Original research is also presented, focusing on two samples of substantiated adult-child incest cases. These samples are analyzed with an emphasis on adding to our knowledge of risk factors—visible signals that incest may be occurring in a given family. The ultimate objective of this research on risk factors is to raise an informed consciousness, so that community professionals as well as concerned lay persons can be better prepared to recognize and report suspected cases. A knowledge of risk factors is also conducive to targeting prevention and intervention efforts. To complete the attack on the problem, we conclude with a full examination of treatment and intervention issues, including debates, problems, and recommended practice guidelines.

SCOPE OF THE ORIGINAL RESEARCH

Legal definitions of incest, sexual abuse, and related offenses vary significantly from state to state. The two samples forming the basis for our original research are from Mississippi and Virginia, respectively. In accordance with legal statutes, we report the numbers of cases classified respectively as incest, sexual abuse, or rape. However, as social scientists, we accept and utilize the general concept that any form of erotic sexual action or behavior between and among family members, other than spouses, is incest. Further, we regard all adult-child incest as sexual abuse. In these terms, every case to be described from these samples is both incest *and* child sexual abuse. A limitation of these two samples is that they are restricted to cases that came to the attention of public authorities. The flip side of this limitation is an asset, however, since these cases were substantiated and described on the basis of on-site investigations. Thus, we were not obliged to rely upon the candor, memory, and comprehension of the victims regarding either the nature of the incest or the concomitant socioeconomic factors, personality variables, family dynamics, and so on.

The two samples presented in this work contain the full range of adult-child incest cases, including father-son, father-daughter, stepfather-daughter, both parent figures-daughter, both parent figures-son, mother-daughter, mother-son, uncle-niece, stepfather-son, grandfather-granddaughter, and uncle-nephew. Nevertheless, like many other incest researchers, we will often concentrate upon father-daughter incest. Due to its numerically high report rates, it is currently assumed to be the most prevalent form of incest (Herman and Hirschman, 1977; Sagarin, 1977; Finkelhor, 1979a; Justice and Justice, 1979)–though the question of the disproportionate reporting of stepfather-daughter incest will also be addressed.

OUTLINE OF CHAPTERS

Chapter 2 provides an overview of historical factors leading to the recognition of child abuse as a social problem, including technological and cultural changes leading to the peculiarly modern view of the child as a worthy and important being with full human rights.

Chapter 3 contains an extensive examination of theories concerning the origin and functional significance of the incest taboo, the question of an incest avoidance tendency, and explanations for the incestuous victimization of children. Included in this chapter are criticisms of theories where deemed appropriate.

Chapter 4 is a review of descriptive research on the incestuous victimization of children. In addition to a summary of findings, the review is a critical examination of research biases, sampling and measurement problems, lapses of definition, and other research limitations.

Chapter 5 synthesizes the research literature reviewed in Chapter 4, presenting an empirically grounded model of adult-child incest. We present a model which eschews oversimplification and attempts to treat adult-child (specifically, father-daughter) incest as the multifaceted, complex situation that in reality it is. The synthesis and explanatory potential represented by this model are achieved by drawing on ecological theories, conflict theory, exchange theory, and the literature on family power. Once constructed, we apply this model to address issues of prediction, prevention, and intervention.

Chapter 6 details findings from data on a small sample of substantiated, investigated adult-child incest cases reported to welfare officials in Mississippi during the calendar year 1979. Findings are discussed in relation to currently available literature, emphasizing practical guidelines for the citizen concerned about "reasonable cause" to report a suspected case of incest. The chapter concludes with a checklist of risk factors, which, when observed in combinations, should prompt a call to the local protective agency (usually the county department of welfare or social services).

Chapter 7 presents findings from a large sample of substantiated and investigated cases brought to the attention of public officials in Virginia's welfare system during the calendar year 1979. Oriented primarily to the researcher and to other professionals, the findings of this chapter raise doubts about the validity of several of the ostensible risk factors which have been widely publicized on the basis of previous studies. The importance of other risk factors is replicated, however. Implications of the findings for theory building are also examined.

Chapter 8 (authored by Kinly Sturkie) provides a review of the practice (social work and clinical) literature and has three major foci: (1) historical factors leading to the rejection of earlier (Freudian) approaches, which isolated the victim; (2) a discussion of the competing perspectives and ideologies influencing treatment and other practice decisions; and (3) an examination of the major modalities for treating incestuous families. With a healthy disdain for both textbook simplifications and polemical diatribes irrelevant to the realities and needs of the suffering client, Dr. Sturkie acknowledges and attempts to grapple with the many problems one encounters in trying to achieve treatment and intervention goals. He displays a humility born of his own extensive experiences working with incest families, noting that some types of incest are beyond the scope of any existing treatment approach—and recognizing that intervention can sometimes do more harm than good.

Chapter 9 is a conclusion highlighting major findings and issues and providing a summary of recent advances in prevention and intervention. Implications of our findings for existing and alternative theories are also examined. Finally, research priorities and methodological issues are considered.

2

A Brief History of Child Abuse

CHILD ABUSE AS A SOCIAL PROBLEM

As Rose (1957) has noted, a collective interpretation process must occur before any given pattern of activity is singled out and defined as a social problem. As with any other "social object" (Mead, 1934), critical to this process is the emergence of a label or phrase symbolically representing the object and connoting an attitude regarding it. In the case of a social problem, the attitude must be one of concern. Further, the object must be acknowledged as a public as opposed to a private concern, as a problem of major importance and urgency, and as a problem that is at least potentially amenable to solutions.

While the United States has made attempts to halt cruelty to children for over a century, it can be argued that child abuse as a concept signifying a public and pressing problem was "discovered" by Drs. Ray Helfer and C. Henry Kempe in 1962 (Antler, 1981, p. 40). This is not to say that the abuse of children, in or outside of the home, was wholly ignored earlier. Social workers, physicians, teachers, and other professionals in immediate contact with children suffering from harsh and cruel physical mistreatment had long sought to halt such abuses. Further, they had argued that intervention in abusive homes might mitigate against cruelty to children and result in the betterment of society (Antler, 1981, pp. 40-41; Pfohl, 1980). The larger society, however, was not yet receptive to such arguments.

Straus (1974) has traced the heightened concern evidenced through the 1960s and early 1970s over the myriad types of family violence to at least three converging social phenomena. The first was a growing public sensitivity to violence in general as society grappled with the moral dilemmas posed by the Vietnam War and sentiments against what many perceived to be futile and unwarranted violence and death for a cause neither fully articulated nor universally appreciated. This sensitivity to violence at the societal level was further promoted by "political assassinations, rising homicide and assault rates, and violent social and political protests" (Straus, 1974, p. 14).

The second factor was the visibility of the women's movement in tandem with the National Organization for Women's crusade against the battering of women. Third (and probably due in part to the first factor), the consensus model, long dominant in the social sciences, lost acceptance as more social scientists in particular (and concerned groups and segments of society in general) began to lean toward an articulation of a conflict model as more "realistically" depicting the substance of human society in the face of turmoil and rapid social change (Straus, 1974, pp. 14-15). Whereas the previously dominant consensus model had assumed that societies normally tend toward equilibrium with a consensus on values and an harmonious integration of interdependent institutions, the emerging conflict model emphasized the pervasiveness of conflicts between opposing groups who variously benefit or suffer from the existing distribution of social prerogatives, advantages, and power. We would add that the youth movement of the 1960s and the black civil rights movement—both emphasizing the rights of individuals who in the past had marginal statuses—complemented the three factors noted by Straus such that, with the aid of media coverage, society in general developed an acute awareness of human rights, the right to self-determination, and the right to be free from oppression whether de jure or de facto, collective or individual, blatant or subtle.

With the discovery of "the battered child syndrome" (Kempe et al., 1962), attention was called to what would later be referred to as the "cycle of violence": in other words, the tendency of abused children to become child abusers as adults. While the Kempe et al. article focused primarily on the battered child from a medical point of view (for example, seriousness of physical damage, abuse detected through x-rays, and so on), it also pointed out that most abusing parents were not psychopathic (p. 18) and that "often parents are repeating the type of child care practiced on them in their childhood" (p. 24).

Concern over the intergenerational transmission of violence increased awareness of family violence and child abuse in general, serving as a catalyst for researchers and practitioners initiating theory, research, intervention, and prevention efforts. In addition, while child abuse in the earliest part of the 1960s initially gained attention from medical professionals, the tempo quickly heightened. Soon not only medical personnel, but service organizations, social scientists, the media, and the general public had defined child abuse as a major social problem of unknown but substantial magnitude (Gil, 1981, p. 291; Gelles, 1980).

The combined efforts of many individuals, groups, and organizations realized one major milestone in 1973 when the Child Abuse Prevention and Treatment Act was passed by the Congress of the United States. This act made provision for a National Center on Child Abuse and Neglect. In addition, provision was made for research, conferences, and dissemination of information. As a spin-off of the recognition of child abuse as a social problem, every state now has statutes defining child abuse and mandating the reporting and investigation of known or suspected cases (Gil, 1981, pp. 291-92; Vander Mey and Neff, 1982). Further, child abuse is becoming recognized as a worldwide social problem, taking various forms with new forms emerging as countries undergo urbanization, modernization, and rapid social change (Dubanoski and Snyder, 1980; Fraser and Kilbride, 1980; de Silva, 1981; Eisenberg, 1981; Shah, 1984; Mehta, Praphy, and Mistry, 1985).

As noted earlier, while Kempe and his colleagues are credited with the discovery of child abuse in the United States, as a matter of record one should recognize that selected individuals and groups in the United States (and other parts of the world) had not ignored the possibility of harsh treatment of children by family members. Though differing in orientation from the contemporary child-abuse movement, not only individual but collective and organized attempts to intervene on behalf of children did occur prior to 1962.

Pfohl (1980) notes that three reform movements focused attention on harsh treatment of children during the nineteenth and early parts of the twentieth centuries. Although these three movements were mainly concerned with saving the "law-abiding" society from the negative effects of adults reared in violent environments, each was nevertheless an attempt to ameliorate family violence. These three movements were the House of Refuge movement, the Prevention of Cruelty to Children campaigns, and the juvenile court movement. (See also Antler, 1981; Rosenthal and Louis, 1981; and Mulford, 1983 for discussions of some or all of these movements.)

Briefly, the House of Refuge movement originated in response to perceived social problems stemming from rapid industrialization and urbanization. New York opened the first House of Refuge for homeless children and children living in "bad" homes (homes in which there appeared to be neglect of children or homes which otherwise appeared to be conducive to the corrupting of the child's character) in 1825 (Pfohl, 1980, p. 325). Children from bad homes, children who lived on the streets, and children who had violated laws were placed in these houses so that they could be removed from criminal elements and could receive a "proper" rearing. It was felt that this approach would reduce the number of future criminals and would, in essence, save society many dollars and lives. It is noteworthy that persons advocating this housing of neglected children or potentially criminal characters did not differentiate between poverty and neglect and did not define the beating of a child as deviant (Pfohl, 1980, p. 325).

The first Society for the Prevention of Cruelty to Children (SPCC) was formed in 1875 in New York. In response to the discovery of "Little Mary Ellen," a young girl who reportedly was beaten every day by her foster parents, often tied to her bed, and once stabbed in the face with a pair of scissors by her foster mother, the New York Society for the Prevention of Cruelty to Animals attempted to remove Mary Ellen permanently from the foster home. A volunteer church worker, Mrs. Wheeler, was told of Mary Ellen's plight by the child's neighbor. Initial intervention attempts proved futile because there was no law to protect the child, since at that time "criminal" beating of a child was not covered by law and was not, therefore, illegal. With the aid of the Society for the Prevention of Cruelty to Animals, it was successfully argued that "if a child has not rights as a human being, she shall at least have the justice of a cur on the street" (Mulford, 1983, p. 3; see also Pfohl, 1980, pp. 325-26). In essence, the argument was that since a child is a member of the animal kingdom, then the child should at least have as much protection as does any other animal in the kingdom. With Mary Ellen's case serving as a catalyst, New York's concerned citizens formed the SPCC. The emphasis, however, was much the same as with the House of Refuge movement. Members of the SPCC strove to save society from future undesirable human elements by intervening in bad homes or in cases where children appeared to be in the midst of negative influences. Labelling the child as deviant apparently occurred. Parents (or guardians) who had beaten or otherwise neglected and mistreated the children removed from the home by the SPCC were neither prosecuted nor defined as abusive or deviant. Moreover, as with the House of Refuge movement, institutionalization of children was practiced by members of the various SPCCs (Pfohl, 1980; Mulford, 1983).

Both the House of Refuge movement and the SPCCs faltered with the emergence of professional social workers and child psychologists. At odds with these new professionals' emphases on healing families and leaving children with their parents, and faced with declining public interest in funding child-saving projects, these movements met with opposition finalizing their demise with the 1909 White House Conference on Children (Pfohl, 1980). This conference argued against the removal of children from their homes on the basis of parental poverty, advocating instead that services be provided to aid families with few resources or those poor in parenting abilities. This action at the conference owes its debt to the Massachusetts SPCC, which, under the direction of the philanthropist Carl C. Carstens, employed professionals in the fields of social work and child psychology to aid parents in adequately providing for and socializing their children (Mulford, 1983, p. 4). This appears to be the first time any agency began to express concern for the child as an individual with human rights (Antler, 1981).

The first juvenile court was established in 1899 in the state of Illinois (Pfohl, 1980, p. 326). Incorporating the old "poor law" functions of the chancery court, the juvenile court system as established in the United States was given the authority to commit dependent and neglected children (Rosenthal and Louis, 1981, p. 56). Though defined as the protectors of juveniles, initially the juvenile courts committed much the same transgressions against poor youths as had the House of Refuge movement and the SPCCs. That is, the juvenile courts also removed children from "bad" homes, institutionalized them, and labelled them. Once again, abusive parents escaped both prosecution and labelling. The goal, as before, was to save society by stemming the development of lower-class delinquents into adult criminals (Pfohl, 1980, pp. 326-27; Rosenthal and Louis, 1981). It was not until the 1920s that charitable organizations, influenced by the sentiments of social workers and child psychologists, began working with the courts and directing attention to the child and his/her welfare. Further influential factors were the Depression of the 1930s and the passage of the Social Security Act of 1935, which made provision for the funding of child welfare agencies. Child labor was for the first time regulated by federal legislation in 1930. In addition, federal legislation called for the creation of the Children's Bureau, an agency mandated to protect children. This included protection from "abuse, neglect, exploitation or moral hazard" (Pfohl, 1980, p. 328).

As indicated by Antler (1981), early attempts by the Children's Bureau to enact legislation similar to the act passed in 1973 met with opposition from the American Medical Association (AMA). The opposition stemmed from the Children's Bureau's targeting of medical professionals as child-cruelty reporting sources. On the one hand, the AMA reasoned that people needing medical assistance might not seek it for fear of legal reprisals. On the other hand, the AMA felt that having other professionals in addition to physicians designated as responsible for the reporting of suspected abuse of children would enhance intervention while at the same time reducing peoples' reluctance to seek medical attention when necessary (Antler, 1981).

The foregoing discussion is in no wise an attempt to minimize either the contributions of Kempe and his colleagues or the great strides made in grappling with child abuse as a social problem that occurred primarily because of their work on the "battered child syndrome." Instead, the discussion seeks to emphasize that a *unified* effort to deal with child abuse was not made prior to Kempe's work; that larger historical currents heavily influenced the recognition of child abuse; and that earlier attempts to draw attention to and ameliorate the abuse of children were frequently disregarded, met with resistance, or were discussed only among certain select groups of people rather than receiving the mass attention that became possible in the 1960s and 1970s.

Margaret Lynch's (1985) excellent discussion of child abuse before the work of Kempe and his colleagues deserves attention at this juncture. Lynch reviews literature from the writings of medical practitioners to glean historical attitudes regarding the treatment of children.[1] She notes that the earliest known surviving treatise on pediatrics, written about 900 A.D., makes mention of the fact that some children suffering from hernias or "prominence of the umbilicas" may actually have been "struck intentionally" (Lynch, 1985, p. 7). Soranus's *Gynaecology* (second century A.D.) gives attention to violent behaviors of some wet nurses, cautioning that nurses who are ill-tempered might mistreat infants and cause serious if not fatal harm (pp. 7-8). Lynch then takes her analysis, based on available literature,

---

[1] Samuel X. Radbill (1974) has done work similar to this and will be referred to later in this same chapter.

through the seventeenth to the twentieth century, noting evidence that medical practitioners have not only recorded mistreatment of children, physical harm of children, and death of children at the hands of adults, but have also been concerned about the welfare of children vis-á-vis childrearing practices, emotional abuse, and neglect (Lynch, 1985, pp. 8-15).

Lynch's work clearly indicates that the writers cited did not have a wide audience and that their concerns were either not heard or not heeded. It may be that, given the higher rates of illiteracy, the scarcity of books, and the lack of extensive communication systems, people simply were not privy to the advice or guidelines and warnings of learned medical men. On the other hand, Straus's (1974) analysis of the factors heightening awareness of family violence need to be re-called at this point. Perhaps the writings reviewed by Lynch were his-torically premature, arriving at times when they were incompatible with prevailing attitudes, norms, and behaviors.

CHANGING VIEWS OF CHILDREN

The preceding discussion of child abuse as a social problem indi-cates that defining violence toward children as "abuse" was in part due to changes in the acceptance of violent behaviors and also to a shift in the perceptions of the rights of individuals. To extend this discussion, we turn to historical analyses regarding the value of chil-dren and commonly shared assumptions of "proper" childrearing practices. As Gil (1981, p. 306) notes, when speaking of what is re-quired to prevent child abuse, we must redefine childhood and the rights of children, rejecting the notion that children are property and not persons in their own right. Changing these sentiments has been fundamental in the redefinition of traditional child-rearing practices as abusive. Had it not been for a shift in the value of children and con-comitant technological and ideological changes, physical and sexual transgressions against children by adults would even today remain relatively free of sanction.

McCoy's journalistic exposé "Childhood through the Ages" (1983) quotes Tamara Hareven as revealing that perceptions of the value of children and appropriate child-rearing practices have varied among social classes and within societies across time (p. 123). Prior to indus-trialization, and especially before the development and availability of reliable birth control, pregnancy was often accompanied by fear of maternal death, fear of the death of the child, and concern over how to provide for the child should it survive infancy and the early years of childhood. Given the high infant mortality rate, mothers frequently did not become emotionally invested in their infants. Illegitimate children were sometimes the victims of infanticide. Viewed as miniature adults whose primary function, especially in the lower classes, was to become part of the family in economic/work terms, children were defined as moral inferiors to be dealt with sternly and harshly. Physical punishment by parents, kin, and nonkin in the household (boarders, apprentices, servants, and so forth) was neither unusual nor opposed by parents (McCoy, 1983).

In the past, harsh physical discipline has been justified on many grounds, including but not limited to the following:

Children are unruly animals whose strivings for independence or quests for answers to their queries must be repressed.
Children only learn to obey through harsh and regular physical discipline.
Children are evil and must have the evil beaten out of them.
Children learn to respect authority through beatings.
Children are the property of the father, whose authority is absolute, and any challenges to this authority deserve punishment (Radbill, 1974; Leslie, 1982; McCoy, 1983).

At least two interactive influences must be noted in relation to the treatment of children in the United States in historical context. These are religion (specifically, Calvinism) and patriarchy. The Calvinist view of children was that they were "imps of darkness" who needed physical discipline to control their dark and evil natures (Radbill, 1974, p. 174). Fathers as patriarchs (much like the Biblical patriarchs) had far-reaching, almost absolute power over their children, who were considered to be their property. The father, if he so wished, could sell their labor. Apprenticing young children was not uncommon. Further, at least two states, Connecticut and Massachusetts, provided permission to have "persistently" disobedient youths put to death (Leslie, 1982, see especially p. 192).

John Witherspoon's 1802 writings to parents tellingly illustrate the power of the father and the emphasis on obedience of children. He writes, ". . .Establish, as soon as possible, an entire and absolute authority." Interestingly, he continues:

I would have it early, that it may be absolute, and absolute, that it might not be severe. If parents are too long in beginning to expect their indulgence, they will find the task very difficult. Children habituated to indulgence for a few of their first years are exceedingly impatient of restraint, and if they happen to be of stiff or obstinate tempers, can hardly be brought to an entire, at least to a quiet or placid submission. . . .There is not a more disgusting sight than the impotent rage of a parent who has not authority. . . .I would therefore recommend to every parent to begin the establishment of authority much more early than is supposed commonly possible. That is to say, from about the age of eight or nine months. (pp. 143-44)

Differences in child treatment and the extent of patriarchal control (or, rather, the exercise thereof) apparently varied by social class and region through the early years of industrialization. Farm and working-class mill families tended to perceive each family member no longer an infant as a contributing work or economic unit of the family. It was not uncommon for children to work in the fields, the home, the factories, or the mills (Wallace, 1981, pp. 169-70). Money made by children legally belonged to the father (Scott and Wishy, 1982).

Managerial and upper-class parents viewed their children somewhat differently. Whereas the mill worker or farmer assessed the value of his children in terms of potential or actual contributions to the family coffers, men in nonmanual labor classes assessed their children "in terms of the potential alliance implications of marriage" (Wallace, 1981, p. 171).

Wallace provides historical records indicating that daughters of these classes who failed to participate in merger marriages risked being disclaimed by their fathers (Wallace, 1981). As today, managerial and upper-class families in the early days of industrialization held strong vested interests in family lineage, resulting in the placement of women on the periphery of family life, the enhancement of patriarchy, and the employment of childrearing practices (ostensibly nonviolent) that emphasized control of the child to reach the desired goal of a continuance of the patronymic descent group (Wallace, 1981, pp. 171-72; Leslie, 1982, pp. 323-26).

Subsequent changes in the value of children and the treatment of children have been traced to several sources. McCoy feels that the wealthy merchant classes of England and the United States, aided by contraception and the development of a breast-feeding cult in the late seventeenth and early eighteenth centuries, began to stress the importance of "upbringing" and the meeting of a child's developmental needs such that the child-centered family became a reality for all social classes by the end of the Victorian era (McCoy, 1983, p. 128).

The previous discussion on the rights of children and the defining of violence against children as abuse may bring part of McCoy's conclusion into question. However, it has been documented that in all social classes, permissiveness in childrearing practices has arisen concomitantly with urbanization and the availability of contraception (Leslie, 1982). Also, as indicated earlier, women's struggles for freedom drew attention to patriarchy's constraints on children as property.[2]

The availability of contraception has been seen as a necessary condition for the freeing of both women and children from patriarchal control (Gordon, 1981; Easton, 1983). With the option of fewer children and the advent of wanted children, in conjunction with a changing mode of economic production in which the old view of the child as a workhorse became obsolete, children began to be perceived as individuals in their own right, whose childhood years carried consequences for the entire society.

As an aside, it is interesting to note that the rise of rationalism and the decline of religion in the late eighteenth and early nineteenth centuries did not bring attempts to halt harsh discipline of children (Pfohl, 1980, p. 324). The concept of children as property apparently overrode such influences. Instead, a concern for the effects of childrearing practices upon society and the possibility of controlling births, in tandem with women's rights strivings, led to a reckoning of children as humans somewhere around the turn of the twentieth century.

Thus, while it is no doubt correct that social forces in the 1960s set the stage for a reexamination of childrearing practices vis-á-vis the battered child syndrome and for the definition of child abuse as a social problem, it is also true that fundamental preconditions for this development were laid many years in advance.

---

[2] The reader is reminded that the struggle for the rights of women has a long history, officially recognized with the Seneca Falls convention in 1848. Research indicates that early in the 1800s, women concerned for their own rights were equally concerned with the oppression of children in patriarchal societies and families (Gordon, 1981; Easton, 1983).

3

A Review of Theories

INTRODUCTION

For organizational purposes, this chapter will be divided into several sections: anthropological, psychological, sociological, ecological, and feminist perspectives. No special section is provided for the sociobiological theories, which are discussed in the anthropology section since their principal focus of concern is exogamy vis-á-vis incest taboos. Anthropological treatments attempt to explain the incest taboo, incest avoidance, and exogamy more generally. Psychological theories include Freud's impulse theory, J. R. Fox's learning theory, and Ellis's aversion theory. Sociologists such as Parsons and Bales (1955) emphasize normative restraints and positive, nonincestuous sexual socialization of the young as necessary for societal maintenance. Also sociological is the systems approach to family violence (including violence that is sexual in nature) developed by Straus (1973). Ecological approaches to child abuse are based on a structural, sociocultural approach to explaining and predicting child abuse and emphasize intervention and prevention. While an ecological model of incest per se has not yet been developed, ecological models of child abuse in other forms hold promise for understanding incest. Feminists argue that father-daughter incest is a product of a patriarchal family structure.

This chapter, then, reviews theories about incest. To be more specific, however, this chapter reviews theories that look at incest in different ways. Some theorists assume that an actual incest taboo (a sacred interdiction) exists among humans. Others assume that humans (and, for some theorists, other bonding-motivated animals) develop incest barriers as a survival mechanism concomitant with a sexual division of labor. Still others contend that humans have or develop an aversion that prohibits incest. In line with such diversity this chapter attempts to present the various treatments given incest, both as per the writers' academic orientations or identifications, and as per their perceptions regarding the evidence of an incest taboo, incest aversion, or incest barrier and the etiology or importance thereof.

As the preceding paragraph brings out, various theories of incest differ in their conceptions of the "explanadum" or "dependent variable" to be explained. They differ even more sharply in the "explanons" or "independent variables" thought to explain the phenomenon. For example, while anthropologists typically concern themselves with incest, the incest taboo, and incest avoidance as primarily cultural phenomena and investigate these matters in terms of survival mechanisms and family and kin structures, psychological theories approach incest as an individual matter, emphasizing impulses, early-life experiences, neurotic responses, and aversions. Among the latter, Freud's early works (around 1918) are an exception, focusing on structural and cultural as well as biological variables in the origins of the incest taboo. Today, however, writers (for example, Rascovsky and Rascovsky, 1972) using a Freudian perspective tend to emphasize early-life experiences, developmental stages, ego defenses, and other individual variables. Though somewhat lengthy, this chapter encompasses the major theoretical approaches, interpretations, and treatments of "incest", however defined or explained.

While the perception of incest as a social problem requiring intervention is a recent development, attempts to understand incest, and especially the nature and societal importance of mechanisms preventing it, certainly are not. Because the prevention of incest has long been viewed as perhaps the key to civilization (Freud, 1918, 1949; Seligman, 1929), few topics have received more sustained attention by theorists.

ANTHROPOLOGICAL THEORIES

Social Organization Theories

Civilization may be regarded as the measure of the capacity to live in organized groups; to this end natural impulses become modified for social gain. (Seligman, 1932, p. 250)

Those barriers were not consciously formulated, but arose, not specifically to check the lust of the *pater familias*, but in the production of
an harmonious family group, and actually changed it from a natural to
a social group. (Seligman, 1932, p. 276)

Seligman and Levi-Strauss felt that the incest taboo (which is actually a "barrier")[1] arises concomitantly with the civilized development of humans into societal groups and various modes of social living
(Levi-Strauss, 1969; Seligman, 1929, 1932, 1950). Both of these
anthropologists argue that the incest taboo makes the family a discrete
and viable unit of society. Further, since the society cannot exist without individual families, incest weakens the functioning of society in
that bonds are broken by the very act of incest. Incest also impedes
the development of intergroup bonds through marriage and the expansion of the kinship group. Incest undermines the intrafamily system while at the same time threatening essential interfamily bonds,
which are dependent upon exogamous mating patterns. Since a family
is the result of the joining not of two individuals but of two family
systems, incestuous marriages or relationships break the continual and
societally necessary linkages of groups. Internally, the incest taboo
functions to unite the cohabiting individuals in a cooperative fashion,
limiting sex to the married persons only. With incest prohibited, family
members have one less area of conflict and can use their coordinated
efforts for the continuance of survival.

Both Seligman and Levi-Strauss propose that a society depends
upon nuclear family groupings. The incest taboo insures those groupings by decreasing conflict among the group's members. Levi-Strauss
stresses that "natural man" mated indiscriminately (with no regard
to blood lines) and promiscuously. When mankind began to live in
separated groupings based on taboos, however, nuclear families were
created. At the same time, the maintenance of the larger society (the
arrangement of intergroup relationships) was enhanced, since each
nuclear family became dependent upon others for survival. Via the
creation of the incest taboos, then, natural man became social man.

---

[1] Both Seligman and Levi-Strauss felt that humans actually invented an incest
"barrier" rather than having any naturally arising or developing incest taboo.
The point is significant in that these two anthropologists imply no natural aversion; rather, the implication is that humans found it necessary to construct strong
barriers against a tendency for indiscriminate sexual activity in order to survive
as a species. Attention is not given to moral ideas surrounding sexual interaction.
To the contrary, emphasis is placed on constructing such barriers so as to enhance
survival by bonding with members of other groups.

The most important taboo is the incest taboo, which creates interdependent nuclear families and a cooperative, dependent basis for survival.

In conjunction with his discussion of the incest taboo as a mechanism for facilitating cooperation and interdependence, Levi-Strauss has referred to the incest taboo as part of the "rule of the gift" (1969, p. 481). He says that men foster interdependence by exchanging the females' sexuality or sexual potential (through marriage) with other men. That is, females are gifts men give to one another so as to create the interdependence necessary for survival.[2] In sum, Levi-Strauss feels that in developing human social organization, the incest taboo functions to provide females as special types of gifts in group exchange relationships.

Leslie White (1948) submits as his basic premise the notion that human behavior is culturally determined. His writings converge with the works of Levi-Strauss and Seligman in that incest taboos are viewed as cultural inventions used to diminish familial competition and encourage multiple group coordination.

In a slightly different vein, Pierre van den Berghe suggests that humans as social animals try to maintain an "optimum balance between inbreeding and outbreeding" (1980, p. 151). He feels that incest avoidance is natural (inherent in human nature), though this avoidance is expressed through incest taboos (p. 156). His vehicle for understanding how societies organize their groups is grounded in anthropological examinations and interpretations of marriage rules, specifically exogamy. This is combined with a Darwinian "survival-of-the-fittest" interpretation of human development. Noting, as did Seligman, that incest taboos and rules of exogamy are not the same, van den Berghe states that while incest avoidance reduces inbreeding, some rules of exogamy do not. Acknowledging, from anthropological evidence, that inbreeding is greatest in the least structured (stratified) societies, and also in the highest strata of stratified societies, van den Berghe argues that marriage rules follow a fitness maxim. That is, men control and allocate between themselves the reproductive potential of women so as to make optimal use of genetic factors in perpetuating strong ("fit") genetic makeups.

Certainly, it seems logical that humans would develop schemas and exchanges of sorts so as to foster intergroup coordination, diminish

---

[2] The exchanging of gifts has been noted in social science literature as a way to facilitate cooperation and cohesion (Malinowski, 1927, 1929; Gouldner, 1960).

intergroup conflict, and enhance survival chances. That females were used in exchanges stands to reason in male-dominated societies. However, one must ask at least two questions of van den Berghe. If humans have a natural incest avoidance tendency, why did it have to be expressed in taboos—or even in some marriage rules? Further, if marriage rules allow for certain types of incest, especially among the highest strata of society, what does this say about the premise that humans have a natural incest avoidance tendency?

Biological Impossibility Theory

Miriam K. Slater (1959) proffers the theory that, due to short life spans and rapid aging of primitive people, incest was impossible and exogamy was necessary. She contends that by the time a child was sexually mature, the parents were dead. Further, since children were not born close together (due to a long breast-feeding period), brother-sister incest was impossible because one child would reach maturity and be getting older before the next child reached maturity. Thus, exogamy became the mating rule for primitive peoples. Slater goes on to argue that even when life spans became longer, incest did not occur because a cultural custom of exogamy was already strongly rooted. Thus, she implies that a rule of exogamy rather than an incest taboo evolved among humans.

The first criticism of this argument is that breast-feeding does not necessarily prohibit pregnancy. Second, Slater is of course looking at incest in terms of marriage—and only secondarily in terms of sexual behaviors. Third, she ignores the possibility of sex between an immature child and a mature adult. Slater states that the possibility of incest between an older brother and a younger sister should be discounted since by the time the sister reaches sexual maturity the brother will have become sexually mature and will have made a marriage arrangement. If we accept Slater's life-span theory, then we would share her assumption that the bearing of children spawned by siblings would probably be unusual—but certainly not impossible. Moreover, incest itself would be neither. First, we know that incest between immature children and mature adults can and does occur.[3] Second, Kinsey's data (1948, 53) document the ability of prepubescent children to be sexually responsive and active. Though we are asking

---

[3] In fact, the surprising frequency of adult-child incest, even in modern societies where Slater assumes her rule of exogamy to be firmly established, is the raison d'etre for the present authors' entire examination of these questions.

readers to take a sort of quantum leap and apply Kinsey's data to primitive peoples, there is little reason to doubt that primitive people also had the capacity to be sexually responsive without being sexually mature. Thus, in a society not yet having rules of exogamy or incest taboos, as Slater supposes, what would make adult-child incest (sexual relations) impossible or even unusual?

Aversion Theory

Seymour Parker (1976) argues that although cultures differ from each other in many ways, the incest taboo is a universal phenomenon. In contrast to this statement, Edward Westermarck, approximately 80 years earlier, proposed that incest should not be viewed so much a taboo as an aversion. In his *History of Human Marriage*, Westermarck (1898) explicated the idea that individuals who live in close association with each other (as, for example, nuclear family members), and who share in the everyday tasks of living, tend to develop sexual aversions to each other.

While much incest literature challenges Westermarck's theory, it is not without some support. When studying sexual relations in Japanese and Chinese minor marriages (where the wife was reared in her prospective husband's immediate family), Arthur P. Wolf (1972) found that the couple typically did not engage in marital coitus. Rather, these couples often were involved in extramarital relations and rarely consummated their marriages.

Shepher (1971), relying upon his study of all marriages of second-generation kibbutz adults and an intensive, longitudinal study of 65 second-generation kibbutz adolescents and adults, found no heterosexual activity among the adolescents and no marriages among the adults. He argues that, from his data, one could conclude that the social arrangements and norms are such that, early in childhood, the kibbutz dwellers experience imprinting that defines sexual activity with other kibbutz peers as taboo. In other words, Shepher posits that in the process of communal socialization, sexual avoidance and exogamy are imprinted; the imprinting occurs at an early age, and, once established, the imprinting has a lasting quality that endures throughout adolescence and adulthood (Shepher, 1971, p. 302). Thus, Shepher's study leads him to utilize not only the basic concepts or ideas employed by Westermarck, but also to rely upon learning theory, which is biologically grounded in conditioning of the individual in line with environmental constraints.

Parker (1976), somewhat differently than Westermarck, assumes that an incest avoidance tendency preceded what would later become an incest taboo. This avoidance functioned to direct people to realms of interaction other than those of the immediate family. This interaction led to the forming of bonds that enhanced the survival chances of the groups and of the society.

The aversion theory can be challenged along lines similar to those noted in conjunction with van den Berghe's work. In addition, the assumption that persons who interact daily and share mundane tasks develop an aversion to one another is questionable in light of more recent research demonstrating that familiarity tends to enhance attraction and may function to create circumstances conducive to sexual involvement (Byrne, 1971; Rubin, 1973; Hendrick and Hendrick, 1983).

Genetic Theory

Lindzey (1967), Campbell (1966), and Aberle et al. (1963) propose a genetic theory of the origin of the incest taboo. The genetic theory states that the incest taboo originated as a means of enhancing human development and civilization by adding stronger genetic makeups in new generations than the makeups that would emerge if humans were to inbreed. At the same time, mating outside the family decreased infant mortality, mutations, and birth defects, which result from the breeding of people with similar genetic makeups. Support for this theory comes from research done by Adams and Neel (1967) and Seemanova (1971). These researchers found evidence indicating that there are greater incidences of physical defects, mutations, and mental and cognitive impairments among offspring of incestuous unions than among offspring of nonincestuous unions.

A criticism of this theory is that the assumption that primitive people were cognizant of these negative effects and could link them as stated seems doubtful (Lester, 1972; Harris, 1975). On the other hand, certain functionalist orientations maintain that social systems operate *sui generis*, tending to preserve functional patterns quite apart from the cognizance of their individual members (see Durkheim, 1938 and 1947).

Role Confusion Theory

Bronislaw Malinowski (1927, 1929) argues that a cultural explanation of the incest taboo lies in the area of role confusion and family disruption. Since incest was conducive to the disruption of family life, it became prohibited (Nimkoff, 1947). Malinowski reasons that as society emerged, the development of distinct role functions facilitated the survival of the society. A division of labor and associated division of roles was necessary. This division of labor allowed for hunting and gathering and the care of helpless infants, thus permitting the survival of the society. The need to survive linked people together in units involving more than one nuclear family. To insure the filling and enactment of these roles, and the maintenance of linkages with other groups, the incest taboo was created. By prohibiting incest, a division of labor ensued, permitting the functioning of the family as a productive economic unit (while at the same time the family members were forced to create and maintain relationships and bonds with other nuclear families). Thus, there was no role confusion and societal survival was insured.

Focusing even more squarely on the issue of role confusion, Coult (1963) proposes that incest taboos function to avoid the confusion of multiple kin roles. Coult concludes that marriage rules serve to prevent a person, or a series of family members, from having several family roles within one kin structure. Thus, role differentiation predominates and role conflict is avoided. With the avoidance of role conflict, families are relieved of disintegrating confusions and incompatabilities.

PSYCHOLOGICAL THEORIES

Freud's Impulse Theory

In contrast to Westermarck, Freud proposed that humans have an impulse or inclination to engage in incestuous behaviors. Freud theorized that humans originally lived in a "primal horde," ruled by a tyrannical patriarch. This patriarch drove away all of his sons and mated with his daughters. The sons, seeing this, banded together, killed the father, and ceremoniously ate him. Shortly thereafter, the sons realized that jealousy and competition among the males for their sisters might cause total destruction. They also felt guilt and remorse over killing and eating their father. So, the brothers instituted the incest taboo (Freud, 1949 [1930]; 1950 [1918]). In other words, their guilt and remorse, coupled with their fears of total destruction by male competition and jealousy, prompted them to institute a taboo against incest. While it has been argued that Freud intended to indicate that the first taboo was against cannibalism (Reed, 1975), most other writers using Freud's work interpret his primal-horde story to indicate the origins of the incest taboo as an interdiction against certain sexual pairings.

Freud also termed the inclination to initiate or to engage in incest an "infantile feature," most commonly found in the "mental lives of neurotics" (1950 [1918], p. 17). He felt that all young males experience the Oedipus complex—desire for their mothers. However, due to their age and size, the males are frustrated in their attempts to consummate their desires. At the same time, they fear their fathers and experience a concern that their fathers, realizing their desires, might castrate them. Young females experience a sexual desire for their fathers. Both males and females tend initially to identify with and desire the opposite-sex parent. Females, like the males, realize their futile situations and undergo a "reaction formation"—that is, instead of admitting hatred of the same-sex parent, the child will identify with and become affectionate toward the same-sex parent. At the same time, male and female children repress their impulsive sexual desires for the opposite-sex parent. Freud felt that as adults, if humans perpetuated incest, it was because they were neurotic and unable to restrain long-repressed impulse inclinations (Freud, 1950 [1918]; 1962 [1905]). Freud finally decided that women patients who told him they had been incest victims were lying to themselves and fantasizing (see also Taubman, 1984).

Robin Fox (1980) argues along similar lines. He assumes that younger and adult males competed with one another for sex and marriage with females. Further, females, utilizing their sexual and reproductive potentials, controlled men by encouraging competition. Through this triangulated competition, human societies organized themselves and evoked controls and balances over incest tendencies and behaviors. While Fox's treatment is somewhat sociobiological in nature, he ultimately relegates incest to the realm of Oedipal impulses and female fantasies.

Rascovsky and Rascovsky (1972) rely heavily upon the works of Freud to articulate explanations for incest prohibitions and the sociocultural consequences thereof. In addition, they focus on the prohibition of filicide. Their assumption is that humans have innate sexual instincts which are controlled through incest prohibitions. Three consequences of incest prohibitions are proposed: "rules of exogamy and subsequent enlargement of social groups; sublimation of incest impulses, subsequently, a redirection of incestuous drives toward acceptable social relationships; and, intergenerational transmission of the human experience, facilitating participation in the socialization of the young" (Rascovsky and Rascovsky, 1972, p. 272).

This socialization ostensibly carries with it strong elements of intimidation so as to control the incest impulses of children by instilling in them an "extreme paranoid" condition (p. 275). Further, utilizing Freudian terminology, Rascovsky and Rascovsky describe the incest taboo as functioning such that parents (often envious of their children) transfer the guilt from their own incestuous desires onto their children and punish the children for both the parents' own and the children's (as perceived by the parents) incestuous inclinations. The children blame themselves, often suffering castration and persecution anxiety. The entire process is obfuscated by denial, leaving intact parental supremacy (pp. 274-75).

Many aspects of Freud's incest theories have been roundly and tellingly criticized in relationship to the empirical evidence (Janeway, 1981). We leave the empirical indictment against Freud and his followers up to Janeway and those similarly qualified (Rush, 1980, for example). We would like to note, however, that Freudian interpretations of incest do tend to blame the victim. As noted earlier, Freud concluded that incest reports were often delusions, with the purported victim projecting her own desires onto the parent. Further, even when the fact of actual incest behavior is incontrovertible, Freudian interpretations, premised on the Oedipus complex, have tended to exonerate the father, placing the blame on the "seductive" daughter (Bender and Blau, 1937; Sloane and Karpinski, 1942; Weiss et al., 1955).

A final theory does Freud one better and provides "food for thought," as it were. Evelyn Reed (1975) has argued that the incest taboo was not originally a taboo against incest. Rather, she contends that the incest taboo was first a "social law of supreme force" (p. 19). Further, while only one clause in the taboo was directed against sex, the most important clause revolved around food. Reed declares that the incest taboo was actually a taboo against cannibalism (Reed, 1975, p. 22).

Ellis's Aversion Theory

Like Westermarck, Havelock Ellis (1906) suggested that humans develop an aversion to incest. Ellis felt that due to long-term association and the sharing of mundane tasks, the levels of sexual arousal in the nuclear family become depressed. The same criticisms raised in response to Westermarck and to Slater apply to Ellis's argument. Much evidence indicates that familiarity does not necessarily nor inevitably breed discontent; rather, the opposite appears to happen (Rubin, 1973, pp. 113-33). While Ellis's work appears to add nothing once one has read the anthropological literature, his theory should be noted for at least two reasons. First, he is one of the very early psychologists, a pioneer at least in the area of sex research and theory. Second, it is interesting to note the convergence of ideation between Ellis and several anthropologists. Such a convergence does not, however, establish the validity of the aversion theory. It remains equally plausible that families would not be able to accomplish the sharing of mundane tasks were it not for the prior establishment of an incest proscription.

J. R. Fox's Learning Theory

J. R. Fox (1962; see also Shapiro, 1980), following Westermarck's lead, theorizes that siblings learn a sexual aversion to one another. In early childhood, he argues, siblings engage in mutual stimulation, but the siblings become frustrated due to their physical inability to consummate their desires. Repeated frustration leads to sexual aversion to each other, since every sex play experience ends up being more painful than pleasurable. Fox concluded that incest will not occur due to the mutual sexual aversion of siblings learned during prepubescent years.

Fox's learning theory, like other theories based upon the idea of aversion or avoidance, is compromised in the face of the results of the Kinsey studies (1948, 1953). As an aside, it is interesting to note that aversion therapy and aversion techniques are today being used to reduce recidivism rates among adult incest perpetrators and child molesters (Forward and Buck, 1978; Quinsey, 1977). That is, some therapists are attempting to deliberately instill an aversion to incest and to child molestation in previous offenders.

SOCIOLOGICAL THEORY AND APPROACHES

Socialization/Role Strain Theory

Talcott Parsons (1954, 1964) and Robert Bales (Parsons and Bales, 1955) argue that the primary function of the nuclear family is the socialization of children. Incest disrupts functioning because the incest results in role confusion and role strain. Because it is dysfunctional, incest is taboo. The family is not a society unto itself; rather, it is a unit of society. The family's major function in society is that of transmitting the basic values and norms of the family and the society to the young—in other words, "latent pattern maintenance." As a dependent unit (dependent upon other families and institutions), a nuclear family must avoid role strain. The family must avoid incest and rely on exogamous marriage to insure survival of the society.

While the foregoing adds nothing to earlier anthropological accounts, Parsons and Bales (1955) go on to contend that a nuclear family imposes a monopoly over genital eroticism. Second, always in the mother-child relationship and to some extent in the father-child relationship, pregenital eroticism is positively institutionalized. (By gratifying some of the child's erotic needs, parents are better able to channel the child in the desired direction throughout the socialization process.) Third, overt expressions of eroticism are taboo between post-Oedipal children and parents. Fourth, no homosexuality is allowed. It is argued that this system within the family is not wholly a repressive institutionalization of sexuality; there is a systematic combination of controlled expressiveness and regulatory prohibition (Parsons, 1964).

Parsons and Bales contend that the family functions such that children are taught their "appropriate" roles; at the same time the "id" in children and parents is repressed (Parsons and Bales, 1955). That is, parents provide sex role models for their children (most control their own impulses in order to do so), and children are encouraged to develop heterosexual affiliations outside the nuclear family. Parsons and Bales (1955) postulate that only in marriages where parents have conflicts with one another are erotic attachments to the parents promoted or rewarded.

In the same vein, Gagnon and Simon (1967) contend that the incest taboo exists primarily because status and role expectations cannot be met if there are incestuous relations within the family. When roles and responsibilities are not clearly defined, socialization of the child does not follow "normative" patterns of growth and personality development.

These theorists assume the primacy of the nuclear family and imply the need to preserve the status quo. Maintaining the family institution and the society as a whole tends to be equated with the preservation of existing task allocations and other roles. Further, implied within the works of Parsons and Bales is the assumption that humans are rational and will do whatever should be done to avoid disintegration or destruction of the society as a system. (For further criticisms of Parsonian and other functionalist thought, see Turner, 1978.)

Taking to task the foregoing sociologists (and, by logical exten-sion, Seligman, Levi-Strauss, and indeed the majority of anthropol-ogists who have addressed these issues), Bagley (1969) argues that theorists err in assuming that the cause of the incest taboo lies in the fact that families are not independent societies and therefore prohibit incest for survival purposes. Rather, argues Bagley, it is sometimes functional for a family to ignore any incest taboo. When this happens, the family becomes an entity unto itself, with its own rules and modes of functioning, wherein incest may be morally approved of by the members comprising the entity (Bagley, 1969, p. 507).[4] In short, al-though prohibiting incest may be functional for the larger society, at least one researcher contends that it is not necessarily functional for an individual family.

Other Sociological Explanations

For the main part, contemporary sociologists focus on incest as child abuse rather than on the origins and significance of the incest taboo. Increasingly, sociologists are coming to the conclusion that incest is not rare—nor has it ever been (Rush, 1980; Gordon and O'Keefe, 1984). There is a pressing need to move beyond explana-tions for cultural proscriptions against incest, turning attention to factors which lead many adults, especially adult males, to violate these proscriptions. Finkelhor (1978a, 1980a, 1980b) and Vander Mey and Neff (see Chapters four and five), for example, have attempted to ar-ticulate family factors and victim and perpetrator characteristics which, based on frequency of report in incest cases, may function as part of the incest scenario. Such factors include patriarchal fathers, powerless mothers, parental alcohol abuse, parents' lack of under-standing of child development, parental history of abuse as a child, social isolation, inadequate housing, inadequate income, reconstituted family structure (with a stepfather present), and marital discord (Finkelhor, 1978, 1980a; Vander Mey and Neff, 1984).

Straus (1973) has articulated a general systems approach as a model for the explanation of family violence. Though his focus of concern was primarily physical violence, included in his explanatory model was sexual abuse. He included in his systems approach family variables, individual family member characteristics, precipitating

---

[4] This line of reasoning has also been argued by those favoring the sexualized family (see Summit and Kryso, 1978).

factors, and societal variables, along with consequences of violence for individuals, families, and societies. Propositions related to this systems approach include the following:

> There is no single "cause" of family violence; children in violent homes may learn violence as an acceptable behavior; violence may be rewarding to the perpetrator if desired results are obtained; since family violence is counternormative, the violence may create conflict; and labelling a person violent may facilitate the perpetuation of a self-fulfilling prophecy. (Straus, 1973)

Straus concludes that the systems approach can account for the onset and perpetuation of family violence. Thus, family violence is a function of individual, family, and societal factors. Finally, there is no one unique combination of these factors which is *the* incest scenario; the risk of incest increases as any one or more parts of the family system become(s) weakened or thrown out of balance.

ECOLOGICAL APPROACHES

> Research on the ecology of human development requires investigations that go beyond the immediate setting containing the person to examine the larger contexts, both formal and informal, that affect the immediate setting. (Bronfenbrenner, 1977, p. 527)

Bronfenbrenner's (1977) articulation of an ecological approach to human development has had a far-reaching impact upon explanatory models of child abuse. Emphasizing the interactive nature between growing human beings and changing environments (p. 513), Bronfenbrenner challenges his readers to grapple with the fact that understanding human behavior requires more than "the direct observation of behaviors on the part of one or two persons in the same place" (p. 514). His argument, in essence, is that environment and social locations, with myriad patterns of organization, bear significant relationship to human beings' behavior and personalities. Frustrated with laboratory experiments whose results frequently display little resemblance to "real life," Bronfenbrenner advocates the use of models that encompass all of the many points of influence in human life. These include: the *macrosystem* (general prototypes, "overarching institutional patterns of the culture or subculture," p. 515); the *microsystem* (the "complex of relations. . .in an immediate setting," p. 514); the *mesosystem* ("interrelationships among major settings" in which a person exists at points in his/her life, p. 515); and the *exosystem* (an extension of the mesosystem—those social structures in which a person is not located, but which influence him, p. 515). Quite simply, Bronfenbrenner argues that questions of human behavior should be examined in social context, appreciating the various levels and types of influence (informal, formal, institutional, and cultural) that have an impact upon humans and their behavior.

James Garbarino (1976), relying upon Bronfenbrenner's earlier attempts to articulate an ecological model of human development, develops an ecological, explanatory model of child abuse/maltreatment. Based on his analysis of child-abuse cases in New York (state), Garbarino found that "the ecological context generated by economic and educational resources is an important factor of child abuse/maltreatment" (Garbarino, 1976, p. 183). Economic disadvantages, stress, isolation, and lack of resources are noted by Garbarino as crucial determining factors predisposing mothers to be abusive toward their children. He suggests that economic improvement and increases in resources might ameliorate the abusive situation.

Garbarino and Crouter (1978) examined child abuse in community context. Examining socioeconomic, demographic, and attitudinal variables in relation to child-abuse cases (p. 608), they found that not only were these variables correlated to child abuse, but that stress, geographic mobility, and negative attributes of or attitudes toward the neighborhood also bore significant relationships to child abuse (p. 609). Their conclusion is that the quality of life of families, resources of families, and family support systems must be assessed so as to provide timely intervention (p. 614).

Garbarino and Sherman (1980) matched a pair of neighborhoods on socioeconomic factors to identify the "socioeconomic, demographic, and attitudinal correlates of neighborhood differences in the rate of child abuse and neglect" (p. 188). One neighborhood had low reported rates of child abuse, and the other had high rates. Their argument is that while an individual family may be high risk for child abuse, the neighborhood also has a great influence. The neighborhood deemed high risk (having high rates of child abuse) was characterized as being "socially impoverished" (p. 192). That is, in the high-risk neighborhood, the neighborhood's public image was poor, neighbors did not engage in much "neighboring," and there were few informal support systems for the residents (p. 192). Conversely, Garbarino and Sherman found that in the low-risk neighborhood, parents used the neighborhood as a resource. Mothers swapped child supervision and babysitting duties, thus creating collective competence among families.

There was far more reciprocity among families in the low-risk compared to the high-risk neighborhood (p. 192). In addition, mothers in the low-risk neighborhood were more likely to include professionals in their support system (p. 193). Garbarino and Sherman contend that the support available in the low-risk neighborhood created a less stressful[5] environment; hence, the neighborhood itself served to mitigate against child abuse and maltreatment.

Recently, Howze and Kotch (1984) have articulated an ecological approach to child abuse and neglect that is based on the work of Garbarino and his various coauthors. Elaborating on Garbarino's breakdown of the cultural milieu, social environment, and familial and individual characteristics (p. 403), they graphically depict their own theoretical model of child maltreatment (p. 406). In addition to Garbarino's four components of the ecosystem, they include in their model social support system/social network, life events, the interpretation of life events, and perceived stress (p. 406). Their work is important, not only for methodological and theoretical reasons, but also because Howze and Kotch emphasize the importance of social support. Since researchers continuously pinpoint stress, social isolation, and lack of resources/social support as predisposing a child to higher risk of abuse, the ecological model clearly holds promise for an understanding of the etiology of child abuse as well as potential avenues for intervention and prevention.

At this juncture, several points need to be made. First, and perhaps most obvious, an ecological approach to incest has not yet been fully articulated. Second, incest is *not* the same thing as physical child abuse. Incest is different from physical abuse and neglect and has its own special dynamics. Third, however, several characteristics of incest families overlap with characteristics of families who physically abuse their children (for example, alcohol abuse, social isolation, crowding, role confusion, low socioeconomic status, and intergenerational transmission of violent and abusive behavior: see Chapter 4 for more descriptions of incest families). Thus, an ecological approach, though somewhat deterministic, holds great promise for explaining and predicting incest. Further, an ecological approach to incest, grounded in empirical research, may enhance expedient intervention and prevention in families at high risk for incest.

---

[5] The importance of stress as a factor in child abuse has been indicated by other researchers, including Garbarino and Ebata (1983).

FEMINIST INTERPRETATIONS

Susan Brownmiller (1975) takes issue with the term incest. She argues that it implies mutuality. Her preference is to call incestuous victimization of children "father rape" (p. 281). From a feminist perspective, she feels that in patriarchal societies women were "man's original corporal property" and children "wholly owned subsidiaries" (p. 281). She notes that while incest taboos may be ancient, there operates in society an even older social law—absolute rule by the father.

Finkelhor (1978a) has criticized Brownmiller's "father rape" terminology. He says that rape and incest are not analogous because incest is protracted rather than a single event, as rape tends to be. In addition, Finkelhor argues that incest is not rape because force is typically not used—children usually submit passively.

While in another writing Finkelhor acknowledges the fact that force is not usually needed since parental authority is sufficient (1978b), he fails to see that, as a violation of intimacy, adult-child incest is very much in line with rape. In fact, one might argue that adult-child incest, which violates a child's trust and exploits the child's dependence upon and faith in the father as a teacher and guide, is one of the most heinous forms of rape. It appears untenable to argue that incest is not rape because physical force is not used. It is rape because a parent abuses his position of dominance, sexually exploiting a child while at the same time disrupting a child's sense of security and progress toward autonomy (which families are supposed to foster). There is psychological and emotional coercion. The very fact that incest typically is protracted points to the father's dominance and exemplifies incest as a special type of rape—a type in which the victim is trapped and finds it difficult to halt recurring episodes. The fact that physical force is not used does not mean that the victim has not been dominated or violated. The dynamics of power and differential access to and utilization of resources in a family must not be overlooked (confer Sprey, 1979). It is not a difficult matter for a parent to subjugate a child to do his will by threatening to withdraw privileges or love. Knowledge, age, size, intellect, vocabulary, dependence, trust, authority, and material resources are all on the side of the father. Physical force in incest, in view of the parent's greater store of resources, need only be used as a last resort—to frighten a child threatening to disclose the situation or to reestablish any perceived loss of power in the process of involving the child in this counternormative "family secret."

On the other hand, feminist arguments contain other components we find problematic, oversimplified, or misleading. Herman and Hirschman (1977) view all existing societies as patriarchal and contend that in such a system women and children are basically property. They argue that in such societies men determine the value of women and children. If Levi-Strauss and other anthropologists are correct, this contention is valid only with reference to primitive societies. Its validity with reference to modern, postindustrial societies, as presented by Herman and Hirschman and other feminists, is open for debate.[6] Less problematic is Herman and Hirschman's observation that anthropologists and Freudians have long assumed that males instituted the incest taboo, while we know that females violate it least.

Herman and Hirschman feel that father-daughter incest is peculiar to patriarchal systems. They suggest that if fathers were not the dominant, authoritarian figures that they are, father-daughter incest would not occur. They conclude that as long as male supremacy is the norm in the family system, father-daughter incest will occur. The females in this system have no recourse, no power, no bargaining lever. While the present authors are sympathetic with their argument, it must be remembered that if one examines power relationships from a resource perspective, one must also consider such mediating influences as comparative resources (for example, the child may expose the victimization or may threaten to do so), and cultural and subcultural norms governing allocation and use/misuse of personal power (see Rodman, 1972).

Frances and Frances (1976) have utilized Freudian works to posit that there is asymmetry in the incest taboo (p. 243). Their argument is that since boys suffer more from castration anxiety and since dominance is related to masculine behavior, males are predisposed to initiate dominant relationships, including adult male/immature female incest. Further, consistent with this same argument, mother-son incest is essentially obviated. However, it should be noted that Frances and Frances actually combine Freudian writings with an incest barrier assumption. They assume that there is a tendency among bonding-motivated mammals to create incest barriers that promote affiliations

---

[6] Actually, this is a very complex issue. In Chapter 2, we presented evidence indicating that the breakdown of patriarchy enhanced children's rights and diminished the perception of children as property. However, even with the decline of patriarchy, child sexual abuse occurs. There appears to be a need to refine this argument vis-á-vis class/culture contexts, since male dominance prevails more in some groups than in others—as research on contemporary incest cases indicates.

with other groups, enhancing survival of the species. They ground their argument in examples from a variety of animals in the wild who have developed patterns of mating that exclude incestuous pairings.

Herman with Hirschman (1981), expanding on their 1977 article, take to task the Frances and Frances asymmetry thesis. They argue that the differential internalization of the incest taboo between males and females is a function of the patriarchal family. The patriarchal family subjugates women, designates child care as women's work, and produces women who seek definition of self and estimations of self-worth from dominant males (p. 58). They contend that nurturing females, though provided ample opportunity to exploit children, do not do so because another product of the patriarchal family is a woman who not only nurtures, but develops concern and sympathy for those weaker than herself.

It should be noted that Frances and Frances (1982) have responded to Herman and Hirschman's criticisms of their incest barrier and asymmetry ideas. According to Frances and Frances, Herman and Hirschman fail to recognize that animals in the wild have been documented as developing such barriers. Further, Frances and Frances contend that Herman and Hirschman err by omitting the role of evolution in human social structures, preferring instead to focus on incestuous victimization in contemporary society as a political and economic issue.

Justice and Justice (1979) have illustrated that incest is sometimes a matter of circumstance or opportunity. Certainly, it stands to reason that families with male-dominant authority structures facilitate such circumstances and opportunities. Moreover, research indicates that extreme male authoritarianism/dominance and female subservience are often found in incest families (Weinberg, 1955; Tormes, 1968; Maisch, 1972; Cormier, Kennedy, and Sancowicz, 1973; Weber, 1977; Justice and Justice, 1979; Julian, Mohr, and Lapp, 1980). Taken by itself, however, the feminist explanation for adult-child incest boils down to one factor (patriarchy), and monocausal theories are notoriously incompatible with the complexity of human social life.

SUMMARY AND CONCLUSION

Though lengthy, this presentation of theories by no means exhausts all writings pertaining to explanations for incest or various aspects of incest. However, it does indicate the range of approaches available in the literature. It also indicates that various theorists concern themselves with different aspects of incest. Undoubtedly, as more data are collected on incest families, more theories may arise or older theories may need to be altered to accommodate research findings. Perhaps this study, with its emphasis upon the social context and demographic characteristics of incest families, may assist others to develop theories of incest that are more comprehensive in the variables they incorporate.

In addition, we would argue that as more data become available, researchers should begin to answer two questions. First, is there really an incest taboo or aversion? Certainly there is a normative proscription against incest. Yet, in light of the frequency with which this norm is violated, the fact that such violations are ordinarily protracted (Weinberg, 1955; Maisch, 1972; Tormes, 1968; Justice and Justice, 1979; Julian, Mohr, and Lapp, 1980), and the fact that violations appear to have been even more common in the preindustrial past (Rush, 1980; Gordon and O'Keefe, 1984), isn't it time to question the assumption that this normative proscription is accompanied by fears of terrible supernatural reprisals (Webster's first definition of "taboo," in *New Collegiate Dictionary*, 1979), or by an aversion that revolts and nauseates at the very contemplation of one's participation in the behavior (as is the case, for example, when a Westerner imagines himself eating human flesh)?

Second, would dropping the questionable assumption that there is an incest taboo or aversion contribute to the development of more effective theoretical principles by which to understand, predict, and prevent incestuous behavior? It may be that a gestalt change is needed in our orientation to this problem. So long as we think of incest as a taboo or an aversion, we tend to ask, "Why would any parent have a sexual desire for his own child?" "What would cause such an unnatural urge?" If, however, there is no such taboo or aversion, then the appropriate question may be, "What prevents most fathers from acting on the occasional sexual attraction or interest they may feel toward their daughters?" That is, what are the effective barriers against incest and how can we strengthen them, add to them, and insure that they are in place throughout all segments of our society?

4

Previous Research and Research Issues[1]

This review of research is subdivided into a variety of topics so as to address the most commonly asked questions regarding incest.[1] It is designed to answer such questions as: who perpetrates or colludes, what are the characteristics of victims and families, and what are the consequences or effects for the victim? Drawing upon research conducted in the fields of sociology, psychology, social work, and journalism, this chapter emphasizes findings that have been replicated in several independent studies. Criticisms and limitations of the available research are noted where appropriate. Research in the general area of child abuse is included where applicable.

LEGAL AND SOCIAL AMBIGUITIES IN THE DEFINITION OF INCEST

Even though every state now has guidelines regarding incest as sexual abuse, and though most people in the United States view incest as victimization when it occurs between a parent and child, there remains a tremendous "gray area" in relation to a social and a legal definition of incest. While Jean Renvoize (1978) is correct in stating

[1] This chapter is an update and revision of "Adult-Child Incest: A Review of Research and Treatment" by Brenda J. Vander Mey and Ronald L. Neff. 1982. *Adolescence* 17 (Winter): 717-35. Reprinted with permission from the publisher.

that the laws (especially the legal sanctions) surrounding incest reflect public opinion about incest violations, Lester (1972), Heider (1969), and Herman (1981) note that states differ markedly in their legal definitions of incest. Most states originally had statutes covering incestuous marriage only. These laws varied by state in terms of permitted and forbidden marriage partners based on kin and blood ties. More recently, states have begun to define adult-child incest as a type of child abuse and a punishable offense, but they still differ as to what constitutes incest and the differentiation between incest, sexual victimization of children, and rape (most states say only completed intercourse is rape). Finally, despite a modest but convergent trend in the direction of more severe penalties and more frequent prosecution, there is still little standardization in sanctions across the states.

Mississippi's statutes and its arrest and sentencing practices exemplify most states' ambiguities regarding adult-child incest. Mississippi has legal codes for adult incest, defined in terms of intercourse and/or marriage when the adults are legally blood related (Mississippi 1972 Annotated Code, 97-29-20; 93-1-1; 93-7-1, c., 1973). These codes delineate reasons for annulment of marriage or prohibition of intercourse and marriage between legally related adults. Further, Mississippi law differentiates between incest, which is defined as intercourse between legally related persons (child and adult), and other behaviors incestuous in nature between and among legally related persons (child and adult). These other behaviors (for example, fondling, indecent exposure, talking "dirty" to a child) all come under the rubric of child sexual abuse. Incest, intercourse between an adult and a child legally related, is codified as a special and more serious form of child sexual abuse (McCormick, 1981a; see also Mississippi Youth Court Act, 43-21-105 of the Supplement to the Mississippi 1972 Annotated Code, Volume II, 1980, and all cross-references therein). Incest, in Mississippi, can also be legally defined as rape, and when so defined carries a heavier penalty than incest or child sexual abuse. In Mississippi, a rape conviction can carry a life sentence. If the victim should die during or as a result of a rape, the perpetrator can be charged with capital murder and, if found guilty, may be subject to the death sentence (McCormick, 1981b). When incest is perpetrated against a teenage daughter, the offending father is likely to get a fine and a light jail sentence if any sentence at all. However, if the child is relatively young (prepubertal or infant), the felony charge of rape is usually applied (McCormick, 1981b). The rationale behind this is that the older child is perhaps less damaged and less violated by the incest than is the younger child (McCormick, 1981b).

David Finkelhor (1979a) studied occurrences of childhood incest and sexual abuse as per college students' reports. Following the reports, Finkelhor personally interviewed many alleged victims. When speaking to incest and to other types of sexual abuse of children, Finkelhor treats the categories separately. However, he notes that much of the incest which occurs is with young children. He also points out that incest does not always involve intercourse, since the age and size of the child sometimes prohibits actual sexual intercourse (penetration). Finkelhor makes it clear that most sexual victimization of children is incestuous in nature, that is, it is usually more of a "family affair" than something initiated by a stranger. From this and other evidence, he concludes that especially for females (over 90 percent of his study's victims were females) the family, including steprelations, is a "sexually dangerous arena" (Finkelhor, 1979a, pp. 83-88).

In a 1980 grant-announcement bulletin, the National Center on Child Abuse and Neglect presented its definition of child sexual abuse (U.S. Department of Health, Education, and Welfare (HEW), 1980, p. vii). The definition of child sexual abuse given by the center included "contacts or interactions between a child and an adult in which the child is used for sexual stimulation of the perpetrator or another person." Sexual abuse may also, according to the center, "be committed by a person under the age of 18, when that person is significantly older than the victim. . . or is in a position of power or control over the child." The center included as perpetrators in intrafamily abuse anyone who victimizes a child and is a parental figure or a "significant other" in the child's intrafamily life. This points to one of the most important aspects of incest involving children: the perpetrator is a parent or some other significant other in the child's intrafamily life and stands in a position of power over the child.

Thus, we can see that there are no clearcut or standard definitions of adult-child incest and child sexual abuse. Just as public opinions vary as to what constitutes incest, so do state statutes. In addition, legal adjudication and sentencing of perpetrators differ by age of victim and seriousness (intercourse versus no intercourse) of the offenses (see especially Herman, 1981). At the same time, however, it remains the case that socially and legally, adult sexual contact with children is seen as deviant and as something that is punishable throughout the United States.

Finally, it should be noted that while states vary on legal definitions of incest, when it results in the victimization of a child, *most researchers include as incest all forms of sexual contact, sexual ex-*

ploitation (*through pornography and so forth*), *and sexual overtures initiated by any adult who is related to the child by family ties or through surrogate family ties* (*the adult shares a primary group relationship with the child*). Further, researchers generally agree that all forms of erotic action or behavior (verbal and nonverbal, physical, visual, and so on) between and among family members other than marital partners is incest, and that incest on the part of the perpetrator is sexual deviance (Gagnon and Simon, 1967; Tormes, 1968; Meiselman, 1978; Justice and Justice, 1979; and Renvoize, 1978).

ESTIMATES OF ACTUAL OCCURRENCES OF INCEST

Ellen Weber's article, "Incest: Sexual Abuse Begins at Home" (1977), is based upon findings from a survey of sexual molestations of children in 1967. The survey was conducted in New York City by the American Humane Association. From the survey, Weber reported that only 25 percent of all sexual assaults of females under the age of 18 are perpetrated by strangers, and that in 35 percent of the cases the incident(s) occurred in the victim's home.

Finkelhor is no doubt correct when he states that "there are no precise and reliable figures on the incidence of child sexual abuse in the United States" (1984a, p. 18). Finkelhor notes that while the American Humane Association has seen a startling increase in the number of sexual-abuse cases reported to authorities nationwide (a tenfold increase from 1976 to 1982), numerous unreported cases remain. Relying upon findings from one National Incidence study, Finkelhor extrapolates that in 1979 there were an estimated 44,700 sexual-abuse cases *known* to authorities (p. 19). In addition, it can be estimated that anywhere from 9 to 54 percent of all adult U.S. women and from 3 to 9 percent of all adult U.S. men were sexually abused as children (Finkelhor, 1984a, p. 20).

Sarafino (1979) attempts to estimate the actual number of cases of sexual abuse against children in the United States. For a one-year period, the total reported sexual offenses against children in Brooklyn, N.Y., Connecticut, Minneapolis, and Washington, D.C. was 2,324. Sarafino uses these data to calculate sexual offenses per 100,000 children, using 1970 census data. In 1970, the combined rate per 100,000 children was 122.5. The national population of children was approximately 61,000,000. Applying the combined rate to the number of children in the United States, Sarafino estimates that there are 74,725 reported cases of sexual victimization of children in the United States every year. Assuming that the unreported rate is three to four times that of the reported rate, Sarafino multiplies 74,725 by 3.5 to yield an estimate of 261,500 unreported cases. Adding this figure to the figure of 74,725 reported cases, he arrives at an estimate of 336,200 sexual offenses against children per year (Sarafino, 1979, pp. 129-30).

IMPEDIMENTS TO REPORTING OF INCEST

Many females hesitate to report incest incidents[2] due to shame, embarrassment, or fear of repercussions (Weber, 1977; Sarafino, 1979; Renvoize, 1978). Following his study of incest cases (N=3) that came to the attention of court authorities after the victims became pregnant by their fathers, Sholevar (1975) suggested that incest may be underreported due to the lack of victim pregnancy. That is, Sholevar suggests that pregnancy prompts reporting and that lack of pregnancy may prohibit reporting (in other words, no pregnancy—no proof for provocation). Of course, it should go without saying that collusive mothers or participant mothers also would avoid or prohibit reporting the incest (Justice and Justice, 1979; Tormes, 1968; and later portions of this chapter).

Cantwell (1981) has found that many victims do not report incest abuse for many years not only because their home is the only place where their needs for survival (food, clothing, and shelter) are being met, but also because incestuous fathers credibly threaten the incest victim. Cantwell found that the most common threat was that of physical punishment. In addition, some victims have been told by their fathers that they (the victims) would go to jail for such behavior if it were to be known. The fathers apparently and easily convinced the children that they were as culpable as the fathers themselves. Some fathers convinced the girls that the relationship was good and good for them (the girls). Other victims were convinced by their fathers that this relationship would keep the family together or that, by participating, the girls were protecting younger sisters from father-daughter relationships (Cantwell, 1981, p. 78). The most frightening and awesome threat revealed through Cantwell's research was "If you tell, I'll kill your mother" (Cantwell, 1981, p. 78).

The absence of a uniform code or legal definition for incest further impedes the collection of accurate statistics on its occurrence

---

[2] Incest is usually not a "one-time thing." The father usually starts with sexual stimulation, fondling, and sexual talk and finally builds up to intercourse over a period of months or years. Intercourse usually occurs over a period of years.

(Keefe, 1979). Fontana (1984, p. 14) states that the lack of clarity regarding what constitutes sexual abuse makes many mandated sources unsure of what would be a "reasonable cause" to contact authorities. This is sometimes confounded by an historical tendency to disbelieve children on the assumption that the child may be fantasizing. Fortunately, this tendency is dissipating (Faller, 1984).

In counseling and/or interviewing alleged and substantiated incest victims, many researchers have noted that collusive or participant mothers are not the only mothers whose actions or attitudes keep the incest from being reported. Some mothers abort reporting attempts due to fear of the perpetrator or loss of income, jealousy of the child, disbelief of the child, and/or loyalty to the perpetrator (Renvoize, 1978; Justice and Justice, 1979; Browning and Boatman, 1977; Weinberg, 1955). In earlier years, many times counselors or caseworkers would dismiss the child's report of incest as mere verbalization of Oedipal or Electra fantasies (Rosenfeld, 1979). Thus, reporting may be inhibited by the emotions of the victims, the emotions or wishes of the mother, mandated reporting sources who are unsure of what is sufficient cause to contact authorities, or, especially in prior decades, by Freudian assumptions.

AGE OF INCEST VICTIMS

From the 1967 New York City survey described earlier, Weber (1977) says that the average age of incest victims is 11 years (she does not define "average"). Lucy Berliner cites the Sexual Assault Center of Harborview Medical Center in Seattle as claiming that 81 percent of incest victims are 12 years of age or younger at the onset of incest (Berliner, 1977). (Unfortunately, Berliner does not describe the data base for this figure.)[3]

Burgess, Holmstrom, and McCausland studied 44 cases of attempted and completed incest which were reported after victims visited Boston City Hospital's Pediatric Walk-In Clinic. The study took place over a period of four years. The authors found that 27.7 percent of the victims were age 1-5; 25.0 percent were age 6-9; 31.8 percent were age 10-13, and 15.9 percent were age 14-16 (Burgess, Holmstrom, and McCausland, 1977, p. 237). Further, 95.4 percent of the victims were females.

---

[3] Berliner's statement is significant in that she reports the ages at onset, acknowledging the protracted nature of incest. Most research only reflects the victim's age at the time the incest was reported, without addressing the duration of the incest (see Julian, Mohr, and Lapp, 1980, p. 22).

In their analysis of 291 reported cases of sexual offenses against children in Minnesota in 1970, Jaffe, Dynneson, and ten Bensel (1975) report the mean age of the child victim to be 10.7 years. It must be noted that in Minnesota an individual is legally a child if he/she is under 16 years of age (Jaffe, Dynneson, and ten Bensel, 1975, p. 689). Thus, the minor status prohibited inclusion of children ages 16-18 and artificially lowered the mean age to some degree. The Jaffe, Dynnesson, and ten Bensel study is also helpful in that a breakdown of the forms of the sexual abuse was provided, including rape (6 percent), intercourse (3 percent), sodomy (3 percent), and indecent liberties (39 percent) (p. 690). Unfortunately, the authors were not able to secure information regarding the relationship of perpetrators to victims. Thus, there is no indication as to what proportion of the cases were incestuous. The study does provide information on a more alarming dimension, however; 2 percent of the sexual abuse cases involved the death of the victim.

Thus, the available literature leads us to conclude that incest typically begins at an early age (prepubertal) and is protracted in nature. That the victims' age at the time of report is most often the early teen years may reflect the fact that it is not until the late preteen and early teen years that children begin to rely upon peers for definitions of "right" and "wrong." At this time, a victim may have her suspicions confirmed that incest is wrong and may use this information as well as her advancing cognitive and emotional age as resources in reporting the incest (Cormier, Kennedy, and Sancowicz, 1973). This interpretation converges with the fact that it is typically the victim who must initiate the report. That is, rather than a mother, teacher, medical professional, or other third party, the victim herself is the most frequent source of the initial report (Vander May and Neff, 1984).

SEX OF INCEST VICTIM

While male victimization certainly occurs, the preponderance of reported incest victims are females. In the study of patients visiting a pediatric walk-in clinic described earlier, Burgess et al. (1978) report that 95.45 percent of the perpetration was against female children. Using records of cases reported to three different agencies in Boston from 1880-1960 (data were collected for each census year, plus four noncensus, war/stress years), Gordon and O'Keefe (1984, p. 28) found that 10 percent of their randomly chosen cases (N=502) involved incest. In these cases, 93 out of 97 (95.88 percent) of the child partners were female. Other studies suggest that the figure of 95 percent may be exceptionally high, but the predominance of female victims is recognized throughout the literature (Weinberg, 1955; Maisch, 1972; Herman and Hirschman, 1977; Rush, 1980; Finkelhor, 1984), with females consistently comprising over 80 percent of the published samples. In addition, of course, all of these studies indicate that males predominate as perpetrators.

Another perspective on the pervasiveness of male-to-female sexual victimization is provided by Dubanoski and McIntosh (1984). Analyzing child-abuse reports in Hawaii that came to the attention of authorities from January 1978 to February 1981, these authors noted that, on the one hand, when fathers and mothers abused their sons, the abuse was most often physical. On the other hand, when fathers abused their daughters, 90 percent of the time the abuse was sexual in nature (Dubanoski and McIntosh, 1984, p. 57).

FATHERS VERSUS STEPFATHERS AS INCEST PERPETRATORS

If one were to analyze the social norms and psychological bonds of the father and stepfather roles, one would expect that stepfathers would be more likely to be incest perpetrators. There is more social distance and no real blood ties involved in the stepfather relationship. Ignoring percentages for a moment, it should be emphasized, first of all, that the biological father is the most frequent perpetrator (Machotka, Pittman, and Flomenshaft, 1967; Specktor, 1979; Finkelhor, 1979a; Meiselman, 1978; Julian, Mohr, and Lapp, 1980; Renvoize, 1978). However, Sagarin (1977) argues that if more cases were reported, stepfather-daughter incest would appear proportionately more often. Sagarin reasons that since there are fewer households with stepfathers, and since Maisch's data (1972) showed almost the same number of stepfather-daughter as father-daughter incest cases, it follows that stepfather-daughter cases occur at proportionately higher rates.

Russell (1984) and Giles-Sims and Finkelhor (1984) represent the most recent attempts to deal directly with the question of biological father versus stepfather incest-perpetrator prevalence. Russell analyzed interviews with a random sample of 930 adult women residing in the San Francisco area in 1978. Her analysis revealed that one out of every six women who had had a stepfather as a primary parent was sexually abused by him during her childhood. In contrast, approximately one out of every forty women who had had a biological father as a primary parent was the target of child sexual abuse perpetrated by him (Russell, 1984, p. 21). In addition, Russell's analysis indicated that in terms of seriousness (from least serious to very serious),[4] 47 percent of the stepfather-perpetrated incest was *very serious* while 26 percent of the father-perpetrated incestuous abuse fell into the same category (p. 19).

Utilizing data from the 1981 National Incidence (NI) study, Giles-Sims and Finkelhor (1984) found that of the sexual abuse cases, 30 percent were perpetrated by stepfathers and 28 percent by fathers (p. 408). At the same time, however, Giles-Sims and Finkelhor do note that if one takes into consideration that stepfamilies are disproportionately located in the lower classes and that the lower classes are overrepresented in reports to authorities, then the NI study may not demonstrate a higher percentage of stepfathers after all. Be that as it may, the Russell and Giles-Sims and Finkelhor research can be taken to indicate that stepchildren are located in situations at higher risk for sexual abuse than children who live with their biological fathers.

INCEST AS A CLASS AND CULTURAL PHENOMENON

There has been a tendency to assume that incest is indigenous to society's lower classes (Riemer, 1940; Kaufman, Peck, and Tagiuri, 1954; Scott, 1977). However, in working with female psychiatric patients who reported childhood incest (N=6) as adults, Rosenfeld (1979) found no evidence that incest is correlated to social class. Rosenfeld gives no criteria for determining social class, and his conclusion, as he indicates, is tentative at best given the convenient and very small sample. Rosenfeld's methodology is further compromised by the probable higher-class bias of psychiatric patients, as well as by the fact that the measurement of the incest depended solely on victim self-reports.

Gagnon interviewed 333 females who reported prepubertal sexual incidents, predominately incestuous in nature. Over 70 percent of these females had some college education at the time of the interviews. Acknowledging the college-educated bias, Gagnon compares his findings with those of other studies. He concludes that sexual offenses

---

[4] From Russell's study (1984, p. 19), *least serious* sexual abuse covered nonforceful, intentional (clothed) kissing and touching; *serious* sexual abuse ranged from forced digital penetration to nonforceful unclothed breast contact and simulated intercourse; and *very serious* sexual abuse ranged from forced penile-vaginal intercourse to nonforceful oral and anal intercourse.

against middle-class females are typically less severe than those committed against lower-class females. Gagnon also notes that there is a proportionately higher rate of reported offenses by lower-class men than by middle-class men (Gagnon, 1965, pp. 190-91). Like Rosenfeld, however, he does not define what he means by "lower" or "middle" class.

In their descriptive study of 665 substantiated reported cases of father-daughter incest (1976-78) in 34 states, Valerie Julian and co-authors found that while the median income in the United States during the study's duration was $18,723, the median income for incest families was between $9,000 and $10,999 (Julian, Mohr, and Lapp, 1980, p. 22). Further, while 65 percent of the U.S. adult male population had a high school diploma, only 41.5 percent of the incest perpetrators had graduated from high school (p. 24). Although the authors caution that lower socioeconomic status may not cause incest, they do feel that social class may be correlated with incest occurrences.

As Justice and Justice (1979) note, there is potential for incest in any family. Indeed, Finkelhor's (1979a) survey of college students found that 20 percent of female victims came from homes with incomes of $20,000 or more. On the other hand, given that a few of Finkelhor's respondents claimed to have been seriously victimized (involved in incestuous intercourse), his data shed little light on the correlation of social class to seriousness of the offense.

While in the past researchers have emphasized that the disproportionate representation of poor families in officially reported samples may be sheerly the product of their greater involvement with and scrutiny by public agencies, it is time to rethink this line of reasoning. First of all, surveys of general populations (Finkelhor, 1979a; Kercher and McShane, 1984) also show a disproportionate frequency of incest in the lower classes. Moreover, as Pelton (1978) notes, research strongly indicates a link between poverty and other types of child abuse, in part due to the increased family stress created by the exigencies of everyday life in poverty. Especially with regard to incest as child abuse, one must seriously consider the greater prevalence of male-dominated families and the greater acceptance of coercion in the "subculture of violence" typically associated with family life in the lower classes (Pelton, 1978; Eisenberg, 1981).

Eisenberg (1981, p. 303) argues that if we are "to prevent—or at least to diminish—child abuse and neglect, our first task is to identify (a) the sociocultural factors which contribute to their prevalence and (b) the populations at special risk." Essentially arguing for employment of an ecological approach to child abuse, Eisenberg acknowledges the direct contribution of poverty to child abuse.[5] Moreover, he is acutely aware of other correlates of lower-class membership (cultural dimensions) that play a part in child abuse. Male dominance, wife abuse, general family violence, relative family isolation, and lack of mother-child bonding are identified by Eisenberg as prominent factors conducive to child abuse in the lower classes. When one places Eisenberg's discussion alongside evidence on the intergenerational dimensions of incest victimization (Goodwin, McCarty, and DiVasto, 1981), one becomes cognizant of the need to view incest, like other forms of child abuse, within the context of family culture as well as family socioeconomic status. Thus, while child abuse (including incest) may be a potential in any family, it is clear that children in the lower classes are more at risk for virtually all types of abuse. Further, lower-class children are more at risk for serious (in other words, more physically damaging or psychologically devastating) victimization (Nixon et al., 1981).

The above statement can quite easily and legitimately be criticized as indicative of our values and our middle-class biases. We justify our stance on the grounds that the literature clearly indicates that lower-class children are consistently overrepresented as victims of child abuse, and, further, as victims of serious abuse. At the same time, we acknowledge the complexity of child abuse taken in cultural context. Korbin (1980) cautions that the definition of child abuse must be examined in cultural context at three levels. These three levels are: acceptable childrearing practices of a group; idiosyncratic departures from subculturally acceptable standards; and societal-level conceptions of abuse and neglect of children (p. 3). That childrearing practices vary between cultures is readily accepted. As Kagan (1983) emphasizes, many different approaches to childrearing are viable, and a child's developmental needs vary with the milieu to which the child must adapt. Korbin feels that it is at this second level that an adequate and more absolute (nonethnocentric) definition of child abuse emerges. At this level, child abuse is defined in terms of "departure from culturally and socially acceptable standards that results in harm to a child or compromises his or her physical, emotional, cognitive, social or cultural development" (Korbin, 1980, p. 4). Given that incest poses potential problems for victims in terms of at least emotional, social,

---

[5] The reader is referred back to the discussion of ecological approaches in Chapter 3 for elaboration.

and cultural development, and, further, that incest may become an intergenerational aspect of certain families, and still further, that this serious type of child abuse has been documented as being more prevalent in the lower classes, it would be irresponsible to sweep these findings under the rug. A generalized indictment of lower-class lifestyles is certainly not justified by these findings. Rather, a sensitivity to the greater problems faced by the lower classes and the lower-class child's heightened risk of harmful mistreatment is sorely needed.

CHARACTERISTICS OF INCEST PERPETRATORS

Perpetrators range on a continuum from very little education, little or no income, and inadequate social adjustment to high school or college education, median income or above, seemingly adequate social adjustment and participation, and apparently stable marriages and home lives. Kaufman, Peck, and Tagiuri (1954) characterized father perpetrators as individuals from poverty-stricken backgrounds and as alcohol abusers with little education who had been inadequately housed and received little warmth or understanding from their parents (p. 268). The fathers had unstable employment records and were depicted as generally irresponsible. Cavallin (1966) described incestuous fathers as paranoiac, with anxiety emanating from a fear of being homosexual. Raphling, Carpenter, and Davis (1967) portrayed incest fathers as frustrated men sexually rejected by unloving and hostile wives. Lukianowicz (1972) noted habitual unemployment as characteristic of incest perpetrators, but contended that none of the perpetrators were psychotic or neurotic. Riemer (1940), Maisch (1972), and Weinberg (1955) all reported little education, broken homes as children, and domineering, tyrannical personalities as features common to incest fathers. Cormier, Kennedy, and Sancowicz (1973, p. 101) found that, typically, while the incest father is "fully exploiting his position as the authoritarian head of the home, he also acts as the caricature of an adolescent." They noted that the father may try to woo the daughter with promises. He also may use threats or blackmail. If all else fails, he may resort to violence, forcing the desired results.

Justice and Justice (1979) and Meiselman (1978) describe samples in which the incest perpetrators did not follow one "type." Some indeed did appear to act like adolescents. Some had low self-esteem. Others, however, had elevated self-esteem. Panton (1979) compared the score results from the Minnesota Multiphasic Personality Inventory (MMPI) given to 35 males convicted of incest and 28 males convicted of nonincestuous sexual molestation of children. Neither group appeared overly predisposed to use violence to force their victims. Both groups had mean scores indicating that they were self-alienated, despondent, rigid, inhibited, insecure, and fearful of inadequate functioning in heterosexual relationships. Incest perpetrators were more socially introverted and the nonincestuous child molesters were more psychosexually immature (Panton, 1979, p. 335).

Flanzer and Sturkie (1983) did a study of 76 families who abused their adolescent children, comparing these families with comparable nonabusive families. The focus of the study was to investigate the role of alcohol use/abuse in connection with the abuse of adolescent children.[6] One finding was that abusing families were poorer and had myriad problems besides alcohol use or adolescent abuse. For example, abusing fathers tended to have low self-esteem. It was not unusual for all members of the family to engage in acts of aggression against one another. Rivalries were fairly common. Marital discord was frequently noted. Though this study concentrated on physical abuse of adolescents, 10 adolescents were found to be victims of sexual abuse. The researchers found no relationship between parental drinking and sexual abuse (Flanzer and Sturkie, 1983, p. 55). Recognizing that their finding runs counter to popular conception, the authors remind their readers that most incest offenders for whom alcohol abuse has been seen as characteristic were institutionalized and adjudicated. The fathers in the authors' study were members of the *general* population. On the other hand, 10 is a very small sample and by no means definitive. Further attention to the alcohol issue is needed. We will return to this issue in Chapters 6 and 7.

INCEST PERPETRATORS BY CATEGORY OF INCEST TYPE

Summit and Kryso (1978, p. 239) find that the two common and crucial characteristics of fathers who go from "loving sensuality to abusive sexuality" are poor impulse control and the confusion of roles. Perhaps some of the uncertainty regarding incest perpetrator characteristics is related to the fact that not only does incest vary by severity,

---

[6] This was part of the Arkansas Alcohol/Child Abuse Demonstration Project. Other questions besides the relationship between alcohol use and adolescent abuse were addressed, with a general emphasis on treatment of families and training of professional staff (p. 11). A copy of this report can be obtained by writing to Dr. D. K. Sturkie, Department of Sociology, Martin Hall, Clemson University, Clemson, SC 29631.

it also varies by type. Much of the variation is related to the degree of perpetrator and family pathology and social isolation. Drawing upon their clinical experience, Summit and Kryso present a "clinical spectrum" of incest, ranging from incidental sexual contact to perverse incest. The categories within the range depicted by Summit and Kryso will be reviewed below so as to further acknowledge the complexity of incestuous abuse of children vis-à-vis perpetrator characteristics.

The ten categories in the Summit-Kryso clinical spectrum are, in order: incidental sexual contact; ideological sexual contact; psychotic intrusion; rustic environment; true endogamous incest; misogynous incest; imperious incest; pedophilic incest; child rape; and perverse incest. Since it is not our intention to rewrite Summit and Kryso's work, we will provide only a synopsis. Our emphasis is placed on illuminating their articulation of degrees of seriousness, degrees of pathology of the perpetrator, and differences in the contexts and motivations for the incest.

Incidental sexual contact is comprised of parents' attempts to divert their own sexual curiosity or impulses toward their children (p. 240). Parents in this category attempt to control themselves by doing such things as bathing children of the opposite sex, wrestling with their children, withdrawing from an older child, erotically intruding upon the child by inappropriate kissing or touching of the child, or engaging in voyeurism.

Ideological sexual contact involves parental encouragement of parent-child sexual contact, with the underlying rationalization that the experiences are constructive elements of child development (p. 241). The dilemma here is that while explicit behavior is being promoted by the parent, it is done without intending to harm the child (p. 241). Summit and Kryso note that some groups (for example, the Rene Guyon Society) have advocated sexualization of children by parents so as to ameliorate the consequences of repression and guilt regarding sex.

The category of psychotic intrusion is felt to be rare in prevalence. Noting that most sexual abusers are not psychotic, Summit and Kryso feel that children rarely fall prey to adults who suffer from psychotic levels of confusion in which children are the object of the confusion (p. 242).

The rustic environment category deals with the "local yokel" stereotype of incest as an element confined to rural, backreach areas. While this backwoods acceptance of incest is mainly a joke theme, Summit and Kryso have on rare occasions encountered families who perceive incest as normal. These families usually come from isolated areas and appear naive or ignorant of sanctions against incest (p. 242). We would point out, however, that Meiselman (1978) indicates that no groups actually accept incest as "normal"; rather, in some isolated areas, sanctions against incest are not as strongly endorsed as in populated areas.

True endogamous incest appears typically among nonimpulsive people who are otherwise socially well adjusted (p. 242). Fathers tend to initiate an erotic relationship with the daughter, disrupting normative role interaction and enactment. In this situation, there is triangulation in the father-daughter-wife relations. Wives tend to be emotionally and sexually distant with their husbands and disenchanted with their marriages (p. 243). Though the father does not usually premeditate incest, there is a gradual buildup of flirtation with the daughter, with incest resulting from a sexualization of the relationship. The father typically reincarnates his youth and his bride-to-be through his relationship with the daughter. Typically, the daughter has assumed the wife/mother domestic role prior to the incest. There evolves a situation in which the daughter uses her power over the father to transcend parental limits on her behavior. The father may retaliate by restricting her freedom or by initiating incest with his younger daughters (p. 245).

It is at this level of incest that pathological disruptions of family life and lasting negative effects of incest begin to escalate. When the daughter seeks the mother's intervention, the mother may blame the daughter or deny the credibility of the daughter's story. Even if she believes the daughter, she may not intervene for fear of losing the father's income (p. 244). Daughters who experience sexualization of their childhood and sexual definitions of self may later enter into relationships characterized by betrayal, loveless sexual bargaining, distrust, rejection, and punishment.

Misogynous incest is characterized by the father's pathological hatred of women. Women are objects to be abused and used—physically and sexually (p. 245). Daughters are seen as possessions to be used as the father sees fit. An end result of misogynous incest may be a tendency on the part of the daughter to marry abusive men. These daughters, as wives, typically take a (learned) helplessness role, failing to protect their own children and placing their children at risk for physical and sexual abuse (p. 245).

In imperious incest, elements of the ideological, rustic environment, and misogynous incest appear (p. 245). Fathers who engage in imperious incest are extremely authoritarian, frequently very self-righteous, and enamored of an emperor role for themselves. The element in common with the rustic environment type of incest is that these families tend to be socially (though not necessarily geographically) isolated, frequently at the father's choosing. Imperious incest perpetrators see themselves as religious figureheads and exercise absolute or nearly absolute control over every family member. Weinberg's (1955) classic analysis of incest cases in Illinois portrayed the two defining features (a tyrannically authoritarian father and social isolation of the family) of this type of incest as the majority pattern for incest families. (Weinberg's study is discussed more fully in a later section of this chapter.)

The pedophilic incest perpetrator, for a variety of reasons, prefers sexual contact with very young children (p. 246).[7] Intercourse is rare. While most pedophiles are nonviolent, there are those who rape children. The child rapist is typically very violent, brutal, antisocial, and has poor impulse control (p. 246). Raping children gives him feelings of power and confirmation of his masculinity that contact with adult women cannot (p. 246). His fear of discovery, however, places the child at risk for serious physical abuse (p. 246). Unfortunately, women married to child rapists are typically passive and dependent and often are characterized by learned helplessness. Typically unsympathetic to her child, this mother fails to intervene or to protect the child.

A perverse incest perpetrator pornographically exploits children, forcing them to engage in bizarre sexual activity to fulfill the adult's fantasies (p. 247). The child's plight is perceived as secondary to the needs of the perpetrator.

Although other typologies of incest may be equally valid, Summit and Kryso's analysis is important in understanding the existence of variations in motivational dynamics, degrees of severity, family characteristics, the mother's role, and effects on victims. Figure 4.1 is a diagram of Summit and Kryso's categories of incest, arranged by de-

---

[7] Araji and Finkelhor (1985) provide a thorough review of literature on pedophilia, indicating that pedophiles are not one "type" and that, further, pedophilia is a complex and multifaceted phenomenon. Sturkie's discussion in Chapter 8 elaborates on these and other issues surrounding pedophilia.

Figure 4.1 Ten Categories of Incest: Arranged by Pathology and Seriousness

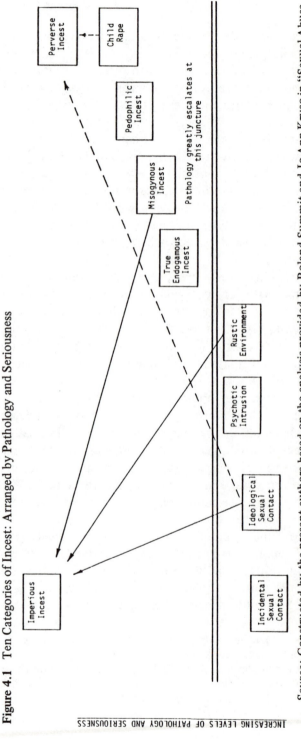

Source: Constructed by the present authors based on the analysis provided by Roland Summit and Jo Ann Kryso in "Sexual Abuse of Children: A Clinical Spectrum," *American Journal of Orthopsychiatry* 48 (1978): 237-51.

gree of pathology, seriousness of perpetrators' intentions, and possible harm to victims.

CHARACTERISTICS OF MOTHERS IN INCEST FAMILIES

Mothers are generally not participants in father-daughter incest; they are usually absent (at the time of the incest occurrences), helpless, oblivious, denying, or (rarely) collusive (Justice and Justice, 1979; Gelinas, 1983). A mother is considered collusive when she passively suspects or knows about the incest and/or relinquishes the role of wife to her daughter, thus inducing incest through role swapping with the daughter (Spencer, 1978; Meiselman, 1978; Finkelhor, 1979). In bizarre cases, the mother may even physically restrain the daughter while the act is occurring (Forward and Buck, 1979). In this case, the mother is not collusive; she is a participant. Mothers are also participants when they engage in heterosexual incest with their sons and/or homosexual incest with their daughters (Maisch, 1972; Weinberg, 1955; Justice and Justice, 1979).

Cormier, Kennedy, and Sancowicz (1973, p. 102) characterize the wives in father-daughter incest families as frigid, unloving, and hostile. Some are seen as passive and submissive, afraid to confront their husbands. Others are seen as good, though unresponsive, wives. Lukianowicz (1972, p. 305) describes the wives as honest, hard-working, long-suffering women who have to contend with unemployed, inefficient, and aggressive husbands. Some of these women are seen as dependent, infantile, and still attached to their mothers. Lukianowicz notes that many wives are cognizant of the incest but do nothing—out of fear of losing the emotional or financial support of their husbands. In terms of personality, the wives in Lukianowicz's study run the continuum of normal, no deviation (12) to frigid (2) to excessively anxious (3) (Lukianowicz, 1972, p. 306).

Kaufman, Peck, and Tagiuri (1954, p. 269) portray the wives in incest families as women who have been deserted by their fathers. Their mothers were stern and demanding, hostile and controlling. Their mothers displaced their hurt feelings onto their daughters. Not surprisingly, these wives often left home at an early age without completing their educations. Having many unmet childhood needs, their emotional problems became compounded when they married infantile and dependent men. Kaufman, Peck, and Tagiuri perceive a cycle of sorts operating between these women's childhoods and their own treatment of their abused daughters. These women appear to be harsh, unemotional, and very dependent, often swapping their wife/mother roles with the role of their daughters.

Sholevar (1975) gives much the same picture in his study of incest, emphasizing the self-centered nature of these cold women who still seek to gratify needs left unmet by a disorganized and truncated childhood. Garrett and Wright (1975) note the martyr role many incest wives play. They contend that incest wives perceive themselves to have been victims in childhood, deprived of happiness, support, and warmth. As wives, they see themselves as being victims once again. They have many responsibilities and receive little if any support from their children or husbands.

Summit and Kryso (1978) have noted that with the more pathological and serious types of incest, mothers may be unsympathetic, retiring, passive, dependent on the perpetrator, or may seek abusive men who betray and reject them. The seeking of betrayal or rejection along with passive dependence and failure to protect her children may in fact stem from her own experiences of sexual and physical abuse as a child. In her study of battered women, Lenore Walker (1984) found that almost 50 percent of the battered women in her study had been sexually molested in childhood (p. 52). Further, Walker also found that some of the battered women knew that their batterer also sexually molested, assaulted, or fondled their children (p. 51). Goodwin, McCarty, and DiVasto (1981, p. 87) found that in their sample of 100 mothers of incest victims, 24 percent of the mothers reported having been incest victims as children. On the other hand, only 3 percent of the 500 mothers in their control sample of nonabused children reported incestuous victimization as children (p. 87). Another 14 percent of the mothers of incest victims reported "some type of sexual stress in childhood" (p. 91). Thus, 38 percent of the mothers of incest victims were victims of incest or other childhood sexual stresses. This compares with a 24 percent reporting rate of stressful sexual childhood experiences among mothers in the control sample (p. 89). The Goodwin, McCarty, and DiVasto study also revealed these important findings:

> There were significantly more incest victims in the control group who reported the victimization to a parent. Mothers of incest victims who themselves had been incest victims had less education than incest victims from the control group, and mothers who had been incest victims and whose children were victims of physical and sexual abuse were them-

selves sexually abused at an earlier age than were women in the control group. (Goodwin, McCarty, and DiVasto, 1981, p. 92)

Goodwin, Cormier, and Owen's (1983) subsequent study of grand-father-granddaughter (N=10) incest cases revealed that not only did the mothers in every case report the incest, but also that six of the mothers had been incestuously victimized by the same perpetrator as were their children (p. 163). This study of trigenerational incest revealed that most of the grandfather perpetrators had victimized several children (several daughters and granddaughters, a niece, a neighbor child, and so on) over a span of 10-30 years. None of the mothers who were incestuously victimized, however, had reported the incest while it was occurring, nor had there been any official intervention on their behalf. Several cases illustrated the protracted nature of incest as earlier described. Chaotic and disorganized family dynamics were also quite frequent among the families of trigenerational incest.

Thus, research indicates that many mothers of incest victims have unmet childhood needs, are dependent upon or fearful of the perpetrator, and are likely to have been victims of physical and sexual abuse as children (see also Gelinas, 1983). It may be that battered women place their children at risk for sexual as well as physical abuse. In fact, previous childhood experiences of mothers may be as important as the father's childhood milieu in predisposing a child to a high risk of incestuous victimization. Although the mechanisms by which incest is intergenerationally transmitted remain unclear, the fact of this transmission is evident. More research is needed to untangle these dynamics.

SPECIAL CHARACTERISTICS OF INCEST VICTIMS

Lauretta Bender and Abram Blau (1937) were the first Americans to report case studies of children who had had sexual relations with adults. They studied 16 children who were admitted to Bellevue Hospital's Children's Ward, Psychiatric Division. The children ranged in age from five to twelve. They were brought to the hospital because of their self-reports of sexual relations with an adult. Five children were males. Bender and Blau reported that a "striking characteristic shown by these children was that they had unusually attractive and charming personalities" (Bender and Blau, 1937, p. 511). Bender and Blau also noted that these children were generally attracted to adults, hyperactive, and physically normal (no defects or handicaps). Some of them were very cooperative or took an active role (were seductive) in the sexual relations reported. The authors felt that the children should not be treated as totally innocent parties since they may have behaved alluringly or seductively, or may even have initiated the sexual relations.

Cantwell (1981, p. 79) succinctly and appropriately counters Bender and Blau's rationale by stating that seductiveness on the part of the sexually abused child is a result of the sexual victimization itself. The child becomes sexualized through the sexual abuse. Further, the child's definition of self is primarily sexual because the sexually abused child has been treated as a sexual object and learns to relate to herself and to others in this way. This, according to Janeway (1981), is one of the "costs" of incest.

Sloane and Karpinski (1942), in a study of five postpubertal females who had experienced incest, concluded that the females were compliant, since the incest occurred over a long period of time. The researchers often referred to their subjects with such terms as "delinquent" or "promiscuous," implying that these personality characteristics were in part responsible for the incest. Sloane and Karpinski, using Freudian analysis, spoke of "incest impulses" and "ego mechanisms" as aspects of some of the females' personalities. They indicated that the females in the incest relationships helped "cause" the incest by their particular personality traits.

Like Bender and Blau and Sloane and Karpinski, Weiss et al. (1955) approached the sexual victimization of children from a psychoanalytic perspective. In a study of 73 females victimized by adults, Weiss and coauthors indicated that 44 (60.27 percent) of the females could be deemed as "participating." Females were described as participating when they did not fight, submitted passively, acted "seductively," or utilized parental conflicts for their own sexual advantages. Interestingly, all other females' cases were classified as "accidental" (28.77 percent) or as "undetermined" (10.96 percent). No incidents were listed as "perpetrated" by adults. The emphasis, instead, was upon the females' personality traits and behaviors which might have precipitated the sexual encounter(s). It should be noted that 49.32 percent of these females experienced sexual relationships that were incestuous.

Few researchers today would look only at personality characteristics of the victims, especially in such an accusatory fashion as the authors cited above. Instead, researchers are also looking at physical and/or mental characteristics of children which make them "high risk"—more vulnerable, more accessible, and less able to defend themselves or to report the incident(s).

Browning and Boatman's (1977, p. 71) study of 14 reported incest cases at the University of Oregon's Health Sciences Center, Child Psychiatry Clinic, indicated that certain children may indeed be "high risk" for abuse. Three of the children (21.45 percent) had physical or mental abnormalities. One was a deaf-mute; one was retarded; and one was disfigured by burns. Four children (28.57 percent) had been conceived out of wedlock. Another child had been abandoned by her mother when she was an infant. All of the children were females. All but one were firstborn children. The remaining child was not firstborn, but her older sister, who was firstborn, reported the victimization of her sister because she too had been victimized by their father.[8]

Tormes (1968, p. 26) also found that in 16 of the 20 cases of incest she studied in New York, the female victim was either the oldest child (50 percent) or the firstborn girl preceded by males (30 percent). None of the youngest females in the incest families studied by Tormes were victimized.

Relying upon data collected from 1970-76 in Ramsey County, Minnesota, Peggy Specktor (1979, p. 9) reports that the oldest girls were nearly always the first victims of incest in their families (note: no N given). Tormes implied that a high-risk female is one who is in a very large family where the parents married young and have been married a relatively long time. This is especially the case if the female is the first child born (Tormes, 1968).

Though it is problematic to conclude that victims' attributes, real or imagined, "cause" incest, it can be valuable to inventory victim characteristics so that the helping professions and concerned citizens may have an understanding of cues that a child is at risk. When combined with behavioral cues (for example, child's grades are dropping; child displays sexual acting-out behaviors; child has an unkempt appearance and uncaring attitude; and child is secretive about her home life), parental cues (for example, the father is authoritarian and overly restrictive of the child's activities), and situational cues (for example, the family is socially isolated), the foregoing ascribed characteristics

---

[8] Successive victimization of daughters is not uncommon. (See Weinberg, 1955; Maisch, 1972; Meiselman, 1978; Renvoize, 1978; Justice and Justice, 1979; and Finkelhor, 1979a.)

should prompt a call to authorities who can investigate the home. We will elaborate on these and other risk factors in Chapters 6 and 7.

CHARACTERISTICS AND DYNAMICS OF INCEST FAMILIES

In his study of 203 cases of incest in Illinois, Weinberg (1955) investigated home conditions and family dynamics to inventory elements possibly conducive to incest. In father-daughter incest, he found that fathers typically were dominant. This father dominance was "not necessarily manifested by the father's earning power but by his intimidation of and emotional sway over the other family members" (Weinberg, 1955, p. 250). Weinberg also found that the majority of father perpetrators were socially distant though sexually familiar with their daughters. He found that a majority of the mothers were indifferent to the daughters' plights. In one of the cases studied, Weinberg noted that the mother and father both openly acknowledged that the father was having intercourse with the daughter. The mother suggested that he use a "protector." The father, perceiving the daughter to be promiscuous, did not feel obligated to do so (p. 116). In another case, the father reigned supreme as a disciplinary and religious figure in his family. He totally isolated his family members from social contacts by threatening (and credibly so) physical punishment and spiritual repercussions for interactions with other people. In this case, the mother was fully aware of the incest and accepted it as part of the father's right (pp. 68-69).

Violent and alcoholic fathers were predominant in the father-daughter cases. Further, Weinberg noted normative and role "disorganization" in many of the father-daughter incest families. Fathers went around the house nude or seminude; slept with their daughters; watched their daughters dress and bathe; were open about parental sexual relations (one father woke his daughter and demanded that she watch the parents engage in intercourse); or did not control impulsive behaviors. Many of the families lacked clear role definitions and expectations for family members. Young daughters frequently did all or most of the housekeeping chores. Mothers often encouraged the father, implicitly or explicitly, to go elsewhere for sex. Many fathers saw themselves as supreme authorities with the right to do as they wished with family members. In the isolated families, daughters often did not resist or defend themselves because the parents had not encouraged or permitted the learning of the greater society's norms and values. In these families, the daughters did not have concrete evidence that the incest was "wrong" (though many intuitively felt it to be). Weinberg concluded that in many father-daughter incest families, normlessness and valuelessness prevail.

Maisch (1972), in his study of incest in the Federal Republic of Germany (N=65), found a variety of home factors that he deemed conducive to or favoring the initiation and establishment of father-daughter incest. Those factors included: father drinking alcohol; wife ill or not at home; father and daughter sharing the same sleeping quarters; overcrowded living conditions; passive behavior on the victim's part; fear of family dissolution on the victim's part; acquiescence to the father as an authority figure; disbelief by the mother; authoritarian, tyrannical fathers; wives who reject or refuse sexual intercourse with the husband; and wife's acceptance of the incest relationship (Maisch, 1972, pp. 174-82).

The mother/wife acquiescing to the incest is more common than one might expect. In Tormes's study of 20 incest cases, 8 mothers saw the incest occur or knew beyond a doubt that incest was occurring, but did nothing to intervene until the daughters became pregnant (Tormes, 1968, pp. 11-13).

Though the potential for incest is there in any family, many researchers caution that families where there is alcoholism on the part of the fathers, authoritarian fathers, and social isolation represent high-risk incest situations (Specktor, 1979; Tormes, 1968; Justice and Justice, 1979; Renvoize, 1978).

If we combine these findings on family dynamics with those reviewed in the preceding sections on the characteristics of the parents in incest homes, several convergent dimensions stand out. The first is pronounced father dominance. Incest homes tend to involve extreme inequality in the relationship between the mother and the father. Typically, incest families are characterized by each members' unquestioned acceptance of the father's prerogative to define other members' roles and to intrude at will in all aspects of any family member's life. Many factors contribute to this unrestrained father dominance. Among them are subcultural norms and beliefs prescribing authority and decision-making competence to males in general and to fathers in particular. Equally important is the lopsided dependence of the mother on the father, due in part to her psychological characteristics (including passivity and a learned helplessness), in part to her objective resource limitations (especially the mother's lack of significant marketable skills for earning potential), in part to a subculture encouraging the housewife versus breadwinner division of labor in gender roles, and in part to a social isolation of the family, which severely limits the mother's access to outside support systems in the form of neighbors, extended family, and community organizations and facilities. A final and very significant contributing factor to the father's excessive dominance in many incest families (though not all—see Chapter 8 for a discussion of mother dominance in incest families) is a subcultural tolerance of violence.

Perhaps equally as important as the father's dominance in homes disposed to incest is the prior incest and/or other sexual abuse of the mother as a child. The mechanism of this intergenerational transmission is unclear. Incest is not, with rare exceptions, transmitted to the daughter by the mother actively encouraging either the daughter or the father toward such involvements. However, the mother's emotional scars may tend to limit and color her own sexual responsiveness such that the father-mother sexual relationship is not satisfying or affectionally bonded over the long term. Further, the mother may unknowingly provide her daughter with an image of sexuality and of men "who want just one thing from a woman," thereby contributing to her daughter's vulnerability to sexual victimization by her father and by other males as well. None of this is clear, however, and more research on the intergenerational dimension of incest is clearly needed.

The father's experiences in his family of orientation are also of preeminent importance. In this instance it does not appear that having suffered or even witnessed sexual abuse in his own youth is typical. Rather, his family background problems are more often a matter of emotional deprivation and harsh physical discipline. The result, we would argue, is not only a predisposition toward aggressive assertion of authority, but also a failure to have experienced precisely the warm and intimate sharing experiences that are necessary to develop some of the normal features of humanness. It is only out of supportive and emotionally rewarding "we" experiences that a child can become an adult capable of truly altruistic and empathic responses (Cooley, 1964). In short, due at least in part to their emotionally deprived backgrounds, these fathers appear unable to care for others—even their own children—enough to override and control the pursuit of their own selfish needs and desires.

Reflecting on these family and parental characteristics and the package they create when combined may take one a great distance toward overcoming the initial sense of disbelief that is felt when confronted with the fact that many fathers, often beset with myriad personal troubles of their own, sexually victimize their daughters.

The works of Summit and Kryso (1978) and Cantwell (1981) present evidence indicating that the incest victim's family tends to victimize her because of her incestuous relationship with her father. Once her involvement is known, other male family members may define her as a temptress, dangerously attractive or alluring (Summit and Kryso, 1978). With knowledge that the girl is no longer a virgin, and in fact has had intercourse with her own father, other male relatives may initiate sexual relations with her. Further, male and female family members and kin may label her as a "slut" or a "whore" (Summit and Kryso, 1978, p. 244; Cantwell, 1981, p. 79). Siblings may "scapegoat" the victim, blaming her for the incest and for other family problems (Gelinas, 1983, p. 325). In essence, family members may blame the victim, reduce her to an object, and fail to intervene for her safety or her mental and social health.

Given the volume of research on perpetrator, mother, victim, and family characteristics which we have surveyed, and the diversity of descriptions given, we have drawn a composite of the most frequently noted characteristics (see Figure 4.2). We have drawn arrows indicating interactions or possible interactions between characteristics of the various actors so as to graphically depict how a child might become an incest victim. Not at this time intended to be a causal model of the incest family as a system in miniature, the figure does sum up characteristics noted in the literature in an explanatory fashion.

SHORT- AND LONG-TERM CONSEQUENCES OF INCEST FOR THE VICTIM

In general, researchers attend more to the long- rather than the short-term effects of incest. Long-term consequences for the victim are those behaviors, attitudes, or opinions that the victim has or displays years after the incident(s) of incest: effects that are due directly or indirectly to the incest. Short-term consequences are those effects that the victim experiences or displays during and/or immediately after the incest and/or its disclosure. The most consistent short-term effects are emotional. The victim feels rejected, used, trapped, confused, humiliated, betrayed, disgraced, and fearful. Other than these emotional difficulties, the victim may suffer somatic symptoms or may suffer in social ways as well. It is not uncommon for the victim to be subjected to the perpetrator's jealousy. He may restrict her social activities (Justice and Justice, 1979). Also, should the victim attempt to halt the incest, the perpetrator may resort to violence, or the threat of violence, to make her continue it (Weber, 1977).

Figure 4.2 General Characteristics of Incest Perpetrators, Victims, Mothers, and Families

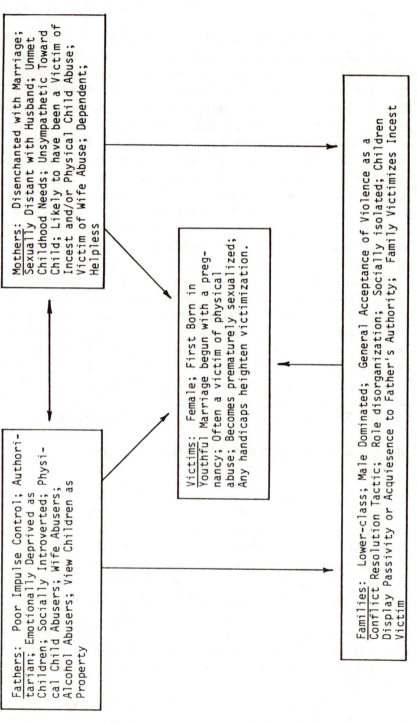

Mothers: Disenchanted with Marriage; Sexually Distant with Husband; Unmet Childhood Needs; Unsympathetic Toward Child; Likely to have been a Victim of Incest and/or Physical Child Abuse; Victim of Wife Abuse; Dependent; Helpless

Fathers: Poor Impulse Control; Authoritarian; Emotionally Deprived as Children; Socially Introverted; Physical Child Abusers; Wife Abusers; Alcohol Abusers; View Children as Property

Victims: Female; First Born in Youthful Marriage begun with a pregnancy; Often a victim of physical abuse; Becomes prematurely sexualized; Any handicaps heighten victimization.

Families: Lower-class; Male Dominated; General Acceptance of Violence as a Conflict Resolution Tactic; Role disorganization; Socially isolated; Children Display Passivity or Acquiesence to Father's Authority; Family Victimizes Incest Victim

Source: Based on a review of incest research literature. Arrows are drawn to indicate individual and family characteristics that probably interact so as to predispose the victim to incest and enhance the entrenchment of ongoing incest victimization.

68

Long-term effects go beyond just the emotions of the victim to various behavioral manifestations of these emotions. Often these behaviors prove to be deviant, antisocial, and/or illegal. Promiscuity, inability to assume a wife/mother role, alcoholism, drug abuse, prostitution, sexual dysfunctioning, delinquency, depression, and suicide have all been found to be correlated with incest (Weber, 1977; K. James, 1977; J. James and Meyerding, 1977; Meiselman, 1978; Justice and Justice, 1979; Specktor, 1979; Silbert and Pines, 1981; Goodwin, 1981; Gelinas, 1983). Many of these behaviors may be attempts to adjust to the memory of the incest or to assuage or deny its emotional scars. Promiscuity, drug abuse, and delinquency have also been identified as coping mechanisms of teenagers during an incestuous relationship.

There are those, however, who contend that the negative effects of incest victimization are often short-lived and minimal—or totally nonexistent. Lukianowicz (1972, pp. 302-3) classified the effects on female incest victims (N=26) into four categories: girls who later became promiscuous; girls who became frigid; girls who became neurotic; and girls who showed no ill effects. There were six girls who were classified as having suffered no effects. One female is quoted as saying that she enjoyed the relationship. This group is perceived by Lukianowicz as confirming Bender and Blau's (1937) contention that children do not necessarily suffer adverse effects from sexual encounters with adults (Lukianowicz, 1972, p. 307).

Koch (1980, p. 647) argues that effects on the child victim are variable, depending upon age of onset, nature, and duration of the incest. Koch states that some children are not affected at all. Lewis and Sarrel (1969) indicate that form of attack and age of victim are important variables in determining the effects of sexual assault on the child victim. Infants may suffer lack of trust, insecurity, and inability to successfully complete certain developmental tasks. Adolescents (Lewis and Sarrell assume that adolescents may provoke the sexual incidents) may become disillusioned. Adolescent males engaged in homosexual activity may feel dirty and unsure of their sexuality. Lewis and Sarrel state that children involved in sex with an adult may suffer somatic symptoms, may suffer anxiety, or may create a "mutually sadistic, ambivalent, as well as seductive relationship between parent and child" (p. 619).

Rosenfeld (1977, p. 799) argues that the effects of experiencing sex with an adult are subtle and varied. He contends that it is difficult to separate the effects of the sexual abuse from the disruption and disorganization of the family. In addition, there may initially be no effect. The victim may not register the impact of the situation until adulthood.

Thus, just as we lack a clear picture regarding the intergenerational dynamics of incest, we have no definite answers as to the effects of incest on child victims. Apparently, we cannot clearly and unequivocally state that incest is traumatic for all victims. However, it appears that for many victims, incest can be and often is permanently scarring.

Finkelhor (1978b, 1980b) has speculated as to the effect of the sexual revolution and society's perceptions of incest's effects. Sensitive to the fact that some people have been advocating adult-child incest as a healthy way to introduce children to their sexuality (in other words, sexualizing the family), he attempts to grapple with sexual liberation as it pertains to children. Striving for sexual equality helped lead many individuals and groups to become concerned about child sexual abuse. Some have argued in favor of the sexualized family (for instance, Nobile, 1978). Others advocate educating children about sexual facts and demystifying sex while at the same time protecting children from sexual exploitation (Oremland and Oremland, 1977; see also the discussion by Summit and Kryso, 1978).

The concerns surrounding the sexualized family are legal as well as social and moral. However, even if some people can engage in positive sexualization of their family members, there will remain those children who are forced into abusive incest. The effects of incest on these children should not be dismissed or obscured by ideological discussions of the benefits of the sexualized family.[9]

Others have emphasized that the effects of incest on family organization, role enactment, and the social training of children cannot be dismissed lightly (Summit and Kryso, 1978; LaBarbera, Martin, and Dozier, 1980; Goodwin, McCarty, and DiVasto, 1981; Gelinas, 1983). We would add that the traumatic emotional effects of incest should not be treated lightly either. The book *Sexual Abuse of Children: Selected Readings* (U.S. Government Printing Office, 1980) is replete with evidence that incest is normally traumatizing, can fill a victim with self-hate, and is often a haunting experience that mentally keeps occurring for the victim long after the actual incidents have ceased.

---

[9]We are not saying that Finkelhor is advocating the sexualized family. He examines it in relation to sexual liberation and the concern over child sexual abuse.

CONCLUSIONS

Drawing from the research reported from a cross section of disciplines and grounded in a variety of evidence ranging from surveys to clinical interviews to onsite investigations of homes, this chapter has reviewed answers the research literature provides to the most frequently asked questions concerning incest. There is much social and legal ambiguity about what constitutes incest. Incest is usally a protracted situation that ordinarily begins in a relatively mild form when the victim is quite young. There appear to be different types of incest, such as pedophilic, misogynous, or imperious. Incest is not one phenomenon, but apparently varies along a continuum of seriousness and perpetrator motivation. Probably least serious is incidental sexual contact, with child rape, perverse incest, and imperious incest appearing to be the most serious types.

Incest typically is not reported until the victim reaches puberty, at which time young people begin to base their definitions of "right" and "wrong" substantially on feedback from their peers. Victims are predominately female and perpetrators are overwhelmingly male. Biological father-daughter incest is the most frequently reported, though stepfather-stepdaughter cases are disproportionately represented in both official reports and surveys.

Incest is not restricted to the lower classes, though there does appear to be an inverse relationship between social class and incest. This may be a real relationship, or it may be a function of class differences in resorting to the authorities concerning family matters. When cultural features of lower-class family life are considered (for example, male dominance, subculture of violence, intergenerational episodes of physical and sexual abuse of children, wife abuse, social isolation, and so on), one must begin to rethink the argument that the over-representation of the lower classes in child-abuse reports is due solely to their greater likelihood of coming to the attention of authorities. In the next few years, as abuse reports from the community at large continue to increase, we may begin to answer this question.

Incest is not rare, nor has it ever been. And, while there is ambiguity regarding many of the characteristics of perpetrators, some attributes have been consistently replicated. Perpetrators tend to be authoritarian males, abusers of alcohol, and persons who define the world outside the home in negative terms. Mothers may be collusive, oblivious, helpless, or denying. Many researchers have suggested that mothers of incest victims typically have unmet childhood needs, are hostile and frigid, and are passive and subservient in relation to their husbands. They are often described as playing a martyr role. Evidence is accumulating which suggests that the mothers of incest victims not infrequently were also victims of incest and physical child abuse. It is believed by some that these mothers are, as a result of such negative childhood experiences, ill equipped to be mothers and wives and frequently tend to marry abusive men who are the type to place their children at risk for physical and sexual abuse.

While earlier research tended to portray victims as seductive provacateers, more recent research indicates that birth order, family configuration factors, personality, physical appearance, and socioeconomic factors may predispose children to being at risk for incestuous victimization.

Though some writers continue to argue that the effects of adult-child incest are typically minimal or nonexistent, the weight of the evidence and the great majority of the authors argue against that comforting opinion. Incest is associated with antisocial, deviant, illegal, and/or self-destructive coping mechanisms in many victims. Finally, though some have viewed sexual liberation as giving rise to the sexualized family, others have expressed concern that advocating and defending such ideals may obfuscate the reality experienced by most incest victims and their family members.

5

A Grounded Theoretical Model

As the preceding chapter testifies, recent research has made great strides in addressing the "what, when, where, and who" of adult-child incest. What remains almost wholly unaddressed is the mind-boggling question of "why." First of all, incest as child abuse is not a simple phenomenon with a clear-cut pattern or dynamic. Because of its many variations, social scientists and practitioners attempting to predict, prevent, or intervene in high-risk or actual incest families find themselves confronted with a dizzying array of correlates and potential causes. Independent of this is a culturally based emotional response. The perpetration of adult-child incest is so offensive and disturbing to our everyday assumptions that there is an immediate tendency to define such behaviors as "beyond me." In a word, it is so shocking that we literally prefer to deny that it can be understood. Certainly, introspective interpretation, or *verstehen*, one of the most frequent and valuable first steps toward a causal analysis in the social sciences (Weber, 1968), is very difficult with this behavior. Finally, research in this area, though currently burgeoning, is so recent that there has been little time to assimilate and attempt to synthesize it—a precondition for building inductively based explanatory models.

Much of the descriptive work has now been done, however; the preceding chapters have provided a degree of the necessary organization and some synthesis of the findings. In this context, *grounded theory* (Glaser and Strauss, 1967), building inductively from specific observations to general statements, becomes possible. There is much debate in the social sciences over the comparative efficiency and power of this relatively inductive versus more deductive approach to theory building (Reynolds, 1971), and we would not argue that the grounded or more inductive approach is always preferable. In the case of a counterintuitive phenomenon such as incest, however, the grounded approach has much to recommend it. With this in mind, we have been working toward a grounded explanatory model of father-daughter incest (Vander Mey, 1981b; revised, 1985). This chapter presents a further elaboration and refinement of this model.

An eclectic approach is best suited for such an undertaking. Our focus is specifically upon father-daughter incest, and our product is an eclectic, resource-based explanation. Drawing from the research literature and incorporating elements from the ecological approach to child abuse, conflict theory, exchange theory, resource theory, feminist interpretations, and Denzin's (1984) phenomenological approach to family violence, this model depicts contributing factors to and mitigating factors against father-daughter incest. The model is diagrammed in Figure 5.1. A discussion of the model follows.

We find at least four levels of actors' milieus which must be appreciated in order to understand incest. These are the society, the neighborhood, the family (including the marital dyad), and the father-daughter dyad. A person has several different spheres of interaction, and no sphere operates without influence from the others. Incest is not simply a product of the structure of the father-daughter dyad, but the latter is partially a product of factors in the remainder of the family unit, in the neighborhood, and in the culture of the society at large. Thus a comprehensive examination of factors that may contribute to father-daughter incest must examine all of these levels.

It is equally important to attempt to answer the question "Why *not* incest?" That is, if all or many of the factors considered to make a family at risk for incest are present, why is it that incest sometimes does not occur? Accordingly, we discuss "mitigating factors"—factors that may deter, prevent, or obviate incest abuse in high-risk situations. In addition to enhancing our grasp of naturally occurring family situations, attention to these mitigating factors may suggest avenues for changing at-risk situations such that incest will be less likely to occur.[1]

---

[1] As indicated, this model is based upon an examination of previous research and theoretical literature. Especially important in relation to the mitigating factors are works by persons advocating an ecological approach to child abuse (Gar-

THE SOCIETAL LEVEL

The term "violence" is applicable not only to acts of physical aggression, but also to acts of sexual aggression. Incest is an act of sexual aggression. We live in a society that has high incidence rates of both physical aggression and sexual aggression (see any recent Uniform Crime Report). Even a cursory examination of popular movies, television programs, novels, and magazines reveals a high tolerance of violence. Acts of physical and sexual aggression help sell these media products by adding excitement to the products. Rush (1980) reviewed movies depicting incest themes and acts of sexual and physical aggression against women and children. She feels that the popularity of these movies indicates not only a tolerance for violence, but also a preference for and enjoyment of such activities. Pornography, especially "chicken porn" (pornography in which children are the focus of attention), flourishes (Pierce, 1984). Frequently, pornographic movies and magazines include heavy doses of scenes of sexual violence with children as victims. Incest themes are common (Pierce, 1984).

The degree to which a society reveres the privacy of the family is another important factor to consider in incest abuse, since it is possible for families to become relatively closed systems. Without outside scrutiny and input, adults may construct reality in whatever manner emerges or as they see fit. This reverence of family privacy accounts for the "nobody's business" response to early abuse intervention efforts (Specktor, 1979). A concern over extreme family privacy has been expressed in child-abuse literature, which indicates social isolation as a predisposing factor in child abuse.

The ascription of an inferior status to women and children is of both theoretical and pragmatic concern due to its impact upon the rights and welfare of women and children in male-dominated societies. As with the other societal level variables, this ascription of inferiority must be measured in degrees. As women have gained more freedom and children's rights have become a public concern, the relative power of men over women and children has diminished. Violence toward women and children by males is no longer accepted carte blanche. However, vestiges of patriarchy remain in our society and carry consequences for women and children in relation to acts of sexual and physical aggression perpetrated against them by men.

---

barino and his various coauthors, as reviewed in Chapter 3; Howze and Kotch, 1984) and Straus's suggestions from his analysis of stress and child abuse (Straus, 1980).

Figure 5.1 An Eclectic, Resource-Based Explanation of Father-Daughter Incest

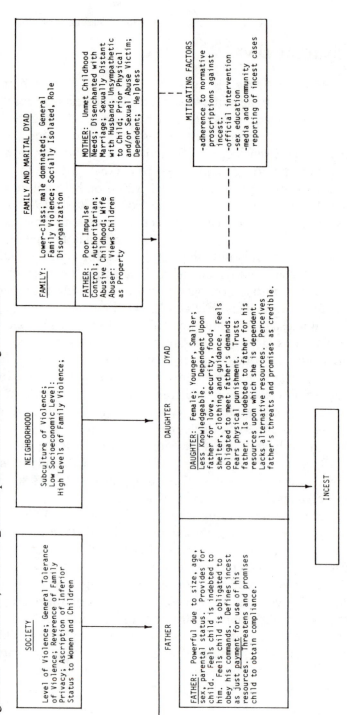

Source: Compiled by the authors.

76

THE NEIGHBORHOOD

The neighborhood serves as the immediate link between the family and the society. We are often evaluated (and evaluate ourselves) in terms of where we live. Our neighborhoods are identified by the community at large in relation to type of housing, quality of housing, socioeconomic level, occupational status of the residents, and reputation of the inhabitants. This reputation of inhabitants may result in the labelling of a neighborhood as "good" if homes are well kept up, inhabitants are industrious, and violent behavior and criminal activity are low or nonexistent. A "bad" neighborhood is usually one in which the housing is of poor quality and poorly maintained, there is much cramping of dwellings and inhabitants, the inhabitants are considered to be of questionable character, and the area itself is perceived to be characterized by violence and criminal activity. Though partly due to self-fulfilling prophecies, neighborhoods perceived as "good" or "bad" do tend to have corresponding effects on the families within them. Good neighborhoods tend to serve as support systems for inhabitants, providing a feeling of positive self-worth; security; and a trust in, acceptance of, and identification with the other residents that facilitates personal and organizational sharing of resources. Conversely, bad neighborhoods are conducive to negative self-esteem, fear of interaction, lack of resident reciprocity, and a tendency toward negativism and fatalism on the part of the residents. As can be seen, for example, in older ethnic communities, even a neighborhood considered bad on economic and status measures such as income level and quality of housing may be experienced as good by residents because there is solidarity, reciprocity, and neighborliness among inhabitants (Garbarino and Sherman, 1980).

In neighborhoods characterized by a subculture of violence, lack of neighborliness (friendliness, reciprocity, and support among inhabitants), and lower socioeconomic levels, the probability of high levels of family problems is heightened. Basically, the reality defined by the neighborhood milieu positively endorses a "fend-for-yourself" mentality among persons in general, including family members. In these neighborhoods, children are at a heightened risk for physical and and sexual abuse. Support for this argument comes from Ditson and Shay's (1984) analysis of child-abuse reports (255 neglect cases; 57 physical-abuse cases; and 33 sexual-abuse cases). Ditson and Shay were able to geographically map occurrences reported. One finding was that 63 percent of the reports involved low-income families receiving Aid for Families with Dependent Children (p. 506). Directing attention to the importance of the ecological or emergent properties of neighborhoods as sociological realities beyond the characteristics of individuals, Ditson and Shay's findings indicated a need to improve the "web of caring" (support systems, involvements, and intervention) (p. 508). Further, one police officer reviewing their findings commented that the child-abuse report mapping results were identical to the city crime map! In short, there are apparent links between a neighborhood's subculture of violence, its lack of neighborliness, and both physical and sexual child abuse.

THE MARITAL DYAD AND THE FAMILY

As indicated in Chapter 4, characteristics and dynamics of the family and marital dyad may predispose children to incest. Authoritarian fathers with poor impulse control who were abused as children, abuse alcohol, view children as property, have a poor sexual and marital relationship with their wives, or are sexually attracted to children place their children at risk for incest abuse when mitigating factors are not present. The child's risk for incest is heightened when mothers married to these types of men are dissatisfied with the marriage; feel sexually distant (uninterested, bored, unaroused, affectionally removed) with their husbands; feel that they have needs not fulfilled in childhood (for example, wasn't loved, was abused, grew up too fast, was robbed of childhood); have been victims of sexual and physical abuse as children; are current victims of wife abuse; feel dependent and helpless; and lack sympathy toward their children. These mothers may feel that they cannot protect their children. They may fear reprisals from the husband. Mothers whose lives have been characterized by truncated childhoods, abusive childhoods, and male domination may place their children at risk for incest because their own despair renders them powerless. In addition, they may be ignorant of support systems or may fail to recognize resources they themselves have or can utilize to improve their marital and family circumstances. Psychologically defeated, they tend to passively accept negative outcomes, including actual or potential violence in their homes.

Families in which there is general family violence, male dominance, social isolation, role disorganization, and a low socioeconomic level (inadequate income, unstable employment, less education) predispose children to incest abuse,[2] especially if the marital dyad is poorly bonded affectionally and sexually. A note of caution must be reiterated at this point. Simply being in the lower ranges of the socioeconomic spectrum does not automatically predispose a child to the risk of incest. The entire family milieu and separate but interacting characteristics of family members must be considered, as must factors at other levels of the model.

THE FATHER-DAUGHTER DYAD

Dynamics of the father-daughter dyad in incest cases are most practically dealt with by examining the power (resource) differential between these two actors in the context of the other levels previously presented. Finkelhor (1984b) identifies the following preconditions as sufficient and necessary for the building of a theoretical model of child sexual abuse.

1. A potential offender needs to have some motivation to abuse a child sexually.
2. A potential offender has to overcome internal inhibitions against acting on that motivation.
3. A potential offender has to overcome external impediments to committing sexual abuse.
4. A potential offender or some other factor has to undermine or overcome a child's possible resistance to the sexual abuse. (Finkelhor, 1984b, p. 53)

Most of these preconditions for a model explaining child sexual abuse have already been considered in our model of incest. For example, living in a society in which pornographic exploitation of children exists, inhabiting a neighborhood that is characterized by high levels of violence, having a marriage in which one's wife is sexually distant, and/or feeling a personal sexual attraction to children certainly provide motivation to sexually abuse and exploit one's children. Because of his lack of effective performance vis-á-vis the competitive occupational world outside the home, the father may be further motivated to incestuously abuse his child so that he may feel powerful. If one

---

[2]Note that we say the child is *predisposed* to incest. Our point is that myriad factors interact to make a situation volatile enough for incest abuse to become a reality. Thus, one factor alone is usually not sufficient to create a situation of risk.

has few sources of power outside one's own family life, and one can rationalize that incest is a just reward for resources used by the child (thereby overcoming inhibitions or blockage), then the power and re-source differential between a father and daughter map out a course conducive to incest. In addition, the abuse of alcohol may make incest seem even more positive (and excusable) to the perpetrator. Certainly, persons with authoritarian personalities who have little impulse con-trol and live in neighborhoods and families such as those earlier de-scribed would find few internal or external controls to impede their abusive behaviors. In families where mothers do not protect their chil-dren, are unsympathetic toward their children, and are sexually dis-tant with their husbands, controls on the perpetrator are few or absent. Similarly, in neighborhoods where reciprocity among inhabitants is absent, where there are high levels of violence, and where few support systems exist, external impediments to abusive acts within one's own family do not appear real or threatening.

Thus, our model provides, from the research, clear answers to Finkelhor's first three pre-conditions: motivation to abuse, lack of internal inhibitions, and lack of external impediments. Because they are only analytically separable, the following section will deal at times with these preconditions again; but it will focus primarily on factors related to the fourth precondition: undermining or overcoming the child's resistance to abuse.

POWER AND RESOURCES IN THE FATHER-DAUGHTER RELATIONSHIP

Incest as child abuse occurs when a person who holds a position of power in a child's intrafamily life sexually victimizes that child. From a Marxist perspective, we can say that the child is open to ex-ploitation because of the inequality of the relationship. The power of the perpetrator springs from many sources, primarily revolving around the resource differential between the parent and the child. In fact, the act of subjugating a person to one's will may itself be a source of power for the perpetrator, as illustrated in the following statement:

> These aggressors who pursue power through incest are often violent men.
> . . .They assert their manhood by tyrannizing their families. Physical
> threats or abuse are the only tools by which they can persuade them-
> selves of their potency. . . .To him (the perpetrator) sex and violence
> are equivalent means to the same end—power. (Forward and Buck, 1978,
> p. 33)

Marx and Engels, separately and jointly, have noted the conflict inherent within marriage and the family due to the sex and class stratification within marriages and families (Marx, 1906; Engels, 1942; Marx and Engels, 1947). That is, in marriage and family no less than in other areas of social life, social inequalities engender opposing interests and thus conflict. Georg Simmel noted that the most intense conflict occurs in primary groups (Simmel, 1955; Wolff, 1950). The family is considered the most primary of all groups. Modern theorists such as Sprey (1971; 1979) and Goode (1971) also see the family as having more potential for intense conflict than any other group.

Sprey and Goode have taken somewhat divergent paths in their respective applications of a conflict perspective to family life. Goode leans toward a classically Marxist interpretation: he perceives the family as a system in which there is unequal distribution of power—usually in favor of the father (Goode, 1971).

Sprey (1971, 1979) takes more of an exchange type of approach. He sees family conflict as a process in which all members have some types of power and negotiate for their best interests. It is possible, according to Sprey, to reach a consensus or otherwise maintain boundaries and thus decrease or temporarily eliminate the conflict. While we concur with Sprey that power in families should not be viewed as a static concept, we find that Goode's treatment of power and conflict are more applicable to power differentials between fathers and daughters in the context of sexual abuse. Power is the "capability to achieve intended effects" (Scanzoni, 1979, p. 302). More specifically, as outlined by Max Weber (1947, p. 151) power is the "probability that an actor within a social relationship will be in a position to carry out his own will *despite resistance*" (emphasis added). Our contention is that the resource differential between father and daughter is such that "bargaining"—at least while the child is young—is minimized and, in the absence of support from her mother or outsiders, the child has no alternative but to comply with her father's demands. Thus, there is less exchange and more potential for exploitation in the relationship.

Our argument is that the incest perpetrator uses illegitimate power when initiating incest. The submission on the part of the daughter, in most cases, cannot be viewed as voluntary (Maisch, 1972; Weinberg, 1955; Finkelhor, 1979b; Dubanoski and McIntosh, 1984). The daughter submits to incest so as to avoid physical abuse, to avoid punishment predicated in threats, and/or to fulfill a sense of obligation to the father because he is her parent and provides for her (Cantwell, 1981; Scanzoni, 1979). Regarding the sense of obligation, it should be noted that the incestuous father often makes the daughter feel obligated to him because of what he has provided for her and the time, energy, and money (his resources) that he has spent on her welfare.[3]

That the daughter would rather not submit is indicated by findings that the father usually uses threats or promises, or attempts in other ways to force or constrain the daughter to feel obligated to him. That is, the daughter usually feels that she has no choice but to submit, though the acts are not to her liking (Maisch, 1972; Brownmiller, 1975; Weber, 1977; Meiselman, 1978; Cantwell, 1981).

The power dynamics that force the child into helpless submission to undesired acts are graphically illustrated by the words of the incest victims themselves:

> He'd pat me when I was in my pajamas and stuff like that. I didn't like it. I felt ashamed. That first time, he came in and started feeling under my pajamas. I was half asleep and didn't know what was happening. He was drunk, and, when he's drunk, he's scary. Before I knew it, he was on top of me, and I kept telling him no, but he said he'd hurt me if I didn't do it. I told him I didn't want to, and he said he was just showing me how. I didn't like it. It hurt. (Anonymous, "What It Was Like to Be an Incest Victim," in Jones, Jenstrom, and MacFarlane, 1980, p. 104)

> If I could wake myself up before he got to my room, I would often scream as though I was having a nightmare (thinking that he couldn't do anything if I woke up the rest of the family). They would wake up, but he would just wait until they were all asleep again and then he would come back for me. I also tried sleeping with my sister, but he would carry me out to the couch in the living room and tell the others I'd been sleepwalking if I was there in the morning. (Barbara Meyers, Incest: If You Think the Word Is Ugly, Look at Its Effects," in Jones, Jenstrom, and MacFarlane, 1980, p. 102)

> Primarily, it was oral sex that he had us do at that very young age. It was done innocently by us, without knowledge of wrong-doing. We didn't like doing this for him, but we thought it was a way of life that was not discussed. As time went on, it was the only way he would buy us a doll or shoes, and later, give us our allowances each week. (Anonymous, "It Hurts to Remember: A Milwaukee Woman's Story," in Jones, Jenstrom, and MacFarlane, 1980, p. 109)

---

[3] Of course, the child will already have an a priori, naive trust and feelings of obligation to her father simply because he is her father. Thus, part of her compliance will occur almost naturally as a learned response to her father as an authority figure. The situation becomes more intense when fathers make explicit the daughter's dependence upon them and obligations to them.

The nature and bases of power in the family will be examined in the following sections, which deal with dominance-subjugation, threats and promises, and stratification.

Dominance-subjugation

Weber defined domination as "the probability that a command will be obeyed" (Weber, 1947, p. 153). Though incest is certainly not just a simple matter of dominance-subjugation, it would be an error not to perceive this dynamic as an aspect of father-daughter incest. Goode (1971, p. 624) states that the family is a power system. Collins acknowledges that "the family is a structure of dominance. . . and we are beginning to see that it enforces a great deal of inequality" (Collins, 1975, p. 225). Further, Goode (1971, p. 628) recognizes that it is usually the father who has the greater strength and who commands more power in the family than does anyone else. Though speaking of prostitution and using a somewhat different perspective, Davis (1937, p. 745) argues that there is a system of dominance operating between the sexes. In this system, the males have dominance over the females and stronger males have dominance over weaker males as well. This dominance of males over females, especially within families, and especially in relation to fathers and children, reflects the larger social order. Denzin highlights a possible negative consequence of such a system of dominance when he states that "violence toward children and women is a pervasive feature of sexual divisions of labor which place females and children in subordinate positions to adult males" (Denzin, 1984, p. 90).

In a family, the father is generally dominant due to being male, being the father, being the predominant breadwinner, and being older and larger (see Goode, 1971, p. 628). All of these attributes are resources that the child does not have. The father has power over the child. This power does not emanate just from the father's age or from the fact that he is the father. The father has power over the child because when the child was a helpless and dependent infant and young child, the child relied upon the father for food, shelter, protection, and direction. Over a period of years, the child has actually come into a situation of "owing" the father for her survival and station in life. While the larger society may argue that the father "owes" the child because he is the adult, is the father, and is socially expected to provide for the child, the abusive father is not responsive to these external definitions. In this context, the reality of the situation is that the child has, over the years, incurred debts of various types to the father; whether or not the child has to pay these debts through incest is up to the father. If he is motivated to sexually abuse the child, finds few or no external impediments to this abuse, and overcomes his own inhibitions toward incest, then the dependent child is obliged to comply with his wishes.

Peter Blau's (1964) treatment of power will help to clarify what has just been said. Blau states, "A person who gives others valuable gifts or renders them important services makes a claim for superior status by obligating them to himself" (p. 108). Further:

> By supplying services in demand to others, a person establishes power over them. If he regularly renders needed services they cannot readily obtain elsewhere, others become dependent on and obligated to him for these services, and unless they can furnish other benefits to him that produce interdependence by making him equally dependent on them, their unilateral dependence obligates them to comply with his requests lest he cease to continue to meet their needs. (Blau, 1964, p. 118)

This is the situation in the relationship between a father and a child. The child is indeed obligated to the father. The father provides for the child what the child cannot provide for herself: tangible and intangible services and resources for which the child has no immediate alternative sources. This dependent position obligates the child to compliance quite apart from any norms of authority or propriety operating in the larger society.

Threats and Promises

As Sprey notes, threats and promises are very similar—the difference is that threats imply punishment for noncompliance while promises offer some type of reward for compliance (Sprey, 1979, p. 138). Threats and promises are both coercive devices. Blau's statement on the matter makes clear the connection between threats and promises:

> Providing needed benefits others cannot easily do without is undoubtedly the most prevalent way of attaining power, through not the only one, since it can also be attained by threatening to deprive others of benefits they currently enjoy unless they submit. The threat of punishment although it exerts the most severe restraints, creates the dependence that is the root of power indirectly, while the recurrent essential rewards that can be withheld do so directly. (Blau, 1984, p. 118)

It seems safe to say that promises and threats play essentially the same role in exacting compliance. Actually, promises can be perceived as "nice threats" in the sense that implied within a promise is the underlying message that if one does not comply, one will not get a reward; thus, one is threatened with punishment in the sense that one may be deprived of a reward. Threats and promises have many applications in the undermining of a child's resistance to incest. For example, a father who has a history of beating his daughter may promise not to beat her if she submits to him sexually. Implied within that promise is the threat of continued beating if she does not submit. Another example, typical of father-daughter incest, is the situation where the father promises the daughter that she may visit a friend or purchase a new dress if she is sexually compliant. Inherent within the promise of reward is the threat that the daughter will be punished by not being allowed to visit her friend or purchase a new dress (in other words, will suffer a withdrawal of reward) if she fails to comply.

To illustrate the blatant power of such threats and promises the words of an incest victim are once again poignantly clear:

> For example, he would pull over on a side street when we were going grocery shopping, or he would promise us a doll or toy and demand sex on the way to the store. I remember when I was about seven, my father ejaculated in my mouth. He leaned back and laughed at me while I spit. I think I have hated to look at him since. That ordeal was the beginning of my rebellion and disrespect. By the time I was about 12, I had begun going to the theater on Friday evenings with a few of my girlfriends. Each Friday, my father would be conveniently located in the basement. If I wanted my allowance, I had to go to him for it. (Anonymous, "It Hurts to Remember: a Milwaukee Woman's Story," in Jones, Jenstrom, and McFarlane, 1980, p. 104)

The father also has ready access, whether explicit or implicit, to an awesome threat of love deprivation or the withholding of love for noncompliance (Collins, 1975, pp. 267-68). The father as a significant other is aware that the child is dependent upon his love for security, for acceptance, and for positive feelings of self. Of course, as Cantwell (1981) indicates, the threats may be so traumatizing to a child that all resistance is obliterated, especially when the father threatens such things as imprisonment of the victim, harsh physical punishment, divorce, or fatal harm to the victim's mother.

The threat-promise system is, of course, intimately bound up with the dominance-subjugation system. As noted by Kenneth Boulding (1970, pp. 24-25), whether or not a threat is likely to be carried out depends upon two things: the threat's credibility and the threatener's capability. The credibility of a threat is dependent upon whether or not the threatener has followed through with his threats in the past. Threat credibility is assessed by the person being threatened. If the threatener in the past has carried through when the threatened party did not comply, the threatened party will see little if any reason to doubt the threatener now (Boulding, 1970, pp. 24-25). In the context of incest, the father who adds up all the costs of carrying out his threats will usually find that the costs are not very great. That is, he is capable of carrying out his threats and can do so with little or no repercussions. Thus, he need not bluff. Most of the costs are incurred by the victim, since she is the powerless one. In addition, the more dependent the threatened person is upon the threatener, the more capable will be the threatener of articulating credible threats and promises, and the more likely it is that the threatened will obey the demands of the threatener.

It should be noted that how indebted, dependent, and obligated a child is to her father is partially dependent upon her knowledge. Especially important is her exposure to alternate viewpoints regarding parent-child relationships, her relationship with her mother and other family members, her knowledge of family life in her society and in other families in her community, and her awareness of alternative resources at her disposal. If these factors are positive, the child can challenge the father's threats and his assessment of reality. Here we find the dynamic dimension of power in parent-child relationships. As the child grows older and acquires other sources of information regarding acceptable father-daughter interactions, she can use her increasing general knowledge, age, and physical maturity as resources to diminish the father's hold over her, and any further advances by the father may be resisted. While a very young child's naive trust in her father increases her vulnerability, an older child whose trust has been violated is more likely, with the resources available to her, to challenge her father. (As will be seen in Chapter 6 and 7, this point is fundamental in understanding the dynamics typically involved in ending the abuse. It is sad yet documented that it is not the mother, another relative, a neighbor, or a teacher, but the victim herself who most frequently reports the abuse to the authorities. More often, we suspect, the abuse is never reported at all, but it is still the victim who is finally able to credibly threaten such a report, often to protect a younger sister, or who runs away, marries early, or otherwise escapes from the situation.)

Stratification in Families

Though we have touched on stratification in families in the discussions above, we feel that a systematic discussion is in order.

Collins (1975, pp. 228-85) uses sex and age stratification factors to explain the class system of the family. He makes the statement that the resources are distributed unequally between males and females because males are larger and stronger, and females are made vulnerable due to the bearing of and caring for children. Applied to the case of father-daughter incest, the female's sex only complicates the situation since, as a child, she is already in an indebted-obligated situation in which the father is, as previously discussed, dominant. Collins notes that, from a Marxian perspective, this male domination of family life by relative size and strength is furthered by economic conditions, in which men have the upper hand (Collins, 1975, pp. 222, 234). Even when the mother works, the ideology of the male as the breadwinner and naysayer tends to maintain the father's dominance (Collins, 1979, pp. 234, 237-54). For a daughter, of course, economic dependence enhances the father's dominance and firmly establishes her in a subordinate position. She does not own the house, the furniture, or the car. She does not own her own clothes and she is not (nor can she be) self-supporting.

Collins contends that, as with sex stratification, the resources that the different age groups have will determine their power over others and their ability to formulate ideologies and make them reality (Collins, 1975, p. 259). There are three resources associated with age stratification: time advantage, size and strength, and physical attractiveness (Collins, 1975, pp. 265-66).

In relation to father-daughter incest, the father has the time advantage because he has lived longer, has had more experience, has established himself, and has accumulated more knowledge with the passage of time. The resources of size and strength are readily apparent. When the father is incestuously oriented toward the daughter, her physical attractiveness to him is a power resource on her side. It is the only card she holds, however, and by no means enough to offset his advantages.

A qualification should be stipulated. While Collins's analysis of family stratification applies with great face validity in families that are male-dominated and traditional in their sex-role orientations, it does not apply as well in families that are equalitarian or quasi-equalitarian. Scanzoni (1979; see also Rodman, 1972) reviews research indicating that in more equalitarian, less patriarchal families (that is, "gender role modern" families) women have more power. This is crucial to a potential child incest victim. When mothers have more power, the daughter is far less vulnerable. First, the mother herself, with her greater power in the family, may serve as a resource for the daughter. Second, if a family is not patriarchal, power is more evenly distributed among family members. Children therefore stand to have more power and be less dominated, less obligated, and less dependent, which in turn makes them less vulnerable to exploitation by adult family members. Further, equalitarian families tend to be higher in socioeconomic standing, and men with more resources are less likely to resort to family violence as a means to experience power (Goode, 1971; Rodman, 1972). Finally, more equalitarian families are less likely to be socially isolated. Thus, daughters in these families have greater knowledge of life in other families and access to alternative support networks in the neighborhood and community.

To summarize the various levels of analysis in this model, the incestuous dyad must, first, be seen as arising within the society's power structure and view of parent-child and male-female relationships. Second, the neighborhood and the family and marital dyad directly impinge upon the father-daughter dyad. Certainly the father's power and his use and misuse of this power must be considered within the context of the other levels of influence. We must also remember that a child's power is not static—it increases as the child ages, thus diminishing the father's hold over her as time goes by. Finally, even if the father-daughter relationship is one in which the father is predisposed to exploit his power advantage, outside influences may effectively intercede on behalf of the actual or potential victim. Thus, our analysis is useful for explaining at the micro level how and why incest may be initiated by fathers. However, an adequate treatment of incest must also be measured and evaluated in the larger context of the family, neighborhood, society, and any possible mitigating factors.

MITIGATING FACTORS

Mitigating factors are conditions that, even when most of the preconditions for incest have been met, serve to decrease the likelihood of incest. In cases where incest has occurred, mitigating factors serve to prevent further episodes. Logically, any mitigating factors must be found or introduced someplace within the four-level life-milieu scheme already discussed. We wish to focus attention on the concept of mitigating factors not because they are beyond or independent of the four life spheres thus far discussed, but strictly for heuristic purposes. By reversing the question at this point from "Why incest?" to "Why not incest?" we can highlight promising avenues for prevention and intervention.

Because most of these factors have been anticipated directly or indirectly earlier in this chapter, they will be presented here in summary form.

Even in the face of motivation and opportunity, adherence to normative proscriptions against incest is a deterrent. ("I want to, I could, but I shouldn't.") This holds for situations in which most of the four preconditions for incest have been met and also for those in which the risk of incest (say, as an "accident" caused by opportunity and a temporary suspension of inhibitions) is nominal. In cases where fathers do not acknowledge and accept such normative proscriptions, and where other risk factors are present, incest is far more likely. Adherence to the normative proscriptions is by no means an absolute bulwark, of course, as a would-be perpetrator may rationalize that his is an exceptional case. It is an important deterrent, however, and often absent in incest cases, especially in extremely isolated families where the father, sometimes assuming the role of religious leader, defines the family's norms in explicit rejection of the ways of the larger society (Weinberg, 1955; Maisch, 1972).

The applied implications here are straightforward. Contrary to traditional assumptions, we cannot safely assume that an ubiquitous incest taboo obviates any need to educate people regarding the necessity to refrain from incestuous contacts with their children. Nearly all perpetrators know that the society defines incest as wrong. More is needed, however. In the face of stresses, pedophilic sexual predilections, violent communities, distant relationships with wives, and the other predisposing conditions discussed earlier, this societal definition needs reinforcement. Just as public service messages tell us not to drink and drive, similar messages are warranted proscribing child abuse, including incest. Especially in the case of incest, the fact that abuse causes severe and lasting emotional damage to the child is not self-evident. Neither is the fact that regardless of the child's behavior, alluring as it may appear, the responsibility for incest and its damage to the child lies entirely with the parent. Both the harm to the child and the parent's responsibility should be emphasized in these messages.

Social support networks of various types can mitigate against incest. First of all, support networks help reinforce the norms of the larger society. Further, support networks serve as resources when stress is too much or one begins to feel motivated to engage in counternormative behaviors. Alcoholics Anonymous serves this purpose for its participants. As noted in Chapter 8 on intervention and treatment for abuse victims and abusive families, various agencies are available for potential or actual perpetrators and victims as well as for other family members. Active community organizations are also important in providing more general types of support and reducing the potential victim's as well as the mother's sense of dependence on the father. Close ties with relatives outside the nuclear family may serve the same purpose. The extent to which these outside supports are available varies greatly from community to community. It should be emphasized that this variable is readily amenable to positive change. Establishing and promoting community awareness of abuse hotlines, shelters, and community counseling centers present key avenues for prevention (Andrews and Linden, 1984). Elementary-school sex and health education that incorporates material on sexual abuse and how to respond to it is a vital part of such a community effort.

Official intervention, of course, is an obvious mitigating factor, although most of the time this would mitigate only against recidivism by known or suspected perpetrators. However, the *threat* of official intervention serves as an additional and more powerful factor. In the past, this threat was virtually nil. Today, with increasing media coverage of intervention in incest cases, it may be a significant deterrent. Certainly, it could become a very significant deterrent if intervention efforts are sufficiently funded and publicized. The largest obstacle to achieving this outcome is lack of financial support, public and private. Presently, most child protection departments are woefully understaffed and overextended.

Sex education is potentially the single most effective factor mitigating against incest. For this potential to be realized, the sex education must include information regarding sexual parameters and what to do if an adult does things not permissible. Even sex education that focuses only on informing children of the names of the body parts, menstruation, sexual reproduction, and the like will increase a child's awareness regarding her body as normal and as her own.

Finally, as noted in discussing other mitigating factors, media and community reporting of incest cases draws public attention to the seriousness of incest abuse and what to do if you know or suspect a case. With the help of the media, suspicious mothers and potential and actual victims can use their knowledge to deter a perpetrator. Further, others in the community may be prompted to report suspicious cases, thus serving as a resource for the victim. In addition, the media coverage of the topic, by itself, serves to inform and to warn potential perpetrators.

These mitigating factors may serve to prevent incest even in high-risk situations. A father fearful of going to prison on a child sexual-abuse charge may find that news coverage of other cases brought to trial serves to constrain him from acting upon his inclinations. A father who has been clearly informed of the damage incest causes to children is, even when other factors conducive to incest are present, less a candidate for incest perpetration than is a father who is not only sexually attracted to children but who also has only a hazy conception that incest is immoral. Daughters knowledgeable about sexual physiology and the facts of child molestation (including the fact that it is a crime) can be expected to discourage all but the most dedicated pedophile. Social support networks of various kinds can reduce vulnerability and increase reporting.

A moral point deserves emphasis as we close this chapter. The responsibility to prevent and intervene in child abuse lies with all adults (Mayhall and Norgard, 1983). Especially when they are informed, all adults can serve as mitigating resources.

6

Risk Factors: A Guide for the Concerned Citizen[1]

INTRODUCTION

The earliest studies of actual incest cases focused primarily on the victims. Further, the emphasis in those early studies was on the victim's personality characteristics, which, as previously discussed, were often interpreted with a seduction-by-the-child explanation for the incest (Bender and Blau, 1937; Sloane and Karpinski, 1941; Weiss et al., 1955). However, in line with trends in the study of other forms of child abuse (Bourne and Newberger, 1979; Cohn, 1979; Gelles, 1978, 1980; Kruger et al., 1979; Straus, Gelles, and Steinmetz, 1980; Mayhall and Norgard, 1983), the emphasis in current empirical literature is on attempts to describe the incest family in multidimensional terms. Many studies have shown that not only the victim's, but both the perpetrator's and the collusive and/or intimidated mother's personality, can shed light on the nature and etiology of adult-child incest. Similarly, a variety of contextual variables—socioeconomic factors, family power structure, birth order and other family configuration variables, and situational variables (for example, overcrowding,

---

[1] The findings discussed in this chapter were presented in "Adult-Child Incest: A Sample of Substantiated Cases" by Brenda J. Vander Mey and Ronald L. Neff. 1984. *Family Relations* 33: 549-57. Reprinted by permission. Copyrighted 1984 by the National Council on Family Relations, St. Paul, Minnesota.

social isolation)—have been implicated as contributing factors (see Chapter 4). Perhaps the most immediate practical benefit of this greatly expanded investigative scope has been the ability to provide community practitioners and other concerned citizens with a growing list of indices by which to recognize high-risk families. As Garbarino and Ebata (1983, p. 779) state, "Perhaps the most important aspect of basic research that can shed light on group differences in risk for abuse and neglect is the study of factors creating either special vulnerability or resistance to particular *forms* of child maltreatment."

Though noted earlier, it bears repeating that most law enforcement, educational, medical, and welfare personnel are legally required to report a case of suspected sexual abuse. Morally, it should be added, any responsible adult has the obligation to report a suspected case.

Because the list of risk factors is quite extensive, we caution the reader at the outset that observing any single factor (for example, the family appears to be socially isolated) should not be cause for alarm. It is when several risk factors are observed in the same family that one should heed the warning signs and respond accordingly (Vander Mey, 1981a). The best place to call is the county welfare department. The report will not of itself result in legal or therapeutic intervention in the family. First, the intake personnel will evaluate the reliability of the call, trying to screen out those that apparently for, say, revenge purposes alone (though some people call to get revenge who know that incest has indeed been occurring in a family). If the report appears to have substance, trained social service workers will conduct a careful investigation. Action will be taken only if the occurrence of abuse is confirmed or strongly suspected.

This chapter reports the results of a study of incest families in the state of Mississippi. The foundation for the chapter's conclusions is much broader, however. The findings from the Mississippi sample are interpreted and supplemented by reference to previous studies. Our findings confirm many of the risk factors suggested by earlier studies and identify some additional factors that may belong on the list.

It should be noted that the research reported here is based on systematic investigations of an exceptionally comprehensive range of potential risk factors. Moreover, the sexual abuse has been substantiated in all cases by intensive interviews with perpetrators, victims, other family members, friends, and neighbors, as well as by medical examinations when appropriate. Finally, the measurement of the risk factors was also verified in onsite investigations, a method more reliable than depending on the respondent or alleged perpetrator to be candid in a survey. Thus, unlike many previous survey-based or clinical studies, a heavy reliance upon the memory, candor, and comprehension of the victim was obviated.

METHODS

This sample consisted of 15 reports involving 26 victims. Although other types of abuse were also involved in many cases, sexual abuse perpetrated by a parent or parent figure was specifically indicated for all 26 victims. The 15 reports were drawn at random from a total of 73 sexual-abuse reports filed with the Mississippi State Department of Public Welfare during the calendar year 1979.[2] Located in the capitol city of Jackson, the State Department of Public Welfare serves as the mandated collection center for information on all cases of child abuse reported to the county Departments of Social Services (DSS), the courts, and/or law enforcement agencies in Mississippi. All 15 reports have been substantiated by the county DSS that served as the intake agency.[3]

All reports were filed on the American Humane Association's National Standard Form 0024. The form includes an item under which success or failure to substantiate the abuse is recorded. Descriptive items address a wide range of family factors (broken homes, new baby/pregnancy in the family, physical abuse of spouse, parental history of abuse as a child, recent relocation, inadequate housing, social isolation, and so on) that may be present along with the abuse. Also covered on the form are sex and ethnicity of victim(s) and perpetrator(s); relationship of perpetrator(s) to victim(s); marital status of parents or parent substitutes; special characteristics or incapacities (mental retardation, physical handicap, emotional disturbance, alcohol dependency, and so on) of the parents or parent substitutes and the involved children; source of initial report; agency receiving the initial report; specific nature and severity of the abuse; any other (nonsexual) abuse or neglect also present; family constellation in terms of number of children, their ages, and so on; education and occupation of both the father and mother or their substitutes; family income and any income supplement; disposition of the child or children; services provided and any legal action(s) taken.

---

[2] A total of 20 reports were randomly selected. The 15 described herein fell into the category of sexual abuse perpetrated by a parent or parent figure.

[3] The substantiation procedure entails an official investigation of the home, interviews with other family members, teachers, friends, and so on, along with a medical examination when applicable.

The interreporter reliability of this instrument has been evaluated by Seaberg and Gillespie (1978), who presented 40 reporters with written case summaries, about 1,000 words in length, describing fictitious abuse cases. All reporters were persons employed in service agencies regularly in contact with child abuse and neglect, and each worked independently in coding the information. Although interreporter reliability was found to be problematic from summaries describing cases of mild and diffuse (low-specificity) abuse, such as emotional neglect, cases of severe and highly specific abuse, such as incest, resulted in generally high interreporter agreement. The lowest reliability estimates in these instances were obtained on items dealing with special characteristics of the victim and family problems. In absolute terms, however, these were at acceptable levels. Specifically, the percentage of reporters agreeing with the modal code on items pertaining to special characteristics of victims ranged from 62.5 to 100, with a mean of 93.6 percent (only one item, diagnosed mentally retarded, obtained a value below 95 percent). The percentage agreeing with the modal code on items pertaining to family problems ranged from 55 to 100, with a mean of 80.9 percent. Those family problem items with reliability estimates below 75 percent were family discord (65 percent), insufficient income (60 percent), heavy continuous child care (67.5 percent), alcohol dependence (65 percent), and mental health problem (55 percent).

In contrast to reliability, no measure of the validity of this instrument is available. It should be noted, however, that all cases in this sample were coded on the basis of information obtained from more than one source (rather than relying solely on the information supplied by a victim or perpetrator, for example). Further, all investigations included at least one visit to the home. It is felt that these factors enhanced the validity of the coding.

There is one obvious limitation of the present sample: its size. Because of the severe underreporting of incest cases at that time, small samples, usually smaller than the present study, are characteristic of research in this area (Williams and Money, 1980). We address this problem by discussing the cases in the context of the larger literature, effectively pooling these cases with those described in earlier studies.

FINDINGS

Ages of Victims and Perpetrators

Table 6.1 provides the ages of victims and perpetrators. (Data were missing on one perpetrator's age, though all victims' ages were

Table 6.1 Characteristics of Victims and Perpetrators

Victims			Perpetrators		
Characteristic	Percent[a]	N	Characteristic	Percent[a]	N
Age Range			*Age Range*[b]		
3-5	3.8	1	23-25	7.1	1
6-8	15.4	4	26-28	0.0	0
9-11	11.5	3	29-31	21.4	3
12-14	34.6	9	32-34	14.3	2
15-17	26.9	7	35-37	14.3	2
18-20	7.7	2	38-40	14.3	2
			41-43	14.3	2
			44-46	0.0	0
			47-49	0.0	0
			50-52+	14.3	2
Sex			*Sex*		
Male	15.4	4	Male	93.3	14
Female	84.6	22	Female	6.7	1
Race			*Race*		
White	84.6	22	White	73.3	11
Black	15.4	4	Black	26.7	4
Special Characteristics[c]					
Only child	21.7	5			
Oldest child	21.7	5			
Only female	13.0	3			
Youngest child	13.0	3			
Step/foster child	30.4	7			
Emotionally disturbed	4.3	1			
None	13.0	3			

Source: Compiled by the authors.

[a]Percentages may not sum to 100 due to rounding or (in the case of victim special characteristics) multiple scoring.

[b]One report did not include age of perpetrator; thus percentages are computed on the available N of 14.

[c]There were three victims for whom data on special characteristics were missing. Thus percentages are computed by dividing by the available N of 23.

recorded.) The median age of the perpetrators at the time of report was 37. However, the modal age of the perpetrators was substantially lower: 30. Both the median and the modal age of the victims at the time of report was 14.[4]

Victim-Perpetrator Dynamics

The perpetrator group was comprised of 14 males and 1 female. The majority (73.3 percent) of the perpetrators were white. There were no interracial families or family-like arrangements and hence no cases of interracial incest (Table 6.1).

A detailed breakdown of the types of perpetrator-victim relationships is provided in Table 6.2. The most frequently occurring relationship was father-daughter (53.8 percent). Foster or stepfather-daughter combinations were next, with a total of six occurrences (23.1 percent). There were three incidences of father-son incest. Finally, the reports included one incidence each of incest between a mother and her daughter, a stepfather and his stepson, and a mother's lover and her daughter. There were no cases of mother-son incest.

Three reports involved a perpetrator who victimized both male and female children. However, most (84.6 percent) of the victims were females. Moreover, no male victimization occurred where there was not also a female victim.

Nearly two-thirds (64.5 percent) of the children were victimized by their biological fathers. Seven children (26.9 percent) were victims of their stepfathers or foster fathers.

Three reports involved a second perpetrator. A second perpetrator is anyone who is collusive, participating, or knows about the abuse and does nothing to stop it. In each instance, the second perpetrator was a white female, the mother of the victim(s) involved. It should be noted that in two cases the mother was mentally retarded; and in the last case parental capacities were limited due to alcohol dependence, mental health problems, fighting between spouses, and a childhood history of abuse on both the parents' parts.

As Table 6.2 shows, twelve victims (46.2 percent) experienced incestuous fondling; five (19.2 percent) were female victims of incestuous intercourse; three (11.5 percent) of the victims were forced to

---

[4] Due to the typically protracted nature of incest and incestuous abuse, we stress that these age values reflect only ages at the time of report—not necessarily ages at the time of onset.

Table 6.2 Dynamics, Dispositions, Services, and Legal Actions

Category	Percent[a]	n(of victims)
Classification		
Father-daughter	53.8	14
Father-son	11.5	3
Mother-daughter	3.8	1
Step/foster father-daughter	23.1	6
Step/foster father-son	3.8	1
Mother's lover-daughter	3.8	1
Type of Sexual Abuse		
Fondling	46.2	12
Intercourse	19.2	5
Threats	3.8	1
Molesting	7.7	2
Oral sex-child to adult	3.9	1
Masturbation of adult	11.5	3
Abuse not specified	7.7	2
Disposition		
Child at home	26.9	7
Disposition pending	34.6	9
Voluntary placement out of home	30.8	8
Court ordered placement out of home	34.6	9
Services[b]		
Casework counseling	95.0	19
Health services	65.0	13
Shelter services	10.0	2
Legal Action[c]		
Juvenile court petition	11.1	2
Juvenile court petition and other protective services	16.7	3
Criminal action taken	55.6	10
Action pending further investigation	5.6	1
Other protective services	11.1	2

Source: Compiled by the authors.
[a]Percentages may not sum to 100 due to rounding or multiple scoring.
[b]Two reports with a total of 6 victims lacked data on services.
[c]Four reports with a total of 8 victims lacked data on legal action.

masturbate an adult; and two children (7.7 percent) were molested. One victim was threatened (she ran away and told authorities before her stepfather could act upon his threats). The final victim was forced to perform oral sex on her mother's lover (in this case, the mother was deemed the second perpetrator).

As indicated in an earlier discussion about Mississippi's legal handling of incest and rape, the charge of rape is usually applied in incest cases where the victim is young or has been extensively victimized. In this sample, three cases led to a charge of rape. In one case, a 23-year-old black male raped his 7-year-old daughter. In another, a 10-year-old black female was raped by her 32-year-old stepfather. In the last case, an 8-year-old white female was forced to have intercourse with her 30-year-old stepfather.

Special Characteristics of Victims

By referring back to Table 6.1, it can be seen that the most frequently occurring special characteristic was being a stepchild or foster child. Nevertheless, the majority (69.6 percent) were neither step nor foster children. Three children each were the only female in the family or the youngest child. Three others had no special characteristics noted. One child was emotionally disturbed. No victims had special physical defects or chronic illnesses.

Source and Recipient of Initial Report

The most frequent source of initial report was the victim (33.3 percent). Law enforcement, hospital/clinic personnel, and "other" registered a tally of two each. Anonymous, school personnel, other relative, and sibling were each initial sources once (6.7 percent each). On the receiving end, the county Department of Social Services (DSS) received the bulk of the initial reports (eleven or 73.3 percent). Courts and law enforcement agencies each received 13.3 percent of the initial reports.

Other (Nonsexual) Abuse/Neglect

Some 67 percent of the reports involved substantiated nonsexual abuse/neglect in addition to the sexual abuse. Physical abuse (30.0 percent) and emotional neglect (40.0 percent) were the most frequently reported. Other types of nonsexual abuse/neglect included no supervision (20.0 percent); cuts and welts (20.0 percent); and locking/out (10.0 percent). Although most of the extrasexual abuse was passive in nature (a matter of neglect), 14.3 percent of the reports involved victims whose injuries were classified as serious/hospitalized. Of course, injuries requiring hospitalization were not necessarily instances of other (nonsexual) abuse. One victim, a three-year-old female, was taken to the hospital to have her vagina restructured due to sexual assaults perpetrated by her mother.

Socioeconomic Factors

There was a trimodal family income of $0-2,999; $5,000-6,999; and $13,000-15,999. However, the largest number of victims, eight, occurred at the very bottom of the distribution: $0-2,999. The median family income per report was $7,000-8,999. This was also the median family income per victim.

Thirteen victims (50.0 percent) lived in families receiving some form of federal or other public income assistance. When an income supplement was received, the most frequent type was Aid to Families with Dependent Children (AFDC).

The modal and median occupation group of the perpetrators per report and per victim was unskilled labor. No perpetrators were involved in business, professional, agricultural, or technical occupations. Interestingly, only 14.3 percent of the perpetrators were unemployed. The median education level for perpetrators per report and per victim was some high school.

Family Factors

Table 6.3 presents various family factors identified in investigations of the home environment. Broken family was the most frequent family problem, present in 71.4 percent of the reports. Likewise, more victims (17) lived in homes that were broken than in families with any other single problem. Financial problems were evident in 50.0 percent of the families encompassing 66.7 percent of the victims. Close to half (42.9 percent) of the victims also experienced a home life where there was physical abuse of a spouse or fighting between spouses.

Nearly half of the reports (and 69.2 percent of the victims) involved families where there was alcohol dependency on the part of at least one parent. Nine victims (34.6 percent) had a parent or parents with police/court records. Six victims (23.1 percent) had a parent or parents "who were mentally retarded. Six others had a parent or parents" with mental health problems. One third (33.3 percent) of the

Table 6.3 Family Factors Per Report and Victim

Factor	Report n	Percent[a]	Victim n	Percent[a]
Family Problems[b]				
Broken family	10	71.4	17	81.0
Insufficient income/misuse of income	7	50.0	14	66.7
Family discord	5	35.7	10	47.6
Physical abuse of spouse/fighting	4	28.6	9	42.9
Parental history of abuse	2	14.3	7	33.3
Heavy continuous child care	2	14.3	2	9.5
Parental Incapacity				
Mentally retarded	2	13.3	6	23.1
Lack parenting skills	5	33.3	5	19.2
Alcohol dependence	7	46.7	18	69.2
Mental health problem	2	13.3	6	23.1
Police record	4	26.7	9	34.6
No tolerance	2	13.3	2	7.7
Environmental Factors				
Inadequate	6	40.0	13	50.0
Social isolation	3	20.0	8	30.8
Recent relocation	2	13.3	7	26.9
Marital Status[b]				
Divorced/separated	3	21.4	3	14.3
Legal marriage	8	57.1	10	47.6
Consensual union	1	7.1	1	4.8
Widow/widower	2	14.3	7	33.3

Source: Compiled by the authors.

[a]Percentages may not sum to 100 due to rounding or multiple scoring.

[b]One report, with five victims, lacked data on family problems and marital status.

reports indicated that the parent or parents present in the home lacked parenting skills. On the other hand, only two families could be characterized as having parents with "no tolerance."

Six reports (40.0 percent) involved families with inadequate housing. Moreover, multiple victims were more likely to be found in these homes (50.0 percent of the victims were inadequately housed). Eight victims (30.8 percent) were in families suffering from social isolation, and seven (26.9 percent) of the victims had experienced recent relocations.

Dispositions, Services, and Legal Actions

As noted in Table 6.2, dispositions were still pending for nine victims (34.6 percent) at the time the report was filed with the authorities. Most of these victims (seven) were still in the home at the time of the report. Another nine victims experienced court-ordered placement out of the home.

Table 6.2 also shows breakdowns of the types of services provided and legal actions taken. One or more specific services were provided to thirteen of the fifteen families, entailing twenty of the twenty-six victims. Of these, nineteen of the victims (95 percent) were in families who received casework counseling. Thirteen (65 percent) of the victims were in families who received health services. Thus, when services were provided, both counseling and health services were usually needed. Finally, two families (two victims) were provided shelter services.

Eleven reports (with eighteen victims) resulted in legal actions. Within these, ten of the victims lived in three families where criminal action was taken against the perpetrator(s). In three other families (three victims), a juvenile court petition was filed and other protective services were provided on behalf of the victims. Juvenile court petitions were the only legal actions taken on behalf of two other victims; another two victims were provided with other protective services only. In one case, involving one victim, legal action was still pending at the time the report was filed.

DISCUSSION

Reaffirming one of the most consistent findings in other studies (Finkelhor, 1979a; Julian, Mohr, and Lapp, 1980; Machotka, Pittman, and Flomenshaft, 1967; Maisch, 1972; Renvoize, 1978; Justice and Justice, 1979), this sample involved predominantly father-daughter incest/sexual abuse. Unlike many other studies, this sample also included a mother-daughter case, a stepfather-son case, and three cases of father-son sexual abuse. It should be noted, however, that all cases of male-male sexual abuse occurred in conjunction with male-female sexual abuse. It may well be that in the absence of the female(s), the abuse of the male would not have occurred or would not have been reported. In regard to the dynamics which may partially explain why males were also abused, the three father-son cases all occurred in large families with alcoholic fathers (in one, the mother was deceased). In the stepfather-son case, the stepfather forced the male child and his two sisters to masturbate him (the adult). The mother-daughter case was a surprise since very little has been said in the literature regarding mother-daughter incest (Meiselman, 1978), except in cases where the mother was in collusion with the father or other adult male (Forward and Buck, 1978). In fact, cases in which the mother is the sole perpetrator, in relation to either a daughter or a son, have been completely absent in most samples (Finkelhor, 1979; Weinberg, 1955; Vander Mey and Neff, 1982). In the case reported here, the mother had less than three years of formal education, had an extremely low income, and was found to be mentally retarded.

There were three mothers who acted as second or collusive perpetrators in the sexual abuse. The extent of their collusion was not always clear, though it appeared that none of these mothers had taken action to halt the father's or lover's behaviors toward the victims. In two of these three cases, the mothers were found to be mentally retarded. It is also noteworthy that one of the two cases in which the mother was mentally retarded was the only case involving clear evidence of the mother playing an actively collusive role in the sexual abuse (the mother forced the child to perform oral sex on her lover). The other case of retardation on the part of the mother involved a mother with education in the zero-to-three years range and a father who was reportedly an alcoholic. There were also mental health problems indicated on the part of the parents in this case. In the last report, the mother and father were high school graduates, had an income in the $20,000-24,999 range, but had such parental limitations or incapacities as lack of tolerance to children, alcohol dependence, and childhood histories of abuse. Thus, all three of these cases entailed factors that may help explain why the mother colluded. Most of the factors and situations noted in these three reports generally coincide with previously published descriptions of families with collusive or participant mothers (Maisch, 1972; Tormes, 1968; Weinberg, 1955). The only factor not previously singled out is mental retardation on the part of the mother. This may indeed be a factor predisposing children to vulnerability to incest/sexual abuse because of the mother's limited ability to socialize her children, to effectively contend with the father or father figure, and to grasp the full extent and significance of the abuse. Mental retardation is obviously conducive to the tyrannical father dominance frequently observed in incest families (Specktor, 1979). The number of cases in this sample is very small, but the fact that two out of three mothers were classified as mentally retarded may point to a significant risk factor.

The victim as the most frequent source of initial report was not an unusual finding and reinforced other research on this matter (Julian,

Mohr, and Lapp, 1980; Maisch, 1972; Tormes, 1968; Weinberg, 1955). That a sizeable minority of the initial reports came from persons outside the family (hospital personnel, teachers, and so on) could possibly be taken as an encouraging indication that the mandated reporting laws are becoming effective, and/or that a significant number of persons outside the family are trained and responsible regarding such matters. It was not surprising that the county Departments of Social Services received the bulk of the reports since those agencies are the most noted for dealing with such problems.

The class attributes of the families indicated a decided concentration in the lower classes, with the modal number of victims at the very bottom of the distribution. This finding converges with nearly all other studies that have reported information on socioeconomic location. In studies of officially investigated cases, including the present sample, such a finding could be a spurious result of class-linked biases in coming to the attention of public welfare agencies. As explicated earlier (see Chapter 4), however, similar findings have arisen in surveys of general populations. Further, resource problems, stresses, and subcultural factors theoretically conducive to incest as well as other types of family violence lead us to suspect that this concentration in the lower classes is substantially real.

The family configuration variables in this sample suggest that more attention should be addressed to this factor. Earlier research has pointed to a high risk for the female who is the firstborn or the only child (Browning and Boatman, 1977; Tormes, 1968) and for the child who is the first female preceded by one or more males (Specktor, 1979; Tormes, 1968). The present data seem to replicate these findings, but suggest that being the youngest child may also signal a heightened risk factor.

That over half of the incest reports involved families in which the parents or parent figures had a legal marriage supports the emerging impression that incest abuse occurs most often in families in which two parents or parent figures are present (Finkelhor, 1979a; Justice and Justice, 1979; Weinberg, 1955). However, a large proportion of the victims (81 percent) lived in families designated as "broken." Families were considered broken if there was or had been no legal union, or if there had been any previous separation, divorce, or death of spouse. Thus, some victims in this sample have been categorized as residing in "broken families" although a legal marriage was present by the time of the report.

Table 6.4   Adult-Child Incest Risk Factor/Indicator List

Father dominance/authoritarianism[b,c,d,g,h,i,k,l]	Mother failing to perform in mother/housewife role[b,c,f,g,k,m]
Father abusing alcohol[d,e,g,h,i,k,l,n]	Female child has assumed housekeeping role[c,f,m]
Father abused as a child[e,n]	Mother relying on female child to meet her friendship/counseling needs[f,m]
Father reared in harsh emotional environment[c,h,m]	Mental health problems on part of mother[a,c]
Faulty stress management on part of father[g]	Mental retardation of mother[n]
Father with police record[n]	Oldest or only daughter[c,k,l,n]
Lack of parenting skills[n]	Youngest daughter[n]
Physical abuse of children/spouse[e,i,l,m,n]	Firstborn child[a,l,n]
Handicapped (physical or mental) child[a]	Broken or reconstituted family[e,f,n]
Child displaying acting-out behaviors[k]	Child and father sleep in same room[g,m]
Child secretive about home activities[k]	Family discord[c,e,n]
Child with low self-esteem[k]	Child not socializing with peers[k]
Child with unkempt appearance and uncaring attitude[k]	Child fearful of family dissolution[c,g]
Withdrawn child[k]	Child with dropping academic achievement[k]
Social isolation[c,d,e,g,i,k,l,m,n]	Child's social activities severely restricted by father[b,d,k,l]
Inadequate housing[c,g,m,n]	Youthful marriage begun with pregnancy followed by more births in fairly rapid succession[l]
Recent relocation[c,g,l,n]	
Mother absent (divorced, deserted, deceased)[c,g,m]	

Source: Compiled by the authors.

[a] Browning and Boatman, 1977
[b] Cormier, Kennedy, and Sancowicz, 1973
[c] Henderson, 1980
[d] Justice and Justice, 1979
[e] Julian, Mohr, and Lapp, 1980
[f] Machotka, Pittman, and Flomenhaft, 1967
[g] Maisch, 1972
[h] Meiselman, 1978
[i] Renvoize, 1978
[j] Sagarin, 1977
[k] Specktor, 1979
[l] Tormes, 1978
[m] Weinberg, 1955
[n] Present study

Family problems, environmental factors, other abuse, and parental incapacities were largely typical of earlier research (see Vander Mey and Neff, 1982), adding further documentation to the growing recognition that incest tends to be embedded in families with other problems in addition to sexual abuse. This study, as others, indicates that these factors—especially when found in combination—signal families that are high risks in regard to incest. One note of caution in relation to this statement: it is virtually impossible to sort out which factors are antecedent to the others, which may be "intervening" factors, and which may be spurious in relation to causal issues. That is, it is difficult to identify the truly active factor or factors predisposing a family to sexual abuse. Moreover, some of these factors may be consequences of the sexual abuse as often as the reverse. From the standpoint of intervention and prevention, however, those concerned with the identification of potential or actual incest/sexual abuse families may be well advised to inventory family factors noted in this and similar studies. The present sample is of particular value because the incest has been substantiated in every instance, thereby avoiding reliance upon victim post factum reports. In addition, an exceptionally full range of potentially predisposing factors have been systematically inventoried and verified in onsite investigations.

APPLICATION: AN INVENTORY OF RISK FACTORS AND INDICATORS

Several researchers have called for treatment and prevention of adult-child incest (Giarretto, Giarretto, and Sgroi, 1978; Herman and Hirschman, 1977; Sgroi, 1975). Some have indicated risk factors that may signal potential or actual incest/sexual abuse (Maisch, 1972; Specktor, 1979; Tormes, 1968; Vander Mey, 1981a; Vander Mey and Neff, 1982). Drawing on these resources and the findings from the current study, the inventory of risk factors/indicators (Table 6.4) may aid helping professionals and the concerned citizen in detecting actual or potential incest/sexual abuse. Observation of any single factor or indicator on this list may not be significant. It is when they are found in combinations that a high risk exists (Specktor, 1979; Vander Mey, 1981).

7

Risk Factors Reexamined: More Evidence for the Researcher

What social, demographic, personality, and situational factors are associated with adult-child incest? This question was addressed in the preceding chapter. The present chapter readdresses the same question, approaching it from a different standpoint. The objective of Chapter 6 was to provide interested lay persons information which may assist them in identifying and reporting suspected cases. In the interest of stemming as much victimization as possible, the operative premise of Chapter 6 was to err on the conservative side. In short, from the standpoint of alerting the public and thus increasing reporting and intervention, any characteristic or circumstance that research has identified as a *possible* risk factor was included in the list provided in Chapter 6.

As a practical guide for reporting, we do not feel that the inventory of risk factors in Chapter 6 is overly inclusive. We noted, first of all, that the citizen should become alarmed only after observing more than one of the factors on the list. Further, once a suspected case is reported to local authorities, an onsite investigation will be conducted. Legal or therapeutic action will not be taken unless the investigation reveals a need for it.

On the other hand, from the standpoint of advancing our knowledge and adhering to the canons of science, these risk factors are in need of further scrutiny. Addressed to the researcher and concerned with issues of methodological rigor, the present chapter proceeds more critically. Nearly all of the previous research on adult-child incest, including the data set analyzed in Chapter 6, has been based on very small samples. This chapter presents evidence from a larger sample. Some of the risk factors that have been suggested on the basis of small samples appear, in view of this larger sample, in need of reassessment. The importance of other previously identified risk factors, however, is reaffirmed.

BACKGROUND

Sample size has been a serious limitation in nearly all of the empirical studies in this area. Case studies with sample sizes of less than 20 have not been uncommon (see Vander Mey and Neff, 1982). As of 1980, very few studies conducted with samples of 100 or more incest victims had been published. Two outstanding exceptions were Finkelhor's (1979a) retrospective study of college students and Weinberg's (1955) Illinois study. Finkelhor's study identified 211 alleged incest victims (151 females, 60 males) and was a very important study indicating that over one out of every five college students reported "incestuous" (with relatives or near-relatives) experiences as a child. The great bulk of these reports, however, involved episodic and relatively mild child-child (siblings or cousins) events. In fact, Finkelhor's sample included only five father-daughter cases, two stepfather-daughter cases, one grandfather-daughter case, and no father-son, stepfather-son, or mother-son cases (Finkelhor, 1979a, p. 87). While Weinberg's study is now dated (1955), it remains an important work in this area. Weinberg started with 203 cases of incest reported to various authorities in Illinois and followed up, when possible, with interviews (159 families) of the victim(s), perpetrator(s), nonperpetrating parent(s), and/or other family member(s).

Recently, the National Incidence (NI) Study, drawing on a probability sample of a wide variety of agencies (county child protective services, police, probation departments, sheriff's offices, coroner's offices, public health departments, public schools, hospitals, mental health departments, and social service agencies) gathered, through sending forms to these agencies, basic data on 17,645 reported cases of child abuse and neglect, of which 7 percent were categorized as sexual abuse (Finkelhor and Hotaling, 1984, p. 24). While a landmark study for certain purposes, the NI study suffered from inconsistencies across the agencies in the definitions of child abuse and neglect, especially in the cases of child sexual abuse (pp. 25-26). Further, beyond age, relationship to perpetrator, and type of abusive act, little information was reported concerning the issue of risk factors.

Like Weinberg's study, the research reported here is based not only on a relatively large sample, but also on examinations of a very broad spectrum of potential risk factors. In common with the cases presented in Chapter 6, the sexual abuse has been substantiated in all instances. Substantiation was predicated on interviews with perpetrators, victims, other family members, neighbors, relatives, and so on and supplemented by medical examinations when appropriate. As explicated in Chapter 6, we feel that this triangulated approach to measurement provides both more reliable and more valid information than that obtained by studies relying exclusively or predominately on victim self-reports. On the other hand, the sample presented here consists solely of cases that have been reported to authorities. Although this is a characteristic shared with most other studies, it is an important limitation. It may bias the sample toward the lower socioeconomic classes who are, in other respects, more likely to utilize or to be monitored by welfare and law enforcement agencies. At the same time, it should be noted that this limitation is not as restricting as one might expect. In fact, in this and other samples of reported cases (for example, the sample presented in Chapter 6), there are families from all economic, educational, and occupational levels.

METHODS

This sample consists of 163 victims of incest whose situations were brought to the attention of protective service workers in Virginia in 1979. As with the sample presented in Chapter 6, other (nonincestuous) abuse was also evident in many cases. Nevertheless, adult-child incest (vaginal or anal intercourse, prostitution, cunnilingus, fellatio, fondling, simulated intercourse, or pornography/pornographic exploitation) was specifically indicated for all victims. These cases were identified from a total of 522 sexual-abuse cases (substantiated and unsubstantiated, incestuous and nonincestuous) reported to the Department of Public Welfare, Child Protective Services across the state of Virginia. All cases described herein were ultimately classified as substantiated ("clear and convincing evidence" of the abuse) by local Child Protective Services personnel.

FINDINGS

Age of Victim

As detailed in Table 7.1, this sample consisted primarily of pre-pubertal (ages 9-11) and teenage victims. Interestingly, the bulk of the victims (66.9 percent) were in the age categories of 12-14 and 15-17. While our first sample (Chapter 6) found a modal age category of 12-14, this larger sample indicates a modal age of 15-17. We hasten to add that these ages reflect only the age at the time of report. As noted before, incest is typically a protracted involvement, beginning before the child reaches the age of nine. It is not typically reported, however, until the victim reaches adolescence, when contacts away from the family of orientation lead to a fuller understanding of sexuality and moral ideas surrounding it (Weinberg, 1955; Tormes, 1968).

Victim-Perpetrator Relationships

A total of 210 perpetrators (155 males, 55 females) incestuously victimized the 163 children in this sample (see Table 7.1). For a third of the victims (33.7 percent), one or more female perpetrator(s) were involved. In the majority of the cases, however, the female perpetrator appeared to be in collusion with a male, as indicated by the fact that the first perpetrator reported was a male in 93.2 percent of the cases. Nevertheless, the first perpetrator was a women in 6.8 percent of the cases. With a woman actively involved in 33.7 percent of the cases, the amount of culpable female participation in this sample is not negligible.

Table 7.2 provides a breakdown of the specific family relationships of victims and perpetrators. It must be remembered that some victims were abused by more than one perpetrator. Accordingly, the categories of victim-perpetrator relationships are not mutually exclusive and the percentages sum to more than 100.

In order of incidence, biological father-daughter incest was the most frequent (reported for 66.3 percent or 108 of the 163 victims). Significantly, the situation of both parents sexually abusing a female child was second in order of prevalence (25.8 percent or 42 victims). Next was stepfather-daughter incest (19.6 percent or 32 victims). There were 18 male children (11.0 percent of the victims) who were sexually abused by their biological fathers. Another 12 males (7.4 percent of the victims) were abused by both parents. Nearly as frequent was mother-daughter incest (11 victims or 6.7 percent of the

Table 7.1 Victim and Perpetrator Characteristics

VICTIMS

Characteristic	Percent[a]	N	Characteristic	Percent[a]	N
Age Range			*Special Characteristics*[b]		
0-2	.6	1	None or Unknown	71.8*	117
3-5	3.0	5	Emotionally Disturbed	17.2	28
6-8	4.9	8	Behavior Problem(s)	11.7	19
9-11	15.3	25	School Problem(s)	8.0	13
12-14	25.2	41	Parents Perceive		
15-17	41.7	68	Special Problem(s)	4.9	8
18-20+	9.2	15	Learning Disabilities	3.7	6
			Mentally Retarded[c]	1.8	3
Sex[c]			Unwanted Pregnancy	1.8	3
Male	16.7	27	Physical Handicap	1.2	2
Female	83.3	135	Juvenile Court	1.2	2
			Other	1.2	2
Race[d]			Chronic Illness	.6	1
White	84.3	134			
Black	14.5	23			
Oriental	.6	1			
Other	.6	1			

PERPETRATORS

Sex of First Perpetrator			*Sex of All Known Perpetrators*[e]		
Male	93.2	150	Male	95.1	155
Female	6.8	11	Female	33.7	55

Source: Compiled by the authors.

[a]Percentages may not sum to 100 due to rounding; computed on N(163) of available data.

[b]Multiple scoring occurred in some cases. Thus percentages do not sum to 100.

[c]Data on sex was missing for one victim. Percentages are based on the available N of 162.

[d]Data on race of victim was missing for four victims. Percentages are based on available N of 159.

[e]There may be more than one perpetrator. Percentages are based on victim N of 163.

Table 7.2 Dynamics, Dispositions, and Legal Actions

Category[a]	Percent[b]	N
Father-daughter	66.3	108
Both parent figures-daughter	25.8	42
Stepfather-stepdaughter	19.6	32
Father-son	11.0	18
Both parent figures-son	7.4	12
Mother-daughter	6.7	11
Foster father-daughter	3.1	5
Uncle-niece	3.1	5
Stepfather-son	2.5	4
Mother-son	1.8	3
Grandfather-granddaughter	.6	1
Uncle-nephew	.6	1
Unknown (missing data)	4.9	8
Dispositions[b]		
Service Plan Achieved	39.3	64
Case Remains Open	31.9	52
Court Placement of Child	15.3	25
Family Referral Service	5.5	9
Referred to Other Agency	5.5	9
Referred to Other Child Welfare Agency	2.5	4
Family Missing	2.5	4
Referred to Other Locality	1.2	2
Legal Actions[b]		
No Action Noted	51.5	84
Referred to Free Legal Services Attorney	30.7	50
Court Petitioned	19.6	32
Criminal Action	19.0	31
Hearing Held	12.3	20
Committed to Local Agency	11.0	18
Court Assigned to Care of Parent	9.8	16
Temporary Custody Pending	9.2	15
72-hour Protection	5.5	9

Source: Compiled by the authors.

[a] Relationship classifications are not mutually exclusive. The same victim may have been victimized by father, mother, and uncle, for example. This victim would show up under the father-daughter, mother-daughter, both parents-daughter, and uncle-niece classifications. Thus, the percentages sum to more than 100. (The data set does not permit the identification of exactly how many victims fall into a given category of multiple victimization; only Ns for each individual classification category are obtainable.)

[b] Due to multiple scoring, percentages do not sum to 100. Percentages are computed on the victim N of 163.

sample). Uncle-niece and foster father-daughter incest occurred with 5 victims (3.1 percent) each. Stepfathers victimized 4 males (2.5 percent). Another 3 males were victimized by their mothers (1.8 percent); and 1 male was victimized by his uncle (.6 percent). Finally, 1 victim was found to have been victimized by her grandfather. Data on the exact relationship between the child victim and the adult perpetrator was missing for 4.9 percent of the victims.

Special Characteristics of the Victims

Among victims for whom a special characteristic was noted, the most frequently occurring feature was being emotionally disturbed (17.2 percent of the sample; see Table 7.1). The next most frequently noted special characteristic was behavior problems on the part of the child. There were 19 children (11.7 percent) who had behavior problems. A child is classified as emotionally disturbed in this data set when faced with factors that limit his/her ability to perceive the world accurately, to control impulses, to learn, and/or to establish relationships with peers at the level usually expected of children his/her age. A child with behavior problems is one who immaturely reacts to stress in an excited and ineffective manner (Child Protective Services Information System [CPSIS] Users Guide, 1979, p. 21).

The third most often observed special characteristic of the victim was school problems (13 victims, or 8.0 percent). This means that the child has difficulty adjusting to school, either academically, socially, or in relation to attendance and discipline (CPSIS Users Guide, 1979, p. 21). In the cases of 8 victims (4.9 percent) the parent(s) perceived that the child had one or more special problems—even though professional diagnoses did not confirm the parent(s)' suspicions about the child.

Another 6 victims (3.9 percent) were reported to have learning difficulties—some type of mental or physical condition making it difficult or impossible for the child to learn or acquire skills without specialized treatment. All children were diagnosed by professionals before the decision was made to report this special characteristic (CPSIS Users Guide, 1979, p. 21).

In addition, 3 children (1.8 percent) were considered to have an intellectual performance level far enough below normal to be labelled mentally retarded. Another 3 children were unwanted when they were born. There were 2 children (1.2 percent) who were impaired to the point of being considered physically handicapped, had previously been brought to the attention of juvenile courts for status or delinquent offenses, or had other, unspecified special characteristics. Only 1 child (.6 percent) suffered a chronic illness.

Source of Report

Table 7.3 presents a breakdown on the source first bringing the case to the attention of the Child Protective Services. The most frequent source of report was a parent or guardian (15.3 percent). This modal category is closely followed by public school personnel (14.7 percent), law enforcement officials (13.5 percent), and, notably, self-referral by the victim (12.9 percent). The remaining cases (43.6 percent) are widely dispersed over a surprising variety of sources, none individually accounting for more than 6.7 percent of the cases.

Other (Nonincestuous) Abuse/Neglect

As shown in Table 7.4, for nearly one-quarter (21.5 percent) of the victims other (nonincestuous) sexual abuse was discovered. In

Table 7.3 Source of Report

Source	Percent*	N
Parent; guardian	15.3	25
Public school	14.7	24
Law enforcement	13.5	22
Self-referral	12.9	21
Friend; neighbor	6.7	11
Hospital; clinic	5.5	9
Relative	4.9	8
Anonymous	4.3	7
Public social service	3.7	6
Courts	3.7	6
Other	3.7	6
Doctor; nurse	2.5	4
Unknown	1.8	3
Private social service	1.8	3
Youth Services	1.8	3
Landlord	1.2	2
Sibling	.6	1
Babysitter	.6	1
Public health worker	.6	1

Source: Compiled by the authors.
*Percentages may not sum to 100 due to rounding.

Table 7.4 Other (Nonincestuous) Abuse/Neglect

Item	Percent[a]	N
Type Abuse[b]		
Emotional neglect	25.8	42
Other sexual abuse	21.5	35
Lack of supervision	8.0	13
Bizarre discipline	6.1	10
Medical neglect	3.7	6
Lack of food, clothing	1.8	3
Educational neglect	1.8	3
Bruises, cuts	1.2	2
Bone fracture	.6	1
Manner of Infliction[b]		
Other	21.5	35
Beating	6.1	10
Exposure to elements	1.2	2

Source: Compiled by the authors.

[a]Percentages are based on N of 163 and may not sum to 100.

[b]Other abuse was not reported for all victims, though some victims suffered multiple nonincestuous abuse.

short, the incest was markedly coincident with other sexual abuse. Emotional neglect was evident in still a larger percentage of the cases (25.8 percent). On the other hand, violence and neglect of food, clothing, medical or other needs were detected with surprising infrequency. In fact, beyond sexual abuse and emotional neglect, only lack of supervision (8.0 percent) and bizarre discipline (6.1 percent) were noted in more than 4 percent of the cases. Information on the "manner of infliction" indicates that detected abuse traceable to beating the child was evident in only ten cases (6.1 percent).

Socioeconomic Factors

Table 7.5 shows the employment status of household heads. Well over half (60.1 percent) of the victims' household heads were working full-time at the time of the report. Some 24 household heads (14.7 percent) were unemployed and 9 (5.5 percent) were working part-time at the time of the report. There was no employment status data available for 32 (19.6 percent) of the household heads.

Table 7.5 Socioeconomic Factors of Victims' Families

Factor	Percent[a]	N	Factor	Percent[a]	N
Household Income			*Income Source*[b]		
0 to 5,000	3.7	6	Employment	66.3	108
5,001 to 10,000	12.3	20	Unknown	19.0	31
10,001 to 20,000	14.1	23	ADC, AFDC	7.4	12
20,001 to 30,000	3.7	6	Social security	4.3	7
Over 30,000	1.2	2	None	1.8	3
Unknown	65.0	106	Other	1.2	2
Education[b]			*Occupation*[b]		
Unknown	51.5	84	None	12.9	21
Part elementary	4.3	7	Labor	28.8	47
Elementary	2.5	4	Agriculture	.6	1
Part high school	6.7	11	Service work	3.1	5
GED	3.1	5	Clerical work	2.5	4
High school graduate	8.6	14	Craftsman	2.5	4
Partial college	1.8	3	Sales	3.1	5
Technical school	1.2	2	Military	18.4	30
College graduate	1.8	3	Manager, administrator	2.5	4
Post graduate work	1.8	3	Professional, technical	.6	1
None	16.6	27	Other	3.7	6
			Unknown	21.5	35
Employment Status[b]					
Unknown	19.6	32			
Unemployed	14.7	24			
Part-time	5.5	9			
Full-time	60.1	98			

Source: Compiled by the authors.
[a]Percentages may not sum to 100 due to rounding.
[b]Information and statistics based on household head data.

Two-thirds (66.3 percent or 108) of the household heads secured their income from employment, and 12 victims' homes received Aid to Dependent Children (ADC) or Aid to Families with Dependent Children (AFDC). A little less than 5 percent of the victims lived in homes where social security was a source of income. Another 3 victims (1.8 percent) were living in homes where there was no apparent source of income at all at the time of report, and 2 victims (1.2 percent lived in homes drawing their income from a source other than those noted above. There was no data available on source of household income for 31 (19.0 percent) of the victims.

Referring again to Table 7.5, it is readily apparent that the modal occupational category for the victims' household head was labor. For 30 of the victims (18.4 percent), the household head was employed by the military as an active member of one of the armed forces. The household head for 6 (3.7 percent) of the victims had an occupation that was classified as "other," indicating that the occupation did not fit any of the traditional categories. There were 5 (3.1 percent) household heads involved in service work and 5 were involved in sales. Another 4 (2.5 percent) each were occupied in clerical work, a craftsman occupation, and management or administration. There was 1 household head engaged in agriculture and another in the professional, technical category. A total of 21 (12.9 percent) of the household heads were unemployed and indicated no occupational identification. Finally, occupational data were missing for 35 (21.5 percent) of the cases.

In contrast to the data on other variables, it is unfortunately the case that information on family income and the educational attainment of the household head is severely limited in this data set. Specifically, data is entirely missing (reported as "unknown") on the household income for 65.0 percent (106) of the victims. Educational attainment of the head of the household is missing for 84 victims (51.5 percent). Thus, the following figures are reported as suggestive at best, considering the high probability of systematic differences between the reported and the missing cases.

As shown in Table 7.5, of the 57 victims for whom family income was reported, 23 (40.4 percent) lived in households with incomes in the $10,001 to $20,000 range. Another 20 victims (35.1 percent) lived in households with incomes in the $5,001 to $10,000 range. There were 6 (10.5 percent) who lived in households in the $0 to $5,000 range. Probably the most significant finding on this variable is that 6 other victims lived in households with incomes in the $20,001 to $30,000 range, and 2 victims (3.5 percent) lived in households with incomes of over $30,000. In short, affluent families were not immune. On the other hand, compared with Census information regarding family income in Virginia in 1979 (U.S. Bureau of Census, 1983), there is a decided overrepresentation of lower-income families in this data set. According to Census data, in 1979 7.1 percent of all families in Virginia had incomes less than $5,000; 12.7 percent had incomes in the $5,000 to $10,000 range; and 30.17 percent had incomes in the $10,000 to $20,000 range. Based on the data available, this data set provides further support for the conclusion that lower-class families are overrepresented in incest samples. Likewise, affluent families, though not immune, are underrepresented. Over 20 percent of families in Virginia in 1979 had incomes in excess of $30,000 (U.S. Bureau of Census, 1983), while the available data indicates that only 3.5 percent of the incest reports came from families in this income range.

Of the 79 victims for whom data on the education variable was available, total lack of education ("none") was reported for 27 (34.2 percent) of their household heads. Another 14 household heads (17.7 percent) were high school graduates and 11 (13.9 percent) had achieved a partial high school education. In addition, 7 (8.9 percent) of the household heads had partially completed elementary school, while another 5 (6.3 percent) had a high school equivalent General Education Diploma (GED). Another 4 (5.1 percent) had elementary school educations; and 3 (3.8 percent) each had partial college, college diplomas, or postgraduate work. Finally, 2 household heads (2.5 percent) had technical school as their highest level of educational attainment.

Family Types

Marital status and type of household are analyzed in Table 7.6. There were 27 victims (16.6 percent) who lived in homes broken by a divorce or separation. However, a large majority of the victims (68.1 percent) were living with parents whose marriages were legally intact. A still larger proportion (73.6 percent) of the victimization occurred in households with two parent figures. Single-parent households, which made up approximately 12.6 percent of all households in the United States in 1978 (Melville, 1980), are only slightly overrepresented in this incest sample (12.9 percent).

"Living together" arrangements (1.2 percent) appear to be distinctly underrepresented in this sample. But, with the marital status recorded as "unknown" in 12.9 percent of the cases, the actual cohabitation percentage may be considerably higher.

Family Problems

Family problems are also presented in Table 7.6. Breakdowns are provided under two overall headings: "internal" (domestic or personality) and "external" (situational, job, financial, or legal). Marital problems and family discord, evident in 50.9 percent and 42.3 percent of the cases respectively, are the leading internal problems. Also

Table 7.6 Family Types and Family Problems

Item	Percent[a]	N	Item	Percent[a]	N
Marital Status			*Household type*		
Married	68.1	111	Two parent figures	73.6	120
Separated	11.7	19	Single parent	12.9	21
Divorced	4.9	8	Extended	3.7	6
Living together	1.2	2	Unknown	9.8	16
Single	1.2	2			
Unknown	12.9	21			
Internal Problems[b]			*External Problems*[b]		
Marital problems	50.9	83	Money management	15.3	25
Family discord	42.3	69	Job-related	9.2	15
Mental health	33.7	55	Criminal justice	8.6	14
Lack understanding of			Social isolation	6.7	11
child development	13.5	22	Insufficient income	6.1	10
Physical abuse of spouse	12.9	21	Housing problem	3.1	5
Alcoholism	12.3	20	Recent relocation	1.8	3
Physical health	11.0	18	Legal problem, civil	.6	1
Parent abused as a child	9.8	16	None or unknown	69.9	114
Heavy child care	6.1	10			
Drug dependency	5.5	9			
Over-zealous discipline	5.5	9			
Mentally retarded parent	1.2	2			
None or unknown	27.6	45			

Source: Compiled by the authors.
[a]Percentages may not sum to 100 due to rounding.
[b]Multiple scoring in some cases.

very frequent are mental health problems, indicated in 33.7 percent of the cases. At the next level of incidence, lack of understanding of child development (13.5 percent), physical abuse of spouse (12.9 percent), alcoholism (12.3 percent), physical health problems (11.0 percent), and parent abused as a child (9.8 percent) are all moderately frequent concomitants of the incest behavior. Heavy child care (6.1 percent), drug dependency (5.5 percent), and overzealous discipline (5.5 percent) are less frequent. It is noteworthy that mental retardation of one or both parent figures was evident in only 1.2 percent of the cases.

The leading external problem was money management (15.3 percent). Job-related problems (9.2 percent), criminal justice problems

(8.6 percent), social isolation (6.7 percent), and insufficient income (6.1 percent) were observed less often. Given their emphasis in the literature, the apparent infrequency of the latter two problems raises questions. The same is true for the reported frequency of housing problems (only 3.1 percent of the cases). These and related concerns will be addressed in the discussion section to follow.

DISCUSSION

Consistent with the sample reported in Chapter 6 and indeed virtually all published reports (Weinberg, 1955; Maisch, 1972; Renvoize, 1978; Justice and Justice, 1979; Julian, Mohr, and Lapp, 1980), father-daughter and step/foster father-daughter cases comprised the bulk of the sample, with father-daughter cases the most frequent. Also consistent with other studies (Meiselman, 1978; Weinberg, 1955; Finkelhor, 1979a), mother-son cases were by far the least frequent type of victimization within the nuclear family. Female perpetration was not negligible, however. Whereas only 3 mothers sexually abused their sons, 11 mother-daughter cases were included in the sample. In addition, 42 female victims and 12 male victims were abused by both parent figures.

The fact that the father-son and stepfather-son cases (a total of 22) outnumbered not only the mother-son but also the both parents-son cases (a total of 15 in the latter two categories) supports the conclusion (Finkelhor, 1979a; Rush, 1980) that the majority of male victims are homosexual targets. And, while Gordon and O'Keefe (1984) surmised from their research that incestuous victimization of males may not be problematic, its frequency in the present sample leads us to contend that it is a problem of considerable magnitude. The difference commanding this divergence of views may be a function of the time periods of the analyses. With our sample collected at a time when consciousness-raising about incest was becoming more widespread, the possibility of homosexual victimization of males may have become more salient to mandated reporting sources, and, probably more important, to the professionals who investigate the home after the report. Because most of the officially reported male victims of adult-child incest reside in homes where there are also female victims (Vander Mey and Neff, 1984), it is highly probable that most male victims are discovered by authorities while investigating a report of suspected female victimization.

The finding that the victim was one of the most frequent sources of the initial report replicates other research on this matter and, in fact, seriously understates the proportion of victim-initiated interventions, inasmuch as law enforcement officials, public school personnel, and other sources may contact the Child Protective Services only after the victim reports the abuse to them (Weinberg, 1955; Tormes, 1968; Julian, Mohr, and Lapp, 1980; Vander Mey and Neff, 1982).

"Parent or guardian" was the modal source of the report. Nevertheless, the percentage of cases reported by this source (15.3 percent) is far lower than one might expect considering the physical location of the activity and the difficulty of hiding recurrent dyadic absences within a nuclear family. This low percentage of reporting by a parent or guardian should not be attributed to the absence of a second parent figure. As noted earlier, adult-child incest typically occurs in a family with two parent figures in residence. The explanation lies instead in the psychological dynamics of the incestuous family. As noted in Chapter 4, there is typically an extreme father dominance in incest families, with the mother having assumed a passive martyr role including varying degrees of learned helplessness. In short, the father perpetrator is typically a dominating force in the family, often to tyrannical proportions, and the mother is too intimidated and psychologically defeated to initiate an action as confrontational as a report to the authorities. Even in the face of overwhelming evidence, she is more likely to deny the incest, often sincerely believing that it is not occurring (Cormier, Kennedy, and Sancowicz, 1973; Tormes, 1968; Meiselman, 1978; Herman and Hirschman, 1977). Further, the marked incidence of perpetration by both parents or parent figures (33 percent in this sample) suggests that, when the incest is acknowledged, the initially innocent spouse may be more likely to collude with the perpetrator than to report him.

The employment status, income source, and occupational distributions in this sample are largely consistent with the socioeconomic patterns noted in the literature. On the one hand, the facts are markedly at odds with the old stereotypic assumption, characteristically encouraged in polite society even today (Sagarin, 1977; Specktor, 1979), that a strong biological or social (Gordon and O'Keefe, 1984) aversion prevents incest except among the degenerate lower classes. More to the point, most incest families are not part of a submerged *lumpenproletariat*. The majority (66.3 percent in this sample) are families with income derived from employment, usually (60.1 percent in this sample) from full-time employment. This leads us to agree with Gordon and O'Keefe (1984) that incest is not typically a product of abject poverty, nor are incest perpetrators typically so disturbed or incompetent that they cannot function in the larger society. On the other hand, in this as in other incest samples (Riemer, 1940; Weinberg, 1955; Maisch, 1972; Sagarin, 1977; Specktor, 1979), the lower socio-economic levels are consistently and decidedly overrepresented.

Further, we would reiterate that when family factors were investigated, it was found that 12.9 percent of the household heads in this sample were unemployed. In addition, the leading external family problem was reported to be money management. Thus, while we can appreciate Gordon and O'Keefe's statement, we must at the same time keep in mind that employment and financial problems are not absent in many incest families.

An apparent exception to these stratification findings arises in the case of race. White families accounted for 84.3 percent of the cases in this incest sample. Blacks accounted for only 14.5 percent. Despite the lower socioeconomic skew of the sample, this is an over-representation of whites and an underrepresentation of blacks—even in comparison to the Virginia population as a whole. As of the 1970 census, whites accounted for 80.9 percent and blacks for 18.5 percent of the population of Virginia (U.S. Bureau of Census, 1972). This racial exception to the stratification picture of incest replicates previous studies (Julian, Mohr, and Lapp, 1980; Vander Mey and Neff, 1984), and some speculation as to its cause may thus be warranted. We would note that this may well reflect a real difference because extreme father-dominance, less frequent in black than in white families (Willie and Greenblatt, 1978), appears to be one of the most frequent correlates of adult-child incest (Weinberg, 1955; Maisch, 1972; Vander Mey and Neff, 1984; Gordon and O'Keefe, 1984). On the other hand, all or part of this finding may represent a reporting artifact, traceable to an actual and/or anticipated lesser responsiveness on the part of authorities to signs or complaints of incest in black families. Certainly, racial differences in incest, real and perceived, need to be more fully researched.

Counter to persistent stereotypes but consistent with findings reported in Chapter 6 and in previous studies (Justice and Justice, 1979; Weinberg, 1955), the majority (68.1 percent) of the victims lived with parents who shared a legal marriage. This finding should not, however, be construed as contradicting the assumption that marital instability increases the risk of incest (see Giles-Sims and Finkelhor,

1984). It should be recalled that in the sample described in the preceding chapter, 81 percent of the victims lived in families characterized by marital instability—not typically because a legal union was lacking at the time, but more frequently because there was no legal union earlier in the same nuclear family, or because at least one of the parents had experienced separation, divorce, or death of a spouse in the past. We concur with Finkelhor (1980a, p. 269) that courting mothers may place their children at risk for sexual victimization by bringing home sexually opportunistic males. In short, marital instability may be an historical antecedent in many cases, although a legal marriage in present by the time of the report (Vander Mey and Neff, 1984).

REPLICATED AND NONREPLICATED RISK FACTORS

This study replicates a high-to-moderate coincidence between adult-child incest and emotional disturbance exhibited by the child, behavior problems exhibited by the child, emotional neglect of the child by his/her parents, other sexual abuse suffered by the child, marital problems or other discord in the child's family, parental mental health problems, parental ignorance in the areas of child development, physical spouse abuse, alcoholism, physical health problems in the family, a parent who was abused as a child, unemployment, and money-management problems. We caution the reader to appreciate the fact that some of these correlates, especially in the case of victim characteristics, may be consequences of rather than antecedents to the the sexual abuse (Kaufman, Peck, and Tagiuri, 1954; Weber, 1977; Vander Mey and Neff, 1982). Other correlates (for example, physical abuse of spouse) may be neither cause nor consequence of the incest, but the result of a third variable (for example, extreme father dominance, a violent subculture, or a violent and unbonded community lacking social support networks) causally related to both.

Several risk factors emphasized in the literature may be less important than earlier studies, based on smaller samples, have suggested. In particular, the incidence of housing problems; insufficient income; heavy child care; social isolation; recent relocation; parental perception of the child as retarded, different, or otherwise abnormal; a child from an unwanted pregnancy; and a child with a juvenile court history are all quite low. These and similar factors have long been associated with a stress theory explanation for various types of family violence and deviance (Gelles, 1980). Their low incidence in this sample does not lend support to such a theory, at least not in relationship to adult-child incest.

Rather than a stress theory emphasizing the family's encounters with demanding problems, it may be that an ecological model focused on neighborhood and subcultural definitions of appropriate *responses* to stressors—as well as the presence or absence of neighborhood support networks, self-esteem, and other factors pertaining to one's resources for coping—is more germane to the problem. As Straus (1980, p. 83) has written in discussing the findings from another study, "Most of the parents in this sample who experienced a high degree of stress did *not* abuse a child. A critical question is brought to light by this fact. What accounts for the fact that some people respond to stress by violence, whereas others do not?" This same question must be asked of inappropriate sexual responses.

The answer may lie with ecological and resource factors as elaborated earlier in Chapter 5. Positive neighborhoods and supportive experiences in one's family of origin provide the individual with feelings of self-worth; security; trust; acceptance and identification with neighbors and extended kin, which facilitate prosocial responses; a sharing of resources; and a confidence that problems can be solved. Conversely, harsh, distant, and trustless relationships in one's family of origin, along with current entrapment in a "bad" neighborhood, are conducive to negative self-esteem; violent and counterproductive coping strategies (for example, alcoholism and denial), and a tendency toward negativism and fatalism.

In line with this argument, it should be noted that the concomitants to incest in this sample, consistent with a theory emphasizing stressors or encounters with demanding problems, do lend support to the importance of resource and coping patterns. The data do not include measures of neighborhood or extended family support networks, but marital problems, family discord, mental health problems, ignorance of child development, and physical abuse of spouse, all prevalent in this sample, are indicative of resource and coping deficiencies.

It should be underscored that none of the concomitants to incest identified in this study, no matter how frequent its coincidence with the abuse, can be confidently interpreted as a causal agent precipitating or contributing to the abuse. Longitudinal studies will be necessary to resolve etiological issues. Nevertheless, the present study can suggest some empirically grounded leads as to which variables are worthy of the major investment necessary for a longitudinal examination. Any of the risk factors addressed in this chapter might be causally related to incest, but only those with at least a moderately strong coincidence with the abuse offer much promise for theory building—and thus for effective treatment and prevention.

Issues of causality, theory, treatment, and prevention have not been central to this chapter, however. Our principal concern has been with the identification of recurring signs—risk factors that signal a likelihood of incest. While the approach taken in Chapter 6, a very comprehensive listing of possible signs, fills a need for increasing initial reports, the more critical approach of the present chapter can contribute to the task of the professional who must investigate the report. For example, such a reexamination of risk factors can contribute, with the assistance of clinicians, to a sharpening of the diagnostic instruments used in child-abuse investigations.

8

Treating Incest Victims and Their Families

Kinly Sturkie, Ph.D.

The primary purpose of this volume is to review, integrate, and extend the current body of knowledge regarding incestuous families. In the sociological and psychological traditions, the preceding chapters have attempted to comprehend and explain the phenomenological why of incest behavior. This chapter, in contrast, is primarily concerned with incest as a practical problem. It makes the shift to focusing on incest as an issue of social intervention rather than academic inquiry, thereby making the issues of genesis secondary to the issues of change.

It is important not to overdetermine the distinction between theoretical knowledge and practical knowledge. At the same time, it is also important to note that this chapter's purpose, and therefore its orientation to knowledge building, is somewhat different from that which is found in the earlier chapters. Knowledge regarding the genesis of a problem is usually developed by isolating factors that are common in many different instances of the problem. This knowledge is developed from what has been called a nomothetic perspective (Gelles, 1982). Clinical practice, on the other hand, often focuses on the differences that occur in several instances of the same problem. The knowledge used in this case is developed from what has been called an idiographic perspective (Gelles, 1982). The practical result is that some empirical and theoretical knowledge regarding incestuous families is simply not relevant for clinical purposes and may even be mis-leading. At the same time, some impressionistic data drawn from practice experience, although clinically relevant, might be of little value in a basic science paradigm.

This chapter begins by briefly reviewing those historical events that led to an intensified interest in treating incestuous families, em-phasizing the ways these events shaped the major treatment philoso-phies subsequently emerging in the field. A basic model for treating incestuous families is then presented, and the dilemmas inherent in the intervention process are described. In the concluding sections, specific techniques for assessing and treating child and adolescent in-cest victims and their families are detailed.

PROMINENT TREATMENT PHILOSOPHIES

In order to fully understand the major trends, themes, and, par-ticularly, controversies in the current treatment literature, it is im-portant to have a familiarity with the historical context within which this literature has evolved. Even the most cursory review of this litera-ture reveals marked variation in both general philosophies and specific techniques of intervention. The purpose of this section, then, is to explore the ideological as well as the clinical sources of that variation.

The idea of defining incest as a "therapeutic" problem can be traced to the very roots of Western psychiatry and the psychoanalytic tradition of Sigmund Freud (Rosenfeld, 1977). One of the important by-products of Freud's early work was the "psychologization" of what had previously been regarded primarily as anthropological or moral problems, thereby opening the door to the possibility of a thera-peutic approach to intervention. In this sense, Freud provided an in-valuable service to the field. However, as has been extensively docu-mented, Freud's particular conception of the causes and frequency of incest, and how one should respond to reports of it, spawned a destructive legacy that would influence the conduct of treatment professionals for many decades (Rush, 1980; Herman, 1981; and Masson, 1984). In brief, because of Freud's work, there has been a proclivity within the helping professionals to deny or discount allega-tions of incest when they have been reported. Freud's work also re-sulted in an equally destructive tendency to blame the victim for its occurrence when evidence of incestuous contact could not be ignored.

Following Freud's writings, both the theoretical and practice litera-ture relating to incest developed slowly through the 1930s, 1940s, and

1950s (see, for example, Bender and Blau, 1937; Sloane and Karpinski, 1942; Kaufman, Peck, and Tagiuri, 1954; and Weinberg, 1955). Interest in incest greatly intensified during the 1960s and 1970s, however, as the result of several directly related and coincidental events. First, both professional and public interest in the topic of child maltreatment was rekindled with the 1962 publication of the now classic paper, "The Battered Child Syndrome," by Henry Kempe and his associates (Pfohl, 1977). This article catalyzed a burgeoning interest in all forms of child maltreatment, eventually contributing to the exploration of child sexual abuse—what was later to be termed the "last frontier" in child abuse (Sgroi, 1975).

This same historical period also witnessed a revitalization of the women's movement and the emergence of an influential feminist literature. One critical aspect of this literature was its provision of a revisionist view of rape and other sexual crimes for which the victim had traditionally been regarded as at least partially culpable. This literature further served as an impetus for feminist reinterpretations of sexual crimes against other victims, including children, and a reexamination and criticism of the traditional approaches to intervening in these problems (Brownmiller, 1975; Herman and Hirschman, 1977; Rush, 1980; McIntyre, 1981; Herman, 1981).

Still another major historical factor influencing the intensification of interest in incest, particularly as a therapeutic problem, was the emergence of the family therapy movement. As interest in family therapy expanded through the late 1960s and early 1970s, virtually every problem that had been the province of traditional, individual psychiatry was reexamined and reinterpreted from a family perspective. This resulted in a considerable expansion of the incest treatment literature from a family perspective (see, for example, Lustig et al., 1966; Machotka, Pittman, and Flomenshaft, 1967; Raphling, Carpenter, and Davis, 1967; Eist and Mandel, 1968).

The emerging feminist and family therapy literatures were similar in that each developed primarily in reaction to traditional Freudian doctrines regarding the theory of the unconscious and the methods of clinical practice that derived from this theory. For example, both stringently objected to the idea that intrapsychic conflicts were somehow more important than current interpersonal reality for the purposes of understanding human behavior and emotional distress. The feminists seized upon and challenged what came to be known commonly as the "Freudian Cover-Up" (Rush, 1980)—the psychoanalytic assertion that clients who reported incidents of incestuous behavior were, in actuality, merely reifying the remnants of an Oedipal fantasy rather than reporting actual life events. Similarly, the family therapy field was developing as a challenge to the psychoanalytic preoccupation with the unconscious and many of its corollary clinical principles. These included the ideas that therapy should be reflective rather than directive, and that only one client should be seen at a time as a way of protecting the client's curative transference relationship with the analyst (Bowen, 1972; Haley, 1972; Napier and Whitaker, 1978).

Despite a shared antagonism to Freudian doctrine, the subsequent developments of the family therapy and feminist literatures were markedly different. While the family therapy field aspired to the development of a new epistemology for psychiatry, the feminists pursued broader social themes. While the family therapists sought to provide a new science of relationships, the feminists sought to provide a new ideology of relationships. As a result, the two groups moved away from Freudian doctrine in decidedly divergent directions, ultimately arriving at very different conclusions about the nature of incest and the most appropriate ways to intervene in incestuous families.

The family therapy field became steeped in concepts drawn from general systems theory, which emphasized part-whole relationships and ecological fields. Though there has never been a definitive family theory of incest per se (see Chapter 3), most family systems conceptions have been based in an epistemology of interrelatedness, and the view of the incestuous family that emerged from this literature included what might be termed the collusion doctrine. This doctrine was clearly articulated in a paper by Machotka, Pittman, and Flomenshaft (1967), for example, in which they suggested that "incest—as much as any other behavior, pathological or not—appears to be determined by an interpersonal triangle" (p. 98). This triangle, as these authors envisaged it, included an "incest-prone" father who was often sexually estranged from his wife, a wife who felt worthless as a woman and who was estranged from her daughter, and a daughter who vengefully perceived her mother as cruel and unjust. What resulted from this constellation of relationships was sexual intimacy involving the father and daughter which the mother simultaneously, collusively denied. A central element of this doctrine was that the mother's denial served as the "cornerstone in the pathological family system," simultaneously helping to create and to maintain the economy of relationships. That this perspective achieved the status of immutable doctrine in some practice settings cannot be overemphasized. For example, almost a decade and a half after the publication of Machotka,

Pittman, and Flomenshaft's paper, Faller (1981), in a major text on child abuse and neglect, asserted that "it is well known that incest is a family affair, not merely a situation of a father who molests his daughter" (p. 149).

The feminist analyses of family relationships, in contrast, were based on a doctrine of exploitation (rather than connectedness) and asserted that the "cornerstone" of the pathological family system was not the collusive mother but patriarchal society (McIntyre, 1981; Herman, 1981). From the feminist perspective, the collusion doctrine, like psychiatry's earlier concept of the schizophrenogenic mother, was simply the old misogyny dressed up in new clothes. Those conceptions of incest that attributed even partial culpability for the behavior to the nonparticipating mother were regarded as providing just one more variation on an enduring cultural theme in which women were somehow made responsible for the sexual conduct of men. From the feminist perspective, then, the family theorists were merely reinforcing a misogynistic ideology with the fabric of pseudoscience—much as the followers of Freud had done before them.

The competing family-system and feminist-revisionist conceptions of incest have been elaborated because each has left an indelible mark on the major philosophies of assessment and treatment evidenced in the current literature. The degree to which professionals regard incest as a familial conspiracy or a problem which the offender imposes on others in great part determines and organizes the therapeutic response. As Star (1983) has succinctly put it, in the fields of domestic violence and sexual abuse, conceptions of "problem-ownership" shape the methods and content of intervention. At one extreme, one encounters family-system approaches, which emphasize a relational focus, including an exploration of the "mutual needs" that are met by the incestuous behavior for all family members. In these approaches, the issues of collusion (by the mother) and complicity (by the daughter) are addressed explicitly (see, for example, Constantine, 1982; Aponte, 1982). At the other extreme, one encounters what have been termed the advocacy approaches, which focus more on the exploitive nature of the father or other offender's behavior and *his* need for therapy to resolve the sexual and social problems to which he has subjected others. These approaches tend to emphasize the importance of providing services that empower and protect the victim and other family members.

Mediating between these more extreme approaches, one will also encounter a more pragmatic amalgam that has been the primary extension of the child protection movement. Because of its historical link with the juvenile and family courts, the child protection approach has often relied upon judicial support while intervening in incestuous families. This is akin to the advocacy approaches. Because of the great professional prestige of the family therapists, however, many of their ideas have also been incorporated into the protective services literature. This tendency to emphasize certain aspects of the family-oriented approaches may also have been enhanced by the fact that professionals in the child protection field may simultaneously be involved in cases of physical child maltreatment in which both parents are perpetrators, the mother is the sole perpetrator, or there is clear collusion between the parents.

In the subsequent sections of this chapter, a variety of methods for intervening in incestuous families are described. As these methods are presented, it is important to keep in mind that they have been influenced as much by broad trends in psychiatry and society at large as they have been by the characteristics and functioning of the incestuous families themselves. The bridge between theory and actual practice is often tentative, inexact, and incomplete, though both practitioners and clients are still expected to cross it. The crossing is sometimes unsuccessful, however, due in part to the fact that the family is made to fit the conceptual bridge, rather than vice versa.

As a final introductory comment, the terms "incest" and "incestuous families" have been and will continue to be used freely throughout this chapter. At the same time, it is a central premise of the chapter that these terms, as such, are not clinically meaningful and may actually be counterproductive. As will be detailed in the next section, there are at least a half dozen different forms of father-daughter incest alone, some of which bear little or no resemblance to incest as it has often been stereotypically viewed. This recognition is critical for members of the service delivery community inasmuch as each of the major treatment philosophies presented earlier may be relevant only in response to particular forms of incest. This recognition should also caution us that certain forms of incest are treatable using the methodologies and technologies that are currently available, while others simply are not.

FORMS OF INCESTUOUS MOLESTATION

The very existence of the diverse treatment philosophies just reviewed leads one to conclude that either the proponents of each have selectively focused on different aspects of the same problem, or this problem exists in a number of distinguishable forms. Both conclusions are no doubt true. The previous section argued that the politics of therapy, as much as the families themselves, influence our conceptions of incest. In this section, the idea that the same problem exists in a variety of forms is explored.

Almost a decade ago, Roland Summit and JoAnn Kryso (1978) offered a typology of forms of child molestation that has immense heuristic value for the purposes of assessing and treating incestuous families. In particular, this typology emphasizes the special features of the various forms of incest, which require different tactics and strategies of intervention.

The major forms of incest as described by Summit and Kryso (1978) have been summarized in chart form (see Figure 8.1). (These were also described in Chapter 4.) Though there are multiple factors that distinguish these forms, Figure 8.1 is organized in terms of only two: the degree to which the relationship between the offender and the victim was primarily exploitive or predatory, and the degree to which the incestuous behavior was primarily motivated by issues of sexual arousal and gratification or by some other nonsexual needs.

Probably the most prominent form of incest is what Summit and Kryso term "true endogamous incest." A hallmark of this form of incest is that it "develops as a surprisingly subtle distortion of normal family relationships" (p. 53). Essentially, the father turns to his daughter for affection that he feels is unavailable to him from his wife or others. To use the language of Araji and Finkelhor (1985), the father experiences "emotional congruence" with his daughter, while simultaneously feeling "blocked" from achieving nurturance from other sources, particularly his spouse. Furthermore, as in the pattern most commonly described by Machotka, Pittman, and Flomenshaft (1967) and others, a systemic consequence of the father-daughter liaison is that the mother may be spared unwanted intimate contact with her husband. Sexual gratification, per se, is of a relatively low influence compared with feelings of nurturance and affection as initial motivating factors in this form of incest.

Though emotional congruity and blockage are fundamental in the initial genesis of this form of incest, it is clinically important not to assume that it is primarily these nonsexual motivations which maintain the behavior. As is axiomatic in the psychotherapy field, what maintains and perpetuates any symptom or problem behavior may have little to do with its original or ultimate cause. More specifically, a need for emotional connectedness may initially move the "incest-

Figure 8.1 Forms of Incestuous Molestation

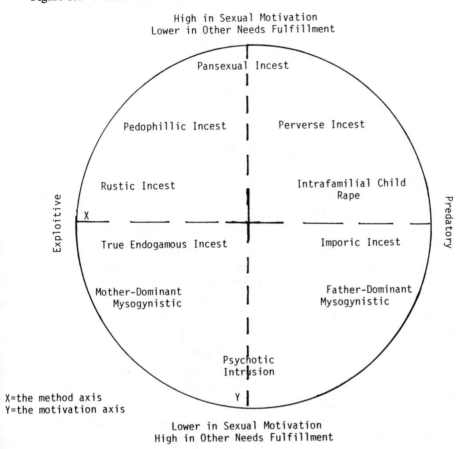

High in Sexual Motivation
Lower in Other Needs Fulfillment

Pansexual Incest

Pedophillic Incest   Perverse Incest

Rustic Incest   Intrafamilial Child
                       Rape

X

True Endogamous Incest   Imporic Incest

Mother-Dominant   Father-Dominant
Mysogynistic   Mysogynistic

Psychotic
Intrusion

Y

Exploitive

Predatory

X=the method axis
Y=the motivation axis

Lower in Sexual Motivation
High in Other Needs Fulfillment

Source: Provided by the author.

prone" father to eroticize his relationship with his daughter. However, the degree to which sexual gratification serves to maintain the relationship should not be underestimated.

Groth has often used a specific metaphor in addressing this issue.

Although it is a sexual offense, incest, like other forms of sexual assault, is not primarily motivated by sexual desire. The sexual offender is not committing his crimes to achieve sexual pleasure any more than an alcoholic is drinking to quench a thirst. Incest is sexual behavior in the service of nonsexual needs. It is the use of a sexual relationship to express a variety of unresolved problems or unmet needs in the psychology of the offender that have less to do with sensual pleasure and more to do with issues surrounding competency, adequacy, worth, recognition, validation, status, alienation, and identity. (Groth, 1982, pp. 227-28)

Groth's conception of incest is clearly psychodynamically based. Incest is viewed as an interpersonal expression of and resolution for intrapsychic conflicts. In this formulation, the sexual gratification that the father derives from the relationship is only a "secondary gain." Another explanation, however, is that the incestuous contacts are maintained primarily by the sexual gratification they afford. Regardless of why one initially drinks alcohol or eroticizes an adult-child relationship, each set of behaviors is clearly maintained by the immediate physiological and emotional changes which they produce. Each set of behaviors affords relief from current stress. Just as importantly, the behaviors make the user feel better emotionally and physically. These changes are only temporary, however. To further extend Groth's substance-abuse metaphor, many true endogamous offenders experience an erotic "hangover." After a molestation incident they are depressed about the behavior, are filled with self-loathing, and swear never to engage in the behavior again. Molesting becomes an uncontrollable compulsion, however, because of the relative availability of the victim and what Marques, Pithers and Marlatt (1984) acronymistically term "PIG": the problem of immediate gratification.

In short, every sexual behavior is multifaceted, meets a number of different needs, and has a variety of personal and social meanings (Simon and Gagnon, 1970; Finkelhor, 1984b). For the purposes of intervention, however, it is critical not to minimize the magnitude of the overtly sexual component of incest, even in cases of true endogamous incest in which other offender needs and other relational issues are clearly involved.

Another form of incest that is initially motivated by nonsexual needs is imperious incest. This form of incest is prompted by the offender's need to function as an emperor: to dominate and maintain absolute control over the other persons in his social sphere. The father in these families typically plays out "an incredible caricature of the male chauvinist role" (p. 57). He may require unyielding obedience from everyone, imprison his family by physically or emotionally isolating it, and regard everyone and everything as a personal resource that he can use at his whim with impunity. In one imperious incest family, for example, the family was required by the father to live in a remote rural area and the wife was refused "the privilege" of obtaining a driver's license, even though the father owned three cars, a motorcycle, and a van. This father usually molested his daughter while his wife made a two-hour trek, by foot, to the grocery store. In a less exaggerated case, an imperious stepfather, who ran a successful small business, molested all three of his wife's teenage daughters. He had run for several political offices, though he never won, and he ran "his" family with an iron fist. Though he confessed to the molestation, he continually expressed more concern over the fact that the revelation had hung "an ax over his head" than sorrow for his offenses. He was highly sensitive to the potential for abusive power, since he so consummately abused it himself. Thus, he greatly feared the power afforded his stepdaughters through the revelation (see Herman, 1981; Sgroi, 1982).

Some imperious fathers are also physically and emotionally abusive to their spouses and children. However, spousal and child maltreatment are also hallmarks of father-dominant misogynistic incest. Rather than being rooted in a more general need to control as in imperious incest, the offender's physical and sexual abusiveness in father-dominant misogynistic incest derives more specifically from a fear and hatred of women.

Stern and Meyer (1980), among others, have also noted that incest may occur in families that are mother-dominant. In these families, the father's feelings of inadequacy (which are also observed in other forms of incest) may be intricately linked with a fear and hatred of women. Unable to directly confront these feelings with his wife, the offender "passive-aggressively" directs them toward the daughter, who is simultaneously dominated and punished through the sexual liaisons. The degradation of her daughter also allows the father to punish his wife. In one family, for example, a misogynistic father who was a successful but highly anxious businessman began molesting his six-year-old daughter after his outgoing wife became widely known in the community for her work on behalf of abused and neglected children.

Children are also sometimes (though rarely) molested by family members who are psychotic and who might not engage in this behavior otherwise. In one case, a teenage son killed his mother, with whom he had been having intercourse. The mother had had a long history of major psychiatric problems, and the son, who was also psychotic, killed her in the belief that she was stealing his body fluids.

As indicated in Figure 8.1, several forms of incest appear to be primarily motivated *and* maintained by sexual issues. The first is pedophilic incest, in which the offender's principal object of sexual gratification is children. Of course, the majority of what have been termed fixated pedophiles (Groth, 1978) never marry because their sexual preoccupation with children and their accompanying emotional inability to relate to agemates hamper the possibility. Some pedophiles do marry, however, as a way of providing protection for themselves from the negative social sanctions imposed on persons who are not sexually normative, and as a way of achieving easy access to child victims. In one case, for example, a woman discovered after three months of marriage that her two daughters were being molested by their stepfather. She had chronic health problems that made her sexually unavailable to her husband, as well as physically and emotionally unavailable to her children. She reported the molestation immediately, however, and entered therapy distraught and self-blaming. Only later did she learn that her husband had been married twice before, each time to women with young daughters whom he had molested, and that he had molested other children as well.

Two other closely related forms of incest are what Summit and Kryso term perverse incest and child rape. A third category, pansexual incest, is also included. A hallmark of perverse incest is its "frankly erotic" quality: there is a seeming need for the offender "to go beyond the limits of acceptable sexual practice and to explore whatever is most forbidden" (1978, p. 56). In one case, for example, a father who eventually molested two of his three children initiated his older son into the world of sexual perversion by sticking his finger in a cat's anus (which the father found erotically exhilarating). Revelation regarding his sexual liaisons with his children came only after one of the children was observed engaging in the same activity. In another case involving bestiality, it was learned after a father impregnated his fourteen-year-old daughter that he had also been molesting his ten-year-old son and had been seen attempting to copulate with a dog. Throughout this period, he also maintained multiple daily sexual liaisons with his wife.

Most perverse incest offenders manifest what Summit and Kryso term "polymorphous perversity." The narrower category of pansexual incest is included to designate those offenders who simply don't distinguish between sex involving children and sex involving adults. They manifest a special form of "bi-" or "tri-sexuality" in which normal adult heterosexual contacts are enjoyed along with adult homosexual and pedophilic liaisons. These offenders are typically hypersexual, but do not always require perversity to achieve sexual gratification.

There are also cases of intrafamilial child rape, which seemingly occur in the absence of some of the other dynamics that have been described. In one case, for example, a stepfather who enjoyed getting high by "huffing" gasoline (inhaling the fumes) raped his six-year-old stepdaughter after returning from an evening with his friends. In other cases, child rape can also represent sexualized aggression and is closely related to imperious or misogynistic incest.

Finally, for some persons who live in remote areas, xenophobia, ambiguous rules regarding sexual contact, and limited sanctions result in incest (Meiselman, 1978). This has been termed rustic incest (Summit and Kryso, 1978).

Being able to recognize and distinguish these forms of incest is an essential practitioner skill for a number of reasons. First, as was noted earlier, there is a relatively poor prognosis for treating some forms using the traditional modes of psychotherapy, and those forms that are treatable may require different forms of intervention. Second, the recognition that there are multiple forms of incest brings the long-debated issue of maternal collusion into a different light. In some forms (true endogamous incest, for example), maternal collusion may be an issue; in some others (pansexual, for example), it usually is not. Also, as will be elaborated later, in some cases of incest the mother may be causally relevant in terms of explaining the problem but not morally responsible for the purposes of intervention. The confusion of these two issues has been a major stumbling block in the field. Third, as is discussed in the subsequent sections on treatment, understanding the form of incest in which a child has been involved helps the practitioner to better understand which treatment themes might be most relevant in psychotherapy with her.

DILEMMAS OF INTERVENTION

Because of the relatively brief period of time in which comprehensive treatment services have been available for the incest victim and his or her family, it is not possible to assert that there is a best way to provide services. It is something of a maxim in the field, however, that work with incestuous families, regardless of the form of incest, virtually always entails far more than the implementation of the traditional forms of psychotherapy (Giarretto, 1976; Burgess, Groth, Holmstrom, and Sgroi, 1978; Conte and Berliner, 1981; Sgroi, 1982). The very nature of the problem requires the cooperative involvement of professionals from a number of fields and disciplines, and the terms "treatment" and "intervention," therefore, typically connote a broad spectrum of services. It has also been widely recognized that the members of incestuous families commonly do not enter, or remain in, treatment voluntarily. Thus, the concept of "treatment" as it is used in this literature necessarily includes services that, at least initially, are provided coercively (see, for example, Giarretto, 1976; Giarretto, Giarretto, and Sgroi, 1978; Herman, 1981; Sgroi, 1982).

Though the community response to incest requires the utilization of a complex service-delivery system, there are a number of problems and dilemmas inherent in its use. The first and most obvious problem is related to the sheer size of this system and the level of cooperation and coordination necessary to make it work. Simply arranging a regular time and a place for professionals to get together to synthesize information and review problem-resolution strategies may be an insidiously complicated task. Many failures to successfully intervene in incestuous families are clearly attributable to problems and conflicts in the service-delivery system itself. Such conflicts undermine specific interventive efforts, drive treatable families away, and allow unmotivated families to terminate prematurely.

A still greater problem, however, relates to the fact that the basic philosophies of some of the major component agencies are often fundamentally different. To cite the most common illustration of these differences, when an incestuous father enters the service-delivery system, he is likely to encounter representatives of the child protective service field who inform him that it is in his child's and his family's best interest to accept full responsibility for the sexual contacts, eventually apologizing to the child. In this context, the child is defined as the victim and is accorded the principal benefits of treatment services. At the same time, however, the father may be simultaneously involved in the judicial system. Within this context, he may be encouraged by counsel to admit nothing, and it may even be argued that it is he who is the victim.

The other side of this dilemma, which is potentially more destructive, directly affects the child. It has long been recognized that it is necessary to take legal action in incest families to physically and emotionally safeguard the child-victim. Legal action is often essential to limit access between the offender and the victim and to establish access between the family and the service-delivery system. Again, it is not typical for an incestuous family to initiate and continue in treatment services without a community mandate. At the same time, however, the very act of obtaining this mandate through the judiciary, which is intended to protect the victim, may serve only to further victimize her, despite the fact that these problems are recognized and addressed in advance. Even though a number of innovative programs for preparing and handling child-victims have been developed, and even though procedures for obtaining child testimony have been modified (see Berliner and Stevens, 1976; Ordway, 1983), the essential dilemma the child faces remains unchanged as a function of philosophical and procedural differences between service components. Schultz (1973) suggested more than a decade ago that it may ultimately be more damaging for many children to be involved in a legal proceeding than not to be. Though there have subsequently been efforts to determine *how* child witnesses should participate within judicial proceedings, no empirically based criteria have been developed for helping to determine which children would best be served by *not* having to participate.

Though it is clearly of secondary importance, it must also be remembered that the process of negotiating the complex service-delivery system exacts a toll on the professional as well. It has been observed that large carnivores (such as tigers), who mark their territory by piddling along a perimeter, contort their faces when they broach the territory of another and encounter the other's scent. This contortion is called a Flehmen grimace. A similar grimace is also observed when professionals are required to cross professional boundaries and enter fields in which procedures, languages, and fundamental values may differ and outcomes may seem irrelevant, if not destructive. For example, members of the judicial system are sometimes horrified with the flimsy evidence on which some mental health professionals are willing to "convict" an alleged incest offender. Some mental health professionals, on the other hand, are sometimes angered and dismayed over the fact that hours may be spent haggling over technical issues during a judicial hearing when such issues may ultimately have only minimal bearing on the plight and wellbeing of a particular child.

METHODS OF INTERVENTION

A plethora of methods has been utilized to treat the members of incestuous families, both separately and collectively. Though a review of these methods reveals that few have been rigorously, empirically evaluated (Conte, 1984), some basic conventions regarding the intervention process have emerged as a result of practice experience, testimonial endorsement, and a small body of evaluative research (see, for example, Kroth, 1979). In a new field, practice experience and testimonial endorsement are important in that they keep practitioners from duplicating the same mistakes. At the same time, practitioners must be sensitive to what Gelles (1982) has termed the "Woozle Effect," in which generalities based on just a few cases are "woozled" around until they achieve the status of law.

The first task in the intervention process is for the professional to examine his or her own feelings about incest (Giarretto, 1976) and his or her willingness to accept and acknowledge that it has occurred (Sgroi, 1975). These tasks are difficult enough when discussing the problem of incest in the abstract; they are even more difficult when one deals with any particular child-victim and his or her family. It cannot be overemphasized that the leap from dealing with incest as a phenomenological problem to dealing with incest as an immediate practice problem is a monumental one. Incestuous families frozen in academic paradigms rarely resemble incestuous families actively negotiating their life courses, and even the most informed, experienced practitioner may find the business of recognizing, acknowledging, and dealing with incest to be far more complex and troubling than he or she ever anticipated.

The next step in the intervention process is the investigation of the incest allegation. The crucial tasks at this stage are establishing an initial working alliance with the victim and his or her family members, collecting and assessing data about the allegation, assuring the physical and emotional well-being of the victim, and dealing with the myriad crises associated with disclosure (Burgess, Holmstrom, and McCausland, 1978; McCarty, 1981; Topper and Aldrich, 1981; Sgroi, 1982; and Faller, 1984).

A major practical dilemma in the field involves the kinds of data that the professional must collect during the investigation. It is a common observation that because of the secretive nature of incest, there are rarely witnesses to it. Further, since incestuous offenders tend not to physically overpower their victims to achieve sexual access (they tend to exert psychological pressure or manipulate them), there are usually no unequivocal physical signs of abuse such as genital bruising or tearing. Even when these signs are present, medical professionals may be unwilling to state that adult sexual involvement with the child was necessarily the cause of the trauma. The practical result is that acceptance or rejection of the allegation must usually be based primarily on the verbal reports of the principals and other indirect, rather than direct, evidence.

One form of indirect evidence that professionals typically collect involves behavioral and emotional indicators. With the exception of precocious sexual knowledge and behavior, however, few of these indicators are unequivocally informative since many of these symptoms and behaviors may also be manifested by children undergoing other life crises and transitions (such as parental divorce). Practitioners may also look for other indicators such as "typical family dynamics" (for example, overinvolvement with and possessiveness of a daughter by her father in conjunction with marital estrangement). Again, however, these dynamics may be present in nonincestuous families, and there are also forms of incest in which these dynamics are essentially irrelevant.

Professionals typically attempt to resolve these investigatory problems by collecting and integrating several different kinds of data, culled using different methods and drawn from a variety of sources. These methods include using drawings, anatomically correct dolls, and other "play" procedures, polygraph examinations, collateral interviews, and the like. However, the necessity of having to rely primarily on indirect evidence means that the allegation is virtually always subject to dispute, and the struggle to establish proof—on both sides— inevitably further traumatizes the victim.

Another practical dilemma in having to rely on indirect evidence to support an allegation is that the offender may also use indirect evidence in an attempt to disprove the allegation. For example, incestuous fathers sometimes attempt to establish that they have not been sexually involved with their child by presenting psychological test results (such as an Minnesota Multiphasic Personality Inventory (MMPI) profile) suggesting that they are not capable of such behavior. Some judges allow these test results to be entered as evidence in judicial proceedings, even though it has never been empirically established that such paper and pencil tests can validly and reliably discriminate all forms of incestuous offenders from nonoffending fathers. Even when the limitiations of the testing process and the findings are openly acknowledged, the scientific authority implicit in this formal process may sway professionals and members of the community at large (jurors, for example), who are confused by the allegations anyway, or worse, do not want to believe them.

At a more philosophical level, as in any other activity involving the collection and interpretation of data, it is imperative that the practitioner be sensitive to the relative probabilities and implications of making what are commonly termed Type I and Type II errors. Stated simply, making a Type I error entails rejecting a true assertion. In the context of a child sexual-abuse investigation, this would involve failure to accept a child's allegation when, in fact, the behavior was occurring. In contrast, making a Type II error involves failing to reject a false assertion. Within the context of an incest investigation, this would mean accepting an allegation from a child when the behavior was not occurring.

Due to the Freudian legacy in psychiatry noted earlier, a tendency for adults to band together in self-protection (Summit, 1983), and the generally troubling nature of this problem, decades of professionals were more willing to make a Type I than a Type II error during incest investigations. The practical result was that countless children who made reports of incestuous molestation were not believed and, no doubt, countless others—anticipating the adult response—never reported their victimization (Finkelhor, 1979a; Meiselman, 1978). In more recent years, however, many child-oriented professionals have demonstrated a preference for risking a Type II error. This shifting orientation has been spurred by the recognition that children virtually never lie in this regard (a position which is empirically based) and a preference for erring on the side of the child if an error is to occur (a position which is value-based). However, this shift is more evident in particular segments of the field than in others. Again, the judicial system remains organized in such a way as to increase the likelihood of a Type I error occurring relative to the position of the child-victim. The judicial protections afforded persons accused of being incest offenders are critical and necessary. False accusations do occasionally arise, though it is virtually always a vindictive adult, not a child, who is the source of the accusation. For example, there are many special problems in investigating incest allegations that arise in the context of custody disputes (Rosenfeld, Nadelson, and Krieger, 1979; Mrazek, 1981). For the purposes of the initial investigation within the child protective services field, however, it is critical that the practitioner have both an orientation and a set of practice skills that decrease, in particular, the potential for a Type I error.

One final dilemma which may arise in the context of the investigation should be noted. This dilemma emerges when there is an attempt to pursue treatment without ever having a formal finding of sexual abuse. For example, the attorney for a father accused of incest may approach the "authorities" suggesting that his client is willing to acknowledge that there are problems in his family, and is willing to participate in court-ordered treatment. At the same time, however, the father may continue to deny the occurrence of any sexual behavior. In such cases, when treatment is ordered with no finding of

Figure 8.2 A Treatment Model for Incestuous Families

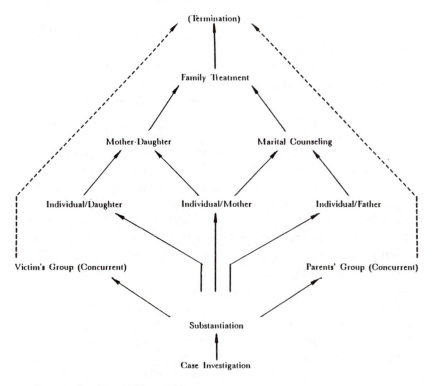

Source: Sturkie, 1983, p. 300.

abuse, the courts may be inadvertently colluding with an offender, and intervention often fails.

The third step in the intervention process involves the provision of ongoing crisis, psychotherapeutic, and other supportive and concrete services for the victim and her family. Families seeking reconstitution are usually involved in a variety of methods of therapy, and there are many alternative ways to sequence these methods. One sequencing model, developed by Giarretto, Giarretto and their colleagues (1976, 1978), has been widely duplicated in the field. In this model, family members are initially seen individually and then progress through meetings involving critical family dyads (see Figure 8.2). Treatment terminates with conjoint sessions involving all family members. Throughout the course of this progression, the members may also be concurrently involved in therapeutic, educational, and self-help groups.

Those incestuous families in which reconstitution is not a goal, or in which the father or father-substitute is not the offender, follow a slightly modified progression.

Psychotherapy with the members of incestuous families usually begins with individual therapy for a number of reasons. First, by definition, the members of these families have poor interpersonal boundaries. Working with members individually facilitates the development of these boundaries by maintaining—spatially and through the therapeutic process—a singular focus on that family member. Second, as will be elaborated, the issue of personal responsibility relative to the incest is usually at the forefront for all family members, whether each endeavors to disown responsibility or appropriately or inappropriately attempts to take it all. The complex and personally threatening task of exploring responsibility best takes place individually at first, particularly in those families in which the offender has been exonerated and the victim has been blamed. Also, during the period immediately following revelation, there may be tremendous pressure on the victim to withdraw the allegation. Since this pressure is so great and retractions so common, Summit (1983) has suggested that dealing with retractions should be regarded as a normal part of the intervention process. There may also be pressure on other family members, including the mother, to side with the offender against the child (Burgess, Holstrom, and McCausland, 1978). At this juncture, individual therapy is a much more emotionally neutral context than is family therapy for family members to work through their ambivalences, sort out their allegiances, and effectively problem-solve.

Many forms of group treatment have also been advocated for the family members (Kempe and Mrazek, 1981; Delson and Clark, 1981; Blink and Porter, 1982; Sturkie, 1983). Group treatment has been advocated for child and adolescent victims, for example, because the fact of having been molested often results in feelings of being "different." These feelings, in turn, may negatively impinge upon peer relationships. Structured contact and sharing with persons who have had similar experiences is therefore beneficial. The group experience is also more "open" and less "secretive" than individual therapy which, with its shroud of confidentiality and the adult therapist being one-up in a power relationship, contains many of the same elements as the incestuous relationship (Herman, 1981). Adjunctive group therapy can therefore serve to "balance" the secretive nature of individual treatment.

Group treatment is also utilized with offenders. As was noted earlier, a parallel has often been drawn between child molestation and substance abuse. Each involves a control disorder which cannot be cured, but which can be managed through lifelong abstinence (Herman, 1981; Groth, 1982). Thus, a self-help, group-based model such as that developed by Alcoholics Anonymous has been used with incest offenders. Within these groups, mutual support is provided among members, while the minimization and denial that are hallmarks of both problems is simultaneously confronted.

A group treatment approach with mothers has also been advocated, since the group affords a new network for these persons, who may be socially isolated. The women in such groups can also share and problem-solve with one another in a cooperative fashion. This experience may represent a major opportunity for women whose feminine relationships have often been markedly competitive (Herman, 1981; Sgroi, 1982).

Regardless of the degree to which one embraces the collusion doctrine, it can be acknowledged that "incestuous behavior is not likely to occur when parents enjoy mutually beneficial relations" (Giarretto, 1976, p. 151). Thus, following individual therapy, marital work is imperative in cases of incest in which the family is seeking reconstitution. This therapy can be either problem-oriented—focusing, for example, on the sharing of affection, sexual functioning, and the like (Justice and Justice, 1981)—or more growth-oriented, dealing with the typical problems in living that married couples encounter. The primary goal of this therapy is the general enhancement of the marital relationship and the "de-triangulating" of the child-victim.

Estrangement between the mother and child-victim is also often observed in most forms of incest (Herman and Hirschman, 1977). Therefore, before a successful full or even partial family reconstitution can occur, these feelings must be addressed through mother-daughter dyad meetings. These meetings are the most crucial element in developing a workable, ongoing child-protection plan, particularly in imperious and misogynistic, father-dominant families.

The process of psychotherapy typically concludes with family therapy. It is crucial to keep in mind that premature conjoint sessions in some forms of incest (for example, imperious and father-dominant misogynistic) have a monstrous potential for thwarting the change process. The father or other offender's willingness to accept full responsibility for eroticizing the relationship is a sine qua non for these meetings. Following his acceptance of this responsibility through a therapeutic apology to the victim, these sessions can begin to address the myriad other practical and emotional problems associated with the development and maintenance of the incest behavior.

SPECIFIC ISSUES IN ASSESSMENT AND TREATMENT: THE INCEST OFFENDER

Nowhere is the ongoing controversy on the causes of child sexual abuse more clearly manifested than in the literature on treating the incest offender. Since incest is variously viewed by some professionals as a sexual problem to be grouped with rape and the other paraphilias, by others as a form of family violence to be grouped with spousal abuse and physical child maltreatment, and by still others as but one of many different symptoms that a dysfunctional family system can generate, it is not surprising that the forms of intervention which have been advocated for incest offenders are radically different.

Therapeutic responses to incest have proliferated in the field in recent years, based on psychodynamic, behavioral, social learning, family therapy, and biomedical formulations. These include the more traditional therapies, which seek to promote self-understanding; educational programs, which attempt to enhance the offender's empathy for the victim and help him better understand the effects of his behavior; skills-training approaches, in which the offender learns how to appropriately ask for attention and affection and deal with rejection; and approaches intended to change and reduce patterns of deviant sexual arousal (Silver, 1976; Becker, et al., 1978; Marshall and Barbaree, 1978; Margues, Pithers, and Marlatt, 1984; and Frank and Watson, 1985). These approaches are obviously varied, focusing in some cases almost solely on the offender's sexual thoughts and behaviors, and in other cases on the needs and deficits that are presumed to underlie the thoughts and behaviors. What unifies the approaches, however, is the attempt to provide both offender treatment and social control. Intervention strategies also include what Money (1984) has termed "penile incarceration" in prisons and in psychiatric treatment programs, and biomedical procedures including psychosurgery, castration, and chemotherapy (Heim, 1981; Heim and Hursch, 1979; Schmidt and Schorsch, 1981; Spodak et al., 1977; Star, 1983; and Money, 1980). Before reviewing some major themes in offender intervention, it might be useful to first examine in more detail some of the current ideas and research findings that have spawned these diverse approaches.

As was suggested earlier, one of the consequences of the far-ranging influence of family conceptions of incest has been a tendency for some practitioners to regard incest as being a phenomenon distinctly separate from the other pedophilias (Conte, 1984). An expanding body of theoretical and empirical literature suggests, however, that this presumption might not be fully correct. At the very least, there has been a trend in more recent years to view the various forms of child sexual abuse in a more unified way (Finkelhor, 1984b).

The press for a unified approach to examining and treating sexual offenses toward children has developed from a number of diverse sources. First, it has commonly been observed that there is a disproportionately high rate of male offenders in incest cases (Meiselman, 1978). It has also been noted that this difference is consonant with the disproportionately high rate for males of all other forms of psychosexual deviation as compared with females. As Money and Ehrhardt (1972) have observed, "the majority of the paraphilias are found exclusively as distortions of the male's gender identity, not the woman's" (p. 148).

Second, it has been posited that this disproportion stems only partially from the politics of family life and the complexities of human social development. It is significant that the processes through which males and females develop their gender identities are asymmetrical. Males must negotiate a more complex developmental course and there is, therefore, the potential for a greater number of "errors." Of equal significance, however, is the fact that the asymmetry in social development parallels asymmetry in anatomical development. Masculinity is additive, and, physiologically, it is also more difficult to create a male than a female (Money, 1980). In short, both asymmetries work against the male. As Money and Ehrhardt (1972) bluntly put it, "Nature makes more mistakes in males." The subsequent outcome is a condition that they term the "psychosexual frailty of the male" (Money and Ehrhardt, 1972; Money and Tucker, 1975; Money, 1980). The behavioral consequence of this frailty is that males consistently breach sexual norms, including prohibitions against incest, far more often than females do. It has also been noted that this is not simply a human phenomenon. Frances and Frances (1976) have emphasized that virtually all bonding-motivated animals have evolved an incest barrier. Even when this barrier is breached in subhuman species, it is virtually always the male who breaches it. Incestuous behavior, then, may be the product of a primitive propensity most evident in males that simultaneously exacerbates and transcends the complexities of modern life.

It has also been demonstrated experimentally that incestuous fathers may not be as different from other child sexual offenders as the family systems theories imply. Abel and his collaborators (1979), for example, compared the sexual arousal patterns of a group of institutionalized male heterosexual pedophiles with a group of heterosexual incestuous fathers. The subjects listened to seven taped vignettes involving varying degrees and kinds of sexual contact between a female child and a male adult. The sexual arousal of these two groups was measured using self-report and physiological response. Based on these measures, the researchers found that the arousal pattern of the incestuous fathers was "identical to that of the heterosexual pedophiles . . ." (p. 19). The researchers further speculated that ". . . it may be that sex with a girl relative is primarily motivated by their (the offender's) sexual preference for young girls, and that the reported distorted family dynamics are the aftermath of the incestuous offender's attempts to involve himself with the most readily available young female, his own daughter, stepdaughter, etcetera" (p. 19). In related research, Panton (1979) compared the MMPI profiles of a group of institutionalized heterosexual pedophiles with a group of incest offenders. He found no significant differences between the two groups except on a social introversion-extroversion scale. Again, the factor that appeared to distinguish the two groups was not the nature of their sexual interest but a variable relating to partner availability.

The research further suggests that incest fathers, often presumed to be deprived of sexual access to their wives, have a variety of potential sexual outlets but still choose their children (Groth et al., 1978). Goodwin and her colleagues (1983) also studied a cohort of ten grandfathers who molested their granddaughters and found that eight of the ten had a history of molesting other children. As was noted earlier, some offenders even have ongoing sexual relations with animals during the period in which they are molesting their children.

These findings underscore the point made earlier that though sexual gratification is only secondary in the genesis of some forms of incest, it is clearly primary in others. They also emphasize the fact that family dynamics are essentially irrelevant in some forms. It is therefore critical that an accurate assessment of the kind of incest be made before one embarks on intervention.

In addition to understanding his motivation for the incest, a comprehensive assessment of the offender includes a full exploration of his psychological and social functioning (Abel et al., 1979; Groth, 1978, 1979, 1982). In the initial stages of intervention, these issues include understanding the current emotional, physical, and sexual threat that he poses to his victim and determining the form of intervention, if any, he is most likely to benefit from. During this period particular attention is focused upon the nature and duration of the sexual involvement, the overall quality of the offender's relationship with the victim, and the method or methods employed for gaining and maintaining the victim's compliance. As was implied in the earlier discussions, factors often associated with a higher probability for recidivism include the occurrence of bizarre or ritualistic sexual behavior during the molestation, the use of violence or the threat of violence to gain compliance from the victim, a history of other criminal and predatory behavior, a history of sexual involvement with other children, and a history of substance misuse, among others (Groth, 1982).

The central theme in any psychotherapy with the incestuous offender is his taking full responsibility for the sexual contact. In some cases, the offender eroticizes normal child behavior. In others, he responds to what he perceives to be provocative behavior. In still others, he may distort a request for affection into an invitation for sexual involvement. In any case, "the major clinical issue . . . is not what the victim allegedly did but how the offender behaved" (Groth, 1982, p. 234).

Summit and Kryso (1978) have elaborated this point, noting that even in cases of true endogamous incest

> the father is the key to the disturbed dynamics and is responsible for the choice to eroticize the relationship with the daughter. Whatever else is said in sympathy with his motivations and regardless of the contributions of the wife and daughter, that responsibility must be emphasized in any therapeutic encounter.

The genuine assumption of responsibility and its expression in the form of a therapeutic apology is often difficult to achieve in certain forms of incest, and the practitioner should, therefore, not be too impatient to achieve them. For example, if the incest behavior derives primarily from a hatred of women or a more general desire to dominate and control those in one's intimate sphere, the offender may continue to regard his behavior as justified. An ongoing problem in "therapy" with some character-disordered offenders is that the therapist (or other members of a therapy group) might simply teach the offender what he is supposed to say. The strength of any apology must therefore be viewed within the context of the nature of the offense. In the case of pedophilic incest, the offender may feel very close to the victim and the apology may be genuine. Nonetheless, there is still a high probability of recidivism.

Ongoing therapeutic involvement with incestuous fathers must also focus on self-management and impulse control and the ways these are manifested within the context of therapy, within the workplace, and at home. Silver (1976), Herman (1981), and Marques, Pithers, and Marlatt (1984), among others, emphasize the importance of the therapist not allowing even the most microscopic behaviors that might be indicative of poor self-management (for example, being late or missing therapy sessions) to go by without being acknowledged and addressed. As in therapy with other client groups, process issues duplicate and intermingle with content issues and must remain a focus of intervention. If a father in an imperious family attempts to decide that non-involved siblings don't need to come to the sessions, or if a father in a true endogamous family attempts to sit by his daughter and not with his wife, or if the father in a mother-dominant misogynistic family attempts to avoid dealing with a female therapist, these issues immediately become grist for the sessions inasmuch as they duplicate the problems that helped create the incest.

Since some forms of incest are primarily motivated by nonsexual desires, and since many offenders have had more or less normal heterosexual relations for some period in their lives but have regressed to child molestation under stress, therapy must also be supportive and explicitly address these stress issues. Manifestations of poor stress management, for example, substance misuse, may be indicative of a weakening ability to abstain from molestation. Marques, Pithers, and Marlatt (1984), for example, have developed a relapse prevention program that is intended to help the offender monitor and manage his own functioning and capacity for recidivism.

Still another issue to be addressed in therapy with offenders is their own perceptions of the causes of the incestuous behavior. As has been noted, some offenders feel extremely guilty following each molestation incident but continue to compulsively engage in the behavior. Though the exploration of the causes of this compulsion is not sufficient to end the behavior, many offenders view this as a necessary task in intervention. Self-exploration and understanding lead to renewed self-trust, which is critical since many offenders trust themselves as little as their victims do.

Whatever theme is being pursued, because of the nature of this problem, more directive forms of therapy may ultimately prove to be more efficacious than reflective approaches. For example, instead of simply discussing the offender's perceptions of the causes of the abuse within the therapy sessions, the therapist may ask the offender to make an audio tape of his discussing this issue with his wife at home. The therapist and the offender may then listen to and discuss the tape in a subsequent session. Not only do tapings and other directive forms of intervention help the therapist monitor important offender relationships; they also emphasize that what happens outside of the therapy room is at least as important as what happens within it.

As was noted earlier, regardless of the form of incest, the issues of sexual arousal and gratification have to be addressed explicitly in treatment. However, these issues are paramount in those forms of incest that are more heavily anchored in sexual needs (see Figure 8.1). In these cases, deviant sexual arousal patterns should be reduced by means of satiation procedures; thought-stoppage and fantasy interruption techniques; methods for avoiding deviant erotic stimuli (such as pornography) and normal stimuli to which the offender responds deviantly; and aversion procedures (such as exposure to noxious odors while engaging in fantasies involving the problem behaviors). It is also emphasized that exploratory research is currently being carried out on the use of pharmacological interventions with sexual offenders. Money (1980, 1984), for example, has described the use of medroxyprogesterone acetate and suggests that it has met with some success in preliminary field testing. Psychiatry witnessed the rise of the family theories of schizophrenia (Boszormenyi-Nagy and Framo, 1965), only to discover that therapy approaches based primarily on verbal exchange simply were not adequate in and of themselves to manage this illness. Chemotherapy and the psychotherapies are now commonly used adjunctively in the treatment of schizophrenia. It seems inevitable that psychopharmacological approaches will eventually be used adjunctively in the treatment of certain forms of incest (pedophilic, perverse), if not most of them. It might also be noted that a secondary effect of using chemotherapy approaches is that the very process of intervening in this way further underscores the issue of problem ownership.

SPECIFIC ISSUES IN ASSESSMENT AND TREATMENT: THE INCEST VICTIM[1]

As is elaborated in Chapter 3, being sexually abused within one's family typically has a number of grave emotional and behavioral im-

---

[1] This section includes updated and revised material that was originally published in Kinly Sturkie, 1983, "Structured Group Treatment of Sexually Abused Children," *Health and Social Work* 8 (Fall): 299-308.

plications for the child or adolescent victim. To be sure, certain symptoms are so commonly encountered in work with these children that they warrant special attention by the professional. It is also emphasized, however, that constellations of symptoms do vary considerably from victim to victim depending on the precipitants for the incest, the nature and duration of the sexual contact, the victim's sex, the victim's age and level of cognitive and emotional development, the nature of the victim's relationship to the offender, and other variables. Particular victims may also not experience distress in particular areas, though one should never assume that a child is undistressed simply because symptomatology is not readily observable. It is the nature of the problem that some victims learn to function as if everything is alright when, in fact, it isn't.

The purpose of this section is to describe some of the common treatment issues confronting the child and his or her therapist, and some of the techniques in the field that are used to address these issues. For the purpose of this discussion, these issues are dealt with under the headings of emotional well-being, behavioral well-being, and physical well-being. These are also presented in a checklist form in Appendix I.

Issues of Emotional Well-Being

Supporting the Child and the Allegation

Despite the fact that children rarely fabricate reports of sexual abuse, and despite the increasing attention this problem has received in the popular media, children who report incestuous relationships are often not believed by significant others, including their mothers, even after full revelation to community agencies. A principal issue of therapeutic involvement with a child, then, entails providing acceptance and support for both the child and her allegation.

One may begin to broach this theme in either individual or group treatment with an exploration of how it feels to be believed or not be believed, to discuss whose fault it is when a parent does not believe, and to examine the social, psychological, and economic reasons why a parent might not believe. Children often display an unexpectedly sophisticated understanding of these reasons. Therapy can also provide a context for the victims to vent their feelings of frustration and bewilderment when they have not been believed.

In a therapy group, victims may also be encouraged to develop scenarios in which parents (also played by children) are approached with an allegation of sexual abuse. The "parents" may then respond appropriately and inappropriately to the child's report. This activity is intended to help victims contribute to the development of their own protection plan by examining with the therapist and the other group members the alternative actions that are available to them depending on parental response (Grando et al., 1979).

Alleviating Feelings of Guilt and Responsibility

Children are notoriously egocentric. They tend to blame themselves for major disruptions in their social existence including events such as parental divorce, death, or even illness, for which they bear no responsibility. It is not surprising, then, that victims of incest often self-prescribe blame. This problem is exacerbated by the fact that the offending father may blame the child for their sexual contacts. For example, he may attribute his advances to what he regards as provocative clothing or behavior on a daughter's part, or he may distort a child's normal wishes and invitations for affection as being invitations for sexual intimacy. He may then point to the child's behavior as the cause of the intimacy. These excuses may seem absurdly flimsy after revelation, but as Summit (1983) has pointed out, since no child can be prepared for the fact of sexual abuse, he or she will usually accept the adult construction that is offered for it.

Within the context of treatment, the themes of guilt and responsibility may be dealt with in a variety of ways. First, through education and discussion, child-clients can repeatedly be given the explicit message that if an adult and a child are engaged in sexual activity, it is the adult's sole responsibility (Finkelhor, 1979b). One may also discuss with victims whether or not they have been accused of being seductive and reassure them that this accusation is only a mechanism by which adults protect themselves and avoid their own responsibility.

The revelation of incest often precipitates a division of loyalties within families in which the significant others in the child's life take conflicting positions on who should and who should not be supported (Burgess, Holmstrom, and McCausland, 1978). The child, by virtue of having had the courage to report or substantiate the molestation, may feel responsible for creating conflict in her nuclear and extended families. Therefore, victims may be encouraged to express the feelings associated with these conflicts, particularly the fear of abandonment. In a group setting, these feelings may often be universalized.

A number of perpetrators are very gentle with their victims, sexualize their relationship with the victim very gradually, and begin the victimization process when the child is extremely young, naive, and unsophisticated. For some victims, then, the experience is not traumatic, and may even by physically pleasurable. When the revelation of the abuse occurs, however, the victim may feel guilty regarding the physically pleasurable aspects of the abuse due to the responses of significant others and professionals. To deal with these feelings of guilt, the therapist may employ a technique developed by Rosensweig-Smith (1979). The child-victim is informed that sexual arousal is a physical response that one's body makes occur automatically. An analogy can then be made to the body's response to tickling. The victim is reminded that if she is tickled, she will probably laugh and respond physically in a number of ways (jerk, twitch) whether she wishes to or not. In the same way, even after one learns that sexual activity involving children and adults is not right, one may still find it sexually arousing. Since this response is automatic, it is not something about which one should feel guilty.

Some children also express guilt or remorse for not having been better able to defend themselves—for not fighting, for example, or for not having said no. These children are supportively given the message that it is extremely hard for a child to say no to an adult, especially when there is the possibility of physical danger or she is threatened with the withdrawal of love or security. The therapist then endeavors to help the child externalize these feelings, in other words, to redefine them as anger and to express them as such.

Porter, Blink, and Sgroi (1982) also note that incest victims may experience guilt over the special status that they may have held in their family, or for special favors, privileges, or material items that accrued to them as confounding factors in the secrecy pact. This guilt, too, must be addressed if present, concurrently focusing on related disruptions in sibling relationships.

Of course, guilt and responsibility are sophisticated concepts that are even difficult to deal with in therapeutic work with adults. The concepts are therefore extremely illusive in child therapy. When broaching these themes with children, it is often necessary to use concrete metaphors. For example, if in a therapy group a child offers comments that suggest she feels responsible for emotionally carrying her parents, she might be asked to physically carry the therapist across the room. The members of the group can then be asked to discuss with one another what this exercise means.

Addressing the Bonds of Secrecy

> She was ready to die at any time, she said, because what men and boys thought about her and tried to do to her made her so ashamed. One of the first things she was going to do when she got to heaven, she said, was to ask somebody what was written on her face and why it had been put there. (Kurt Vonnegut in *Deadeye Dick*)

It is a cruel irony that victims of child sexual abuse, especially incest, are often forced into secrecy regarding the abuse experiences while at the same time they fear that peers and others can "magically" recognize them as victims. The fear that others may know may either lead the child to withdraw from peer relationships or, in an attempt to master the anxiety associated with being recognized, inappropriately divulge the details of her victimization. In one case, for example, it was arranged for two sisters who had been molested by their stepfather to go to summer camp for two weeks. The first hour she was in her cabin, the younger sister announced (much to the chagrin of her older sister) what had happened to her. This not only affected her peer relationships, but also led to enhanced feelings of responsibility when her camp counselor accused her of bragging about the incidents. In fact, this was her inept way of attempting to deal with her feelings of differentness. Another principal goal of treatment, then, is to reinforce and support the revelation of abuse (having told despite being cautioned not to), while at the same time emphasizing that the child has the most power to determine who outside the family and the treatment setting will know or not know about the abuse.

Learning to appropriately discuss the secret is accomplished in a group setting by having each participant discuss her own abuse experiences only when she is ready. In addition to practicing appropriate sharing, this serves to universalize and, therefore, destigmatize the abuse for the participants.

Due to pressure from the perpetrator to keep the abuse a secret, victims often develop what may be termed a *cover-up deportment*. Stated simply, a cover-up deportment is a child's having learned to act as if everything is fine when, in fact, it is not. Unfortunately, this survival skill may lead to a general inability to identify and express particular feelings. In either an individual or group context, then, a number of games may be employed in which the children are encouraged to express, label, and even exaggerate feeling states. The utilization of these games is intended to promote general emotional growth in addition to helping break the bonds of forced secrecy required by the cover-up deportment.

A fundamental question relevant to all psychotherapy with children is "when is enough, enough?" Deciding when to terminate is always a difficult decision, but it is even more complex in relation to victims of incest, who may manifest the cover-up deportment or pseudomaturity. Child therapy is often terminated when the child is exhibiting no problematic behaviors or is voicing no concerns. Some incest victims may do neither but still be experiencing a number of unresolved conflicts. Both child-victims and their parents may also assert that having to participate in therapy only serves to keep the wounds open. Though there are situations in which children leave therapy because their parents have not adequately worked through their own issues (Sgroi, 1982), there are also situations in which it is more beneficial for the child to move on and interminable therapy may actually be counterproductive. Again, these are very difficult clinical judgements, which must be made on a case-by-case basis.

Finally, a number of incest victims report experiencing nightmares and troubling secret thoughts (including rational and irrational fears) that derive from the abuse experience. Therapy, therefore, may also employ sharing games. In a group, for example, each child can identify a trusted individual, both within and outside of the group, with whom she can share and discuss troubling thoughts if they should arise. These sharing games enhance peer relationships as well as helping to facilitate the child's identifying a trusted adult or adults who can be made a part of the protection plan.

Anger

As has been noted, the requirement that the victim counterfeit her feelings due to pressure by the perpetrator may lead to a general inhibition or inappropriate expression of affective content. Though feeling states are often dealt with throughout the course of treatment, repressed anger is so prevalent in sexual-abuse victims that particular time should be set aside for the purposes of exploring this anger and granting permission for and facilitating its expression when present.

It is important to explore potential anger at the offender and, when relevant, the mother or other significant caretaker who the child may believe abandoned her. A number of writers have noted that incest victims are frequently more angry at their mothers than they are at the offender, even when the offender is their father (Herman, 1981; Meiselman, 1978). The anger derives from the child's inference, correct or not, that her mother failed to take protective action though she knew of the molestation or should have been able to recognize cues that the victimization was occurring. Though there has been considerable debate about this issue in the literature in recent years, whether or not mothers should have been able to identify the symptoms of abuse, for the purposes of intervention, is somewhat irrelevant. Though in some cases the therapist may help the child appropriately redirect and refocus her anger, even misdirected anger is real and it is beneficial to the child to help her express it. Role playing what the child would like to say to her mother also helps prepare her for the later, critical mother-daughter dyad sessions.

Active expression of the anger toward the perpetrator is accomplished through a variety of techniques. First, as has been noted, a number of the victims knew that they were not physically or psychologically capable of saying no to the perpetrator but later expressed remorse for not having been better able to protect themselves. In the context of a group, then, the children may be encouraged to scream what they would like to have said to the perpetrator. The wish to fight back is also actualized through the hitting of pillows and yelling "no!". In addition to allowing the victims to vent their anger, this symbolic control of the perpetrator is intended to enhance the child's sense of body integrity and safety.

At the same time, it is critical not to require the child to be angry if she is not. Some victims are romantically infatuated with the perpetrator and may experience no anger even though the relationship is exploitive and extractive. Furthermore, the relationship may be sexually pleasurable for some children or the only source of nurturance they believe is available to them. As Herman (1981) has emphasized, it is critical that anger not be presented as the only "innocent" response.

Though helping incest victims to recognize and express anger is often an important theme in treatment, the practitioner will also occasionally encounter adolescents who are so angry regarding their abuse that it is debilitating. The therapeutic task in this case is to help the client find a way to live with this anger. For example, one older adolescent remained furious with both her parents for years following the revelation of her abuse because they had simultaneously abandoned her and minimized the significance of the molestation that she had experienced. On several occasions she confronted them, but rather than provide her with the apology she so desperately wanted, they simply told her to stop dwelling on it. This further intensified her anger, which, at the same time, she thought was only making her situation worse. Since it was evident she could not give up her anger, even though it was a problem for her, her therapist reframed the anger by encouraging her not to give it up. To give up the anger, the therapist reasoned, would be to follow her parents' directive to quit dwelling on the problem. In this way, the disturbing anger was made acceptable.

Powerlessness

Children who have been sexually abused have often been physically overpowered, or psychologically intimidated, and have had their trust in adults exploited. These experiences may lead to feelings of helplessness and lack of control which, if not confronted, may persist for many years. A major goal of treatment, then, is to empower the victims.

A first step in the empowerment process in a group setting is to use the participants to help each other identify various areas of their lives in which they have control. This may include, for example, reviewing that they have a significant amount of power in determining who knows and who does not know about their sexual experiences. The group participants may also be encouraged at an age-appropriate level to examine the quality of their relationships in general, including how they make contact with others, whether they are quiet or outgoing, and so on.

Issues of Behavioral Well-Being

Maladaptive Behavior with Peers and Adults

Power is a double-edged sword, and it is not uncommon for children who have been victimized to develop certain survival skills that were adaptive in one setting but are maladaptive and self-defeating in others. Some children, for example, have learned that the only way they can survive with adults is to be what is commonly termed "manipulative" and "deceptive." The utilization of a supportive relationship or a group process aids in the examination and confrontation of inappropriate behaviors. Occasionally contingency management and other behavior modification procedures may be needed for the development of new, prosocial behaviors.

Sexual Precociousness

Children who have been sexually exploited often learn to relate to adults only in sexual ways. Adults may label this behavior seductive, but as Burgess and Groth (1980) have pointed out, it is more appropriately characterized as "sexually stylized behavior." Victims may engage in precocious sexual activities with classmates, friends, or siblings or may approach adults in a sexual manner. Thus, both individual and group treatment may be utilized to educate victims about what is appropriate and inappropriate touching within the family and without. In this connection, group members, for example, may discuss how to express affection without making sexual contact. Issues of precocious dress and the overuse of make-up may also be broached. Even in the context of a good therapeutic relationship or well-functioning group, these are usually very threatening topics for the victims, who may disavow the connection between their dress and deportment and abuse.

Related Developmental Issues

Child sexual-abuse victims are not immune to the other problems that may befall children and adolescents. As has been noted, some victims have been poorly parented in general and require work in the areas of peer relationships, adult-child relationships, school performance, and the like. Also, any major life change may be hard for a child even when excellent social and family supports are available; child sexual-abuse victims frequently find themselves having to change schools, friends, and recreational activities with relatively few supports, as a result of a move into the foster-care system. During the first few weeks a child is in an alternative care system, therapy may be the most stable aspect of her social existence. Thus, therapy can serve as an important forum for dealing with the variety of feelings and adjustment problems evoked by the social and emotional upheaval associated with revelation and intervention.

Surviving Court

Many child sexual-abuse victims have one or more court experiences, which are scary at best and traumatizing at worst. These court experiences are related to juvenile court dependency and neglect proceedings, appearances in criminal proceedings, or both. Furthermore, most children still active in treatment have the expectation that they will have to return to court at some point—frequently as the sole witness to their victimization. It is therefore useful for the victim-witness advocacy procedures noted earlier to be used in the preparation of the child for a court appearance. A group may also serve as an important context for sharing the anxieties surrounding a court appearance, providing mutual support, and making predictions about what is likely and not likely to happen. Victims may also wish to role play the entire court proceeding with various group members serving as the prosecutor, defense attorney, judge, and even the perpetrator.

Physical Well-Being

Victims of child sexual abuse have been physically invaded as well as psychologically compromised and exploited. Thus, they may lose a sense of ownership of their bodies and a concomitant loss of the sense of territorial security that should come from being at home. It is extremely common, for example, for victims to describe feelings of dissociating from their bodies during a molestation incident, to believe they had no right to limit access to their bodies by others, and to dread having to spend time at home. Because of the physical trauma that may accompany abuse, and because of society's view of children who have been involved in a sexual relationship, the child may also regard herself as unclean and as undesirable in any way that is nonexploitive and nondebasing. Blink and Porter (1982) have referred to this as the "damaged goods syndrome." Thus, a primary purpose of treatment is to reestablish the child's sense of body integrity as well as her general sense of physical safety.

There may be a tendency to regard a child who has been involved in an ongoing sexual relationship as being far more knowledgeable about anatomy than she or he actually is. An adult survivor of an incestuous relationship once told her therapist that she became pregnant through that relationship. Though she had engaged in intercourse with her father for over two years, she did not know the mechanism of pregnancy. When the fetus "quickened," she thought she had something so wrong with her inside that she was going to die. One starting point for attempting to reestablish body integrity, then, is basic sex education—or, more accurately, reeducation—regarding basic physiological functions and their connection to feelings of love and affection. With latency-aged children, for example, this might begin simply with drawing, labelling, and discussing the human body, particularly in the context of group treatment.

Despite the potentially young age and limited intellectual capabilities of some victims, it may be useful to use the terminology "body integrity." Exploring and describing what this term means serves as one vehicle to communicate the idea that one's body is one's own and no one, not even an adult, has the right to touch particular areas without permission. This point may also be emphasized through a number of experiential activities including pushing away individuals who try to invade one's body space, practicing yelling no, and the like. These experiential activities also give rise to more general "protection issues," in which victims may identify and share techniques they have developed to enhance their own physical safety and avoid threatening adults.

For older adolescent victims, the issues relating to physical well-being are often crystallized by dating experiences in which the victim may have to confront issues of sexuality. The issues involved in learning to say no within this context are critically important in that it is hoped that this skill can be generalized to other relationships in the future.

A NOTE ON INTERVENING WITH
NONPARTICIPATING MOTHERS

A major consequence of the tension between the treatment philosophies proffered by the family theorists and those proffered by the feminists was the crystallization of the need to clearly distinguish the issues of systemic causality and moral responsibility in the assessment of incestuous families. With their emphasis on "circular causality," many family models—regardless of the referring problem—have had a tendency for the therapist "to spread the blame around." As was noted earlier, however, this orientation to the problem of incest has the unfortunate result of placing the mothers in these families in the untenable position of being made responsible for their husbands' sexual conduct. On the other hand, the clinical finding that some mothers have known about, and even encouraged, sexual liaisons in their families has been so ubiquitous that it should not be ignored. To overlook or to rationalize this finding would be tantamount to ignoring the nature of the emperor's new clothes.

These conflicting "realities" about the mothers in incest families have stemmed partially from a failure to adequately distinguish different forms of incest. However, they also seem to have derived from an implicit equating of systems causality and personal responsibility. To cite an example, a practitioner seeing a true endogamous, father-daughter incest family might learn that in the months immediately preceding the onset of the incest, the mother refused to engage in intercourse with her husband. The practitioner may also learn that to decrease marital conflict and to avoid her spouse, the mother asked to be transferred to the night shift at her job. It might further be revealed that the mother's relationship with her daughter was an openly conflictual one, which duplicated a conflictual relationship that she had had with her own mother. From one perspective, it might be argued that it is naive not to regard the mother's behavior as being causally relevant in the development and maintenance of the incest, since the molestation might not have occurred if the mother had been responsive to her husband or if she had been emotionally or physically available to her daughter. From the other perspective, however, to suggest that the mother contributed causally to the problem, ipso facto, partially exonerates the father. Persons with this view regard moral responsibility almost as if it were a quantifiable commodity and suggest that any responsibility ascribed to the mother inevitably decreases the responsibility that the father must bear.

The models for incest that are currently being developed (see, for example, Chapter 5 of this volume and Finkelhor, 1984b) make it clear that causality and responsibility are really separate dimensions of the same problem. In fact, the father can be regarded as being fully culpable for the sexual contact, while the causal relevance of the mother can also be acknowledged. This is equivalent to acknowledging that a child's inability to protect him or herself may be a causal factor in incestuous molestation, though it is never the child's responsibility if he or she is involved in a sexual relationship with an adult (Finkelhor, 1984b).

A central premise of this chapter is that no preconception should be imposed on any incestuous family involved in treatment. Every "fact" about incestuous families that has emerged from the literature should serve only to generate clinical hypotheses, which can subsequently be supported or jettisoned during the course of intervention. The nature of the mother's involvement, in particular, should never be dealt with presumptively. Rather, her relationships with other family members in general and the incestuous behavior in particular must be thoroughly explored. One way of beginning this exploration is to examine her level of acceptance of the allegation, the nature of her acknowledgement of the allegation, and the form of action that she took in response to it (Sturkie, 1982). These issues are presented in Figure 8.3.

Upon being informed that incest is occurring within her family, or upon encountering cues or clues that raise this possibility for her, the nonparticipating mother must decide for herself whether or not to accept that this behavior has occurred. The myriad reasons why she might not accept the allegation have been widely described. For

Figure 8.3 Maternal Responses to the Allegation of Incest

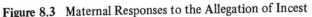

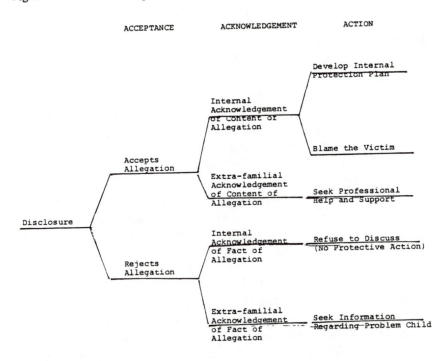

ACCEPTANCE   ACKNOWLEDGEMENT   ACTION

Develop Internal Protection Plan

Internal Acknowledgement of Content of Allegation

Blame the Victim

Accepts Allegation

Extra-familial Acknowledgement of Content of Allegation

Seek Professional Help and Support

Disclosure

Internal Acknowledgement of Fact of Allegation

Refuse to Discuss (No Protective Action)

Rejects Allegation

Extra-familial Acknowledgement of Fact of Allegation

Seek Information Regarding Problem Child

Source: Sturkie, 1982.

example, if the incestuous relationship has been truly secretive (because her daughter has actively worked to protect her from the knowledge), the mother may not be able to accept that such behavior could have gone on without her knowing about it, or she may not be able to believe that she could marry a man who was capable of such behavior. In short, she consciously refuses to accept the allegation. On the other hand, if she had been sexually abused herself, she might not be able to accept that she could have permitted the same fate that had befallen her to befall her daughter. Or, she may be panicked at the prospects of having to attempt to economically provide for her family, particularly if she has lived in a father-dominant, misogynistic or imperious family and has never been permitted to cultivate her competencies. In these latter examples, the rejection may be more a function of unconscious denial. Of course, there are also mothers who simply do not know whom to believe and fail to accept the allegation by default.

After the mother establishes a personal conviction regarding whether or not to accept the allegation, she must then choose to acknowledge it either solely within the confines of her family (internally) or within and outside of the family (externally). If she does not accept the allegation, she may acknowledge it only internally. Her course of action may then be to refuse to discuss it any further. She may also not accept the allegation but still acknowledge it externally. This situation is exemplified by the mother whose action is to seek professional advice on why a child would concoct such a preposterous story.

Mothers who accept the allegation can also acknowledge it only within the families, or within and outside as well. There are undoubtedly many mothers who validate the allegation within their families but do not inform outside authorities. Their action is to develop an internal protection plan. Reports of incest survivors also indicate that there are mothers who accept the allegation but acknowledge it only internally by blaming the child for the behavior.

Finally, there are mothers who accept the allegation and acknowledge it internally and externally through eliciting help from friends, extended family, or the professional community. Still other mothers do not accept the allegation but acknowledge it externally by coalescing with the offender and abandoning the victim.

Figure 8.3 has been included to emphasize the diversity of maternal responses that are possible following disclosure and the importance of adequately assessing any particular mother's response. From a practice standpoint, the form of maternal response may make some forms of intervention more appropriate and some particular therapeutic themes more germane. For example, though support groups made up of mothers who have previously dealt with the pain of disclosure may be useful in most cases, these are almost essential in cases involving mothers who do not accept the allegation. If the rejection of the allegation is seemingly rooted in a history of having been molested herself, the group may have a therapeutic focus helping the mother work through her own unresolved issues as a way of helping her close the wounds, which will in turn help her be available to her daughter. If the rejection is manifested by the mother's attempt to find out why her daughter would make something up, the therapeutic experience may be more educationally oriented and present-focused, dealing solely with the present issues involved in disclosure.

Mother-daughter dyad meetings are also a common element of therapeutic intervention in incest families; however, they may have particular salience in those families in which the allegation is accepted but only acknowledged, initially, internally. In cases in which the victim is blamed for the occurrence of the behavior, or in cases in which an internally developed protection plan is developed only to subsequently fail, mother-daughter dyad meetings are often the most crucial aspect of the entire treatment enterprise. It is common within these cases that the victim is angrier at her mother than at the sexually offending parent. Professionals should be careful not to chastise mothers who have attempted to resolve the problem internally, only to subsequently fail. A sensitive professional should recognize the myriad reasons why some mothers elect not to involve outsiders, and the simple lack of professional involvement should never be regarded as "no action," in and of itself.

Recognizing that many mothers do accept, fully acknowledge, and take decisive action in response to disclosure should also serve as a reminder that a supportive parent may be the best therapist a child-victim may have. Sgroi (1982), among others, maintains that children have a right to professional services. At the same time, professionals must remember that in many cases they simply cannot offer children more than a competent parent can. In these cases, the professional serves primarily in a consultative role, coaching the mother on how to deal with her child.

SUMMARY

The purpose of this chapter has been to describe the major treatment methods currently evidenced in the practice literature and the treatment ideologies that underpin them. It has been emphasized that this form of therapy is manifestly difficult due both to the complexity of the problem and the service-delivery system necessary to address it. Great strides have been made in distinguishing the various forms of incest, the causal factors surrounding them, and the potential needs of the various family members following revelation. Much work still remains to be done in terms of treatment methodology, however, particularly in work with incest offenders.

9
Conclusion

In 1897, near the very beginning of his psychological writings, Sigmund Freud argued that "incest is anti-social and civilization consists of a progressive renunciation of it" (Freud, 1954). Following this lead many social theorists have offered anthropological, biological, psychological, or sociological explanations for the avoidance of incest as a taboo, an aversion, or a sociocultural barrier. At the same time, however, the fact that incest actually occurs was long ignored or obscured. Certainly, attempts to study actual cases of incest behavior were not deemed necessary. After all, most of the traditional theories portrayed incest as virtually unheard of in civilized settings. In sum, it was assumed to be nonproblematic. In that context, a social scientist who might venture to study incest cases would have run a serious risk of being viewed as a crackpot or a sensationalist, drawing attention to the exceptional rather than identifying regularities affording the basis for laws or principles of human behavior. The lingering Victorian legacy also mitigated against research on sexual topics. Thus, until very recently, academics, much like the lay public, tended to deny or evade the reality of incest (Masters and Johnson, 1976) or to assume that it occurs only among the degenerate lower classes (Sagarin, 1977; Riemer, 1940; Specktor, 1979).

Following the lead of research and practice concerned with other types of child abuse and neglect, the study of incest as an actual occur-

166

rence has finally emerged as a significant research effort. A substantial body of descriptive literature is now available. It is no exaggeration to say that turning to the empirical study of incest has brought an awakening. Long considered to be nearly unthinkable, recent findings indicate that the incestuous violation of children is one of the more frequent types of child abuse. In fact, child sexual abuse perpetrated by a stranger or an extrafamilial acquaintance is the exception. In the majority of reported sexual-abuse cases, the perpetrator is the child's father, step or foster father, mother's boyfriend/lover, or other parental figure (Weber, 1977; Finkelhor and Hotaling, 1984). Moreover, although rates of step and foster father perpetration are disproportionately high (higher than the incidences of step or foster fatherhood in the general population), in most samples the most frequent perpetrator is the biological father (Julian, Mohr, and Lapp, 1980; Justice and Justice, 1979; Maisch, 1972; Renvoize, 1978; Sagarin, 1977).

Reversing the traditional emphasis, most social scientists today are more concerned with the perpetration of incest than with the nature or functional significance of an incest taboo or aversion. Further, while social science attention to incest as a taboo or an aversion was highly theoretical, the current research effort is conspicuously atheoretical. Although this may have been healthy at the onset, freeing those who turned to the study of incest as child abuse from preconceived and problematic formulations (for example, Freudian assumptions), research unguided by theoretical considerations soon becomes unwieldy and stale, a noncumulative array of answers to unrelated questions. In fact, in this as in other areas of child-abuse and family-violence literature, the most pressing unmet need is for well-developed and empirically grounded theory (Gelles, 1980, 1982).

In the opinion of the present authors most of the traditional incest theories, which predate the availability of any significant amount of research evidence, are dead ends. Nearly all of these theories start with the premise, implicit or explicit, that there is an incest taboo or aversion to be explained. In light of the evidence now available, we submit that the premise should be questioned. Certainly there is a normative proscription or prohibition against incest. But more than that is suggested when one speaks of a taboo or an aversion. Webster's first definition of taboo is "a prohibition against touching, saying, or doing something for fear of immediate harm from a mysterious superhuman force" (*Webster's New Collegiate Dictionary*, 1979). As elaborated in Chapter 3, we find it difficult to juxtapose that concept with the available evidence on adult-child incest. Given the frequency with which the incest prohibition is violated, the fact that such violations are ordinarily protracted, and the fact that violations appear to have been even more frequent in our preindustrial past (Rush, 1980), we question the assumption that this normative prohibition is accompanied by fears of immediate supernatural harm. As to the aversion thesis, while some evidence suggests that familiarity may detract from sexual interest (Shepher, 1971), other evidence suggests that the reverse is often the case (Rubin, 1973; Byrne, 1971; Hendrick and Hendrick, 1983).

The issues here are not merely academic. As noted in Chapter 3, thinking of incest as a taboo or an aversion leaves one focused on the question of why anyone would even so much as feel a sexual interest in his own child. In short, this relegates incest to the realm of the bizarre—provoking the assumption that the parent in question must have bizarre personality problems. As noted in Chapter 4, however, research indicates that very few incest perpetrators are psychotic. We propose an alternative orientation to the problem. Namely, it may be that many if not most fathers experience an occasional sexual desire in response to their daughters. They do not act on that impulse—because of certain barriers. Perhaps one of the most important barriers is a strong concern for the daughter's welfare. Partially because of harsh, unemotional, and unsupportive environments in their own childhoods, and partially because of subcultural factors, incest perpetrators have often failed to develop the capacity for such altruistic responses—even in relation to their own children. For many other perpetrators it appears that what is good for the daughter can readily be redefined in a fashion congruent with their own desires (Nobile, 1978). That is, rationalization occurs. From this orientation, then, the key questions become: What are the effective external barriers? How can we strengthen those barriers, add to them, and insure that they are in place throughout all segments of our society?

Although this orientation to the problem challenges the fundamental assumptions of most traditional (taboo and aversion) theoretical orientations, it is congruent with exchange, resource, ecological, and feminist orientations. Especially among the feminists (Brownmiller, 1975; Rush, 1980; Janeway, 1981), there is clearly a recognition that incest taboos or aversions are, at best, weak and easily overcome—not the fundamental reactions assumed in Freudian and other traditional theories. Further, all of the contemporary perspectives converge on the importance of resources and power, emphases we find propitious for synthesizing the now extensive research findings on the concomitants and dynamics of incestuous child abuse. Thus, for example, extreme father dominance, a passive mother characterized by learned helplessness, a mother who herself has been a victim of child sexual abuse and/or is emotionally and sexually distant with the father, a neighborhood lacking in social support networks, a subculture of violence, a father abusing alcohol, and a father reared in a harsh, unemotional environment—all have implications for the breakdown of normal barriers to incestuous behavior.

Accordingly, we have drawn on these contemporary perspectives to propose (see Chapter 5) an eclectic, resource-based model that not only synthesizes the available research findings on the complex assortment of apparently predisposing factors, but addresses their interplay in power and resource dynamics within the four life spheres defining the social environment of the actors. In addition, the proposed model speaks to factors that can mitigate against incest even in high-risk situations, yielding implications for prevention and intervention. Given that every individual has several spheres of interaction, that a combination of risk factors are typically present in an incest family, and that there are several different kinds of incest families, the model eschews oversimplification and attempts to grapple with adult-child incest (specifically, father-daughter incest) in its complex reality.

Though quite extensive, the existing research literature on incestuous child abuse has many limitations. Moreover, these limitations are most glaring precisely on the dimension of separating causes from mere correlates of the abuse. Thus, we certainly do not conceive the model herein proposed as a definitive portrait. Ferreting out causal connections is by far the most difficult task in the process of science, however, and the higher levels of confidence in causal conclusions can be obtained only by the testing of a priori hypotheses (Kerlinger, 1973). In short, constructing the theoretical models from which hypotheses can be derived is a critical step in the pursuit of a rigorous etiological understanding of any phenomenon. It is hoped that this model will stimulate such hypothesis-testing efforts, virtually nonexistent in the current literature on incestuous child abuse, provoking modifications or alternative frameworks as the results unfold.

Although substantial confidence in this or any model of adult-child incest must await further research in this field, the model presented does provide an interim basis, extensively grounded in the available research findings, for addressing applied issues of prevention and intervention. Among the applied implications of this model is the conclusion that we cannot safely assume that a purported incest taboo obviates any need to educate people regarding the importance of re-fraining from incestuous contacts with their children. Just as public-service messages warn us against drinking and driving, similar messages are needed proscribing incestuous child abuse. Unlike physical child abuse, the fact that incest causes severe and lasting emotional damage to the child is not self-evident. Neither is the fact that, however allur-ing the child's behavior may appear, the responsibility for avoiding incest and thus its damage to the child lies wholly with the adult. Both the costs to the child and the parent's accountability, moral as well as legal, should be articulated in those messages.

Another implication (following from evidence on the absence of social support networks in neighborhoods beset by high levels of fam-ily violence including child abuse) is that instituting and publicizing abuse hotlines, shelters, and community counseling centers constitute prime prevention initiatives.

Far greater financial support for official intervention is also needed. Presently, most child protective agencies are painfully understaffed and overextended. While funding will never be sufficient to directly confront all perpetrators, a substantial increase in funding, coupled with adequate media coverage, could elevate what is now only a minor threat to a would-be perpetrator to a major barrier against incest.

Sex education, incorporating material on molestation and how to respond when an adult violates the boundaries, is almost certainly the single most effective deterrent to child sexual abuse, including incest. Nevertheless, the overwhelming resource and power advantages of the parent, in relationship to the child, must caution us that enlightening the child is by no means a panacea. Ultimately, every responsible adult should serve as a barrier mitigating against incest in his or her com-munity.

On this score, it is encouraging to note that reports to authorities have increased in recent years (Fontana, 1984; Finkelhor, 1984b). Nevertheless, the impediments to reporting have by no means been eliminated. One of the major obstacles to reporting is that concerned citizens and mandated sources are unsure as to what constitutes reason-able cause to contact officials or agencies. Responding to this problem, a few researchers, drawing upon analyses of case reports, have at-tempted to articulate risk factors coincident with incest (Finkelhor, 1980a; Specktor, 1979). Generally sensitive to the finding that incest families typically have more "problems" than incest, they caution that a single factor may not signal risk, though a *combination* of factors warrants investigation. Historically, two of the most acknowledged risk factors have been extreme father dominance and alcohol abuse by the father. Recent evidence documents the validity of these signals. Other factors noted include inadequate housing, marital discord, a marriage begun with a pregnancy with several births in rapid succession, passive mothers, mothers with unmet childhood needs, and fathers reared in harsh, unemotional environments.

Other guidelines for identifying high-risk families have been emphasized in this work (see Chapters 6 and 7). A teacher may be able to spot a possible or potential incest victim by noting the following in the child: depression; drop in academic performance; truancy; non-involvement in social activities with other children; overrestrictive demands on the child from the parents; poor self-image as reflected in modes of dress or lack of good hygiene (Specktor, 1979, p. 12). High-risk families are often those voluntarily and/or geographically isolated and those with rigid boundaries on their activities and interactions with persons other than immediate family members. In high-risk families, the mother is often extremely dependent upon the father emotionally, socially, and financially. She may also relinquish her mother/wife role to the daughter. The father is characteristically overrestrictive and controlling of the other members' behaviors and social activities. His behavior often appears tyrannical—absolutely and arbitrarily ruling the life routines of every member of the family. Perhaps the most readily identifiable feature of an incestuous or potentially incestuous father is his lack of impulse control (Specktor, 1979, p. 14; Summit and Kryso, 1978).

Mayhall and Norgard (1983, Chapter 14) contend that prevention and intervention responsibilities should be shared. Concerned adults, mandated sources, and law enforcement, counseling, and social service agencies need to coordinate their efforts to be more effective. In addition, Fontana (1984) and various others (Finkelhor, 1980a; Specktor, 1979; Herman and Hirschman, 1977; Vander Mey and Neff, 1982, 1984) have requested more research, more clarification of definitions and risk factors, and more evaluation of treatment programs so as to further the effectiveness of those sharing responsibility for victims and families. And, while Herman and Hirschman (1977) see consciousness raising and eradication of the patriarchal family as the fundamental answers to incest perpetration, it must be realized that these two things take time; and, as Fontana (1984) and Mayhall and Norgard (1983) emphasize, action is needed immediately. The bureaucratic maze needs to be simplified. Lines of communication between individuals and agencies need to be open and accessible. Information must be broadly disseminated.

One suggestion in line with this would be to commercialize research publications on incest and make them readable and affordable to the general public. Researchers should not talk among themselves exclusively, publishing only in professional journals to be read by other academicians or their students. By making research findings readily accessible, not only is informed consciousness raising enhanced, but an informed public may emerge ready to act and to help shoulder the responsibility. We agree with Mayhall and Norgard (1983, pp. 355-56) when they state, ". . . Every person shares the responsibility for the existence of abuse and neglect in our society and for prevention and treatment. Every person has power to effect positive and negative change. Every person is also affected by the decisions of others."

All states have laws defining parties responsible for reporting suspected child abuse and neglect (Sgroi, 1975). Usually, these sources are termed "mandated" sources or "adjudicated adults." For example, Mississippi legislators (House Bill No. 1065, Mississippi Legislature, Regular Session, 1975) have amended Section 43-41-11 of the Mississippi 1972 Annotated Code such that the following persons are required to report to the county welfare agency any suspected abuse or neglect of children, or any case where he/she has observed child abuse or neglect: dentist, intern, resident, registered nurse, psychologist, teacher, social worker, school principal, child caregiver, minister, or any law enforcement officer. If any of these persons are working in a school, hospital, child care center or other similar institution dealing with children, the person should make all reports to either his/her immediate supervisor or to the director of the institution. Failure to report renders the adjudicated adult legally liable for the abuse and/or neglect of the child or children concerned. Those who report are immune from legal liability and their identities are kept confidential. What constitutes reasonable cause, however, is not delineated in the statute.

While monies are very limited, at least one group has found ways to circumambulate this problem by drawing upon local agencies and voluntary organizations and resources, using the media to mobilize a community effort to halt, prevent, and/or intervene in incest cases (Andrews and Linden, 1984). Incorporation of incest information and intervention training into the education of family social-service professionals is also critical to the goals of community mobilization (Krenk, 1984).

In terms of prevention, Justice and Justice (1979) stress that it is important for parents to avoid nudity with pubertal and near-pubertal children; that mothers act as role models for their daughters and define permissible limits of sexual behavior with fathers; that parents avoid (routinely) sleeping with children; and that parents refrain from flirting with children (Justice and Justice, 1979, p. 17). Rosenfeld suggests that other preventive measures include privacy, no overstimulation of the child by the parents, and changes in family affection patterns as the child grows older (1977, pp. 233-34).

From a feminist perspective, consciousness raising may prevent some incest, but father-daughter incest can be eradicated only with the disappearance of male supremacy. For some feminists, eliminating male dominance from the culture is both necessary and sufficient for eradicating father-daughter incest. The argument is that incest occurs in patriarchal systems where fathers exercise their power and thereby initiate such prohibited relationships. The father has the power and the ability to exploit the daughter due to the structure of the family and of the society. Thus, if male supremacy and patriarchal families were nonexistent, father-daughter incest would also vanish (Herman and Hirschman, 1977; Brownmiller, 1975; Janeway, 1981). Such simplified, monocausal analyses are notoriously incompatible with the complexities of human social life. However, in light of the findings on the typical characteristics of father perpetrators (dominating, authoritarian), it is surely correct to argue that patriarchal norms and family patterns are a major contributing factor. From a pragmatic standpoint, our own suggestion would be to increase the availability of parenting skills classes oriented toward a positive valuation of all members of the family.

Numerous authors have advocated a variety of types of treatments and counseling for victims and families (Giarretto, Giarretto, and Sgroi, 1978; Forward and Buck, 1978; Berliner and Stevens, 1976; Burgess et al., 1978; Carrozza and Heirsteiner, 1983). With children, Burgess, Holmstrom, and McCausland (1978) have shown the expediency of using play therapy. What children cannot communicate with words, they can often depict in play; or, in play, what they have been emotionally unable to discuss may surface. CSATP (Child Sexual Abuse Treatment Program) uses some humanistic psychology, and Parents Anonymous (for abusive or potentially abusive parents and their spouses) uses psychodrama (Giarretto, Giarretto, and Sgroi, 1978; Forward and Buck, 1978). With institutionalized incest perpetrators and child molesters, aversion techniques have been employed (Quinsey, 1977). Forward and Buck (1978) note that gestalt therapy, transactional analysis, behavior modification, crisis intervention and psychoanalysis are also being used. Burgess, Holmstrom, and McCausland (1978) surveyed many of the available counseling approaches and stressed that a social network model should be implemented for many cases. Finally, religious counseling has been suggested for some cases (Specktor, 1979).

One intriguing aspect of the Arkansas CSATP (Sturkie, 1983), which utilizes Berliner and Stevens's (1976) victim advocacy program, is that the personnel at the Arkansas CSATP have the victims role play the court appearance sequence. The victims play at being the judge, offender, defense attorney, and prosecutor. In addition to preparing victims for their court appearances, role playing allows victims to gain power over their perpetrators in a symbolic fashion—vicariously reversing the original power differential they confronted as victims and thereby enhancing personal autonomy and body integrity.

Carrozza and Heirsteiner (1983) have described group art/therapy sessions conducted on an after-school basis. Through art, talking, and listening, the therapists attempt to move the girls through five stages: gathering; self-disclosure; regression; reconstruction; and ending. The objectives are to facilitate the development of an internal locus of control and to free the expression of anger, joy, jealousy, hostility, and so on concerning herself, the perpetrator, her victimization, and her family life. By drawing and exchanging pictures of one another, the children are provided images of themselves as they appear to others and a more realistic orientation to themselves and the world. Carrozza and Heirsteiner feel that the art/communcation sessions are conducive to developing independence, positive self-image, resistance to further exploitation, improved academic performance, and renewed interest in extracurricular activities (1983, p. 173).

Critical analyses of the various treatment approaches are almost nonexistent. One exception is found in a feminist critique by Herman and Hirschman (1977), who argue that psychoanalytic approaches to incest are futile if not counterproductive. They contend that psychoanalytic therapy isolates the female victim and focuses on her own guilt, feelings of inadequacy, and emotional problems. Herman and Hirschman advocate consciousness raising, which brings the female victims together and gives them a common identity and a sense of mutual support. Consciousness raising is seen as a positive approach to incest treatment and intervention because it makes incest a public concern, taking the burdens of guilt and shame off the victims. This general approach is consistent with the positive effects reported by

Sturkie (1983). Not only does it appear that some families can be reconstituted incest-free, but victims can become more socially competent and less prone to further sexual victimizations.

Sturkie's discussion in the present volume (Chapter 8) illuminates both the complexity and the frustrations entailed in "treating" incest families. First of all, if one hopes to "successfully" treat (in other words, insure an establishment of and adherence to normative proscriptions against) incest one must necessarily take an idiographic (Gelles, 1982) approach to the problem. In practice settings, some theory and conclusions based on a nomothetic approach to the problem are at least misleading and at worst irrelevant. Persons working with incest families must operate under the assumption that while there may be many similarities among incest families (for example, authoritarian fathers, poor impulse control on the father's part, alcohol abuse, and role disorganization of the family), one must also recognize and work through family differences. These differences include the father's motivation, the mother's orientation to the child and the father, the child's age and precocity, levels of role disorganization, severity of abusive pathology, or degree of pedophilic attraction to children. The possible combinations of social, psychological, and ecological problems are infinite.

Given this understanding, practitioners have the unenviable task of deciding not only the "best" or most appropriate treatment modality for entire families, but also the best treatment for dyads within the family and individual victims, mothers, and perpetrators. In order to do this, practitioners must delve into the assumptions and ideologies that serve as the foundation for any given treatment modality. They must assess the degree of pathology of a given family, the severity of the abuse, and the motivation of the offender (Summit and Kryso, 1978)—as well as family and individual differences in responsiveness to any particular type of therapy.

In sum, many people have begun to identify and publicize ways to prevent, treat, or halt incest. The major outreach effort has been directed toward sensitizing people, especially mandated community professionals, to indices by which high-risk families can be detected. Sex education has been seen as the principal preventive weapon. Although, as underscored in Chapter 8, many incest families appear beyond the scope of any existing treatment program, successful treatment is a realistic goal in the majority of cases. Achieving this goal is fraught with obstacles, however, including contradictory objectives pursued by various agencies in the intervention program. It is heartening to observe that so much has been implemented since Henry and Anna Giarretto established the first Child Sexual Abuse Program (CSATP) in Santa Clara County, California in 1971.[1]

The enumeration of potential risk factors has been seen, as this work also advocates, as a positive approach to raising consciousness and increasing the tendency among adults to respond responsibly by reporting suspect incest cases, thus facilitating at least intervention if not some prevention. Further, incest is being treated through self-help groups of parents and children who have experienced incest, again with reported success.

In terms of basic research, there is a need for larger samples, comparison samples, cross-cultural research, more triangulated measurement of antecedents and effects, longitudinal designs, and a greater reliance on substantiated cases of incest in descriptive research. Though small and convenient samples, clinical and caseworker observations, and unsubstantiated self-reports offer insights into the dynamics and consequences of adult-child incest, more rigorous methodology is needed to confirm suggestive findings and to resolve contradictory arguments about the relative importance and frequency of various contributing factors as well as the frequency and extent of damage resulting to the child.

There is also a clear need for research that will allow us to move beyond educated guesses as to the ratio of reported to unreported cases of adult-child incest. Better records, standardization of definitions, standardization of investigation and reporting procedures, and improvement of national report-collection systems are needed to facilitate unambiguous comparisons and to clarify the numbers of reported cases. There is a growing appreciation that survey methodology is the best approach for ascertaining the prevalence of unreported cases. Only a few surveys have so far been conducted, however. Most needed are surveys of the general population incorporating incest/sexual abuse questions (perhaps adding items to the National Opinion Research Center (NORC) General Social Survey, for example).

---

[1] It should be noted, however, that neither the educational, the counseling, nor the self-help approaches have been evaluated by rigorous experimental designs incorporating random assignment and control groups. Though such evaluations may be resisted, without them there can be no confidence that the victims and potential victims in need of effective assistance are actually receiving it.

A concerted effort by all adults in the society is needed to combat this severe form of child abuse. This effort must engage informed persons who understand incest as a type of child abuse without one cause or consequence, without one form or solution.

Appendix

Assessment and Treatment Issues with Child and Adolescent Victims of Incest: A Therapeutic Checklist

ISSUES OF EMOTIONAL WELL-BEING

1. Feelings of rejection, isolation, and abandonment
   A. as a function of victim status
   B. associated with having one's allegation not being accepted by parents, professionals, and/or others
   C. resulting from physical removal following disclosure, or resulting from other social disruption
   D. associated with the crystallization of the offender's warning

2. Feelings of responsibility
   A. for the molestation incidents,
      1. deriving from normal developmental processes
      2. deriving from accusations from the offender
      3. deriving from significant others and/or professionals who may have blamed the child
   B. for the division of loyalties—in the family and/or extended family—precipitated by the revelation

3. Feelings of guilt
   A. associated with legal sanctions against the offender and/or with "destroying the family"
   B. associated with the physically pleasurable aspects of the abuse
   C. associated with the special status, privileges, and/or material items resulting from victimization
   D. for not having adequately defended oneself and/or other siblings

179

4. Fear and anxiety
   A. fear and anxiety associated with not being believed
   B. exacerbated anxiety related to the nature and timing of the revelation
   C. fear and anxiety associated with being recognizable as child sexual-abuse victim:
      1. inappropriate secrecy and withdrawal from peers and others
      2. inappropriate disclosure as a mode of dealing with anxiety
   D. fear of abandonment and/or family dissolution
   E. fear of reprisal by the offender or others
   F. fear and anxiety associated with judicial appearances
   G. "nongrounded" fears and anxiety manifested in sleep disturbances, restlessness, shortened attention span, and related symptomatology often exhibited by children

5. Anger
   A. overt anger at the offending parent/other offender
   B. overt anger at nonparticipating parent or others who were perceived by the child as being nonprotective due to failure to accept the allegation and/or failure to recognize the signs of undisclosed abuse
   C. covert anger expressed through symptoms of depression
   D. covert anger/feelings of responsibility expressed through self-destructive behaviors and acting-out
   E. confusion related to anger projected by others

6. Powerlessness
   A. powerlessness as manifested through depression
   B. overcompliance; hypervigilance
   C. impaired ability to trust manifested in relationships with
      1. adults (including professionals)
      2. peers
      3. self (including the "cover-up" deportment and limited emotional expression; low self-esteem)

ISSUES OF PHYSICAL WELL-BEING

1. Loss of sense of ownership of one's body

2. Loss of sense of territorial security, which should be associated with being at home
3. Fear of immediate and long-term physical damage associated with the abuse
4. Loss of bodily esteem
   A. feelings of disgust and loathing
   B. fear of being regarded by others as soiled (the damaged-goods syndrome)

ISSUES OF BEHAVIORAL AND INTERPERSONAL FUNCTIONING

1. Sexual functioning
   A. precocious, promiscuous, and/or indiscriminate sexual behavior initiated by peers, self, and/or others
   B. sexual victimization of peers, siblings, or younger children
   C. sexually stylized behavior (seductive behavior) with adults
   D. inappropriate or precocious dress or other quasi-sexual presentations

2. Related developmental issues
   A. developmental fixation or regression associated both with the molestation and the process of intervention (for example, school performance, encopresis, emotional neediness)
   B. precocious social functioning including pseudomaturity
   C. distortions in expectations for relationships
   D. underparenting and poor socialization

References

Abel, Gene; Judith V. Becker; William Murphy; and Barry Flanagan. 1979. "Identifying Dangerous Child Molesters." Paper presented at the 11th Banff Conference on Behavior Modification, March.

Aberle, David F.; Urie Bronfenbrenner; Eckhard M. Hess; Daniel R. Miller; David M. Schneider; and Hames N. Spuhler. 1963. "The Incest Taboo and the Mating Patterns of Animals." *American Anthropologist* 65:253-65.

Adams, M. S., and J. V. Neel. 1967. "Children of Incest." *Pediatrics* 40:55.

Andrews, Duane R., and Rhonda Linden. 1984. "Preventing Rural Child Abuse: Progress in Spite of Cutbacks." *Child Welfare* 63 (September-October):443-52.

Antler, Stephen. 1981. "The Rediscovery of Child Abuse." In *The Social Context of Child Abuse*, edited by Leroy H. Pelton, pp. 39-54. New York: Human Sciences Press.

Aponte, Harry. 1982. "The Person of the Therapist." *The Family Therapy Networker* 6:19-21, 46.

Araji, Sharon, and David Finkelhor. 1985. "Explanations of Pedophilia: A Review of Empirical Research." *Bulletin of the American Academy of Psychiatry and Law* 13:17-37.

Associated Press. 1985. "Reports of Child Sexual Abuse Soared in 1984." *The Greenville News and Greenville Piedmont* (Greenville, SC), February 7, p. 30a.

Bagley, Christopher. 1969. "Incest Behavior and Incest Taboo." *Social Problems* 16:505-19.

Bakan, David. 1971. *Slaughter of the Innocents A Study of the Battered Child Phenomenon*. Boston: Beacon Press.

Becker, Judith, et al. 1978. "Evaluating the Social Skills of Sexual Aggressives." *Criminal Justice and Behavior* 5:357-67.

Bender, Lauretta, and Abram Blau. 1937. "The Reaction of Children to Sexual Relations with Adults." *Journal of American Orthopsychiatry* 7 (October): 500-18.

Berliner, Lucy. 1977. "Child Sexual Abuse: What Happens Next?" *Victimology: An International Journal* 2:327-31.

Berliner, Lucy, and D. Stevens. 1976. "Special Techniques for Interviewing Child Witnesses." Seattle, Washington: Haborview Medical Center.

Blau, Peter. 1964. *Exchange and Power in Social Life*. New York: John Wiley & Sons.

Blink, L., and F. Porter. 1982. "Group Therapy with Female Adolescent Sexual Abuse Victims." In *Handbook of Clinical Intervention in Child Sexual Abuse*, edited by Suzanne Sgroi, pp. 147-76. Lexington: Lexington Books.

Boulding, Kenneth E. 1970. *A Primer on Social Dynamics: History as Dialectics and Development*. New York: The Free Press.

Bourne, Richard, and Eli H. Newberger, eds. 1979. *Critical Perspectives on Child Abuse*. Lexington: D.C. Heath and Company.

Boszormenyi-Nagy, I. and J. Framo, editors. 1965. *Intensive Family Therapy*. New York: Harper and Row.

Bowen, Murray. 1972. "Family Therapy and Family Group Therapy." In *Family Therapy in Clinical Practice*. New York: Jason Aronson. 183-240.

Brenton, Myron. 1977. "What Can Be Done About Child Abuse?" *Today's Education* 66:51-53.

Bronfenbrenner, Urie. 1977. "Toward an Experimental Ecology of Human Development." *American Psychologist* 32:513-31.

Browning, Diane H., and Bonnie Boatman. 1977. "Incest: Children at Risk." *American Journal of Psychiatry* 134 (January-June):69-72.

Brownmiller, Susan. 1975. *Against Our Will: Men, Women and Rape*. New York: Simon and Schuster.

Burgess, Ann Wolbert, and Nicholas Groth. 1980. "Child Sexual Abuse." Keynote speech presented at the Third National Symposium on Violence in Families, Hot Springs, Arkansas.

Burgess, Ann Wolbert, and Lynda Lytle Holmstrom. 1979. *Rape: Crisis and Recovery*. Bowie, MD.: R.T. Brady.

Burgess, Ann Wolbert, and Lynda Lytle Holmstrom. 1978. "The Child and Family During the Court Process." In *Sexual Assault of Children and Adolescents*, edited by Ann Wolbert Burgess et al., pp. 205-30. Lexington: Lexington Books.

Burgess, Ann Wolbert; Linda Lytle Holmstrom; and Maureen P. McCausland. 1978. "Divided Loyalty in Incest Cases." In *Sexual Assault of Children and Adolescents*, edited by Ann Wolbert Burgess et al., pp. 115-26. Lexington: Lexington Books.

———. 1977. "Child Sexual Assault by a Family Member: Decisions After Disclosure." *Victimology: An International Journal* 2:236-50.

Burgess, Ann Wolbert; Nicholas Groth; Lynda Lytle Holmstrom; and Suzanne M. Sgroi, eds. 1978. *Sexual Assault of Children and Adolescents*. Lexington: Lexington Books.

Byrne, Donn. 1971. *The Attraction Paradigm*. New York: Academic Press.

Campbell, Bernard. 1966. *Human Evolution*. Chicago: Aldine Publishing Company.

Cantwell, Hendrika B. 1981. "Sexual Abuse of Children in Denver, 1979: Reviewed with Implications for Pediatric Intervention and Possible Prevention." *Child Abuse and Neglect* 8:75-85.

Carrozza, Phyllis, and Catherine L. Heirsteiner. 1983. "Young Female Incest Victims in Treatment: Stages of Growth Seen with a Group Art Therapy Model." *Clinical Social Work Journal* 10:165-75.

Carruthers, E. A. 1973. "The Net of Incest." *Yale Review* 63:211-27.

Cavallin, Hector. 1966. "Incestuous Fathers: A Clinical Report." *American Journal of Psychiatry* 122:1132-38.

Cohn, Anne Harris. 1979. "Effective treatment of child abuse and neglect." *Social Work* 24:513-19.

Collins, Randall. 1975. *Conflict Sociology: Toward an Explanatory Science.* New York: Academic Press.

Constantine, Larry. 1982. "Letter to the Editor." *American Journal of Orthopsychiatry* 52:748-49.

Conte, J. 1984. "Progress in Treating the Sexual Abuse of Children." *Social Work* 29:258-63.

Conte, J., and Lucy Berliner. 1981. "Sexual Abuse of Children: Implications for Practice." *Social Casework* 62:601-06.

Cooley, Charles Horton. 1964. *Human Nature and the Social Order.* New York: Schocken.

Cormier, Bruno N.; Miriam Kennedy; and Jadwiga Sancowicz. 1973. "Psychodynamics of Father-Daughter Incest." In *Deviance and the Family*, edited by Clifton D. Bryant and J. Gipson Wells, pp. 97-116. Philadelphia: F. A. Davis Co.

Coser, Lewis A. 1977. *Masters of Sociological Thought.* 2d ed. New York: Harcourt Brace Jovanovich.

Coult, Allan D. 1963. "Causality and Cross-sex Prohibition." *American Anthropologist* 65:266-67.

Courtois, Christine A. 1979. "Victims of Rape and Incest." *The Counseling Psychologist* 8:38-40.

CPSIS Users Guide. 1979. Child Protective Services Information System Users Guide. Richmond, VA: Department of Welfare, Bureau of Child Protective Services, Commonwealth of Virginia.

Davis, Kingsly. 1937. "The Sociology of Prostitution." *American Sociological Review* 2:744-55.

de Francis, Vincent. 1969. *Protecting the Child Victim of Sex Crimes.* Denver: American Humane Association, Children's Division.

Delson, N., and M. Clark. 1981. "Group Psychotherapy with Sexually Molested Children." *Child Welfare* 60:175-82.

Denzin, Norman K. 1984. "Toward a Phenomenology of Domestic, Family Violence." *American Journal of Sociology* 90:483-513.

de Silva, Wimala. 1981. "Some Cultural and Economic Factors Leading to Neglect, Abuse and Violence in Respect of Children within the Family in Sri Lanka." *Child Abuse and Neglect* 5:391-405.

Ditson, Joan, and Sharon Shay. 1984. "Use of a Home-based Computer to Analyze Community Data from Reported Cases of Child Abuse and Neglect." *Child Abuse and Neglect* 8:503-9.

Dubanoski, Richard A. 1981. "Child Maltreatment in European- and Hawaiian-Americans." *Child Abuse and Neglect* 5:457-65.

Dubanoski, Richard A., and Sally R. McIntosh. 1984. "Child Abuse and Neglect in Military and Civilian Families." *Child Abuse and Neglect* 8:55-67.

Dubanoski, Richard A., and Karen Snyder. 1980. "Patterns of Child Abuse and Neglect in Japanese- and Samoan-Americans." *Child Abuse and Neglect* 4: 217-25.

Duke, James T. 1976. *Conflict and Power in Social Life*. Provo, Utah: Brigham Young University.

Durkheim, Emile. 1938. *The Rules of Sociological Method*. Edited and Translated by George E. G. Gatlin. Chicago: The University of Chicago Press and Glencoe: The Free Press.

_____. 1947. *The Elementary Forms of Religious Life: A Study in Religious Sociology*. Translated by Joseph Ward Swain. Glencoe: The Free Press.

Easton, Barbara. 1983. "Feminism and the Contemporary Family." In *Everyday Family Life*, edited by Brenda J. Vander Mey, Ronald L. Neff, and David H. Demo, pp. 97-120. Minneapolis: Burgess Publishing Company.

Eisenberg, Leon. 1981. "Cross-Cultural and Historical Perspectives on Child Abuse and Neglect." *Child Abuse and Neglect* 5:299-308.

Eist, H.I., and A. Mandel. 1968. "Family Treatment of Ongoing Incest Behavior." *Family Process* 7:216-32.

Ellis, Havelock. 1906. *Sexual Selection in Man*. Philadelphia: F.A. Davis.

Engels, Frederick. 1942. *The Origins of the Family and the State*. New York: International Publishers.

Erchak, Gerald M. 1981. "The Escalation and Maintenance of Child Abuse: A Cybernetic Model." *Child Abuse and Neglect* 5:153-57.

Faller, Kathleen Coulborn. 1981. *Social Work With Abused and Neglected Children*. New York: Free Press.

_____. 1984. "Is the Child Victim of Sexual Abuse Telling the Truth?" *Child Abuse and Neglect* 8:473-81.

Feldman-Summers, S., and M. Edgar. 1979. "Childhood Molestation: Variables Related to Differential Impacts on Psychosexual Functioning in Adult Women." *Journal of Abnormal Psychology* 88:407-17.

Finkelhor, David. 1984a. "How Widespread is Child Sexual Abuse?" *Children Today* 13:18-20.

_____. 1984b. *Child Sexual Abuse: New Research and Theory*. New York: The Free Press.

_____. 1980a. "Risk Factors in the Sexual Victimization of Children." *Child Abuse and Neglect* 4:265-73.

_____. 1980b. "Sexual Socialization in America: High Risk for Sexual Abuse." In *Childhood and Sexuality: Proceedings of the International Symposium*, edited by Jean-Marc Sampon, pp. 641-48. Montreal: Editions Etudes Vivantes.

_____. 1979a. *Sexually Victimized Children*. New York: The Free Press.

_____. 1979b. "What's Wrong with Sex between Adults and Children?" *American Journal of Orthopsychiatry* 49:692-97.

_____. 1978a. "Psychological, Cultural and Family Factors in Incest and Family Sexual Abuse." *Journal of Marriage and Family Counseling* 4:41-49.

_____. 1978b. "Social Forces in the Formulation of the Problems of Sexual Abuse." Paper V55, Family Violence Research Program. Durham, N.H.: University of New Hampshire, November.

Finkelhor, David, and Gerald T. Hotaling. 1984. "Sexual Abuse in the National Incidence Study of Child Abuse and Neglect." *Child Abuse and Neglect* 8: 23-33.

Flanzer, Jerry P., and D. Kinly Sturkie III. 1983. *Arkansas Alcohol/Child Abuse Demonstration Project*. Final Report. Little Rock, Arkansas: Graduate School of Social Work, University of Arkansas at Little Rock.

Fontana, Vincent. 1984. "When Systems Fail: Protecting the Victim of Child Sexual Abuse." *Children Today* 13:14-18.

Forward, Susan, and Craig Buck. 1978. *Betrayal of Innocence Incest and its Destruction*. New York: Penguin.

Fox, J.R. 1962. "Sibling Incest." *British Journal of Sociology* 13:128-50.

Fox, Robin. 1980. *The Red Lamp of Incest*. New York: E.P. Dutton and Company.

Frances, Vera, and A. Frances. 1976. "The Incest Taboo and Family Structure." *Family Process* 15:235-44.

_____. 1982. "Review of Judith Lewis Herman's (with Lisa Hirschman) *Father-Daughter Incest*." *Family Process* 21:258-60.

Frank, James, and Al Watson. 1985. *Treating Sex Offenders: A Research Overview and Program Manual*. Columbia, S.C.: South Carolina Department of Corrections.

Fraser, Gertrude, and Philip L. Kilbride. 1980. "Child Abuse and Neglect—Rare, but Perhaps Increasing, Phenomena among the Samia of Kenya." *Child Abuse and Neglect* 4:227-32.

Freud, Sigmund. 1962 (1905). *Three Essays on the Theory of Sexuality*. New York: Avon Books.

_____. 1954 (1895). *The Origins of Psycho-Analysis*. New York: Basic Books.

_____. 1950 (1918). *Totem and Taboo*. London: Routledge and Kegan Paul.

_____. 1949 (1930). *Civilization and Its Discontents*. Translated by Joan Riviere. London: The Hogarth Press.

Gagnon, John H. 1965. "Female Victims of Sex Offenses." *Social Problems* 12: 176-92.

Gagnon, John H., and William Simon. 1967. *Sexual Deviance*. New York: Harper and Row.

Garbarino, James. 1976. "A Preliminary Study of Some Ecological Correlates of Child Abuse: The Impact of Socioeconomic Stress on Mothers." *Child Development* 47:178-85.

Garbarino, James, and Ann Crouter. 1978. "Defining Community Context for Parent-Child Relationships." *Child Development* 49:604-16.

Garbarino, James, and Aaron Ebata. 1983. "The Significance of Ethnic and Cultural Differences in Child Maltreatment." *Journal of Marriage and the Family* 45:773-83.

Garbarino, James, and Deborah Sherman. 1980. "High-risk Neighborhoods and High-Risk Families: The Human Ecology of Child Maltreatment." *Child Development* 51:188-98.

Garrett, T. B., and Richard Wright. 1975. "Wives of Rapists and Incest Offenders." *Journal of Sex Research* 2:149-57.

Gelinas, Denise J. 1983. "The Persisting Negative Effects of Incest." *Psychiatry* 46:312-32.

Gelles, Richard J. 1982. "Applying Research on Family Violence to Clinical Practice." *Journal of Marriage and the Family* 44:9-20.

————. 1980. "Violence in the Family: A Review of Research in the Seventies." *Journal of Marriage and the Family* 42:873-85.

————. 1978. "Violence toward Children in the United States." *American Journal of Orthopsychiatry* 48:580-92.

Gentry, Charles E. 1978. "Incestuous Abuse of Children: The Need for an Objective View." *Child Welfare* 62:355-64.

Giarretto, Henry. 1976. "Humanistic Treatment of Father-Daughter Incest." In *Child Abuse and Neglect: The Family and the Community*, edited by Ray Helfer and Henry Kempe, pp. 143-58. Cambridge, Mass.: Ballinger.

Giarretto, Henry; Anna Giarretto; and Suzanne M. Sgroi. 1978. "Coordinated Community Treatment of Incest." In *Sexual Assault of Children and Adolescents*, edited by Ann Wolbert Burgess et al., pp. 231-40. Lexington: Lexington Books.

Gil, David. 1981. "The United States Versus Child Abuse." In *The Social Context of Child Abuse*, edited by Leroy H. Pelton, pp. 291-324. New York: Human Sciences Press.

————. 1970. *Violence Against Children: Physical Abuse in the United States*. Cambridge, Mass.: Harvard University Press.

Giles-Sims, Jean, and David Finkelhor. 1984. "Child Abuse in Stepfamilies." *Family Relations* 33:407-13.

Glaser, B. G., and A. L. Strauss. 1967. *The Discovery of Grounded Theory*. Chicago: Aldine.

Goode, William J. 1971. "Force and Violence in the Family." *Journal of Marriage and the Family* 33:624-36.

Goodwin, Jean. 1981. "Suicide Attempts in Sexual Abuse Victims and Their Mothers." *Child Abuse and Neglect* 5:217-21.

Goodwin, Jean; Lawrence Cormier; and John Owen. 1983. "Grandfather-Granddaughter Incest: A Trigenerational View." *Child Abuse and Neglect* 7:163-70.

Goodwin, Jean; Teresita McCarty; and Peter DiVasto. 1981. "Prior Incest in Mothers of Abused Children." *Child Abuse and Neglect* 5:87-95.

Gordon, Linda. 1981. "Voluntary Motherhood: The Beginnings of the Birth-Control Movement." In *Family Life in America 1620-2000*, edited by Mel Albin and Dominick Cavallo, pp. 131-47. St. James, New York: Revisionary Press.

Gordon, Linda, and Paul O'Keefe. 1984. "Incest as a Form of Family Violence: Evidence from Historical Records." *Journal of Marriage and the Family* 46: 27-34.

Gouldner, Alvin W. 1960. "The Norm of Reciprocity: A Preliminary Statement." *American Sociological Review* 25:161-78.

Grando, Roy; Helena Yiori; Keith Noble; and Betsy Sukowicz. 1980. "Incest: The Stressful Process of Therapy." Unpublished paper. Springfield, Mo.: D. E. Burrell Community Mental Health Center, Inc.

Groth, Nicholas. 1982. "The Incest Offender." In *Handbook of Clinical Intervention in Child Sexual Abuse*, edited by S. Sgroi, pp. 215-39. Lexington, Mass.: D.C. Heath.

_____. 1979. *Men Who Rape*. New York: Plenum.

_____. 1978. "Guidelines for the Assessment and Management of the Offender." In *Sexual Assault of Children and Adolescents*, edited by A. W. Burgess et al., pp. 25-42. Lexington, Mass.: Lexington Books.

Groth, Nicholas; Ann Wolbert Burgess; H. Jean Birnbaum; and Thomas S. Gary. 1978. "A Study of the Child Molester: Myths and Realities." *LAE Journal of the American Criminal Justice Association* 41:17-22.

Haley, Jay. 1972. "A Review of the Family Therapy Field." In *Changing Families*, edited by J. Haley, pp. 1-12. New York: Grune and Stratton.

Harris, Marvin. 1975. *Culture People and Nature*. 2d ed. New York: Crowell Publishers.

Heider, Carl G. 1969. "Anthropological Models of Incest Laws in the United States." *American Anthropologist* 71:693-701.

Heim, Nikolaus. 1981. "Sexual Behavior of Castrated Sex Offenders." *Archives of Sexual Behavior* 10:11-19.

Heim, Nikolaus, and Carolyn J. Hursch. 1979. "Castration for Sex Offenders: Treatment or Punishment?" *Archives of Sexual Behavior* 8:281-99.

Henderson, D. J. 1980. "Incest: A Synthesis of Data." In *Traumatic Abuse and Neglect of Children at Home*, edited by G. J. Williams and J. Money. Baltimore: Johns Hopkins University Press.

Hendrick, Clyde, and Susan Hendrick. 1983. *Liking, Loving and Relating*. Monterey, Calif.: Brooks/Cole Publishing Company.

Herman, Judith (in collaboration with Lisa Hirschman). 1981. *Father-Daughter Incest*. Cambridge, Mass.: Harvard University Press.

Herman, Judith, and Lisa Hirschman. 1977. "Father-Daughter Incest." *Signs: An International Journal of Women in Culture and Society* 2:735-56.

Howze, Dorothy C. and Jonathon B. Kotch. 1984. "Disentagling Life Events, Stress and Social Support: Implications for the Primary Prevention of Child Abuse and Neglect." *Child Abuse and Neglect* 8:401-9.

Jaffe, Arthur C.; Lucille Dynneson; and Robert W. ten Bensel. 1975. "Sexual Abuse of Children." *American Journal of Diseases of Children* 129 (June): 689-92.

James, Jennifer, and Jane Meyerding. 1977. "Early Sexual Experience as a Factor in Prostitution." *Archives of Sexual Behavior* 7:31-42.

James, Kathleen Leigh. 1977. "Incest: The Teenager's Perspective." *Psychotherapy: Theory, Research and Practice* 14:146-55.

Janeway, Elizabeth. 1981. "Incest: A Rational Look at the Oldest Taboo." *Ms. Magazine*, November, pp. 61-64, 81, 109.

Jones, Barbara McComb; Linda L. Jenstrom, and Kee MacFarlane, eds. 1980. *Sexual Abuse of Children: Selected Readings*. Washington, D.C.: U.S. Department of Health and Human Services: Administration for Children, Youth and Families. Children's Bureau National Center on Child Abuse and Neglect. Publication no. (OHDS) 78-30161. Issued November.

Jones, Ernest. 1913. "A Review of Von Otto Rank's *Daz Inzest–Motiv in Dichtung und Sage*." *Journal of Abnormal Psychiatry* 8:68-69.

Julian, Valerie; Cynthia Mohr; and Jane Lapp. 1980. "Father-Daughter Incest: A Descriptive Analysis." In *Sexual Abuse of Children: Implications for Treatment*, edited by Wayne M. Holder, pp. 735-56. Denver: American Humane Association, Child Protective Division.

Justice, Blair, and Rita Justice. 1979. *The Broken Taboo: Sex in the Family*. New York: Human Sciences Press.

Kagan, Jerome. 1983. "The Psychological Requirements for Human Development." In *Everyday Family Life*, edited by Brenda J. Vander Mey, Ronald L. Neff, and David H. Demo, pp. 136-49. Minneapolis: Burgess Publishing Company.

Kaufman, Irving; Alice L. Peck; and Consuelo K. Tagiuri. 1954. "The Family Constellation and Overt Incestuous Relations between Fathers and Daughters." *American Journal of Orthopedic Psychiatry* 54:266-79.

Keefe, Mary. 1978. "Police Investigation in Child Sexual Assault." In *Sexual Assault of Children and Adolescents,* edited by Ann Wolbert Burgess, A. Nicholas Groth and Lynda Lytle Holmstrom, pp. 159-70. Lexington: Lexington Books.

Kempe, C. Henry; Frederic N. Silverman; F. Brandt; William Droegemueller; and Henry K. Silver. 1962. "The Battered Child Syndrome." *Journal of the American Medical Association* 181:17-24.

Kercher, Glen A., and Merilyn McShane. 1984. "The Prevalence of Child Sexual Victimization in an Adult Sample of Texas Residents." *Child Abuse and Neglect* 8:495-501.

Kerlinger, Fred N. 1973. *Foundations of Behavioral Research*. 2d ed. New York: Holt, Rinehart and Winston.

King County Rape Relief. 1979. "He Told Me Not to Tell." Seattle, Washington.

Kinsey, Alfred C.; Wardell B. Pomeroy; Clyde E. Martin; and Paul H. Gebhard. 1953. *Sexual Behavior in the Human Female*. Philadelphia: W. B. Saunders.

———. 1948. *Sexual Behavior in the Human Male*. Philadelphia: W. B. Saunders.

Kjonstad, Asbjorn. 1981. "Child Abuse and Neglect: Viewed in Relation to 12 Fundamental Principles in a Western Social and Legal System." *Child Abuse and Neglect* 5:421-29.

Koch, Michael. 1980. "Sexual Abuse in Children." *Adolescence* 15:643-48.

Korbin, Jill E. 1980. "The Cultural Context of Child Abuse and Neglect." *Child Abuse and Neglect* 4:3-13.

Krenk, Christopher J. 1984. "Training Residence Staff for Child Abuse Treatment." *Child Welfare* 58:167-73.

Kroth, Jerome. 1979. *Child Sexual Abuse: An Analysis of a Family Program.* Springfield: Charles Thomas.

Kruger, Lois; Dori Moore; Patricia Schmidt; and Ronna Weins. 1979. "Group Work with Abusive Parents." *Social Work* 24:337-38.

LaBarbera, Joseph D.; James E. Martin; and J. Emmett Dozier. 1980. "Child Psychiatrists' View of Father-Daughter Incest." *Child Abuse and Neglect* 4:147-51.

Leslie, Gerald R. 1982. *The Family in Social Context.* 5th ed. New York: Oxford University Press.

Lester, David. 1972. "Incest." *The Journal of Sex Research* 8:268-85.

Levi-Strauss, Claude. 1969. *The Elementary Structure of Kinship.* Boston: Beacon Press.

Lewis, Melvin, and Philip M. Sarrel. 1969. "Some Psychological Aspects of Seduction, Incest and Rape in Childhood." *American Academy of Child Psychiatry Journal* 8:606-19.

Lindzey, Gardner. 1967. "Some Remarks Concerning Incest, the Incest Taboo and Psychoanalytic Theory." *American Psychologist* 22:1051-59.

Lukianowicz, N. 1972. "Incest I: Paternal Incest." *British Journal of Sociology* 120:301-313.

Lustig, Noel et al. 1966. "Incest: A Family Group Survival Pattern." *Archives of General Psychiatry* 14:31-40.

Lynch, Margaret A. 1985. "Child Abuse Before Kempe: An Historical Literature Review." *Child Abuse and Neglect* 9:7-15.

Machotka, Paul; Frank S. Pittman; and Kalman Flomenshaft. 1967. "Incest as a Family Affair." *Family Process* 6 (March):98-116.

Maisch, Herbert. 1972. *Incest.* New York: Stein and Day.

Malinowski, Bronislaw. 1929. *The Sexual Life of Savages in North-Western Melanesia.* London: Routledge and Kegan Paul.

———. 1927. *Sex and Repression in Savage Society.* London: Routledge and Kegan Paul.

Marques, J.; W. Pithers; and A. Marlatt. 1984. "Relapse Prevention: A Self-Control Program for Sex Offenders." *Appendix to Report to California State Legislature.*

Marshall, W. L., and H. E. Barbaree. 1978. "The Reduction of Deviant Arousal: Satiation Treatment for Sexual Aggressors." *Criminal Justice and Behavior.* 5:294-303.

Marx, Karl. 1906. *Capital*. Chicago: C. H. Kerr.

Marx, Karl, and Frederick Engels. 1971. *The Communist Manifesto*. New York: International Publishers.

―――. 1947. *The German Ideology*. New York: International Publishers.

Masson, Jeffrey. 1984. *The Assault on Truth: Freud's Suppression of the Seduction Theory*. New York: Farrar, Straus, and Giroux.

Masters, William and Virginia E. Johnson. 1976. "Incest: The Ultimate Sexual Taboo." *Redbook*, 146 (April), pp. 54-58.

Mayhall, Pamela D., and Katherine Eastlack Norgard. 1983. *Child Abuse and Neglect: Sharing Responsibility*. New York: John Wiley and Sons.

McCarty, Loretta. 1981. "Investigation of Incest: Opportunity to Motivate Families to Seek Help." *Child Welfare* 60:679-89.

McCormick, Michael. 1981a. Personal interview by telephone. April 6. Starkville, Miss.

―――. 1981b. Personal interview by telephone. April 8. Starkville, Miss.

McCoy, Elin. 1983. "Childhood through the Ages." In *Everyday Family Life*, edited by Brenda J. Vander Mey, Ronald L. Neff, and David H. Demo, pp. 121-29. Minneapolis: Burgess Publishing Company.

McIntyre, Kevin. 1981. "Role of Mothers in Father-Daughter Incest: A Feminist Analysis." *Social Work* 26:462-66.

Mead, George Herbert. 1934. *Mind, Self and Society*. Chicago, Ill.: University of Chicago Press.

Mehta, Meenaksi N.; S. V. Praphy; and H. N. Mistry. 1985. "Child Abuse in Bombay." *Child Abuse and Neglect* 9:107-11.

Meiselman, Karin. 1978. *Incest: A Psychological Study of Causes and Effects with Treatment Recommendations*. San Francisco: Jossey-Bass.

Melville, Keith. 1980. *Marriage and Family Today*. 2d ed. New York: Random House.

Mississippi Legislature, The. 1975. *House Bill No. 1065*. Regular Session, 1975: 1-9.

Mississippi, The State of. 1980. "Youth Court Act, 32-21-105." *Cumulative Supplement to Mississippi Code 1972*. Volume 11. Rochester, NY: The Lawyers Cooperative Publishing Company.

―――. 1973. *Mississippi Code 1972 Annotated*. Volume 10. Atlanta: The Harrison Company. Rochester, NY: The Lawyers Cooperative Publishing Company.

Money, John. 1984. "Paraphilias: Phenomenology and Classification." *American Journal of Psychotherapy* 38:164-79.

―――. 1980. *Love and Love Sickness*. Baltimore: The Johns Hopkins University Press.

Money, John, and Anke Ehrhardt. 1972. *Man and Woman, Boy and Girl*. Baltimore: The Johns Hopkins University Press.

Money, John, and P. Tucker. 1975. *Sexual Signatures*. New York: Little, Brown and Company.

Mrazek, David. 1981. "The Child Psychiatric Examination of the Sexually Abused Child." In *Sexually Abused Children and Their Families*, edited by P. Mrazek and H. Kempe, pp. 143-54. Oxford: Pergamon Press.

Mrazek, Patricia. 1981. "Group Psychotherapy with Sexually Abused Children." In *Sexually Abused Children and Their Families*, edited by P. Mrazek and Henry Kempe, pp. 199-210. Oxford: Pergamon Press.

Mulford, Robert M. 1983. "Historical Perspective." In *Child Abuse and Neglect: A Guide With Case Studies for Treating the Child and Family*, edited by Nancy B. Ebeling and Deborah A. Hill, pp. 1-9. Boston: John Wright PSG Inc.

Napier, A., and C. Whitaker. 1978. *The Family Crucible*. New York: Harper and Row.

National Center on Child Abuse and Neglect. 1981. *Study Findings: National Study of the Incidence and Severity of Child Abuse and Neglect*. DHHS Publication (HDS) 81-30325. Washington, DC: U.S. Government Printing Office.

Newberger, Eli H., and Richard Bourne. 1980. "The Medicalization and Legalization of Child Abuse." In *Child Abuse: Commission and Omission*, edited by Joanne Valiant Cook and Roy Tyler Bowles, pp. 377-93. Toronto: Buttersworth.

Nimkoff, Meyer F. 1947. *Marriage and the Family*. Boston: Houghton Mifflin.

Nixon, James; John Pearn; Ian Wilkey; and Gwynneth Petrie. 1981. "Social Class and Violent Child Death: An Analysis of Fatal Nonaccidental Injury, Murder and Fatal Child Neglect." *Child Abuse and Neglect* 5:111-16.

Nobile, Philip. 1978. "The Last Taboo." *Penthouse*, January, p. 117.

Ordway, Dustin. 1983. "Reforming Judicial Procedures for Handling Parent-Child Incest." *Child Welfare* 62:68-75.

Oremland, Evelyn K., and Jerome Oremland. 1977. *The Sexual and Gender Development of Young Children: The Role of Education*. Cambridge: Ballinger.

Panton, James H. 1979. "MMPI Profile Configurations Associated with Incestuous and Non-Incestuous Child Molesting." *Psychological Reports* 45:335-38.

Parker, Seymour. 1976. "The Precultural Basis of the Incest Taboo: Toward a Biosocial Theory." *American Anthropologist* 78:285-305.

Parsons, Talcott. 1964. *Social Structure and Personality*. New York: The Free Press.

_____. 1954. "The Incest Taboo in Relation to Social Structure and the Socialization of the Child." *British Journal of Sociology* 5:101-17.

Parsons, Talcott, and Robert F. Bales. 1955. *Family, Socialization and Interaction*. Glencoe: The Free Press.

Pelton, Leroy H. 1978. "Child Abuse and Neglect: The Myth of Classlessness." *American Journal of Orthopsychiatry* 48:608-17.

Pfohl, Stephen J. 1980. "The 'Discovery' of Child Abuse." In *Child Abuse: Commission and Omission*, edited by Joanne Valiant Cook and Roy Tyler Bowles, pp. 323-39. Toronto: Buttersworth.

Pfohl, Stephen J. 1977. "The Discovery of Child Abuse." *Social Problems* 24(3): 310-23.

Pierce, Robert Lee. 1984. "Child Pornography: A Hidden Dimension of Child Abuse." *Child Abuse and Neglect* 8:483-92.

Porter, F.; L. Blink; and S. Sgroi. 1982. "Treatment of the Sexually Abused Child." In *Handbook of Clinical Intervention in Child Sexual Abuse*, edited by Suzanne Sgroi, pp. 109-38. Lexington, Mass.: D. C. Heath.

Quinsey, Vernon L. 1977. "The Assessment and Treatment of Child Molesters: A Review." *Canadian Psychological Review* 18:204-20.

Radbill, Samuel X. 1974. "A History of Child Abuse and Infanticide." In *Violence in the Family*, edited by Suzanne K. Steinmetz and Murray A. Straus, pp. 173-79. New York: Dodd, Mead and Company.

Rascovsky, Arnaldo, and Matilde Rascovsky. 1972. "The Prohibition of Incest, Filicide and the Sociocultural Process." *International Journal of Psycho-Analysis* 53:271-76.

Raphling, D. L.; B. L. Carpenter; and A. Davis. 1967. "Incest: A Geneaological Study." *Archives of General Psychiatry* 16 (April):505-11.

Reed, Evelyn. 1975. *Woman's Evolution From Matriarchal Clan to Patriarchal Family*. New York and Toronto: Pathfinder Press.

Renvoize, Jean. 1978. *Web of Violence: A Study of Family Violence*. London: Routledge and Kegan Paul.

Reynolds, Paul D. 1971. *A Primer in Theory Construction*. Indianapolis: Bobbs-Merrill.

Riemer, Svend. 1940. "A Research Note on Incest." *American Journal of Sociology* 45:565-71.

Rodman, Hyman. 1972. "Marital Power and the Theory of Resources in Cultural Context." *Journal of Comparative Family Studies* 3 (Spring):50-69.

Rose, Arnold M. 1957. "Theory for the Study of Social Problems." *Journal of Social Problems* 4:189-99.

Rosenfeld, Alvin A. 1979. "Incidence of a History of Incest Among 18 Female Psychiatric Patients." *American Journal of Psychiatry* 136:791-95.

————. 1977. "Sexual Misuse and the Family." *Victimology: An International Journal* 2:226-35.

Rosenfeld, A.; C. Nadelson; and M. Krieger. 1979. "Fantasy and Reality in Patient's Reports of Incest." *Journal of Clinical Psychiatry* 40:159-64.

Rosensweig-Smith, J. 1979. "Human Sexuality Concerns in the Treatment of Child Sexual Abuse." Paper delivered at the Second National Symposium on Violence in Families. Hot Springs, Arkansas. October.

Rosenthal, Margurite, and James A. Louis. 1981. "The Law's Evolving Role in Child Abuse and Neglect." In *The Social Context of Child Abuse*, edited by Leroy H. Pelton, pp. 55-89. New York: Human Sciences Press.

Rubin, Zick. 1973. *Liking and Loving: An Invitation to Social Psychology*. New York: Holt, Rinehart and Winston.

Rush, Florence. 1980. *The Best Kept Secret*: *Sexual Abuse of Children*. New York: McGraw-Hill.

Russell, Diane E. H. 1984. "The Prevalence and Seriousness of Incestuous Abuse: Stepfathers Vs. Biological Fathers." *Child Abuse and Neglect* 8:15-22.

Sagarin, Edward. 1977. "Incest: Problems of Definition and Frequency." *The Journal of Sex Research* 13:126-35.

Sarafino, Edward. 1979. "Estimates of Sexual Offenses against Children." *Child Welfare* 58:127-33.

Scanzoni, John. 1979. "Social Processes and Power in Families. In *Contemporary Theories About the Family*, edited by Wesley R. Burr, Reuben Hill, F. Ivan Nye, and Ira L. Reiss, pp. 295-316. New York: The Free Press.

Schmidt, Gunter, and Eberhard Schorsch. 1981. "Psychosurgery of Sexually Deviant Patients." *Archives of Sexual Behavior* 10:301-23.

Schultz, Leroy. 1973. "The Child Sex Victim." *Child Welfare* 52:147-57.

Scott, Donald M., and Bernard Wishy, eds. 1982. *American Families*: *A Documentary History*. New York: Harper and Row.

Scott, Edward M. 1977. "The Sexual Offender." *International Journal of Offender Therapy and Comparative Criminology* 21:255-63.

Seaberg, J. R., and D. F. Gillespie. 1978. "A National Child Abuse and Neglect Data Bank: Inter-Reporter Reliability." Unpublished manuscript prepared for the Center for Social Welfare Research, School of Social Work, University of Washington. Seattle.

Seemanova, Eva. 1971. "A Study of Children of Incestuous Matings." *Human Heredity* 21:108-28.

Seligman, Brenda Z. 1950. "The Problem of Incest and Exogamy: A Restatement." *American Anthropologist* 52:305-16.

_____. 1932. "The Incest Barrier: Its Role in Social Organization." *British Journal of Psychology* 22:250-276.

_____. 1929. "Incest and Descent: Their Influence on Social Organization." *Royal Anthropological Institute of Great Britain* 59 (January-June):231-72.

Sgroi, Suzanne. 1982. *Handbook of Clinical Intervention in Child Sexual Abuse*. Lexington: D.C. Heath.

_____. 1975. "Sexual Molestation of Children: The Last Frontier in Child Abuse." *Children Today*, May-June, pp. 18-21+.

Shah, P. M. 1984. "The Health Care of Working Children." *Child Abuse and Neglect* 8:541-44.

Shapiro, Judith. 1980. "Incestuous Sheets: A Review of Fox's *Red Lamp of Incest*." *Psychology Today*, October, pp. 110-14.

Shepher, Joseph. 1971. "Mate Selection Among Second Generation Kibbutz Adolescents and Adults: Incest Avoidance and Negative Imprinting." *Archives of Sexual Behavior* 1:293-307.

Sholevar, G. Pirooz. 1975. "A Family Therapist Looks at the Problem of Incest." *American Academy of Psychiatry and the Law Bulletin* 3:25-31.

Silbert, Mimi H., and Ayala M. Pines. 1981. "Sexual Child Abuse as an Antecedent to Prostitution." *Child Abuse and Neglect* 5:407-11.

Silver, Steven. 1976. "Outpatient Treatment for Sexual Offenders." *Social Work* 21:130-40.

Simmel, Georg. 1955. *Conflict and the Web of Group Affiliations*. New York: The Free Press.

Simon, W., and J. Gagnon. 1970. *The Sexual Scene*. New Brunswick: Transactions, Inc.

Slater, Miriam Krieselman. 1959. "Ecological Factors in the Origin of Incest." *American Anthropologist* 61:1042-59.

Sloane, Paul, and Eva Karpinski. 1942. "Effects of Incest on the Participants." *American Journal of Orthopsychiatry* 12:666-73.

Specktor, Peggy. 1979. *Incest: Confronting the Silent Crime*. Minneapolis: Minnesota Program for Victims of Sexual Abuse.

Spencer, Joyce. 1978. "Father-Daughter Incest: A Clinical View from the Corrections Field." *Child Welfare* 57:585-87.

Spodak, Michael; Ann Falck; and Jonas Rappeport. 1978. "The Hormonal Treatment of Paraphiliacs with Depo-Provera." *Criminal Justice and Behavior* 5: 304-14.

Sprey, Jetse. 1979. "Conflict Theory and the Study of Marriage and Family." In *Contemporary Theories About the Family*, Volume II, edited by Wesley R. Burr, Reuben Hill, F. Ivan Nye, and Ira L. Reiss, pp. 130-59. New York: The Free Press.

_____. 1971. "On the Management of Conflict in Families." *Journal of Marriage and the Family* 33:722-33.

Star, Barbara. 1983. *Helping The Abuser*. New York: Family Service Association of America.

Stern, M. J., and L. Yeyer. 1980. "Family and Couple Interaction Patterns in Cases of Father/Daughter Incest." In *Sexual Abuse of Children: Selected Readings*, pp. 83-86. Washington: Department of Health and Human Services.

Straus, Murray. 1980. "Stress and Physical Child Abuse." *Child Abuse and Neglect* 4:75-88.

_____. 1974. "Forword." In *The Violent Home: A Study of Physical Aggression Between Husbands and Wives*, edited by Richard J. Gelles, pp. 13-17. Beverly Hills, Calif.: Sage Publications.

_____. 1973. "A General Systems Theory Approach to a Theory of Violence between Family Members." *Social Science Information* 12:105-25.

Straus, Murray A.; Richard J. Gelles; and Suzanne K. Steinmetz. 1980. *Behind Closed Doors: Violence in the American Family*. Garden City, NY: Anchor Press.

Sturkie, Kinly. 1984. "Family Therapy of a Domestic Violence Service Delivery System." *Clinical Social Work Journal* 12:78-84.

_____. 1983. "Structured Group Treatment of Sexually Abused Children." *Health and Social Work* 8:299-308.

———. 1982. "Non-Participating Mothers in Incest Families: A Review of the Literature and Beyond." Paper presented at the Second National Conference on the Sexual Victimization of Children, Washington, D.C.

Summit, Roland. 1983. "The Child Sexual Abuse Accomodation Syndrome." *Child Abuse and Neglect* 7:177-93.

Summit, Roland, and JoAnn Kryso. 1978. "Sexual Abuse of Children: A Clinical Spectrum." *American Journal of Orthopsychiatry* 48:237-51.

Taubman, Stan. 1984. "Incest in Context." *Social Work* 29:35-40.

Topper, A., and D. Aldrich. 1981. "Incest: Intake and Investigation." In *Sexually Abused Children and Families*, edited by P. Mrazek and H. Kempe, pp. 109-27. Oxford: Pergamon Press.

Tormes, Y. 1968. *Child Victims of Incest*. Denver: The American Humane Association, Children's Division.

Tsai, Mavis; Shirley Feldman-Summers; and Margaret Edgar. 1979. "Childhood Molestation: Variables Related to Differential Impacts on Psychosexual Functioning in Adult Women." *Journal of Abnormal Psychology* 88:407-17.

Turner, Jonathon. 1978. *The Structure of Sociological Theory*. Rev. ed. Homewood, Ill.: The Dorsey Press.

U.S. Bureau of Census. 1983. *1980 Census of the Population, Volume 1. Characteristics of the Population*. Chapter D. *Detailed Population Characteristics Part 48 Virginia*. PC80-1-D48. Washington, D.C.: U.S. Department of Commerce, Bureau of the Census.

———. 1972. *1970 Population, General Population Characteristics*. Final Report PC(1)-B1, United States Summary. Washington, DC: U.S. Government Printing Office.

U.S. Department of Health, Education and Welfare. 1980. Grant Announcement. Washington, D.C.: Office of Human Development Services: Administration for Children, Youth and Families.

van den Berghe, Pierre. 1980. "Incest and Exogamy: A Sociobiological Reconsideration." *Ethology and Sociobiology* 1:151-62.

Vander Mey, Brenda J. 1981a. *Aggravated Father-Daughter Incest and Sexual Abuse: A Quest for Facts Based Upon a Sample of Substantiated Cases in Mississippi*. Unpublished master's thesis, Mississippi State University, Department of Sociology and Anthropology.

———. 1981b. "Father-Daughter Incest: A Conflict Approach." Working paper. Department of Sociology, Clemson University, Clemson, S.C. Revised 1985.

Vander Mey, Brenda J., and Ronald L. Neff. 1984. "Adult-Child Incest: A Sample of Substantiated Cases." *Family Relations* 33:549-57.

———. 1982. "Adult-Child Incest: A Review of Research and Treatment." *Adolescence* 17 (Winter):717-35.

Walker, Lenore E. 1984. *The Battered Woman Syndrome*. New York: Springer Publishing Company.

Wallace, Anthony F. C. 1981. "Childhood, Work, and Family Life in a 19th-Century Cotton Mill Town." In *Family Life in America 1620-2000*, edited by

Mel Albin and Dominick Cavallo, pp. 169-183. St. James, New York: Revisionary Press.

Weber, Ellen. 1977. "Incest: Sexual Abuse Begins at Home." *Ms. Magazine*, April, pp. 64-76.

Weber, Max. 1968. *Economy and Society: An Outine of Interpretive Sociology.* Volume 3. Edited by G. Roth and C. Wittich. New York: Bedminster Press.

———. 1947. *The Theory of Social and Economic Organization.* Edited by Talcott Parsons. New York: Oxford University Press.

Weinberg, S. Kirson. 1955. *Incest Behavior.* New York: Citadel Press.

Weiss, Joseph; Estelle Rogers; Miriam R. Darwin; and Charles E. Dutton. 1955. "A Study of Girl Sex Victims." *Psychiatric Quarterly* 29:1-27.

Westermarck, Edward. 1922 (1898). *The History of Human Marriage.* Volume 2. New York: The Allerton Book Company.

White, Leslie A. 1948. "The Definition and Prohibition of Incest." *American Anthropologist* 50:416-35.

Williams, Gertrude J., and John Money, eds. 1980. *Traumatic Abuse and Neglect of Children at Home.* Baltimore: The Johns Hopkins University Press.

Willie, Charles V., and Susan L. Greenblatt. 1978. "Four 'Classic' Studies of Power Relationships in Black Families: A Review and Look to the Future." *Journal of Marriage and the Family* 40:691-94.

Witherspoon, John A. 1982 (1802). "Letters on Education." In *American Families: A Documentary History*, edited by Donald M. Scott and Bernard Wishy, pp. 143-49. New York: Harper and Row.

Wolf, Arthur P. 1972. "Childhood Association and Sexual Attraction: A Further Test of the Westermarck Hypothesis." *American Anthropologist* 70:503-15.

Wolff, Kurt A., ed. 1950. *The Sociology of Georg Simmel.* New York: The Free Press.

Author Index

Subject Index

mothers, characteristics of, 34-36,
40, 56-61, 64, 66, 71-72, 102-03;
and prohibition of incest report,
46, 56, 59-60
motivation for incest, 55, 59, 79-80,
134, 148, 150

National Center on Child Abuse and
Neglect, 44
National Incidence (NI) Study, 5, 45,
50, 108
National Organization for Women,
13
neighborhood, and child abuse, 36-
37; and incest, 74-75, 77, 88,
124, 170
New York, SPCC, 15; study, 36, 45
nomothetic perspective, 126, 175

Oedipus Complex, 31

Parents Anonymous, 173
patriarchal family, the, 40
patriarchy, and child rearing, 19-20;
and history of sexual exploitation,
7-8; and incest, 38-40. See also
Male Dominance.
pedophiles, 53-54, 135-36, 148
pedophilic incest, 55, 57, 71, 135-36
perpetrator characteristics, 34, 53-59,
64-65, 69, 71-72, 110
perverse incest, 55, 57, 71, 135-
36
phenomenological analysis, 73-74, 83,
126
physical abuse, and incest, 57, 64,
146; of mothers, 60
physical well-being, 152, 160-61
pornography, 7, 75. See also Child
Rape.
poverty, 16-17; and child abuse, 15,
51-52; and perpetrators, 53
power, 2, 6, 38-39, 56, 75, 80-83,
87-88
powerlessness, 158. See also Power.

pregnancy, and reports of incest,
46, 65; and victims, 160
prevention, 173-75
primal horde, 29-30
promises, 53, 83-86. See also Threats.
psychopharmacological approaches,
151-52
psychotherapy, 149-50
psychotic intrusion, 55

rape, 7; incest as, 38, 43, 57, 99
religion, 57, 64. See also Calvinism.
Rene Guyon Society, 55
reporting, and actual abuse rates, 5-
6; by victim, 48; impediments to,
46-47, 170; increase in, 5, 170
researcher objectivity, 3-4
resources, mandated, 14, 16-17, 47,
171-72; of fathers, 39, 80-83, 87;
of mothers, 77, 87-88; of victims,
48, 80-83, 86-88, 124
responsibility, issue of, 149, 153-
55
risk factors, defined, 9; enumerated,
34, 63-65, 79, 93, 104, 106, 123,
170-71
role conflict, 29
role confusion, 28-29, 54-57
rule of the gift, 25
rustic environment, 55-56, 137

samples, limiations of, 108; types of
in incest research, 4
secrecy, 155-56
self esteem, and neighborhoods, 77;
of perpetrators, 54
self report, 4
seriousness, degree of, by incest type,
55-59, 71; and social class, 52;
and victimization, 50-51, 99-100
service delivery system, 138
sex education, 90, 160-61, 170, 175
sexual abuse, and equality, 70; history of, 6-9; types of, 48. See also
Incest.

About the Authors

Brenda J. Vander Mey, Ph.D., is an assistant professor of sociology at Clemson University, Clemson, South Carolina. A family sociologist, she has written several journal articles and numerous professional papers on the topic of incest abuse. Her current research endeavors are oriented toward an in-depth study of the sexual victimization of male children by family members.

Ronald L. Neff, Ph.D., is assistant professor in the department of sociology and anthropology, Mississippi State University and senior research associate with the Mississippi Alcohol Safety Education Program. Trained in social psychology and small group dynamics at the University of Iowa, his research interests range from the precipitants and scars of child and wife abuse to the special characteristics of the chronic drunken driver. In addition to consulting and conducting applied research for state, local, and federal agencies, Dr. Neff has authored numerous papers for professional associations and societies and has published in a number of professional journals

Kinly Sturkie, Ph.D., teaches in the department of sociology at Clemson University. Professor Sturkie earned a doctorate in social work from the University of Southern California, received a certificate in child sexual abuse treatment from the Institute for the Community as Extended Family, San Jose, California, and has served on the staffs of two child sexual abuse projects.

M.

O

J

R